SECOND EDITION

ETHICAL AND PROFESSIONAL ISSUES IN COUNSELING

R. ROCCO COTTONE
University of Missouri–St. Louis

VILIA M. TARVYDAS
The University of Iowa

Merrill
Prentice Hall

Upper Saddle River, New Jersey
Columbus, Ohio

Library of Congress Cataloging-in-Publication Data

Cottone, R. Rocco.

    Ethical and professional issues in counseling / by R. Rocco Cottone and Vilia M.
Tarvydas.—2nd ed.

      p. cm.

    Includes bibliographical references and index.

    ISBN 0-13-026852-6 (pbk.)

    1. Counselors—Professional ethics. I. Tarvydas, Vilia M. II. Title.

BF637.C6 C625 2003

174'.915—dc21

2001058723

Vice President and Publisher: Jeffery W. Johnston
Executive Editor: Kevin M. Davis
Associate Editor: Christina Kalisch Tawney
Editorial Assistant: Autumn Crisp
Production Editor: Mary Harlan
Production Coordination: Lea Baranowski, Carlisle Publishers Services
Design Coordinator: Diane C. Lorenzo
Cover Design: Thomas Borah
Cover Image: SuperStock; © 2002 Artists Rights Society (ARS), New York/ADAGP, Paris.
Text Design and Illustrations: Carlisle Publishers Services
Production Manager: Laura Messerly
Director of Marketing: Ann Castel Davis
Marketing Manager: Amy June
Marketing Coordinator: Tyra Cooper

This book was set in Garamond by Carlisle Communications, Ltd. It was printed and bound by Courier Kendallville, Inc. The cover was printed by Phoenix Color Corp.

Pearson Education Ltd.
Pearson Education Australia Pty. Limited
Pearson Education Singapore Pte. Ltd.
Pearson Education North Asia Ltd.
Pearson Education Canada, Ltd.
Pearson Educación de Mexico, S.A. de C.V.
Pearson Education—Japan
Pearson Education Malaysia Pte. Ltd.
Pearson Education, *Upper Saddle River, New Jersey*

10 9 8 7 6 5 4 3 2 1
ISBN: 0-13-026852-6

Dedications

To my five children, who, in every moment, show me the meaning of unconditional love: Christopher Rocco, Laura Kristina, Maria Francesca, Torre Alexander, and Cristiana Danielle.   R.R.C.

To my husband, George; his love, sensitivity, sacrifice, and dedication to me and our family have embodied what an ethical life truly means.

To my son, Ted, who makes my life joyful and spirited and gives me a true appreciation of what love, heart, and fresh insights can do to make life fully meaningful.

To my students and clients over the years; their wisdom, courage, and willingness to teach me have immeasurably enriched my life, both personally and professionally.   V.M.T.

Preface

We welcome you to the second edition of *Ethical and Professional Issues in Counseling*. We are flattered by the success of the first edition, especially in light of the highly competitive ethics text market in counseling and psychology. Accordingly, we have done much to make the second edition even more attractive to students and faculty members. We hope you find the new edition useful, scholarly, and up to date.

CHANGES TO THE SECOND EDITION

Significant changes we have made are:

1. We added two new chapters, one about ethics and multiculturalism (Chapter 11) and a second about office and administrative practices (Chapter 8). The new chapter on multiculturalism provides a review of crucial matters in this emerging focus of counseling practice. The chapter on office and administrative practices gives specific guidance on how to manage an office or counseling practice in an ethically sensitive way. These areas have been neglected in many textbooks on ethics.

2. We substantially revised the technology (Chapter 10), decision-making (Chapter 6), and supervision (Chapter 19) chapters. In the first edition, the technology chapter received excellent reviews, and we are pleased that David Peterson, the chapter author, has provided an up-to-date revision in this area of quickly emerging applications. The technology chapter captures new information and new standards as the profession has begun to recognize and to address ethical problems that arise from use of technology in counseling and counseling psychology. The revised decision-making chapter provides a great number of references, and it outlines nearly all of the models in the literature to the date of publication. Readers now have access to information on many ethical decision-making models. Two models are outlined in detail, and readers are able to compare, to contrast, and to use the models as guides if they so choose. There has been a total revision of the supervision chapter by two leading authorities on the topic. We believe this area of ethics is important because many counselors, soon after obtaining credentials, are asked to provide supervision to students and candidates for licensure or specialty certification.

3. We split the chapter on career and rehabilitation counseling into two chapters—one on each specialty. Career counseling is now covered in Chapter 15 and rehabilitation counseling is now explored in Chapter 17. This division more clearly differentiates the specialty areas and provides a more comprehensive presentation of ethical dilemmas specific to each area.

   We also split the first chapter into two chapters, with Chapter 1 introducing ethical and legal issues and Chapter 2 delineating all of the major mental health professions, for example, counseling, psychology, psychiatry, social work, marriage and family therapy, and psychiatric nursing.

4. The chapter on health care settings (Chapter 9) has been substantially revised and focuses on health care issues that confront counselors regardless of setting. Emphasis is now placed upon ethical issues rather than setting. Sections have been added on topics of high impact and interest, such as genetics, eugenics, abortion, complementary and alternative

medical approaches, and rational suicide. The discussion on managed care has been updated and expanded.

We believe these changes make the textbook stronger, more comprehensive, and more focused on the ethical issues faced by counselors and counseling psychologists in daily practice.

We have also made some changes to make the text more user friendly. These changes include the following:

1. We added objectives at the beginning of each chapter so readers can see at a glance what can be learned by a thorough reading of the chapter. The objectives are clearly linked to competency requirements associated with program accreditation and specialty certification in the field.
2. Wherever possible we tried to be consistent in use of terms and definitions in the text. The glossary has been updated and is a useful tool for students needing ready access to definitions of major terms.
3. We have updated and expanded source materials associated with the text. Through the Merrill/Prentice Hall Companion Website, students and faculty have ready access to support materials and information.
4. We deleted a cumbersome chapter on theoretical and philosophical issues, choosing to infuse that information less obtrusively in other chapters.

All in all, we believe we have made the textbook more thorough, reader friendly, and scholarly. We hope that you find the text a valuable tool as you explore the area of ethical, legal, and professional issues in counseling and counseling psychology.

ACKNOWLEDGMENTS

As with any major project, no two individuals work without the support of a number of people. Professional colleagues, students, family members, and friends all have an influence on the contents of a textbook such as this. We are very fortunate to be able to enlist a group of contributors, each providing expertise in a specialty area that supplements our areas of expertise. We could not have produced a work of a high caliber (to which we aspired) without their help. In those chapters with contributing authors, the names of the authors are provided at the beginning of the chapter, and they should be given full credit in any citation of their work.

We are grateful to the following reviewers for their valuable suggestions: Jo Ann Abe, Southern Connecticut State University; Deborah Barlieb, Kutztown University of Pennsylvania; Al Carlozzi, Oklahoma State University; Joseph Guido, Providence College; Chris A. Ike, Fayetteville State University; Terrance L. Peterson, St. Cloud State University; Bonnie J. Rubenstein, University of Rochester; Todd T. Russell, Texas A & M International University; Simeon Schlossberg, Western Maryland College; and Sangeeta Singg, Angelo State University.

We also appreciate our professional colleagues, especially those at the University of Iowa and the University of Missouri–St. Louis (UM–St. Louis). Without the support of our faculty colleagues and department chairs (Dennis Maki at Iowa and Therese Cristiani at UM–St. Louis), we could not have devoted the time and effort to this textbook or its revision.

Our students, of course, are our inspiration. They inspire us to try to touch their lives, as they are incredibly bright, caring, and dedicated people. We hope to instill readers with ethical sensitivity and a firm knowledge of ethical standards and ethical issues so that they may be able to enter the profession with confidence and pride. This book was born of a desire to assist professional counselors and counseling psychologists in establishing a professional identity. Our students have clearly and positively influenced this book.

We have also been fortunate to have an editor and an editorial staff that have been supportive and patient. Kevin Davis, of Merrill/Prentice Hall, and his staff have provided us with much guidance and good advice. We also thank Christina Tawney, for her help in coordinating the publication of the second edition. It has been a pleasure to work with Kevin, Christina, and others on the Merrill/Prentice Hall staff.

Finally, our families are the foundation of what we do. We find the support from our spouses (George and Molly) unconditional, and we are blessed with their love, patience, and understanding.

And to the readers, thank you for allowing us the opportunity to revise this book and, hopefully, to make it a mainstay text in the area of ethical and professional issues in counseling and counseling psychology.

R. Rocco Cottone

Vilia M. Tarvydas

Discover the Companion Website Accompanying This Book

THE PRENTICE HALL COMPANION WEBSITE: A VIRTUAL LEARNING ENVIRONMENT

Technology is a constantly growing and changing aspect of our field that is creating a need for content and resources. To address this emerging need, Prentice Hall has developed an online learning environment for students and professors alike—Companion Websites—to support our textbooks.

In creating a Companion Website, our goal is to build on and enhance what the textbook already offers. For this reason, the content for each user-friendly Website is organized by topic and provides the professor and student with a variety of meaningful resources. Common features of a Companion Website include:

For the Professor—

Every Companion Website integrates **Syllabus Manager™,** an online syllabus creation and management utility.

- **Syllabus Manager™** provides you, the instructor, with an easy, step-by-step process to create and revise syllabi, with direct links into Companion Website and other online content without having to learn HTML.
- Students may logon to your syllabus during any study session. All they need to know is the web address for the Companion Website and the password you've assigned to your syllabus.
- After you have created a syllabus using **Syllabus Manager™,** students may enter the syllabus for their course section from any point in the Companion Website.
- Clicking on a date, the student is shown the list of activities for the assignment. The activities for each assignment are linked directly to actual content, saving time for students.

- Adding assignments consists of clicking on the desired due date, then filling in the details of the assignment—name of the assignment, instructions, and whether it is a one-time or repeating assignment.
- In addition, links to other activities can be created easily. If the activity is online, a URL can be entered in the space provided, and it will be linked automatically in the final syllabus.
- Your completed syllabus is hosted on our servers, allowing convenient updates from any computer on the Internet. Changes you make to your syllabus are immediately available to your students at their next logon.

For the Student—

- **Counseling Topics**—17 core counseling topics represent the diversity and scope of today's counseling field.
- **Annotated Bibliography**—includes seminal foundational works and key current works.
- **Web Destinations**—lists significant and up-to-date practitioner and client sites.
- **Professional Development**—provides helpful information regarding professional organizations and codes of ethics.
- **Electronic Bluebook**—send homework or essays directly to your instructor's email with this paperless form.
- **Message Board**—serves as a virtual bulletin board to post—or respond to—questions or comments to/from a national audience.
- **Chat**—real-time chat with anyone who is using the text anywhere in the country—ideal for discussion and study groups, class projects, etc.

To take advantage of these and other resources, please visit the *Ethical and Professional Issues in Counseling,* Second Edition, Companion Website at

www.prenhall.com/cottone

About the Authors

R. Rocco Cottone, Ph.D., is a Professor of Counseling and Family Therapy and Coordinator of the Doctoral Programs in the Division of Counseling and Family Therapy at the University of Missouri–St. Louis. He earned a Ph.D. at Saint Louis University and an M.Ed. in counseling from the University of Missouri–Columbia. He is certified in rehabilitation counseling, family therapy, and professional psychology. He is a member of the American Counseling Association and the American Psychological Association, and a Clinical Member of the American Association for Marriage and Family Therapy. He holds licenses in counseling and psychology.

Vilia M. Tarvydas, Ph.D., LMHC, CRC, is a Professor and Program Coordinator of The Graduate Programs in Rehabilitation at The University of Iowa. She has a Ph.D. in rehabilitation psychology from the University of Wisconsin–Madison and an M.S. in rehabilitation counseling from the University of Wisconsin–Milwaukee. She is a licensed psychologist in Wisconsin and a licensed mental health counselor in Iowa. She was a Program Director for a brain injury rehabilitation center and has practiced as a psychologist in a hospital setting. Dr. Tarvydas is a Past President of the American Rehabilitation Counseling Association, was Vice-Chair of the Commission on Rehabilitation Counseling Certification, and served as

Chair of its Ethics Committee. She has been awarded the Eda Holt Lifetime Achievement in Rehabilitation Award. Dr. Tarvydas is currently Vice-Chair of the Iowa State Board of Behavioral Science Examiners, and a member of the American Counseling Association's Ethics Committee.

CONTRIBUTORS

Janine M. Bernard, Ph.D., NCC, ACS, is a Professor and Chair of the Counseling and Human Services Department at Syracuse University. Dr. Bernard received her Ph.D. in counselor education from Purdue University and her M.A. in counseling and personnel services from the University of Connecticut. Dr. Bernard is an Approved Clinical Supervisor and has written extensively in the area of clinical supervision. She is also a Past Chair of the National Board for Certified Counselors.

Ronald E. Claus, M.Ed., is a Ph.D. candidate in the counseling doctoral program at the University of Missouri–St. Louis. He is a Research Scientist with the Missouri Institute of Mental Health in St. Louis.

Donna A. Henderson, Ph.D., is an Associate Professor in the counselor education program at Wake Forest University. She has a Ph.D. from The University of Tennessee at Knoxville in counselor education and an M.A. in teaching from James Madison University. She is a licensed professional counselor and a licensed school counselor in North Carolina. Dr. Henderson is also active in the Southern Association of Counselor Education and Supervision. She is a former high school counselor and has taught English and language arts in grades 7 through 12.

Dennis R. Maki, Ph.D., CRC, LMHC, ACS, is a Professor in The Graduate Programs in Rehabilitation and Chair of the Division of Counseling, Rehabilitation and Student Development at The University of Iowa. Dr. Maki received his Ph.D. from the University of Wisconsin–Madison in rehabilitation counseling psychology and his M.A. in rehabilitation counseling from Michigan State University. He is a past president of the American Rehabilitation Counseling Association and current chair of the Council on Rehabilitation Education. Dr. Maki is an Approved Clinical Supervisor and is a consistent contributor to the professional literature in the areas of clinical supervision, assessment, rehabilitation counselor education, and cross-cultural issues related to disability and rehabilitation.

Christine Malaski, M.S., OTR/L, is a doctoral student in the rehabilitation counselor education program at The University of Iowa. Ms. Malaski has an M.S. in occupational therapy from Western Michigan University and is an Assistant Professor of occupational therapy at St. Ambrose University, Davenport, Iowa.

Susan McGuire, M.Ed., NCC, MAC, is President of Diversified Counseling Services in St. Charles, Missouri. She is a specialist working in the area of addictions, with special emphasis on work with gambling addictions and ex-offenders. She is a doctoral candidate in counselor education and supervision at the University of Missouri–St. Louis.

Barbara Wolf O'Rourke, Ph.D., RN, is an adjunct faculty member with The University of Iowa Graduate Programs in Rehabilitation. Dr. O'Rourke has a Ph.D. in rehabilitation psychology, an M.A. in counseling and human development, and a B.S.N. in nursing, all from The University of Iowa. She is involved in private practice as a rehabilitation psychologist and practices as a psychiatric nurse at Mercy Hospital in Iowa City, Iowa.

David B. Peterson, Ph.D., CRC, NCC, LP, is Program Director of the Graduate Programs in Rehabilitation Counseling at New York University. He began his academic career at the Graduate Programs in Rehabilitation at The University of Iowa. Dr. Peterson completed his Ph.D. in rehabilitation psychology at the University of Wisconsin–Madison and his master's degree in deafness rehabilitation counseling from Northern Illinois University. In addition, he has an applied degree in electronic engineering technology and has worked in the aerospace industry. His research interests include computer-based training and computer-assisted instruction in rehabilitation counseling with foci on clinical problem solving in case management and ethical decision making.

Mark Pope, Ed.D., NCC, NCCC, RPCC, is an Associate Professor of Counseling in the Division of Counseling and Family Therapy at the University of Missouri–St. Louis. Dr. Pope is a past president of the National Career Development Association. He holds licenses in counseling and psychology. He is a member of the APA, ACA, NCDA, and the Society for Vocational Psychology. Dr. Pope was elected to serve as president of the American Counseling Association in 2004.

Tarrell Awe Agahe Portman, Ph.D., LMHC, NCC, is an Assistant Professor in the Division of Counseling, Rehabilitation and Student Development at The University of Iowa. She teaches in the M.A. school counseling program and the Ph.D. counselor education program. She is a licensed teacher and K–12 school counselor in Missouri and Iowa. Dr. Portman's research agenda is in the area of multiculturalism, specifically with American Indian women.

Contents

PART 3

PART 4

PART 6
Conclusion 413

PART I

Overview of Ethical, Professional, and Legal Issues in Counseling

1. Introduction to Ethical Issues in Counseling

2. Counseling and the Mental Health Professions

3. Introduction to Ethical Principles and Standards in Counseling

4. Ethics and the Law

CHAPTER 1

Introduction to Ethical Issues in Counseling

Objectives
■ ■ ■ ■ ■ ■ ■ ■ ■ ■
After reading this chapter, you should be able to:

- Understand ethical terminology and define an "ethical dilemma."
- Distinguish "philosophical" ethics and morality from "professional" ethics and morality.
- Distinguish professionally mandated ethics from legally mandated ethical standards.
- Explain the importance of professional organizations, especially those that define and enforce ethical standards.
- Define the terms "licensure," "certification," and "accreditation," and identify acceptable certification and accreditation bodies in counseling and psychology.
- Explain the system of ethics governance in counseling.

■ ■ ■ ■ ■ ■ ■ ■ ■ ■

INTRODUCTION

Aside from counseling theory, there is probably no other area of study that is more related to the everyday practice of counseling than the area of professional ethics. Counselors are frequently confronted with ethical dilemmas. An **ethical dilemma**[1] is a circumstance that stymies or confuses the counselor because (a) there are competing or conflicting ethical standards that apply, (b) there is a conflict between what is ethical and moral, (c) the situation is such that complexities make application of ethical standards unclear, or (d) some other circumstance prevents a clear application of standards. Counselors who are faced with an ethical dilemma must be alert to ethical and legal standards. They must be educated as to what is considered acceptable and competent counseling practice. They should be educated about the ethical nuances involved in practice with special populations or in types of specialty practice. They must have a sense of their own morals and how those

---

[1]Boldfaced words in Parts I though IV are defined in the Glossary.

morals interplay with professional standards. Counselors must know when serious ethical dilemmas arise so that they may make informed and ethical decisions. In day-to-day practice, this means counselors must, from the very beginning of each case, act in a way that is ethically sensitive.

Ethical standards do not arise in a vacuum. They derive from the judgments of individuals who are members of established and respected professional associations, such as the American Counseling Association (ACA) or the American Psychological Association (APA). These professional associations act much like the guilds of old, representing individuals of related professional interests. Not only do professional organizations provide a meeting ground for practitioners, educators, and researchers, they also play a political role in advocating for the profession. These organizations must communicate to many audiences that the represented professionals are competent, needed, and guided by standards (e.g., ethical codes) that act to minimize or prevent harm to the individuals they serve. A profession without enforceable ethical standards is a questionable profession. Therefore, counselors must be alert to political and professional issues in counseling, psychology, and the other mental health professions.

This text focuses on ethical and professional issues in counseling (as a separate profession) and counseling psychology (as a specialty within the profession of psychology). Part I introduces ethical and professional issues, presents definitions and case-related scenarios, and introduces several key legal issues. Part II focuses on values clarification and ethical decision making and presents two ethical decision-making models. Part III introduces issues that arise in work settings: "ethical climate" in the workplace and administrative practices as they relate to ethical and legal issues. Part IV presents emerging issues and current challenges in the field, including technology issues and those that arise in medical or behavioral health settings. Part V provides detailed and targeted summaries of ethical issues and standards in several of the major specialties of counseling, such as school, marriage and family, rehabilitation, career, addictions, and mental health counseling. Finally, Part VI reviews the role of the counselor as an ethical practitioner, including the counselor's duties and responsibilities in ethically compromising circumstances. This text provides the professional counselor with more than a cursory review of ethical issues; its purpose is to instill ethical responsibility through informed practice.

DEFINING ETHICS

The terminology related to **ethics** is sometimes confusing because the technical definitions used by philosophers and the definitions used by the lay public and mental health professionals do not match perfectly. "Ethics" in philosophy generally refers to theories about what is acceptable behavior. When the term "philosophical ethics" is used, it implies a discussion of theory. Many theories are related to ethics, and the behaviors that are defined as "good" or "right" that derive from one theory may be quite different than those that derive from another theory. For example, Friedrich Nietzsche, a 19th-century German philosopher, developed a theory of "evolutionary naturalism," wherein right and wrong result from what is naturally selected (following Darwin's theory of evolution). What is "weak" in terms of survival is not valued by a literal interpretation of Nietzsche's (1888/1968a; 1891/1968b) work. In *The Antichrist,* Nietzsche (1888/1968a) stated: "The weak and the failures shall perish. . . . And they shall even be given every possible assistance" (p. 570). Immanuel Kant's (undated, 1949) "categorical imperative" stands in contrast. In his view, the decision maker must consider that the decision may become a universal standard—even applying to the decision maker. Kant's "categorical imperative" has been trivialized to the golden rule—do unto others as you would have others do unto you. Consider how a person with a serious disability would view these two philosophies. By one philosophy, the disabled person would be viewed as dispensable; by the other philosophy, the person may be viewed as valuable. In some ways, what is good according to Nietzsche's theory is in conflict with Kant's. So what is right or valuable by one theory may not be right or valuable by another theory. Ethical theory ultimately directs interpretation of what is "good" or "bad." These examples demonstrate that philosophical ethics is theoretical. The study of philosophical ethics shows that what is defined as a "good act" clearly derives from the theoretical orientation.

In philosophy, the term "morality" stands in contrast to ethics. Morality relates more to the application of ethical principles than to actual specified actions. Johnson (1999) stated:

Philosophers have generally, for purposes of clarity, confined the usage of the terms *morals* and *morality* to the realm of practice. When they say that someone is morally good, they mean that the actions of that person are praiseworthy. *Ethics* is a term that refers not directly to practice but rather to theory. Philosophers would not ordinarily say that someone is an ethically good person, but rather a good ethicist, meaning that the person's theories about ethics are worthy of serious consideration. This difference in usage, although generally accepted in philosophical circles, is not followed by people in general. In particular, the terms *ethics* and *ethical* are often used in place of *morality* and *moral*. For instance, we commonly speak of business *ethics* rather than business *morality* and we ask of someone's action "Was that *ethical?*" rather than "Was that *moral?*". (p. 2)

So, in philosophy, when an act is in question, it is a moral question. Whether the act is considered moral depends on the ethical theory that is applied.

Outside of philosophical circles, ethics and morality are intermixed and difficult to distinguish (Johnson, 1999). This is especially true when considering the professional ethics of counselors and psychologists. In fact, the philosophical definitions just described almost seem at odds with the application of these terms in professional ethics. One often hears the term, "professional ethics," meaning that a practitioner is *acting* according to standards of practice defined as acceptable by the profession. (Remember, "actions" in philosophy were reserved for "morals.") The term "moral" often implies that a person has a firm philosophical foundation, even a grounding in religious dogma or standards. In common parlance, when one says someone has morals, it means the person is guided by higher principles. So, in common usage, the terms are almost used to mean the opposite of what is acceptable in the discipline of philosophy.

For clarity, this text uses the term *ethics* as it applies to philosophy. As related to the discipline of philosophy, it is identified as "philosophical ethics." In those cases, the discussion will center on ethics as theory (as in the case of Nietzsche or Kant). When the term *ethics* is used without the qualifier (philosophical), it is used to mean *professional ethics*. Thus, when the term *ethics* stands alone, the reference is to professional ethics and the actions of professionals according to standards applied by the profession. When the term *morality* is used to apply to philosophy, as related to the discipline of philosophy, it is identified as "philosophical morality." When the term *morality* (or *morals*) is used without the qualifier (philosophical), it is used to mean morality in the everyday sense. So when the term *morals* or *morality* stands alone, the reference is to principles or beliefs that guide an individual, sometimes deriving from a religious standard. The definitions, then, are as follows:

- **Philosophical ethics**—the theoretical analysis of what is "good," "right," or "worthy."
- **Professional ethics** or **ethics**—acceptable or good practice according to agreed-upon rules or standards of practice established by a profession, as in counseling or psychology.
- **Philosophical morality**—assessment of actions of a person against a theory in philosophical ethics. Philosophical morality always refers to an act.
- **Morality**—the principles that guide an individual, sometimes deriving from a religious standard; sometimes referred to as moral principles.

In this text, the terms *ethics* and *morality* are addressed more often than are their philosophical alternatives. This is a text on professional ethics and practice, and, although reference is made to philosophical ethics and philosophical morality, the focus is clearly on the applied practice of ethics in counseling and psychology.

To further clarify the use of these terms, consider the following examples. What is ethical (even legal) practice in medicine may be immoral by certain religious standards (e.g., abortion). What is ethical in counseling practice also may be immoral by certain religious standards. For example, a fundamentalist Christian may be faced with a dilemma in counseling gay partners about their sexuality. A Roman Catholic counselor may be uncomfortable providing birth control information to a teenage client. In professional practice in the United States, ethics is separated from morality at the level of professional and legal directives. Consider the situation presented in Box 1.1 to assist in exploring your moral positions. Professional and legal standards tend to correspond to what is "ethical." However, individual professionals may choose not to separate the moral from the ethical; for example, some physicians may refuse to perform abortions on moral grounds.

PROFESSIONAL ETHICS VERSUS LEGALLY MANDATED ETHICS

Now that the terms *ethics* and *morals* have been clarified, a distinction also must be drawn between what is considered "professional" ethics and "legally-mandated" ethics. In the United States, professionals such as counselors or psychologists are directed and bound by the ethical standards of the professional organization or organizations to which they belong. Most counselors are members of the American Counseling Association (ACA). Counseling psychologists may have member-

Box 1.1   A Clarification of Morals Exercise

What are your morals? As part of the self-exploration process that is critical to anticipating how you will handle ethical dilemmas, take a few minutes to define and assess some of your basic moral principles—those principles that guide you broadly in your daily life. Consider also that these moral principles may translate to specific actions as you are faced with difficult choices as a counselor. For example, what is your stand on abortion? Is it guided by a religious standard? Would you counsel someone considering an abortion? Consider another moral issue: the taking of another person's life. What is your moral stance? Is it ever justifiable to take another person's life? If you believe taking a life can be justified, under what circumstances is it justified? Under what conditions would you counsel a client who has taken someone's life in a way that you do not believe is justifiable? Consider sexual relations outside of marriage. Are they acceptable or unacceptable? Does your religion guide you on this matter? Would you "keep the secret" from a spouse while counseling a person who admits, without remorse, to an extramarital sexual relationship? Attempt to define several guiding and absolute principles that influence you in your day-to-day life. What are the foundations of these beliefs? Finally, consider circumstances that would modify your stance.

ship in either the ACA or the American Psychological Association (APA), or both. The ACA and the APA are professional organizations that provide a forum for counselors to address their educational, personal, and professional needs. The ACA has affiliate organizations, and the APA has divisions devoted to specialty interests. For example, two affiliate organizations of the ACA are the American Rehabilitation Counseling Association (ARCA) and the International Association for Marriage and Family Counseling (IAMFC). Rehabilitation counselors and marriage/family counselors attend the ACA conference and also attend meetings and professional presentations sponsored by their respective affiliate groups and the ACA as a whole. The APA is similar— divisions of the association (e.g., counseling psychology, rehabilitation psychology, or family psychology) organize activities and presentations for the national APA conference. The ACA and APA also make malpractice and other types of personal insurance available to members. Additionally, the ACA and the APA have established professional standards through committees that oversee ethical rules (including disciplinary procedures) and practice. (Both the ACA and the APA ethics codes are in the appendix at the end of this text.)

The ACA and APA codes of ethics direct members who are faced with an ethical concern or ethical dilemma. Such a circumstance requires a professional to decide if an action is right or wrong (before or at the time of the act) when competing or mutually exclusive ethical, moral, or legal standards are involved. (Remember the definition of an ethical dilemma discussed in the first paragraph of this chapter.) Competing standards of right and wrong may be at the root of an ethical dilemma. The ACA and APA codes of ethics are *professional* ethical standards.

Counselors who are licensed to practice counseling by one of the licensing states (46 of the 50 states in the United States as of this writing) and psychologists licensed to practice psychology (in any of the 50 states) are also directed by the ethical code referenced in the relevant state's licensure statute. In fact, one of the main reasons for the licensure of professions (such as counseling or psychology) is to protect the public from unqualified or unethical practitioners. Counselors or counseling psychologists who act unethically, as judged by a licensure authority according to the authority's accepted standards, are subject to penalties as severe as suspension or revocation of a professional license. **Licensure** allows a person to practice a profession and prevents the practice of a profession by those who are unlicensed (Anderson, 1996; Dorken, 1976). **Revocation** of a license, therefore, is a loss of the right to practice in the state's jurisdiction. **Suspension** of a license is a temporary loss of the right to practice the profession within the jurisdiction. Licenses are not easy to attain. To be licensed as a professional counselor in most states requires a master's degree with one or more years of supervised professional (post-degree) practice; licensure candidates must also pass a stringent examination. The standards in psychology are similar, except a doctoral degree is almost always required. Consequently, the prospect of losing a professional license means the loss of livelihood. Whereas a breach of the code of ethics of a professional organization (such as the ACA or APA) can result in professional censure or even loss of membership, the breach of an ethical standard required by regulatory law may result in the loss of a license to practice and/or other legal penalty. The distinction, therefore, between professional and legal ethical standards is a crucial one.

In some cases, state licensure statutes or regulations simply reference the professional association's code of ethics. Most states develop their own standards, but ethical standards in licensure statutes are usually similar to (or based in large part on) those of the professional association. In counseling, the American Association of State Counseling Boards (AASCB) provides guidance to individual state licensure boards on matters related to ethical standards and enforcement. Members of the AASCB are representatives from state licensure boards. This organization works to enhance the consistency of standards in licensing counselors among all states. It also addresses issues of **reciprocity** of licensure (Altekruse, 2001). Licensing reciprocity is a process whereby a licensed counselor's credentials in one state are recognized by another state for licensure purposes without additional imposed requirements. In psychology, the Association for State and Provincial Psychology Boards (ASPPB), a group made up of state psychology licensing board representatives, has its own code of ethics. (See Sinclair [1996] for a comparison of the ASPPB code of conduct and the APA and Canadian Psychological Association codes of ethics.) The ASPPB has also set up a credential bank for individuals who meet quality licensure standards to facilitate reciprocity between states—the Certificate of Professional Qualification (CPQ) in psychology. The CPQ is accepted by many states as a credential that meets licensure standards. These important license-related organizations establish the ethical and professional training standards required to be admitted and retained in the professions.

Counselors need to know both the professional and legal ethical standards that direct their practices. Professionals are obligated to know these standards beyond the knowledge gained by a cursory reading of a code. Counselors should commit to memory the general principles that operate in ethical practice, and they should regularly discuss with other counselors or psychologists how such principles apply to professional practice. (see Box 1.2 for a statement made by a counselor who volunteered to share his own experience related to a serious breach of professional ethics.) Chapter 3 provides a summary of ethical issues and the standards involved and presents case scenarios with practice-relevant contexts for understanding these standards. Chapter 4 contains a summary of legal issues.

Box 1.2   Ethical Errors: Serious and Painful—A Letter from a Counselor Accused of Serious Ethical Misconduct

I remember the day all too well. It was the worst day of my professional life. "My God! What have I done?" Panic surged through my body. My mind raced with worry on the day my boss confronted me with my worst nightmare. He informed me that a former client of mine had accused me of the most serious of ethical violations. Specifically, I was being accused of having a detrimental relationship with this client—a sexual relationship. My boss had tears in his eyes as if he was saying, "Please tell me it isn't true." But, I could not deny the truth. I had been denying the truth for 10 months. It was time to come clean and try to salvage what little integrity I had left. This is my story. It is serious and extraordinarily painful. I hurt many people. My behavior was completely irresponsible. I have lived through it, and I keep what I did in front of me as a teaching tool. I can never forget what I did, or I may become vulnerable again. It doesn't really matter what is known intellectually about ethical errors. Anyone can read and understand that there are certain things that must not be done, and there are many gray areas as well. But what happens when the human, vulnerable side surfaces? What happens when buttons get pushed and countertransference issues arise? I hope what happens is that the truth is faced, that a boss or trusted colleague is consulted, or that personal counseling is undertaken. I didn't face the truth. As a result, I had to talk to a lawyer, to an ethics committee, and to my insurance company. I lost my job, my license, and lots of money. This was certainly an expensive lesson. What I did was wrong. My punishment was deserved.

What I gained from this ordeal was something very important: I gained myself. I'm sure most students of counseling and most practicing professionals have heard the many reasons why people pursue counseling professionally, including meeting one's own personal needs.

This was certainly true for me. My need was to be needed. Therefore, I've been vulnerable to needy clients. When clients were hurting, I wanted to rescue and take care of them. I knew this prior to acting out, but I didn't know how strong this need was and how I could lose myself and my professional boundaries.

One of the many ironies is that I could see what was happening. I remember reviewing the ethical guidelines concerning potentially detrimental relationships. I even informed my spouse that I was attracted to a client prior to acting out. But I was blinded by needs. I needed help, but was ashamed to ask for it. My denial took over and deception began. I held this shameful secret inside. My strong word of caution: Don't keep secrets. Secrets have powerful and destructive energy.

All counselors will be faced with ethical dilemmas throughout their careers. There are no simple answers and no complete guidebook to inform how to respond to the many difficult and ambiguous situations. Experience is a great teacher, but it cannot help with every possible concern. Furthermore, experience often teaches the hard way, by giving the test first, followed by the lesson.

There is little guidance to help those who have been cited for ethical misconduct or legal wrongdoing. A legal specialist for psychologists and counselors informed me that approximately 50 percent of mental health professionals will face some ethical or legal hardship during the course of their careers. How does one prepare for this behaviorally and emotionally? It is all too easy to say, "Just don't make any ethical mistakes." This statement is unrealistic and naive. Like shadows, mistakes lurk in the darkness and catch a person off guard, when one is most vulnerable.

If for some reason you are accused of some wrongdoing, whether you are guilty or not, it will most likely shock your system. Be prepared for an emotional roller coaster. Get help, but be cautious. Get a lawyer if necessary; inform your insurance company if your lawyer recommends that you do so (make sure you carry insurance); and be careful about what you tell friends, family, and colleagues. By all means, talk to a therapist if you are personally struggling.

I experienced a plethora of emotions. That dear old question, "How did it make you feel?" certainly became real for me. I was angry at my client, at first, for turning me in; after all, my client was a willing participant who encouraged my involvement. My denial was still strong for the only person I should have been angry at—myself. A client places a counselor in an authority position whether welcomed or not. I abused my position. I should have been angry at myself for allowing this to happen.

Once I was able to accept complete responsibility for what I did, I could begin to grieve. These were extraordinarily tough days. I had to endure many losses. I experienced many days of depression. For months I was completely ashamed of myself as a human being and could not imagine ever counseling again. Eventually, I realized that although I did a terrible thing, I was not a terrible person. I was a counselor who let personal issues get in the way of my professional responsibilities. Today I am very remorseful for what I did, and I am fortunate that I received a great deal of support when I began to tell the truth.

Not all people forgave me for what I did, and I understand this. I am very sorry for my behavior and I wish I could make amends to all those who suffered. I have developed many resources to help me personally, especially when I'm feeling stressed and overwhelmed, and I use my resources rather than just talk about them. I encourage all counselors to do the same. My resources are personal therapy, a 12-step program, my spouse, and a personal accountability program. It is very easy for counselors to talk and to listen, but more difficult for them to do their own personal work. Frankly, I believe that many counselors are compulsive about their jobs while neglecting themselves personally. Regardless, counselors owe it to their clients, to their profession, to their families, and most of all, to themselves, to take care of themselves.

Well, that is my story. I wouldn't wish it upon anyone. I have to live with myself every day knowing what I did. Sometimes it is very difficult and painful for me. But it is important for me to keep my pain and my story in front of me. I need to remind myself of what I did so I can prevent myself from ever doing it again. Mistakes are best prevented by taking an honest accounting of one's life and one's situation. Be alert to "red flags," and consult supervisors, colleagues, friends, or a therapist if personal needs begin to blind you to your professional responsibilities.

I wish you well on your journey.

ETHICS GOVERNANCE[2]

Some means to govern ethical practice are necessary to give meaning to professional standards and to enhance the societal stature of the profession. These governance processes guide counselors through education and socialization in their professional role and, subsequently, discipline them if they do not practice within the proscribed standards. Ethical standards of practice can be thought of as being either *mandatory* or *aspirational* in the level of direction they provide the practitioner (Corey, Corey, & Callanan, 1998). The most basic level of ethical functioning is guided by **mandatory ethics,** wherein individuals focus on compliance with the law and the dictates of the professional codes of ethics that apply to their practice. At this level, counselors are concerned with remaining safe from legal action and professional censure. At the more ethically sophisticated level, the **aspirational** level, individuals additionally reflect on the effects of the situation on the welfare of their clients and the effects of their actions on the profession as a whole.

These same concepts of mandatory and aspirational ethics can be applied to counseling's standards of practice. It is important to reiterate that specific codes of ethics are binding only on persons who hold that particular credential or membership. If a credential holder or a member of a professional group violates an applicable code of ethics, the organization has the responsibility to provide a disciplinary procedure to enforce its standards. In the case of a professional association, the ultimate sanction would typically be loss of membership, with possible referral of the findings of an ethics committee to other professional or legal jurisdictions. This referral may be accomplished by providing information to the AASCB or the ASPPB for dissemination to member licensing boards. For example, the AASCB has a Disciplinary Information Network (DIN) that provides to affiliate member licensure boards or organizations information on individuals who have been disciplined by an organization or state licensure board. The ACA and several specialty credentialing bodies are members. For a credentialing body such as the National Board of Certified Coun-

selors (NBCC), the largest certifying body for professional counselors, or for a counselor licensure board in one of the licensing states, violators could face the more serious option of certificate or license revocation, thus possibly removing their ability to practice. Less serious levels of sanction, such as a reprimand or a period of probation, are also utilized. In the case of a reprimand or probation, there is often an additional requirement for educational or rehabilitative remedies, such as taking an educational course on ethics, treatment of an addiction, supervised practice, or other remedies to assist counselors in regaining an appropriate level of functioning ethically and/or personally. The assessment of the level of seriousness of the ethical violation will affect the actual choice of sanction once an individual is found to be in violation of the code of ethics. Factors often considered include whether the act was intentional, the degree of risk or actual harm to the client, the motivation or ability of the violator to change, and the recidivism of the violator (Koocher & Keith-Spiegel, 1998).

Responsible practitioners supplement the mandatory level of ethics awareness with advanced knowledge of the scholarly literature on accepted ethical practice. They also consult colleagues who may have experience addressing challenging ethical circumstances and who are respected in the community as ethically wise practitioners. In addition, they may gain guidance from other codes of ethics and specialty guidelines. Sophisticated practitioners will seek these sources to supplement the required mandatory ethical standards with the more aspirational principles. In fact, for certain situations, the course of action suggested by the aspirational guidelines may contradict or exceed those required by mandatory standards. Such situations create stressful ethical dilemmas and place practitioners in need of means to reconcile them responsibly (see Chapters 5 and 6 for further guidance on making ethical decisions when involved in ethical dilemmas).

There are several levels of ethics governance for counselors and various organizations are involved at different levels. These organizations, taken as a whole, constitute an interconnected network of entities that performs a diversity of functions. Each entity plays a role in the creation of a system of ethics governance.

Colleges and universities provide professional education and research services. Professional programs at universities or colleges in counseling or psychology usually operate under the review of professional accrediting organizations. **Accreditation** allows for clear recognition of a program (its nature, intent, and qual-

---

[2]This section was adapted from "Standards of Practice: Legal and Ethical" by Vilia M. Tarvydas in D. R. Maki & T. F. Riggar (Eds.), (1997), *Rehabilitation Counseling: Profession and Practice.* Copyright © 1997 by Springer Publishing Company. Used by permission of Springer Publishing Company, Inc., New York 10012.

ity). The review process is a means to certify that the school program meets standards set by the accrediting body. **Professional accreditation** is the process whereby a college or university professional program (e.g., counseling or psychology) voluntarily undergoes review by an accrediting body, such as the Commission on Rehabilitation Education (CORE) or the Commission on the Accreditation of Counseling and Related Educational Programs (CACREP) or the APA (1995). CORE, CACREP, and the APA are professional accrediting bodies that evaluate graduate education programs in rehabilitation counseling, counseling, and counseling psychology, respectively. **Professional accrediting bodies** essentially qualify educational programs as meeting standards beyond those required of colleges or universities to offer degrees; they certify that the educational institution meets these high professional standards. Professional accrediting bodies have the broadest function to provide aspirational educational guidance in ethics. They help to establish the structural foundation for ethical governance. Additionally, they help to build the theoretical and research base for understanding ethical issues, decision-making processes, and ethical educational methods. These aspects of the aspirational knowledge base are needed to support ethical development of a profession. Colleges and universities also ensure that proper preservice education and professional socialization occur to inculcate future practitioners and educators with the proper ethics base. Educators play an important part in role modeling and supporting ethical analysis and ethical behavior in teaching, supervision, and actual clinical practice. Educational institutions also serve as a resource to other professional organizations and regulatory bodies to provide teaching, research, and service that support aspirational and mandatory ethical practice.

The next level is comprised of the professional organizations with aspirational codes of ethics but with no internal mandatory enforcement mechanisms. The International Association for Marriage and Family Counseling or the Association for Specialist in Group Work (ASGW), as divisions of the ACA, are examples. For such organizations, the primary task is to encourage aspirational ethical practice of their members and the application of ethical standards in specific specialty contexts. Mandatory enforcement is not undertaken by such professional organizations due to factors such as lack of (a) appropriate consumer access and protection in the disciplinary process, (b) appropriate remedies for serious infractions, and (c) substantial financial, staff, and professional resources necessary for respon-

sible enforcement. In some cases, the mandatory enforcement function of the organization is referred to a parent organization (e.g., to ACA in the case of the IAMFC or the ASGW) or the complainant is referred to another appropriate jurisdiction (e.g., a state licensure board) to initiate a disciplinary process.

Nonetheless, professional organizations with aspirational codes perform several significant functions within the ethics governance structure. They typically provide their members with supplemental codes of ethics that extend and illuminate other, more general codes. Such documents provide guidelines for ethical practice for particular, frequently encountered ethical issues or professional activities. For rehabilitation counselors such issues might be (a) assessment of persons with functional limitations due to disability, (b) interdisciplinary team practice issues, (c) managed care practice, and (d) the responsibility of advocacy for persons with disabilities. A supplemental code may take the form of guidelines for practice that address specialty setting or function-specific issues, as is done in the APA (such as the *Guidelines for Computer-based Tests and Their Interpretation* [APA, 1986]). In addition to maintaining supplementary, specialty ethical standards or guidelines, some professional organizations at the aspirational level collect information regarding ethical trends and needs for revision of either the specialty or generalist ethics codes. Their leaders also participate in revision and writing for both types of codes. These organizations identify and supply qualified professionals to serve on the various mandatory enforcement bodies. They provide educational programs to extend the knowledge base and to define better quality ethical practice, performing significant educational and socialization functions. A new and innovative role for these organizations, one that is potentially most meaningful, is identifying or providing remediation or rehabilitation programs for impaired professionals who have been found in violation (or are at risk for violation) of ethical standards.

At the third level of ethical governance are professional organizations that maintain and enforce a mandatory code of ethics (such as the ACA or the APA). These organizations provide an entry-level mandatory code and enforcement process for their members and, in the case of the ACA, enforce the standards or guidelines of affiliate (specialty) organizations. Organizations at this level consult with certification and licensing bodies and the specialty professional organizations to ensure active participation of all parties in ethics enforcement. They also provide educational programs to increase practitioner knowledge.

(Box 1.3 provides an exploration of how one state has interpreted the general professional standard forbidding sexual intimacies with clients.) The next level of ethics governance includes professional regulatory bodies that either certify or license professionals, and those that constitute the pre-eminent enforcers of a mandatory code. National certification bodies, such as the NBCC and Commission on Rehabilitation Counselor Certification (CRCC), as well as state counselor and psychology licensure boards, operate at this level. They perform a pivotal role in the promulgation and enforcement of ethical standards. They do not develop completely novel internal standards; rather, they draw their specific codes of ethical standards from the organizations that constitute the professional body or their constituent counseling communities, and then regulate based on the profession's own internal standards. They also may provide information and consultation to professional organizations in revising and maintaining current codes of ethics. Beyond their ethical regulatory function, these bodies encourage ethical proficiency of their licensees and certificate holders by requiring graduate degree program education and continuing (postgraduate) education, often in the area of ethics.

The courts are at the pinnacle of the ethics governance hierarchy. One of the primary mechanisms for this type of governance is adjudication of malpractice in the civil courts. In **malpractice** actions, establishing a violation of duty is one of the central points. The standard for determining what constitutes "good professional practice," as applied to the matter at hand, is required. "Good professional practice" is sometimes hard to de-

fine and requires many types of considerations. It is not unusual to call various expert witnesses to testify regarding such practices. Additionally, one party to the action might attempt to establish that a blatant violation of the general rules of the profession occurred by reference to the profession's ethical standards (Thompson, 1990).

Another standard of practice applied in court may be consideration of whether the action or service in question was within the **scope of practice** of both the profession and the individual, the extent and limits of activities considered "acceptable" by individuals licensed or certified in a profession or specialty. Licensed counselors or psychologists in many states are governed by the scope of practice described in state statutes, and licensees may be required to declare their personal scopes of practice at the time they are licensed or when renewing a license (e.g., marriage and family counseling or counseling psychology). Practitioners are ethically bound to limit their own scope of practice to areas within those of the profession and in specialties within which they have obtained appropriate training and supervision. They must be able to demonstrate that they are competent to practice by virtue of appropriate education, supervision, and professional experience.

This six-level professional governance structure constitutes a network of mandatory and aspirational ethics. An interactive system of research, education, and enforcement shapes and regulates the ethical practice of counselors. This structure provides a system of knowledge, traditions, rules, and laws, but does not provide practitioners with possibly the most crucial

Box 1.3 Ethics Governance and One State's Standard

To consider ethics governance related to mandatory licensure standards, consider a State of Missouri dictate that addresses sexual intimacies with clients. The ethics code referenced in the rules and regulations of the Missouri State Committee for Professional Counselors has a stipulation that bans "sexual intimacies" with clients. The standard, however, defines "sexual intimacies" very broadly, including sexual intercourse and sodomy, of course, but also including "hugging or caressing by either the licensed professional counselor or the client" or "touching" a person's "legs, stomach, chest, breasts, genitals or buttocks." Has the Missouri dictate gone too far, or is it right on target? If a counselor touches someone's knee, should that be considered unethical? How about a hug abruptly initiated by a client leaving the office—is that unethical? How about a counselor hugging a distressed child in a school context? Remember, this is a mandatory standard, and a person's license is at risk if there is a breach of ethical standards.

tool for ethical practice—knowledge and experience in applying their ethical decisions.

Although professionals may sometimes become caught up in the technicalities of ethics governance, it is important to keep in mind that preventing harm to others and benefiting them through a professional relationship is what "professional ethics" is all about. Lest readers lose sight of the powerful influence they have on people's lives, it is crucial to keep the client's welfare in mind. Box 1.4 is a statement by a former client of a psychologist who breached the detrimental relationship ban of his profession. The statement was volunteered by the victim and is published with her full permission. It is disguised to prevent identification, but is a true account of her feelings through the process of her personal relationship with the psychologist.

Box 1.4   A Client's Story

For about a year, I sat "in the chair," trying to understand what had brought me to therapy. Across from me sat my therapist, my confidant, my partner in piecing together the puzzle that had become my life. I began by explaining that I was hurting inside because of the young woman I had become. I felt angry, defensive, alone. I had detached myself from all those who were dear to me, except for my family. They, however, were kept at arm's length. My temper had become short and my list of reasons for not going out with my friends had become long. I was confused by these changes in myself because I was unable to identify the source. I was sad about the changes because I did not like living such a negative, un-peopled existence. This existence was nothing like what I had lived the previous 22 years.

The day I realized why I was "in the chair" remains etched vividly in my mind. With bowed head and long curls hiding my face, I choked out the words with humiliation, shame, fear, and pain: *I was raped.* I told the therapist the story from the beginning—a story which began as one of friendship, laughter, and fun. Then I recounted how suddenly, without warning, the man I had chosen to call friend turned into someone I no longer knew. I told of the day he hovered above my head with eyes full of hate as he spoke with venom, and how because of shock and fear, I could not move. He hurt me with his body and he hurt me with his words. I described how it seemed like hours later, that he dropped me off in front of my apartment. It was at that time that he grabbed the back of my head once again, pressed his mouth angrily onto mine and told me he'd like to do that again sometime—that it was fun.

The pain I went through by finally acknowledging the rape was deep. Making sense of how it had affected my life forced me to open myself up to feel all that the experience was for me. I told the therapist that I felt robbed. I was robbed of my virginity and robbed of my innocence. Perhaps most critical, however, was that I felt I was robbed of my confidence. I felt I could no longer judge who or what was safe. This rapist had been my friend for months. I had gone willingly to his apartment. I completely trusted the boundary I felt existed between us. Then he raped me. Then, he acted like it wasn't rape. Instead, he acted as if I had an equal role in creating what had happened.

My sense of industry and self-power were badly shaken. I trudged through it all with the therapist. He was the only one who knew my secret and as such, I funneled my only bit of trust into the therapeutic relationship. As I worked through the details of the rape, I began focusing on *self* and my interaction with others. In an attempt to learn to trust again but this time with wisdom, I opened my life completely to the therapist. I chiseled away at the walls that I had built as a means of protection.

After several years of being in and out of therapy with this man, in one session, he said he'd like to have a beer with me. At this point, I trusted him implicitly. He had validated my feelings through the therapeutic relationship and I felt very connected to him. I agreed to have a

continued

beer with him. A decision could not be made as to where we would go that next week, so he suggested we just meet in his office. The following week, he brought a six pack of beer and I "sat in the chair." I remember feeling drawn to him on some level. I think the connection was so strong for me because of the work we had done together in therapy. He had become the only man I trusted aside from those in my family. On another level, I knew it was wrong for me to have a beer with my therapist. I also felt it was wrong for me to feel an attraction to him.

I continued seeing him therapeutically after that, but there was no more alcohol involved. After several months, I terminated the therapeutic relationship for good. I felt I was ready to build healthy relationships without being too fearful of making a decision that was unsafe or wrong for me.

Several years later, I wrote my then ex-therapist a note explaining my marriage was ending. After getting the note, my ex-therapist called and asked me to go get a beer. Again, the decision was made to meet at his office. Again, he brought the beer. Again, I sat "in the chair." After catching up for several hours, it was time to go. We stood up and hugged one another, which we had never done before. After a few minutes, he looked down on me and kissed me. The embrace became very sexual very quickly. As his hands moved to places previously associated with pain, I was not sure how to respond. I was certainly shocked and a little scared that he was touching me in this way. I kept my arms around his waist, not touching him in a sexual way. In addition to feeling shocked and a bit scared, because of my past, I also wanted so desperately for someone I trusted to touch me in a loving way that was full of care and tenderness. Based upon the words he whispered in my ear, it seemed he wanted to show me what tender, loving touch was like. I did not stop him from touching me. I was a willing participant, but also felt uneasy for I knew it was wrong for both of us to be doing.

I could not sleep that night. I was so full of self-condemnation—it horrified me to consider what my loved ones would think if they knew I had engaged in this type of relationship with my ex-therapist. For days afterward, when it entered my mind, a chill ran through my body. I was shocked that it had even happened.

After a few weeks, he called again. This time, he would come to my apartment. His visits became weekly. By this time, we were in a mutually sexual relationship. I could hardly fathom the fact that my ex-therapist and I were touching one another in a sexual way. It seemed the more he needed to be with me, the less comfortable I felt with what was happening. It seemed strange inside to think that the person I had needed for so long in therapy could somehow need something from me.

Several times, I expressed my difficulty with the situation and that I felt it wasn't right. His response at those times was related to us both being adults and it said implicitly that we were making the *choice* to be there with one another. As his comfort level began to increase as the relationship wore on, he began to speak his mind and act more freely. My unease became increasingly worse. Eventually, there were times when he touched me in a way that was painful, and he spoke to me in language that was crude. None of this felt loving. When I continued to bring up my uneasiness, he continued to tell me that we were adults. At this point, he was clearly no longer validating my experience. It was like I was not allowed to discuss this with him. The power differential was still present, despite the fact that the therapeutic relationship had ended. I couldn't help but feel that if I had received these types of responses from a man other than my ex-therapist, my response or action would have been much different.

I finally recognized the physical and emotional pain I was in due to this relationship. I ended my involvement with my ex-therapist and was overwhelmed by the fall-out. I felt angry, defensive, alone. I had detached myself from other individuals who were dear to me. I was ashamed, humiliated, full of guilt, and full of pain. Perhaps most importantly, however, was that my sense of being able to judge who or what was safe for myself was shaken. This man had been my therapist. I had trusted him for years. I completely trusted the boundary I thought existed between us. In this case, it was a trust that I was safe from harm with him. I don't think he intended to hurt me, but his involvement with me re-injured me related to my original therapeutic issues.

The torment I have put myself through for getting involved with my ex-therapist is enormous. The anger I felt once I understood the clearly existing power differential has left me feeling victimized to some degree. Even as I was ending the relationship, I felt unable to share the full range of my feelings and the impact the relationship had on me and my life. It was as if I could not talk to him in that way because of who he was.

I am not comfortable simply labeling myself as a victim in this incident. I engaged in the relationship willingly. However, as my ex-therapist, he was well aware of my need for loving, physical touch. He was well aware of my fear of trusting men, as well as trusting myself to make good choices about men. I am being honest in saying I feel that a seduction occurred. The very issues which brought me to therapy were those which he sought to fill through a physical relationship with me. Despite my willingness to become involved with this man, he had an ethical responsibility to keep it from happening, whether he was attracted to me or not. The legal ethical guidelines for psychologists in his state ban sexual intimacies with former clients for five years. Our relationship occurred well within five years of our last official therapeutic contact.

In my opinion, this type of relationship should never occur between a previous client and therapist, regardless of the elapsed time. The therapist potentially knows everything about the client—strengths and vulnerabilities. The difference in power exists long after the therapeutic relationship ends. While my ex-therapist suggested that I had an equal role in the choice to get involved by saying we were both adults, I now believe the responsibility weighs more heavily on his shoulders, as the professional.

So I write this story now—a story which began as one of trust, professionalism, and growth. Then, the man I had called "confidant" and "therapist" turned into someone I no longer knew. He became a lover. He hurt me with his words and he hurt me with his body. Together, we shattered what had become whole in me. I am on a new path to putting the pieces back together, but I am no longer "in the chair."

CHAPTER SUMMARY

Knowledge of professional ethics is crucial to the everyday practice of counseling. Counselors who are faced with an ethical dilemma must be alert to ethical and legal standards. Professional organizations provide standards and codes that guide mental health professionals.

Philosophical ethics is the theoretical analysis of what is good, right, or worthy. Professional ethics is acceptable or good practice according to agreed-on rules or standards of practice established by a profession. Philosophical morality is the assessment of actions of a person against a theory in philosophical ethics and always refers to an act. Morality refers to the principles that guide an individual and often derive from a religious standard.

Licensure allows a person to practice a profession and prevents the practice of a profession by those who are unlicensed. Licenses can be revoked or suspended for violation of codes of ethics.

A five-level professional structure governs ethics for counselors: (1) colleges/universities; (2) professional organizations with aspirational codes of ethics but without internal enforcement mechanisms; (3) professional organizations that maintain and enforce a mandatory code of ethics; (4) enforce mandatory codes; and (5) the courts.

REFERENCES

Altekruse, M. K. (2001). *Counselor portability*. Presentation made to the American Association of State Counseling Boards. (Available from Dr. Altekruse at NTU, P. O. Box 311337, Denton, TX 76203-1337.)

American Psychological Association. (1986). *American Psychological Association guidelines for computer-based tests and interpretations*. Washington, D.C.: Author.

American Psychological Association, Office of Program Consultation and Accreditation. (1995). *Guidelines and principles for accreditation of programs in professional psychology*. Washington, D.C.: Author.

Anderson, B. S. (1996). *The counselor and the law* (4th ed.). Alexandria, VA: American Counseling Association.

Corey, G., Corey, M. S., & Callanan, P. (1998). *Issues and ethics in the helping professions* (5th ed.). Pacific Grove, CA: Brooks/Cole.

Dorken, H. (1976). *The professional psychologist*. San Francisco: Jossey-Bass.

Johnson, O. A. (1999). Ethics: Selections from classical and contemporary writers. Fort Worth, TX: Harcourt Brace.

Kant, I. (undated, 1949). *Critique of practical reason and other writings in moral philosophy* (L. W. Beck, Trans.). Chicago: University of Chicago Press.

Koocher, G. P., & Keith-Spiegel, P. (1998). *Ethics in psychology* (2nd ed.). New York: Oxford University Press.

Nietzsche, F. (1968a). The Antichrist. In W. Kaufmann (Ed. & Trans.), *The portable Nietzsche* (pp. 565–656). New York: Penguin. (Original work written in 1888).

Nietzsche, F. (1968b). Thus Spake Zarathustra. In W. Kaufmann (Ed. & Trans.), *The portable Nietzsche* (pp. 565–656). New York: Penguin. (Original work written in 1891).

Sinclair, C. (1996). A comparison of codes of professional conduct and ethics. In Bass et al. (Eds.), *Professional conduct and discipline in psychology*. Washington, D.C.: American Psychological Association.

Thompson, A. (1990). *Guide to ethical practice in psychotherapy*. New York: Wiley.

ACA Code of Ethics and Standards of Practice

To review this information, please see Appendix A beginning on page 420 of this book.

Ethics Principles of Psychologists and Code of Conduct

To review this information, please see Appendix B beginning on page 435 of this book.

CHAPTER 2

Counseling and the Mental Health Professions

Objectives
■ ■ ■ ■ ■ ■ ■ ■ ■ ■ ■

After reading this chapter, you should be able to:

- Provide a brief history of the counseling profession.
- Distinguish counseling from counseling psychology.
- Summarize education requirements, post-degree training, licensure, certification, and scope of practice for the mental health professions.

■ ■ ■ ■ ■ ■ ■ ■ ■ ■ ■

INTRODUCTION

Membership in a "profession" offers an individual status and responsibility. Law and medicine, both considered models of professionalism, are founded on a body of knowledge, technique, and practice. They are grounded in academic studies, have a scholarly base, and provide guidance to practitioners in the form of ethical and moral standards (e.g., medicine's Hippocratic oath). They allow practitioners several avenues of practice, even independent or freestanding practice. Over time, both psychology and counseling have become established as independent professions, technically on par with medicine and law. To present oneself as a counselor or psychologist means that the individual has accomplished much—graduate education, post-graduate training, admission to the profession by competitive examination, and linkage to a professional community with strict ethical standards. There is pride in such accomplishment.

Today, counseling and psychology are not alone in the mental health enterprise. There are a number of competitive mental health professions, each with its own history and traditions. It is important for any practicing mental health professional to be alert to the mental health professions and the standards of each. Medicine's specialty of psychiatry is the oldest established mental health profession. The youngest, in terms of pervasive legislative support, is marriage and family therapy. Social work and psychiatric nursing are two other mental health professions. Professionals with these affiliations make up the core of mental health providers.

In the mental health service arena, the core mental health professions both compete and cooperate. In all types of practice, it is likely that counselors will work with other mental health professions in the best interest of their clients. For example, many clients served by counselors in private practice may receive medication from a physician (either a primary care provider or a psychiatrist). It is crucial for independently practicing counselors to have working relationships with the prescribing physician. Many managed care organizations require nonphysician providers to have established cooperative service arrangements with board certified psychiatrists. Counselors working in agencies often work with a team of professionals assigned to the care of individual clients. Team members need to be alert to the limits of practice of other professionals. They also need to know the specialized skills associated with professional affiliation. It is unlikely that counselors will be involved in cases in which they are the only provider of mental health services.

COUNSELING AND COUNSELING PSYCHOLOGY

Counseling and counseling psychology were once considered sister occupations. They developed side-by-side as advances occurred in measurement/assessment, counseling theory, and mental health services. Counseling emerged from (and is still deeply embedded in) the educational setting, whereas psychology emerged as an academic discipline with applications in mental health settings. The first psychological clinic was founded in 1896 at the University of Pennsylvania (Fowler, 1996). Psychology's professional development preceded counseling by approximately 20 or 30 years, especially as related to licensure and independent mental health practice. The psychology specialty of **counseling psychology** is a bridge that spans the two professions; counseling psychology also acts as a boundary marker between them. If there is any doubt that the professions of counseling and psychology overlap in regard to activities and scope of practice, counseling psychology acts as a symbol of their similarity. On the other hand, if there are any doubts that the former sister occupations have emerged as discrete and competitive mental health professions, licensure standards of the two groups stand as distinguishing criteria. Although counseling psychologists may qualify for licenses in either psychology or counseling, requisite coursework or other requirements may be different between the two professions, requiring the licensure applicant to seek training beyond courses required for a degree. Master's-level counselors do not

meet licensure standards for psychology in states that adopt American Psychological Association (APA) standards, which require a doctoral degree in psychology. Even doctoral-level-trained counselors find it difficult to meet psychology licensure standards, as degree requirements for psychology clearly require a degree title in "psychology" (counseling, education, or counselor education doctorates do not qualify). The provinces of the professions have been defined.

Gelso and Fretz (1992) defined several unifying themes of counseling psychology that apply to counseling as well: (a) "the focus on intact, as opposed to severely disturbed, personalities"; (b) "the focus on people's assets and strengths and on positive mental health *regardless* of the degree of disturbance"; (c) an emphasis on brief interventions; (d) "an emphasis on person-environment interactions, rather than an exclusive focus on either the person or the environment"; and (e) "an emphasis on educational and career development of individuals and on educational and vocational environments" (pp. 7–9).

In regard to practice, there is little that differentiates the licensed professional counselor from the licensed psychologist. Both provide counseling (or psychotherapy). Both professional licenses typically allow for assessment of individuals with standardized measurement instruments, such as intelligence tests or personality tests. Both licensed professional counselors and licensed psychologists provide individual or group treatments. The two professions compete in the same market of mental health services. Of all the mental health professions, counseling and psychology are probably the most similar in philosophy and practice.

Counseling is not as closely aligned, either philosophically or historically, to the other mental health professions: psychiatry, social work, marital and family therapy, and psychiatric nursing. The following section describes credentials in counseling and the other mental health professions.

THE MENTAL HEALTH PROFESSIONS

Beyond having a good understanding of the ethical principles that direct the professions of counseling and psychology, it is important to be well acquainted with the other mental health professions. It is especially important to know each profession's *credentials* and **limits of practice** (the boundaries that demarcate the acceptable activities associated with a profession).

The following section summarizes professional identification and practice-related issues in counseling, psychology, and the other established mental health professions.

Counseling

Counseling is an emerging mental health profession that developed from the field of professional education. At the time of this writing, 46 states regulate the independent practice of counseling, which essentially enables the practice outside of schools or other educational settings. Because of counseling's historical linkage to schools, most professional counselors are educated in college or university departments or schools of education (where they usually have the option of receiving training to become school or nonschool community counselors).

The standard educational credential is the master's degree in counseling. Typically, the specific degree titles are the Master of Education (M.Ed.), the Master of Arts (M.A.) in education or counseling, the Master of Science (M.S.) in education or counseling, or the Master of Counseling (M.C.) degree. Doctoral-level practitioners may hold the Doctor of Philosophy (Ph.D.) in education or counseling. The Ph.D. is considered the highest academic degree in the United States, and traditionally has been viewed as a research degree and a practitioner degree in the mental health field. Some practitioners may hold the Doctor of Education (Ed.D.) in counseling, which is considered a professional degree in education, much like the Doctor of Medicine (M.D.) credential is a professional degree in medicine. Most schools or colleges at research universities offer the Ph.D. or the Ed.D. with an option of the Ph.D. While there is a trend away from the Ed.D. at large research universities, it is offered by increasing numbers of comprehensive (nonresearch) universities (Osguthorpe & Wong, 1991).

In most states, certified school counselors must have a master's degree plus documentation of specific coursework in education. Certification is usually granted to individual school counselors and is regulated by the state's department of education. Certification as a school counselor by such a department usually allows counseling practice *only* within elementary, middle, and secondary schools within the state. School certification in no way implies that the counselor has been credentialed to practice counseling independently (i.e., in private practice for a fee).

The independent practice of counseling is typically regulated by state licensure statutes. *Licensure* is a type of regulation that may restrict both the use of a professional title, such as "counselor," and the practice of counseling in fee-for-service, independent practice. **Independent practice** is the practice of counseling outside of an exempt institutional or other setting (exempt from oversight by the licensure authority). For example, counselors working for a state government may be exempt from the licensing requirement. Because the state hires counselors based on some standard, and their practice is supervised and monitored by the authority of the state agency, it may be unnecessary to require that these employees meet additional state licensure requirements. Exemptions from licensure, if any, vary from state to state, and counselors should know the generally accepted exemptions to identify counselors who are practicing legally or illegally. In many states, counselors employed by a state's mental health, vocational rehabilitation, or family services agency may not be required by statute to be licensed by the regulatory board. They may practice counseling consistent with and within the bounds of their employment; however, a counselor who works in an exempt setting as an employee is not able to practice independently for a fee outside of that employment. A private practice as a second job, no matter how small the practice, remains under the jurisdiction of the licensure authority.

Each licensure statute defines the nature and limits of counseling practice controlled by the law *and* defines exceptions (exempt practice). For example, Christian Science practitioners are often exempted—as long as they practice within the bounds of religious doctrine, they may counsel Christian Scientists about religious and personal issues. Typical exemptions include pastoral counselors, state and/or federal employees, school counselors (as long as they are certified by the state's department of education), hypnotists, and substance abuse treatment personnel. Each state's exemptions may be unique to the politics involved in passing the licensure statute in that state. Exemptions are usually listed in the statute itself.

Counselor licensure for independent practice in most states requires a relevant master's degree from an acceptable educational institution with coursework in identified core areas (such as assessment, group counseling, counseling ethics, and counseling theories). States often require one or two years of postmaster's degree supervised experience. Additionally, the license candidate must pass an examination of knowledge in the core areas of counseling by achieving an acceptable passing, or "cut," score, which is usually at or near the national mean. The newly licensed professional counselor (often designated "L.P.C." or other letters representing the state's title) is then allowed to charge clients for providing counseling services *independent* of any institutional oversight. Although practice is considered "independent," licensed professional counselors are obligated to follow ethical and legal rules set forth by the state's licensure board, which has the right to suspend or revoke the license for unethical or illegal practice. Additionally, some licensure boards require continuing education of licensed professionals and may impose other requirements to maintain a license. Licensure boards often adopt nationally accepted ethical codes, often the ACA's code or some derivative, and adopt administrative or disciplinary rules that constitute mandatory standards of practice to protect consumers.

In addition to licensure of independent practice and state regulation or certification of counselors in the schools, another type of credential is sought by mental health professionals—specialty certification.

Specialty certification (such as in the specialties of rehabilitation, mental health, family, or addiction counseling) is a voluntary means for professionals to identify themselves as trained and qualified specialists. Overseen by freestanding, nongovernmental, and national specialty certification boards, specialty certification identifies professionals who hold specialized training or experience in a circumscribed practice of counseling, usually assisting a unique subpopulation of clients. For example, certified rehabilitation counselors (CRCs) specialize in assisting individuals with disabilities; marriage or family counseling specialists serve couples or families. Specialists often limit their practices to clients who need their particular type of treatment. In effect, specialty certification is a means to identify and to designate counselors who have met specialty standards and who, to some degree, limit their practices to those activities consistent with the specialty.

Many specialty certification boards are given approval or credibility by a large, national professional association. In counseling, the Commission on Rehabilitation Counselor Certification (CRCC) certifies rehabilitation counselors. CRCC was organized with the support of the American Rehabilitation Counseling Association, an affiliate of what is now the ACA, and in conjunction with the National Rehabilitation Counseling Association (NRCA), a division of the National Rehabilitation Association. These organizations currently have seats on the commission. The CRC credential is the oldest and most widely recognized professional counseling specialty designation. The National Board

of Certified Counselors (NBCC) is the largest recognized specialty board in professional counseling. NBCC certifies general counselor and several specialty practitioners, such as addiction counselors and mental health counselors. (See Box 2.1 for information on contacting the ACA, NBCC, CRCC, and AASCB.)

Ordinarily, specialty certification requirements are equivalent to or more stringent than licensure standards. However, some counselors may be certified by a specialty board but may not be licensed to practice independently. Specialty certification is simply a way of identifying a practitioner's level of training and limits of practice; it is not a legal right to practice for a fee. Many counselors employed by a state government's vocational rehabilitation agency (usually a license-exempt setting) attain the CRC credential to demonstrate their commitment and allegiance to their specialty, even though they may be required by law to restrict their practice to their state government job (if they are not licensed).

The mental health field has seen a proliferation of questionable certifications. Anyone can set up a specialty certification by incorporating a "board," getting a post office box, and developing application forms. A number of boards advertised in professional newspapers and journals have questionable or nonexistent connections to legitimate professional organizations. These boards may charge exorbitant fees to provide impressive-sounding credentials. However, most professionals consider such certification as worthless, except perhaps in deceiving the public. Wise and ethical practitioners seek certification only by specialty boards that are well respected in the professional community and have established relationships with recognized organizations that represent a profession (such as the ACA). Practitioners who purchase credentials from freestanding and unrecognized certification bodies to imply a level of expertise or training may be considered unethical, if such an action misrepresents their professional qualifications.

The terms most commonly used to describe specialty designation in the counseling and mental health professions are **certification, board certification,** or **diplomate** (such as the diplomate of the American Board of Professional Psychology).

Psychiatry

Psychiatry, the oldest recognized mental health profession, is a medical specialty. All psychiatrists must be physicians and, therefore, must have a medical or equivalent degree. Two academic-professional degrees in the United States allow for licensure as a fully qual-

Box 2.1   Counseling Professional Organizations and Credentialing Bodies

The largest professional group representing professional counselors is the American Counseling Association (ACA), 5999 Stevenson Avenue, Alexandria, VA 22304-3300; phone 703-823-9800; the ACA Web site is www.counseling.org. The National Board of Certified Counselors (NBCC) is located at 3-D Terrace Way, Greensboro, NC 27403-3660; phone 910-547-0607; the NBCC Web site is www.nbcc.org. The address of the Commission on Rehabilitation Counselor Certification (CRCC) is 1835 Rohlwing Road, Suite E, Rolling Meadows, IL 60008; phone 847-394-2104; the CRCC Web site is www.crccertification.com. The address of the American Association of State Counseling Boards (AASCB) is 3-A Terrace Way, Greensboro, NC 27403-3660; phone 336-547-0914; the AASCB Web site is http://www.aascb.org.

ified physician—the Doctor of Medicine (M.D.) and the Doctor of Osteopathy (D.O.). The Doctor of Chiropractic (D.C.) degree, which sometimes allows for the title of "Chiropractic Physician," is not consistent with licensure for the full range of treatments typically associated with medical practice (e.g., chiropractors in most states are not allowed to prescribe medication). Graduates of medical schools outside the United States may have the M.D. degree or some variation, but once they pass a state's licensure standards for the Doctor of Medicine, they may legitimately use the "M.D." designation after their names.

The Doctor of Osteopathy (D.O.) degree is awarded by schools of osteopathy. Such schools are typically not associated with universities. Osteopathy is considered an alternative to the traditional training model of the profession of medicine, which is technically called "allopathy." It is a relatively young profession, developed as an offshoot of medicine based on philosophical differences. Osteopaths believe that physical structure is often implicated in the disease process, and physical manipulation is a primary osteopathic treatment. Additionally, osteopaths focus on the individual patient more holistically and view medication as an adjunct to other treatments. There is separate licensure for osteopathic physicians. Regardless, osteopaths are licensed to provide the full range of medical treatment, including surgery and the prescription of medication. In a substantial portion of academic curricula and in actual practice, there may be little that distinguishes an osteopathic physician from an allopathic physician. In fact, some D.O.'s specialize in psychiatry, seeking additional residency training after the education required for licensure as an osteopath.

A licensed physician must have the appropriate degree from an accepted school of medicine or osteopathy. Additionally, a one-year, general medical "internship" must be completed in a hospital. Candi-

dates are granted a license to practice as a physician upon completion of the internship and after passing the required licensure examinations (sometimes called "state board" examinations). This license allows the physician to perform all medical procedures and to prescribe medicine. Licensed physicians can practice independently—that is, in private practice. However, many hospitals will not grant a physician **hospital privileges** (the right to admit patients to and treat patients in the hospital) without post-internship training. Hospitals usually require a physician to show evidence of three or more years of additional training in a specialty—a residency. A **specialty residency** is a three year or more, hospital based training program that prepares the physician to practice diagnosis, general treatment, and specialty procedures in a specific area of medical practice, such as orthopedic surgery, internal medicine (diagnostics), pediatrics, dermatology, family practice, or psychiatry. There are many specialties in medicine and osteopathy. Physicians who have completed a specialty residency can legitimately claim to be specialists and can perform procedures, usually within hospitals where they have been granted hospital privileges. Many physicians who have completed specialty residencies also seek **specialty designation**—certification through a national specialty certifying board. Specialty designation through such a board has become the benchmark for advanced specialty practice.

The national certifying body in psychiatry is the American Board of Psychiatry and Neurology (ABPN; see Box 2.2). Physicians who have been licensed and have completed an approved (by the relevant specialty board) specialty residency may then sit for a specialty examination, a rigorous test of knowledge within the specialty. Upon passing the test, physicians are granted "diplomate" status—essentially receiving a diploma

---

Box 2.2   Psychiatry Professional Organizations and Credentialing Bodies

The largest professional association representing psychiatrists is the American Medical Association (AMA). Specifically related to psychiatry, however, the American Psychiatric Association (APA) is the largest professional group representing psychiatrists. The American Psychiatric Association is located at 1400 K Street, N.W., Washington, D.C. 20005; phone 202-682-6000; the APA Web site is www.psych.org. The American Board of Psychiatry and Neurology (ABPN) address is 500 Lake Cook Road, Suite 335, Deerfield, IL 60015-5249; phone 847-945-7900; the APBN Web site is www.abpn.com.

---

of completion of specialty training. Diplomates of a specialty board may describe themselves as "board certified" specialists.

It is not necessary to be a board certified specialist to practice a specialty. However, to legitimately and ethically practice a specialty, a physician should have at least completed an approved specialty residency. Many psychiatrists practice without the ABPN designation.

Board certification is no guarantee of competence, just as not having board certification is no indication of incompetence. However, board certification helps to identify duly trained and knowledgeable specialty practitioners.

Psychiatrists can perform physically intrusive procedures (e.g., surgery, blood tests, etc.), electroconvulsive therapy (ECT), psychotherapy, and medicinal treatment or pharmacotherapy. Additionally, by virtue of their general medical training, they may practice any and all procedures within general medicine. This training allows the psychiatrist to be uniquely qualified to understand and address the biochemical and medical aspects of mental disorders. By nature of their training, psychiatrists have a knowledge base to understand and to treat any co-morbid physical illness in individuals with mental disorders.

Psychology

Psychologists, unlike psychiatrists, cannot prescribe medications or perform other treatments or diagnostic procedures that are intrusive or insultive of the physical structure of the body. (It is noteworthy, however, that some psychologists, at the direction of some leaders of the APA, are actively petitioning state legislatures for the right to prescribe medication.) Psychologists, like counselors, can assess individuals with normative tests (such as IQ, aptitude, personality, or interest tests). Psychiatrists are not typically trained in psychometrics

or psychological testing procedures and interpretation, and they should not be involved in such activity without appropriate training and supervision. Psychiatrists, psychologists, and counselors, however, are all trained and licensed to perform psychotherapy or counseling.

Psychologists must be educated to the level of the academic doctorate (Doctor of Philosophy, Ph.D.; Doctor of Education, Ed.D.; or Doctor of Psychology, Psy.D.). The Psy.D. is usually awarded by freestanding, nonuniversity-affiliated schools of psychology; as such, institutions granting the Psy.D. degree typically do not seek to prepare psychologists for potential research or academic roles. Freestanding schools of psychology primarily train individuals for clinical practice. The Ph.D. is usually awarded in clinical psychology or counseling psychology at university colleges of arts and science. Schools of education at universities or colleges may award the Ph.D. or the Ed.D. in counseling, educational, or school psychology. Any of these psychology degrees, if obtained from a legitimately accredited college or university, may signify doctoral-level training in psychology. Increasingly, however, the preferred national standard for academic psychology programs is accreditation through the American Psychological Association's Committee on Accreditation.

To become licensed as a psychologist, candidates must complete the doctorate from an appropriately accredited program and perform one or two years of postdoctoral experience supervised by a licensed psychologist in a psychology service delivery program that is accepted or approved by the state licensure authority. Additionally, candidates must pass a stringent licensure examination. Once licensed, psychologists can independently provide the full range of psychological delivery services for a fee.

Psychologists may become board certified through the American Board of Professional Psychology (ABPP), which has linkage to the APA, or by the American Board of Psychological Specialties (ABPS), which has linkage

Box 2.3   Psychology Professional Organizations and Credentialing Bodies

The address of the American Psychological Association (APA) is 750 First Street, N.E., Washington, D.C. 20002-4242; phone 800-374-2721; the APA Web site is www.apa.org. The American Board of Professional Psychology (ABPP) is located at 514 E. Capital Avenue, Jefferson City, MO 65101; phone 573-634-5607; the ABPP Web site is www.abpp.org. The address of the American Board of Psychological Specialties (ABPS) is C/O the ACFE, 2750 E. Sunshine, Springfield, MO 65804; phone 417-881-3818; the ABPS Web site is www.acfe.com.

to the American College of Forensic Examiners (see Box 2.3). "Forensics" is a term that pertains to legal issues or testimony in legal proceedings as an expert witness. The ABPP is the older, more recognized and respected clinical credential, whereas the ABPS primarily identifies a specialist in expert witness testimony. Specialties designated by either the ABPP or the ABPS include clinical, counseling, family, rehabilitation, and neuropsychology. ABPP specialty certification requires up to five years of postdoctoral specialized experience under the supervision of a board certified specialist, plus an acceptable score on an examination of knowledge in the specialty.

The largest professional association representing psychologists in the United States is the American Psychological Association (APA).

Marriage and Family Therapy

Marriage and family therapists are licensed in 44 states (as of this writing). Marital therapy focuses on concerns experienced by couples. The focus is on the relationship itself, with an implied obligation to assist the partners to solve problems so they can maintain their relationship. Family therapy is a treatment approach that treats social concerns or individual problems (including psychopathology) within the context of the family (whether defined by genetics, law, common law, or choice) or recognized household. Other individuals may be involved in a family's problem and may be asked to participate in treatment; for example, a dating partner of a household member may be asked to attend a session.

Marital and family therapists are trained to treat relationships from a dyad (a two-person system) to a family system of three (a triad) or more individuals. Unlike other mental health professions that focus primarily on individual treatment, marital and family therapists are trained in theories of relationships and relationship treatment, which typically are grounded in social systems theory (Cottone, 1992). This unique theoretical and clinical training constitutes a critical difference in how therapists conceptualize and practice their profession; relationships clearly become the focus.

There is controversy over the existence of marriage and family therapy as a separate or independent mental health profession. Larger, more inclusive professions, such as psychology and counseling, have taken the stance that marital therapy and family therapy are actually treatment approaches that counselors or psychologists may choose with appropriate training and experience. They argue that marriage and family therapy is not a profession unto itself, but rather reflects a body of specialized techniques. Accordingly, freestanding licenses for marriage and family therapists are criticized by some psychologists and counselors who believe that any trained psychiatrist, psychologist, or counselor with specialty training can practice marital and family therapy. Because marital and family therapy is within the scope of practice of the other mental health professions in many states (e.g., counseling or psychology), it is considered a specialty of those professions rather than a separate profession.

Marriage and family therapists represented by the American Association for Marriage and Family Therapy (AAMFT; see Box 2.4) have taken the position that specialty training and specialty designation are not enough. They argue that in-depth, master's-level professional training is needed, primarily with grounding in social systems theory. Further, they have argued convincingly before state legislators that marriage and family therapy should be licensed as a freestanding mental health profession. As a result, many states license marriage and family therapy separately from other mental health professions.

To be licensed as a marriage and family therapist requires a master's degree in marital and family therapy (or a closely related degree), with specialized coursework in systems theory, marital and family treatment approaches, and marital and family therapy ethics, among more general areas. The college or university degrees

---

Box 2.4   Marriage and Family Therapy Professional Organizations and Credentialing Bodies

The address of the American Association for Marriage and Family Therapy (AAMFT) is 1133 15th Street, N.W., Suite 300, Washington, D.C. 20005-2710; phone 202-452-0109; the AAMFT Web site is www.aamft.org. The International Association of Marriage and Family Counselors is an affiliate of the American Counseling Association and can be contacted through the ACA at 5999 Stevenson Avenue, Alexandria, VA 22304-3300; phone 703-823-9800; the ACA Web site is www.counseling.org. The National Academy for Certified Family Therapists (NACFT) is located at 50 South Steele Street, Suite 222, Denver, CO 80209-2807; phone 303-377-1970; the NACFT Web site is www.nacft.com.

---

most often awarded are the Master of Science (M.S.) or Master of Arts (M.A.). One or two years of post-master's supervision of practice is also required. Upon completion of the supervised experience, applicants must pass an examination covering core knowledge areas.

Currently, there are no formally credentialed subspecialties of marriage and family therapy and, consequently, there are no specialty designations. In time, there will likely be specialty boards in marriage counseling, family work, children's issues, and other areas addressed by marriage and family therapists.

The AAMFT has a restricted membership composed of already licensed or highly trained and supervised professionals. The AAMFT offers an advanced membership level (clinical member), which acts much like a credential because the criteria for "clinical membership" are stringent. Interestingly, no examination is required to become a clinical member of the AAMFT. Rather, it requires two years of close supervision by an AAMFT "approved supervisor" once candidates have completed basic master's-level coursework. The emphasis on the supervisory relationship, rather than on an examination, appears to reflect the overall emphasis of the profession on "relationship."

Psychiatric Nursing

Psychiatric nursing has established itself as a mental health specialty through general certification in psychiatric and mental health nursing and through advanced "clinical specialist" certification as a mental health nurse. Training for the general practice of nursing requires at least two years of college-level preparation leading to state "registration" as a nurse (a registered nurse, R.N.). This registration is akin to state licensure of other health professions. To become a registered nurse, an individual must have an acceptable degree in nursing and must pass an examination over nursing theory and practice and

meet other registration requirements. There are three educational routes to meet educational requirements: the two-year associate's degree; the three-year diploma from a hospital-based "school" of nursing; and the bachelor's degree in nursing from a college- or university-affiliated nursing school. There is a trend away from the associate's degree and toward the bachelor of nursing degree as an entry-level training requirement.

Registered nurses are allowed to provide the full range of nursing services, primarily treating patients under the direction of a physician. However, in the psychiatric nursing area, certified "clinical specialists" in mental health nursing are master's-degree-trained nurses who have completed specialized coursework in psychotherapeutic approaches. Certified clinical specialists in mental health nursing make the case that they are trained to the level necessary to provide mental health treatments independent of physician oversight. Nurses are not licensed to administer psychological or educational tests or to independently prescribe medications.

The primary certifying body for professional nurses is the American Nurses Credentialing Center (ANCC; see Box 2.5). The ANCC was established under the auspices of the American Nursing Association (ANA). Over 90,000 nurses are certified by the ANCC. The ANCC certifies only those nurses holding the baccalaureate in nursing, regardless of state registration to practice nursing. Synopses of the two certifications in mental health nursing provided by the ANCC are as follows:

1. *"Psychiatric and mental health nurse" certification.* Generally, this level of certification requires the R.N., documented experience in psychiatric nursing, 30 contact hours of continuing education in coursework relevant to mental health practice, and a passing score on an examination over topics including theories/concepts, psychopathology, treatment modalities and nursing interventions, and professional issues and trends.

2. *The "clinical specialist" certification in either adult or child/adolescent psychiatric and mental health nursing.* Generally, this level of certification requires the R.N., documented experience in psychiatric nursing, documentation of experience in treatment modalities, a master's degree in psychiatric nursing or a closely related field, post-master's experience in psychiatric nursing, and a passing score on an examination that includes theories, psychopathology, treatment modalities, trends and issues, and other areas.

In addition to the ANA, the National League for Nursing (NLN) is respected as a professional nursing organization.

Social Work

Generally, social workers trained to the level of the master's degree specialize in one of two areas: public policy or clinical social work. In the mental health field, the clinical or psychiatric social worker is trained to practice as an independent mental health professional.

The degree required for independent practice in clinical social work is the Master of Social Work (M.S.W.) degree, which generally requires 60 to 72 semester hours of graduate coursework. Individuals seeking to be mental health professionals usually follow a graduate coursework track that focuses on psychotherapeutic treatment (rather than on social policy). Social workers often are trained to provide group and family treatments as well as individual psychotherapy, depending on the focus of the degree program. Social workers are not trained or licensed to administer psychological or educational tests or to prescribe psychotropic medications.

Licensure of social workers generally requires the M.S.W. and one to two years of post-master's supervised experience. A passing score on a licensure examination covering social work theory and practice often is required. Psychotherapy, group therapy, and couple or family therapy are all within the scope of practice of most social work licenses.

Master's-level-trained social workers who wish to be certified may seek credentialing through the Academy of Certified Social Workers (ACSW), which then allows its initials to be used after a social worker's name to designate advanced certification. The ACSW is a widely recognized and respected social work credential and is awarded under the direction of the National Association of Social Workers (NASW; see Box 2.6). The NASW is the largest national organization representing social workers. To be an ACSW, one must have a master's degree in social work, two years of post-master's paid experience in social work practice under supervision of a social worker, and an acceptable score on an examination over social work knowledge in assessment and service planning, intervention, professional development, ethical standards, and administration. The ACSW is a generic credential and does not necessarily reflect qualifications in "clinical" practice.

Social workers who are specialists in clinical practice may seek listing in the NASW "Register of Clinical Social Workers." There are two levels of certification in the "clinical" category: the "Qualified Clinical Social Worker" and the "Diplomate in Clinical Social Work." Both clinical credentials require a master's or doctoral degree in social work from a program accredited by the Council on Social Work Education, the social work accrediting body. Additionally, the ACSW credential or state licensure in social work and two years of supervised experience in "clinical" social work are needed. No examination is needed for the "Qualified Clinical Social Worker" credential, but candidates must pass an advanced examination to be a "Diplomate." The diplomate credential also requires three additional years of practice.

There is one other social work certification—the "School Social Work Specialist." This specialist must have a master's degree in social work from an accredited program, two years of postgraduate supervised school social work experience, and a passing score on a specialty test for school social workers. The ACSW is not needed.

Box 2.6 Social Work Professional Organization and Credentialing Body

The address of the National Association for Social Work (NASW) is 750 First Street N.E., Suite 700, Washington, D.C. 20002-4241; phone 202-408-8600 or 1-800-638-8799; the NASW Web site is www.naswdc.org.

Social work has established itself as a viable mental health profession. In fact, by level of education, it is the profession that competes most closely with master's-level professional counseling. Counselors and social workers may compete for similar jobs in mental health centers, hospitals, educational institutions, and other settings not requiring doctoral-trained professionals.

CHAPTER SUMMARY

Psychiatrists are licensed physicians that hold either the M.D. or D.O. degree. Candidates are granted a license to practice as a physician upon completion of an internship and after passing licensure (state board) exams. A specialty residency is usually a three-year, hospital-based training program that prepares the physician to practice diagnosis, general treatment, and specialty procedures. A specialty designation is certification through a national specialty certifying board. Professional organizations and credentialing bodies for psychiatrists include the AMA, the APA, and the ABPN.

Psychologists treat individuals with psychotherapy and counseling, and assess individuals with IQ, aptitude, personality, and interest tests. They cannot prescribe medications or perform treatments or intrusive diagnostic procedures. Psychologists must be educated to the level of the academic doctorate and must perform one or two years of postdoctoral experience supervised by licensed psychologists. They must pass a stringent licensure exam. Counseling psychologists provide counseling and psychotherapy and assess individuals with standardized measurement instruments, such as intelligence tests and personality tests in both individual and group treatment. Professional counselors hold a master's degree in counseling. Doctoral-level practitioners may hold a Ph.D. in education or counseling; some practitioners may hold an Ed.D. in counseling. Certified school counselors require a master's degree plus specific coursework in education. Licensure is a type of regulation that restricts both the use of a professional title and the practice of counseling in fee-for-service independent practice. Specialty certification is a voluntary means for professionals to identify themselves as trained and qualified specialists that is overseen by national specialty certification boards. Professional organizations and credentialing bodies for counselors include the ACA, the NBCC, and the CRCC. Professional organizations and credentialing bodies for psychologists include the APA, the ABPP, and the ABPS.

Marriage and family therapists focus on relationship concerns experienced by couples or families. A master's degree, specialized coursework, and one or two years of post-master's supervision of practice, and successful completion of an exam are required. Professional organizations and credentialing bodies for marriage and family therapists include the AAMFT, the ACA, and the NACFT.

Psychiatric nurses are master's-degree-trained nurses with specialized coursework in psychotherapeutic approaches. Two certifications are provided: psychiatric and mental health nurse, and clinical specialist. Professional organizations and credentialing bodies for psychiatric nurses include the NLN and the ANA.

Social workers generally specialize in public policy or clinical social work. A master's degree and one to two years of post-master's degree supervised experience are required. The NASW is the professional organization and credentialing body for social workers.

REFERENCES

Cottone, R. R. (1992). *Theories and paradigms of counseling and psychotherapy.* Needham Heights, MA: Allyn & Bacon.

Fowler, R. D. (1996, June). Clinical psychology celebrates its 100th. *The APA Monitor, 27*(6), 3.

Gelso, C. J., & Fretz, B. R. (1992). *Counseling psychology.* Fort Worth, TX: Harcourt Brace Jovanovich.

Osguthorpe, R. T., & Wong, M. J. (1991). *The Ph.D. versus the Ed.D.: Time for a decision.* Provo, UT: Brigham Young University. (ERIC Document Reproduction Services No. ED 339685)

CHAPTER 3

Introduction to Ethical Principles and Standards in Counseling

Objectives

▪ ▪ ▪ ▪ ▪ ▪ ▪ ▪ ▪ ▪ ▪

After reading this chapter, you should be able to:

- Explain the five "ethical principles" that guide the helping professions: autonomy, nonmaleficence, beneficence, justice, and fidelity.
- Understand the specific standards commonly found in ethical codes that guide practices in counseling and psychology, including confidentiality, privacy, privileged communication, avoiding potentially detrimental counselor-client relationships, informed consent, responsibility, and competence.

▪ ▪ ▪ ▪ ▪ ▪ ▪ ▪ ▪ ▪ ▪

INTRODUCTION

Counselors must deal with a variety of ethical issues and dilemmas. Specific standards guide their practice, including confidentiality and privacy, privileged communication, avoidance of potentially detrimental counselor-client relationships, informed consent, professional responsibility, and competence. Several basic ethical guidelines have evolved in the helping professions, primarily deriving from the field of biomedical ethics. Five ethical principles guide ethical standards in the field of counseling: autonomy, nonmaleficence, beneficence, justice, and fidelity.

ETHICAL PRINCIPLES

In the most recent edition of *Principles of Biomedical Ethics* (Fourth Edition), Beauchamp and Childress (1994) described four general principles of ethical medical practice. They stated:

> The four clusters of principles are (1) respect for autonomy (a norm of respecting the decision-making capacities of autonomous persons), (2) nonmaleficence (a norm of avoiding the causation of harm), (3) beneficence (a group of norms for providing benefits and balancing benefits against risks and costs), and (4) justice (a group of norms for distributing benefits, risks, and costs fairly). (p. 38)

These four ethical principles have been applied to other human service professions since the first edition (1979) of the Beauchamp and Childress book. In counseling, the principles are recognized as foundational guidelines for the specific ethical standards that address everyday practice. In fact, Kitchener (1984) published a seminal work applying the four ethical principles plus the "ethical rule" of *fidelity* to counseling psychology. According to Beauchamp and Childress, fidelity involves being true to one's word, and it also implies "trust" in the professional providing services and "loyalty" to the person being served. For example, Beauchamp and Childress (1994) stated: "Abandonment is a breach of fidelity, an infidelity amounting to disloyalty" (p. 430). A counselor should not abandon (discontinue services without adequate cause) a client in the middle of a contracted service. Kitchener believed that the four ethical principles (autonomy, nonmaleficence, beneficence, and justice) and the ethical rule of fidelity were foundational to ethical standards in counseling. In the literature of counseling, there has been widespread acceptance of these foundational principles, and, following Kitchener's lead, the rule of "fidelity" has been uncritically incorporated as an equal "principle" to the other four principles originally defined by Beauchamp and Childress.

Consider the five foundational principles listed in Box 3.1 as you read the following sections. Each standard is, to some degree, an application of one or more of the guiding ethical principles.

ETHICAL STANDARDS IN COUNSELING

Confidentiality and Privacy

The APA and ACA codes of ethics address the issue of privacy as related to confidentiality. The concepts are related, but there are differences. Privacy is a broader issue—counselors and psychologists, by nature of their work, are privy to the most personal and intimate information about their clients. The very fact of attending counseling is a very private matter to some individuals. U.S. culture generally respects the fact that individuals have a privacy right to maintain certain personal information—meaning it is not to be shared in an open forum. **Privacy** is the client's right to keep the counseling relationship a secret. Privacy relates not only to communications made by counselors, but also to the disposal of records, not being identified in a waiting room, tape recordings, use of credit cards for billing, use of computer services for scoring of tests or billing, and other documentary or business activities of the counselor. For example, if a client pays for services with a credit card, and the counselor lists a counseling agency name or profession on the receipt, the credit card company effectively has information that the individual paid for services to a counselor, which is a breach of privacy. If sessions are scheduled in a way that others may observe clients in a waiting room, privacy may be compromised. Both the ACA and APA codes of ethics state that an individual's privacy should be respected. Counselors must be mindful of this overriding standard.

Confidentiality more specifically addresses information communicated in the counseling context and was developed as something akin to an antigossip guarantee. **Confidentiality** is "the obligation of professionals to respect the privacy of clients and the information they provide" (Handelsman, 1987, p. 33). When information is communicated in the privacy of the formal counselor-client relationship, it is to be maintained as a secret within that relationship. Confidentiality is an ethical concept almost universally referenced in both professional association codes of ethics and legal ethical standards. When confidentiality is referenced by law or statute, it is referred to as "legal confidentiality." *Legal confidentiality* is a mandate that prevents the discussion of private communications

---

Box 3.1 A Simplified Summary of the Five Ethical Principles

Autonomy—To allow opportunity for self-determination and unfettered decision making; to honor the right to individual decision making

Nonmaleficence—"Primum non nocere" ("First let us do no harm"); to act so that harm is not done to clients

Beneficence—To do good; to help clients and benefit them

Justice—To be fair and egalitarian

Fidelity—To be loyal, honest, and to keep promises

(with a counselor in a professional context) from being revealed to other individuals. Counselors cannot reveal to other individuals what is communicated in counseling without potential penalty of law. Confidentiality guaranteed by a professional association alone (nonlegal confidentiality) does not carry the weight of law; however, it does carry the weight of the professional association, which can censure members or remove them from association membership. Confidentiality is a guarantee to clients that what they communicate privately in professional counseling will be held "in confidence"—for the ears and eyes of the counselor alone, unless clients specifically release the counselor from the promise.

There are limits and exceptions to both professionally mandated and legal confidentiality. In a classic court case, *Tarasoff v. the California Board of Regents* (VandeCreek & Knapp, 1993), a judgment was made that a psychologist had the "duty to warn" an endangered party when a counseling client made a direct threat on a life. In this case, the psychologist, a counselor at a University of California counseling center, warned the police of the threat. Unfortunately, he failed to warn the threatened individual, whom the client later murdered. The judgment stated that in such cases, confidentiality is overridden by the **duty to warn**—to inform endangered individuals of an identifiable threat (see the related discussion in Chapter 4). Threats to individuals should not be taken lightly; the authorities *and* the potential victim must be warned. Most ethical codes in psychology and counseling incorporate the practices suggested by the Tarasoff decision, and counselors should be alert to this limit of confidentiality.

Other common limits to confidentiality typically referenced in professional codes or statutes involve the following:

1. Required revelation to authorities of any case of substantiated or suspected child abuse or neglect;

2. Required revelation to authorities of intent to do harm to an individual or to society (e.g., through an illegal act);

3. Required revelation of counseling information to a parent or legal guardian of a client who is a minor child, on the request of the parent or legal guardian; and

4. In-case consultation with other professionals or students of counseling (often, however, identifying information must be disguised).

Counselors should inform clients prior to counseling of any professional and/or legal limits to the confidential relationship. Otherwise, they may share confidential information with others only with the direct written consent of clients.

From 1 July 1999 to 30 June 2000, there were more questions to the ACA ethics committee about "confidentiality" than any other ethical standard (Brown, 2001). Of 605 inquires, 231 were directly related to issues of confidentiality.

Confidentiality is not only a legal issue at the state level; federal laws and regulations also address it. A federal law prohibits the disclosure of information of individuals treated for chemical dependency (see Chapter 18). On 13 June 1996, the U.S. Supreme Court ruled that communications between psychotherapists and their clients are confidential and privileged. The decision specifically extended federal privilege, which, according to the ACA (1996), "already applies to psychiatrists and psychologists." The actual Supreme Court case extended privilege to a licensed social worker, which, according to the ACA (1996), "leave[s] the door open for inclusion of other providers of psychotherapy" (p. 10). The Supreme Court decision adds credence to a generally respected concept of confidentiality in counseling and psychology. On 14 April 2001, the United States Department of Health and Human Services instituted a rule providing new federal standards for the privacy of health records. That federal rule requires separate authorization by the patient for the release of psychotherapy case notes, such as information about medication prescription, medication monitoring, start and stop times of counseling sessions, type and frequency of treatment, and test results and summaries may be released with a standard request. However, the actual psychotherapy case notes, which often contain intimate details about a client's life, can be released only with separate specific consent of the client (New Patient Records Privacy Rule, 2001). Program benefits cannot be denied for a client's refusal to release the specific psychotherapy case notes. Compliance with the rule is required by 14 April 2003. Counselors or psychologists in private practice will also be required to follow the rule. Obviously, this rule protects undue invasion of a client's privacy.

Although confidentiality appears to be a straightforward concept, challenging situations may arise that make judgments difficult (see Box 3.2). One area of contemporary concern is related to individuals with human immunodeficiency virus (HIV) who may transmit the virus to others through intimate relations. Should the counselor breach confidentiality and warn a partner of

Box 3.2　Questions for Reflection

What value is the counseling profession if counseled individuals cannot be assured of confidentiality? If confidentiality cannot be guaranteed for an individual (or a group of individuals), what is the risk of nontreatment? Will individuals choose not to seek counseling if their confidentiality is not guaranteed? What is the risk to society if such individuals do not seek counseling?

an HIV-positive individual? Does Tarasoff apply? What are a counselor's responsibilities? These questions have received attention in the literature (e.g., Cohen, 1990; Harding, Gray, & Neal, 1993; Schlossberger & Hecker, 1996; Stanard & Hazler, 1995), but there are no clear answers. The ACA and APA codes do not give unquestionable guidance. However, an evolving norm to break confidentiality appears to be emerging in recent legal case law if the following criteria are met: (a) there is an identifiable party at risk; (b) there is a significant risk of infection; (c) a warning is likely to be effective in preventing infection; and (d) efforts to get the infected individual to reveal the infection to the endangered party have failed (see Reaves, 1999). Revelation appears justified if the criteria are met. Like all complicated legal matters, there have been exceptions to the prevailing case law. In a Texas Supreme Court ruling (*Santa Rosa Health Care Corporation v. Garcia* [1998]), a provider was not held responsible to inform the wife of a hemophiliac of her possible exposure to HIV. The issue becomes a balancing act. Which is most critical—the risk of a life, the risk to society, or the risk of a most basic ethical standard at the foundation of a profession?

Acceptable ethical standards are often established after a serious concern has been raised in the literature or in the courts. Counselors must remain current with the professional literature to ensure that they are alert to potential ethical dilemmas; by doing so they can act to prevent a breach of ethics before it happens.

CASE SCENARIO 3-1

Confidentiality

The mother of a 21-year-old female client calls, concerned about her daughter, and wishes to share information with the counselor about the daughter's status. In the course of the conversation between the mother and the counselor, the mother asks about the daughter's progress in counseling. Should the counselor answer?

NO.　The counselor should not answer without specific written consent from the client that allows communications

with the mother. In fact, counselors should not even acknowledge that they are seeing any clients to anyone over the phone, especially without the client's written consent. This is true of anyone seeking information about an individual's participation in counseling, even an identified lawyer or judge. Counselors should be leery about communicating about clients over the phone on incoming calls, but may more safely communicate to individuals on calls they place with the permission of their clients.

CASE SCENARIO 3-2

Confidentiality

A counselor at a party meets a social worker who referred a client to the counselor. The social worker begins to discuss the client with the counselor while other individuals are milling around. Should the counselor discuss the case?

NO.　The counselor should communicate to the social worker that they should not talk about cases at the party. With appropriate permission from the client, they should talk about the case only in a private, professional (not social) context. At that time, they should discuss only information directly pertinent to the social worker's role in the case and allowed by client consent. It is also prudent in this day of advanced technology (e.g., e-mail and cellular phones) to evaluate the privacy of any professional conversation, however proper, to ensure that confidentiality or privacy is not unintentionally breached.

CASE SCENARIO 3-3

Confidentiality

The spouse of a counselor meets the counselor at the counselor's office and sees a client walk out of the counseling office. The spouse asks, "What's his problem?" Should the counselor discuss the case with the spouse?

NO.　A counselor's confidentiality does not extend to a spouse. In some cases, it does extend to coworkers in agencies or to other professional colleagues, but even in these cases, the coworkers or colleagues must be informed of the confidential nature of the information and must guarantee that they will maintain confidentiality.

Regardless, the service-providing counselor is ultimately responsible ethically if confidentiality is breached.

CASE SCENARIO 3-4

Confidentiality

A counselor has had a rough day and goes to a local cosmetology salon after work. The counselor begins discussing tough cases with the cosmetologist but is careful to disguise names and identifying information about specific clients. Has anything unethical occurred?

YES. If it is possible that someone can identify a client by context, confidentiality has been breached. If, for example, a relative or friend of a client overhears such a conversation and can piece together the information, thereby identifying the client, an unethical act has occurred. Only in certain professional situations can a general discussion of disguised cases be ethical, such as a professor's discussion of a case in a relevant college class. Even if the risk of identifying a client is not significant, any practice of public discussion of cases is generally harmful of the trust of confidentiality. It risks decreasing the confidence of the lay public in the profession of counseling and subjects both clients and other counselors to misunderstanding or even ridicule.

Privileged Communication

Privileged communication is a legal right of clients found in state or federal statutes. **Privileged communication** is a client's right to prevent the revelation of confidential information in a legal proceeding (e.g., in a legal hearing or courtroom). A counselor cannot be forced to testify on a client's case if the privilege stands. Privileged communication is owned by the client, and only the client can waive the privilege allowing testimony (Hummel, Talbutt, & Alexander, 1985; Reaves, 1999). Privileged communication, being a legal right, is not found in professional codes of ethics; it is statutory.

Like confidentiality, there are limits to privileged communication. In many states, stipulations override any psychotherapist or counselor privileged communication in cases of substantiated or suspected child abuse or neglect. In such cases, a judge can order a counselor to testify on otherwise confidential information. Such disclosure is not illegal, and the counselor is given immunity from prosecution (i.e., cannot be found guilty of breaching privileged communication). Privilege also may not stand when a client sues a counselor.

In some states, communications are "privileged" in civil but not criminal cases by licensure statute. If a client is charged with a felony and goes to criminal court, attorneys can request the counseling case files and the judge can order the counselor to testify. Such a request to testify is called a **subpoena,** an order to appear in a legal hearing with all requested information. On the other hand, when a civil court (not a criminal court) such as a divorce court subpoenas a counselor, the counselor must refuse to testify about a client's case on the grounds of the client's lawful right to privileged communication. Other examples of civil cases in which a counselor cannot testify include workers' compensation disability/injury hearings, social security disability hearings, child custody hearings, termination of parental rights hearings (unless there is an allegation of child abuse or neglect and an exemption to privileged communication), and other legal proceedings in which a crime allegedly has not been committed. As with confidentiality, counselors must know the limits of privileged communication written into licensure laws or other state statutes. (See the general review of privileged communications laws across several mental health professions by Herlihy & Sheeley, 1987.) The ethics committee of a state counseling association or a licensure board of a state can help a counselor identify those laws that affect professional practice. Most ethical codes require that counselors respect the laws in the jurisdiction within which they practice.

The U.S. Supreme Court ruled in the *Jaffee v. Redmond* (1996) case that communications between licensed psychotherapists and their patients are privileged communications. This ruling was groundbreaking because it has federal implications (not limited to one state) and because it was liberal in its definition of psychotherapist and psychotherapy. The privilege was applied to a client who was seeing a licensed clinical social worker. Remley, Herlihy, and Herlihy (1997) stated:

> The *Jaffee* decision has created an interpretation and generalization problem because state statutes have established privilege for the clients of specified licensed mental health professionals, whereas the Supreme Court decision has created a privilege for the "patients" of "psychotherapists." Because there is no definition of "psychotherapist" in federal law, federal courts will probably review state statutes to determine whether licensed mental health professionals are psychotherapists when determining whether their clients have privilege. No state currently licenses psychotherapists; rather, licensure is accorded to counselors, psychiatrists, psychologists, social workers, and others who may provide psychotherapy services. Whether privilege will be extended to clients of licensed counselors in federal courts in the future may depend on whether licensed counselors are recognized by the courts as "psychotherapists." The

---

Box 3.3   Questions for Reflection

Confidentiality and privileged communication are related concepts, although privileged communication applies strictly to legal settings (e.g., preventing revelation of confidential information before the courts). Which of the five ethical principles underpin the concepts of confidentiality and privileged communication (autonomy, nonmaleficence, beneficence, justice, or fidelity)?

Jaffee decision may force the counseling profession to formulate a clear answer to the currently debated questions of whether counseling and psychotherapy are synonymous or separate and distinct activities, and whether counselors are willing to call themselves psychotherapists.

Only time will tell the implications of the *Jaffee v. Redmond* decision for the counseling profession.

CASE SCENARIO 3-5

Privileged Communication

A vocational rehabilitation counselor is hired by a workers' compensation insurance company to assess an alleged injured worker. The insurance claims adjuster refers the case and is suspicious that the claimant is malingering (faking an injury or illness) to collect workers' compensation injury benefits. The claims adjuster requests that the counselor evaluate the client to plan and to recommend rehabilitation services, if necessary. The counselor does not explain any limits of confidentiality and does not have the claimant sign a waiver of privileged communication. Counseling clients in the counselor's state are afforded privileged communication in civil legal proceedings. Later, the counselor is asked to testify on the case by a workers' compensation administrative law judge. The counselor was hired by the workers' compensation insurance company, so the counseling information is owned by the insurance carrier. Therefore, the counselor must testify. True or false?

FALSE.   The client/claimant owns the privilege, and only the client can waive the privilege in a civil case. If it appears that court testimony is going to be part of a case assessment, the counselor should obtain a written waiver of privileged communication before assessing the client. This issue also involves another ethical standard, informed consent, which we address later in this chapter.

CASE SCENARIO 3-6

Privileged Communication

A marriage counselor sees a husband and wife in counseling conjointly. The counselor is subpoenaed by a judge regarding divorce proceedings at the request of the husband's attorney. The husband claims that the counselor had evidence of the wife's mental instability from previous medical and hospital records as well as from observation of the wife in marriage counseling. The husband believes the marriage counselor can testify as to the effects of the wife's mental disorder on the marriage. The husband waives privileged communication. The counselor refuses to testify on the basis of the privileged communication of the wife. Is the counselor acting legally?

IT DEPENDS.   In some states, privileged communication stands only in cases in which there has been one-on-one communication between a client and a therapist. If other persons are present (as in group counseling or marriage, couple, or family counseling) the privilege may not stand. Whether privilege stands depends on how the statute is written and on past case law. In some states, relationship theory and family counseling are referenced into the definition of practice in the psychology or counselor licensure statute. Therefore, it can be assumed by the law itself that privilege extends to circumstances involving relational treatment or family counseling. If there is no state case law on this issue, a final conclusion on this issue is not possible. A counselor who is unsure whether privileged communication applies should consult or hire an attorney before attending any legal proceeding, thereby seeking representation on that issue before the court.

CASE SCENARIO 3-7

Privileged Communication

An allegation of child abuse is made against a counselor's client, who is the parent of the child in question. The counselor is subpoenaed by a hearing officer to attend a parental rights termination hearing. The counselor must go to testify. True or false?

TRUE.   In states where privileged communication is overridden by licensure or other statutes in cases of child abuse or neglect, the counselor should appear and be prepared to testify in those cases. However, the counselor should alert the judge or hearing officer of the client's right to privileged communication and should formally request that the privilege be overridden as a part of the record, based on the relevant statute.

Detrimental Counselor-Client Relationships

Historical Use of the Terms "Dual" and "Multiple" Relationships.   The literature of the mental health professions historically associated the term **dual relationship** with a misuse of therapist power or authority. Such relationships led to situations wherein the therapist not only served as a professional helper, but also established a second role with the client that was always viewed as harmful. This is reflected in the older codes of ethics; for example, the outdated American Association for Marriage and Family Therapy (AAMFT) "Code of Ethics" stated that therapists "make every effort to avoid dual relationships with clients that could impair professional judgment or increase the risk of exploitation" (AAMFT, 1991). The American Counseling Association (ACA, 1995) code stated that "dual relationships" should be avoided "when possible." The term "dual relationship" has lost favor in the recent literature because it is unclear and, to some degree, misleading. For example, every counselor in private practice is in a dual (or for that matter, "multiple") relationship with clients by nature of counseling. The counselor is a professional helper and is also involved in a contracted financial arrangement and a record-keeping arrangement. The therapist in private practice is at least involved in three professional relationships with clients: helper, business service provider, and record keeper. The term "dual relationship," therefore, is not necessarily a negative term, and most codes acknowledge this by qualifying any discussion of dual relationships with a statement addressing "exploitation" of clients. A dual relationship that is an exploitive relationship is wrong. Across the board, codes of ethics place a ban on "exploitation" of clients. Unfortunately, the term "dual relationship," in and of itself, holds an undeserved negative connotation, and the newer codes of ethics have begun to modify terminology in discussing these matters. However, revisions often hold to the "dual relationship" tradition, but focus on banning all interactions outside of counseling at the expense of potentially beneficial interactions.

Ethical breaches in this area of counseling are the most prevalent and potentially damaging to clients and the profession of counseling as a whole. The position of the authors is that part of the problem may be related to unclear or inexact terminology and ethical guidance on the "dual relationship" issue. Accordingly, we make some sweeping recommendations related to terminology as applied to this area of ethics.

Perhaps part of the negative connotation associated with the term "dual" relationship has to do with the associated concern of exploitive sexual relationships. Ethical codes in the mental health professions ban sexual relationships with current clients, and, in the case of former clients, ban involvement for a period two to five years subsequent to professional involvement. There is unanimous agreement among ethical codes: *sexual intimacies with clients are unethical.* In states where psychotherapeutic practice is regulated, such relationships are also illegal. They are considered a breach of the most basic trust between a mental health professional and a client. This ban is not just a moral issue; research evidence indicates that such relationships are damaging to clients (see the discussion in Pope, 1988 and the study by Bouhoutsos, Holroyd, Lerman, Forer, & Greenberg, 1983). There are no compelling reasons in defense of sexual relations with current or recent clients. Counselors would have difficulty defending themselves in cases of substantiated or acknowledged sexual activity of this sort. In any discussion of potentially detrimental relationships with clients or former clients, sexual intimacies stand alone and deserve to be addressed directly and unequivocally. Related to legal repercussions of sexual relations with clients, Reaves (1999) stated, "the largest civil judgments have been reserved for those professionals that engage in such heinous conduct" (p. 23). Both the ACA and APA codes of ethics make it clear in freestanding sections that sexual intimacies with clients are unethical. The codes ban sexual intimacy with former clients for a period of time, but allow for professional scrutiny even after that time has passed.

Licensure boards often report that mental health professionals have had licenses suspended or revoked on the basis of improper sexual intimacies with patients or trainees under their supervision. The sexual contact issue between patients and counselors is very commonly the charge that leads to suspension or revocation of a professional license on ethical grounds. The Association of State and Provincial Psychology Boards (ASPPB, the professional association of licensure boards), which keeps statistics on disciplinary actions of its boards, reported that the highest number of reported disciplinary actions against psychologists fit into the category of "sexual/dual relationship with patient"; 715 of 2206 disciplinary actions were in the sexual/dual relationship category (ASPPB, 2001).

Aside from the issue of sexual intimacies with current or former clients, the term "multiple" relationships has gained favor recently, implying two or more therapist-client relationships. The term is used in the more recent ethical code revisions. Typically, the term "multiple relationship" is linked to the issue of exploitation or harm to clients. Exploitive or harmful multiple roles are considered unethical.

Harmful versus Nonharmful Interactions.   Although it is wise to avoid potentially detrimental relationships with clients or trainees, not all relationships with clients outside of counseling are technically illegal or unethical (see the analysis by Anderson & Kitchener, 1998). Certainly an unplanned, accidental social contact is not unethical; for example, a counselor could hardly be blamed for running into a client at a party or athletic event. Other cases also may not be unethical:

1. A professor of counseling is impressed by a student. After the student graduates, she hires him to work in a counseling service that she owns.
2. A supervisor of counselor licensure candidates gets to know his supervisees over several years of supervision. Friendships develop that last beyond the formal supervision agreement.
3. A counselor encounters a former client whose counseling was terminated several years earlier. The counselor remembers that the client provided a professional service, which he currently needs. He then negotiates to purchase the services from the former client.

These relationships are not illegal or technically unethical, but still warrant scrutiny. Counselors generally know if a relationship holds the potential of harming the client, impairing professional objectivity, or compromising the client's best interests or well-being (Kitchener, 1988). Counselors should also consider the appearance of impropriety as well as the unintended level of coercion or influence they may have on impressionable clients. The general rule is *avoid potentially detrimental relationships,* or, if such a relationship is imminent, clearly examine the ethical or legal ramifications.

Some have argued that a total ban on relationships outside the contracted therapeutic relationship is unjustified. Lazarus (2001) has been a vocal critic of such bans in psychotherapy in general. Tomm (1993), in the specialty of marriage and family counseling, has also been adamant in arguing against a total ban on extratherapy interactions. Their positions are founded on personal experiences wherein clients or trainees actually benefited by interactions outside of the counseling or supervising process. Both have made compelling arguments that an outright ban on all nontreatment (or nonsupervision) interaction misses the point—the issue is really detriment or exploitation by unethical practitioners. They argue that the focus should be on banning exploitation or harmful interactions, not on banning all nonprofessional interactions. For example, should a counselor feel guilty about buying Girl Scout cookies from a client? Technically, this could be viewed as unethical, but it certainly is not likely to be harmful, and in some sense, it might be beneficial to the client. Although buying cookies from a client can be viewed as a trite example, there are many examples wherein therapists are put in positions of interacting with clients in ways that are innocent to the therapeutic relationship and may actually be beneficial to the client—attending a ceremony or family funeral, accompanying a client on an anxiety-producing activity, purchasing a product or service in a way that does not compromise counseling. An outright ban appears to be unjustified.

However, there may be a slippery slope. Haug (1993) has made a case that involvement in interactions outside of counseling with a client may lead to potentially detrimental relationships (one step on a slippery slope may lead to a fall). By banning all extra-therapeutic interactions, ethical authorities may act to prevent truly harmful ethical breaches.

Counselors and therapists are human. No licensure board or ethical authority can control feelings. Pope, Keith-Spiegel, and Tabachnick (1986) found that "attraction to clients is a prevalent experience among both male and female psychologists" (p. 155). *Feelings* may develop and may be uncontrollable, but there are controls on *actions* of professionals. The issue really relates to the potential harm of a client or trainee. The basic question is, "Is the client/trainee in danger of physical or emotional harm?" But even that question is not answered easily. In a survey of male counselors, Thoreson and his associates found that "although relatively few respondents (1.7%) reported having engaged in sexual misconduct with clients during a professional relationship, the prevalence rate increased to 17% when the definition of sexual misconduct was expanded to include (a) students and students under supervision, and (b) occurrences of sexual misconduct after the professional relationship" (Thoreson, Shaughnessy, Heppner, & Cook, 1993, p. 429). In a later survey of female counselors, "Counselors viewed sexual contact in current professional relationships as less ethical than contact in subsequent relationships, although relationships with former clients were seen as less ethical than relationships with former trainees. Compared with male counselors from a previous study, female counselors were less likely to report sexual contact in their professional roles" (Thoreson, Shaughnessy, &

Frazier, 1995, p. 84). There may be differences of opinion about the level of unethical practice depending on the gender of the individual questioned. Counselor trainees need to be alert to the issues. Educators should train mental health professionals about ways to handle attraction and sexual feelings toward clients ethically (Harris, 2001; Vasquez, 1988).

As to whether there is danger of physical or emotional harm, a healthy friendship that develops during a formal counseling or supervisory relationship and lasts beyond the formal contracted services may not be considered harmful. Sexual intimacies are another matter. To reiterate, research shows that clients most usually are in danger of emotional harm when involved sexually with a counselor or therapist (Bouhoutsos et al., 1983; Pope, 1988). To cross the line of sexual intimacy is a misuse of power for the therapist. Clients must be viewed, to some degree, as emotionally vulnerable by nature of their status. Seduction by clients is considered a symptom of some emotional disorders. Counselors must take extra precautions against any semblance of nonprofessional relationships.

If there is any question that the therapist may be "set up" by a client, or if there is discomfort regarding a counseling relationship, the counselor should take reasonable precautions. Strategies to consider include leaving the door slightly opened so that a secretary or colleague can see in the office, but in a way that the voice is somehow screened to maintain confidentiality; taping all sessions with client consent; and inviting a second therapist to do co-therapy with the client's permission. Just as care must be taken to protect clients from potential harm from interactions with counselors, care must also be taken to protect counselors from the malicious intentions of some clients.

Controversy exists over the issue of potential harm related to the use of touch in therapy. Some psychotherapeutic techniques actually encourage touch between therapists and clients. Other techniques may involve deep muscle massage or physical contact. Therapists who use these techniques believe that touch is therapeutic. Regardless, the ethical codes clearly ban sexual intimacy—any sexual contact is unacceptable. Therapists who use touch as part of their therapeutic repertoire should use it cautiously and appropriately. Hand-holding may be acceptable; touching a person's knee or thigh can be considered crossing the ethical line. Having a witness available during treatments may also prevent the misinterpretation of touch in therapy or may minimize the therapist's legal vulnerability. Counselors should review state statutes and standards

related to physical contact between counselors and clients if they plan to use such modalities. Some state guidelines are stricter than others.

Relationships with clients that are not officially considered "counseling" are controversial. Current standards related to "dual," "multiple," or "exploitive" relationships appear to be inadequate in addressing concerns raised in the professional literature.

A Need for Clearer Standards.   The high number of complaints, questions, and infractions in the category of "dual" or "multiple" roles in counseling may be related to confusion over the terms. The terms "dual," "multiple," and "exploitive" relationships are inexact. *Although there is historical linkage to these terms, they should be abandoned.* Inexact terminology and ambiguous or equivocal standards are problematic for the ethics committees of credentialing bodies. The recommended standards in Box 3.4 are more exacting, using behavioral-specific terminology. The recommended standards avoid the terms *dual, multiple,* and *exploitive.* Nonprofessional relationships are separated from contiguous professional relationships (such as counseling a group and an individual at the same time, or when there is a role change during the counseling process such as going from marriage counseling to individual counseling). Several standards that relate to interactions with clients, former clients, trainees, and research participants are consistent. There is less room for equivocation as to whether a counselor has been exploitive or blinded by impaired judgment. The focus becomes detriment to clients. The recommended standards also allow for potentially beneficial relationships with clients other than the contracted therapeutic relationship, with the client's written permission, clear forethought, and adequate consideration before the relationship is initiated.

Although no ethical standards can give absolute guidance in every case of an ethical dilemma, clear guidance on matters involving potentially detrimental counselor-client relationships appears warranted, especially in light of the number of infractions in this area. Therefore, the recommended standards are offered with the intention of facilitating educated discussion, dialogue, and debate on these matters. The question is, "Is there a better way to communicate right and wrong when it comes to interaction with clients in and outside of the therapeutic relationship?"

Differences in the Proposed Standards and Traditional Standards Banning Potentially Detrimental Relationships.   The following differences exist between the traditional standards on the "dual

Box 3.4 Recommended Standards—Potentially Detrimental Counselor Relationships

1. Sexual, intimate, or romantic counselor-client relationships

   a. Sexual, intimate, or romantic counselor-client interactions or relationships with current clients or their family members are banned.

   b. Sexual, intimate, or romantic counselor-client interactions or relationships with former clients or their family members are banned for a period of five years following the last professional contact.

2. Counselor-client, nonprofessional relationships (other than sexual, intimate, or romantic interactions or relationships)

   a. Counselor-client, nonprofessional relationships with clients, former clients, or their family members should be avoided.

   b. When a counselor-client, nonprofessional relationship or interaction with a client or former client (for a period of five years after the last professional contact) may be potentially beneficial to the client or former client, the counselor must document in case records prior to the interaction or relationship the rationale for such an interaction or relationship, the potential benefit, and anticipated consequences for the client or former client and other individuals significantly involved with the client or former client. Such interactions or relationships should be initiated with appropriate written client consent. (Examples include, but are not limited to: attending a graduation, wedding, or other formal ceremony; attending a funeral for a family member; purchasing a service or product provided by a client or former client; visiting an ill family member; accompanying a client on an activity that would be otherwise distressing.) When unintentional harm or injury occurs to the client or former client, or to an individual significantly involved with the client or former client, due to the nonprofessional interaction or relationship, the counselor must show evidence of an attempt to remedy such harm or injury. This standard in no way relieves the counselor of legal liability for harm or injury to clients.

3. Counselor-client, contiguous professional relationships

   When a counselor is involved in more than one counseling modality with a client (e.g., counseling an individual and a group contiguously) or changes counseling modality from the originally contracted relationships, the client is allowed fully informed written consent and the right to refuse services related to a contiguous modality or a change in modality. Clients must be fully informed of any anticipated consequences (e.g., financial, legal, personal, or therapeutic) of counselor contiguous modalities or changes in the way counseling is accomplished. Examples of modality changes include: (a) changing from individual to marital or family counseling; (b) changing from an evaluative to a therapeutic role or vice versa; and (c) changing from a counselor to a researcher role (i.e., enlisting clients as research participants).

4. Counselor-trainee (supervisee or student) relationships

   a. Sexual, intimate, or romantic counselor-trainee interactions or relationships with current trainees are banned.

   b. Counselors must not provide counseling services to their current trainees.

   c. Counselor-trainee, nonprofessional or contiguous professional relationships should be avoided.

   d. When a counselor-trainee, nonprofessional or contiguous professional relationship or interaction may be potentially beneficial to the trainee, the counselor must document

Chapter 3   Introduction to Ethical Principles and Standards in Counseling   ■   35

in appropriate training records prior to the interaction or relationship the rationale for such an interaction or relationship, the potential benefit, and the anticipated consequences for the trainee and other individuals significantly involved with the trainee. Such interactions or relationships should be initiated with appropriate trainee written consent. (Examples include, but are not limited to: attending a graduation, wedding, or other formal ceremony; attending a funeral of a family member; purchasing a service or product provided by the trainee; visiting an ill family member; accompanying and providing support to a trainee during a nonprofessional activity or an activity tangential to the professional role; co-authoring a research or case study report.) When unintentional harm or injury occurs to the trainee or to an individual significantly involved with the trainee, due to the nonprofessional or contiguous professional interaction or relationship, the counselor must show evidence of an attempt to remedy such harm or injury. This standard in no way relieves the counselor of legal liability for harm or injury to trainees.

5. Counselor-research participant relationships (When research participants are former clients or when research activity includes the provision of counseling services, standards 1b and 2b also apply.)

   a. Sexual, intimate, or romantic counselor-research participant interactions or relationships with current research participants are banned.

   b. Counselor-research participant, nonprofessional relationships should be avoided.

   c. When a counselor-research participant, nonprofessional relationship or interaction may be potentially beneficial to the research participant, the counselor must document in case records prior to the interaction or relationship the rationale for such an interaction or relationship, the potential benefit, and anticipated consequences for the research participant and other individuals significantly involved with the research participant. Such interactions or relationships should be initiated with appropriate written consent. When unintentional harm or injury occurs to the research participant or to an individual significantly involved with the research participant, due to the nonprofessional interaction or relationship, the counselor must show evidence of an attempt to remedy such harm or injury. This standard in no way relieves the counselor of legal liability for harm or injury to research participants.

Box 3.5   Questions for Reflection

Are the recommended standards in Box 3.4 clearer than the standards in the current ACA and APA codes of ethics? What problems can be anticipated with the recommended standards? Are there gaps or inconsistencies in the current ACA or APA standards? Are there gaps or inconsistencies in the recommended standards?

relationship" issue and the recommended standards in Box 3.4:

1. The recommended standards expand the ban on sexual relationships to intimate and/or romantic interactions.

2. The recommended standards unequivocally ban sexual, intimate, or romantic interactions for a five-year period for clients and former clients. There is no "gray area" of potential dispute over whether a client has been harmed or exploited after a period of two years since the last professional contact (past standards

allowed for such behavior so long as it was not exploitive or harmful two years subsequent to the end of counseling).

3. The recommended standards separate nonprofessional interactions and contiguous professional interactions, giving clarity on such matters. For example, if a client is involved in group counseling and is seen contiguously in individual counseling, ethical dilemmas may arise (see Chapter 16). If there is a change in counseling modality (from individual to group or family counseling), counselors need specific guidance on how to handle these contiguous professional relationships. In the past, contiguous professional relationships and nonprofessional relationships were not distinguished in the "dual relationship" language.

4. Although nonprofessional relations should be avoided, the recommended standards do not ban potentially beneficial relationships or interactions with clients as long as there is forethought and the client provides written consent. Counselors no longer need to be leery about overtures to clients if the proposed interaction is potentially beneficial and if precautions are taken to prevent a "slippery slope." Client written permission, which is required of all professional activities, should be required in this area as well. Counselors must not be relieved of any responsibility for inadvertent harm done by their actions.

5. The recommended standards use the term *trainee* to mean both students and supervisees and give clear guidance to the extent of acceptable relations with trainees. Trainees are not considered vulnerable by nature of a mental illness or the presence of a close therapeutic relationship with the supervisor or educator, so relationships subsequent to the training are not banned.

6. The recommended standards related to research participants are clear and fully consistent with the other standards in the category.

Overall, the standards in Box 3.4 are recommended as one possible means to clarify an ethical standard that sorely needs clarification.

Confronting Counselors in Potentially Detrimental Relationships with Clients or Trainees. As with breaches of all ethical standards, counselors who are aware of colleagues who are involved in potentially detrimental relationships with clients or trainees are obligated to confront the counselor in question. Most ethical codes allow a counselor *first* to confront the suspected unethical practitioner to attempt to rectify

the problem before being obligated to report the concern formally to a legal or ethical authority. Colleagues have great potential influence over perpetrators of unethical behavior by addressing ethical concerns openly and by re-educating (or educating, in some cases) the unethical parties of her ethical obligations. However, colleagues should report to authorities serious infractions or persistent concerns subsequent to re-educating or warning the perpetrator. In most cases, the reporting party is legally or professionally protected from retribution (e.g., immunity from any sort of counter legal suit). It is a professional counselor's responsibility to confront an unethical colleague. Borderline ethical concerns or dilemmas warrant discussion of the concerns, as well as consultation with an authority on ethical matters (e.g., a member of a professional association's ethical practice committee).

Counselors need to be cautious about potentially detrimental relationships with clients or trainees. Concerned counselors should first discuss ethical standards with another knowledgeable professional. A clear breach of standards warrants a means of rectification other than official report. Consultation with authorities is warranted if the concerns are persistent or of a serious or sexual nature.

Informed Consent

Informed consent is the client's right to agree to participate in counseling, assessment, or other professional procedures or services after such services are fully explained and understood. Caudill (1998) stated:

> The premise, established in the 1972 case of *Cobb versus Grant* and the 1980 case of *Truman versus Thomas,* behind informed consent is that a patient should have access to all meaningful information in order to formulate an intelligent decision about whether to proceed with a particular course of treatment of a medical or psychological condition. The doctrine was originally defined with reference to medical care, where the options were generally quite clear and susceptible to formula application. (There are only so many ways to set a broken bone or to treat an infection). (p. 7)

However, there may be complications when this concept is applied to counseling. Caudill (1998) continued:

> The application of informed consent to psychotherapy, however, has led to some degree of confusion and murkiness. One of the problems in this regard is that unlike medicine, in the field of psychotherapy there are over 100 theoretical orientations and schools of thought.

> ## Box 3.6   Questions for Reflection
>
> What ethical principle(s) is(are) at the root of the standards in Box 3.4 relate to avoiding potentially detrimental relationships with clients—autonomy, nonmaleficence, beneficence, justice, or fidelity?

Thus, a therapist with a Freudian theoretical orientation will approach a problem markedly differently than one with a cognitive behavioral orientation. (p. 7)

Regardless, clients have the right to know the potential benefits or detriments of therapy or counseling. They should be fully informed of significant facts about procedures, what typically occurs, and the probable outcomes before treatment. Clients should be informed of the credentials or training of treating professionals, especially as related to specialized procedures. There should be no counselor coercion involved in a decision to undergo treatment. Alternative treatments, or alternatives to treatment, should also be addressed (see Caudill [1998] and Handelsman & Galvin [1988], for specific issues related to content and format of informed consent procedures).

Counselors generally present this information to clients in writing. The information should be clear and presented at a level that the client can understand (Handelsman, Kemper, Kesson-Craig, McLain, & Johnsrud, 1986). Counselors should ensure that clients are intellectually and emotionally able to understand the information provided so that they can make a true voluntary judgment (Handelsman & Galvin, 1988). Essentially, clients have freedom of choice to participate in counseling services.

Handelsman and Galvin (1988) provided a format for informed consent that lists questions the client can pose to the therapist. This format fosters open discussion of therapeutic issues and helps to establish a professional relationship and rapport. More recently, Handelsman (2001) makes a compelling argument that informed consent should be considered a process, not an event. The consent process should be incorporated into the treatment process.

Informed consent alone does not legitimize treatment approaches. Caudill (1998) stated:

Of course, the fact that informed consent is given does not legitimize treatment approaches which are illegal or unethical. For example, in California there was a case in which therapists allegedly used a technique that in-

volved beating the patient. In fact, they had informed consent forms which purported to authorize such treatment. In *Rains versus Superior Court* (1984), a California appellate court essentially held that it didn't matter what the consent form said, no such treatment was permissible. In addition, the cases are quite clear that an informed consent form will not legitimize treatment by an individual who does not have the requisite professional license. (p. 7)

Informed consent provisions do not override the responsibility of counselors to be nonmaleficent and to provide competent services.

Obtaining informed consent is not as serious a concern when clients are of legal (adult) age to consent and when they voluntarily seek treatment. However, it becomes a more serious concern when a client is a minor, when clients may not be fully competent to consent to treatment, or when there is a third-party referral. A **third-party** referral source is another individual, an agency, or an organization that directs the client to the provider of services. Clients referred by a third party sometimes go willingly and voluntarily submit to treatment. Other times, therapy is **compulsory,** meaning it is required for some legal reason. Compulsory therapy is initiated by a third-party referral source, usually as a form of rehabilitation or ongoing assessment when (a) the client has been involved with, is accused of, or is guilty of an illegal or potentially harmful act, or when (b) treatment is viewed as a means to return a person to gainful activity when the person is receiving benefits or services for disability or other conditions. Examples of compulsory counseling are (a) a judge-ordered referral of an ex-offender who, as part of rehabilitation, must undergo counseling; (b) a workers' compensation company-referred injured client who is at risk of losing benefits and is required to undergo vocational assessment; (c) a chemically dependent parent who is at risk of losing her children through parental rights termination unless there is sobriety; and (d) a misbehaving child who is required to undergo assessment or therapy as a condition for return to school or other settings. In all of these cases, a third party requests evaluation or correction of the client's problem or condition. It is a client's right to consent to counseling. Even in cases of compulsory counseling, clients have the right to refuse services. If legal issues are involved, clients have the right to know if their counselor will testify on the case. If a counselor may be called to testify, the client must waive privileged communication, if applicable, and must be informed of the possible outcomes *before* accepting counseling services.

Minor children involved in counseling technically do not have the right to consent to treatment; their parents or legal guardians have the right to consent for them. This is true in most states, but there are exceptions. Some states (by statute) allow minor children to seek counseling related to birth control, venereal disease, pregnancy/abortion, or substance abuse/dependence treatment without the consent of a parent or legal guardian. Barring such exceptions, parents or legal guardians not only have the right to consent to their children's counseling, they also, in most cases, may have the right to know what occurs in counseling and they may request termination of counseling at any time.

It is therapeutically and ethically wise for the counselor to consult a minor about treatment issues and to enlist the minor's participation when parental or guardian consent is given, even if there are limits to the confidential relationship. The limits of confidentiality must be addressed with the minor in a way that the minor understands: The minor must know that what is discussed in counseling can be shared with the parent or legal guardian.

Some counselors attempt to get a verbal or written agreement from parents or legal guardians that they will respect the minor's right to confidentiality. This is no guarantee, however. Unless there is clear statutory provision and case law for a parent or legal guardian's ability to waive both informed consent and access to case information, such agreements must be viewed as tenuous, or even potentially misleading. Separate agreements that waive parental rights to informed consent or access to files may not be upheld legally. Certainly a parent or legal guardian would have the right to cancel such an arrangement at any time.

Obtaining informed consent is even more complicated when elderly or disabled persons are involved (Pepper-Smith, Harvey, Silberfeld, Stein & Rutman, 1992). Can an elderly person with serious mental deterioration (e.g., dementia) consent to psychological or counseling assessment or treatment? Can a relative be consulted or informed? Many elderly clients may have diminished capacity to make informed judgments, yet they may be considered legally "competent." These clients may be in vulnerable circumstances if an unscrupulous practitioner is involved. It is wise to obtain consent to inform and to consult with involved family members or to do family intervention in most cases in which a person's ability to make judgments is diminished. Such a person's "informed consent" to treatment may be in order technically. However, ethically, the involvement of family members may be necessary to ensure appropriate treatment when there is no legal guardian.

CASE SCENARIO 3-8

Informed Consent

A physician writes an order for a counselor to assess the IQ of a geriatric patient at a hospital. The patient consents. The IQ test and a thorough mental status assessment produce results of diminished capacity, but overall the IQ is in the low borderline range of measured intelligence. The counselor sends the bill for the assessment to Medicare and sends a co-payment bill to the spouse of the patient, who protests both the rationale for the test and the bill itself. The spouse claims that she should have been informed. Was anything done unethically in this case?

IT DEPENDS. The question on this case is, "Were the IQ testing and mental status assessment necessary for diagnostic or treatment reasons?" If so, nothing was done illegally, although a professional consult with a second opinion would be recommended, and appropriate consultation with family members (with permission) seems justified.

CASE SCENARIO 3-9

Informed Consent

A husband and wife attend their first marriage counseling session. They are never informed about the potential length of treatment, the probable results, or alternative treatments. The counselor simply begins doing treatment. Is this ethical?

NO.   Most codes of ethics either explicitly or indirectly require: (a) the counselor to formally present procedure-relevant information; and (b) the client to formally consent before treatment is initiated.

Professional Responsibility

Professional responsibility is the counselor's obligation to clients and to the counseling profession. It relates to the appropriateness of professional actions. In all cases, a professional counselor's responsibility is to advance the welfare of clients (Margolin, 1982). Counselors must not discriminate against those who seek their services. They cannot subjugate their obligations to their clients for the sake of monetary or other rewards. Professional counselors are also obligated to end their services if it becomes clear they are not helping or benefiting their clients.

Professional counselors are obligated to their employers as well as to their clients. They have a responsibility to serve their employers in a way that demonstrates competence and ethical sensitivity. Sometimes, however, conflicts arise between employing institutions and the best interests of clients. If such conflicts jeopardize the integrity of professional services rendered to clients, the counselor has an obligation to attempt to remedy the compromising conditions. When a reconciliation of institutional and professional conflicts is not forthcoming, the counselor has an obligation to terminate the affiliation with the employing institution, rather than to persist or compound the injustice. Just as physicians should not compromise the health and safety of their patients in a hospital that provides less than minimal standard care, counselors should refuse to treat clients in settings where clients' best interests are in conflict with institutional interests. Professional counselors should always seek to develop treatment (work) environments where the employing institution's goals and objectives are consistent with a primary responsibility for competent and timely service to clients. (See the related discussion in Chapter 8 on office and administrative practices.)

It is also important to recognize that the client is the *person who is served,* not the person or institution paying the bill (Cottone, 1982). Inexperienced or uninformed counselors or counselors who are unduly influenced by their business interests often mistakenly feel that their obligation is to the paying party. The counselor's principal obligation is *always* to the person receiving services—the client or counselee—unless there is potential danger to another individual or to society. In such a case, the counselor has a duty to warn the endangered party and the authorities. The presence of a third party (a person or institution) paying for services does not diminish, redirect, or in any way compromise the counselor's primary obligation to the counselee.

There may be limits to confidentiality or privileged communication if there is a third-party payer. In such cases, clients must be fully informed prior to the onset of treatment of any limits to confidentiality or privileged communication to ensure informed consent. Clients have the right to refuse treatment, even with the presence of a third-party payer, and counselors must respect clients' rights to refuse treatment. Counselors have a clear responsibility to persons who receive their counseling services.

Persons who refuse treatment when there is third-party oversight may suffer consequences directly related to the relationship between the client and the overseeing person or agency (e.g., a third-party referral source or payer). Those consequences should be clearly circumscribed to the client's relationship with the third party and should not impinge on the client's relationship with the counselor. Counselors have a primary responsibility to assess or treat fully informed clients competently and to communicate their findings only with the client's consent.

CASE SCENARIO 3-10

Responsibility

A counselor receives a referral from a friendly caseworker at the state family services agency. The caseworker communicates with the counselor that he is counseling a woman who is "disturbed." He wants her evaluated presumably for treatment potential, but notes that the information is really needed for possible parental rights termination. The counselor receives many cases from the referring caseworker at the family services agency, and the counselor agrees to assess the referred individual, saying "I'll see what I can do." The client comes with the full intention of later receiving counseling under the auspices of the family service agency. Instead, the client is evaluated and never scheduled for later treatment, and the counselor's report appears as evidence in a parental rights termination hearing. Is this unethical?

PROBABLY.   Assuming that the counselor informed the client of limits to confidentiality and/or privileged communication, this is still a probable breach of responsibility. This is especially true if the findings were in any way influenced by the prior stated intent of the caseworker to seek parental rights termination. The client should have been fully informed of the intent of the evaluation and its potential uses. Additionally, the evaluation should be as objective as possible in its recommendations, using standard and accepted means of assessment.

CASE SCENARIO 3-11

Responsibility

A school counselor/evaluator is given a case referred by a teacher who is a close friend. The teacher communicates to the counselor that the student is a "BD" (behavior-disordered) student and the teacher wants this child "out of my classroom" and "placed in special education." The counselor finds that much of the problem may be "embedded in" and "specific to" the teacher-student relationship, meaning there is less support for a diagnosis of BD in other settings. Yet the teacher has documented well the misbehavior of this student. The counselor recommends to the special education panel that a diagnosis/classification of BD is warranted. Is this ethical?

POSSIBLY.   The counselor has an obligation to assess, historically and otherwise, the student's behavior in other settings with other authority figures. If the counselor's recommendation is primarily based on the friend's documentation and without otherwise independent competent assessment of competing outcome/recommendations, there is a breach of responsibility and probably a case of professional incompetence.

CASE SCENARIO 3-12

Responsibility

A researcher does a followup study on a previously tested hypothesis. The outcome conflicts with the prior conclusion and statistical findings. The researcher writes an article on the initial findings, but fails to acknowledge the followup study. The researcher also fails to acknowledge the work of one of her students who collected the data during the original study. The report is later published. Is this unethical?

YES.   There is a breach of "responsibility" on two counts. First, the researcher has an obligation to report the findings of the followup study, even if it means the article might not be published. This omission is a breach of responsibility to the profession. Secondly, there is a breach of responsibility to the student who assisted in the study. The student should receive acknowledgment formally on the manuscript.

Competence

Professional "competence" focuses on two aspects of professional practice: (a) the quality of provided services and (b) the boundaries or scope of professional activity. Boundaries of professional activities involve whether the professional is trained, experienced, and licensed appropriately to perform certain procedures or treatments. **Counselor competence,** in the ethical sense, means that the counselor or therapist is capable of performing a minimum quality of service and that the service provided is clearly within the limits of her training, experience, and practice as defined in professional standards or regulatory statutes. A counselor who tells a client not to take prescribed medication is unethical and is practicing illegally (literally practicing medicine without a license). A counselor who uses hypnotic technique may well be within the ethical and legal bounds of the counseling profession, depending on the counselor's past training and experience with hypnotic technique and regulation of hypnosis by statute. Both the quality issue and the scope of practice issue are implied in any discussion of professional competence.

Similarly, professional counselors or therapists who may be licensed to practice certain procedures or techniques should not perform those activities without appropriate specialized training in the area of practice in question. In some cases, they may request a professional consult with a specialist. A **professional consultation** is a paid, formal arrangement wherein a consulting counselor obtains a second opinion, professional advice, or even supervision (to the extent of possible co-therapy) on an issue of concern from a knowledgeable, competent colleague. A licensed counselor with a rehabilitation counseling degree who does marriage counseling without ever having had a course or supervision in marriage counseling is practicing unethically (literally crossing the border of professional competence). In such cases, the rehabilitation

---

Box 3.9   Questions for Reflection

Which ethical principle(s) appear(s) foundational to the concept of professional competence—autonomy, nonmaleficence, beneficence, justice, or fidelity?

---

counselor has an obligation to refer the client to or consult with an appropriately trained and credentialed marriage counselor. Likewise, a marriage counselor should not suddenly begin chemical dependency treatment with a substance-dependent client without specialized training in chemical dependency; referral to or consultation with an appropriately trained rehabilitation counselor is in order. Just because a professional is licensed to perform a procedure does not mean he or she can ethically perform the procedure. All physicians are *licensed* to do brain surgery, yet only those who have specialized training or experience in the procedure should be actively and independently doing it.

CASE SCENARIO 3-13

Professional Competence

A school counselor has a client who is showing excessive anxiety; the counselor later learns that the client has been diagnosed by a psychiatrist as having "generalized anxiety disorder." The school counselor begins to arrange individual sessions of counseling and performs a technique called *systematic desensitization*, a behavioral technique used to ameliorate symptoms such as phobic anxiety when the anxiety results from the presentation of a specific object or situation. Is the counselor practicing unethically?

POSSIBLY NOT.   If the anxiety is specifically school-related and the counselor has been trained and supervised successfully in systematic desensitization, this activity is within the realm of competent practice. School anxieties, such as a phobia to testing or speaking in public, are treatable ethically by appropriately trained school counselors. On the other hand, if the phobia is not school-related, or if the counselor is attempting to treat the generalized anxiety disorder, this is questionable practice. It is generally understood that generalized anxiety disorder is not best treated by systematic desensitization. Also, the psychiatrist, if he or she was treating the client actively, should have been consulted, even regarding treatment of a circumscribed school phobia.

CASE SCENARIO 3-14

Professional Competence

A marriage counselor is counseling a couple that is having sexual difficulties. The problem is a complicated one, and the counselor's interventions have not produced a desirable outcome. The counselor has explained to the couple that although he has training to address certain sexual problems, he does not view himself as a sex therapist. Regardless, the husband and wife implore the counselor to continue treatment. They do not want to start over with another professional. The counselor continues to counsel the couple. Is this unethical?

PROBABLY.   If other trained sex therapists are available, the counselor should either refer the couple to a sex therapist or professionally consult with one. On the other hand, if no other professional is available, the counselor has an obligation to immediately seek appropriate training or guidance and to serve the couple as best as possible.

CHAPTER SUMMARY

Five principles guide ethical standards in the helping professions: autonomy, nonmaleficence, beneficence, justice, and fidelity. Counselors must abide by the ethical standards of confidentiality/privacy, privileged communication, avoidance of potentially detrimental relationships, informed consent, professional responsibility, and competence.

Confidentiality is the obligation of professionals to respect the privacy of clients and the information they provide. Counselors cannot reveal to others what is communicated in counseling without potential penalty of law, where there is legal confidentiality.

Privileged communication is a client's right to prevent the revelation of confidential information in a legal proceeding. A counselor cannot be forced to testify on a client's case if the privilege stands.

Potentially detrimental relationships may involve sexual, intimate, romantic, or inappropriate (1) counselor-client interaction; (2) counselor-client, nonprofessional relationships; (3) counselor-client, contiguous professional relationships; (4) counselor-trainee relationships; and (5) counselor-research participant relationships. Mental health professionals engaged in such relationships may face license suspension/revocation and legal consequences.

Informed consent is the client's right to agree to participate in counseling, assessment, or other professional procedures and services after such services are fully explained and understood. Clients must be fully informed of significant facts about procedures and possible outcomes before treatment.

Professional responsibility is the counselor's obligation to clients and to the counseling profession. Counselors have a primary responsibility to advance the welfare of their clients. They also bear responsibility to serve their employers in a way that demonstrates competence and ethical sensitivity.

Counselor competence means that the counselor or therapist is capable of performing a minimum quality of service and that the service is clearly within the limits of the counselor's training, experience, and practice as defined in professional standards or regulatory statutes. Counselors without specialized training in a particular area should refer clients to appropriately trained professionals.

REFERENCES

American Association for Marriage and Family Therapy. (1991). *Code of ethics.* Washington, DC: Author.

American Counseling Association. (1995, June). Code of Ethics and Standards of Practice. *Counseling Today, 37*(12), 33–40.

American Counseling Association. (1996, July). Supreme Court extends confidentiality privilege. *Counseling Today, 39*(1), 1, 6, 10.

Anderson, S. K., & Kitchener, K. S. (1998). Nonsexual posttherapy relatioships: A conceptual framework to assess ethical risks. *Professional Psychology: Research and Practice, 29,* 91–99.

Association of State and Provincial Psychology Boards. (2001). *Ethics, law and avoiding liability in the practice of psychology.* Montgomery, AL: Author.

Beauchamp, T. L., & Childress, J. F. (1994). *Principles of biomedical ethics* (4th ed.). New York: Oxford University Press.

Bouhoutsos, J., Holroyd, J., Lerman, H., Forer, B. R., & Greenberg, M. (1983). Sexual intimacy between psychotherapists and patients. *Professional Psychology: Research and Practice, 14,* 185–196.

Brown, S. P. (2001). Report of the ACA ethics committee: 1999–2000. *Journal of Counseling and Development, 79,* 251–252.

Caudill, O. B. (1998, February/March). The hidden issue of informed consent. *Family Therapy News,* p. 7.

Cohen, E. D. (1990). Confidentiality, counseling, and clients who have AIDS: Ethical foundations of a model rule. *Journal of Counseling and Development, 68,* 282–286.

Cottone, R. R. (1982). Ethical issues in private-for-profit rehabilitation. *Journal of Applied Rehabilitation Counseling, 13*(3), 14–17, 24.

Handelsman, M. M. (1987). Confidentiality: The ethical baby in the legal bathwater. *Journal of Applied Rehabilitation Counseling, 18*(4), 33–34.

Handelsman, M. M. (2001). Accurate and effective informed consent. In E. Welfel & E. Ingersoll (Eds.), *The mental health desk reference: A sourcebook for counselors and therapists.* New York: Wiley.

Handelsman, M. M., & Galvin, M. D. (1988). Facilitating informed consent for outpatient psychotherapy: A suggested written format. *Professional Psychology: Research and Practice, 19,* 223–225.

Handelsman, M. M., Kemper, M. B., Kesson-Craig, P., McLain, J., & Johnsrud, C. (1986). Use, content, and readability of written informed consent forms for treatment. *Professional Psychology: Research and Practice, 17,* 514–518.

Harding, A. K., Gray, L. A., & Neal, M. (1993). Confidentiality limits with clients who have HIV: A review of ethical and legal guidelines and professional policies. *Journal of Counseling and Development, 71,* 297–305.

Harris, S. M. (2001). Teaching family therapists about sexual attraction in therapy. *Journal of Marital and Family Therapy, 27,* 123–128.

Haug, I. (1993). *AAMFT luncheon plenary on "Dual Relationships: Sex, Power, and Exploitation."* (Audiotape cassette recording published through the AAMFT Resource Link). Norcross, GA (1-800-241-7785).

Herlihy, B., & Sheeley, V. L. (1987). Privileged communication in selected helping professions: A comparison among statutes. *Journal of Counseling and Development, 65,* 479–483.

Hummel, D. L., Talbutt, L. C., & Alexander, M. D. (1985). *Law and ethics in counseling.* New York: Van Nostrand Reinhold.

Jaffee v. Redmond et al. 1996 WL 315841 (U.S. June 13, 1996).

Kitchener, K. S. (1984). Intuition, critical evaluation, and ethical principles: The foundations for ethical decisions in counseling psychology. *Counseling Psychologist, 12,* 43–55.

Kitchener, K. S. (1988). Dual role relationships: What makes them so problematic? *Journal of Counseling and Development, 67,* 217–221.

Lazarus, A. A. (2001, January/February). Not all "dual relationships" are taboo: Some tend to enhance treatment outcomes. *The National Psychologist, 10*(1), 16.

Margolin, G. (1982). Ethical and legal considerations in marital and family therapy. *American Psychologist, 37,* 788–801.

New patient records privacy rule takes effect. (2001, Spring). *Practitioner Update, 9*(1), 1, 4.

Pepper-Smith, R., Harvey, W. R., Silberfeld, M., Stein, E., & Rutman, D. (1992). Consent to a competency assessment. *International Journal of Law and Psychiatry, 15,* 13–23.

Pope, K. S. (1988). How clients are harmed by sexual contact with mental health professionals: The syndrome and its prevalence. *Journal of Counseling and Development, 67,* 222–226.

Pope, K. S., Keith-Spiegel, P., & Tabachnick, B. G. (1986). Sexual attraction to clients: The human therapist and the (sometimes) inhuman training system. *American Psychologist, 41,* 147–158.

Reaves, R. P. (1999). *Avoiding liability in mental health practice.* Montgomery, AL: Association of State and Provincial Psychology Boards.

Remly, T. P., Herlihy, B., & Herlihy, S. B. (1997). The U. S. Supreme Court decision in *Jaffee v. Redmond:* Implications for counselors. *Journal of Counseling and Development, 75,* 213–218.

Santa Rosa Health Care Corporation v. Garcia, 964 S.W.2nd 940 (Texas, 1998).

Schossberger, E., & Heckler, L. (1996). HIV and family therapists' duty to warn: A legal and ethical analysis. *Journal of Marital and Family Therapy, 22,* 27–40.

Stanard, R., & Hazler, R. (1995). Legal and ethical implications of HIV and duty to warn for counselors: Does Tarasoff apply? *Journal of Counseling and Development, 73,* 397–400.

Thoreson, R. W., Shaughnessy, P., & Frazier, P. A. (1995). Sexual contact during and after professional relationships: Practices and attitudes of female counselors. *Journal of Counseling and Development, 74,* 84–89.

Thoreson, R. W., Shaughnessy, P., Heppner, P. P., & Cook, S. W. (1993). Sexual contact during and after the professional relationship: Attitudes and practices of male counselors. *Journal of Counseling and Development, 71,* 429–434.

Tomm, C. (1993). *AAMFT luncheon plenary on "Dual Relationships: Sex, Power, and Exploitation."* (Audiotape cassette recording published through the AAMFT Resource Link). Norcross, GA (1-800-241-7785).

VandeCreek, L., & Knapp, S. (1993). *Tarasoff and beyond: Legal and clinical considerations in the treatment of life-endangering patients* (2nd ed.). Sarasota, FL: Professional Resource Press.

Vasquez, M. J. T. (1988). Counselor-client sexual contact: Implications for ethics training. *Journal of Counseling and Development, 67,* 238–241.

CHAPTER 4

Ethics and the Law

Objectives
■ ■ ■ ■ ■ ■ ■ ■ ■ ■ ■

After reading this chapter, you should be able to:

- Describe the complex relationship between ethics and the law.
- Identify the four legal mechanisms that are relevant to the practice of counseling: Professional ethics committees, state licensure boards, criminal courts, and civil courts.
- Explain the key challenges facing counselors during the four phases of the counseling relationship, including: counselor competency, informed consent, confidentiality and privileged communication, exceptions to confidentiality, recordkeeping, dangerousness and crisis concerns, and termination issues.

■ ■ ■ ■ ■ ■ ■ ■ ■ ■ ■

INTRODUCTION

Many counselors find the relationship between their clinical practices and the dictates of the law unsettling, and this relationship makes them feel vulnerable. In the past, it was not uncommon for counselors simply to hope that their basically sound clinical methods would be congruent with appropriate legal practices. Such a reactive posture is no longer adequate for professional counselors, who now need to understand and actively manage the legal aspects of their practices.

Counseling has become a dynamic, well-recognized profession. As a result, counselors have taken on increasingly responsible roles in terms of the independence of their practices and how their work affects their clients. The standing of counselors as independent and responsible professionals has been recognized legally by 46 states and the District of Columbia through counselor licensure (at the time of this writing). It is not unusual for counselors to be involved in such highly charged events as diagnosing their clients as having a serious mental disorder, recommending that custody of a child be terminated, testifying at a hearing regarding the effects of spousal abuse, or counseling an adult with mild mental retardation regarding reproductive rights and options. Counselors also provide forensic services related to their counseling expertise in countless civil, criminal, and administrative hearings. It is only reasonable to assume that with increased visibility and professional status, counselors will be held legally accountable for their actions. More im-

Box 4.1   Question for Reflection

Examine the current ACA and APA codes of ethics and law. They address the relationship between ethics and law. How are practitioners directed by these codes?

portantly, counselors must understand and protect the legal rights of their clients.

Counselors must approach the relationship between law and ethics with a constructive and clearheaded perspective. Many years ago, Ware (1971) considered the relationship between law and professional judgment in reconciling legislated and ethical standards of conduct. She noted that both tend to remain broad and open to situational interpretation, and she provided advice that continues to be meaningful to the profession's contemporary legal environment: Beware the tendency to look to other professions for standards to reconcile these conflicts. Noting counselors' emerging interest in the law, Ware described the phenomenon as a function of two factors: (1) a hope that the law would relieve counselors from the pressure to resolve complex or vague professional dilemmas; and (2) a fear that counselors might be sued regarding some legal violation. Ware concluded that although knowledge of legal standards is necessary to address issues in a balanced way, it would be unwise to rest too much hope on legal remedy or to fear the law too greatly. This goal for ethical decision making of knowledge and respect in balance with all clinically relevant factors is the approach taken in Tarvydas's Integrative Decision-Making Model of Ethical Behavior (see Chapter 6).

THE RELATIONSHIP BETWEEN LAW AND ETHICS

Both law and ethics have effects on the counselor-client relationship. Generally, the law is supportive or neutral in dealing with professional ethical codes and standards. The legal structure is neutral in most instances, allowing the profession to govern its practitioners' conduct and practices. Only in instances in which public health, safety, or welfare is threatened does the legal system tend to intervene and override the ethical codes of the profession. Counselors must have a situation-specific interpretation of both legal and ethical regulatory standards to conduct well-informed practice. Codes of ethics are not intended to

supersede the law, but rather to clarify existing law and policy. (This close relationship between societal morals and values and professional values will receive detailed discussion in Chapter 5.) When instances occur in which ethical standards conflict with the law, it is difficult to reconcile legislated and ethical standards of conduct. Both standards are broad and open to situational interpretation, so counseling organizations need to work with bar associations, legislatures, the judiciary, and their own memberships to educate and to achieve better standards.

Counselors must think dynamically about the relationships among the law, the ethical standards of their profession, and their individual professional ethical and moral consciences. On rare occasions, counselors may be required to exercise personal and professional judgment when the legal and ethical requirement are at odds. The codes of ethics for the mental health professions offer limited guidance in this instance (see Box 4.1). The APA code of ethics provides no overall requirement to abide by any legal statute or administrative rule. It does contain several specific standards requiring conformity with legal requirements related to referral practices, fee practices, research and practices with research animals, and familiarity with rules concerning forensic work. Typically, ethical standards generally state that in cases of conflict, practitioners should make the parties aware of the conflict and their commitment to the ethical standards and attempt to resolve the conflict in a responsible manner. Other codes of ethics sometimes defer to the law (Remley, 1996).

Even when the code of ethics states that the professional should abide by the dictates of the law, the problem of what should be done in a specific instance of conflict is not resolved for two reasons: (1) It is the responsibility of the professional to weigh all aspects of a situation, determine which ethical and legal standards apply in general, and decide how they apply in this instance. Clients vary and each set of circumstances adds situational complexity to the interpretation. Counselors must exercise their judgment regarding the issues and concerns embedded in the situation. Through this interpretation, counselors can assess the appropriateness and applicability of the ethical and legal

TABLE 4–1 Interactions between Ethics and the Law

	Example	
1. Ethical & Legal	Following a just law	Keeping a client's confidences that are also protected by law from disclosure
2. Ethical & Illegal	Disobeying an unjust law	Refusing to breach promised confidentiality even though ordered to by court
3. Ethical & Alegal	Doing good where no law applies	Offering free service to poor clients
4. Unethical & Legal	Following an unjust law	Following the Federal Trade Commission's edict that ethical codes cannot prohibit the use of testimonials in ads for counseling services
5. Unethical & Illegal	Breaking a just law	Disclosing confidential information protected by law from disclosure
6. Unethical & Alegal	Doing harm that no law prohibits	Promoting client dependency to enhance one's own feeling of power

Note: Adapted from *Guide to Ethical Practice in Psychotherapy* by A. Thompson, 1990, New York: John Wiley & Sons. Copyright 1990 by John Wiley & Sons. Adapted by permission.

standards. It can be argued that the norm of engaging in such a level of independent judgment with the intent of upholding the principles and standards of the profession distinguishes a true profession from a skilled occupation. (2) Even after thorough efforts to resolve the conflict lawfully, the legal option for action may not be in the best ethical interests of the client—the counselor's primary ethical obligation. Authorities on moral development and ethical decision-making theory recognize that the best solution to an ethical dilemma may violate the law in the interests of a higher moral or conscience level of analysis (Kohlberg, 1964, 1981; Van Hoose & Paradise, 1979). These models are discussed in greater detail in Chapter 5. It is generally accepted that counselors and other professionals have a strong prima facie obligation to abide by the legal requirements of a situation. **Prima facie,** a Latin phrase, means that the obligation in question must be considered in every case and set aside only if valid and compelling reasons to do so are present in a specific instance. These reasons would involve ethical or legal reasons of greater importance than the specific legal rule in question.

Thompson (1990) noted that there are six interactions between ethics and the law. The examples listed in Table 4–1 illustrate the distinctions.

When counselors are faced with an apparent conflict between ethics and the law, you must take steps to resolve it. They must recognize that forces other than law and ethics may clash to create conflict. For example, employer policies and procedures, accreditation rules, or funding source rules might be at issue rather than the law. Remley (1996) recommended the following steps to guide the counselor in such conflicts:

1. Identify the force that is at issue regarding the counselor's behavior . . .
2. If a legal question exists, legal advice should be obtained . . .
3. If there is a problem in applying an ethical standard to a particular situation or in understanding the requirements of an ethical standard, the best action a counselor could take is to consult with colleagues and with those perceived to be experts in the counseling field . . .
4. If a force other than law or ethics (for example, an employer, an accrediting body, or a funding agency) is suggesting that a counselor take some action he or she perceives to be illegal, the counselor should seek legal advice to determine whether such action is indeed illegal. (p. 288)

Counselors must involve themselves in efforts to change laws that they believe place their clients at risk or cause them injury or harm. This determination often is not easy for counselors to make. For example, state law might force counselors to report the physical abuses of children as soon as they become aware of the abuses. This action might be taken despite the fact that the child must return home at the end of the session pending an investigation and might be in even more danger of serious harm in retaliation for reporting the abuse to the counselor.

At its best, the legal system has stimulated the mental health professions to enhance their ethical standards. The careful ethical practices commonly used by counselors to warn and to protect potential victims of their dangerous clients are owed to the lessons learned in the landmark decisions surrounding the *Tarasoff v. the Regents of the University of California* (1974) court case (see Chapter 3). That decision and the related rulings that followed it are now collectively known as the *Tarasoff doctrine.* They have occasioned intense professional review and, in general, have positively influenced the growth of ethical standards and counseling interventions with dangerous clients for almost the past three decades.

LEGAL MECHANISMS

Society holds all mental health professionals accountable for maintaining proper clinical and ethical standards of practice through four legal mechanisms: professional ethics committees, state licensure boards, criminal courts, and civil courts (Pope & Vasquez, 1998).

Counselors and other mental health professionals are not expected to have expert knowledge of legal concepts and mechanisms and how they apply to their work at the same level as would an attorney. In fact, they are expected to have no special legal knowledge beyond that of a competent layperson (Shea, 1985), but they must seek legal opinions as needed. Nevertheless, counselors are aided by knowledge of the basic legal mechanisms that govern their practices. Such knowledge might allow them to avoid important missteps, anticipate possible legal entanglements, and react more appropriately to legal processes should the need arise.

The U.S. Constitution and federal, state, and local levels are the essential levels of legal authority (Remley, 1996). Laws pertaining to particular matters often differ from jurisdiction to jurisdiction. These differences can be quite striking from state to state, potentially leading to radically different implications for lawful, proper conduct in the same situation. For instance, the issues of privacy and confidentiality for clients who are HIV positive receive radically different treatment in the laws of various state jurisdictions. (See Burris [2001] for an excellent discussion of legal considerations that relate to working with clients who are HIV positive.)

A number of useful resources about state statutes, federal law, and court rulings that are relevant to counselors and other mental health professionals are available. Helpful references include the series of volumes published by the American Psychological Association on state laws for mental health professionals, additional information on legal aspects of practice offered by Remley and Herlihy (2001), and a comprehensive overview of legal issues for the helping professions by Swenson (1997). In addition, the Internet provides a number of useful sites to research state and other legal information. These resources allow counselors to become more intelligent consumers of legal services to understand their clients' legal situations.

Legal consultation is often imperative to understand the "terms of art" used in law, whose meanings vary from common understanding. The law itself varies from state to state—either in terms of the specific laws enacted by state legislatures or the way the courts within local jurisdictions have interpreted it in specific cases. The body of court rulings that interpret a law establishes what is known as case law. **Case law** provides precedents that are relevant to the law's interpretation in specific circumstances and jurisdictions and contributes to the evolution of a legal concept. Counselors must determine what laws and interpretations are relevant for any legal issues raised in the state and local jurisdictions in which they practice. For instance, all 50 states have some form of law that requires mandatory reporting of child abuse by mental health and other professionals. However, the definition of child abuse, the evidence necessary to report it, and the manner and timing of its reporting vary. Some states do not differentiate between neglect and abuse, but others do (Fischer & Sorenson, 1985). While counselors are not expected to have advanced legal knowledge, they are obligated to have basic knowledge of their own state statutes and case law related to their profession.

Laws are also classified as civil or criminal. **Civil law** involves the obligation of citizens to one another. The obligation must be asserted by the individual before the obligation is enforced by the government (Remley, 1996). A civil matter involves an offense to an individual. The remedy is some form of compensation to the victim (Keary, 1985). Malpractice, the most common cause of legal liability for mental health practitioners, is a type of civil action (see Chapter 1).

Criminal law involves conduct required of all citizens or prohibited to all and is enforced by the government's legal authorities. In criminal matters, the state punishes the violator; punishments may involve imprisonment, fines, or death (Remley, 1996). Criminal actions against counselors in matters unrelated to their professional roles are likely just as common as those for members of the general public. The most frequent type of professionally related criminal offense for psychotherapists is fraud related to third-party billings (Pope & Vasquez, 1998). Engaging in sexual intimacy with a client is also a criminal offense in some states, including Colorado, Wisconsin, Minnesota, Missouri, Texas, Washington, and Florida (Corey, Corey, & Callanan, 1998).

The legal system embodies what society considers a minimum level of acceptable behavior on the part of its citizens. Professional organizations generally wish to strive for higher standards of behavior in professional practice and enforce these standards upon their members. However, no society will delegate all authority for such enforcement solely to the profession because it must continue to protect the rights and well-being of its citizenry. Thus, ethical and legal standards should be complementary in most instances, although both require different interpretations to be fully understood.

COMMON LEGAL CONCERNS

Any number of possible legal issues exist that may affect counselors in the course of their service to clients. The most frequent legal concerns are fewer and more predictable due to counselors' increased awareness of the ethical aspects of counseling practice. Practitioners should recognize the more frequent issues and develop a well-informed approach to handling them—a series of "conceptual templates for legal risk situations." By doing so, inexperienced counselors can anticipate and handle many of the standard issues more capably and know the initial steps to take when confronted with the more serious, complex situations. Such a proactive mental structure is important for better management of legal risk and liability exposure. DePauw (1986) provided a useful template for anticipating important ethical concerns in counseling practice, proposing that counselors adopt a standard, natural timeline perspective for ethical considerations. The timeline approach alerts the counselor to specific problems as they arise within the stages of client service. This approach allows counselors to anticipate the natural rhythm of issues in their individual relationships with clients. DePauw incorporated many of the key challenges in client services and noted ethical matters in four phases of the counseling relationship:

I. *Initiation Phase Issues*
  A. Precounseling considerations
    1. advertising
    2. avoiding misuse of institutional affiliations
    3. financial arrangements
    4. donated services
  B. Service provision issues
    1. adequacy of counselor skills, experience, and training (competency)
    2. better service option for client
    3. concurrent counselor involvement
    4. conflicting dual relationships
  C. Informed consent issues
    1. structures to educate regarding purposes, goals, and techniques
    2. explanation of rules of procedure and limitations
    3. supervision and consultation release concerns
    4. experimental methods of treatment
II. *Ongoing Counseling Issues*
  A. Confidentiality
  B. Special issues of confidentiality
    1. children
    2. groups
  C. Consultation
  D. Recordkeeping
III. *Dangerousness and Crisis Concerns*
  A. Threat to self
  B. Threat to others
  C. Child abuse
  D. Gray areas (e.g., HIV/AIDS and dying client issues)
IV. *Termination Phase Issues*

FIGURE 4–1. Timeline Perspective on Ethical and Legal Considerations
Note: From "Avoiding Ethical Violations: A Timeline Perspective for Individual Counseling" by M. E. DePauw, 1986. *Journal of Counseling & Development, 64*(5), 303–305. Copyright 1986 by American Counseling Association. Reprinted by permission.

1. initiation phase issues
2. ongoing counseling issues
3. dangerousness and crisis concerns
4. termination phase considerations

Figure 4–1 presents the issues considered within each phase.

Initiation Phase Issues

The initiation phase includes the areas of precounseling, service provision, and informed consent. During this phase, counselors reach out to potential clients and ready them to enter into counseling relationships appropriately prepared and informed.

Counselor Competency.   It is critical for the well-being of clients that counselors possess adequate skills, experience, and training to serve them competently. Additionally, it is important that counselors assure themselves and their clients that they have these necessary qualities. By doing so, counselors limit their liability and observe any regulations that require them to practice only within a specific scope of practice.

Counseling and other professional licensure laws commonly include definitions of the profession, as well as the practice and procedures of the profession. Taken together, these statutory definitions, and any regulations that may pertain to them, define the scope of practice for the profession within a jurisdiction. The definitions are usually drawn from those established by the profession's organizations at the national level. For example, the American Counseling Association (ACA) has used its model counselor licensure bill to encourage a more regularized structure for individual state laws. At this writing, both ACA and the American Association of State Counseling Boards (AASCB) have had joint discussions to consider ways to establish shared model standards for counselor licensure. They have established a task force to develop basic standards for counseling credentialing that address a shared definition of professional counseling. If this model is established, it will provide mechanisms to better assist counselors who are licensed in one state to be able to move to another state and have their credentials accepted; this mechanism is called **portability.** Enhancing portability of counselor licensure credentials is a critical issue for the progress of counselor professionalization that hinges on a shared understanding of the counselor's scope of practice and the core requirements for counselor licensure.

A *scope of practice* is a statement of the extent and limit of practices considered acceptable to become licensed or certified professionals. More broadly defined, it is a recognized area of proficiency or competence gained through appropriate education and experience. In most cases, the scope of practice is related closely to the profession's definition of its areas of competency. Professionals licensed under a specific law may operate within the limits of the scope of practice as described within that jurisdiction's law and regulations.

The professional scope of practice is different than the individual counselor's scope of practice, although they do overlap. An individual's scope of practice is based on one's own knowledge and skills gained through education and professional experience. Counselors are bound ethically to limit their practice to the scope of practice for which they are prepared within the profession's larger scope. In addition, the licensure regulations of many states require that professionals must identify their personal scope of practice and stipulate that they will practice within this area. Sometimes this includes the provision of a written statement of the scope of practice to the licensure board. This statement then constitutes the appropriate legal and ethical limitations to the counselor's practice.

Counselors should not provide or supervise services to clients outside their area of expertise. Their scopes of practice should be made clear to prospective clients before they are accepted into practice. Referral to another professional is appropriate if the client's problem falls outside the counselor's scope of practice (Anderson, 1996). If counselors work with clients or techniques outside their areas of competency, they could be disciplined if the licensure board becomes aware of it, or the work might become a negative factor in a malpractice lawsuit if it can be demonstrated that the counselors used techniques for which they were not trained that resulted in harm to the clients.

Another important concern for all counselors, regardless of their level of skill or experience, is to responsibly maintain or add to their levels of competence. Both new counselors and experienced counselors may need to add a skill or area of practice to their professional practice capabilities. Licensing and certification bodies expect counselors who hold their credentials to engage in continuing education to maintain or add knowledge and skills, learn new procedures, and learn about needs of changing client populations. Counselors often enter into new practice areas with some concern and trepidation about how to gain the necessary competencies without unduly exposing their clients to risk or ineffective service. An individualized, systematic, and developmental continuing education program that includes specific personal professional goals and activities to meet these goals is an indispensable tool to enhance competency levels. Responsible professionals have a rich number of in-service, continuing education workshops, university courses, and programs to form an initial basis

Box 4.2 Question for Reflection

What should a classically trained school counselor, supervised in a school setting and licensed to practice independently in a state, do before setting up a private practice in marriage counseling?

of learning new information. Many of these activities are offered through distance education programs for those who cannot participate through traditional means like conferences and on-location workshops. In addition, it is critical to practice new skills until they are mastered with the supervision or collaboration of a colleague who is skilled in the new area of competence. It is important to look for a balance of didactic and practice activities, as well as proper supervision, to assure that the counselor has adequately achieved the desired level of competency in the new skill area.

Informed Consent Issues. Clients have the right to make informed choices about their care. Counselors have the legal duty to provide their clients with sufficient information and to make sure they fully understand it before making their decisions. This practice originated within medical treatment settings and has come to be known as *informed consent*—the client's right to agree to participate in counseling, assessment, or professional procedures or services after such services are fully described and explained in a manner that is comprehensible to the client.

As the counselor and the client enter into the counseling relationship, they enter into a contractual relationship as well. This contract may be formal if it is written, or it may be spoken between the two parties. Both parties to the relationship must understand the basic aspects of the situation into which they may enter. Documentation is important to clarify what the counselor is, and is not, promising to do for the client. If one party thinks that the other party has not provided the items that were agreed on, that person may consider the contract violated—a legal charge called **breach of contract.**

Counselors should begin the informed consent process by engaging in a screening or precounseling consultation—this might be an aspect of the initial intake meeting. An initial precounseling consultation is an excellent tool to assure that adequate and attentive initial preparation is available to both parties. At that time, certain basic information about the client's issues and objectives for counseling and the counselor's competency must be discussed to ascertain if the counselor

is the appropriate helper for this individual client (Anderson, 1996).

Although there are many types of information that the counselor would be wise to provide to the client, some basic issues should be part of a thorough precounseling consent process. Discussing the common limits to confidentiality is particularly important at this initiation of counseling stage (see Chapter 3). Bertram and Wheeler (1994) include 20 topics on their checklist for a written informed consent for treatment (see Appendix A at the end of this chapter). This document provides a thorough and useful format. Additionally, the counselor should discuss the same information with the client to reinforce the client's understanding of what is likely to occur in counseling. Generally, a written consent to treatment or a related document (i.e., professional disclosure statement or therapeutic contract) should address areas such as: (a) the therapeutic process, (b) background of the therapist, (c) costs involved in therapy, (d) length of therapy and termination, (e) consultation with colleagues, (f) interruptions in therapy (e.g., vacations, illness), (g) client's right of access to files, (h) rights pertaining to diagnostic labeling, (i) nature and purpose of confidentiality, (j) audiotape or videotape recording, (k) the benefits and risks of treatment, and (l) alternatives to traditional therapy (Corey, Corey, & Callanan, 1998). Many of these areas are ethically required according to professional codes of ethics. For example, code of ethics typically oblige the counselor to disclose: (a) the implications of diagnosis, (b) the intended use of tests and reports, (c) the limitations of confidentiality, (d) the clients' rights to participate in ongoing counseling plans, and (e) the clients' rights to refuse services and be advised of the consequences of refusal. These professional disclosure statements are important, useful documents for both the counselor and the client. They constitute a legal contract and are often signed by both parties (Remley & Herlihy, 2001). In addition, any written contract or document should be periodically discussed and updated to fit the current nature of the agreed-upon work in which the counselor and client are engaged.

Box 4.3   Question for Reflection

How do the current ACA and APA codes of ethics address requirements of informed consent? What specifically must be addressed in the informed consent process?

Shaw and Tarvydas (2001) have noted several benefits of using professional disclosure forms, including: (a) promoting client comprehension, (b) increasing client responsibility, (c) reducing the likelihood of client exploitation through a "contract" format, (d) reducing future conflicts because of misperceptions, (e) protection of counselors against malpractice suits, (f) encouraging self-scrutiny by health care professionals, and (g) increasing the autonomy of clients by making them less dependent on the counselor for information. Yet, in reviewing the literature on utilization of these forms in the mental health professions, Shaw and Tarvydas also found that many professionals do not use them.

Informed consent requires the presence of three legal elements: capacity, comprehension of information, and voluntariness. The person must (1) possess the ability to make a rational decision **(capacity);** (2) have sufficient information and be able to understand it **(comprehension);** and (3) give consent by acting freely in the decision-making process **(voluntariness)** (Bray, Shepard, & Hayes, 1985). Counselors should obtain written, informed consent before proceeding with the client and make every effort to ensure that this consent is genuine and valid.

Several issues may arise that call this consent into question. Remember that **client competency** is not an all-or-nothing quality. Clients must be competent to make decisions for themselves, a precondition for being able to consent autonomously (Beauchamp & Childress, 1994). The criteria for the ability to make a decision also vary by the context or criteria of the decision to be made (Beauchamp & Childress, 1994). For example, an individual may be able to think rationally enough to decide whether to wear a coat on a given day, but may not be competent to decide whether to sell the family business. Limitations in competency may be temporary or permanent. Factors that might affect competency temporarily include intoxication or a severe psychological trauma, such as rape. More permanent conditions that affect a person's competency might include dementia (a loss of intelligence due to physical-organic factors) or severe mental retardation. Other cognitive or emotional states have less consistent or unclear effects on competency, such as major depression or judgment deficits after a trau-

matic brain injury. If counselors are in doubt about the ability of clients to make rational decisions, and evaluation of competency is not within the scope of counseling practice, they should seek consultation with other professionals able to make such determinations. If a person is judged to be incompetent, a legal guardian or parent can provide consent. Counselors should always determine if their clients have guardians who must be involved in decision making, and the type of guardianship involved. A guardianship may extend to all areas of a client's life or may be specific to one area, such as financial or medical matters.

Several informed consent issues beyond client competency are of concern. Counselors have a major responsibility for the client's comprehension or understanding of the matter at hand. Counselors must ensure they provide information in a manner that maximizes the client's ability to understand it and its implications. The counselor must know the client's communication and learning styles and the conditions necessary for the individual to understand the information. The counselor must tailor the discussion to meet those needs. Some issues to be considered include the client's (a) verbal (oral and reading) and cognitive abilities, (b) ability to see or hear, (c) emotional state, (d) language of first choice, (e) degree of fatigue or illness, and (f) distractibility or attentional ability. The same information may need to be presented several ways (e.g., discussed, demonstrated, or written), repeated several times or on different occasions, or even provided by different persons. Counselors should be increasingly focused on awareness of the needs of clients from diverse cultural backgrounds to assure they obtain informed consent. Some cultures are more collectivistic in their worldview. A client arriving at an individual choice without consulting elders or other family members may violate the norms of the client's culture and place the counseling relationship in a precarious state (Remley & Herlihy, 2001).

Counselors must take special care with any forms used. They must be free of jargon, written at an appropriate reading grade level, and legible. The client must be literate in the language used on the form. An analysis of mandated consent to psychotherapy forms used in Colorado (Handelsman, Martinez, Geisendorfer, & Jordan,

1995) found that the forms' average readability level reached upper college grades. Additionally, the majority of the forms contained legally mandated information, but fewer contained ethically desirable information.

Counselors must realize that no specific approach to informed consent works for all clients. They must use their professional sensitivity and judgment to find the correct method in each case. The client is dependent upon the counselor in this matter. Research has shown some positive results of proper informed consent procedures in counseling and psychotherapy. Results include clients' decreased anxiety, increased compliance with treatment, increased alertness to problems in treatment, and more rapid recovery (Pope & Vasquez, 1991; Shaw & Tarvydas, 2001).

Ongoing Counseling Issues

At this point in the process, the counselor and client are engaged in the ongoing work they have outlined. Two common issues with legal aspects are especially important in this phase: confidentiality and record-keeping (consult Chapter 8 for further information about the proper maintenance of records and files used in counseling).

Confidentiality and Privileged Communication. Confidentiality and privileged communication are among the most troublesome areas of practice for mental health professionals (see Chapter 3). A national study found that almost two-thirds of psychologists (61.9%) unintentionally violated client confidentiality (Pope, Tabachnick, & Keith-Spiegel, 1987). Anderson (1996) described the issues of confidentiality as confusing and of concern to counselors.

The ethical obligations of confidentiality and privileged communication derive from the ethical principles of fidelity (being loyal and keeping promises), autonomy, and the principle of nonmaleficence, (refraining from doing harm to another). These principles support the counselor's duty to keep client information private and not reveal what is said or done within the counseling relationship. This promise of privacy to the client allows for the openness of communication and trust—the most basic and essential component of the therapeutic relationship.

The related concept of privileged communication provides clients the legal right that their confidential communications cannot be revealed in a legal proceeding. It derives from English common law in recognizing that clients must have the ability to talk freely to their attorneys if they are to defend themselves effec-

tively in criminal legal proceedings (Anderson, 1996). Additionally, state statutes have established privileged communication similar to that of the attorney-client privilege for some professionals. Over time, privileged communication has been applied through common law or state statute to limited types of relationships, beginning with priest-penitent, attorney-client, and husband-wife relationships and gradually extending to those of physician-patient, psychologist-client, social worker-client, and counselor-client. In the case of the mental health professions, privilege applies only to licensed therapists. Recent studies have documented that counselor-client privilege exists in all but one state that licenses counselors (Glosoff, Herlihy, & Spence, 2000), and in all 50 states for psychologists (Glosoff, Herlihy, Herlihy, & Spence, 1997). In that sense, counselor licensure statutes that include proper protections are an important tool to assist the counselor in protecting client confidentiality.

This extension of the protection to mental health professionals appears to have continued with the recent Supreme Court decision in *Jaffee v. Redmond* (Remley, Herlihy, & Herlihy, 1997). This decision upheld the ability of licensed psychotherapists to maintain the confidences of their clients in federal court cases. The case involved the ability of a clinical social worker licensed in Illinois to assert privilege for communications between herself and her client in a lawsuit. The client, Mary Lu Redmond, was a police officer who killed Ricky Allen, Sr. after responding to reports of a fight in progress. She found Allen allegedly poised to stab another individual. Carrie Jaffee, the administrator of the Allen estate, brought the lawsuit against Redmond, the City of Hoffman Estates, and its police department, alleging excessive force had been used in the incident. In the course of the legal proceedings, the family petitioned to obtain notes made by the therapist in counseling sessions with Redmond after the incident. Redmond and the therapist refused to provide the notes. The judge instructed the jury to assume the notes were unfavorable to Redmond, and the plaintiff won the case. On appeal in the U.S. Court of Appeals for the 7th Circuit, the jury verdict was thrown out and the case was remanded for new trial. The court opinion stated that the trial court had erred by not offering protection to confidential communications. Jaffee appealed this decision to the U.S. Supreme Court, which upheld a strict standard of privileged communication in its 13 June 1996 ruling. The arguments made before the highest court by ACA and APA in friend-of-the-court briefs stem from four longstanding criteria that support the granting of privilege in the legal system. According to Wigmore (1961), the four criteria are:

1. The communications must originate in confidence that they will not be disclosed.
2. This element of confidentiality must be essential to the full and satisfactory maintenance of the relationship between the parties.
3. The relationship must be one that, in the opinion of the community, ought to be fostered.
4. The injury that would be inflicted to the relationship by the disclosure of the communications must be greater than the benefit gained for the correct disposal of litigation.

The *Jaffee v. Redmond* ruling applies only within the federal court system, but it does extend psychotherapist privilege to another group of licensed professionals—clinical social workers. Leadership in the counseling profession noted the following:

> With this recognition of licensed clinical social workers and the previous recognition of clinical psychologists and psychiatrists, counselors are the largest remaining group of licensed professionals providing psychotherapeutic services that is not explicitly recognized by federal courts. The Supreme Court used the term psychotherapist in its decision and counselors must be considered psychotherapists if they are to be covered by the Jaffee ruling. (National Board for Counselor Certification, 1996, p. 4)

The Supreme Court mentioned state licensure of clinical social workers as a key factor in its decision. State licensure, inclusion of the profession in the privilege statutes of each state, and establishment of uniform qualifications for professionals to be considered psychotherapists appear to be important elements in advancing privileged communication status to counselors in the future (NBCC, 1996). Some authorities predict this landmark ruling may establish further privilege for licensed counselor-client relationships in future cases (Remley & Herlihy, 2001).

Special Issues and Exceptions to Confidentiality. The ethical obligation of counselors to assure clients of confidentiality, and the clients' related legal right of privilege, are basic to counseling. Many circumstances vary for counseling in different specialized areas of practice, and issues of confidentiality and privilege express themselves somewhat differently across these situations. Special circumstances related to confidentiality and privilege include counseling with persons who

have HIV or AIDS (see Chapter 9), families or couples (see Chapter 12), minors or school settings (see Chapter 13), people with disabilities (see Chapters 14 and 17), groups (see Chapter 16), and clients in drug or alcohol treatment facilities (see Chapter 18). The rapid increase and extensive use of electronic and other technological devices in counseling settings has also created challenging problems for maintaining client confidentiality (see Chapter 10).

There are several exceptions to the general requirement of counselors to hold client communications confidential. Arthur and Swanson (1993) noted the following:

1. Client is dangerous to self or others.
2. Client waives confidentiality and privilege by requesting a release of information.
3. Counselor receives a court order requiring the release of information.
4. Counselor is involved in systematic clinical supervision.
5. Client's information and paper work are processed by clerical workers for routine purposes, and client has been informed of this arrangement prior to counseling.
6. Counselor-required legal or clinical consultation, and client is informed of this counselor right before counseling.
7. The issue of the client's mental health is raised by client in a legal proceeding, such as a custody lawsuit.
8. Counseling occurs with a third party in the room, as in group or family counseling.
9. Client is a minor (younger than age 18).
10. Client information is made available within the agency or institution as part of the treatment process, with the client receiving precounseling notification of this practice.
11. Information is shared within a penal institution as part of the operation of the institution or the case process.
12. Client discloses the information to advance a criminal or fraudulent activity.
13. Child abuse is suspected by the counselor.

Other exceptions to confidentiality exist for psychologists and counselors who serve in the military. In this highly specialized setting, the mental health professional is obliged to report threats to military installations, weapons, and military integrity, even when these do not imply specific threats to specific persons.

Two additional concerns arise for all counselors who are faced with the legal system's demands for information they view as confidential: subpoenas and court appearances. A legally inexperienced counselor's first impulse upon receiving a subpoena might be to surrender all materials requested in the subpoena. This well-meaning response would not be proper because the ethical and legal duty to protect a client's confidentiality requires that the counselor make appropriate attempts to preserve client privacy.

A *subpoena* (see Chapter 3) is a court order to appear in a legal hearing—a court appearance or a deposition—with all requested information. The counselor might be questioned or subpoenaed documents might be examined. Often, subpoenas are drafted broadly to capture any information that might be of assistance to a party to the legal proceeding requesting the information—a "fishing trip" for anything potentially helpful. Counselors should be familiar with state statutes regarding privilege that might apply in their jurisdiction (Anderson, 1996). Arthur and Swanson (1993) and Anderson (1996) provide more specific recommendations to respond to a subpoena (Figure 4–2).

An order to appear in court if the counselor's client is a defendant in a lawsuit presents a similar set of challenges. Counselors should protect their clients' confidences in a manner consistent with the earlier information. Judges can compel counselors to answer questions in legal proceedings even though counselors may argue that it is their ethical responsibility to preserve client confidentiality. If that occurs, Anderson (1996) has several additional suggestions: (a) answer truthfully, but do not volunteer information beyond what is specifically requested, (b) the counselor should be protected in the hearing by an attorney (the counselor's or the client's) and should follow the attorney's direction, and (c) discuss the concerns regarding confidentiality with the attorney before the hearing and prepare for the actual testimony to be provided.

1. Do not respond to the subpoena automatically. Be sure that all staff members know proper procedures for responding.
2. Determine if the subpoena was requested by a current or former client or his or her attorney. Legally, this would require you to produce the documents or testify as directed. However, it is ethically important that you review any concerns you might have about detrimental aspects of this information with these parties so that they may exercise truly informed judgment about proceeding with this request.
3. Consult with your attorney and the client's attorney, after obtaining the client's permission to do so, regarding the situation. If the judgment is that you should respond to the subpoena, obtain written release of information forms specifying what will be released, and to whom, from all clients whose information will be revealed.
4. If it is determined that you should not respond, ask the client's attorney to file a motion to quash the subpoena. In this case, a judge will hear the concerns about the detrimental effects of revealing the materials and privately view them to rule on whether the counselor should be compelled to respond to the subpoena or to further limit the information provided.
5. NEVER ignore a subpoena or defy it without taking some of the measures described here and without legal assistance.
6. Be sure to keep thorough documentation in the client's record of all interactions with the client or the client's attorney in this matter, as well as copies of all subpoenas, releases of information, court rulings, and official communications.

FIGURE 4–2. Considerations in Responding to a Subpoena

Recordkeeping. The importance of observing minimum acceptable standards of clinical recordkeeping should be obvious. Case records have been reported to be one of the top five areas of legal liability for counselors (Snider, 1987). Mitchell (2001) described common ways to guarantee a lawsuit, many of which are documentation related (see Figure 4–3).

Unfortunately, formal training in case-recording methods and procedures is usually limited in the professional education of most counselors. These matters are considered to be primarily a part of students' clinical experiences. While good methods may certainly be learned in this manner, the resulting training is typically varied in terms of content, depth, and method. Counselors must educate themselves on the best practices in recordkeeping in mental health professions and thoroughly acquaint themselves with the methods and requirements of the system and practices used in their own setting. Good, basic introductions to client case-recording methods are provided by Mitchell (2001), Remley and Herlihy (2001), and Piazza and Baruth (1990). Counselors working in schools that receive federal funding should be aware that educational and other records are covered by the Family Educational Rights and Privacy Act (FERPA), which provides rights of access to educational records to students and their parents, and defines *educational record* as any

- Document that something needs to be done; then do not do it.
- Do not keep records current.
- Do not obtain complete assessments or develop a comprehensive treatment plan.
- Establish policies and procedures, but do not follow them.
- Do not review or audit your records.
- Nurture a dependent relationship and then cut it off quickly.
- Combine a suicidal client with a provider who has a reputation for sexual impropriety.

FIGURE 4–3.   Ways to Guarantee a Lawsuit

Note: Taken from *Documentation in Counseling Records* (p. 11) by R. Mitchell, 2001, Alexandria, VA: American Counseling Association. Copyright 2001 by American Counseling Association. Reprinted by permission.

record kept by employees of an educational institution. Anderson (1996) further states that "records made by and kept in the sole possession of" a professional such as a physician, psychologist, or other recognized professional "are excluded from the disclosure requirements, except that notes may be provided to other treating professionals or reviewed by a physician of the student's choice" (p. 38). For further information regarding issues of confidentiality in the schools, refer to Chapter 13.

The issue of adequate recordkeeping is considered so important in the practice of psychology that the American Psychological Association (1993) has adopted *Record Keeping Guidelines*. In addition to considering the principles and purpose underlying clinical records, the guidelines provide specific recommendations in the following areas: content, construction and control, retention of records, procedures with outdated records, and disclosure of recordkeeping procedures. The considerations relevant to electronic recordkeeping are discussed in Chapter 10.

It is beyond the scope of this discussion to introduce the technical methods involved in good clinical recordkeeping practices. However, Arthur and Swanson (1993) make several legally relevant points: (1) Security of files must be maintained; files must not be left where they can be accessed by unauthorized persons. (2) Notes should be written in nontechnical, clear, and objective statements with behavioral descriptions. Any subjective or evaluative statements involving professional judgments should be so designated and written in a separate section clearly set aside from factual content. (3) All client records should be written with the understanding that

they might be seen by the client, a court, or some other authorized person. (4) Only information that is necessary and appropriate to the reason the client is receiving services should be documented. Remley (1990) cautioned that counselors should document critical incidents or interactions with clients extensively. Examples include emergencies; circumstances in which clients will not follow recommendations, thereby risking a negative outcome or endangering themselves; or when litigation appears possible. Good recording practices enhance the quality of clinical analysis and service and protect both the client and the counselor.

Dangerousness and Crisis Concerns

At any point in working with a client, even as early as the first contact, crises and dangerous circumstances may arise. Such situations need to be dealt with effectively to prevent harm to the client and any other parties at risk. The *Tarasoff* court decision (see Chapter 3) and other related cases have shaped our understanding of how counselors should proceed. The *Tarasoff* case is arguably the best-known case in mental health and counseling history. Prior to this decision, the core ethical tendency was preserving client confidentiality. The results of this case made it clear that therapists had a legal obligation to third parties who are at risk of serious harm from dangerous clients. The California Supreme Court noted in its decision that "the protective privilege ends where the public peril begins" (*Tarasoff v. Regents of the University of California*, 1976, p. 347). As a result of the original *Tarasoff* decision (1974), the court held that an affirmative duty existed to warn the identifiable victim despite the client's right to confidentiality. This ruling established that "liability would attach where the psychotherapist *reasonably believed, or should have believed*, that the client posed a serious danger *to an identifiable potential victim*" (Anderson, 1996, p. 29, italics in original). This doctrine has come to be known as the *duty to warn*. The *Tarasoff* decision is binding only in California—other state courts do not have to follow its dictates. However, it has been an influential case; many other state and federal courts follow this ruling. Because determining the specific duty imposed on the psychotherapist in a particular jurisdiction is so confusing, 23 states have passed laws to define how the duty to warn and protect should be discharged. These laws generally establish: (a) when the duty arises, (b) the manner in which the psychotherapist may fulfill this duty, and (c) established immunity to the professional for violating client confidences to discharge the duty to protect (see Burris [2001] for a detailed presentation of these laws). Counselors should educate themselves about the legal requirements in their local jurisdictions for the duty to warn and protect others from dangerous clients.

The 1976 *Tarasoff* ruling (known as *Tarasoff II*) was an appeal of the original 1974 *Tarasoff* decision (*Tarasoff I*). The defendants alleged that the parents of the client did not have a legal claim in the matter but rather were private third parties and not clients of the therapist. The California Supreme Court reconsidered the case and found that the parents could sue the defendants. *Tarasoff II* effectively expanded the original decision from the more limited duty to warn to a more inclusive "duty to protect." In the **duty to protect** standard, warning the intended victim is only one option available to the therapist to protect others from a dangerous client (VandeCreek, Bennett, & Bricklin, 1994). Other interventions with the potential to be equally effective may be used to control the potential of dangerous behavior. These interventions include (a) voluntary or civil commitment of the client, (b) an increase or change in medication to control the condition creating the danger, (c) an increase in the frequency of sessions or supervision, or (d) referral of the client to another provider with better potential to control the violent behavior. Clearly, this does not absolve the therapist from the responsibility to exercise due care and proper professional judgment in assessing and attempting to protect potential victims from dangerous clients. It does expand the range of options to meet the needs of the public for protection and of the client to receive care that does not automatically expose the therapeutic relationship to the same level of potential harm (VandeCreek et al., 1994). Assessing the degree of dangerousness or risk presented by a client has always been acknowledged as a difficult and not necessarily successful task, even for skilled therapists. Counselors must carefully determine whether they possess the clinical skills and competency to do so. If they do not, they must immediately involve supervisors and/or other appropriately skilled colleagues in such a manner to ensure safety of all parties concerned. Efforts to accurately gather important information and consultation are very important for any clinician, regardless of skill and experience level, to most accurately assess degree of risk (Kitchener, 2000). When assessing the potential for harm, many ethicists use a model of risk assessment developed by Beauchamp and Childress (1994). This approach assesses two elements of harm: the probability of harm (high or low) and the magnitude of harm (major or minor) likely. The need to breach confidentiality to protect others is highest when there is a

- As in all other situations, discuss the issue fully and openly with clients.
- Inform clients of the counselor's legal responsibility to warn others.
- Inform your supervisor of the potentially dangerous situation. If there is no supervisor, consult with another professional.
- Notify the person who might be responsible for the client or contact the police.
- Notify the intended victim.
- Explore other options, which may include commitment to an appropriate psychiatric facility.

FIGURE 4–4. Steps to Protect Others When Working with a Dangerous Client

Note: From *The ACA Legal Series: Confidentiality and Privileged Communication* (p. 22) by G. L. Arthur & C. D. Swanson, 1993, Alexandria, VA: American Counseling Association. Copyright 1993 by American Counseling Association. Reprinted by permission.

high potential for harm and the magnitude of the harm is major. Conversely, if the possibility of harm is minor and the type of harm is minor, the counselor is in a clearer position to preserve client confidentiality while resolving the situation. Figure 4–4 presents recommended steps for the counselor to take if the client has been assessed as dangerous.

Several subsequent court decisions have expanded and clarified the duty to protect from dangerous clients. For example, victims who are not specifically identified but are foreseeable, likely targets of client violence, such as family members and others in close proximity to an identifiable victim, should be warned (*Hedlund v. Superior Court*, 1983; *Jablonski v. United States*, 1983). Counselors should educate themselves on additional rulings that influence their duty to protect their clients and people around them from harm. State and federal courts continue to struggle with how this important issue should be resolved in particular circumstances. Costa and Altekruse (1994) provide a set of practical guidelines for dealing with duty-to-warn situations, emphasizing practical issues in their application.

Another court case has established that a parallel duty exists to violate confidentiality if a client is judged to be at risk for self-harm. *Eisel v. Board of Education of Montgomery County* was a 1991 decision by the Maryland Court of Appeals that established the duty to protect for school counselors. This case involved a child who threatened suicide in the presence of schoolmates, who reported the threats to their parents, who notified the school counselors. The counselors interviewed the child, who denied the threats. Counselors did not notify the child's parents or school administration. After the child did commit suicide, the father sued the counselors and the school, alleging breach of duty to intervene to prevent the suicide (Anderson, 1996). This case and others led Anderson (1996) to caution that counselors do have a duty to protect their clients from harming themselves if it is foreseeable (see the guidelines for dealing with suicidal clients).

In more recent years, a significant amount of legal attention has focused on whether or not confidentiality of an HIV-positive client can be breached if his behavior puts unknowing others at serious risk for infection. Because social stigma and discrimination may cause serious harm to people with HIV disease, many states have passed stringent laws to protect the confidentiality and privacy of people who are HIV positive. Release of information may be permitted under narrowly defined circumstances, often only by physicians and often related to threats posed by the client. A state statute may impose a duty to warn (as in 23 states) and a state law may require nondisclosure of HIV-related information (Burris, 2001). The complexities of how to proceed in such contradictory instances when both legal dictates exist make it clear that counselors should obtain legal counsel to assist them in understanding their legal obligations. Counselors should review how the laws and cases in their own jurisdictions are pertinent to their work with people who are HIV positive *before* they are directly faced with them in the counseling relationship.

Termination Phase Issues

In the final phase of counseling, the focus shifts to ensuring that the client is prepared for the transition out of counseling or into a new relationship if a referral is made. Clearly, termination is a right of both the counselor and the client. The stage should have been set for the length and nature of the relationship, beginning with the process of informed consent and continuing through the therapy and subsequent reevaluations of the nature of the counseling relationship. If a client requires additional therapy or counseling beyond the counselor's scope of competence, the counselor is ethically responsibile to refer the client properly and ensure that his counseling needs are met after the conclusion of the first relationship. The counselor might consider documenting the referral arrangements in a follow-up letter summarizing the arrangements or names of individuals to whom referral might be made to record the transition precautions.

Counselors should take particular caution in two instances at termination. First, clients with serious, unresolved clinical conditions that require further intervention should not be terminated. If their care is beyond the abilities of the counselor, a referral may be made, but counseling must be continued until the referral transition occurs. Second, caution must be exercised in situations in which the counselor works for an institution, such as a managed care system, that mandates termination after a specified number of sessions, whether or not the client's condition is resolved sufficiently. If a client is terminated prematurely by the counselor, a malpractice suit may be filed for abandonment or failure to treat or refer. The counselor should seek to continue treatment, at least until appropriate alternate treatment can be arranged (Bennett, Bryant, VandenBos, & Greenwood, 1990).

Pressure on counselors and mental health professionals to terminate services prematurely may become one of the most prominent ethical and legal issues in mental health care (see Chapter 8 for discussion of the administrative aspects of financial and termination issues). The temptation to terminate a client may be great when a provider's fees run out, the client cannot afford further care, or the client amasses an increasingly large bill. If the client is in need of further treatment, the therapist is obligated to meet that need until it is resolved or a referral can be arranged. The more appropriate route to dealing with this issue is for the counselor and the client to fully understand the financial conditions and limitations involved and determine whether the client's resources will be sufficient for the duration of the counseling relationship. Counselors are not obligated to accept a client into counseling if this situation does not seem workable at the outset. The potential client may be better served by seeking counseling with an agency that has the potential to carry out a reasonable treatment plan.

CHAPTER SUMMARY

Counselors must have a situation-specific interpretation of both legal and ethical regulatory standards to conduct well-informed practice. They must weigh all aspects of a situation, determine which ethical and legal standards apply in general, and decide how they apply in a particular instance.

Society holds all mental health professionals accountable for maintaining proper clinical and ethical standards of practice through four legal mechanisms: professional ethics committees, state licensure boards, criminal courts, and civil courts.

The counseling relationship has four phases: (1) initiation phase, (2) ongoing counselor phase, (3) dangerousness and crisis concerns phase, and (4) termination phase. Each phase faces key challenges, including counselor competency, informed consent, confidentiality and privileged communication, exceptions to confidentiality, record keeping, dangerousness, and termination issues.

REFERENCES

American Psychological Association. (1993). Record keeping guidelines. *American Psychologist, 48*, 984–986.

Anderson, B. S. (1996). *The counselor and the law* (4th ed.). Alexandria, VA: American Counseling Association.

Arthur, G. L., & Swanson, C. D. (1993). *The ACA legal series: Confidentiality and privileged communication.* Alexandria, VA: American Counseling Association.

Beauchamp, T. L., & Childress, J. F. (1994). *Principles of biomedical ethics* (5th ed.). Oxford: Oxford University Press.

Bennett, B. E., Bryant, B. K., VandenBos, G. R., & Greenwood, A. (1990). *Professional liability and risk management.* Washington, DC: American Psychological Association.

Bertram, B., & Wheeler, A. M. (1994). *Legal aspects of counseling: Avoiding lawsuits and legal problems.* Workshop materials. Alexandria, VA: American Counseling Association.

Bray, J. H., Shepard, J. N., & Hayes, J. R. (1985). Legal and ethical issues in informed consent to psychotherapy. *The American Journal of Family Therapy, 13*(2), 56–60.

Burris, S. (2001). Clinical decision making in the shadow of law. In J.R. Anderson & B. Barret (Eds.), *Ethics in HIV-related psychotherapy: Clinical decision making in complex cases* (pp. 99–129). Washington, DC: American Psychological Association.

Commission on Rehabilitation Counselor Certification. (2001). *Code of professional ethics for rehabilitation counselors.* Rolling Meadows, IL: Author.

Corey, G., Corey, M., & Callanan, P. (1998). *Issues and ethics in the helping professions* (5th ed). Pacific Grove, CA: Brooks/Cole.

Costa, L., & Altekruse, M. (1994). Duty-to-warn guidelines for mental health counselors. *Journal of Counseling & Development, 72*, 346–350.

DePauw, M. E. (1986). Avoiding ethical violations: A timeline perspective for individual counseling. *Journal of Counseling & Development, 69*, 3–36.

Eisel v. Board of Education of Montgomery County, 324 Md. 376, 597 A, 2d 447 (Md. Ct. App. 1991).

Fischer, L., & Sorenson, G. P. (1985). *School law for counselors, psychologists, and social workers.* New York: Longman.

Glosoff, H. L., Herlihy, B., & Spence, B. (2000). Privileged communication in the counselor-client relationship. *Journal of Counseling & Development, 78,* 454–462.

Glosoff, H. L., Herlihy, S., Herlihy, B., & Spence, B. (1997). Privileged communication in the psychologist-client relationship. *Professional Psychology: Research and Practice, 28*, 573–581.

Handelsman, M. M., Martinez, A., Geisendorfer, S., & Jordan, L. (1995). Does legally mandated consent to psychotherapy ensure ethical appropriateness? *Ethics and Behavior, 5*(2), 119–129.

Hedlund v. Superior Court of Orange County, 669 P.2d41, 191 Cal. Rptr. 805 (1983).

Jablonski v. United States, 712 F.2d 391 (9th Cir., 1983).

Jaffee v. Redmond et al., WL 315841 (U.S. June 13, 1996).

Keary, A. O. (1985). Criminal law and procedure. In N. T. Sidney (Ed.), *Law and ethics: A guide for the health professional* (pp. 63–102). New York: Human Sciences.

Kitchener, K. S. (2000). *Foundations of ethical practice, research, and teaching in psychology.* Mahway, NJ: Lawrence Erlbaum Associates.

Kohlberg, L. (1964). Development of moral character and moral ecology. In M. L. Hoffman & L. W. Hoffman (Eds.), *Review of child development research:* Vol. I. New York: Russell Sage Foundation.

Kohlberg, L. (1981). *Philosophy of moral development.* San Francisco: Harper & Row.

Mitchell, R. W. (2001). *Documentation of counseling records* (2nd ed.). (AACD Legal Series). Alexandria, VA: American Counseling Association.

National Board for Counselor Certification. (1996, Summer). Jaffee v. Redmond: A primer on privilege. *NBCC NewsNotes, 13,* 1–4.

Piazza, N. J., & Baruth, N. E. (1990). Client record guidelines. *Journal of Counseling & Development, 68*, 313–316.

Pope, K., Tabachnick, B., & Keith-Spiegel, P. (1987). Ethics of practice: The beliefs and behavior of psychologists as therapists. *American Psychologist, 42*, 993–1006.

Pope, K., & Vasquez, M. J. T. (1998). *Ethics in psychotherapy and counseling* (2nd ed.). San Francisco: Jossey-Bass.

Remley, T. P., Jr. (1990). Counseling records: Legal and ethical issues. In B. Herlihy & L. Golden (Eds.), *ACA Ethical standards casebook* (4th ed., pp. 162–169). Alexandria, VA: American Counseling Association.

Remley, T. P., Jr. (1996). The relationship between law and ethics. In B. Herlihy & G. Corey (Eds.), *ACA ethical standards casebook* (5th ed., pp. 285–292). Alexandria, VA: American Counseling Association.

Remley, T. P., & Herlihy, B. (2001). *Ethical, legal, and professional issues in counseling.* Upper Saddle River, NJ: Merrill/Prentice-Hall.

Remley, T. P., Jr., Herlihy, B., & Herlihy, S. B. (1997). The U.S. Supreme Court decision in Jaffee v. Redmond: Implications for counselors. *Journal of Counseling and Development, 75*, 213–218.

Shaw, L. R., & Tarvydas, V. (2001). The use of professional disclosure in rehabilitation counseling. *Rehabilitation Counseling Bulletin, 45,* 40–47.

Shea, T. E. (1985). Finding the law: Legal research and citation. In N. T. Sidney (Ed.), *Law and ethics: A guide for the health professional* (pp. 411–424). New York: Human Sciences.

Snider, P. D. (1987). Client records: Inexpensive liability protection for mental health counselors. *Journal of Mental Health Counseling, 9*, 134–141.

Swenson, L. C. (1997). *Psychology and law: For the helping professions.* Pacific Grove, CA: Brooks/Cole Publishing Co.

Tarasoff v. Regents of University of California, 13 C.3d 177, 529 P.2d 553, 118 Cal. Rptr. 129 (1974).

Tarasoff v. Regents of University of California, 17 Cal. App. 3d 425, 551 P.2d 334 (1976).

Thompson, A. (1990). *Guide to ethical practice in psychotherapy.* New York: John Wiley & Sons.

VandeCreek, L., Bennett, B. E., & Bricklin, P. M. (1994). *Risk management with potentially dangerous patients.* Washington, D.C.: APA Insurance Trust.

Van Hoose, W. H., & Paradise, L. V. (1979). *Ethics in counseling and psychotherapy: Perspectives in issues and decision making.* Cranston, RI: Cranston Press.

Ware, M. L. (1971). The law and counselor ethics. *Personnel and Guidance Journal,* 50, 305–310.

Wigmore, J. H. (1961). Evidence in trials at common law. In J. T. McNaughton (Ed.), *Rules of evidence* (Vol. 8, rev. ed.). Boston: Little, Brown.

APPENDIX 4–A

Informed Written Consent for Treatment Checklist

Requirements vary greatly regarding the necessity or the content of an informed written consent for treatment—sometimes referred to as a Fact Sheet. Agency or institutional policies, state counselor licensing laws and rules, and other binding directives often determine the existence or content of this document. The intent of an informed consent document is to define the basic treatment relationship between counselor and client. Misunderstanding and disappointment, which are often the genesis of a liability claim, can be reduced when clients are made knowledgeable of the ground rules of the counseling relationship. Trust and the therapeutic relationship are enhanced when clients understand what is expected or required of a counselor and of themselves in a successful counseling relationship.

The following topics are recommended for consideration when developing an informed written consent for treatment:

1. **Voluntary Participation.** Clients voluntarily agree to treatment and can terminate at any time without penalty.
2. **Client Involvement.** What level of involvement and what type of involvement will be expected from clients?
3. **Counselor Involvement.** What will the counselor provide? How will this be provided? How can the counselor be reached in the event of an emergency?
4. **No Guarantees.** Counselors cannot guarantee results (e.g., become happier, less tense or depressed, save the marriage, stop drug use, obtain a good job).
5. **Risks Associated with Counseling.** Define what, if any, risks are associated with the counselor's particular approach to counseling.
6. **Confidentiality and Privilege.** Specify how confidentiality will be handled in couple counseling, family counseling, child/adolescent counseling, and group counseling situations. How may confidential and privileged information be released?
7. **Exceptions of Confidentiality and Privilege.** Define specific statutory circumstances where confidentiality and privilege cannot be maintained (e.g., abuse reporting).
8. **Counseling Approach or Theory.** What is the counselor's counseling orientation or theoretical belief system? How will that affect treatment?
9. **Counseling and Financial Records.** What will they include? How long will they be maintained? How will they be destroyed?
10. **Ethical Guidelines.** What standard defines the counselor's practice? How might a client obtain a copy of these guidelines?
11. **Licensing Regulations.** What license does the counselor hold? How may a client check on the status of the license?
12. **Credentials.** What education, training, and experience credentials will the counselor need to provide counseling treatment, including any specialty credentials?
13. **Fees and Charges.** What are the specific fees and charges? How will fees be collected? How are financial records maintained?
14. **Insurance Reimbursement.** What responsibility will the counselor take for filing insurance forms? What fees, if any, are associated with insurance filing? How will co-payments be handled?
15. **Responsibility for Payment.** Who is responsible for payment of counseling charges? How will delinquent accounts be handled? What charges will be assessed for delinquent accounts?
16. **Disputes and Complaints.** How will fee or other disputes be resolved? Provide the address and phone number of the state licensing board for complaints if required by state licensing statute.
17. **Cancellation Policy.** How much notice for cancellation of a scheduled appointment is required? What fees will be charged for late cancellation?

18. **Affiliation Relationship.** Describe independent contractor and/or partnership relationship with any other practitioners in office suite.
19. **Supervisory Relationship.** Describe any required supervisory relationship along with reason for the supervision. Provide supervisor's name and credentials.
20. **Colleague Consultation.** Indicate that, in keeping with generally accepted standards of practice, you frequently consult with other mental health professionals regarding the management of cases. The purpose of the consultation is to ensure quality care. Every effort is made to protect the identity of clients.

NOTE: From "Legal Aspects of Counseling: Avoiding Lawsuits and Legal Problems," by B. Bertram & A. M. Wheeler, 1994, Workshop materials, Alexandria, VA: American Counseling Association.

PART II

Values Clarification and Decision Making

CHAPTER 5

Values, Valuing, and Principles in Counseling

Objectives

■ ■ ■ ■ ■ ■ ■ ■ ■ ■

After reading this chapter, you should be able to:

- Explain the value-laden nature of counseling.
- Define and contrast the concepts of ethics, morals, and values.
- Explain the historical and ongoing role of values in the counseling process.
- Identify and discuss the three processes used to examine and work with value systems: values clarification, values conflict resolution and valuing processes, and moral discussion.
- Discuss the five core ethical principles most relevant to counseling practice.
- Explain how the five core ethical principles underlie common counseling practices and codes of ethics.

■ ■ ■ ■ ■ ■ ■ ■ ■ ■

INTRODUCTION

Counselors and their clients focus on issues of value and the meaning of life as they solve problems, develop strategies, and work toward goals. They use their unique interpretations of what is good, bad, right, wrong, joyous, and painful in their experiences to guide them. These understandings, called values, are abstract and difficult to define and communicate. Values must be experienced to be truly grasped. They are powerful and drive our choices about what we wish to do and what we would like to have. They focus our energies and choices. Reflect on the strong emotion and sense of rightness you experience when you hug your child after returning from a long journey; the confusion and disgust you feel as you watch the beating of an individual on television news; or the sense of calm and joy you experience when you see a beautiful sunrise or feel gentle, pine-scented breezes. The beliefs and preferences that underlie these values can be articulated—love of family, respect for life and personal freedom, and respect for nature and our responsibility to care for these resources. Values are formed over the years through our experience of the beliefs, choices, and actions of significant others and through exposure to cultural institutions such as school and places of worship.

Both clients and counselors hold values, whether or not they are able to articulate them in the moment. When clients come to counselors for assistance in making choices or changing their lives, both parties enact values, either knowingly or unknowingly.

Professional ethical principles are drawn from societal values that guide counselors in making difficult choices when working with clients. These principles are the basis of a variety of professional practices and the codes of ethics used in counseling.

Value analysis and choice in ethical decision making are increasingly important. New developments in ethics, such as virtue ethics, multiculturalism, and feminist streams of thought, illustrate how values and worldview-based analysis can be reframed to accommodate the diverse lives and perspectives of all people in counseling.

VALUES: THE BASIC CONCEPTS

Ethics, Morals, and Values

In a sermon given in Georgia on 4 February 1968, during the height of the Civil Rights movement, the Reverend Martin Luther King, Jr. spoke eloquently about what it takes to truly be a helper:

> Everybody can be great because anybody can serve (the Civil Rights movement). You
> don't have to have a college degree to serve, you don't have to make your subject
> and verb agree to serve, you don't have to know about Plato and Aristotle to serve, you
> don't have to know Einstein's "Theory of Relativity" to serve, you don't have to know
> the Second Theory of Thermodynamics and Physics to serve. . . . You only need a heart
> full of grace, a soul generated by love. (King, 1968)

The issues that surround ethical judgment involve a complex interplay of morals, values, and priorities that people hold in relationship to themselves, their colleagues, and other professionals. Ethical principles of practice are interrelated with, but distinguishable from, concepts such as morals, values, and codes of ethics. Taken together, they form the heart and soul of counseling.

Ethics and Morals. *Ethics* has been variously defined. In Chapter 1 the difficulty of distinguishing the concepts of ethics and morality in the arenas of philosophy and professional practice was discussed. Remember, in discussing the practice of professional counseling

and psychology, the term professional ethics carries a meaning more closely related to the concept of philosophical morals; that is, *acting* in accord with standards of professional practice. When reading the professional counseling and psychology literature, the meaning of ethics and morality becomes even more confusing because authors do not have a clear agreement on definition. For example, in the professional counseling and psychology literature, ethics is defined as "a branch of study in philosophy concerning how people ought to act toward each other, pronouncing judgments of value about those actions" (Kitchener, 1984, p.18); and "a hierarchy of values that permits choices to be made based on distinguished levels of right or wrong" (Shertzer & Linden, 1979, p. 510). In describing *morals* in the professional literature, the nature of the concepts takes on a clear connotation of the goodness or badness of human behavior or character (Van Hoose & Kottler, 1985) and implies an element of coercion (Mowrer, 1967). Although ethics also deals with the appropriateness of human action, it connotes more of a basis in reason and objectivity (Van Hoose & Kottler, 1985). In differentiating between ethics and morals, Kitchener (1984) noted that morals are more related to the individual's belief structure, whereas ethics involve the study and evaluation of this belief structure. The importance of this distinction and the evaluative component of ethics become clear when one realizes that "it is critical to differentiate between saying 'X' *believes* a certain action is right or good and that action *is* right or good" (Kitchener, 1984, p. 16). It is not difficult to think of examples of people who are steeped in personally or environmentally distorted thinking: Remember the scientists in charge of the Tuskegee experiment that left black men with syphilis intentionally untreated for decades, or the Reverend Jim Jones, who led the mass suicide of his cult in Guyana. The individuals involved in these, and countless other tragic circumstances, may have acted consistently with their personal moral code, but not ethically, as based on a broader analysis of appropriate behavior. The need for evaluation of personal actions against a broader standard of what is right and good is imperative for the well-being of all.

Values.   Counselors are required to distinguish their personal moral codes from and reconcile them with the profession's values to behave in an ethical manner. However, some experts in the field maintain that the stated attempt to separate moral outlook and choices from professional skills and practices is both deceptive and deleterious to one of psychotherapy's major

Box 5.1   End-of-Life Choices as Enacted Values

Anyone who has worked with or been close to someone who is near death knows that the final choices about how one dies take on stark personal meaning. Being near death is sometimes referred to as "instant values clarification." It is important to discuss your final wishes about terminal care with medical caregivers and family while you are healthy and able to express your desires. By making these decisions before you become ill with a life-threatening condition, your choices will be based on clear thinking and on your personal values about the end of life. An Extended Values History is a tool to assist you and your loved ones in making decisions about the quality of care you desire (or do not desire) if you become terminally ill. Although the document is not legally binding, it is used in conjunction with a legally executed living will and/or durable power of attorney for health care. Go to www.euthanasia.org/vh.html and complete the *Extended Values History*. Discuss your choices and answers with those closest to you. In class, discuss what you discovered about yourself and your values in doing this important bit of personal business.

sources of legitimacy, direction, and power (Frank, 1961; London, 1986). In fact, Doherty (1995) advocated counseling that actively incorporates a moral development perspective. He argued that counselors should urge their clients to adopt a sense of moral responsibility, and that counselors should ascribe to the ideals of commitment, justice, truthfulness, and community in their work with clients. Others have suggested that counseling be seen as an opportunity for moral reflection and encouragement of character development (Griffith & Duesterhaus, 2000). Clearly, counselors must give much thought to understanding the role of morals and values in their work. Most professionals agree that all counseling involves values, no matter how directly or indirectly they are expressed.

Rokeach (1973) defined *value* as "an enduring belief that a specific mode of conduct or end-state of existence is personally or socially preferable to an opposite or converse mode of conduct or end-state of existence" (p.5). Values involve that which is intrinsically worthwhile or worthy of esteem for its own sake, and reflect the value holder's worldview, culture, or understanding of the world. Values arise from individuals' experiences and interactions with their culture, the world, and the people around them, such as their parents, friends, religious leaders, and neighbors. Thus, values vary among individuals, but are likely to vary less among persons growing up within similar systems, such as specific cultures or religions. A value system is a hierarchical ranking of the degree of preference for the values expressed by a particular person or social entity.

Values are often mistakenly thought of as involving a simple expression of personal interest or prefer-

ence, such as a preference for an automatic rather than a standard transmission in a new car. Actually, values are more complex—they involve a set of beliefs that include evaluative, emotional, and existential aspects. There are elements of goodness, obligation, or requirement; positive or negative affective orientation; and a sense of the meaningfulness of the situation or choice attached to the object of the valuing process. Values are not directly observable, but they guide human choice and action through the value preferences expressed in human choices and goals, and they may also be expressed verbally (see activity in Box 5.1).

There are many systems for describing values, including Rokeach's (1973) 18 values that reflect desirable end-states. Allport, Vernon, and Lindzey (1960) saw six basic values or evaluative attitudes reflected in personality types: theoretical, economic, aesthetic, social, political, and religious. Similarly, Frankena (1963) identified eight distinct realms of value, only one of which is related to ethics: morality, art, science, religion, economics, politics, law, and manner or custom. In all of these systems, values can be either *moral* or *nonmoral* in nature—they may or may not involve preferences concerning what is morally right or wrong. For example, a person's choice to become a vegetarian might be based on nonmoral or moral value grounds. It might stem from belief in the importance of social status and a wish to follow the lead of a charismatic friend, or to be "politically correct" (nonmoral values of manner or custom); or the choice might be based on a spiritual belief that all forms of life should be respected and protected from discomfort and violence (moral). Thus, any situation, choice, or action may be valued or prized in a number of disparate and possibly competing ways by different individuals or groups. It also is possible for one individual to hold two or more conflicting values about a particular object or situation, resulting in some level of dissonance if the person becomes aware of the conflicting values. The vegetarian who believes in the sanctity of all life forms may also value respect for family tradition and a mother's wishes (thus eating Thanksgiving turkey once a year at the family gathering).

The process of socializing new students into a profession can also be thought of as introducing them to the profession's specific core values. For example, new students will learn the high value that counselors place on protecting clients' privacy by hearing instructors and fellow students discuss it in class and then observing their clinical supervisors struggle to keep client information confidential by claiming privilege in the face of a subpoena. This socialization process can be seen as a way of assisting these individuals in adopting a specific subculture or worldview that will enhance their professional perspective, judgment, and ability to function responsibly in their new roles. Rokeach and Regan (1980) noted two dimensions of values that are relevant to counseling: (a) standards of competency and standards of morals, and (b) terminal (desirable end-states) and instrumental (behaviors useful to reach end-state) values. Wisdom (more desirable than foolishness), truthfulness (more desirable than deceit), and freedom (more desirable than enslavement) are examples of terminal values. Instrumental values concern those idealized or desirable types of behavior that are useful in attaining the end-state, such as being organized or industrious. They are not necessarily good in and of themselves. For example, the instrumental value of industriousness may serve either a thief or Mother Theresa, but to very different ends. These dimensions add richness to the consideration of ethics concepts. Thus, unethical practices can be seen as stemming from either ignorance or inadequate training and supervision (violations of the value concerning standards of competency), as well as from personal profit motive, need for self-enhancement, or the need to maintain power and status (terminal values). These latter motivations may be related to personal values that are nonmoral values, and are in conflict with the moral values embedded in the profession's values as reflected in its standards regarding particular situations.

Another important differentiation involves acknowledging that some values can be seen as universal, but not necessarily absolute. Historically, anthropologists see such values as the prohibition against killing, a pro-

I. Commitment to something greater than oneself
   To recognize the existence of and be committed to a Supreme Being, higher principle, transcendent purpose or meaning to one's existence
   To seek the truth (or truths)
   To seek justice

II. Self-respect, but with humility, self-discipline, and acceptance of personal responsibility
   To respect and care for oneself
   To not exalt oneself or overindulge—to show humility and avoid gluttony, greed, or other forms of selfishness or self-centeredness
   To act in accordance with one's conscience and to accept responsibility for one's behavior

III. Respect and caring for others (i.e., the Golden Rule)
   To recognize the connectedness between all people
   To serve humankind and to be helpful to individuals
   To be caring, respectful, compassionate, tolerant, and forgiving of others
   To not hurt others (e.g., do not murder, abuse, steal from, cheat, or lie to others)

IV. Caring for other living things and the environment

FIGURE 5–1. The Short List of Universal Moral Values
Source: From "A Short List of Universal Moral Values" by R. T. Kinnier, J. L. Kernes, and T. M. Dautheribes, 2000, *Counseling and Values, 45,* 4–16. Copyright 2000 by American Counseling Association. Reprinted by permission.

hibition on marriage or sexual intercourse between members of the immediate family, respect for ownership of property, and truthfulness as values shared by most human cultures (Brandt, 1959; Kluckhorn, 1951). Nevertheless, culturally permissible exceptions under specific circumstances are allowed, such as killing to defend one's own life or in battle in a war. This acknowledgment is not tantamount to ethical relativism or situational ethics. These exceptions are related to limited circumstances that make the exception permissible. Further, these exceptions are widely understood and supported by the entire cultural group for all people in similar circumstances. In more recent work, the quest to identify universal values relevant to counseling while still respecting human diversity continues. After reviewing the scholarly and religious literature concerning universal values and values central to the major streams of world culture, Kinnier, Kernes, and Dautheribes (2000) compiled a list of universal moral values to use in counseling to assist clients in examining the implications of their value conflicts. Examine these values as presented in Figure 5–1 and think about whether you agree that

abortion	assisted suicide	pre- or extra-marital sex
sexual identity issues	child custody	spousal abuse
substance abuse	illegal means of support	interracial relationships
cross-racial adoption	unsafe sexual activity	child neglect/abuse
controversial religious beliefs	racist behavior/attitudes	dishonesty
birth control	unwed pregnancy	discipline of children
infertility/childlessness	cosmetic surgery	death and dying
unusual sexual practices	gang membership	suicide

FIGURE 5–2. Value-Charged Issues in Counseling

they are universal. How do you feel about using them in counseling? Are they "universal" enough to be used with clients of diverse cultural, ethnic, and religious backgrounds? How might examining them assist both counselor and client in resolving the issues presented in counseling?

VALUES IN COUNSELING

Historical Perspective

Do all members of the human race share common values? To what degree should a counselor's values influence clients? These questions constitute some of the most troublesome debates in counseling and date to the beginning of psychotherapy's development with Sigmund Freud's psychodynamic approach. In his system of therapy, the therapist was to work assiduously to maintain an absolute neutrality of response to the patient, thus providing a "blank screen" on which the patient could project and play out intrapsychic conflicts. The desired result of this process was transference reaction. Patients would project the persona of an important figure from their earlier psychic development and engage this persona in reparatory work by playing out conflicts with this figure in the therapist-patient relationship. It was essential that characteristics of the therapist, including values and morals, were not conveyed to the patient, thereby encouraging the projection process.

The substance of orthodox Freudian psychodynamic therapy as well as the enthusiastic adoption of the objective, scientific paradigm continued to influence the development of all psychotherapy. This legacy resulted in a long-term supposition that counselors and therapists could and should be value-neutral, a belief that persisted into the 1950s (Ginsberg & Herma, 1953; Walters, 1958). Later, professionals began acknowledg-

ing the value-based nature of counseling (Bergin, 1985; London, 1986; Pietrofesa, Hoffman, Splete, & Pinto, 1978). Education and research have continued to value and develop the scientific and technical aspects of professional practice in subsequent decades. However, it is just as critical for counselors to acknowledge and develop the ability to address the moral and value dimensions of their expertise (Corey, Corey, & Callanan, 1998; London, 1986). Herr and Niles (1988) noted that the counselor's values determine the *process* of counseling, whereas the client's values determine the *content* of counseling. In addition, the content of the problem the client brings to counseling may be value-laden in and of itself for both the counselor and client, such as whether or not to have premarital sex. Clients also may attempt to camouflage or avoid certain issues due to struggles with their value systems, such as refusing to discuss their struggles with issues of gender identity. Figure 5–2 provides examples of the myriad value-charged issues that clients may bring to counseling. Counselors should examine their own values and biases in these areas.

QUESTION FOR REFLECTION

Your 16-year-old client informs you that she is pregnant by her 17-year-old-boyfriend. She tells you that she does not love her boyfriend and was thinking about ending the relationship prior to the pregnancy. She wants to have an abortion and needs your help. You are pro-life and do not support abortion; however, you work in a public school that does not have a policy prohibiting counselors from working with students considering abortion. What do you do?

A counselor's personal and professional value systems will influence the course of the counseling interaction through a wide range of mechanisms: (a) if and how the client will be diagnosed, (b) whether certain topics will be focused on or discussed at all through specific direction or more subtle verbal or nonverbal reinforcement, (c) which goals are considered possible or appropriate for the counseling work they will do, and (d) how they will be evaluated (Strupp, 1980).

Counselors' Values in the Relationship

Counselors should become intensely involved in assessing their own values and how they affect the counseling process (Corey, Corey, & Callanan, 1998; Herr & Niles, 1988). It is highly unethical for counselors to *impose* their values on a client (Corey, Corey, & Callanan, 1998). For example, some counselors have pressured homosexual clients who are content with that status to become involved in conversion or reparative *role recovery* therapy. While this may be an appropriate approach for gay clients who are unhappy and wish to become heterosexual in their lifestyle, it is unethical to even subtly coerce clients to undergo therapy they do not desire. However, it may be helpful for the counselor to *disclose* her values. Recent recommendations urge counselors to disclose their values and philosophical orientations directly to clients. This discussion might occur either within the context of specific issues that arise within the course of counseling or as part of the process of informed consent and professional disclosure at the outset of counseling (Tjelveit, 1986). As with any advanced counseling technique, such as confrontation, the counselor should disclose values carefully. This disclosure should be intentional, focused on enhancing the client's process, and presented in an open, non-judgmental manner that carries with it the sense that these values may be accepted or rejected without risking the counseling relationship.

QUESTION FOR REFLECTION

Your client makes this statement in session: "I hate Jews. It's too bad Hitler wasn't able to finish what he started." You are Jewish. What, if anything, do you say in response to this statement?

The client might experience the same personal values held by the counselor, as well as a more general body of shared values. Traditionally, these shared values have been described as *mental health values* (Jensen & Bergin, 1988) or *essential therapeutic values* (Strupp, 1980). A national survey by Jensen and Bergin (1988) examined counselors' degree of consensus with key mental health values including autonomy and independence, skill in interpersonal communication,

honesty, and self-control. They found a substantial consensus among surveyed counselors that these are central counseling values.

The essential therapeutic values described by Strupp (1980) are that people (a) have rights, privileges, and responsibilities; (b) have the right to personal freedom; (c) have responsibilities to others; (d) should be responsible for conducting their own affairs, as much as they are able; (e) should have their individuality respected; (f) should not be dominated, manipulated, coerced, or indoctrinated; and (g) are entitled to make their own mistakes and learn from them. Values may be observed interpersonally within the counseling relationship through studying the perceived operation of (a) **support,** the receiving of encouragement, understanding, and kindness from others; (b) **conformity,** the following of rules and observation of societal regulations; (c) **recognition,** the attraction of favorable notice and being considered important; (d) **independence,** seeing oneself as being free to make one's own decisions and acting autonomously; (e) **benevolence,** the experience of sharing, helping, and acting generously toward others; and (f) **leadership,** the sense of having responsibility, power, and authority over others (Gordon, 1976). Clearly, the values of counselors are expressed through specific behaviors that affect the client in the counseling relationship.

In addition to these more global value orientations, some theoretical orientations embody and promulgate specific philosophical or value positions as part of the therapeutic system. To the degree that counselors follow these specific systems of therapy, they will directly influence the philosophy and values of their clients, hopefully with the client's direct awareness and consent. Examples of such approaches and associated values include (a) Adlerian Psychotherapy's emphasis on social striving and social interest; (b) Reality Therapy and its focus on personal responsibility and the quality of the individual lifestyle; (c) Existential Therapy and its emphasis on learning this particular philosophical system, including such concepts as self-determination and freedom with responsibility; and (d) Ellis's Rational–Emotive Behavior Therapy and its goal of indoctrinating the client with a new set of rational beliefs and values. A counselor's theoretical approach, philosophy, and underlying value system also have an influence on clients. Therefore, the counselor should include these beliefs in the informed consent procedures at the outset of the relationship. These issues should be thoroughly discussed in terms that prospective clients can understand to ensure that they comprehend these aspects of counseling, how the issues might influence their treatment, and whether the values are compatible with their own value system.

When there appears to be serious value incompatibilities or extreme levels of discomfort, counselors must determine if they should continue working with a client or refer the client to someone else who might have a better level of ability or compatibility with which to assist the client. If the counselor is in serious danger of imposing values on the client or is unable to remain objective, the counselor should consider referring the client elsewhere. Counselors often either over- or underestimate their ability to work with clients who cause such reactions in them. In such instances, counselors must make every effort to be honest with themselves. Supervision by a skilled senior colleague is invaluable in this determination. If the counselor is actually placing the client at risk or impeding progress, an appropriate referral made in a positive, constructive manner is necessary. In other instances, proper safeguards such as a skilled supervisor, consultant, or cotherapist can be arranged. Then, with client consent, counseling can proceed effectively. Such situations help counselors increase their ability to understand the viewpoints of others that may be challenging to them.

Research has demonstrated that the degree to which the values of the counselor and client are congruent influences the outcome of the counseling process. For example, clients who adopt values like those of their counselors tended to have more positive outcomes (Beutler, Pollack, & Jobe, 1978; Landfield & Nawas, 1964; Welkowitz, Cohen, & Ortmeyer, 1967). This important effect of differing counselor and client value systems demonstrates the increasing importance of the counselor being culturally sensitive. Counselors must become aware of the value systems of their clients from different cultures and of their own cultural assumptions and biases. They also must be willing and able to apply the skills necessary to accommodate and work across these diverse cultural perspectives (Pederson, 1985; Sue, 1996).

QUESTION FOR REFLECTION

Your client, a member of the Lakota Sioux, recently lost her husband in an automobile accident and is seeing you for counseling. She reports that she saw her deceased husband and he told her to "watch for the eagle." She has been maintaining evening vigils in wait of her husband's request. You become concerned because she seems to be experiencing hallucinations. What will you do?

Values, Cultural Worldviews, and Multiculturalism

A deep appreciation and understanding of the values of various cultural, social, and racial groups may provide a window into the relationship with a client who is from a nonmajority group. (Many of the basic concepts of multiculturalism and the ethical obligations to diverse clients are discussed in Chapter 11.) Counselors must understand how individuals from different cultures see the world and how they value different situations or ways of being—their **worldview**. In our diverse society, we can no longer presume that all people hold common, universal values that will be expressed in the same way. Even when people from diverse cultures do hold common values, they may apply them to specific circumstances very differently. The actual choices and behaviors they choose are more likely culture specific.

The values of different cultures have been described using a variety of dimensions upon which cultural groups may differ. While these various descriptors may be confusing, they do reflect the rich differences in what human beings value and how they see the world. Themes or dimensions for cultural values include nature, time, social relations, activity, humanity, customs, traditions, and religion (Hopkins, 1997). In contrast, Hofstede (1980) researched cultural differences relevant to public life and work behavior and found four major cultural dimensions: (a) power distances, (b) uncertainty avoidance, (c) individualism/collectivism, and (d) masculinity/femininity, or valuing assertiveness and materialism rather than concern for people and quality of life.

Becoming culturally sensitive is not an easy pursuit for counselors and constitutes a life-long area for personal and professional development. Corey, Corey, and Callanan (1998), strident proponents of this type of value learning and exploration, noted that often counselors must challenge the stereotypical beliefs that are common legacies of a Eurocentric majority culture. The stereotypical assumptions they call attention to are that clients: (a) are ready to engage in and value self-disclosure; (b) will be better off if they behave in an assertive manner; (c) believe that self-actualization is important, and that a trusting relationship can be quickly formed; (d) have nonverbal behaviors we can readily understand; and (e) value directness (Corey, Corey, & Callanan, 1998). Counselors must continuously strive to learn more about different cultures and varying value systems related to their clients' lives. Learning about these value themes or dimensions by listening to clients with openness and a desire to enter into their frame of reference is an important obligation.

VALUES CLARIFICATION, VALUING, AND MORAL DISCUSSION

How can counselors best prepare themselves to recognize their values and the implications of these values in their work? This task can be daunting. Three general processes have been developed to assist in this task: (a) values clarification, (b) the valuing process, and (c) moral discussion.

Values Clarification

The work of Raths, Harmin, and Simon (1966, 1978) sparked a tremendously successful movement among educators, counselors, other helping professionals, and even the public that focused attention on the importance and understanding of values. These scholars addressed the vacuum that many people felt in the 1950s in terms of establishing a sense of meaning and the importance of values within their lives and work. This movement appeared to be a reaction to the value-neutral influence of the scientific tradition and the increasing popularity of the humanistic philosophical and therapeutic movements of the late 1950s to the 1970s. The contemporary work of Rogers, Perls, Maslow, and others encouraged self-determination, examination of one's own perspectives, and the search for personal meaning and truth through self-examination (Kinnier, 1995). It is within that context that Raths, Harmin, and Simon (1966) noted that many individuals are unaware of the values they hold and suffer from this lack of focus in their personal and professional relationships and even in the sense of who they are.

Values clarification helps individuals clarify their beliefs through a method that focuses on the *process* surrounding assigning value rather than on the *content* of what is valued (Raths, Harmin, & Simon, 1966). Distinct steps in the values clarification process involve the three main functions of prizing, choosing, and acting on one's values. Values chosen through this process are considered *clarified values.*

Kirschenbaum (2000) became convinced that values clarification should be an element in a more comprehensive approach that includes the original seven valuing processes described by Raths, Harmin, and Si-

I.   *Inculcating*
II. *Modeling*
III. *Facilitating*
    A. *Prizing* beliefs and behaviors
        1. prizing and cherishing
        2. publicly affirming, when appropriate
    B. *Choosing* beliefs and behaviors
        3. choosing from alternatives
        4. choosing after consideration of consequences
        5. choosing freely
    C. *Acting* on beliefs
        6. acting
        7. acting with a pattern, consistency and repetition
IV. *Value-laden skill building*

FIGURE 5–3.   The Comprehensive Values Education Process (Includes the Seven Values Clarification Steps in the Facilitation Process)
Source: Adapted from "From values clarification to character education: A personal journey" by H. Kirschenbaum, 2000, *Journal of Humanistic Counseling, Education and Development, 39,* 20. Copyright 2000 by the American Counseling Association. Reprinted by permission.

mon (1978) that are contained in the facilitating stage of the new model, but also adds the processes of inculcation of positive values and character, modeling of values and character, and skill building necessary to live a satisfying and constructive life (Kirschenbaum, 2000; see Figure 5–3). This recent revision addresses the criticisms of those authorities who faulted values clarification for being concerned only with the process rather than the outcome of the process. Kirschenbaum's more recent revision concerns itself with both the process and the hoped-for outcomes of values education. Box 5.2 lists activities that are consistent with this tradition.

Values Conflict Resolution and Valuing

Values Conflict Resolution.   Clearly, the ways in which human experience can be explored through values clarification are vast. Nevertheless, values clarification began to lose favor during the 1980s. The most common area of concern involves the apparently value-neutral position of the group leader or teacher. Many have voiced concern that this experience may create a permissive, self-absorbed atmosphere, and in its extreme, allow abusive or abhorrent values to go

Box 5.2   What Are Some of My Values?

The following activities are consistent with the values clarification tradition. After completing the activities, discuss your answers in a group. Conduct an open, thought-provoking discussion with your peers, examine the consequences of your position, and publicly affirm your beliefs.

Activity 1. Imagine that your doctor has told you that you have a virulent form of cancer and you will be dead soon. You have decided to write your own eulogy. What are the unique traits or meaningful accomplishments that you especially want to include? Why are they particularly important to you? Which one is the *most important* to you? Why? Which one is most important to your parents? Which one is most important to your spouse, partner, or closest friend? Do these perspectives differ? Why or why not?

Activity 2. Imagine you are in a longstanding relationship with your partner that is very happy, except for one thing—you and your partner are not able to have a biological child despite wanting one badly. You have decided to adopt a child, but are not able to receive a healthy infant of your own race. You are offered the opportunity to choose from among the following babies: a biracial baby, a baby that is moderately mentally retarded, a baby whose biological mother is HIV positive, a 2-year-old who appears to be hyperactive, a child with facial deformities that can only be partially corrected by surgeries, and a toddler who survived the murder–suicide of his biological parents. Would you adopt one of these children or choose not to have a child? If you would adopt, which child would you select and why? For each of the children you did not select, what was your reasoning?

Countless individuals have taken part and benefited from this type of encounter. This approach offers opportunities to examine countless aspects of our personal and professional relationships and lifestyle choices. It is likely to stimulate lively discussion and serious self-examination. The activities can be tailored to the concerns and needs of quite disparate types of people, including counselors. For example:

■ What is your ideal type of client to work with? Why? Your most dreaded? Why?

■ What makes you happiest about your work as a counselor? Over what do you become the most upset or afraid?

■ Who is the living person who has most influenced your work? Why and how?

■ What historical or prominent celebrity figure has most influenced your work? Why and how?

■ What is the greatest boost to your effectiveness and why?

■ What is the biggest threat to your effectiveness and why?

■ What are you proudest of about yourself as a counselor? Ashamed?

---

unchallenged. Kinnier (1995) suggested that religious conservatism, political conservatism, a therapeutic paradigm shift away from humanistic philosophy, and the inherent flaws within the theory itself are the major forces that have dampened earlier enthusiasm for values clarification. He noted that the core concepts are worth retaining, and recommended several changes to resolve specific problems and extend the usefulness of this approach. Kinnier (1995) forwarded the idea of focusing on one concrete and specific values conflict at a time in a specific area of the person's life because people do not effectively evaluate values in single, abstract form. The emphasis should not be on rank-ordering values, but rather on determining which values are in conflict and the degree of conflict, as well as arriving at an overall statement of how the key values in conflict can be reconciled. This would provide a more specific goal to the process—resolution of a specified values conflict—and, thus, Kinnier (1995) suggested how more effective interventions could be tailored to assist in this conflict resolution (Table 5–1). The interventions are divided between rational and intuitive-type foci to accommodate differing personal styles of those in conflict.

In addition to these concerns about how the process was conceptualized and applied, several authorities reviewed the effectiveness of values clarifica-

TABLE 5–1   Strategies for Intrapersonal Values Conflict Resolution

Rational	Intuition-Enhancing
Defining the conflict clearly	Emotional focusing
Gathering information systematically	Brainstorming/Free association
Comparing alternatives & considering consequences logically	Life review
Eliminating alternatives systematically	Psychodrama Guided imagery into hypothetical focus
Being vigilant for maladaptive affect regarding the conflict, resolution, or both (e.g., excessive worry, postdecisional regret, irrational beliefs) and using cognitive restructuring, emotional inoculation, or stress-reduction techniques to counter maladaptive affect	Personal rituals Incubation (e.g.,Vision Quest, Incubation (e.g.,Vision Quest, meditation) Self-confrontational exercises such as the devil's advocate or the two-chair exercise, and confrontation with one's own mortality that involves both rational discourse and a focus on affective reactions

Source: From "A Reconceptualization of Values Clarification: Values Conflict Resolution" by R. T. Kinnier, 1995, *Journal of Counseling & Development, 74,* 18–24. Copyright 1995 by American Counseling Association. Reprinted by permission.

tion in values or moral education. Based on their critical review of the literature in this area, two leading proponents of moral education (Leming, 1993; Lickona, 1991) considered the moral discussion approach of Lawrence Kohlberg (1981) rather than values clarification (Raths, Harmin, & Simon, 1966) to be successful in moral education.

Valuing.   Other issues have arisen as counselors attempt to apply the individualistically oriented concepts of values clarification to group or marriage and family counseling issues. The role of interdependence in healthy human relationships and the social, political, and cultural context of the individual's experience are an important aspect of the counseling therapeutic and theoretical worldviews that are beyond the scope of more limited specialty area perspectives. For example, Sue (1996) noted that counseling practices that impose monocultural value systems or biases on clients from diverse cultural backgrounds are discriminatory and unethical.

Marriage and family counselors have long struggled with issues of reconciling the conceptualization of the individual's values with those in the relationships of the group or family as a wholistic entity. Doherty and Boss (1991) reviewed the literature on value issues and ethics in the practice of marriage and family. They note that the idea of value neutrality on the part of the therapist is no longer viable, and the emphasis in the field should be on accommodating values within the therapeutic process. Thomas (1994) provided a model of value analysis within marriage and family counseling that attempts to meld personal and systematically oriented value systems in address-

ing value dilemmas. He noted that counselors must analyze and reconcile values at (a) the individual level of the counselor microsystem, (b) the family level of the client's microsystem, and (c) the level of the overlapping counseling process itself (mesosystem). These operations are embedded in the context of societal values surrounding the dilemma (macrosystem). While this analysis may be couched in the marriage and family counseling paradigm, it is important for counselors in all settings to consider contextual or hierarchical levels that affect their ethical and values analysis (Tarvydas & Cottone, 1991). Sue (1996) called for a recognition that systems interventions will be necessary for ethical practice as counselors recognize that clients often have experiences embedded in the systems in which they are nested.

Valuing, or the negotiation of values, is a model and practice that has grown out of these concerns for reconciling disparate and often competing values orientations. This model better accommodates forces of social change as expressed in various social and cultural value changes (Huber, 1994). Huber described the valuing process as one in which the counselor:

Negotiates with a client in emphasizing certain values previously de-emphasized, and at the same time in relegating other values to the background. Within the context of the therapist-client negotiation, values evolve with accompanying behavioral changes that are compatible with values changes. Essentially, the therapist and client come together in negotiating a common world of less pain and conflict...Valuing recognizes that when therapist and client come together, they can negotiate a new, common system containing elements of both sub-systems as well as unique properties arising from their interactions. (pp. 235–236)

Counselors must acknowledge several implications in their practice to enact such an approach to reconciling values. Taken together, these assumptions constitute a valuing perspective and worldview that create the conditions for this more interactive alliance around a particular values perspective. Huber (1994) described these key assumptions based on the earlier work of Dell (1983). The practitioner must recognize that:

1. *No such phenomenon as an absolute value* exists that is objectively true or good. Rather, values are a result of the person's processing or reaction of a system's values.
2. All persons must *take responsibility* for selecting, interpreting, and holding their own values; thus, no one can be held ultimately responsible for changing another's values.
3. Therapists must accept responsibility for the tendency to *pathologize their clients,* or to see them in terms of their pathologies or problems, thus de-emphasizing the role of their own values in the process.
4. Counselors must accept that "*what is, is.*" They must allow clients to be accepted for who they are, rather than being judged as bad or sick because of behaviors that do not conform to the counselor's values or preferences.

In addition to these assumptions, values negotiation or valuing involves several process-related components.

The value assumptions just described are only working assumptions and must be examined critically. Nevertheless, these principles, if acknowledged and incorporated within the work of the valuing process, will allow valuing to occur in a constructive and productive manner. The core components of valuing are (a) recognition of mutual obligations and entitlements within the relationships among the parties, or the "give and take" of human interactions; (b) the acknowledgment of those things to which others are entitled and the valid claims of others; and (c) the balance of fairness (Huber, 1994). If obligations, entitlements, and claims are all taken together and are in relative balance, the climate will facilitate the balance of fairness in terms of values issues in the relationship. While attending to these principles and the valuing process within the counseling relationship may appear to add greatly to

its complexity, in reality these considerations recognize and respect the truly shared nature of this important relationship between diverse, autonomous beings. Values issues that arise between counselor and client from the dazzlingly numerous sources of interpersonal diversity are not only accommodated, but have the potential to enrich the counselor and the client, and their relationship, if they are directly addressed within the valuing process.

Moral Discussion and Levels of Development

Kohlberg (1964; 1971), one of the key figures in developmental psychology and the philosophy of morality, has led in the current understanding of the moral development of children and adults. His work provides a way to extend and enrich the important process of values education or clarification by understanding the moral perspectives that underlie these value choices. Kohlberg's work presents a theoretical understanding of how moral reasoning develops and relates values to moral growth. The Kohlberg system removes concerns about the seeming relativity of values in the values clarification by interpreting moral choice within a particular, developmental moral system that holds justice as its core concept. Kohlberg's theory explains value choices within the context of how people develop higher levels of moral judgment (Reimer, Paolitto, & Hersch, 1983).

Kohlberg's work (1964; 1971) is drawn from Piaget's developmental psychology, which focused on the reasoning processes underlying the behavior involved in children's cognitive developmental stages. Similarly, Kohlberg focused specifically on the reasoning processes underlying the behaviors associated with moral development. He also assumed a universal, absolute core of morality that provides structure to this reasoning process. Kohlberg maintained that all human societies believe in certain core moral values, even though there may be moral debates and cultural differences regarding their interpretations: (a) laws and values, (b) conscience, (c) personal roles of affection, (d) authority, (e) civil rights, (f) contract, trust, and justice in exchange, (g) punishment, (h) the value of life, (i) property rights and values, and (j) truth. Kohlberg spent his career studying how moral stages are organized and learned. He proposes that children form their own moral philosophies and systems as they are exposed to and grapple with moral experiences and dilemmas. This process is creative and is an attempt to make sense out of the information, experiences, and culture that surround the individual. It is considered optimal to expose people to these situations and assist them in processing them for themselves within the context of the moral system. Kohlberg and Wasserman (1980) recommended that ethical behavior can best be encouraged by (a) exposing people to the higher stages of moral development; (b) introducing them to irreconcilable ethical dilemmas, thus stimulating awareness and dissatisfaction with the lower, less-sophisticated levels of reasoning; and (c) providing a supportive, therapeutic environment in which the situations and analyses can be processed freely. Van Hoose and Kottler (1985) noted that the counseling session is a likely environment for this process.

QUESTION FOR REFLECTION

You counseled a couple for approximately one year and the marriage ended in divorce. The husband is suing his wife for custody of their two children. You have received a subpoena from the husband's attorney to appear in court to testify about the wife's emotional instability. Although there was evidence of the wife's emotional instability during counseling, you do not think it is serious enough to warrant an "unfit mother" verdict. To complicate matters, you find out that the wife has employed the most incompetent attorney in the city and you are afraid he will not represent her well. What will you do?

Kohlberg's system of moral development stages has been described as Kohlberg's greatest contribution to the study of ethics (Van Hoose & Kottler, 1985). Van Hoose and Paradise (1979) have adapted these stages to describe the stages of ethical orientation for counselors (Figure 5–4). They assumed that counselors, like all persons, initially mature through stages of development within the context of age and situation-specific experiences. They challenged counselors to identify and explore their rationales for particular value or ethical choices. Through insight and self-awareness, counselors reach more sophisticated levels of ethical reasoning. These stages of ethical orientation presented by Van Hoose and Paradise (1979) are (a) punishment, (b) institutional, (c) societal, (d) individual, and (e) principle or conscience. (See Figure 5–4 for descriptions of the stages' characteristics. You may wish to think about the last ethical dilemma you faced, how you responded to it, and your level of thinking on this matter.) The individual's level of ethical orientation can be thought of as forming that person's intuitive sense

Stage I. Punishment Orientation Counselor decisions, suggestions, and courses of action are based on a strict adherence to prevailing rules and standards, i.e., one must be punished for bad behavior and rewarded for good behavior. The primary concern is the strict attention to the physical consequences of the decision.

Stage II. Institutional Orientation Counselor decisions, suggestions, and courses of action are based on a strict adherence to the rules and policies of the institution or agency. The correct posture is based on the expectations of higher authorities.

Stage III. Societal Orientation The maintenance of standards, approval of others, and the laws of society and the public characterize this stage of ethical behavior. Concern is for duty and societal welfare.

Stage IV. Individual Orientation The primary concern of the counselor is for the needs of the individual while avoiding the violation of laws and the rights of others. Concern for law and societal welfare is recognized, but is secondary to the needs of the individual.

Stage V. Principle or Conscience Orientation Concern for the individual is primary with little regard for the legal, professional, or societal consequences. What is right, in accord with self-chosen principles of conscience and internal ethical formulations, determines counselor behavior.

FIGURE 5–4. Stages of Ethical Orientation

Source: From *Ethics in Counseling and Psychotherapy: Perspectives in Issues and Decision Making* (p. 117) by W. H. Van Hoose and L. V. Paradise, 1979, Cranston, RI: The Carroll Press.

of moral judgment. The counselor would use this first general level of orientation or moral thinking to consider ethical dilemmas as described by Kitchener (1984) and discussed within the decision-making arena described in Chapter 6.

In the context of this theoretical framework, a number of assumptions regarding ethical behavior follow: (a) counselor's functioning is not solely at one stage—this functioning may be affected by situational, educational, and other variables; (b) the orientations are qualitatively discrete stages that reflect a continuum of ethical reasoning; (c) the basis for ethical judgment is characterized by the dominant stage of ethical orientation; (d) stages are continuous and overlapping, suggesting development toward higher levels; (e) development in ethical judgment is forward and irreversible, but specific ethical actions need not be so; and (f) internalized ethical conflict may be generated by discrepancies between ethical reasoning and action associated with situational influences (Van Hoose & Paradise, 1979). While all stage theories can be criticized for certain structural limitations (e.g., not accommodating individual variations in patterns of movement between stages), the stages of ethical orientation for counselors presented by Van Hoose and Paradise (1979) continue to provide a useful framework for counselors to think about their moral development. Counselors may be assisted by realizing that there are hierarchically and developmentally ordered benchmarks against which they measure their current ethical reasoning abilities. Additionally, because the theory is oriented toward continued moral development through ongoing education within a specific moral and principled framework, it provides a positive, structured model for professional education and improvement.

APPLYING ETHICAL PRINCIPLES IN COUNSELING

Ethical principles are the higher-order norms or fundamental assumptions that develop and are consistent with a society's moral principles and that constitute higher standards of moral behavior. Counseling and psychology have largely espoused principle ethics, the model of ethical reasoning traditionally dominant in medicine and bioethics. **Principle ethics** involves objectively applying a system of ethical rules and principles to determine what is the right or moral decision about an ethical dilemma. Several ethical principles have risen to prominence over the years as having particular importance for helping with ethical decision making in U.S. culture among helping professions. See Chapter 3 for an introduction to these principals. They are: autonomy, beneficence, nonmaleficence, justice (Beauchamp & Childress, 1983), and fidelity (Kitchener, 1984).

These ethical principles embody lofty concepts as well as practical judgments about those qualities that work to the greater good in society. Principle ethics involve reasoning about the dilemma or choice by *specifying* and *balancing* these principles in an ethical analysis to arrive at an ethical justification for an ultimate solution to the dilemma. **Specifying** involves determining and naming the principles that are involved in the situation being considered. **Balancing** involves weighing which principles are more applicable or im-

portant in the analysis (Meara, Schmidt, & Day, 1996). Several principles or moral obligations are usually involved in a dilemma. They are based on well-accepted and generalizable values in society. These principles are said to have *prima facie* merit in the analysis; that is, these principles must be considered in every case and, if set aside, valid and compelling reasons must be given. Such reasons are usually based on the specific facts in the situation and the greater importance of other core principles to the issue. This process allows for maintaining the general structure of moral obligations within a society without thoughtlessly forcing its members into slavish, absolutist compliance with standards that do not fit specific situations. These five principles form the substrate on which our most enduring professional ethical obligations are based.

Autonomy

Autonomy is a right to self-determination of choice and freedom from the control of others. Kitchener (1984) noted that there is a difference between freedom of action and freedom of choice: While people should have freedom to make choices, their ability to act on these choices is limited by the autonomy of others. If a person's choice abridges the freedom or autonomy of another, as in murder, it would be ethical to deny the autonomy in that instance. Counselors create conditions of autonomy for their clients when they do not interfere unnecessarily in the clients' decisions; when they provide all necessary information to their clients in a manner they can understand; and when it is determined that the clients have the ability to use this information to assess their choices, plan them, and carry them out (Howie, Gatens-Robinson, & Rubin, 1992). The necessary conditions for autonomy are voluntariness, competence, and full disclosure of information. The specific professional practice responsibilities related to this principle are professional disclosure, informed consent, right to privacy and protection of confidentiality, and determination of competency for the types of decisions involved in the situation.

CASE SCENERIO 5-1

Autonomy

A counselor at a community mental health center has been seeing a client for approximately six months. The counselor's client initially presented substance use concerns, but has not been complying with treatment goals for reducing substance use. The psychiatrist who manages the client's medications has suggested to the counselor that this client needs to be in a structured treatment program. At the client's next appointment, the counselor tells the client that arrangments for the client to participate in the agency's treatment program have been made "for her own good." The client is visibly upset at this news and replies that she has no desire to be in the program. The counselor tells the client, "It's too bad, you're already in it." Is this a violation of the client's autonomy?

YES.   The counselor has ignored the client's right to self-determination or autonomy by making a treatment decision for the client without presenting information to the client in order for the client to make her own decisions.

1. The client is *actually* limited in his or her ability to act autonomously and to adequately assess his or her own interest. (The client is seriously depressed, mentally ill, uninformed, coerced, drugged, etc.)
2. The authority to act in the interest of another is based in a knowledge of the conditions promoting the client's *real* interests, which is superior to the client's own knowledge.
3. A serious effort has been made to know the particular personal interest of the client and to take that interest as primary.
4. The risk to the client is real and significant and the loss of autonomy is the minimum necessary to promote the good of the client.

FIGURE 5–5.   Justifications for Paternalistic Beneficent Action

Source: From "Applying Ethical Principles in Rehabilitation Counseling" by J. Howie, E. Gatens-Robinson, and S. E. Rubin, 1992, *Rehabilitation Education, 6,* 45. Copyright 1992 by Elliot and Fitzpatrick. Reprinted by permission.

Beneficence and Nonmaleficence

The principles of beneficence and nonmaleficence are closely related, and in some ways represent different aspects of the same concept. *Beneficence* involves a more active concept of contributing to the well-being of others, whereas nonmaleficence involves being passive or refraining from taking some action that might harm another. At its most basic level, it involves the general social obligation to provide mutual aid to members of our society who are in need of assistance. This obligation for mutual aid applies as long as (a) doing so involves a significant need on the part of the other; (b) the person who might assist the other has some particular qualification, such as knowledge or skill to assist the other; (c) the action would have a high probability of succeeding; and (d) the risk or burden to the person rendering aid is not greater than that to the person needing aid (Beauchamp & Childress, 1983).

In addition to the societal obligation for beneficence, all members of a profession such as counseling have additional obligations to assist their clients. The entire existence of a profession is based on the society's recognition of special skills and knowledge, as well as a purpose to help members of the society with certain types of problems and situations. Important professional duties stemming from beneficence include the obligation to assure that professionals establish, reach, and maintain an appropriate level of competency in terms of their knowledge, skills, and ethical practices. They must balance their decisions to influence the client or actively undertake a course of action that, in their professional judgment, will result in the client's increased growth or well-being against the possibilities that they might, at the same time, sacrifice some of the client's autonomy or do harm to the client. Counselors must not assume a paternalistic or parentlike stance toward their clients. When working with clients of different backgrounds, classes, races, religions, or abilities, counselors must be ever cautious about assuming that they know better than the clients or their families concerning what is in the clients' best interests. Howie, Gatens-Robinson, and Rubin (1992) offer specific guidelines for determining when paternalistic beneficent action might be justified (Figure 5–5). Being an expert does not automatically entitle the professional to the moral authority to take paternalistic action on behalf of a client. Counselors may be making a morally wrong action if they discuss only traditional career choices with female clients. If they assume that female clients would benefit more from traditional career choices than from the challenges of a nontraditional career, they are acting paternalistically.

Nonmaleficence is one of the oldest moral principles in the professions, probably best known as the cornerstone of the Hippocratic oath taken by ancient Greek physicians to "above all, do no harm." *Nonmaleficence* is refraining from any action that might cause harm, in addition to not intentionally harming others. This principle is often considered the most pressing obligation for professionals because their activities have the potential to do either good or harm. As a result of the client's trust and the counselor's advanced knowledge, the counselor often has access to special information or opportunities to injure clients either intentionally or unintentionally.

Kitchener (1984) discussed the responsibilities involved in diagnosis of clients as an especially powerful occasion to help or to harm the client. In conjunction with the client, the counselor must determine whether the benefits of diagnosis outweigh the possible harm of going through the assessment and diagnostic processes. Because diagnosis is related closely to treatment planning, funding, and the effects of labeling, these are important concerns. Kitchener noted that the experience of distress or discomfort is often unavoidable—even necessary—during diagnosis and treatment. This realization may make it difficult to discern what constitutes sufficient level of harm to justify nonpursuit of a particular course in counseling. Even counselors who do not diagnose clients directly are not absolved from concerns about diagnosis and misdiagnosis. In reality, psychiatrists, psychologists, and counselors who assign diagnoses often must rely on a variety of records, comments, evaluations, and judgments that are (or should be) conveyed to them to assist in making an appropriate diagnosis. Counselors must assure that their observations are included in this process, or that an inappropriate diagnosis is reevaluated. The increased use of managed health care and the medical model to access psychotherapy have resulted in heavy pressures on mental health professionals to provide diagnoses for funding of care. These pressures are likely to increase the incidence of misdiagnosis or overdiagnosis, while increasing the possibility of harm to clients.

CASE SCENARIO 5-2

Beneficence

A client comes to a university counseling center with an eating disorder. No one on staff has expertise in this area, but the client is in need of services and is assigned to a female counselor. The counselor is aware that she lacks the knowledge and skills to work effectively with this client's issues, and seeks consultation and supervision from a private practitioner who specializes in eating disorders. Is the counselor acting in the best interest of her client?

YES. This scenario illustrates the principle of beneficence. Counselors are obligated to possess appropriate levels of competence in terms of knowledge and skills to work with particular client issues. When no other qualified counselor is available within a particular agency, it is appropriate and the counselor's ethical obligation to seek consultation and supervision.

CASE SCENARIO 5-3

Nonmaleficence

A counselor in private practice utilizes a particular therapy technique only with his female clients. He firmly believes that clients with past sexual abuse issues can only make

progress in treatment if they have sex with a caring, male counselor. He regularly encourages his female clients to consider, as part of the treatment plan, engaging in sexual relations with him to "work through past trauma." Is this ethical?

NO. This scenario illustrates a violation of the principle of nonmaleficence. There is absolutely no research evidence to suggest that client-counselor sexual relations are therapeutic. Quite to the contrary, sexual relations between client and counselor are considered to be harmful to the client and are a clear ethical violation.

Justice

The concept of *justice* involves fairness and equality in access to resources and treatment. Counselors are obligated to assure that their processes, agencies, and services do not discriminate. They must not operate in a manner that advances discrimination at the hands of others. *Distributive justice* involves access to resources and services that may be considered scarce (Howie, Gatens-Robinson, & Rubin, 1992). All of the policies and rules of agencies, institutions, eligibility criteria, laws, and social policies that affect the mental health practice should meet acceptable criteria for just distribution. If counselors determine that serious inequalities exist, they must determine what types of advocacy (both within and outside of the given system) are needed to address the injustice and undertake advocacy efforts to remediate the situation.

Some criteria for distributive justice that might be considered include (a) equal shares, (b) distribution by need, (c) distribution by motivation or effort, (d) distribution by contribution of person, (e) free market exchange or purchase, and (f) fair opportunity, or equalizing unequal opportunity (Howie, Gatens-Robinson, & Rubin, 1992). The process of determining a model of justice for a particular purpose and justifying that particular approach is a complex and important aspect of enacting the ideal of justice. Counseling practices such as due process considerations, access to grievance processes, and techniques of systems intervention and advocacy are examples of activities related to this principle.

CASE SCENARIO 5-4

Justice

Agency X is located in a small community and provides a variety of psychological, social, and vocational services for its clients. One staff member in particular has expertise in the area of vocational and career counseling. She sees two new clients, both with work-related problems. One client, a well-respected member of the community, is a department head at the county courthouse. The other client works as a night custodian at a local factory and has had some legal difficulties. The counselor recommends a full career assessment for the first client in response to the client's request for career exploration. She tells the second client that career counseling services are not offered at this agency, only job placement. She also tells him that he is experiencing job stress that will soon pass if he "just works hard enough." Is this discriminatory?

YES. This scenario illustrates a violation of the principle of justice. By not making the same recommendation for both clients in response to similar requests for career counseling, the counselor is discriminating against the second client based on his personal characteristics. The counselor is ethically obligated to provide equal access to resources and services to all clients.

Fidelity

Promise keeping, keeping commitments, and honesty and loyalty are characteristics of the principle of *fidelity.* Because the bond of trust in the counseling relationship is considered to be of utmost importance to its effectiveness, this principle holds particular meaning for individuals in counseling and the related professions. Indeed, many theorists, such as Rogers, place particular importance on the healing characteristics engendered by the very qualities nurtured by fidelity. Some interpretations of fidelity emphasize the nature of the promises made to clients and the social contract between professional and client. However, reducing this concept to a legalistic concern that recognizes only specific, direct promises, and not those implied within the nature of the relationship, is inappropriate to the richness of the counselor-client relationship. Such counseling practices as professional disclosure, informed consent, maintenance of confidentiality, misrepresenting or withholding the truth or lying, and avoiding or appropriately dealing with dual/multiple relationships are obligations that flow from the important principle of fidelity.

CASE SCENARIO 5-5

Fidelity

A client in need of a more structured living environment does not fully meet the criteria for admission to the local care facility. The client has been suicidal in the past and seems to again be exhibiting signs of instability, but not at a level severe enough to warrant placement in the care facility or a hospital. Two staff members in a community agency consult with one another and decide to say that

the client is in need of hospitalization for suicidal ideation. The underlying purpose is to have him meet the qualifications for admission into the care facility. Is this in the client's best interest?

NO. This scenario illustrates a violation of the principle of fidelity. Although it may be in the client's best interests to be in the care facility, the staff members are misrepresenting the truth to justify his admission.

Principles, Practices, and Codes of Ethics

The five ethical principles are drawn from broader, sociocultural understandings of what is right and good. Therefore, they have great explanatory power regarding how certain professional practices and rules, such as professional codes of ethics, agree with the common sense and general sense of the moral principles of U.S. society (Figure 5–6). They are at the heart of any well-written ethical rule or common clinical practice.

Even though the various professions and professional specialties in counseling have many codes of ethics, all can be analyzed in terms of the ethical principles upheld by their canons and rules. These codes are surprisingly similar in their basic conceptualizations of ethical practices. Of course, differences exist in specific areas and in how the details of the core obligations are discharged. Nevertheless, it can be said that all mental health professions endorse the core ethical obligations embodied in these five ethical principles.

The practice of selecting a particular rule from a code of ethics to analyze the ethical principles that support it is useful. This activity has been used by the Ethical Case Management Practice Training Program developed by Rubin and associates (Wilson, Rubin, & Millard, 1991). This analysis is helpful in strengthening the counselor's levels of familiarity and comfort with the application of these specific ethical principles. It also strengthens the ability to discern the underlying principles behind any number of ethically charged rules, policies, or client situations (Figure 5–7). Of course, the application of the ethical principles is also a critical stage of the ethical decision-making process as described by many authorities (see Chapter 6).

Other Ethics Approaches

Principle ethics and analysis are powerful tools that the counselor must learn to employ in the ethical decision-making process. Recent trends question the exclusive reliance on principle ethics, most notably those of feminist scholars and authorities in cross-cultural or multicultural

The practices that counselors use every day are based in the ethical obligations they owe their clients. There are also pragmatic and theoretical reasons why these practices are followed. However, if counselors stop and think, they will also hear the "whisper" of one or more ethical obligations to their clients that would be fulfilled if the counselors follow the practice under consideration. Inspect the following list of principles and practices. Can you think of other practices that represent some of the principles? Are there other principles that are related to some of the practices other than those listed here?

Autonomy
Maintaining confidentiality, right to privacy
Obtaining informed consent
Obtaining competency evaluation
Utilizing individualized treatment plans

Nonmaleficence
Avoiding counseling in areas where not competent
Avoiding dual relationships
Providing informed consent prior to procedures that carry risk for the client, so clients may decline if that is their wish, in areas such as diagnosis, research, or psychological testing

Beneficence
Working within limits of/maintaining competence
Heeding the duty to warn/duty to protect
Breaking confidentiality; involuntary hospitalization; initiating guardianship procedures
Terminating or referring clients not benefiting from services

Justice
Challenging biased practices based on race, age, gender, culture, or disability
Offering additional services to those to whom difference is relevant
Assuring services are accessible to public with physical or language barriers
Advocating against discrimination
Doing *pro bono* work

Fidelity
Being loyal to clients
Advocating for clients
Being truthful and honest with clients
Providing full professional disclosure and informed consent
Respecting confidentiality
Being loyal to colleagues and the profession
Being loyal to employers
Keeping contracts

FIGURE 5–6. Counseling Practices and the Ethical Principles that Underlie Them

Check your ability to perceive the principles involved in ethical rules by reviewing the analyses in this activity box. To further your understanding, you might wish to select several additional rules from the ACA code of ethics as well as another code of ethics in which you are interested to practice determining which ethical principles underlie specific rules.

Exercise 1
Ethical Rule: ACA Code of Ethics B.1.a. Counselors respect their clients' right to privacy and avoid illegal and unwarranted disclosures of confidential information.
Ethical Principles: Autonomy, Beneficence, and Fidelity

Exercise 2
Ethical Rule: ACA Code of Ethics E.2.b. Counselors are responsible for the appropriate application, scoring, interpretation, and use of assessment instruments, whether they score and interpret such tests themselves or use computerized services.
Ethical Principles: Nonmaleficence, Beneficence, and possibly Justice if information gained will determine access to resources or services

Exercise 3
Ethical Rule: ACA Code of Ethics A.5.a. In the counseling relationship, counselors are aware of the intimacy and responsibilities inherent in the counseling relationship, maintain respect for clients, and avoid actions that seek to meet their personal needs at the expense of clients.
Ethical Principles: Fidelity and Nonmaleficence

FIGURE 5–7. Ethical Code Rules and Basic Principles

studies. This critique is related to the perception that the cultural assumptions in principle ethics are based heavily on Western, scientific thought and a general individualistic, male-oriented worldview (see Chapter 11).

Since the late 1980s, the study of ethical discourse has been enriched by writings on the ethics of care and virtue ethics. These two perspectives offer alternative perspectives for considering ethical reasoning. Both hold the potential to better accommodate the positions of nonmainstream people, women, and persons from culturally diverse backgrounds. Virtue ethics, the ethics of care, and the multicultural perspective can complement the traditional processes of principle ethics that have provided the bulk of ethical tradition within counseling.

Virtue ethics is very often discussed by contrasting it to the prevailing tradition of principle ethics. In **virtue ethics,** professionals are called upon to aspire toward ideals and develop virtues or traits of character to achieve these ideals (Meara, Schmidt, & Day, 1996). It is the qualities of the person that have merit or work in some particular context; these qualities are often related to matters of right conduct or morality. Virtue ethics focuses on the agent or individual rather than on the action or decision made, as in principle ethics—not "what shall we do?" but rather "who shall we become?" (Kliest & White, 1997, p. 129).

Virtue ethics has two general goals: (1) achieving and maintaining professional competence, and (2) striving for the common good. To accomplish these ends, the professional should cultivate the virtues of prudence, integrity, and respectfulness. Virtuous professionals (a) are motivated to do what is good; (b) possess vision and discernment; (c) realize the role of affect or emotion in assessing or judging proper conduct; (d) have a high degree of self-understanding and awareness; and, most importantly, (e) connect with and understand the mores of their communities and the importance of community in moral decision making, policy setting, and character development; and are alert to the legitimacy of client diversity in these respects (Meara, Schmidt, & Day, 1996). Some authorities see virtue ethics as enhancing ethical practice in multicultural contexts: Practitioners are more sensitive in their conduct because they are rooted in a particular community's wisdom and moral sense (Ibrahim, 1996; Vasqeuz, 1996).

It is important to evaluate critically how virtue ethics can contribute to the ethical tradition of the counseling profession, as well as to consider related concerns. The communities that are a crucial medium for the development of a virtuous ethic can themselves be insular and ethnocentric, thus becoming harmful to others (Kitchener, 1996). Also, the virtue ethics tradition is seen as irrelevant to the adjudication of ethics complaints by licensure boards and ethics committees (Bersoff, 1996). Finally, the professional community has raised concerns that it may be impossible to teach virtues and that selection of virtuous individuals into the professional community may be the necessary approach (Bersoff, 1996; Kitchener, 1996). Nonetheless, many scholars believe that principles and virtues cannot be separated—neither is primary, but each serves to balance the other. Professionals are called upon to perform certain actions to certain kinds of people.

The **ethics of care,** which springs from the feminist scholar Carol Gilligan's (1977) critique of Kohlberg's (1971) work on moral development, is not necessarily a new approach. Her groundbreaking critique noted that Kohlberg's work was based on male, and not female, research participants. Women were generally seen in Kohlbergian research as performing at a lower state of moral maturity—that of conventional-level development. Gilligan stated that because women attend to the influences of relationships in their reasoning, their approach is essentially accommodated by a system of moral development that is relationally—and not justice—based. Thus, caring for others is not interpreted as consistent with the highest level of moral development. As a result, Gilligan and other scholars working in this new perspective developed an approach to ethics: the ethics of care that operates in contrast to the prevailing ethic of justice, or principle ethics. Although many of these scholars were feminists, the area is more properly thought of as the *ethics of care* rather than *feminist ethics* due to its content, applicability across genders, and much broader influence on the study of ethics, such as to the study of ethics within a multicultural context.

Within the ethics of care, the world is seen through a particular "way of knowing" or interpreting experience that emphasizes human connectedness, or a relational perspective; as opposed to seeing it through a lens of scientific knowledge and the laws of nature and man. It emphasizes the social construction of understanding, knowledge, and the participation of a community of "knowers." Within this perspective, great importance is placed on communication with others, and honoring relational obligations or obligations of care inherent in the relationships between people. To fulfill this obligation, one person must be able to take the perspective of and understand the other. This perspective calls upon one to not leave out others to whom one owes social obligation or exclude them from consideration (Noddings, 1992). While the ethics of care has had wide influence, particularly in nursing scholarship, it has received a number of criticisms as well. For example, some feel it could lead to neglecting the care of strangers (Crowley, 1994), exploitation of the caregiver, not distinguishing between right and wrong sufficiently because care is blind (Nelson, 1992), and not having a coherent definition of the ethic of care (Veatch, 1998).

These newer areas of ethics scholarship have done much to enrich the dialogue about ethics, as well as humanizing and diversifying the practice of applied ethics. Any serious area of study requires that scholars and practitioners be alert to new trends and information that result in updating or changing the knowledge base and skills of the field. The multiculturalism movement, virtue ethics, and the ethics of care perform such a service for the study of ethics and substantially enrich counselors' understanding of practicing the profession ethically. In the next chapter you will be introduced to two models of ethical decision making that attempt to respond to these new ways of viewing ethics, Tarvydas' Integrative Decision-Making Model of Ethical Behavior, and Cottone's Social Constructivism Model of Ethical Decision Making. Tarvydas' model incorporates the influences of virtue ethics within the important attitudinal assets that are discussed as permeating the ethical decision making process, and the influence of the ethics of care can be seen in the careful consideration of the perspective of the other and the stakeholders in Stage I, as well as the infusion of contextual analysis throughout Stages III and IV. Cottone's Social Constructivism model is wholly grounded in a foundational theory that views relationships and relational systems as the core of understanding for ethical analysis. These constructivism models are yet another illustration of how virtue ethics and the ethics of care have stimulated new thinking in the understanding of ethics.

CHAPTER SUMMARY

The issues surrounding ethical judgment involve a complex interplay of morals, values, and priorities that people hold in relationship to themselves, their colleagues, and other professionals. Ethics is a branch of study in philosophy concerning how people ought to act toward one another. Morals involve the goodness or badness of human behavior or character. Values are enduring beliefs of what is worthwhile and reflect the value holder's worldview, culture, or understanding of the world.

Values clarification, the valuing process, and moral discussion are general processes that assist counselors in working with clients' value systems. Values clarification involves three steps: prizing, choosing, and acting on one's values. Values chosen through this process are called clarified values. Valuing, or negotiation of values, accommodates forces of social change as expressed in social and cultural value changes. Moral discussion focuses on reasoning processes that underlie behavior associated with moral development.

Ethical principles are the higher-order norms that develop and are consistent with a society's moral principles. Principle ethics applies a system of ethical rules to determine moral decisions in ethical dilemmas. The ethical principles of autonomy, beneficence, nonmaleficence, justice, and fidelity are important in ethical decision making among the helping professions. Autonomy is a client's right to self-determination of choice and freedom from the control of others. Beneficence involves an active concept of contributing to the well-being of others. Nonmaleficence is refraining from any actions that might cause harm. Justice involves fairness and equality in clients' access to resources and treatment. Fidelity is keeping commitments, promises, honesty, and loyalty.

REFERENCES

Allport, G. W., Vernon P. E., & Lindzey, G. (1960). *The study of values.* Boston: Houghton-Mifflin.

Beauchamp, T. L., & Childress, J. F. (1983). *Principles of biomedical ethics.* Oxford, England: Oxford University Press.

Bergin, A. E. (1985). Proposed values for guiding and evaluating psychotherapy. *Counseling and Values, 29,* 99–116.

Bersoff, D. N. (1996). The virtue of principle ethics. *The Counseling Psychologist, 24,* 86–91.

Beutler, L. E., Pollack, S., & Jobe, A. (1978). Acceptance, values, and therapeutic change. *Journal of Consulting and Clinical Psychology, 46,* 198–199.

Brandt, R. (1959). *Ethical theory.* Upper Saddle River, NJ: Prentice Hall.

Corey, B., Corey, M. S., & Callanan, P. (1998). *Issues and ethics in the helping professions* (5th ed.). Pacific Grove, CA: Brooks/Cole.

Crowley, M. A. (1994). The relevance of Noddings' ethics of care to the moral education of nurses. *Journal of Nursing Education, 33*(2), 20–34.

Dell, P. (1983). From pathology to ethics. *The Family Therapy Networker, 7*(6), 29–31, 64.

Doherty, W. J. (1995). *Soul searching: Why psychotherapy must promote moral responsibility.* New York: Basic Books.

Doherty, W., & Boss, P. (1991). Values and ethics in family therapy. In A. S. Gurman & D. P. Kniskern (Eds.), *Handbook of family therapy: vol. 2.* New York: Brunner/Mazel.

Frank, J. (1961). *Persuasion and healing.* New York: Schoken.

Frankena, W. K. (1963). *Ethics.* Upper Saddle River, NJ: Prentice Hall.

Gilligan, C. (1997). In a different voice: Women's conception of the self and of morality. *Harvard Educational Review, 47,* 481–517.

Ginsberg, S. W., & Herma, J. L. (1953). Values and their relationship to psychiatric principles and practice. *American Journal of Psychotherapy, 7,* 536–573.

Gordon, L. V. (1976). *Survey of interpersonal values: Revised manual.* Chicago: Science Research Associates.

Griffith, B. A., & Duesterhaus, M. (2000). Integrating a moral conversation: A framework for counselors. *Journal of Humanistic Counseling, Education and Development, 39,* 47–55.

Herr, E. L., & Niles, S. (1988). The values of counseling: Three domains. *Counseling and Values, 33,* 4–17.

Hofstede, G. (1980). *Culture's consequences: International differences in work values.* Beverly Hills, CA: Sage Publications.

Hopkins, W. E. (1997). *Ethical dimensions of diversity.* Thousand Oaks, CA: Sage Publications.

Howie, J., Gatens-Robinson, E., & Rubin, S. E. (1992). Applying ethical principles in rehabilitation counseling. *Rehabilitation Education, 6,* 41–55.

Huber, C. H. (1994). Ethical, legal, and professional issues in the practice of marriage and family therapy (2nd ed.). Upper Saddle River, NJ: Merrill/Prentice Hall.

Ibrahim, F. A. (1996). A multicultural perspective on principle and virtue ethics. *The Counseling Psychologist, 24,* 78–85.

Jensen, J. P., & Bergin, A. E. (1988). Mental health values of professional therapists: A national interdisciplinary study. *Professional psychology: Research and practice, 19,* 290–297.

King, M. L., Jr. (1968, February 4). Drum Major Instinct sermon. Given at Ebenezer Baptist Church, Atlanta, GA.

Kinnier, R. T. (1995). A reconceptualization of values clarification: Values conflict resolution. *Journal of Counseling & Development, 74,* 18–24.

Kinnier, R. T., Kernes, J. L., & Dautheribes, T. M. (2000). A short list of universal moral values. *Counseling and Values, 45,* 4–16.

Kirschenbaum, H. (2000). From values clarification to character education: A personal journey. *Journal of Humanistic Counseling, Education and Development, 39,* 4–20.

Kitchener, K. S. (1984). Ethics in counseling psychology: Distinctions and directions. *Counseling Psychologist, 12*(3), 43–55.

Kitchener, K. S. (1996). There is more to ethics than principles. *The Counseling Psychologist, 24,* 92–97.

Kleist, D. M., & White, L. J. (1997). The values of counseling: A disparity between a philosophy of prevention in counseling and counselor practice and training. *Counseling and Values, 41,* 128–140.

Kluckhorn, C. (1951). Values and value-orientations in the theory of action: An exploration in definition and clarification. In T. Parsons & E. A. Shils (Eds.), *Toward a general theory of action* (pp. 338–433). Cambridge, MA: Harvard University Press.

Kohlberg, L. (1964). Development of moral character and moral ecology. In M. L. Hoffman & L. W. Hoffman (Eds.), *Review of child development research.* Vol. I. New York: Russell Sage Foundation.

Kohlberg, L. (1971). Moral development and the education of adolescents. In R. Purnell (Ed.), *Adolescents and the American high school.* New York: Holt, Rinehart & Winston.

Kohlberg, L. (1981). *Philosophy of moral development.* San Francisco: Harper & Row.

Kohlberg, L., & Wasserman, E. R. (1980). The cognitive-developmental approach and the practicing counselor: An opportunity for counselors to re-think their roles. *Personnel and Guidance Journal, 59,* 559–568.

Landfield, A. W., & Nawas, M. M. (1964). Psychotherapeutic improvement as a function of communication and adoption of therapist's values. *Journal of Counseling Psychology, 11,* 336–341.

Leming, J. S. (1993). *Character education: Lessons from the past, models for the future.* Camden, ME: The Institute for Global Ethics.

Lickona, T. (1991). *Educating for character.* New York: Bantam.

London, P. (1986). *Modes and morals of psychotherapy* (2nd ed.). New York: Holt, Rinehart & Winston.

Mcara, N. M., Schmidt, L. D., & Day, J. D. (1996). Principles and virtue: A foundation for ethical decisions, policies, and character. *The Counseling Psychologist, 24*(1), 4–77.

Mowrer, O. (1967). *Morality and mental health.* Chicago: Rand McNally.

Nelson, H. L. (1992). Against caring. *The Journal of Clinical Ethics, 3*(1), 8–14.

Noddings, N. (1992). In defense of caring. *The Journal of Clinical Ethics, 3*(1), 14–17.

Pederson, P. (Ed.). (1985). *Handbook of cross-cultural counseling and therapy.* Westport, CT: Greenwood.

Pietrofesa, J. J., Hoffman, A., Splete, H., & Pinto, D. (1978). *Counseling: Theory, research, and practice.* Chicago: Rand McNally.

Raths, L., Harmin, M., & Simon, S. (1966). *Values and teaching: Working with values in the classroom.* Upper Saddle River, NJ: Merrill/Prentice Hall.

Raths, L., Harmin, M., & Simon, S. (1978). *Values and teaching: Working with values in the classroom* (2nd ed.). Upper Saddle River, NJ: Merrill/Prentice Hall.

Reimer, J., Paolitto, D. P., & Hersch, R. H. (1983). *Promoting moral growth: From Piaget to Kohlberg.* New York: Longman.

Rokeach, M. (1973). *The nature of human values.* New York: Free Press.

Rokeach, M., & Regan, J. (1980). The role of values in the counseling situation. *Personnel and Guidance Journal, 58,* 576–583.

Shertzer, B., & Linden, J. (1979). *Fundamentals of individual appraisal: Assessment techniques for counselors.* Boston: Houghton-Mifflin.

Strupp, H. H. (1980). Humanism and psychotherapy: A personal statement of the therapist's essential values. *Psychotherapy: Theory, Research and Practice, 17,* 396–400.

Sue, D. W. (1996). Ethical issues in multicultural counseling. In B. Herlihy, & G. Corey (Eds.), *ACA ethical standards casebook* (5th ed.). Alexandria, VA: American Counseling Association.

Tarvydas, V. M., & Cottone, R. R. (1991). Ethical responses to legislative, organizational, and economic dynamics: A four-level model of ethical practice. *Journal of Applied Rehabilitation Counseling, 22*(4), 11–18.

Thomas, V. (1994). Value analysis: A model of personal and professional ethics in marriage and family counseling. *Counseling and Values, 38,* 193–202.

Tjelveit, A. C. (1986). The ethics of value conversion in psychotherapy: Appropriate and inappropriate therapist influence on client values. *Clinical Psychology Review, 6,* 515–537.

Van Hoose, W. H., & Kottler, J. A. (1985). *Ethical and legal issues in counseling and psychotherapy* (2nd ed.). San Francisco: Jossey-Bass.

Van Hoose, W. H., & Paradise, L. V. (1979). *Ethics in counseling and psychotherapy: Perspectives in issues and decision making.* Cranston, RI: The Carroll Press.

Vasquez, M. (1996). Will virtue ethics improve ethical conduct in multicultural settings and interactions? *The Counseling Psychologist, 24,* 98–104.

Veatch, R. M. (1998). The place of care in ethical theory. *Journal of Medicine and Philosophy, 23*(2), 210–224.

Walters, O. S. (1958). Metaphysics, religion, and psychotherapy. *Journal of Counseling Psychology, 5,* 243–252.

Welkowitz, J., Cohen, J., & Ortmeyer, D. (1967). Value system similarities: Investigation of patient/therapist dyads. *Journal of Consulting Psychology, 31*(1), 48–55.

Wilson, C. A., Rubin, S. E., & Millard, R. P. (1991). Preparing rehabilitation educators to deal with ethical dilemmas. *Journal of Applied Rehabilitation Counseling, 22*(1), 30–33.

CHAPTER 6

Ethical Decision-Making Processes[1]

Vilia M. Tarvydas
R. Rocco Cottone
Ronald E. Claus

Objectives
■ ■ ■ ■ ■ ■ ■ ■ ■ ■ ■
After reading this chapter, you should be able to:

- Explain the decision-making process as a value-laden, but rational, process.
- Cite the literature on decision-making models.
- Summarize the models of ethical decision-making.
- Apply two decision-making models—one based on an integration of current theory and practice, and the other based on a purely theoretical model.

■ ■ ■ ■ ■ ■ ■ ■ ■ ■ ■

INTRODUCTION

This chapter presents a scholarly review of ethical decision-making models. It also presents details of two decision-making models developed by the authors. Tarvydas developed the first model; it is an integration model that blends the best of what is known about decision making in counseling to the date of this writing. An extended example of how this model might be applied to resolve an ethical dilemma is provided. Cottone developed the second model; it is a theoretically-based model designed using a social constructivism philosophy. Beyond showcasing the authors' models, it is hoped you will get a sense of their commitment to applying ethics best practices in the field, and to their theoretical, philosophical, and empirical inclinations. Presenting both models also is intended to give students and professors some choice and flexibility in approaching ethical decision making in and outside of the classroom. The models are quite distinct. It is hoped readers will gain by comparative analysis of the models.

---

[1] Parts of this chapter draw heavily and directly from two works published in the American Counseling Association (ACA) *Journal of Counseling and Development*—Cottone (2001) and Cottone and Claus (2000) with permission of the ACA; and from "Standards of Practice: Legal and Ethical" by V. M. Tarvydas, 1997, in D. R. Maki & T. F. Riggar (Eds.), *Rehabilitation Counseling: Profession and Practice*, Copyright 1997 by Springer Publishing Co. Used by permission.

Box 6.1   Question for Reflection

Reflect on your last major decision, such as choosing an undergraduate or graduate program, becoming engaged or married, making a major purchase, or choosing a job. Think about the process you experienced as you made the decision. Did you do some background research? What individuals were involved in discussion about the decision? What values affected your decision? Who communicated these values to you during your personal development? What social or cultural factors may have influenced your decision? Was the process smooth or abrupt? What emotions did you experience? Did you have a chance to reflect or reconsider your decision after you made it? What actions did you take to implement the decision? Looking back, do you feel it was a wise decision?

ETHICAL JUDGMENT

The practice of counseling is an art as well as a science, requiring the practitioner to make both value-laden and rational decisions. Rather than being incompatible stances, facts and values must be considered together if counselors are to make good decisions. Ethical deliberation blends such elements as (a) personal/moral sensitivity, (b) philosophy of practice, (c) clinical behavioral objectivity, and (d) the responsibility for efficient and competent care of clients.

An ethics code provides counselors with guidance for the specific situations they experience in their practices. However, authorities have long recognized that ethics codes must be general enough to apply across a wide range of practice settings. They also are reactive in nature; that is, they address situations that have already been part of the profession's experience (Kitchener, 1984; Mabe & Rollin, 1986). As a result, even with the knowledge of the profession's code of ethics, counselors may not find sufficient guidance to resolve a dilemma. They may find that the particular situation they face is not addressed in their code, is addressed by more than one code providing conflicting direction, or that conflicting provisions within one code appear to apply to the situation. Thus, counselors must be prepared to exercise their ethical and professional judgment responsibly. *Ethical dilemmas are not so much a failure of ethical codes as a natural and appropriate indicator of the importance of professional judgment.* The need to use ethical judgment is affirmation that one is involved in the "practice of a profession," rather than "doing a job," however skilled.

To exercise professional judgment, counselors must be prepared to recognize underlying ethical principles and conflicts among competing interests, as well as to apply appropriate decision-making skills to resolve the dilemma and act ethically (Francouer, 1983; Kitchener,

1984; Tarvydas, 1987). Fortunately, professionals are assisted in this task by examination and refinement of their ordinary moral sense, as well as the availability of thoughtful models for the ethical decision-making process. Many components of ethical decision making involve teachable, learnable skills to supplement the professional's developing intuitive judgment.

Several models exist that explain and structure the process of ethical decision making. Some are highly theoretical; others are empirical or philosophical. Some are clinically sound approaches derived from practices that have been known to resolve significant ethical dilemmas. Others are based on anecdotal evidence alone—given credence in stories that have become ethical folklore. Because ethical decision making is so critical to the practice of the counseling profession, this chapter provides a thorough scholarly review of the literature on the topic. There are many ethical decision-making models in counseling, but only some are philosophically, empirically, or theoretically founded.

ETHICAL DECISION-MAKING MODELS: A REVIEW OF THE LITERATURE

In 1984, Kitchener published a seminal work related to ethical decision making in counseling and counseling psychology. Kitchener argued that in the absence of clear ethical guidelines, relying on personal value judgments (as some other authors had proposed) was inadequate because "Independent of . . . external considerations, not all value judgments are equally valid" (p. 44). She argued that counseling professionals should "develop a deeper understanding of the basis for ethical decision making" (p. 44). She then presented a model that integrates Hare's (1981) work on levels of moral thinking (intuitive and critical-evaluative), and Beauchamp and Childress's

(1979) suggested ethical "principles" (autonomy, beneficence, nonmaleficence, and justice), and the ethical "rule" of fidelity. Subsequent to Kitchener's 1984 publication, there have been many publications on ethical issues in counseling.

Since Kitchener's (1984) article was published, Beauchamp and Childress's (1979) text, *Principles of Biomedical Ethics*, has been revised several times; it is a highly cited work in its fourth edition (1994) that has laid the groundwork for other authors. Although the Beauchamp and Childress (1994) text is a foundation text that provides guiding principles for ethical decision making, it fails to address decision-making models or processes with any depth. Instead, the authors provide a thorough analysis of ethical theory, including criteria of theory construction and an overview of widely recognized ethical theories (e.g., utilitarianism, Kantianism, and liberal individualism). In a work published in the same year, Beauchamp and Walters (1994) provided a "set of considerations" or "methods" for resolving moral disagreements as a way "of easing and perhaps settling controversies" (p. 4). The methods included: (a) "obtaining objective information," (b) "providing definitional clarity," (c) "adopting a code," (d) "using examples and counterexamples," and (e) "analyzing arguments" (pp. 4–7). Beauchamp and Walters (1994) did not present a review of decision-making processes, but they took a position and presented a basic model for judging ethical decisions. As with the Beauchamp and Childress (1994) and Beauchamp and Walters (1994) works, there was a lack of in-depth discussion of ethical decision-making processes in the literature. Rather, authors simply listed the actual act of making a decision as a step, or they did not list it as a step at all. In either case, they did not address an explanatory framework for the decision process itself. Some models are exceptions (i.e., that explain the actual decision process), especially those involving theoretical and philosophical foundations.

THEORETICALLY OR PHILOSOPHICALLY BASED MODELS OF ETHICAL DECISION MAKING

Several authors made an attempt to ground ethical decision making on some theory or philosophy—notably, Hare's (1991) *The Philosophical Basis of Psychiatric Ethics*, which in its original 1981 form was used by Kitchener as a guiding work. Hare argued that absolute thinking (dealing with rights and duties) and utilitarian thinking (doing the greatest good for the greatest number; considering the interests of patients) were both involved in ethical decision making. He then invoked two levels of moral reasoning to address ethical dilemmas—the "intuitive" and "critical" levels:

> That we have a duty to serve the interests of the patient, and that we have a duty to respect his rights, can both perhaps be ascertained by consulting our intuitions at the bottom level. But if we ask which duty or which intuition ought to carry the day, we need some means other than intuition, some higher kind of thinking (let us call it 'critical moral thinking') to settle the question between them . . . (p. 35)

Hare believed that the "intuitive level, with its prima facie duties and principles, is the main locus of everyday moral decisions" (p. 35). However, he argued that it is "not sufficient" (p. 36), and must be superceded by critical (utilitarian) thinking when "no appeal to intuitions" can "settle the dispute" (p. 38). Although Hare's work was applied to psychiatry, it has direct relevance to counseling. Many have followed the lead of Kitchener and incorporated his ideas in their works.

Rest (1984) produced another work that is cited often in the literature. He published extensively on the topic of developmental issues related to moral reasoning (e.g., Rest, Cooper, Coder, Maganz, & Anderson, 1974; Rest, Davison, & Robbins, 1978). His 1984 work, written specifically for the applied ethics of psychology, drew heavily on theories of moral development (e.g., Kohlberg, 1969, 1980) and research findings (e.g., Schwartz, 1977) to present a four-component model of "processes involved in the production of moral behavior" (p. 19). The components are: (a) "To interpret the situation in terms of how one's actions affect the welfare of others"; (b) "To formulate what a moral course of action would be; to identify the moral ideal in a specific situation"; (c) "To select among competing value outcomes of ideals, the one to act upon; deciding whether or not to try to fulfill one's moral ideal"; (d) "To execute and implement what one intends to do" (p. 20). The four components are not temporally linear, and they are not virtues or traits of individuals. Rather, "they are major units of analysis in tracing out how a particular course of action was produced in the context of a particular situation" (p. 20). Rest argued that "The four component model provides a framework for ordering existing research on moral development, identifying needed research and deriving implications for moral education. There are many directives for the moral education of counselors that come from this research" (p. 27). For instance, he believed an assessment instrument could be developed for each component to assess counseling students entering training or the outcomes of training programs themselves. In a later work, Rest (1994) reviewed the works of Kohlberg and gave an up-to-date summary of research findings related to Kohlberg's theory. He also offered a revision of the four-component model. He defined the four components as "the major determinants of moral behavior" (p. 22), and he summarized the components as: (a) "Moral Sensitivity," (b) "Moral Judgment," (c) "Moral Motivation," and (d) "Moral Character" (pp. 23–24). He stated:

> In summary, moral failure can occur because of deficiency in any component. All four components are determinants of moral action. In fact, there are complex interactions among the four components, and it is not supposed that the four represent a temporal order such that a person performs one, then two, then three, then four—rather the four components comprise a logical analysis of what it takes to behave morally. (p. 24)

Rest's model is clearly theoretically linked to cognitive theory through the works of Kohlberg, and he has one of the most empirically well-grounded approaches for analyzing moral behavior.

Gutheil, Bursztajn, Brodsky, and Alexander (1991), in a text on decision making in psychiatry and law, provided a chapter entitled, "Probability, Decision Analysis, and Conscious Gambling." The chapter reviewed the mechanistic and probabilistic paradigms in science and took a stand that decision making must account for some level of uncertainty (probability). They made an argument in favor of "decision analysis" as a formal decision making tool:

> Decision analysis is a step-by-step procedure enabling us to break down a decision into its components, to lay them out in an orderly fashion, and to trace the sequence of events that might follow from choosing one course of action or another. This procedure offers several benefits. It can help us to make the best possible decision in a given situation. Moreover, it can help us to clarify our values, that is, the preferences among possible outcomes by which we judge what the best decision might be. Decision analysis can also be used to build logic and rationality into our intuitive decision making—to educate our intuition about probabilities and about the paths of contingency by which our actions, in combination with chance or "outside" events, lead to outcomes. (p. 41)

Decision analysis involves several "approaches," including: (a) acknowledging the decision; (b) listing the pros and cons; (c) structuring the decision (including devel-

opment of a decision "tree" to graph decisional paths and subsequent decisional branches); (d) estimating probabilities and values; and (e) calculating expected value. Estimating probabilities by means of a decision tree may involve calculating "the relative frequency with which the event in question occurs over a large number of trials in similar circumstances" (p. 46). The authors contrast decision analysis to decision making as gambling. Their model is clearly linked to nonmechanistic, probability theory in science (e.g., the uncertainty principle).

Two articles integrated Berne's (1972) Transactional Analysis therapeutic approach with ethical decision-making processes. For example, Chang (1994) identified a five-step model of making an ethical decision and emphasized three core values implicit in Transactional Analysis. These values affect the decision-making process through the assumptions that: (a) people are born acceptable or "OK"; (b) clients are capable of understanding their problems and are actively involved in healing; and (c) people can take charge of their lives. Chang addressed the interplay of Transactional Analysis values and other ethical standards or directives. McGrath (1994) believed that Kitchener's (1988) discussion of roles was relevant to Transactional Analysis (TA) because it was common to view TA supervisors also as therapists. Accordingly, role theory would have direct relevance to individual TA therapists making decisions.

Based on a theory of feminism, Hill, Glaser, and Harden (1995) proposed a model for ethical decision making. They value the emotional responses of the counselor and the social context in which the therapeutic relationship takes place. In accord with feminist beliefs regarding power, the client is engaged as fully as possible in the decision-making process. At each step, the feminist model includes a rational-evaluative procedure with corresponding emotional and intuitive queries to assist the counselor. This model includes a review process in which the counselor considers the impact of personal values, the universality of the proposed solution, and the intuitive feel of the proposed solution. Because personal characteristics affect ethical decisions, the authors believe integration of this factor into their model improves the decision-making process.

Betan (1997) proposed a hermeneutic perspective of ethical decision making. He stated that "hermeneutics represents a shift in views of the nature of knowledge and the process of how we come to know" … since … "knowledge is situated in the context of human relationships in which the interpreter (as knowledge is interpretation) participates in narrating meaning" (p. 352). He advocated that hermeneutics adds to, rather than replaces, the principled approaches of Kitchener (1984) and Rest (1984): "The context of the therapeutic relationship and the clinician's psychological needs and dynamics are fundamental considerations in the interpretation and application of ethical principles" (p. 356). Further, he stated:

> A linear, logical-reductionistic approach to ethics, such as that offered by Kitchener (1984) and Rest (1984), can lead to a false dichotomy between the rational and the intuitive, and the universal and the subjective. The key in this hermeneutic approach is to acknowledge the dialectic of the universal and the subjective of human relations, in which each informs the other. That is, our sense of what is universal (in this regard, a standard or principle) is a product of shared subjective experiences, which in turn are embedded in a context of cultural interpretation. (p. 356)

The prima facie obligation of ethical principles asserted by Kitchener must instead, according to Betan, be applied in the context of personal and cultural values. That an ethical truth is constructed in the framework of one's conception of self, others, and the world holds implications for counselor training; counselors must work to gain awareness of ethical dilemmas, their own personal and moral values, and the interaction between ethical principles and context.

Cottone (2001) took an even more radical relational position than that of Betan (1997). Cottone (2001) proposed an ethical decision-making approach based on social constructivism. He argued that decision making is not a psychological process. Rather, decision making always involves interaction with other individuals. Building on the works of Gergen (1985) in social psychology and the works of Maturana (1978, 1988; Maturana & Varela, 1980) in the biology of cognition, Cottone (2001) argued that ethical decisions "are not compelled internally; rather, they are socially compelled" (p. 6). Further, he asserted that ethical decision making occurs in the interactive processes of negotiating, consensualizing, and arbitrating. An individual's psychological process is not involved. The social constructivism perspective of ethical decision making takes the decision out of the "head," so to speak, and places it in the interactive process between people. Cottone's model is presented later in this chapter.

Empirical Findings Related to Theoretically or Philosophically Based Models

Two empirical studies in the published literature had direct theoretical linkage. Cottone, Tarvydas, and House (1994) derived hypotheses about how counseling students in a graduate program make decisions based on social systems theory. According to social systems theory, they posited that "all thinking and decision making would be highly socially and relationally influenced, and both number and types of relationships would potentially influence how individuals act and think" (p. 57). They concluded:

> The results indicate that interpersonal relations influenced the ethical decision making of graduate counseling student participants when they were asked to reconsider a decision. In other words, relationships seem to influence ethical decision making linearly and cumulatively. Additionally, there seems to be an interaction between the number and type of consulted relationships in a way that eludes simple explanation. Although there was only a small interaction effect size, the results support a conclusion that ethical decision making in a reconsideration circumstance is a relatively complex issue, with at least the number and type of relationships interacting. (p. 63)

The results support a conclusion of social influence over ethical choice. The second study was a test of Janis and Mann's (1977) theory of decision making under stress by Hinkeldey and Spokane (1985). Hinkeldey and Spokane concluded that "consistent with Janis and Mann's theory, results showed that decision making was affected negatively by pressure but that participants relied little on legal guidelines in making responses to ethical conflict dilemmas" (p. 240).

Dinger (1997) presented dissertation findings on a study that compared Kitchener's (1984) Ethical Justification model to the A-B-C-D-E worksheet model of Sileo and Kopala (1993) and concluded that the Kitchener model better served participants in identifying the ethical issues presented in different scenarios.

PRACTICE-BASED MODELS OF ETHICAL DECISION MAKING

Some authors have proposed models based on pragmatic procedures derived largely from experience or intended primarily as practical guides for counselors. These models tend to be less theory specific or philosophically pure than those discussed previously. Table 6–1 summarizes practice-based, decision-making models and provides a step-by-step comparative layout. Although the steps may not align perfectly in the table, it does present a basic visual picture that allows

TABLE 6-1 Summary of Several Ethical Decision-Making Models

Corey, Corey, & Callanan (1998)	Forester-Miller & Davis (1996)	Hill, Glaser, & Harden (1995)	Keith-Spiegel & Koocher (1985)	Stadler (1986)	Steinman, Richardson, & McEnroe (1998)	Welfel (1998)
1. Identify the problem	1. Identify the problem	1. Recognize the problem	1. Describe the parameters	1. Identify competing principles	1. Identify the problem	1. Develop ethical sensitivity
2. Identify potential issues involved	2. Apply the ACA code of ethics	2. Define the problem	2. Define the potential issues	2. Secure additional information		2. Define the dilemma & options
3. Review relevant ethical guidelines		3. Consult if needed	3. Consult legal and ethical guidelines	3. Consult with colleagues	2. Identify the relevant ethical standard	3. Refer to professional standards
4. Obtain consultation	3. Determine nature of dilemma		4. Evaluate the rights, responsibilities, & welfare of involved parties	4. Identify hoped-for outcomes	3. Determine possible ethical traps	4. Search out ethics scholarship
5. Consider possible & probable courses of action	4. Generate potential courses of action	4. Develop solutions	5. Generate alternate decisions	5. Brainstorm actions to achieve outcomes	4. Frame preliminary response	5. Apply ethical principles to situation
6. Enumerate consequences of various decisions	5. Consider potential consequences, determine course of action	5. Consult if needed	6. Enumerate the consequences of each decision	6. Evaluate effects of actions	5. Consider consequences of that response	6. Consult with supervisor & peers
			7. Estimate probability for outcomes of each decision	7. Identify competing nonmoral values		
7. Decide on best course of action	6. Evaluate selected course of action	6. Choose a solution	8. Make the decision	8. Choose a course of action	6. Prepare an ethical resolution	7. Deliberate & decide
		7. Review process		9. Test the course of action		
	7. Implement course of action	8. Implement plan and evaluate		10. Identify steps, take action, evaluate	8. Plan and execute the selected action	8. Inform supervisor & take action
		9. Reflection			9. Evaluate course of action	9. Reflect on the experience

for a comparative analysis. (For a more in-depth discussion of these approaches, see the article published by Cottone and Claus [2000].)

Tarvydas's Integrative Decision-Making Model of Ethical Behavior[2]

The Tarvydas Integrative Decision-Making Model of Ethical Behavior incorporates the most prominent principle and virtue aspects of several decision-making approaches and introduces some contextual considerations into the process. Generally, ethical decision-making models can be thought of as having the characteristics of either *principle* or *virtue* ethics (Corey, Corey, & Callanan, 1998). Principle ethics focuses on the objective, rational, and cognitive aspects of the process. Practitioners who adhere to this perspective tend to view the application of universal, impartial ethical principles, rules, codes, and law as the core elements of ethics. Virtue ethics considers the characteristics of the counselors themselves as the critical element for responsible practice. Thus, proponents of virtue ethics approaches tend to concern themselves more with counselors reflecting on and clarifying their moral and value positions. Additionally, they examine other personal issues that might influence their ethical practice, such as unresolved emotional needs that might negatively affect their work with clients. Many argue that it is preferable that ethical decision making include both aspects (Corey, Corey, & Callanan, 1998; Meara, Schmidt, & Day, 1996). Among other positive contributions of such a synergistic approach, Meara, Schmidt, and Day (1996) and Vasquez (1996) speculated that the addition of virtue ethical perspectives would improve ethical conduct in multicultural and diverse interactions and settings. The Tarvydas Integrative Model (Table 6–2) emphasizes the constant process of interaction between the principle and virtue elements, and places a reflective attitude at the heart of the process. The model also focuses on the actual production of ethical behavior within a specified context, rather than prematurely terminating analysis by merely selecting the best ethical course of action. This approach respects the importance of setting and environmental factors that are crucial in counseling. Indeed, in reviewing the various approaches to ethical decision making,

Garcia, Cartwright, Winston, and Borzuchowska (in press) observed that this model uses virtue ethics and behavioral strategies that are consistent with a multicultural approach to counseling and ethical decision making. They proposed an Integrative Transcultural Ethical Decision-Making Model that is based primarily on the Tarvydas Integrative Model.

Conceptual Origins. The Tarvydas Integrative Model builds on several well-known decision-making models used widely by professionals in the mental health and counseling communities. The seminal works of Rest (1984) and Kitchener (1984) are foundational. Rest (1984) provided the Tarvydas Integrative Model, with its core understanding of ethical decision making, as a psychological process that involves distinct cognitive-affective elements interacting in each component. Cognitions and emotions are seen as unavoidably intertwined at each component of the decision-making process and in the production of ethical behavior. Rest (1984) conceptualized ethical decision making as more than a direct expression of moral or value traits or a stage in a moral developmental process. He emphasized considering the completion of ethical behavior as the necessary point for consideration, rather than merely arriving at a cognitive decision or intent to do an ethical act. Therefore, Rest's (1984) ethical decision-making components and many of his considerations are the foundation of the Tarvydas Integrative Model.

Kitchener (1984) provided other core elements to the Tarvydas Integrative Model. She made a use of Hare's (1981) distinction between the intuitive and critical-evaluative levels of ethical decision making, thus providing a forum to incorporate the richness and influence of the everyday personal and professional moral wisdom into the individual professional's process of ethical decision making. This personal and professional wisdom informs the first level of the process—the intuitive level, where both nonconscious and conscious levels of awareness lead to decisions that call into play the individual's existing morals, beliefs, and experiences. These morals, beliefs, and experiences that constitute our ordinary moral sense also include professional learning and experiences. Kitchener noted that the intuitive level of process often is the professional's main decision-making tool when a situation is not perceived as novel, unusual, or requiring an unusual level of care. The intuitive level of analysis always constitutes the first platform of decision making, even when the situation requires the more stringent level of

---

[2]This chapter section draws heavily and directly from "Standards of Practice: Legal and Ethical" by Vilia M. Tarvydas, 1997, in D. R. Maki & T.R. Riggar (Eds.), *Rehabilitation Counseling: Profession and Practice,* Copyright 1997 by Springer Publishing Co. Used by permission.

TABLE 6–2 The Tarvydas Integrative Decision-Making Model of Ethical Behavior

Themes or Attitudes in the Integrative Model

Maintain an attitude of **reflection.**

Address **balance** between issues and parties to the ethical dilemma.

Pay close attention to the **context(s)** of the situation.

Utilize a process of **collaboration** with all rightful parties to the situation.

Stage I. Interpreting the Situation through Awareness and Fact Finding

Component 1	Enhance **sensitivity** and **awareness**
Component 2	Determine the major **stakeholders** and their ethical claims in the situation
Component 3	Engage in the **fact-finding** process

Stage II. Formulating an Ethical Decision

Component 1	**Review** the problem or dilemma
Component 2	Determine what **ethical codes, laws, ethical principles, and institutional policies and procedures** exist that apply to the dilemma
Component 3	Generate possible and probable **courses of action**
Component 4	Consider potential positive and negative **consequences** for each course of action
Component 5	**Consult** with supervisors and other knowledgeable professionals
Component 6	Select the best **ethical course of action**

Stage III. Selecting an Action by Weighing Competing, Nonmoral Values, Personal Blind Spots, or Prejudices

Component 1	Engage in reflective recognition and analysis of **personal competing nonmoral values, personal blind spots, or prejudices**
Component 2	Consider **contextual influences** on values selection at the collegial, team, institutional, and societal levels
Component 3	Select the preferred course of action

Stage IV. Planning and Executing the Selected Course of Action

Component 1	Figure out a reasonable **sequence of concrete actions** to be taken
Component 2	Anticipate and work out personal and contextual **barriers** to effective execution of the plan of action, and effective **countermeasures** for them
Component 3	**Carry out, document, and evaluat**e the course of action as planned

analysis involved in the critical-evaluative level of consideration. Thus, a person's ordinary moral sense is relevant to one's ethical decision-making process, reinforcing the concerns raised by proponents of the virtue ethics perspective.

If the ethical issue is not resolved at the intuitive level, the counselor progresses to Kitchener's (1984) critical-evaluative level of ethical analysis. This level involves three hierarchical stages of examination to resolve the dilemma. At the first stage, the counselor determines if any laws or ethical rules exist that would provide a solution for the dilemma. If they do not exist, or if they exist but provide conflicting dictates, the counselor progresses to the second stage by consider-

ing how the core ethical principles apply to the situation. The seminal work of Beauchamp and Childress (1994) identified autonomy, beneficence, nonmaleficence, and justice as the core ethical principles that govern ethical behavior. Kitchener (1984) subsequently added fidelity to these core principles for helping professionals, resulting in five core ethical principles to be considered in ethical decision making.

If counselors are still uncertain as to the appropriate ethical course of action, they proceed to the third stage—assessing the positions suggested by ethical theory. Patterson (1992) recommended that counselors should be concerned with normative ethical theory and may benefit from considering whether they prefer their action be based on a general or a universal law. Kitchener (1984) suggested applying the "good reasons" approach, in which counselors attempt to make a decision based on what they would wish for themselves or someone dear to them. Another standard suggested by Kitchener is to take the action that will result in the least amount of harm.

The final conceptual influence on the Tarvydas Integrative Model is the four-level model of ethical practice introduced by Tarvydas and Cottone (1991). This approach extends consideration of the contextual forces acting on ethical practice beyond the singular focus of the individual practitioner in relationship to the individual client. The four levels are hierarchical, moving to increasingly broader levels of social contexts within which ethical practice is influenced. The four levels are (1) the clinical counseling level, (2) the clinical interdisciplinary level, (3) the institutional/agency level, and (4) the societal resource/public policy level. The relationships among the levels are seen as interactive. Peak ethical efficiency and lowest levels of ethical stress are reached when each level holds compatible values and standards or endorses a mutually acceptable mechanism for ethical dilemma resolution. The first (or micro) level in the hierarchy is the traditionally central clinical counseling core, in which the counselor-client relationship is the focus. The second level is the clinical interdisciplinary team interaction. At this point, practitioner-to-practitioner dynamics are considered. Team members may be physically dispersed, but functionally remain a team in terms of collaboration or coordinated work with respect to the client's care. Team communications occur by telephone or electronic means, with only infrequent meetings or staffings. Nonetheless, they constitute an important clinical and ethical force in the client's life. Team relationships and leadership, collaboration skills, and the interplay of the differing ethical codes and traditions become important to the process. At the third level, the institutional or agency context and its constraints enter into the process. Dictates of agency policy, practitioner-supervisor style and practices, and staffing patterns are factors that might have an influence. Corporate or administrative operations such as institutional goals, marketing strategies, and corporate oversight processes may also play a role. At the fourth (or macro) level, the effects of overall societal resources and public policy are considered. Social concern for scarce health care resources, the movement to managed care, and the privatization of mental health care are examples of broad themes and related policies that may affect ethical practices at the practitioner level. Societal values related to such areas as independence and self-sufficiency, work and productivity, physical appearance, what constitutes an unacceptable lifestyle, and other types of behavior do influence the work of counselors extensively (Gatens-Robinson & Rubin, 1995). Societal values also are expressed in more concrete ways that may affect counselor practices through such influences as the climate created by local public opinion and various legislative and regulatory codes.

Themes and Attitudes. In addition to the specific elements or steps of the Tarvydas Integrative Model, four underlying themes or attitudes are necessary for the professional counselor. These attitudes involve mindfully attending to the tasks of (a) maintaining a *stance of reflection* concerning one's own conscious awareness of personal issues, values, and decision-making skills, as well as extending effort to understand those of all others concerned with the situation, and their relationship to the decision maker; (b) addressing the *balance* among various issues, people, and perspectives within the process; (c) maintaining an appropriate level of *attention to the context* of the situation in question, allowing awareness of the counselor-client, treatment team, organizational, and societal implications of the ethical elements; and (d) seeking to use a process of *collaboration* with all rightful parties to the decision, but most especially the client.

By adopting these background attitudes of reflection, balance, context, and collaboration, counselors engage in a more thorough process that will help preserve the integrity and dignity of all parties involved. This will be the case even when outcomes are not considered equally positive for all participants in the process, as is often true in a serious dilemma when such attitudes can be particularly meaningful. Indeed, Betan and Stanton (1999) studied students' responses to ethical dilemmas, analyzing how emotions and concerns influence willingness to implement ethical knowledge. They concluded that "subjectivity and emotional involvement are essential tools for determining ethical action, but they must be integrated with rational analysis" (Betan & Stanton, 1999, p. 295).

Reflection is the overriding attitude of importance throughout the enactment of the specific elements of stages and components that constitute the steps of the Tarvydas Integrative Model. Many complex decision-making processes easily become overwhelming, either in their innate complexity or in the real-life press of the speed or intensity of events. In the current approach, the counselor is urged to always "stop and think!" at each point in the process. The order of operations is neither critical nor absolute, or more important than being reflective and invested in a calm, dignified, respectful, and thorough analysis of the situation. It is not until we recognize that we are involved in the process and appreciate its critical aspects that we can call forth other resources to assist the process and persons within it. Such an attitude of reflection will serve the counselor well at all stages of this process.

CASE SCENARIO 6–1

Themes and Attitudes

Jimmy W. is in fifth grade and has been sent to see you, his school counselor, by Mrs. James, his teacher. This has been a difficult year for you professionally and personally. You have felt overwhelmed by an increasing number of students assigned to you. You also have had difficulty concentrating since your rather acrimonious divorce,which was finalized during the summer. Jimmy has continued to do good work in class since his parents' divorce eight months ago. However, Mrs. James has noticed that Jimmy tears up his worksheets and art projects as soon as they are graded and is not showing his usual enthusiasm for school work. She has talked to him about the situation, but Jimmy denies that anything is wrong. Jimmy finally confides to you that his mother will no longer allow him to send letters and his completed school work to his father who lives in another state. He misses his father and his correspondence with him; he also thinks his work is meaningless and not important enough to be seen by his dad. He asks you if you will send his letters and school work to his father occasionally. Jimmy finally gives you permission to discuss his concerns with his mother. Mother angrily forbids you to communicate with Jimmy's father in any way. She informs you that she is the sole custodial parent and guardian, and that Mr. W. moved away rather than "be bothered with the responsibility of Jimmy." She reluctantly allows you to continue counseling Jimmy about his "behavior problems" in school, but tells you not to raise his hopes about seeing or communicating with his father. While you will continue to provide supportive counseling to Jimmy, you consider the matter of contact with Mr. W. closed. By the end of the school year, you have not heard from Mr. or Mrs. W. and Jimmy's problems have not worsened. Were you correct?

PROBABLY NOT. When you stop and reflect on this situation outside of the furor of the meeting with Jimmy and his mom, you realize that two factors probably clouded your thinking. The first factor was your own painful divorce and custody problems. The second factor involved recent situations in which your school principal criticized you before the school staff for refusing to reveal to him confidential information in a controversial case about a student's family financial matters. Your anger at your former spouse and your

fear of the principal have blinded you to other questions you must explore. You may discover that either the mother has incorrectly reported the custody arrangements, or the father does have some legal right to the communication his son desires. Even if Mr. W. does not have a legal right to correspondence from his son, Jimmy's rights and desires must be considered primary, and his father may have some moral claim to continue contact with his son apart from the custody decree specifics. Although counseling must occur with parental consent, it might be possible to counsel Jimmy and his mom to preserve some acceptable type and level of contact with Jimmy's father. A greater ability to communicate might facilitate Jimmy's adjustment and future cooperative communication regarding other aspects of Jimmy's welfare. These deeper considerations would include themes of balancing the moral claims of all parties to the situation regardless of the legal aspects of the situation. It also introduces the attitude of collaboration to the decisions involving Jimmy's well-being. None of these issues would have been available for your consideration unless you had first systematically practiced the attitude of reflection about a decision you initially thought was obvious.

Elements. The specific elements that constitute the operations within the Tarvydas Integrative Model have four main stages with several components and steps within each stage. As previously stated, the concepts summarized in the following sections are primarily from Rest (1984), Kitchener (1984), and Tarvydas and Cottone (1991).

Stage I: Interpreting the Situation Through Awareness and Fact Finding. At this stage, the primary task of counselors is to be sensitive and aware of the needs and welfare of the people around them, and the ethical implications of these situations. This level of awareness allows counselors to imagine and to investigate the effects of the situation on the parties involved and the possible effects of various actions and conditions. This research and awareness must also include emotional as well as cognitive and fact-based considerations. Three components constitute the counselors' operations in this stage.

Component 1 involves enhancing one's sensitivity and awareness. In *Component 2*, the counselor takes an inventory of the people who are major stakeholders in the outcome of the situation. It is important to reflect on any parties who will be affected and play a major role in the client's life, as well as considering what their exact relationship is ethically and legally to the person at the center of the issue—the client. In Case Scenario 6–1, Jimmy may be best served by some contact with his father,

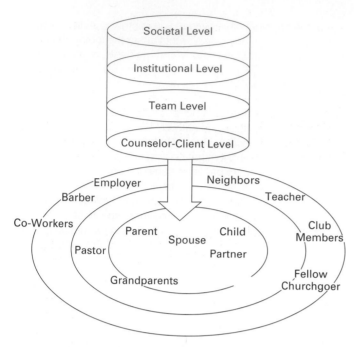

FIGURE 6–1. The Intersection of the Client's Personal World with the Counselor's Professional Hierarchical Contexts

assuming that the father is interested and not abusive. Imagine dropping a rock into a pond: The point of impact is where the central figure, the client, is situated. However, the client is surrounded by people at varying levels of closeness, such as parents, foster parents, intimate partners, spouse, children, employer, friends, and neighbors. They radiate out from the client in decreasing levels of intimacy and responsibility to the client.

Figure 6–1 depicts how the spheres of influence of these stakeholders in the client's life, as well as the stakeholders at each of the four levels in the professional world of the counselor, may intersect. This way of thinking about the relationships between the different stakeholders in the situation allows for a fuller appreciation of the specific people and contexts of the counselor's practice and the client's situation. A number of people and levels of the service hierarchy will (or should) play a part in the ethics decision. These social forces will create both positive and negative influences in the ethical situation and should be taken into account in the ethical analysis. The ethical claims of these parties on the counselor's level of duty are not uniform. Almost all codes of ethics in counseling make it clear that the client is the person to whom the first duty is owed, but there are others to whom the counselor has lesser, but important, levels of duty. It is al-

ways important to determine whether any surrogate decision makers for the client exist, such as a guardian or person with power of attorney, so that they may be brought into the central "circle of duty" early in the process. In Case Scenario 6–1, the mother must be counseled. The noncustodial parent has many rights to contact his son and even decision-making authority in some jurisdictions. It is useful to be sensitive and proactive in working through situations in which the legal relationships involved do not coincide with the social and emotional bonds between the client and other people involved in the dilemma.

In the final element in Stage I, *Component 3*, the counselor undertakes an extensive fact-finding investigation of a scope appropriate to the situation. The nature of the fact-finding process should be carefully considered and is not intended to be a formal investigative or quasi-legal process. The counselor should carefully review, understand the information at hand, and seek out new information. Only information that is appropriately available to a counselor should be involved. The scope and depth of information that would be rightfully available to the counselor is surprising, but it is often underutilized. For example, information might be gained from such sources as further discussion with the client, contacts with family (with appropriate permission of the client), case records, expert consultation and reports, legal resources, or agency policy and procedures. In Case Scenario 6–1, the exact legal nature of the father–son relationship and the mother-father relationship should be explored.

Stage II: Formulating an Ethical Decision. Although this aspect of the process is most widely known by professionals, many may erroneously think it is the end of the process. The central task in this stage is to identify which of the possible ethical courses of action appears to come closest to the moral ideal in the situation under consideration (Rest, 1984). Many decision-making models in other areas of counseling can be applied as a template at this stage, but the following components are drawn from the work of Van Hoose and Kottler (1985).

Component 1 suggests that the counselor review the problem or dilemma to be sure that it is clearly understood in light of any new information obtained in Stage I. In *Component 2*, the counselor researches the standards of law and practice applicable to the situation. This component includes Kitchener's (1984) attention to ethical codes, laws, and ethical principles; and Tarvydas and Cottone's (1991) concern for the team and organizational context in the examination of institutional policies and procedures to make mention of other useful areas for consideration. If you were the counselor in Case Scenario 6–1, at this point you would need to ensure that you were familiar with the requirements of the Family Educational Rights and Privacy Act of 1974 (see Chapter 13). You need to be sure about the protection afforded to your counseling notes and which records about Jimmy would be released to Jimmy's parents upon their request. The counselor would also analyze which of the five core ethical principles (autonomy, beneficience, nonmaleficence, justice, and fidelity) are either supported or compromised by the types of actions that are being contemplated. This operation is formally known as *principle analysis* and is one of the most challenging, yet critical, aspects of the ethical analysis of a dilemma. The core, or main principle, analysis concerns the ethical obligations owed to the client rather than those owed to other parties in the situation. *Component 3* initiates the process of formally envisioning and generating possible and probable courses of action. As with all decision-making processes, it is important not to truncate this exploratory process by prematurely censoring the possibilities, or succumbing to a sense of being too overwhelmed or too limited in options. *Component 4* is the logical outgrowth of considering courses of action—positive and negative consequences are identified and assessed in light of the risks, as well as the material and personal resources available. In *Component 5*, the counselor is reminded to consult with supervisors and trusted, knowledgeable colleagues for guidance, if this has not been done before this point. Professional standards of practice emphasize the importance of appropriate collegial consultation to resolve difficult clinical and ethical dilemmas. Research has also demonstrated that such consultations can have a significant influence on those seeking such consultation (Cottone, Tarvydas, & House, 1994). At this time, it is valuable to review the reasoning employed so far in working through the ethical dilemma, and the solutions and consequences envisioned, to be sure that all potentially useful and appropriate considerations have been taken into account. Finally, the best *ethical course* of action is determined and articulated in *Component 6*. The ethical decision at this stage of the model should be contrasted with the actual decision made by the counselor—that is the product of Stage III.

Stage III: Selecting an Action by Weighing Competing, Nonmoral Values, Personal Blind Spots, and Prejudices. Many people would think the eth-

ical decision-making process is concluded at the end of Stage II. This impression is limited by the realization that many additional forces may affect the counselor. As a result, the counselor may not actually execute the selected ethical course of action. *Component 1* of Stage III interjects a period of reflection and active processing of what the counselor intends to do in view of competing, nonmoral values (Rest, 1984). At this point, the counselor considers any personal factors that might intervene to pull him away from choosing the ethical action or cause that action to be substantially modified. Nonmoral values involve anything that the counselor may prize or desire that is not, in and of itself, a moral value, such as justice, valuing social harmony, spending time with friends or working on one's hobby, or having personal wealth. In this component, counselors are also called upon to examine themselves to determine if they have some personal blind spots or prejudices that might affect their judgment or resolve to do the ethical thing, such as a fear of HIV infection or the conviction that men who are homosexual are also likely to molest children. This portion of the model provides an excellent opportunity for counselors to carefully evaluate whether they have adequately incorporated multicultural considerations and competencies in their work on this ethical dilemma. They need to be sure that they are not operating from a culturally encapsulated frame of reference. In Case Scenario 6–1, the counselor might have realized upon reflection that her need to avoid controversy with the principal, or her identification with Jimmy's mother's anger with her ex-husband (a noncustodial parent), and her wish to be seen as supportive of the rights of a single mother may be competing with her knowledge of what is legally or ethically right.

It is important that counselors allow themselves to become aware of the strength and attractiveness of other values they hold that may influence whether they will discharge their ethical obligations. If they are self-aware, they may more effectively and honestly compensate for their conflicted impulses at this point. They may have a visceral distaste for homosexuals, an overriding need to protect minor children, or a sexual or emotional attraction to a particular client. Counselors may have strong needs for acceptance by peers or supervisors, prestige, influence, to avoid controversy, or to be financially successful. These value orientations may come into conflict with the course of action necessary to proceed ethically and must be reconciled with the ethical requirements if the client is to be served ethically. On the other hand, counselors may place a high value on being moral, ethical, and accepted as respected professionals with high ethical standards. They may value the esteem of colleagues who place a high value on ethical professional behavior. Those forces should enhance the tendency to select ethical behavioral options. (The influence of the ethical climate on the ethical behavior of the counselor is more fully explored in Chapter 7.) The importance of selecting and maintaining ethically sensitized and positive professional and personal cultures is critical to full professional functioning, as the next component suggests.

In *Component 2* of Stage III, counselors systematically inventory the contextual influences on their choices at the collegial, team, institutional, and societal levels. While this is not a simple process of weighing influences, it should serve as an inventory of influences that may be either dysfunctional or constructive for selecting the ethical course over other types of values present in these other interactions. Counselors may also use this type of information to think strategically about the influences they will need to overcome to provide ethical service in the situation. Beyond the immediate situation, it is important to recognize that counselors should control their exposure to contexts that consistently reinforce values that run counter to the dictates of good ethical practices. In Case Scenario 6–1, Jimmy's counselor might be influenced in one direction if she spends most of her personal and professional time with staff who are primarily concerned with getting ahead in the school hierarchy and being seen favorably by the administration, in contrast with having a few strong relationships with colleagues who take great pride in their professional identities and reputations. This problem might result in terminating or curtailing certain relationships, changing employment, or selecting another aspect of counseling service to provide.

Component 3 is the final aspect of Stage III. At this time, the counselor selects the preferred course of action or the behavior that he plans to undertake. This decision may be a reaffirmation of the intention to take the ethical course of action as determined at the conclusion of Stage II. However, it may be some other course of action that may even be unethical or a modified version of the ethical course of action selected in Stage II. Whatever the choice, the counselor selects it after this more extensive reflection on his own competing values and personal blind spots, as well as the contextual influences on him in the situation in question.

Stage IV: Planning and Executing the Selected Course of Action.

Rest (1984) described the essential tasks of this stage as planning to implement and execute what one plans to do. This operation includes *Component 1*, in which the counselor determines a reasonable sequence of concrete actions to be taken. In *Component 2*, the task is to anticipate and work out all personal and contextual barriers to effectively executing the plan. It is useful to prepare countermeasures for barriers that may arise. In Case Scenario 6–1, if Jimmy's father indeed has a legal and ethical right, as well as a personal interest in Jimmy, what barriers might arise if Jimmy is given the opportunity to contact him? It is here that the earlier attention to other stakeholders and their concerns may suggest problems or allies to the process. Additionally, earlier consideration of the contextual influences in Stage III assist the counselor in this type of strategic planning. *Component 3* is the final step of this model. It provides for the execution, documentation, and evaluation of the course of action as planned. Rest (1984) noted that the actual behavioral execution of ethics is often not a simple task, frequently drawing heavily on the personal, emotional qualities and professional and interpersonal skills of the counselor. He mentions such qualities as firmness of resolve, ego strength, and social assertiveness. Countless skills such as persistence, tact, time management, assertiveness skills, team collaboration, and conflict-resolution skills could be added to this list. Considerations are limited only by the characteristics and requirements of the counselor and the specific situation involved. To protect the interests of both counselor and client, document the entire plan and the rationale behind it thoroughly, and take ethical decision-making steps in response to the ethical dilemma as the process unfolds. The information gained in this documentation process will prove critical in evaluating the effectiveness of the entire ethical decision-making process.

Practicing the Tarvydas Integrative Model. Like the basic counseling microskills, the skills of ethical decision making do not come automatically, or even easily, after merely reading concepts in a book. A gradual progression in gaining practical skills and sensitive, accurate ethical knowledge is achieved by solving mock ethical dilemmas; working to address actual ethical dilemmas under the supervision of an ethically knowledgeable instructor, clinical supervisor, master counselor or mentor; and incorporating ethical analysis into the clinical training process.

Case Scenario 6–2 presents a complex ethical case with a full ethical analysis using the Tarvydas Integrative Model and all of its stages and components. The analysis does not represent "the one and only" correct answer to the dilemma presented. Information discovered or concerns raised by other reasonable people can lead to important shifts in the elements of a case. Reasonable professionals can judge and weigh the same ideas or risks differently; there may be several valid conclusions to the same case. This process is not so much about getting the "hidden, correct answer" but rather about going through the process of decision making thoroughly and carefully while exercising due care and good, reasonable professional judgment throughout. By doing so, counselors are more likely to arrive at an explicable judgment that minimizes risk to the client, the counselor, and others. Counselors also benefit from increased confidence and peace of mind in knowing they did their best and used a thorough, thoughtful approach to solving a dilemma that may not have a satisfying solution for the parties involved.

CASE SCENARIO 6–2

ILLUSTRATION OF THE TARVYDAS INTEGRATIVE MODEL FOR ETHICAL BEHAVIOR

Narrative of Case Example

John, a 43-year-old man, is meeting with a counselor at the Department of Correctional Services (DCS). He has recently been released from prison on parole, and is meeting with a counselor voluntarily to deal with some issues of depression. He is currently on medication for depression, and has attempted suicide in the past. He was married to a woman for nine years and they had two children together, now ages 7 and 5. She also had two children from a previous relationship, now ages 12 and 8, whom John also considers to be his children. He and his wife are recently divorced. At first she would not allow the children to visit their dad, but just recently John says they have been talking again, and his ex-wife has started to trust him again and lets the children visit whenever they want to. Just recently, his youngest girl confided in him that their mom and her new friends are still using drugs and also selling them from the house. She had found a syringe at the home that her mom thought was hidden. John is very adamant that he does not want to contact Department of Human Services (DHS) or any other similar agency about this. He had contacted DHS for a similar situation a few years ago, and had a bad experience. DHS had "done nothing," and his ex-wife had found out that he had made the report. She did not let him see the kids for a long time after the incident. He feels that at this point, he can do the most good by keeping a close relationship with his children and a civil relationship with his ex-wife. He is now living a clean and drug-free life, and feels that he is now his ex-

wife's best hope to straighten out. He says if a report is made, the only thing he is sure of is that his ex-wife will not let him see the children, and he does not know if he could live without being part of his children's lives. In this case, the client, John, has his reasons for not wanting to contact DHS, and client autonomy needs to be respected. The client also raises the issue that maybe contacting the authorities really is not in the best interest of the children. John also made some statements regarding not being able to live without being a part of his children's lives, which need to be taken seriously given his suicidal history and current state of depression. On the other hand, the young children are involved in a dangerous situation. There is no report of physical or sexual abuse occurring, yet drug use in the home and young children coming across needles is definitely dangerous and could be considered abuse. At this point the counselor feels there may be a potential dilemma that needs to be explored further.

Stage I: Interpreting the Situation Through Awareness and Fact Finding

The counselor's primary task in Stage 1 is to be sensitive and aware of the needs and welfare of the people involved, and the ethical implications of these situations. This level of awareness allows counselors to imagine and to investigate the effects of the situation on the parties involved and the possible effects of various actions and conditions. This research and awareness must also include emotional as well as cognitive and fact-based considerations.

Component 1: Sensitivity and Awareness   At this point, the counselor talks to the client and gets his impression of who will be affected by this situation, and how they will be affected. The client clearly cares about his children and firmly believes that they will have their best chance if he continues to be a part of their lives. John has no guarantee what would happen if he did contact DHS, and he does not want to take that risk. Given what happened the last time he called, he is very distrustful of the system and his ex-wife's reaction. John also expressed some concerns for his ex-wife, and even though they parted on unfriendly terms, he still seems to care about her and wants what is best for her. He says that they are just starting to talk again, and he feels that he may be the only one who truly understands what she is going through with the drugs. John feels he might be able to help his ex-wife kick the habit. While he admits that he worries what kind of environment his children are living in, John feels that this is the best chance they have.

The counselor also notes that there are four children in the house, of varying ages. While an 18-year-old might understand how dangerous finding a needle in the house really is, a 5-year-old most likely would not. Aside from needles being in the house, there is also the potential for danger from the people who are around the children. If their mother is dealing drugs from the home, it is likely that many of those she sells to are in the house also and around the children.

John says he understands all of this, but still feels that he is making progress with his ex-wife and that he is the best chance for his children. He acknowledges that he is taking on a lot of responsibility, but says that he would do anything for his children and truly believes that he is doing the best for them in the long run.

Component 2: Major Stakeholders and their Ethical Claims
The counselor identifies the parties who will be affected and what their exact relationship is ethically and legally to the person at the center of the issue. There are often others to whom the counselor has lesser, but important, levels of duty, such as parents, intimate partners, spouse, children, employer, friends, neighbors, guardian, or persons with power of attorney. The following list shows all important parties with an ethical or legal claim in this situation.

Parties	Ethical Claim
1. The client	He does not want to contact any authorities
2. The children	They may be in danger, may not know all of their options or how they could get help
3. DCS	The agency is responsible for its counselors, and could be held liable for mistakes made by its employees
4. The counselor	He may be held liable for any harm that befalls the children or the client
5. The ex-wife	She could face an abuse investigation and the subsequent consequences
6. Grandparents	They would most likely get custody of the children if DHS did find abuse

Component 3: Fact-Finding Process   The counselor undertakes an extensive fact-finding investigation of a scope appropriate to the situation by reviewing and understanding current information and seeking out new information. This investigation involves gathering information appropriately available to the counselor either through professional records and channels (with appropriately obtained releases of information), or through public domain information. Sources might include further discussion with the client, contacts with family (with the client's permission), current and old client records in one's own or another agency, expert consultation and reports, legal resources, or agency policy and procedures. List all facts or factual questions the counselor should reasonably be able to research or answer.

A call was made anonymously to DHS to find out if the situation in general fell under the guidelines for mandatory reporters, which it did not. DHS stated that it did not fall under mandatory guidelines because it was third-party information.

The counselor talked to the supervisor and found out that DCS has an unwritten rule, or policy, to convince the client to call authorities and report the situation himself.

The client stated that if DHS was contacted, an investigation was conducted, and action was taken to remove the

children from their mother, the maternal grandparents would probably receive custody. The client stated that he has a good relationship with his ex-wife's parents. He thought that they would allow him to see the children if they did get custody.

The counselor was informed by a supervisor that DHS may not have done anything the last time John reported because there may have been some type of drug investigation going on. If there is a current investigation into drug trafficking or selling, DHS can postpone going into the house for a child abuse charge because the house is under supervision as part of a larger investigation.

Stage II: Formulating an Ethical Decision
The counselor's task in this stage is to identify which of the possible ethical courses of action appears to come closest to the ethical ideal in the situation under consideration.

Component 1: Review Problem or Dilemma   Review the problem or dilemma to be sure it is clearly understood in light of any new information.

This situation does not fall into the category of mandatory reporting, so the counselor is not legally bound to break the client's confidence. However, we now know that the unwritten policy of the counselor's institution (DCS) is to try to convince or coerce the client to call DHS on his own. Thus, we must decide whether to respect the client's wishes not to call DHS or try to coerce the client to call, in accordance with the institution's unwritten policy.

Component 2: Determine Ethical Codes, Laws, Principles
The counselor must determine and research the standards of law (in any and all applicable local jurisdictions) and professional practices applicable to the situation. The latter material includes ethical codes and related standards of care, laws, ethical principles, and institutional policies and procedures. List these here.

Ethical Codes

List any rules or canons from applicable ethics code(s) and provide a summary of the dictate. For counselors, the ACA Code of Ethics and Professional Standards and any applicable specialty standards are recommended. If the counselor is licensed or holds national certification, the codes of ethics that apply to that credential also must be consulted.

ACA Code of Ethics:

Section A.1.a "Primary Responsibility. The primary responsibility of counselors is to respect the dignity and promote the welfare of the clients."

Section A.1.b "Positive Growth and Development. Counselors encourage client growth and development in ways that foster the client's interest and welfare; counselors avoid fostering dependent counseling relationships."

Section B.1.c "Exceptions. The general requirement that counselors keep information confidential does not apply when disclosure is required to prevent clear and imminent danger to the client or to others or when legal requirements demand that confidential information be revealed."

Section D.1.c "Negative Conditions. Counselors alert their employers to conditions that may be potentially disruptive or damaging to the counselor's professional responsibilities or that may limit their effectiveness."

Section D.1.l "Employer Policies. The acceptance of employment in an agency or institution implies that counselors are in agreement with its general policies and principles. Counselors strive to reach agreement with employers as to acceptable standards of conduct that allow for changes in institutional policy conducive to the growth and development of clients."

Laws/Legal Considerations   List any laws or legal considerations that may apply. Research those relevant to your own jurisdiction. The example is provided based upon Iowa law, circa 2000. This example is not to be considered a legal opinion, only an example. For further information, consult legal counsel and resources in your own area.

Iowa Code:

Section 232.69 "Mandatory and permissive reporters-training required." A counselor is considered to be a mandatory reporter "who, in the scope of professional practice or in their employment responsibilities, examines, counsels, or treats a child and reasonably believes a child has suffered abuse." Section 232.68 Included in the definitions of child abuse: "An illegal drug is present in a child's body as a direct and foreseeable consequence of the acts or omissions of the person responsible for the care of the child."

Ethical Principles   List all ethical principles that describe relevant obligations. Describe the courses of action, the principles upheld, the principles compromised, and the obligations. Sometimes this process if referred to as "principle analysis." This is a process wherein ethical principles are specified and subjected to balancing considerations.

Each of the two courses of action can be supported by one or more ethical principles. Contacting authorities could fall under the category of beneficence on the part of the children. Keeping John's confidence could fall under the category of autonomy, for honoring the right to individual decisions. There is also the possibility that both scenarios could fit into the category of nonmaleficence. Not telling anyone could lead to harm for the children in some way. Also, by telling, it is possible that John's fears could materialize and the ex-wife could keep the children away from him. In this way, it may be harmful to John and also to the children if they are not allowed to see their father.

The ethical principles supporting the other course of action will be compromised. If the authorities are notified, the counselor is not respecting the client's autonomy. If authorities are not told, the counselor may be compromising the principles of nonmaleficence toward the children and the concept of beneficence in the same way.

In principle analysis, the principle obligations owed to your client normally outweigh those owed to others. Therefore, they are the only ones frequently considered; or if

those obligations to others are considered, those owed to the client generally supercede them because the counselor incurs these primary obligations by virtue of entering into a professional relationship with the client. The exception to this case would involve obligations to vulnerable others (e.g., small children), and/or those situations in which there is a high degree of serious danger or risk. This reasoning is why this case is a particularly troublesome dilemma.

This situation is an ethical dilemma, not just an ethical issue. An ethical issue has a fairly identifiable course of action that is appropriate, even if taking that action is not necessarily easy in practice (i.e., as in the case of involuntarily committing a seriously suicidal individual).

Action A. Pressuring the Client

Principles Upheld
Beneficence (to children)

Principles Compromised
Beneficence (to client)
Nonmaleficence (to client)
Autonomy (of client)
Fidelity (to client)

Action B. Not Pressuring the Client

Principles Upheld
Nonmaleficence (to client)
Beneficence (to client)
Autonomy (to client)
Fidelity (to client)

Principles Compromised
Beneficence (to children)
Nonmaleficence (to children)

Institutional/Agency Rules or Policies   List any institutional/agency rules or policies that may apply. In the experience of the counselor, the unwritten policy of DCS is to try to coerce the client into reporting the possible child abuse to DHS.

Component 3: Courses of Action   List all possible and probable courses of action. If you can boil this selection down to two opposing options, this strategy is recommended.

Action A: Attempt to coerce the client into reporting.

Action B: Do not try to coerce the client into reporting.

Component 4: Positive and Negative Consequences
Consider potential positive and negative consequences for each course of action in light of the risks.

Action A: Pressure the Client

Positive Consequences
May protect the children from abuse
Follows unwritten DCS policy
Hurts client's trust of counselor
DCS would not step in to coerce the client
Less time for other pressing issues of client
Protects DCS from liability

Negative Consequences
Does not respect client's autonomy or confidentiality
Ex-wife may cut off child visitation

Negative relationship with ex-wife
May evoke suicidal thoughts

Action B: Do Not Pressure the Client

Positive Consequences	Negative Consequences
Respects client's autonomy and confidentiality	Does not protect children from possible abuse
Time for other client issues	Counselor is defying employer (DCS)
Does not evoke suicidal thoughts	DCS might step in and coerce client anyway
Child visitation is preserved	DCS might be liable (if child is harmed)
Positive relationship with ex-wife	

Component 5: Consult with Others   Consult with supervisors and other knowledgeable professionals. Review the reasoning employed so far in working through the ethical dilemma by consulting with others.

Individual	Type of Consultation
1. ACA ethics committee	Review situation, obtain suggestions and opinion
2. Counselors from other corrections agencies	Review situation, obtain suggestions and opinion
3. Other colleagues	Review situation, obtain suggestions and opinion
4. DHS anonymously again	Review situation, obtain suggestions and opinion
5. Attorney	Review situation, obtain suggestions and opinion

Component 6: Determine Best Ethical Action   Select the best ethical course of action.

The best ethical course of action would be not to pressure the client to report to DHS, for the following reasons:

1. More ethical principles support this course of action, especially for the client.
2. More positive than negative consequences are likely to result.
3. The Iowa Code does not consider this a situation of mandatory child abuse reporting because the counselor is not working directly with the children, and the only information is "hearsay."

Stage III: Selecting an Action by Weighing Competing, Non-moral Values, Personal Blind Spots, or Prejudices

In this stage, the counselor must realize the many additional forces that may affect him and tempt him to not actually execute the selected ethical course of action.

Component 1: Competing Values or Concerns   The counselor engages in a period of reflection and active processing of personal competing values (e.g., need to be liked by coworkers or his supervisor, or a desire to be seen as a "team player" so as to be promoted by the supervisor), personal blind spots, or prejudices that may influence whether or not he will discharge his ethical obligations.

These value orientations may either come into conflict with the course of action necessary to proceed ethically or enhance the tendency to select ethical professional behavior.

Conflicting Concerns	Potential Effects
1. Fear of a negative evaluation by employer if he does not follow unwritten policy	loss of job, license, respect; financial consequences
2. Feel the need to protect the children at all costs no matter what the situation	Loss of reputation and seen as a confidentiality risk
3. Fear of legal repercussions if abuse situation is not reported to DHS	Children are harmed, loss of license of job
4. Fear of harm to DCS	Personal mental health; financial impact on agency/self
5. Fear of losing respect of colleagues	Personal mental health, future relationships
6. Feeling that client should not be pressured and has autonomy in the decision	Harm to children; increased client confidence
7. Feeling that counseling session should be used to work on the client's problems (e.g., depression)	DHS not contacted and children are harmed, client benefits from counseling rather than using all of the time trying to convince client to call DHS?

Component 2: Contextual Influences   The counselor systematically inventories the contextual influences on his choices at the collegial, team, institutional, and societal levels. These influences might be either dysfunctional or constructive for selecting the ethical course over other types of values.

Level 1: Clinical
1. Counselor's professors/supervisors have recommended advocating for clients' autonomy in the past.

Level 2: Team
1. A few coworkers note that DHS said that the counselor is not required to report the situation to DHS because it is third-party information.

Level 3: Institutional/Agency
1. DCS has an unwritten policy of convincing the client to report abuse on his own.
2. Counselor's supervisor and most colleagues support the institution's policy and feel that all counselors at DCS should adhere to both written and unwritten policies.

Level 4: Social Policy/General Cultural
1. Society values children and children's welfare.
2. Society has little tolerance for drug abuse or the selling of drugs, especially when children are involved.

3. There is a fear of transmitted diseases in society, especially HIV and AIDS, which can be passed through intravenous drug use.
4. Society has a prejudiced attitude toward ex-cons on parole, and makes little distinction between those who are recovering successfully and those who are not.

Component 3: Select Preferred Action The counselor selects the preferred course of action.

This course of action is to attempt to convince the client to call DHS anonymously. Yet, the counselor still respects the client's autonomy and will not coerce him to report the situation to DHS.

Stage IV: Planning and Executing the Selected Course of Action

In this stage, the counselor plans to implement and execute the selected course of action.

Component 1: Possible Sequences of Actions The counselor determines a reasonable, practical sequence of concrete actions to be taken. List the action steps to be taken.

1. Talk with client about the consequences of his reporting versus not reporting the situation (anonymously, at least) to DHS.
2. Attempt to convince the client to call DHS anonymously for information about what would happen if the situation were reported.
3. If the client does not call, do not continue to convince him any further.
4. If the client does call and receives the information, give support for what he decides to do next.

Component 2: Contextual Barriers and Countermeasures The counselor will need to anticipate and work out all personal and contextual barriers to effectively execute the plan. It is useful to prepare countermeasures for any contextual barriers that may arise.

Possible Barriers	Possible Countermeasures
1. Client does not wish to call	Document the attempts to get him to call and do not press the issue any further
2. Supervisor may want the counselor to continue to coerce the client to call	Counselor could let the supervisor know what she is or is not comfortable doing and apprise someone in authority over the supervisor of the situation
3. DCS may assign the case to someone else	No countermeasure unless client insists upon seeing the current counselor
4. Client's ex-wife may refuse to let him see the children if he reports the situation to DHS	Counselor could encourage the client to speak with an attorney about his rights with the children

Component 3: Carry Out, Document, and Evaluate

This step provides for the execution, documentation, and evaluation of the course of action as planned. Describe here the planned goal(s) and potential types of measurements of plan effectiveness and sources of information.

The counselor would carry out the plan by talking to the client about the consequences of reporting versus not reporting the abusive situation to DHS and attempt to get the client to call for information. If the client decides to call, the counselor would support his next step. The counselor would document the ethical decision-making steps taken. Finally, the counselor would evaluate the effectiveness of the plan of action and the entire ethical decision-making process.

Goal	Measure
1. Review consequences of reporting or not reporting, and attempt to get the client to call DHS for information	Weigh benefits and costs of client's decision, assess client's level of comfortability with either decision
2. Support client if he decides to call	Assess what client needs from counselor
3. Prevent harm to children and help mother	Follow up with treatment referrals for mother and on the children's welfare

This case study was developed by Vilia Tarvydas, Ph.D., LMHC, CRC, and uses the Tarvydas Integrative Decision-Making Model for Ethical Behavior.

Cottone's Social Constructivism Model of Ethical Decision Making

The "social constructivism" model of ethical decision making was first introduced in the literature in 2001. This model is based purely on philosophy, incorporating the ideas of the social constructivism movement into mental health services without integration of other ideas historically valued in the ethical decision-making literature. Whereas the Tarvydas model builds on the best that is known about ethical decision making as a psychological and social process to date, the Cottone model diverges by presenting a model that is incompatible with the emphasis of established models on psychological theory. It is a purely social/relational model.

The term **social constructivism** is used here to represent an intellectual movement in the mental health field that has emerged from both the psychological and systemic-relational paradigms of mental health services (see the related discussions in Lyddon [1995] and Cottone [1992]). Generally, social constructivism implies that what is real is not objective fact;

rather, what is real evolves through interpersonal interaction and agreement as to what is "fact" (Ginter et al., 1996). The radical constructivist position, deriving from the works of von Foerster (1984), von Glasersfeld (1984), and specifically Maturana (Maturana, 1978, 1988; Maturana & Varela, 1980), has been embraced by theorists in the field of marriage and family therapy as an offshoot of social systems theory (a comprehensive theory of relationships). It is a unique, biologically grounded theory (the biology of cognition) that ultimately allows for a biosocial interpretation of what is "real." In essence, biologically based social constructivism argues that all that is known is known through biological and social relationships. Even the biological bases of knowledge are best interpreted as deriving from complex physiological *relations* wherein observing organisms interact to construct a reality. Maturana's work is used as a foundation to argue that the biological system is not a static system that creates language; rather, it is a plastic system that is ever-changing through the influence of social interaction, which is the context for language creation. By contrast, the social constructionist movement in psychology (e.g., Gergen, 1985) is more rooted in the social psychology literature and avoids in-depth theorizing about biological bases. Gergen (1985, 1991, 1994) has thrown down a broad theoretical gauntlet arguing for a social-relational interpretation of human understanding. Gergen (1991) stated: "The reality of the individual is giving way to relational reality" (p. 160). The term "social-constructivism," therefore, is used here to represent the biologically rooted but radical constructivism deriving primarily from the works of Maturana, while acknowledging the seminal works of Gergen, which are grounded in social psychology.

The need for a social constructivism model of ethical decision-making is threefold. First, it provides a distinct view of the decision-making process—it is based purely on a relational view of reality. Other models tend to portray the decision maker as a psychological entity that makes the decision alone or within some social context. For example, Kitchener, in her highly cited 1984 work, described ethical decisions as those involving the decision maker's intuitive and critical evaluative reasoning. In contrast, the social constructivism perspective places the decision in the social context itself, not in the head of the decision maker; decision making becomes an interpersonal process of "negotiating," "consensualizing," and "arbitrating" (three terms defined later in this chapter). A second rationale for developing a social constructivism

model is that it may lead to empirical testing of social versus psychologically based ethical decision-making models. Because a constructivism approach is so unique theoretically, it provides a competitive perspective to more psychologically based models. Critical paradigm experiments (Cottone, 1989a, 1989b) may be designed to test the social perspective against the more traditional psychological perspective. Such experiments help researchers and practitioners weigh the relative merits of one approach against another, providing an empirical foundation that is sorely needed in this area of study. The third rationale for a social constructivism model is its appeal to practitioners as an alternative perspective for framing ethical decisions. Although there is a plethora of ethical decision-making models, this model provides an alternative to psychologically based or hybrid models for practitioners who are more aligned with a systemic or relational worldview. The model is parsimonious and does not involve complex steps or stages, so it may be easier for counselors to implement in the stressful times that accompany an ethical challenge.

Understanding the Application of Social Constructivism to Ethical Decision Making

"Objectivity in Parentheses." What social constructivism means to ethical decision making is that decisions can no longer be viewed as occurring internally. Many other decision-making models portray the decision as the responsibility of the individual decision maker. For example, an individual is asked to decide on a best course of action (Corey, Corey, & Callanan, 1998), select an action by weighing competing values in a given context (Tarvydas model), make the decision (Keith-Spiegel & Koocher, 1985), or deliberate and decide (Welfel, 1998). From a constructivism perspective, decisions are moved out of the intrapsychic process and into the interpersonal realm. As Gergen (1985) wrote:

> From this perspective, knowledge is not something people possess somewhere in their heads, but rather, something people do together. Languages are essentially shared activities. Indeed, until the sounds or markings come to be shared within a community, it is inappropriate to speak of language at all. In effect, we may cease inquiry into the psychological basis of language (which account would inevitably form but a subtext or miniature language) and focus on the performative use of language in human affairs. (p. 270)

Further, Gergen said: "The mind becomes a form of social myth; the self-concept is removed from the head and placed within the sphere of social discourse" (p. 271). From this vantage point, all that is done, all activity, and all to which language is applied, is a reflection of what has been shared previously in the community. Language is not generated spontaneously; it is transmitted socially. All that is done (in language or otherwise) is bound to heritage. Decisions, therefore, cannot be located "in" the individual. Rather, they are in the social matrix.

The social constructivism position is contrary to the positions taken by ethicists in counseling who appear to be bound predominantly to psychological theorizing about how decisions are made. Decision-making models tend to lay out steps for ethical choice (see Cottone & Claus, 2000), but almost across the board they fail to describe adequately how that choice occurs; it somehow disappears into the head (or mind) of the individual making the decision, either intuitively or based on utilitarian values (cf. Hare, 1991). How is it, for example, that values are weighed by the individual? Few models actually answer that question. For example, Gutheil, Bursztajn, Brodsky, and Alexander (1991) grounded their decision model in probability theory and weighing probabilities. With most models, how a decision is made is a psychological mystery.

The social constructivism approach to ethical decision making places the ethical decision out in the open—in the interaction between individuals as they operate in what Maturana (1978) identified as the "consensual domain" (p. 47). A decision is never made in a social vacuum. A decision is always made in interaction with at least one other individual. The interactive aspects of a decision are undeniable. In professional ethics, a decision to enter into an intimate relationship with a client is a decision made in interaction with the client. Likewise, a decision to breach a client's confidentiality is a decision made in relation to a third party. Decisions are not compelled internally; rather, they are compelled socially. This is the social constructivism position.

Some decisions may be viewed as "good" within a social context, while others may be viewed as "bad" within a social context. But that is not to say that decisions are "relative." What differentiates the social constructivism approach from purely relative models of right or wrong (where right and wrong are relative truths) is that the social constructivism approach defines the view within a social consensual domain as

absolutely true within that social context. As Maturana (1988) described it, "objectivity" is "in parentheses," where the parentheses are the boundaries of human interaction. In other words, reality is viewed as socially constructed, and within the social context, it is an absolutist's view. To demonstrate this point, consider that there can be competitive social consensualities—competitive absolute truths, so to speak. Understanding that there can be competitive absolute truths (a logical contradiction) helps to clarify the distinction between social constructivism and objectivism (where there is one absolute truth) and relativism (where truth is relative to each individual). Social constructivism stands apart from objectivism and relativism in the primacy of relationships. In effect, there are pockets of objectivities, and each pocket is demarcated by the group that acts according to what is believed to be true. For example, according to social constructivism, there can be several competitive truths, even competitive "gods." Each of a number of competitive gods represents absolute truth within a social-consensual domain represented by the religion's adherents. Each such god effectively competes for what is absolutely true against other gods (other socially consensually constructed realities). Ironically, some people literally war over some religions; but there is no irony from a social constructivism perspective. In those cases, the warring individuals believe absolutely in the "truths" represented by their god and will fight to the death to preserve such principles.

Just as people fight wars over religion, so too can mental health professionals war over what is considered ethical practice. Past court cases have frequently represented the battlefield. The classic and well-known *Tarasoff* legal decision is a good example. In that case, a University of California therapist took what he believed were acceptable actions to warn authorities of a dangerous client. The therapist took actions that were, up to that moment, directed by the professional consensus as to obligations of counselors in that circumstance. The surprise was that the courts ruled in favor of a different view—siding with the family of the murdered individual targeted by the client—and the courts assessed liability. VandeCreek and Knapp (1993) explained:

> The decision was based, to a large extent, on the affirmative duty to act which arises out of the "special relationship" between a psychotherapist and a patient. According to the common law, an individual usually has no duty to control the behavior of another in order to protect a third

party. Nevertheless, once a "special relationship" has been established, the law may require affirmative obligations. These socially recognized relationships, such as parent to child or possessor of land to renter, imply a legal duty to attempt to protect others from harm, or to warn them of potential harm. (p. 5)

The professionals involved were essentially trying to protect the confidentiality of the client consistent with ethical standards to that date. But, in interaction with the legal system, the actions and the defense did not hold weight. Accordingly, serious implications for professional ethics in counseling derive from a social constructivism perspective because no single, socially constructed ethical stance can be considered inherently better than another—predominance only derives from negotiation, consensus building, and/or arbitration. As with the *Tarasoff* decision, the involved parties were acting according to what was directed socially by the consensus of their communities. The fact that there was an unresolved clash of consensualities led to arbitration.

Conflicting Consensualities. Professionals must identify the levels of consensus that operate around an action or a dilemma. The fact that there is a dilemma means there may be a disagreement—a conflict of consensualities—between groups of people with which the professional has interacted.

The codes of the American Counseling Association (ACA) and the American Psychological Association (APA) reflect consensualities as to what is acceptable practice; membership in either the APA or the ACA indicates interaction with the consensualizing process the association represents. Counselors also interact with clients and client families, lawyers, judges, physicians, and other mental health professionals. Each interaction may represent the coming together of two systems of thought. Each may represent a distinct consensus on an issue. When there is a disagreement over an ethically sensitive issue that is resistant to easy negotiation, there is a conflict of consensualities. Take, for example, one of the most salient cases of a breach of ethical standards—sexual intimacies with a client. The counselor who enters a sexual relationship with a client acts in a way that represents rejection of the professional standard banning sexual intimacies while acting in a way that represents acceptance of the risks of the social/sexual relationship. The sexual relationship may also represent linkage to a system, which may not fit well within the constraints of a secret, professionally banned relationship. For example, the client may have family, friends, or an attorney who advise that such a

relationship is "wrong." When a disagreement arises between the professional and the client's system, a clash of consensualities may result (a disagreement over the nature or course of the relationship), with potential legal and professional threat to the counselor. The decision to enter into such a relationship is an act of vulnerability for the professional—the counselor's livelihood is at stake. Nothing professionally damaging may occur, but there is a possibility that the couple's initial consensus that the relationship exists (or may be acceptable at some level) may deteriorate under the strain of other relationships and competing consensualities that come to bear on their interaction. Of course, there is a consensus established in the professional literature that sexual intimacies with clients are unethical (see the American Counseling Association and American Psychological Association codes in the Appendix found at the end of the book) and harmful (e.g., Bouhoutsos, Holroyd, Lerman, Forer, & Greenberg, 1983; Pope, 1988). Therefore, a counselor would be well served to avoid such a detrimental relationship. There is little support for an offending professional given current ethical and professional standards.

A decision to breach an ethical standard (as with an offending counselor) or the decision to challenge a professional's ethics (as with the educated client) is a decision that derives from past and present interactions. There are no psychological determinants, but only biological and social forces that affect interactions one way or another. In other words, *the actions of the client and the counselor can be completely conceptualized as resulting from physical and social forces,* not psychological needs. The action to mount an ethical challenge to the counselor also derives from physical and social factors impinging the client. What appears to be an ethical (or unethical) decision is simply an action taken in concert with the emerging social consensus of the moment.

Social constructivism ethical decision making means that the professional must avoid linkages of vulnerability and cultivate linkages of professional responsibility. Relationships should be cultivated in accord with the larger socio-legal consensus that pervades professional practice. Ethical decision making occurs well before a crisis of consensualities arises. It is implicit in the professional culture. It means a rich, professional network is established and actions are taken to prevent and to avoid contact with social networks where challenges of "right" and "wrong" must be answered.

So, social constructivism ethical decision making is not classic psychological decision making at all. It is linkage to professional culture. One either does or does not fully enter into a professional culture. Those interactions that help to engage a professional fully in the ethical professional climate are actions of ethical choice. Such activity happens most basically in educational institutions where counselors are introduced by seasoned clinicians to a professional culture and to the rules that guide acceptable practice. At that level, the profession is responsibile for conveying the importance of linkage to a professional culture so that communicating on ethical issues becomes an ongoing activity of the student professional.

The Interpersonal Processes of Negotiating, Consensualizing, and Arbitrating

Counseling practice is complex and ethical dilemmas arise as new challenges confront practitioners. Even a counselor who is closely aligned with an ethically sensitive professional community may face an ethical challenge. Should there be accusations of unethical practice, counselors must act to protect their own and their clients' interests. In such cases, the social constructivism ethical decision-making alternative to psychologically based ethical decision making must occur. It does not occur internally or "in the head." Instead, social constructivism ethical decision making is a process of negotiating (when necessary), consensualizing, and arbitrating (when necessary) that occurs in the interpersonal process of relations that come to bear at critical moments of professional practice.

Negotiating is the process of discussing and debating an issue wherein at least two individuals indicate some degree of disagreement. For example, if a client's attorney contacts a counselor about testifying at a worker's compensation or disability hearing, the counselor should first request permission from the client to release confidential information (in order to talk to the attorney). Next, the counselor should consult with the attorney and negotiate as to whether the testimony is crucial to the client's case. If there is a formal request to testify, a waiver of privileged communication might be necessary, depending on laws in the jurisdiction. If there is a disagreement over the nature of the testimony or its potential effects, the counselor might refuse to testify, recognizing that a court-ordered subpoena might result. Negotiation, therefore, is a process of discussing and debating a position taken by the counselor; negotiation requires operation in language and some level of expressed disagreement.

Consensualizing is a process wherein at least two individuals act in agreement and in coordination on an issue. Consensus is viewed as an ongoing interactive process, not a final outcome or "thing." Cottone (1992) stated: "The idea of consensus must not be viewed solely as a formal language-based activity. In fact, consensus is probably best understood by the actions of individuals as they relate mutually, verbally and non-verbally, within certain interpersonal contexts" (p. 269). Where there is language, social interaction, and co-operation, there is an evolving consensuality. (Notice that the word "co-operation" is hyphenated; the hyphen is purposeful and indicates that individuals operate—act—in a coordinated fashion.) Maturana (1970) described this as the "consensual domain" (p. 50). Individuals who consensualize may have been involved in negotiation, but it is not necessary to negotiate to consensualize. Negotiation requires that there was some degree of disagreement, whereas consensualizing may or may not involve disagreement. For example, if an attorney requests that a counselor testify, the counselor may agree (with minimal discussion or no debate) and may just show up at the scheduled hearing ready to testify. In this case, the attorney and the counselor have consensualized by coordinated action as to the request to testify. Consensualizing is the process of socially constructing a reality. If there is disagreement or discordant action (consensualizing is not evident), arbitration may be necessary.

Arbitrating is a process whereby a negotiator or negotiators seek the judgment of consensually accepted individuals (alone or in groups) who are socially approved as representatives of sociolegal consensus—arbitrators. Arbitrators make judgments in interaction with each other, complainants, defendants, the authority of agreed-upon rules or law, and past judgments (e.g., case law). In most cases, the arbitrator has final say, unless, of course, there is an appeal to a higher consensually accepted arbitrator (e.g., a court of appeals). Arbitrating is the social process that imposes a socially constructed reality.

Response to a Challenge. When a professional is accused or questioned about ethical misconduct, he or she may respond in a way that acknowledges, disputes, or further questions the alleged or questionable behavior. The counselor's response probably derives as much from the nature of the relationship to the accuser or inquirer as to the nature of the alleged misconduct. To deny an accusation of a "nemesis" may prevent meaningful negotiation, even in the case of acceptable conduct, setting up an adversarial circumstance and a clash of consensualities to be settled by consensually agreed-upon higher authorities (e.g., the courts). Denial to a friendly colleague, on the other hand, may bring about negotiation as to whether a breach has occurred (against some agreed-upon standard, such as an ethics code). The moment of accusation or inquiry is a critical moment, and social forces influence what may appear to outsiders as a "decision."

The Social Constructivism Process of Ethical Decision Making When a Concern Arises. At critical moments, such as when a concern arises or when there has been an accusation or inquiry, the ethically sensitive professional operating from a social constructivism mode would take several steps: (a) obtain information from those involved; (b) assess the nature of the relationships operating at that moment in time; (c) consult valued colleagues and professional expert opinion (including ethics codes and literature); (d) negotiate when there is a disagreement; and (e) respond in a way that allows for a reasonable consensus as to what should happen or what really occurred. Every relationship involved must be examined for potential linkage to another (possibly adversarial) system of thought. Additionally, every involved relationship must be assessed for a potential conflict of opinion over what should or did happen. If consensus is not possible, further negotiation, interactive reflection, or arbitration may be necessary. (See Figure 6–2).

After information is obtained, the nature of relationships is assessed and valued colleagues and experts are consulted (Figure 6–2). The interactive process of socially constructing an outcome to an ethical dilemma involves negotiating (if necessary), consensualizing, and arbitrating (if necessary). The ultimate goal is to establish consensus among involved parties about what should or did happen in questionable circumstances. When consensualizing fails, parties may partake in "interactive reflection," a process of conversation with trusted individuals to come to agreement as to whether arbitration should be sought or whether a position needs to be modified to re-enter negotiation. If consensualizing fails after interactive reflection, arbitration is necessary.

"A Truth" Versus "The Truth." Interactions between people can, hopefully, be accounted for by discussion or reasonable negotiation of what should happen (or what actually occurred). Unfortunately, "the truth" may be a matter of dispute. If, in fact, counselors plan to break the rules (or have broken the

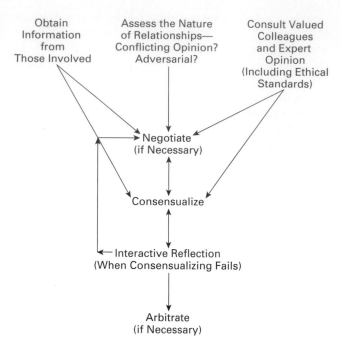

FIGURE 6–2. The Interactive Process of Socially Constructing an Outcome to an Ethical Dilemma

rules), they should accept the consequences of their actions imposed by the sociolegal consensus in the profession and the courts. Otherwise, they might act to protect their own professional interests by denying a wrongdoing, possibly at the expense of clients.

It may be that only a client and a professional know the actions that have occurred. When there is a difference of opinion about an act—a conflict of consensualities—arbitration may be the only answer. In such cases, the "truth" may never be known, even though a judgment may occur. Aside from arbitration, when there is a dispute (i.e., there are competing truths), only in cases of repeated offenses can a "truth" be established. Where there are repeated offenses, such a "truth" is established around the victims, whose stories combine to constitute a systemic imperative for legal or professional action. Some professionals may "come clean" in such a circumstance. Other professionals may resist acceptance of professional or legal mores (or possibly be the victims of a conspiracy, however unlikely). Whatever the professional's action, it reflects the physical and social forces affecting the counselor at that moment in time.

Once an ethical course of action has been chosen, it is wise for counselors to take additional steps in line with the recommendation of Tarvydas (Tarvydas Model

1998) to engage in a period of reflection and active processing of what the counselor intends to do. From a social constructivism position, however, reflection is not a process of mind—rather it is a continued reappraisal of actions in context and in consultation with others who can provide a perspective that represents their linkage to the professional community. It is a continued process of seeking alternative opinions or perspectives. If different perspectives emerge that allow for different views and a negotiated settlement (prior to an arbitrated decision), it is not too late to reappraise the circumstance. In the constructivism model, such reflection takes the form of "interactive reflection."

Case Scenario 6-3 is based on an actual case discussed in a graduate course on ethical issues in counseling. The case demonstrates the interactive processes involved in decision making. Terms associated with the social process of ethical decision making are bracketed as related to the flowchart shown in Figure 6–2.

CASE SCENARIO 6–3

Counseling is provided to a 12-year-old girl through a family counseling agency funded by both private and government funds. The girl lives with her grandmother, who signs the consent for treatment as the child's legal guardian. After several counseling sessions, the grandmother demands to know what the child reported. The child, in counseling, reports to the counselor that the grandmother is not her legal guardian, which is substantiated [assessment of the nature of relationships]. Her mother is identified as legal guardian [assessment of the nature of relationships]. The mother lives 60 miles from the counseling center and has not been involved with the child for some time. The counselor is faced with a dilemma—technically there has been no informed consent because the grandmother fraudulently signed the consent form as the legal guardian. Yet the counselor has an ethical "responsibility" to the child according to ethical standards. The counselor consults the executive director of the agency (a noncounselor) who informs her that counseling cannot continue without informed consent or procedures would be breached, threatening the service contract [consultation of colleagues]. The clinical service supervisor is consulted and informs the counselor that, aside from informed consent, she still has an obligation to the child [consultation of colleagues]. The counselor attempts to seek the mother's permission, but fails on several phone attempts [obtaining information from involved parties]. She even arranged through certified mail to meet the mother, drove 60 miles, and was disappointed when the mother did not show for the scheduled meeting at the arranged site [attempt to negotiate]. The counselor then sought the joint counsel of her clinical supervisor and the executive director [consultation with colleagues]. The executive director took a firm legal stance and directed her not to work with the child without legally executed informed consent by the responsible adult. An agreement was reached among the professionals to request the grandmother's assistance in procuring the informed consent of the mother [consensualizing]. The grandmother agreed [consensualizing], but faced with the noncooperation of the mother [nonconsensus], the grandmother obtained legal custody of the child only after threatening the mother with charges of child neglect [threat of arbitration leading to renegotiation and coordinated action between the mother and grandmother]. Counseling was reinitiated with the consent of the grandmother as the legal guardian. The child was informed that the grandmother had legal access to information provided in counseling.

As Case Scenario 6–3 demonstrates, the outcome of an ethical dilemma is highly social and can be clearly conceptualized as an interactive, not intrapsychic, process.

Concluding Words About Social Constructivism Ethical Decision Making

Gergen (1991) stated: "When individuals declare right and wrong in a given situation they are only acting as local representatives for larger relationships in which they are enmeshed. Their relationships speak through them" (pp. 168–169). The social constructivism approach to ethical decision-making is a purely social interpretation of the decision-making process. The social constructivism decision-making approach is a process of negotiating and consensualizing. All acts occur in a social context. From the constructivism perspective, decisions occur always in interaction. Professionals are less vulnerable to ethical challenges if they are linked to a rich professional culture, which is not supportive of a breach of ethical standards. When concerns arise at crucial moments of professional practice, the social constructivist obtains information from those involved, assesses the nature of relationships operating at that moment, consults valued colleagues and professional expert opinion (including ethical codes), negotiates when necessary, and responds in a way that allows for a reasonable consensus. Where negotiation must occur—when there is a conflict of consensualities—the counselor may accept or challenge an opposing position, knowing that an adversarial relationship may be established and judgment may occur in consensually agreed-upon "courts" of arbitration.

CHAPTER SUMMARY

Counselors must exercise their ethical and professional judgment responsibly. They must recognize an ethical dilemma and apply appropriate decision-making skills to resolve the dilemma. Several models exist that explain and structure the process of ethical decision making: theoretically or philosophically based models and practice-based models.

Theoretically or philosophically based models ground ethical decision making on a theory or philosophy. These models include absolute thinking (Hare); moral reasoning (Rest); decision analysis (Gutheil, Bursztagn, Brodsky, & Alexander); transactional analysis (Berne); feminist (Hill, Glaser, & Harden); hermeneutic (Betan); and social constructivism (Cottone).

Practice-based models are based on pragmatic procedures derived from experience or intended as practical guides for counselors. They are less theory specific or philosophically pure than theoretical models and have characteristics of either principle or virtue ethics. Principle ethics focuses on the objective, rational, and cognitive aspects of a process. Virtue ethics considers the characteristics of the counselors themselves as the critical element for responsible practice. The Tarvydas Integrative Model builds on the Rest and Kitchener models and has a four-level approach: (1) clinical counseling level, (2) clinical interdisciplinary level, (3) institutional/agency level, and (4) societal resource/public policy level. The Tarvydas model has four underlying themes: stance of reflection, balance, attention to the context, and collaboration.

Cottone's social contructivism model provides an alternative to practitioners who are more aligned with a systemic or relational worldview. In this view, decisions are not viewed as occurring internally; decisions are moved out of the intrapsychic process and into the interpersonal realm. Social constructivism ethical decision making is a process of negotiating, consensualizing, and arbitrating. Negotiating is the process of discussing and debating an issue wherein at least two individuals indicate some degree of disagreement. Consenualizing is a process wherein at least two individuals act in agreement and in coordination on an issue. Arbitrating is a process whereby a negotiator seeks the judgment of consensually accepted individuals who are socially approved as representatives of sociolegal consensus. Overall, social constructivism ethical decision-making directs counselors to avoid linkages of vulnerability while cultivating linkages of professional responsibility.

REFERENCES

Beauchamp, T. L., & Childress, J. F. (1979). *Principles of biomedical ethics.* Oxford, England: Oxford University Press.

Beauchamp, T. L., & Childress, J. F. (1994). *Principles of biomedical ethics* (4th ed.). New York: Oxford University Press.

Beauchamp, T. L., & Walters, L. (1994). *Contemporary issues in bioethics* (4th ed.). Belmont, CA: Wadsworth.

Berne, E. (1972). *What do you say after you say hello? The psychology of human destiny.* New York: Grove Press.

Betan, E. J. (1997). Toward a hermeneutic model of ethical decision making in clinical practice. *Ethics and Behavior, 7,* 347–365.

Betan, E. J., & Stanton, A. L. (1999). Fostering ethical willingness: Integrating emotional and contextual awareness with rational analysis. *Professional Psychology: Research and Practice, 30,* 295-301.

Bouhoutsos, J., Holroyd, J., Lerman, H., Forer, B. R., & Greenberg, M. (1983). Sexual intimacy between psychotherapists and patients. *Professional Psychology: Research and Practice, 14,* 185–196.

Chang, V. N. (1994). A transactional analysis decision-making model and ethical hierarchy. *Transactional Analysis Journal, 24,* 15–20.

Corey, G., Corey, M. S., & Callanan, P. (1998). *Issues and ethics in the helping professions* (5th ed.). Pacific Grove, CA: Brooks/Cole.

Cottone, R. R. (1989a). Defining the psychomedical and systemic paradigms in marital and family therapy. *Journal of Marital and Family Therapy, 15,* 225–235.

Cottone, R. R. (1989b). On ethical and contextual research in marital and family therapy: A reply to Taggart. *Journal of Marital and Family Therapy, 15,* 243–248.

Cottone, R. R. (1992). *Theories and paradigms of counseling and psychotherapy.* Needham Heights, MA: Allyn & Bacon.

Cottone, R. R. (2001). A social constructivism model of ethical decision making in counseling. *Journal of Counseling and Development, 79,* 39–45.

Cottone, R. R., & Claus, R. E. (2000). Ethical decision-making models: A review of the literature. *Journal of Counseling & Development, 78,* 275–283.

Cottone, R. R., Tarvydas, V., & House, G. (1994). The effect of number and type of consulted relationships on the ethical decision making of graduate students in counseling. *Counseling and Values, 39,* 56–68.

Dinger, T. J. (1997, April). *Do ethical decision making models really work? An empirical study.* Paper presented at the American Counseling Association world conference, Orlando, FL.

Forester-Miller, H., & Davis, T. E. (1996). *A practitioner's guide to ethical decision-making.* Alexandria, VA: American Counseling Association.

Francouer, R. T. (1983). Teaching decision making in biomedical ethics for the allied health student. *Journal of Allied Health, 12,* 202–209.

Garcia, J., Cartwright, B., Winston, S. M., & Borzuchowska, B. (in press). A transcultural integrative ethical decision-making model in counseling. *Journal of Counseling & Development.*

Gatens-Robinson, E., & Rubin, S. E. (1995). Societal values and ethical commitments that influence rehabilitation service delivery behavior. In S. E. Rubin & R. T. Roessler (Eds.), *Foundations of the vocational rehabilitation process* (pp. 157–174). Austin, TX: Pro-Ed.

Gergen, K. J. (1985). The social constructionist movement in modern psychology. *American Psychologist, 40,* 266–275.

Gergen, K. J. (1991). *The saturated self.* U.S.A.: Basic Books.

Gergen, K. J. (1994). *Toward transformation in social knowledge* (2nd ed.). London: Sage.

Ginter, E. J. (chair), Ellis, A., Guterman, J. T., Ivey, A. E., Lock, D. C., & Rigazio-Digilio, S. A. (1996, April). *Ethical issues in the postmodern era.* Panel discussion conducted at the 1996 world conference of the American Counseling Association, Pittsburgh, PA.

Gutheil, T. G., Bursztajn, H. J., Brodsky, A., & Alexander, V. (1991). *Decision making in psychiatry and the law.* Baltimore, MD: Williams & Wilkins.

Hare, R. (1981). The philosophical basis of psychiatric ethics. In S. Block & P. Chodoff (Eds.), *Psychiatric ethics* (pp. 31–45). Oxford, England: Oxford University Press.

Hare, R. (1991). The philosophical basis of psychiatric ethics. In S. Block & P. Chodoff (Eds.), *Psychiatric ethics* (2nd ed., pp. 33–46). Oxford, England: Oxford University Press.

Hill, M., Glaser, K., & Harden, J. (1995). A feminist model for ethical decision making. In E. J. Rave & C. C. Larsen (Eds.), *Ethical decision making in therapy: Feminist perspectives* (pp. 18–37). New York: Guilford.

Hinkeldey, N. S., & Spokane, A. R. (1985). Effects of pressure and legal guideline clarity on counselor decision making in legal and ethical conflict situations. *Journal of Counseling and Development, 64,* 240–245.

Janis, I. L., & Mann, L. (1977). *Decision-making: A psychological analysis of conflict, choice, and commitment.* New York: The Free Press.

Keith-Spiegel, P., & Koocher, G. P. (1985). *Ethics in psychology.* New York: Random House.

Kitchener, K. S. (1984). Intuition, critical evaluation and ethical principles: The foundation for ethical decisions in counseling psychology. *The Counseling Psychologist, 12*(3), 43–55.

Kitchener, K. S. (1988). Dual role relationships: What makes them so problematic? *Journal of Counseling and Development, 67,* 217-221.

Kohlberg, L. (1969). Stage and sequence: The cognitive-developmental approach to socialization. In D. Soslin (Ed.), *Handbook of socialization theory and research* (pp. 347–480). Chicago: Rand McNally.

Kohlberg, L. (1980). High school democracy and educating a just society. In R. L. Mosher (Ed.), *Moral education: A generation of research and development* (pp. 20–57). New York: Praeger.

Lyddon, W. J. (1995). Forms and facets of constructivist psychology. In R. A. Neimeyer & M. J. Mahoney (Eds.), *Constructivism in psychotherapy* (pp. 69–92). Washington, D.C.: American Psychological Association.

Mabe, A. R., & Rollin, S. A. (1986). The role of a code of ethical standards in counseling. *Journal of Counseling and Development, 64,* 294–297.

Maturana, H. R. (1970). Biology of cognition. In H. R. Maturana & F. J. Varela (1980). *Autopoiesis and cognition: The realization of the living.* Boston: D. Reidel.

Maturana, H. R. (1978). Biology of language: The epistemology of reality. In G. A. Miller & E. Lenneberg (Eds.), *Psychology and biology of language and thought* (pp. 27–63). New York: Academic Press.

Maturana, H. R. (1988). Reality: The search for objectivity or the quest for a compelling argument. *Irish Journal of Psychology, 9*(1), 25–82.

Maturana, H. R., & Varela, F. J. (1980). *Autopoiesis and cognition: The realization of the living.* Boston: D. Reidel.

McGrath, G. (1994). Ethics, boundaries, and contracts: Applying moral principles. *Transactional Analysis Journal, 24,* 6–14.

Meara, N. M., Schmidt, L. D., & Day, J. D. (1996). Principles and virtues: A foundation for ethical decisions, policies and character. *The Counseling Psychologist, 24,* 4–77.

Patterson, J. B. (1992). Ethics and ethical decision making in rehabilitation counseling. In R. M. Parker & E. M. Szymanski (Eds.), *Rehabilitation counseling: Basics and beyond* (pp. 165–193). Austin, TX: Pro-Ed.

Pope, K. S. (1988). How clients are harmed by sexual contact with mental health professionals: The syndrome and its prevalence. *Journal of Counseling and Development, 67,* 222–226.

Rest, J. R. (1984). Research on moral development: Implications for training psychologists. *The Counseling Psychologist, 12*(3), 19–29.

Rest, J. R. (1994). Background: Theory and research. In J. R. Rest & D. Narvaez (Eds.), *Moral development in the professions: Psychology and applied ethics* (pp. 1–26). Hillsdale, NJ: Lawrence Erlbaum Associates.

Rest, J. R., Cooper, D., Coder, R., Maganz, J., & Anderson, D. (1974). Judging the important issues in moral dilemmas—an objective test of development. *Developmental Psychology, 10*(4), 491–501.

Rest, J. R., Davison, M. L., & Robbins, S. (1978). Age trends in judging moral issues: A review of cross-sectional, longitudinal, and sequential studies of the Defining Issues Test. *Child Development, 49*(2), 263–279.

Schwartz, S. H. (1977) Normative influences on altruism. In L. Berkowitz (Ed.), *Advances in experimental social psychology* (Vol. 10, pp. 221–279). New York, NY: Academic Press.

Sileo, F. J., & Kopala, M. (1993). An A-B-C-D-E worksheet for promoting beneficence when considering ethical issues. *Counseling and Values, 37,* 89–95.

Stadler, H. A. (1986). Making hard choices: Clarifying controversial ethical issues. *Counseling and Human Development, 19,* 1–10.

Steinman, S. O., Richardson, N. F., & McEnroe, T. (1998). *The ethical decision-making manual for helping professionals.* Pacific Grove, CA: Brooks/Cole.

Tarvydas, V. M., (1997). Standards of practice: Ethical and legal. In D. R. Maki & T. F. Riggar (Eds.), *Rehabilitation Counseling: Profession and practice* (pp. 72–94). New York: Springer.

Tarvydas, V. M. (1987). Decision-making models in ethics: Models for increased clarity and wisdom. *Journal of Applied Rehabilitation Counseling, 18*(4), 50–52.

Tarvydas, V. M., & Cottone, R. R. (1991). Ethical responses to legislative, organizational and economic dynamics: A four level model of ethical practice. *Journal of Applied Rehabilitation Counseling, 22*(4), 11–18.

Tymchuk, A. J. (1986). Guidelines for ethical decision making. *Canadian Psychology, 27,* 36–43.

Van Hoose, W. H., & Kottler, J. A. (1985). *Ethical and legal issues in counseling and psychotherapy.* San Fransisco: Jossey-Bass.

VandeCreek, L., & Knapp, S. (1993). *Tarasoff and beyond: Legal and clinical considerations in the treatment of life-endangering patients.* Sarasota, FL: Professional Resource Press.

Vasquez, M. J. T. (1996). Will virtue ethics improve ethical conduct in multicultural settings and interactions? *The Counseling Psychologist, 24*, 98–104.

von Foerster, H. (1984). On constructing a reality. In P. Watzlawick (Ed.), *The invented reality* (pp. 41–61). New York: W. W. Norton.

von Glasersfeld, E. (1984). An introduction to radical constructivism. In P. Watzlawick (Ed.), *The invented reality* (pp.17–40). New York: W. W. Norton.

Welfel, E. R. (1998). *Ethics in counseling and psychotherapy: Standards, research, and emerging issues.* Pacific Grove, CA: Brooks/Cole.

PART III

Organizational and Administrative Issues

CHAPTER 7

Ethical Climate

Vilia M. Tarvydas
Barbara J. O'Rourke
Christine Malaski

Objectives
■ ■ ■ ■ ■ ■ ■ ■ ■ ■ ■

After reading this chapter, you should be able to:

- Outline the concepts and elements of organizational culture and explain their effects on the ethical climate of an organization.
- Define "impaired professional" and describe the effects of impairment on professional practice.
- Explain counselor burnout, relate it to job stress, and describe the factors that may increase its incidence or assist in alleviating its detrimental effects.
- Describe professional boundary problems, the types of counselors who may be affected, and some strategies to limit potential problems with professional boundaries.
- Discuss the problems that accompany substance abuse problems among counselors.
- Explain mobbing behavior in the workplace and its effects on workers, its relationship to organizational characteristics, and ways to reduce its incidence.
- Discuss whistle-blowing and its consequences for the whistle-blower and all others involved.

■ ■ ■ ■ ■ ■ ■ ■ ■ ■ ■

INTRODUCTION

Whether counselors realize it or not, they are profoundly influenced by the environments and work cultures in which they practice. If they are unaware of these influences, they are powerless to develop appropriate responses or strategies to respond intentionally to these work culture challenges—or to draw upon the work culture's strengths. Work environments are cultures that create particular ethical climates that influence the quality of service provided to clients. Unethical individuals in the workplace have the ability to influence others to behave unethically, and vice versa.

Ivey (1999) asserted, "Intentionality is a core goal . . . [of effective counseling]" (p. 14). He stated the following:

Intentionality is acting with a sense of capability and deciding from among a range of alternative actions. The intentional individual has more than one action, thought, or behavior to choose from in responding to changing life situations. The intentional individual can generate alternatives in a given situation and approach a problem from different vantage points, using a variety of skills and personal qualities, *adapting styles to suit different individuals and cultures*. (p. 14)

Building on Ivey's concept of intentional, theory-based counseling to include ethical decision making or applied ethics, it is important to understand that an ethical perspective and process must also be skill based and intentional. Further, issues of morality and ethical decision making are ever-present in the machinations of everyday counseling. Every counseling decision contains an ethical or moral aspect, and each of these decisions is embedded in an influencing context. To achieve a more complete approach to intentional counseling, counselors must be equally aware of and proactive about ethical choices in communication techniques.

Research continues to explore significant factors that may influence counselors' degree of effectiveness in ethical decision making. Factors that have been examined include variables related to the individual counselor, such as moral orientation (Liddell, Halpin, & Halpin, 1992), the number and type of consulted relationships (Cottone, Tarvydas, & House, 1994), or level of ethics education (Tarvydas, 1994). Additionally, the effect of context-related factors on ethical decision making is being examined. Factors such as the effect of working in a certain type of environment, such as within a school-based or health care team; or with particular people, such as individuals from numerous disciplines may influence the ethics of practice. The need is great for ongoing research that will continue to identify, clarify, and define factors as they relate to sound, ethical decision making in counseling practice.

Applied ethics in counseling occurs within organizational or institutional settings; for example (a) hospitals, (b) community mental health centers, (c) small, mental health, private practice groups, (d) schools, (e) military settings, and (f) rehabilitation settings. An ethical or unethical climate has effects on the *intentional* ethical decision-making process of counselors. Counselors may face a significant environmental challenge by sharing a work environment with an unethical colleague.

ORGANIZATIONAL CULTURE

More and more, counseling occurs within the context of an organization or institution. To understand more clearly how ethical decision making can be affected by participation in an organizational setting, think of an organization as a type of culture. The use of a cultural perspective can help counselors realize the organization's complexity and the interactive nature of variables within a setting as they influence decision making. This includes a need to understand the unique aspects of group or team experiences. The social, political, and cultural dynamics that occur in a larger organization, like a hospital, also occur within smaller group settings such as a classroom within a school.

Culture

Conceptual models used to develop an understanding of multicultural and cross-cultural counseling suggest that counselors must fully examine the potential influence of their worldview upon their counseling practice (Ivey, 1999). A worldview is made up of the observable artifacts, values, and underlying assumptions held by an individual. Counselors must strive to understand how a developed worldview may influence (a) the decision making of members of any culture, (b) any individual who interacts with members of the culture, and (c) the effects of the interaction between an insider (a member of the culture) and an outsider. Multicultural models typically assume that the counselor is the outsider; however, the converse may also be true. If clients take an active decision-making role regarding their care within a health care team, or if students and their parents construct an education plan, the clients are working to gain acceptance within the team. The team is a cultural group with its own language and style of communicating. The client is the outsider and may feel very uncomfortable about this difference. Counselors' worldviews are shaped partially by their participation in a specific organizational culture. These worldviews may affect their decision making, including the ethical components of those decisions.

Schein (1990), an organizational psychologist, implied that a specified group of people who have had stability over time and a shared history of working together form a culture. The culture is what the group learns over a period of time in regard to problem solving. This type of learning is manifested as observable behaviors—ways of thinking about the world and ways of feeling. More specifically, Schein stated:

> Culture can [now] be defined as (a) a pattern of basic assumptions, (b) invented, discovered, or developed by a given group, (c) as it learns to cope with its problems of external adaptation and internal integration, (d) that has worked well enough to be considered valid, and therefore (e) is to be taught to new members as the (f) correct way to perceive, think, and feel in relation to those problems. (p. 111)

This description of a working culture clearly reflects experiences reported by counselors who have been part of a working group, whether on a school team with one or two members or on a larger team of health care workers. For example, a group of counselors assumes, based on recent complaints about services provided by one member of the group, that discussing appeal procedures with clients sets a tone that encourages client complaints. Consequently, the group falls into the practice of merely handing out the client rights brochure without further discussion with the client. This practice becomes so routine that new staff members are told not to spend valuable time discussing appeal rights with clients. Over time, what effects will this change in the agency culture have on the atmosphere in the agency, on the counselor-client relationship, and on the rights of clients?

Any definable group with a shared history can have a culture within an organization. Therefore, an organization can have many subcultures. Specific units within an agency, or disciplines within the same organization, can have fully functioning subcultures complete with their own language and practices—and degrees of respect for ethical practice standards. They may also have their own set of ethical practice ideals and standards due to different ethical traditions, degrees of education, and exposure to ethical standards.

Ethics and Organizational Culture

Hospital-based practice is a specific type of organizational culture that generally manifests a model of practice reflected by a definable paradigm. The hospital practice model, typically known as the *medical model*, represents the organic paradigm (Cottone, 1992). This model is becoming increasingly prevalent in the behavioral health practices of counselors due to the influence of managed care on all mental health disciplines. The medical model culture is characterized as one in which the physician diagnoses and treats the disease of the client, and the client is re-

lieved of blame. The role of the physician (expert) is often defined as autocratic. The role of both the client and the ancillary staff (including the counselor) is to trust and to cooperate with the physician (expert). The historical shaping of this paradigm was developed from the values and procedures of its religious and military roots. Historically, this paradigm contains a deference and deeply rooted respect for chain-of-command orders over and above individual beliefs. Therefore, this approach represents a parentalistic and hierarchically based framework that has potential for creating ethically based tension. The tension inherent in this culture is encountered when the "order" from the physician (expert) conflicts with the autonomous needs of the client or other caregivers.

Professional roles are constructed in response to institutional expectations and professional practices. Beauchamp and Childress (1994) stated that such roles also incorporate virtues and obligations. Roles encompass social expectations as well as standards and ideals. The hospital culture is an example of an environment or context with definitive ideas about how the helping process should occur.

Case Scenario 7-1

A Cultural Setting

A rehabilitation counselor is asked by a client to represent her at a rehabilitation residential care treatment center's interdisciplinary team meeting. The client's desire is to remain in the center until she feels more able to manage her own care. After careful assessment, the counselor concurs with the client that a delayed discharge would be in her best interest. The client's psychiatrist orders that the client be prepared for discharge immediately. The implicit rule of the organization is that clients belong to the doctors and that the center and its staff are only assisting the physicians in the care of their clients. Dissenting opinions at team meetings are discouraged strongly due to their historically fruitless outcomes and the time they take from the staff. Should the counselor persist in forwarding the desire of the client? How?

YES.   Ethical standards in counseling clearly define counselors' obligation to their clients, and the rehabilitation counselor's code of ethics also requires that the counselor assist clients in advocating for their needs and rights (CRCC, 2001). Further, collaboration is considered a necessary condition for ethical decision making.

Political and moral or ethical problems will arise and persist as long as some professionals make the decisions and order their implementation by others who have not participated in the decision making. Beauchamp and Childress (1994) pointed out that these conflicts are avoidable but must be anticipated and prevented by establishing practices that honor open and collaborative decision making. Obligations of fidelity must be made clear; open routes to collegial dialogue must be valued. If this is not the case, Beauchamp and Childress warned, compassion, while cherished as a core virtue, can also cloud judgment and work against rational and effective decision making. Based on the levels of organizational practice discussed in Tarvydas and Cottone (1991), a useful, ethical decision-making model for use in the larger organizational context is provided in Chapter 6. Given guidelines such as those provided in this model, decision making that involves complexity and conflict can be broken down into manageable tasks that help facilitate collaborative discussion among all rightful parties.

The setting, including the people with whom counselors work, significantly influences ethical decision making. Doherty (1995) summarized this point well:

> Unsupportive and alienating work settings inevitably affect therapists' ability to care, especially for difficult clients at the end of a long workday or workweek. Having our work undermined by other professionals in positions of greater institutional power erodes motivation and investment in clinical care. Seeing too many clients during a workweek does the same, as does having to fit the client's needs to the rigidly enforced restrictions of managed care contracts. Therapists start to go through the motions, it shows, and we know it. We become negative about our clients, we hope for no-shows and cancellations, our natural caring declines, and our ethical caring begins to feel like martyrdom. When such conditions arise, it is time to change the context or get out, in my view, because we cannot sustain the fundamental virtue of caring. (p. 13)

Clearly, the work setting, whether it is an informal group or a more formal organizational structure, influences counselors' decision-making processes significantly.

ORGANIZATIONAL CLIMATE

Several authors have suggested that an organizational climate is the outward manifestation of its culture (Mohan, 1993; Schein, 1990). *Climate* is a metaphor that suggests an image wherein the environment, as the sum total of energy, presents atmospheric conditions as a type of aura. These conditions hold, support, create, and sustain the type of ethical decision making that occurs. An awareness of these conditions is particularly important when counselors confront a decision with an emotional component, such as one that presents an ethical dilemma. Using the atmospheric conditions of our weather example, the climate may be fair or stormy. Bellah, Madsen, Sullivan, Swidler, and Tipton (1985) described this phenomenon as our *moral ecology.*

Organizational climate is how people characterize a system's practices and procedures, such as the sense of safety or fear of retribution that a counselor may feel when faced with big or small decisions within this context. Therefore, the concept of organizational climate—more specifically, the ethical climate—is one level of analysis that can help us understand and explain moral behavior as it is observed. An **ethical climate,** one facet of an organizational climate, describes the shared perceptions that colleagues hold concerning ethical procedures and practices within an organization. It upholds or erodes virtues such as compassion, discernment, truthfulness, and integrity.

The individual and organizational variables that contribute to the ethicality of the climate are complex and multilayered (Tarvydas & Cottone, 1991). The decision maker is faced with individual, client, team, and organizationally contingent factors that must be considered. For example, decisions within an organization are often made by teams or groups rather than by individuals. Such decisions affect the workings of a team or group within the organization significantly. A growing body of literature is examining the dynamics inherent in team-based, ethical decision making (Agich, 1982; Klebe-Trevino, 1986; O'Rourke, 1996). A basic understanding of some of the identified variables, both for the individual and for the team, is essential to intentional ethical counseling within an organizational setting.

Two basic individual skills have been identified as essential to the collaborative process: (a) the ability to assert one's thoughts and ideas, and (b) the ability to clarify the content of others' contributions to the decision-making process (Weiss & Davis, 1985). These basic skills are useful in any decision-making process involving two or more individuals and are particularly important in a hierarchically structured context wherein one person has more power than others.

Given the potential inequities and complexities inherent in making team-based decisions, it is essential that a working team establish a due process in a particular form for its decision-making practices. The mechanism of such a due process must be sensitive to multiple disciplinary perspectives and cultural gender differences, and must be able to facilitate the production of a group decision. Constructing a useful process that is both efficient and equitable is a complex task. For example, the following questions may arise: How do we proceed if a particular professional disagrees with a team decision? Is team consensus necessary to adopt a decision? How do we provide client confidentiality when decisions made about the client occur within a larger organization that has nonprofessional support staff and reporting or billing requirements? What is an appropriate appeals process that is truly accessible to clients? Like the construction of a group culture in group counseling that has established normative behavior, the working relationship of a team develops over time and must be shaped proactively from its beginning.

CASE SCENARIO 7-2

Confidentiality

A school counselor is working with a young woman who has had numerous behavioral problems, including shoplifting. The student has demonstrated significant improvement during the last semester in both her motivation toward school and in her social behavior. Trust was difficult to establish between the girl and her counselor, but they have developed a working relationship. During the annual IEP meeting, one of the girl's teachers suggested that the student might benefit from having a job. There is an opening in the lost-and-found department of the school office. Should the counselor tell the team, which includes the student's mother, that she has concerns about the student's current ability to handle other people's property? What could this disclosure do to the trust that has been built with the client? Should the counselor voice her concerns?

PROBABLY YES.　The counselor has a responsibility to support the young woman and help her achieve her counseling goal of avoiding behavioral problems such as stealing. Allowing her to be placed prematurely in a setting that exposes her to overwhelming triggers for stealing behavior would present considerable therapeutic risk. Another concern involves the degree to which the team understands the critical importance of confidentiality and the team's shared responsibility for assisting the student's progress toward dealing with her behavioral problems. The counselor must be an active participant in setting the climate for these team responsibilities and may have to engage in tactful, active teaching or reminders. This sets the stage for any appropriate client disclosures. If the team is truly to function as a treatment team, important observations should be shared—but with the shared responsibility to

assure that the student's trust and confidentiality are not violated.

Lastly, but most importantly, the integrity of the student must be respected. The counselor must gain the student's permission (and even direct participation) in bringing this concern to the team and her mother. Her ability to directly evaluate the risk to herself and bring the issue to the team might have significant therapeutic benefits. At the outset of counseling, the student should have been informed that information and counselor judgments integral to her case would be shared with the treatment team, thus setting the stage for this discussion. If the student is reluctant and the counselor still thinks the opinion must be shared, the counselor should at least discuss her reasons for the disclosure and its perceived benefits and risks with the student before the team meeting.

Accountability to the Organization

The nature of the counseling environment plays a significant role in counselors' decision-making processes. Ethical standards mandate that counselors are accountable to both their clients and to the organizations in which they work. As a result, it is ethically sound practice for counselors to explore fully and to commit to the mission and standards of practice of any organizations for which they work. Conversely, it is the organization's ethical obligation to fully disclose all relevant information about its mission and practices, including its provision of due process for resolution of conflicts with employees. Counselors who accept a position with an organization enter into a tacit agreement with that organization to honor its values and standards of practice. At the same time, counselors have an obligation to honor their professional code of ethics. Intentional practice is served by having a pre-existing plan to resolve any conflicts between organizational and professional obligations. Institutions have attempted to be more intentional by constructing mechanisms to provide due process through working ethics committees and the use of case consultation meetings. Again, the Tarvydas decisional models described in Chapter 6 are useful tools for any individual counselor seeking to reconcile professional and institutional aspects of ethical dilemmas.

Consider the effect of a specific, overarching philosophy that creates a hospital's climate, such as a religious affiliation. Clinical decisions concerning use of client service options such as provision of pregnancy termination and birth control, or withdrawal of nutrition and hydration from a client in a persistent vegetative state, become enmeshed in the ethical value climate of that particular institution. Extend this consideration to a school environment, such as a gender controversy in providing a support group for gay, lesbian, and bisexual students in a high school. An institution's values and moral orientation are often the overriding aspect of the concerns involved in these situations.

Organizational values and morality subsequently influence the ethical decision-making processes of members. This force is particularly evident when moral obligations and religious standards are in conflict with an institution's espoused ethical practices.

CASE SCENARIO 7-3

Accountability

A counselor is working with a client who has been treated for depression at a local Catholic mental health outpatient clinic. During the course of her treatment, the client disclosed that she had been raped several weeks earlier but is otherwise not sexually active. A pregnancy test reveals that she is pregnant. She is requesting information from the counselor about obtaining a therapeutic abortion. Should the counselor engage in a dialogue about this issue with the client, given that it is strictly forbidden by institutional values?

YES.   As part of informed consent, the counselor must inform the client about the limits of their relationship and offer to help her identify her alternatives.

Climate Factors and Ethical Decisions

Factors in the work environment that influence the ethical decision-making climate of service organizations include the organization's socialization practices, interpersonal relationships with significant others in the workplace (peers and superiors), role perceptions, and individual levels of development of the service providers. Research has examined specific elements of an organizational environment that have shown influence on the ethical behavior of employees. These factors include (a) structure (centralized versus participatory management), (b) ethical climate (reinforceable values; e.g., beneficence), (c) task dimensions, (d) influence of significant others in the environment, (e) role perceptions, and (f) levels of personal development of the individual service provider (Wiles, 1993). These elements include the influence of significant others such as peers and superiors, the opportunity to behave ethically as guided by a code of ethics, and the application of rewards and punishments for both ethical and unethical behavior. Wiles (1993) reviewed the ethical climate lit-

1. Environmental factors (external forces)
2. Organizational factors (organizational culture; organizational socialization; characteristics of the job/task; significant others in the organization)
3. Opportunity and situational factors
4. Individual factors (personal values; societal and familial socialization experiences; ego strength; locus of control; field dependence; personal knowledge and attitudes; age; education; gender; job tenure)
5. Stage of moral development
6. Characteristics of the moral issue
7. Recognition of the moral issue (moral sensitivity)
8. Moral evaluation (includes moral philosophy, ethical decision ideology, and phased decision process)
9. Intentions
10. Behavior
11. Evaluation of the behavior (ability to self-reflect)

FIGURE 7–1.   Factors in Organizational Climates That Affect Individual Decision Making
Source: From *Socialization and Interpersonal Influence on Ethical Decision-Making Climate in Service Organizations* by J. Wiles, 1993, unpublished dissertation. Memphis, TN: University of Memphis.

erature and found that organizationally based ethics decision-making models include 11 specific factors, as noted in Figure 7–1.

Clearly, an ethical climate is constructed as a product of the interaction among the institution, the individual counselor, and numerous contributing influences from both sources. The ACA Code of Ethics recognizes these influences and clearly defines standards of practice regarding personnel administration. It is the responsibility of the individual counselor to address some of these influences before making a working covenant with the institution.

The remainder of this chapter examines factors related to the influence of significant individuals within counselors' work environment who may have been unethical in their behavior or impaired in their ability to practice.

IMPAIRED PROFESSIONALS

The impairment of professionals' ability to function in their professional roles is a growing concern in U.S. society. Impairment should not be seen as being judgmental. Rather, it is a relative term that describes function and is distinct from a disability. A **disability** is an identifiable condition that may be more stable and whose functional limitations, when manifested, are recognized and often overcome with appropriate changes, assistance, or accommodations. In contrast, an **impairment** is an often gradually recognized condition that manifests when an individual attempts to perform some activity. It is not immediately obvious and involves a level of diminished function (obtained by documented evidence). Impairments may be manifested on a continuum by varying degrees of loss of optimal function and can have many causes. A person with a disability may also become impaired, given this perspective. In fact, all counselors are impaired to some degree at some time in their practice. Impairment may be the result of having a headache or the flu. The more dysfunctional and pervasive impairments that can disrupt professional performance typically include unrecognized or untreated chronic physical illness, substance abuse, and emotional or psychological factors such as burnout and sexual acting-out behaviors. Lamb, Cochran, and Jackson (1991) defined impairment broadly as it is applied to psychology interns in the following way:

> An interference in professional functioning that is reflected in one or more of the following ways: (a) an inability or unwillingness to acquire and integrate professional standards into one's repertoire of professional behavior; (b) an inability to acquire professional skills and reach an accepted level. (p. 293)

Ethically, professional impairment is a matter of decreased level of professional competence. The term can be applied to people in various professional roles, including those of student, counselor, and supervisor. Three of the more common issues related to professional impairment are (a) burnout and job stress, (b) violation of professional boundaries, and (c) substance abuse.

Counselors who continue to provide professional services while impaired may be in violation of their ethical code. A counselor who is aware that a colleague or student is providing unethical services but fails to intervene may also be behaving unethically due to failure to address this issue. This failure to act may detract from the quality of client care or actually result in harm to a client.

Awareness that includes a working knowledge of practice standards and a sensitivity to violation of these standards is key to ethical behavior. The impaired professional often provides clues over time that a pattern of problem behavior exists. Typically, the unethical behavior of an impaired colleague is not an isolated occurrence. For example, it is not difficult to imagine a colleague who comes in late frequently, is irritable with other staff members, and often cuts client sessions short. After some time, you and your colleagues are shocked, but not surprised, to discover that the supervisor has found this colleague has not been staying current with his charting and has even falsified some of these documents. Worse yet, there is speculation that he has been seeing one of his clients socially after work.

BURNOUT AND JOB STRESS

According to Skorupa and Agresti (1993), **burnout** is an emotional exhaustion in which the professional no longer has any positive feelings, sympathy, or respect for clients. It is often associated with fatigue, frustration, and apathy that result from prolonged stress and overwork. Burnout is thought to have three distinct factors: (a) emotional exhaustion, including feeling emotionally overextended with work; (b) depersonalization, including having unfeeling or impersonal reactions to clients; and (c) a lack of personal accomplishment or feeling incompetent at your work (Maslach & Jackson, 1986).

Counseling and the work done in the helping and mental health professions are very stressful by their very nature. Counselors work to help clients in very intimate and personal ways, but work with clients whom they cannot and should not control, and within institutions and financial and practical constraints over which they have similarly little control. This uncertainty and lack of control are often coupled with witnessing the emotional ups and downs of clients' lives and working within crisis or traumatic situations. All counselors at some time experience some degree of the signs of burnout. Studies reviewed by Welfel (2002) have shown that about "1 to 5% of those sampled suffer from a full syndrome of burnout, but approximately one-third of the counselors scored high in emotional exhaustion in a number of these studies" (p. 59).

Burnout should be differentiated from job stress. Stadler (1990) noted that "impaired counselors have lost the ability to transcend stressful events" (p. 178). Not all stress is negative or rises to the level that it seriously affects the function of the individuals experiencing it. In fact, stress can be positive and, in its most basic sense, is the individual's reaction to challenges and changes. It can mobilize, focus, and energize the individual's work and responses, hopefully leading to the satisfaction of a job well done or a difficult challenge resolved positively. There are quite a number of resources that counselors can use to enhance their personal and professional well-being in dealing with job stress and preventing burnout. Research has shown that some personal characteristics cast a protective influence over distress. For example, research has shown that for some individuals, the quality of personality hardiness can interrupt the stress-exhaustion process (Maddi & Kobasa, 1984). Nevertheless, preventative steps are important for the well-being of all helping professionals, either to increase their quality of life or to prevent some serious, negative reaction. Brems (2000) has provided a personal and professional self-care plan for counselors, whether they are novices or seasoned professionals. She provides detailed information about the following self-care skills:

Professional Self-Care Skills
- Continuing education
- Consultation and supervision
- Networking
- Stress management strategies

Personal Self-Care Skills
- Healthy personal habits
- Attention to relationships
- Recreational activities
- Relaxation and centeredness
- Self-exploration and awareness

Studies suggest that certain client factors may contribute to therapist burnout. Among these are the number of contact hours with clients and the number of clients in a caseload that present with pervasive stressful behavior, such as aggression or limit testing (Hellman, 1986). These factors are of concern in the increasingly dominant environment of managed care. Interestingly, therapists who work in agency settings were more prone to burnout than those working in private settings (Hellman, 1986). These data indicate the importance of climate conditions on an individual. Implications for ethical practice may include (a) setting limits on the size of a caseload, (b) acknowledging a duty to understand the process of burnout and prevention techniques, (c) conducting research to determine how work settings can affect counselors, and (d) mediating untoward effects of workplace stress on the work of counselors.

CASE SCENARIO 7-4

Burnout?

A social worker with many years of experience is working as your colleague and mentor. You notice that she has be-

come increasingly judgmental. She becomes anxious and rejects her clients when they start to place demands on her or when they "don't do what is good for them." You understand her job-related stresses: All of you are expected to take more and more clients, do more documentation of services, and are no longer offered overtime pay. What strategies can you offer your colleague to help her deal with this situation? Is her behavior severe enough to constitute burnout? Impairment?

YES AND NO. Yes, certainly these are signs of counselor fatigue and high levels of job stress. However, impairment is present only if your colleague's judgmental attitudes influence her actual practice. Approach her as a concerned colleague and remind her of the importance of managing her job-related stress. Support her in identifying and practicing strategies to increase her levels of personal and professional wellness. Since you discover she wants to learn some stress management techniques, you invite her to join your evening meditation class at the Yoga Center.

PROFESSIONAL BOUNDARIES

Professionals who transgress boundaries with clients, students, or participants in research violate clearly stated ethical standards related to detrimental counselor-client relationships (basic concepts related to detrimental counselor-client relationships were discussed in Chapter 3). Supervisors and educators also have responsibilities to avoid conflicting relationships (see Chapter 19). Schoener (1995) clarified detrimental relationships by describing the types of individuals who may become boundary violators. These types describe the predictive traits of professionals who are reported violators. The six traits, are: (1) psychotic and severe borderline disorders, (2) manic disorders, (3) impulse control disorders, (4) chronic neurosis and isolation, (5) situational offenders, and (6) deficits due to naivete (Figure 7–2).

Schoener (1995) called for more sophisticated assessment procedures and asserted that "prior to the last decade, sexual misconduct and other boundary violations by professionals were treated . . . via a combination of reprimand and temporary privilege suspension. [And] only rarely was there a formal evaluation or planned rehabilitation effort" (p. 95). Students and novice practitioners who violate client boundaries typically fall in the naive category. Examine your own boundary awareness by doing the activities in Figure 7–3. Adequate educational opportunities

1. **Psychotic and severe borderline disorders.**
   These professionals tend to have difficulties with boundaries due to problems with impulse control and thinking.
2. **Manic disorders.** This refers to individuals with manic disorders that are not medically managed and have become impulsive.
3. **Impulse control disorders.** These include a wide range of paraphilias (strong attractions to nonsexual objects) and other impulse disorders.
4. **Chronic neurotic and isolated.** Professionals who tend to be emotionally needy on a chronic basis and meet many needs through relationships with clients.
5. **Situational offenders.** These professionals are generally healthy with good practice history, free of boundary problems, but a situational breakdown in judgment or control has occurred, occasionally in response to some life crisis or loss.
6. **Naivete.** In the absence of pathology, these professionals have difficulty understanding and operating within boundaries due to social deficits or the development of inadequate knowledge base.

FIGURE 7–2. Predictive Features of Potential Boundary Violators

Source: From "Thinking About Blowing the Whistle?" by A. G. Felie, 1983, *American Journal of Nursing, 83*, 1541–1542. Reprinted by permission of Lippincott-Raven Publishers, Philadelphia, PA.

to explore these issues and quality supervision are essential to their practice.

There has been a good deal of research on the factors that appear to be related to increased risk of boundary violations. Counselors should be mindful of these characteristics. The professional who seems to be at most risk is a male who is experiencing personal burnout. He may also be professionally isolated and in the midst of a serious life crisis or experiencing distress in his private life (Borys & Pope, 1989; Smith & Fitzpatrick, 1995). A sufficiently impaired individual may meet his personal needs by entering into an inappropriate relationship with his client.

CASE SCENARIO 7-5

Boundary Issues

Last semester, as a graduate assistant, you were supervising a student on a project that reflects your own inter-

ests. You met outside of your scheduled supervisory hour on several occasions and began to know more about each other's personal lives. You really like this student and want to see him succeed. You have just received your class list for the course you are teaching next semester. This student's name is on the list. Do you have any ethical concerns? What actions can you take to ensure that you and the student remain ethical?

YES. Your friendship with this student has the potential either to make objective judgment difficult or to create the appearance of unfairness in the minds of other students. Raise this issue with both the student and the supervising faculty member so that alternate arrangements might be discussed, such as transfer of yourself or the student to another section. It might be possible for the student to continue in your class if you end your social relationship and arrange for more intense faculty review of your grading.

It is natural for counselors to be attracted to clients or to like their company at times. This reaction is not unusual in professionals who are highly interested in people and are motivated to help them. Some basic practices assist counselors in avoiding poor habits or patterns that may gradually facilitate boundary-violating behaviors. Counselors should try to adopt the following practices, which will provide client-centered care and maintain professionalism:

1. Provide individual care—Show compassion, meet the client's needs, show interest in the client but do not promote or encourage a relationship that leads to dependence. Be mindful of cultural and ethnic characteristics.
2. Use good communication skills—Watch the level of disclosure (remember who is giving and who is receiving therapy!), ask colleagues for feedback, and seek feedback from an objective party.
3. Monitor physical boundaries—Watch clothing selection, type of touch (therapeutic touch versus sexual touch), and avoid potentially detrimental relationships.
4. Maintain emotional-psychological boundaries—Avoid enmeshment, power/control issues, and affection. Solve problems *with* the patient, not *for* the patient.
5. Remember your code of ethics—Above all, keep in mind that you are a professional who provides a professional service—keep the focus of therapy as such.

Activity 1: Identifying Boundary Crossings

Place a checkmark on the line if you feel that the behavior described in the statement is crossing a professional boundary. After you complete the checklist on your own, discuss your opinions with your classmates. Use the discussion points that follow to add some others' perspectives to your thinking.

1. _____ You are spending a disproportionate amount of time with one client.
2. _____ You feel that you are the only one who "really understands" the client.
3. _____ A client's significant other brings treats such as cinnamon rolls, garden produce, and cookies to you on a daily basis.
4. _____ You tend to keep secrets with a client or make special plans.
5. _____ You are guarded or defensive when questioned about your interactions or relationship with a client.
6. _____ A client requests you discuss with her your hospitalization for depression. You spend 30 minutes of the therapy session sharing your experience.
7. _____ You ask a client for personal advice in an area in which she is an expert (car dealer, financial planning).
8. _____ Your client wants to introduce her daughter to your son for the purpose of a social relationship.
9. _____ About 6 months after you have counseled a client, she asks you for a date to which you consent. On your first date, she makes sexual advances that you give in to.
10. _____ You give a client a ride home after her counseling session.
11. _____ Your client pages/beeps you to discuss bringing lunch to her home at her expense prior to a home therapy or case management session.

Discussion Points

1. You need to watch the amount of time you spend with your clients. You do not want to make clients over-dependent on you. Meet their needs, but do not foster detrimental dependence.
2. You are not the only person who understands the client. This type of attitude can also foster detrimental dependence.
3. In this situation, you would be well-advised to understand the facility/agency policy regarding accepting gifts. If the policy OKs accepting food from clients and family, share the gifts with other staff and other clients if possible. If other clients observe the gift-giving, they may fear a lower level of care unless they, too, bring gifts. Also, evaluate the possible role of the client's cultural background in offering gifts. Make all reasonable attempts to be sensitive to traditions. Acknowledge the gift but do not make it the center of attention. Treat the gift-giving in a culturally appropriate manner (if relevant in the situation). If your facility does not allow gift-giving, graciously decline the gift and offer the family another option, such as donating the food to a homeless shelter or battered women's shelter.
4. Keeping secrets or making special plans with a client is not viewed as therapeutic. Your fellow clinicians may consider this behavior devious and deceitful.
5. Why are you so defensive? If you have nothing to hide, why the defensiveness? You need to check this out for yourself.
6. Who is giving and who is receiving therapy? Always be mindful of your role—meeting the client's needs, not the client meeting your needs.
7. Again, as in #6, who is giving and who is receiving therapy? You can generalize about the client's occupation and needs as they relate to therapy, but do not ask for or receive advice specifically for yourself at the client's expense.
8. This may be considered breaking a professional boundary and does not relate to therapy goals.
9. You are placing yourself in serious risk of a detrimental counselor-client relationship. What is your role? It is not that of the client's friend. Participating in a social relationship may be considered a boundary violation.
10. Is this part of your job description? In some places, counselors may transport clients in agency vehicles; however, if this is not a part of your job description, you need to consider the numerous liability issues that can arise.
11. Is one of your therapy goals lunch preparation or teaching/reinforcing independent living skills? If so, you need to plan ahead and work with the client. The client should not be buying your meal. If you do get the lunch, how will you bill for the services provided? You can't bill for eating with your client. What are the client's needs and goals for therapy?

continued

FIGURE 7–3.   Boundary Awareness Activities

Activity 2: Test Your Boundary Awareness

Be prepared—your clients may make statements to you like those that follow. Pair up with another student and take turns role-playing counselor and client. The client starts out the interchange with one of the following client statements. After about 2 or 3 minutes of mock dialogue, discuss with your partner how each of you felt and the reactions each of you had during this interchange. Make a particular effort to talk about what conditions might make you, as the counselor, vulnerable to responding in an unprofessional manner and what you, as the client, might be seeking in these interchanges.

My doctor never talks to me!
Have you ever been depressed?
You make me mad.
I want to talk to your supervisor!
Is my case manager any good?
Do you go to church?
You were rude to me, I want another therapist!
You are not helping me!
Will you go to dinner with me?
I hate going to physical therapy.
You are the only person who understands me!
You don't understand me, you've never had cancer!

FIGURE 7–3. Boundary Awareness Activities—*continued*

SUBSTANCE ABUSE

While the etiology of substance dependence and abuse is varied, pre-existing faulty coping mechanisms and certain predictive behaviors seem to precede professional impairment. Knowledge of risk factors related to chemical dependency can aid in early recognition and intervention. The following etiologic factors have been consistently cited in the literature: (a) genetic predisposition, (b) poor coping skills, (c) lack of education about impairment, (d) absence of effective prevention strategies, (e) drug and alcohol availability, (f) the context of a permissive environment, and (g) denial.

Ironically, as with any lethal malady, early diagnosis and intervention are critical, but the hallmark of chemical dependency continues to be denial. Waiting for spontaneous insight from an affected colleague is unconscionable—and unethical. While the workplace is traditionally the last area to be affected, professional competence is affected adversely. Barriers to early recognition of the chemical dependency of a colleague include (a) lack of training in recognition of early signs of abuse, (b) the insidious and confusing effect of the disease's progression on daily function that lends to signs that are easily rationalized away, and (c) the subsequent denial of both the impaired professional and the individual's colleagues.

The task of differentiating impairment from problematic behaviors is difficult. Acting on the conclusion that impairment is imminent is even more difficult. Relatively few counselors have received training in this area. The literature (Skorina, DeSoto, & Bissell, 1990) suggests that counselors tend to underestimate or fail to recognize impairment in colleagues. Therefore, intervention, and the colleague's recovery, may be delayed.

Suggestions for dealing intentionally with potential impairment among one's peers include primary, secondary, and tertiary levels of intervention based on the timing and need of the situation. Primary interventions include involvement in educational programs (e.g., graduate education or in-service programs). These educational programs provide (a) values clarification regarding impairment and the individual conditions that often cause the impairment (e.g., adopting an attitude of assistance and compassion versus one of blame); (b) knowledge of potential signs of impending impairment for each condition; and (c) enactment of prevention strategies that address each area of potential impairment (both individually and institutionally). Secondary interventions include the establishment and knowledge of sound practice standards. These standards include steps to obtain due process for both the individual who may be impaired as well as the individual's colleagues. Tertiary intervention involves understanding and involving the necessary resources to make a direct intervention with an impaired colleague.

CASE SCENARIO 7-6

Substance Abuse

The medical director of the treatment center where you work as a chemical dependency counselor has started to miss the morning staff meetings fairly regularly. He always has a rational explanation. Two weeks ago, an evening nurse confided in you that she thought she smelled alcohol on the doctor's breath as he attended to a client. Is this enough evidence to initiate an intervention with the physician?

NO. Impairment requires the documentation of significantly impaired function. However, there is enough evidence to discuss your concerns with the physician.

MOBBING

In the last decade, the concept of emotional abuse in the workplace began to be recognized, discussed, and treated in the United States. Increased numbers of high-profile, shocking incidents of violence in schools and the workplace caused scholars to consider factors that create negative, and sometimes unbearable, forces acting on individuals. Counselors and the settings in which they work are not immune to these forces. A recent text by Davenport, Distler Schwartz, and Pursell Elliott (1999) described **mobbing** as "workplace expulsion through emotional abuse" (p. 20). These authors noted that the term was derived from its root word, *mob,* meaning a disorderly crowd engaged in lawless violence. The first use of this term, as applied to human behavior, occurred in the 1960s by an Austrian ethnologist, Konrad Lorenz. Lorenz described human behavior as being similar to the behavior that animals show in scaring away an enemy.

Later, Heinesmann, a Swedish physician, researched similar behavior among children that has subsequently been labeled *bullying.* His early work, *Mobbing: Group Violence Among Children,* was published in Sweden in 1972. Until 1982, this concept was used exclusively in the study of children. Leymann (1996) then used the term *mobbing* to describe similar violence among adults in the workplace. He found that work cultures created circumstances wherein marked individuals were labeled as difficult and pushed to the margins of the workgroup culture. Leymann's work has generated much interest in Europe.

According to Davenport et al. (1999), mobbing is an emotional assault that targets an individual via two types of hurtful conduct from work colleagues. One type of misconduct is overt and is considered to be active aggression. The other involves passive tactics that are more covert and often disguised between acts of occasional kindness. Mobbing is a process that happens insidiously over time. Leymann (1996) distinguished five phases in this process: conflict, aggressive acts, management involvement, branding (as "difficult" or "mentally ill"), and expulsion. Other terms have been used for these phenomena: bullying, workplace trauma, harassment, and emotional abuse in the workplace (Keashly, 1998).

Dynamics of the Mobbing Process

Mobbing is the process of an emotional assault (Davenport et al., 1999) that often begins with passive, insidious marking of an individual as a threat to the norms of the organizational culture. The mobbing process is like the process of marking among people with disabilities that has been so well described by Jones et al. (1984) in their classic text, *Social Stigma: The Psychology of Marked Relationships.* This stigmatizing process is always relational. In the classic case, the process begins when an individual's flaw or mark of deviance initiates a pronounced attribution process. The process of attributing certain negative characteristics to the person results in an attack on the person's basic integrity and often results in hostile rejection. The outcome is not necessarily based on who the person actually is, but whom the person may represent to the organizational culture. For example, a counseling intern frequently asks pointed questions about the billing practices of the supervisor and the other counselors in the agency. This intern may eventually be ostracized by all of the counselors as someone who is "holier than thou" and has no potential for the "real" work of counseling.

A distinguishable characteristic of mobbing is the organizational collusion that typically supports this insidious process. Davenport et al. (1999) identified organizational elements that make a working environment vulnerable to participation in mobbing: bad management (e.g., excessive bottom-line orientation at the expense of human resources), stress-intensive workplace, monotony, disbelief or denial by managers, unethical activities, flat organizations, and downsizing/restructuring/merging. These authors asserted that it is the culture of the organization that determines whether mobbing will be allowed to develop or will be extinguished, particularly the organization's ability to handle differences and conflict.

Within this vulnerable organizational context, Davenport et al. (1999) suggested that the complex dynamic that results in mobbing is the outcome of an interaction among five elements: (1) the psychology and the circumstances of the mobbers; (2) the organizational culture and structure; (3) the psychology of the mobbee's personality; (4) the circumstances of the mobbee; and (5) a triggering event, a conflict, and factors outside the organization (i.e., values and norms in U.S. culture).

WHISTLE-BLOWING

Counselors are mandated by their codes of ethics and by state licensure guidelines to report questionable or unethical behavior, yet many are hesitant to become whistle-blowers. **Whistle-blowing** is the ethical reporting of unethical behavior, and it has often been used in a pejorative sense. Collegial support may be mixed when a colleague reports the suspected behavior of a peer.

Mixed support may be particularly evident in hierarchical organizations, such as large bureaucracies or hospitals, if the accused is an administrator, supervisor or physician who also occupies a place on the upper level of the hierarchy, or if the whistle-blowing disrupts the immediate work team in any setting. On the other hand, whistle-blowing can be beneficial and override the negative risks by (a) providing a climate that supports the protection of current and future clients as well as coworkers, (b) facilitating communication among colleagues, and (c) encouraging constructive problem solving. Several laws have been designed to safeguard employees who suspect the unethical behavior of their colleagues. However, court actions suggest that legal protection for whistle-blowers is tentative. For example, a 1981 Michigan state law protects employees who expose illegal or dangerous employee activity from wrongful discharge from any government or private-sector organization. However, as stated in Chapter 3, counselors are obligated to their employers as well as to their clients, making the decisions concerning disclosure ethically complex. The actual experience of becoming a whistle-blower can be a life-changing event if the situation is serious enough. At times, the counselor may receive sufficient support and the process may be difficult, but gratifying. In other instances, the experience can be harrowing even though the counselor may eventually be vindicated. Box 7.1 relates the story of two counselors who "did the right thing" and are proud of it, yet they paid a serious price. Note the characteristic mobbing behaviors that were directed against them in the process.

Ethical codes for counseling disciplines do provide codified standards of behavior for addressing concerns regarding unethical behavior of a colleague. The APA and the ACA codes of ethics provide standards for informal resolution of ethical violations and for reporting ethical violations. They direct the professional first to attempt to resolve the situation by discussing it directly and informally with the other therapist, providing that confidentiality rights of the client are not violated in the process. If the violation is too serious, or is not resolved after this informal discussion, the professional will take further action including possible referral to licensure boards and/or professional organizations' ethics committees for adjudication. This last course of action would not be possible if there are violations of the client's confidentiality rights that cannot be resolved.

In a more general sense, Felie (1983) suggested several guidelines for whether, when, and how to blow the whistle on a colleague if informal routes prove to be ineffective and if the colleague is not of one's own discipline but works as a peer within an organizational setting. She has outlined six steps for addressing the problem (Figure 7–4).

The act of taking a colleague to task for ethically inappropriate behavior is daunting. Nevertheless, counselors have an important obligation to their clients and society at large to protect them and to uphold the trust placed in the profession.

LEGAL ISSUES

The Civil Rights Act of 1967, Title VII, made it unlawful for an employer to discriminate or to fire an individual based on race, color, religion, sex, or national origin. Subsequently, federal and state legislation extended this protection; for example, The Age Discrimination in Employment Act of 1967; The Vocational Rehabilitation Act of 1973; and The Americans with Disabilities Act of 1990. The Supreme Court ruled that Title VII is not limited to tangible discrimination but is also intended to be applied to people who may be subjected to a hostile work environment. For example, the claim of "hostile environment" has been used in litigation involving sexual harassment.

Recent U.S. legislation has attempted to extend compensatory relief to individuals who have suffered significant mental injury as a result of a hostile working

Box 7.1 Two Colleagues Make the Ultimate Ethical Decision

We live in an interdependent world where work and ethics are inextricably linked. Knowing that we are providing a useful service to others lets us routinely deal with difficulties and problems that are part of any job. In our place of work, routine circumstances led to a chain of events that uncovered fraudulent billing practices. We attempted to correct this by working within the corporation. Our attempts to correct unethical and fraudulent activities were "spun" by corporate managers as "politics," described as "trying to get workers" (those who were responsible for the fraudulent activities). We experienced first-hand how a system that had lost its moral compass protects itself through attacks on our professional credibility. We were threatened and isolated. One of us was fired, the other was forced out. Later we found ourselves unemployable. We worried that we had been blacklisted. We can attest that "whistle-blowers suffer certain and severe retaliation from management especially if their information proves to be significant, reveals systematic misconduct, and the practices exposed are part of the regular profit accumulation of the organization" (Rothschild & Miethe, 1999).

We are not experts, but when we found ourselves in a whistle-blower situation, we experienced first-hand the connection between work and ethical expression. We were dumbfounded when the corporation ignored the bad billing practices we had discovered. Instead of backing our efforts, the corporation criticized us for not getting along with subordinates. Overnight everything changed. We went from the model team to troublemakers.

We were disappointed by the behavior of some coworkers. Professional colleagues whom we had once respected became overwhelmed by concerns for job security. We found silence where we had expected support from the organization and other members of the helping professions. We experienced the effects of extreme trauma, shame, fear, loss of confidence, and depression that impacted all of our relationships and family. Despite our own fear of what the future could bring, we summoned our courage and proceeded with integrity. We could do the right thing by having our case heard and decided in a court of law. We took the initiative with energy and conviction, persevering and being willing to hang in there, no matter what.

Having our case heard in a court of law made a big difference. Even if the case had not been won, having a trial was the right thing. The trial was based on evidence and we had the documentation that made the difference. The procedures of the trial were daunting; however, the trial was our only opportunity to make our case to the public. By taking a stand we were effectively cut off from the support systems one traditionally turns to in times of great stress.

Our former boss apparently forgot that he had nominated one of us for Employee of the Year when he testified that that person was always a problem. The CEO was angry and embarrassed when confronted by the evidence. One of our frustrations with the discovery process was that the only documentary evidence of the billing problem came from us. Despite our requests for documentation, the corporation seemed not to have any of the many memos we had generated on the subject. We were appalled to learn that one of the employees we had tried to correct had searched our office and thrown many papers away. Realizing that our concerns about the organization practices needed to be supported by evidence, we carefully documented them in a report to the clinical supervisor as we sought for the identified issues to be addressed by appropriate supervisors in the organization. This report and retention of records of our repeated attempts to seek the support of organization officers in correcting these practices provided the evidence that made the difference. The money won in the lawsuit is a representation of some justice for the individuals involved.

Being a whistle-blower was a life-altering experience. In its entirety, the experience was painful. We had acted in good faith to seek remedies to fraudulent practices and the system did not recognize or honor that effort. The experience also was an opportunity. It gave us a window in time to evaluate our ethics and our values. When work and life are rooted in ethical practice, you have the energy and the vision to do whatever is necessary. We all want to contribute and make a positive difference with our work. We are all drawn to what is good and right and each one of us is capable of making this difference. We found that in our materialistic society, ethical and value-based action is not to be taken for granted and is the only thing that gives authenticity and substance to living and working.

continued

Box 7.1 Two Colleagues Make the Ultimate Ethical Decision—*continued*

A decision to step forward should not be taken without serious consideration. Sound legal advice and documentation is crucial as well. The role of whistle-blower was forced upon us. After the fact, we realized that even though we could not predict what the outcome of our actions might be, our response of finding justice through the legal system was the right and good thing to do. We did not know that it would work out to a positive conclusion. We only knew that it was the right action to take and did so without regrets. We could not turn a blind eye to our professional ethics or the rights of our clients to honest and ethical services. When life and work are guided by ethical values, we are empowered to act responsibly and compassionately, even in the midst of challenging circumstances. Each one of us has the ability to make this difference. Never forget what the priorities are.

1. **Confirm the issue.** Conduct an objective assessment of the situation. Make certain that you are competent to make this determination and that your desire to make this report is not based on personal motives.
2. **Check your perceptions with peers.** Examine them against the norms of your institution and your discipline. Compare the activity against your state's practice guidelines and those of your institution. Does the situation truly exceed acceptable standards? Maintain a nonjudgmental attitude throughout the process.
3. **Involve others in an action plan.** Develop a plan of action for voicing your concerns. Respect your institution's chain of command. Multiple participants are more effective in providing a successful intervention. Have intervention goals established in advance. Anticipate possible reactions.
4. **Set deadlines.** They demonstrate that you are serious. Implement your plan after conferring with your immediate supervisor.
5. **Document details of your discussion.** Include time, date, and the basic content of the conversation. Timing of any intervention is crucial— soon after a precipitant crisis is optimal.
6. **If needed, take the problem upstairs.** If your supervisor dismisses or fails to address the situation, be prepared to move up the organizational ladder.

FIGURE 7–4. Guidelines for Whistle-Blowing
Source: From "Thinking About Blowing the Whistle?" by A. G. Felie, 1983, *American Journal of Nursing, 83,* 1541–1542. Reprinted by permission of Lippincott-Raven Publishers, Philadelphia, PA.

environment. Arizona, California, Iowa, Wisconsin, and Wyoming legally acknowledge that mental injury can result from excessive stress on the job—calling it *mental-health injury.*

This changing legal landscape is also affecting the corporate world. Companies such as Levi Strauss & Co. and the Saturn Corporation are leading the way in establishing company philosophies that support an individual's right to a work environment that is free from mobbing. Davenport et al. (1999) offered a list of twelve components that can create this type of culture (Figure 7–5).

Mental health, rehabilitation, and other helping organizations that employ professionals who work directly with clients should take seriously the need to establish a nonthreatening, positive environment.

Mobbing and whistle-blowing often begin with the presence of an unresolved conflict and the admirable attempt of an individual to resolve the situation. One result of an unresolved situation of conflict may be the act of whistle-blowing. The conflict may actually provide a potentially explosive atmosphere with the fuel it needs to ignite. In turn, the whistle-blower can serve as a target for unresolved hostility, or mobbing.

CHAPTER SUMMARY

Counselors are profoundly influenced by the environments and work cultures in which they practice. Work environments are cultures that create a particular ethical climate that influences the quality of services provided to clients. Ethical and unethical colleagues influence their coworkers to behave ethically and unethically.

1. Mission statement that includes the organizational objectives on how employees are treated; vision and value statements that align all employees
2. Organizational structure; clear reporting levels
3. Job descriptions—defined in terms of duties and responsibilities
4. Personnel policies—comprehensive, consistent, legal, simple, including expected behaviors and standards of ethics
5. Disciplinary issues; dealt with consistently, fairly, and expeditiously
6. Employees buy into the goals and objectives of the organization. They have been educated regarding their role in the achievement of these goals.
7. New employees are not only selected based on their technical qualifications but also on the basis of their emotional intelligence, such as their capacity of dealing with diversity, working in self-directed teams, and managing conflict.
8. Training and staff development—highly valued for all employees. The system meets the needs of the changing organization. Training includes issues of human relations in addition to technical knowledge.
9. Communications—open, honest, effective, and timely
10. Participation, teamwork, creativity, decision-making trust, empowerment; structures that allow for the highest possible degree of employees' personal involvement in achieving the company's goals
11. Conflict resolution/mediation—a mechanism for resolving conflict at all levels. There is a follow-up to ensure that the conflict has really been resolved.
12. EAPs (Employee Assistance Programs) or a comparable program that includes behavioral risk assessment and management (Davenport et al., 1999, p. 142)

FIGURE 7–5.   Ways to Reduce Mobbing

Source: From "Mobbing: Emotional Abuse in the American Workplace" by N. Davenport, R. Distler Schwartz, & G. Pursell Elliot, 1999. Reprinted by permission of Civil Society of Publishing, Ames, IA.

Organizational climate is how people characterize a system's practices and procedures, such as the sense of safety or fear of retribution that a counselor may feel. Ethical climate describes the shared perceptions that colleagues hold concerning ethical procedures and practices within an organization.

A disability is an identifiable condition that may be stable and is often overcome with appropriate changes, assistance, or accommodations. An impairment is a gradually recognized condition that manifests when an individual attempts to perform some activity. Chronic physical illness, substance abuse, burnout, and sexual acting-out behaviors are pervasive impairments that can disrupt professional performance. Substance abuse adversely affects professional competence. Early diagnosis and intervention are essential. Burnout is an emotional exhaustion in which the professional no longer has any positive feelings, sympathy, or respect for clients.

Boundary violations occur when professionals' ethical standards are loose with clients, students, or research participants. Those most likely to violate professional boundaries are those who have psychotic disorders, manic disorders, impulse control disorders, chronic neurosis and isolation, and naivete, and those who are situational offenders.

Mobbing is an emotional assault that targets a work colleague. Organizational elements that contribute to mobbing include bad management, a stress-intensive workplace, monotony, disbelief or denial by managers, unethical activities, flat organizations, and downsizing/restructuring. Whistle-blowing is the ethical reporting of unethical behavior. Whistle-blowing receives mixed support, particularly in hierarchical organizations. It can be beneficial and override the negative risks by providing a protective environment for clients and coworkers and facilitating communication. The experience of becoming a whistle-blower can be a life-changing event.

REFERENCES

Agich, G. J. (Ed.). (1982). *Responsibility in health care.* Boston: D. Reidel.

Beauchamp, T. L., & Childress, J. F. (1994). *Principles of biomedical ethics.* New York & Oxford, England: Oxford University Press.

Bellah, R. N., Madson, R., Sullivan, W. M., Swidler, A., & Tipton, S. M. (1985). *Habits of the heart: Individualism and commitment in American life.* New York: Harper & Row.

Borys, D. S., & Pope, K. S. (1989). Dual relationships between therapist and client: A national study of psychologists, psychiatrists, and social workers. *Professional Psychology: Research and Practice, 20,* 283–293.

Brems, C. (2000). *Dealing with challenges in psychotherapy and counseling.* Pacific Grove, CA: Brooks/Cole.

Commission on Rehabilitation Counselor Certification. (2001). *Code of professional ethics for rehabilitation counselors.* Rolling Meadows, IL: Author.

Cottone, R. R. (1992). *Theories and paradigms of counseling and psychotherapy.* Needham Heights, MA: Allyn & Bacon.

Cottone, R. R., Tarvydas, V., & House, G. (1994). The effect of number and type of consulted relationships on the ethical decision-making of graduate students in counseling. *Counseling and Values, 39,* 56–68.

Davenport, N., Distler Schwartz, R., & Pursell Elliott, G. (1999). *Mobbing: Emotional abuse in the American workplace.* Ames, IA: Civil Society of Publishing.

Doherty, W. J. (1995). *Soul searching: Why psychotherapy must promote moral responsibility.* New York: Basic Books.

Felie, A. G. (1983). The risks of blowing the whistle. *American Journal of Nursing, 83,* 1387.

Helnesmann, P. (1972). *Mobbing: Group violence among children,* Stockholm, Sweden: Natur och Kutlur.

Hellman, J. (1986). The stresses of psychotherapeutic work: A replication and extension. *Journal of Clinical Psychology, 42,* 197–204.

Ivey, A. E. (1999). *Intentional interviewing and counseling: Facilitating client development in a multicultural society* (4th ed.). Pacific Grove, CA: Brooks/Cole.

Jones, E., Farina, A., Hastorf, A., Markus, H., Miller, D., & Scott, R. (1984). *Social stigma: The psychology of marked relationships.* New York: W. H. Freeman and Company.

Keashly, L. (1998). Emotional abuse in the workplace: Conceptual and empirical issues. *Journal of Emotional Abuse, 1*(1), 85–117.

Klebe-Trevino, L. (1986). Ethical decision making in organizations: A person-situation interactionist model. *The Academy of Management Review,* 11, 601–617.

Lamb, D. H, Cochran, D. J., & Jackson, V. (1991). Training and organizational issues associated with identifying and responding to intern impairment. *Professional Psychology: Research and Practice, 22,* 291–296.

Leymann, H. (1996). The content and development of mobbing at work. *European Journal of Work and Organizational Psychology, 5* (2).

Liddell, D. L., Halpin. G., & Halpin, W. G. (1992). The measure of moral orientation: Measuring the ethics of care and justice. *Journal of College Student Development, 33,* 325–330.

Maddi, S. R., & Kobasa, S. C. (1984). *The hardy executive: Health under stress.* Homewood, IL: Dow Jones-Irwin.

Maslach, C., & Jackson, S. E. (1986). *Maslach Burnout Inventory: Manual* (2nd ed.). Palo Alto, CA: Consulting Psychologists Press.

Mohan, J. (1993). The business of medicine. *Sociology, 22,* 648–649.

O'Rourke, B. (1996). *Individual interdisciplinary team members' perception of ethics decision-making context: A descriptive study.* Unpublished doctoral dissertation, University of Iowa, Iowa City.

Rothchild, J., & Miethe, T. D. (1999, February). Whistle-blower disclosures and management retaliation: The battle to control information about organization corruption. *Work & Occupations, 26* (1), 107–128.

Schein, E. H. (1990). Organizational culture. *American Psychologist, 45,* 109–119.

Schoener, R. (1995). Assessment of professionals who have engaged in boundary violations. *Psychiatric Annals, 25,* 95–98.

Skorina, J. K., DeSoto, C. B., & Bissell, L. (1990). Alcoholic psychologists: Routes to recovery. *Professional Psychology: Research and Practice, 21,* 248–251.

Skorupa, J., & Agresti, A. (1993). Ethical beliefs about burnout and continued professional practice. *Professional Psychology: Research and Practice, 24,* 281–285.

Smith, D., & Fitzpatrick, M. (1995). Patient-therapist boundary issues: An integrative review of theory and research. *Professional Psychology: Research and Practice, 26,* 499–506.

Stadler, H. A. (1990). Counselor impairment. In B. Herlihy & L. Golden (Eds.), *Ethical standards casebook.* Alexandria, VA: American Association for Counseling and Development.

Tarvydas, V. M. (1994). Ethical orientations of masters' rehabilitation students. *Rehabilitation Counseling Bulletin, 37,* 202–214.

Tarvydas, V. M., & Cottone, R. R. (1991). Ethical responses to legislative, organizational, and economic dynamics: A four-level model of ethical practice. *Journal of Applied Rehabilitation, 22*(4), 11–17.

Weiss, S. J., & Davis, H. P. (1985). Validity and reliability of the collaborative practice scale. *Nursing Research, 34,* 299–305.

Welfel, E. R. (2002). *Ethics in counseling and psychology: Standards, research, and emerging issues* (2nd ed.). Pacific Grove, CA: Brooks/Cole.

Wiles, J. (1993). Socialization and interpersonal influence on the ethical decision-making climate in service organizations. Unpublished dissertation, University of Memphis, Memphis, TN.

CHAPTER 8

Office, Administrative, and Business Practices

Objectives

▪▪▪▪▪▪▪▪▪▪▪

After reading this chapter, you should be able to:

- Discuss the ethical issues that typically arise from office, administrative, and business practices.
- Explain the major areas of concern that derive from the layout of the professional counseling office, such as privacy and confidentiality issues.
- Discuss how to oversee, manage, and monitor ethically sensitive activities in schools, agencies, and private practices.
- Explain procedures and policies that may be discriminatory or unfair to special populations of clients.
- Identify issues related to billing health insurance and working through managed care providers.

▪▪▪▪▪▪▪▪▪▪▪

INTRODUCTION

One of the most overlooked areas of study in the ethics literature relates to business practices. Yet, business practice is one of the most challenging areas of ethical practice—and one of the areas most challenged by clients and other individuals served by professional counselors. Many of the complaints before licensure boards and certification bodies are about business, administrative, or office practices, such as inadequate recordkeeping or fraudulent acts (e.g., false billing) (Association of State and Provincial Psychology Boards, 2001). Nothing will raise the ire of a client (or third-party payer) more than a bill for unsatisfactory services, a bill that does not reflect the actual services requested or provided, a bill that breaches confidentiality, or a bill that reflects financial irregularities. Generally, counselors are ill-prepared to address these issues and to set standards and office procedures to prevent problems. Classic examples of problematic office practices include: (a) waiting rooms that do not provide any privacy (secretaries discuss issues with clients in the open or there is no discreet entry or exit); (b) use of electronic equipment without adequate encryption (e.g., fax machines, cell phones, intercoms; see Chapter 10); (c) advertising (misrepresentation, for example); (d) fee setting and collection of unpaid bills;

(e) maintenance of records and disposal of confidential records (e.g., shredding of records); (f) referral and termination procedures; (g) poor sound insulation in offices; (h) misrepresentation of credentials to the public (e.g., licensure status); and (i) fraudulent billing practices.

THE LAYOUT OF THE OFFICE

Privacy issues should be utmost in the design of a professional office. A professional supervisor recently visited a student intern at a reputable sex therapy clinic. While waiting in the lobby area, he was able to overhear a secretary asking detailed, intimate questions of a prospective client over the phone. The secretary repeated the prospective client's name, phone number, and address as she recorded them so that everyone in the waiting area could hear. Soundproofing or screening in such a situation is absolutely necessary. Waiting areas should be designed so that people entering or leaving the counseling suites can do so without passing other waiting clients. A separate exit door is ideal, or if space restrictions prevent a separate exit door, scheduling should take place so that a minimal number of people are in the waiting area at one time. Files should not be left out in the open so that visitors in the waiting area can see them, and computer monitors should be turned so that confidential information is not easily viewed by the waiting public. These are basic issues of privacy. Nothing is more disturbing than waiting in a physician's office and having one's medical problems broadcast to everyone present. Counseling clients may have issues even more sensitive than those of patients in a physician's office. Counselors and administrators must be very sensitive to these common breaches of privacy, which can be prevented by careful planning. Counselors are guided by the American Counseling Association (ACA) and American Psychological Association (APA) ethics codes, which make it clear that counselors must respect the privacy of their clients.

Offices should also be organized to provide for the safety of clients and staff. If safety concerns arise from the nature of the clientele, staff should be prepared to deal with emergency situations. Some professionals provide counsel to ex-offenders, individuals with anger or impulse control problems, or individuals with poor or impaired judgment. A rehabilitation counselor in a nonprofit agency was punched in the face by a client diagnosed as having paranoid schizophrenia.

The client reported that he overheard the counselor make a racial slur while the counselor was on the phone trying to assist in job placement of the client. The client had a record of assaulting other individuals for racial slurs, even when no such slurs were heard by bystanders. The client was apparently hallucinating and became violent in response to the hallucinations. Given the client's record, precautions should have been taken in this case. When working with potentially dangerous or violent clients, counselors should establish safety and contingency plans. Procedures for warning or alerting others of potential, imminent, or active crises should be in place. Equipment might be purchased to help to ensure safety (door key pads, warning systems), or offices can be designed to allow visual access (counselor offices with windows to another secure office) so other professional staff can monitor activities. Counselors, staff, and clients should feel safe in the counseling setting, and administrative and professional staff should be alert to potential concerns and methods for preventing problems.

The common practice of sharing office space is another area of concern. Some counselors, by choice or by necessity, share office space—they may see clients at different times during the same day or on different days. In most cases, this arrangement is a matter of economics. Private practitioners in part-time, private practices may be unable to afford an individual office all their own; they may enter into an agreement with a colleague to share costs and space. Some agencies and schools are pressed for space and are unable to provide individual offices for professional staff. Whatever the arrangement, counselors who share space should have a clear agreement about the boundaries related to client information. Unless the counselors are employed by the same agency or school and have their clients' understanding of the organization's right to share information, they must make efforts to secure files and other case-relevant information. Separate storage areas (e.g., file cabinets) should be secured even from colleagues who share space; licenses should be displayed according to law for all of the people who use the office; and procedures for taking calls and messages must be established to provide for maximum security. A formal, written ethics agreement between parties sharing space is also recommended. Extra precautions should be taken to ensure that a client's rights are not compromised because of financial exigency.

Counselors must also be sensitive to accessibility issues—individuals with disabilities often have impairments that affect their mobility. Special parking spaces for those with mobility problems must be provided. Offices and buildings should be designed to maximize the accessibility of individuals with problems negotiating spaces. Elevators should be available in storied buildings, facilities should be wheelchair accessible, and bathrooms must be made accessible. Special accommodations for the hearing or visually impaired should be in place. Sensitivity to disability-related concerns is important when serving individuals in need. In most states, the state department that provides rehabilitation services addresses accessibility issues in establishing and maintaining an office. Offices that receive federal funds must be in compliance with accessibility standards.

QUESTION FOR REFLECTION

You are a counselor in an agency with paper-thin walls. You are counseling a client, and both you and your client are able to overhear a very private counseling session from an adjoining room. What should you do?

Consider the options in this situation. Consult the ethical codes of the ACA and the APA. What is your first course of action? Is additional follow-up activity necessary?

FEE SETTING, BILLING, AND COLLECTIONS

Fee issues are among those that appear to produce the most variability of confidence when practitioners are asked to rate ethical acceptability (Gibson & Pope, 1993). Gibson and Pope (1993), citing their own findings and the work of Pope and Vasquez (1991), concluded, "The topic of fee is one that often evokes feelings of discomfort and may therefore be relatively neglected in training programs" (p. 334).

Counselors should follow some simple advice in establishing their billing and collections policies—be cautious and be fair. If clients or third-party payers feel cheated or slighted, there is potential for conflict. The ACA and APA ethics codes indicate counselors and psychologists should not be discriminatory in setting fees.

A classic area of debate related to fee setting among practicing professionals is the issue of "sliding fee scales." In this system, individuals are required to pay a certain amount for a service based on their income (see Lien, 1993). A person with a very low income may be required to pay an amount less than a person with a high income for an hour of counseling or psychotherapy. There are benefits and problems

with this sort of fee setting (Lien, 1993). Some argue that it provides people with low incomes an opportunity to receive services they otherwise could not afford. Others argue that it is inherently unfair and prejudicial of the wealthy client or the client with insurance or other benefits. It also appears to be in conflict with the ethical code of the ACA, which requires that there be no discrimination against individuals on the basis of socioeconomic status. Some agencies have compromised by charging lower fees for the services of student counselors (pre-degree) or counselors-in-training (degreed, but unlicensed or provisionally licensed professionals working to meet licensure standards). Some still argue that this may provide an inferior (or at least a less clinically savvy) product to the poorer client. It is also possible that if a practitioner receives a lower fee, he or she might be less conscientious.

The flat fee, variable collection procedure is another option. In this system, one fee is charged for all clients, say $100 per hour. All clients are required to pay at least 50 percent of the fee before they leave the office ($50). The remainder is billed to the client. Some clients may choose to pay the total amount at the time of the service; others have insurance that may cover the balance. The procedure is invariable in collection of at least a certain percentage of the fee at the time of service. However, the agency can use discretion in collection of the unpaid balance. Clients who have fewer resources may not be billed on the remainder as often, or may not be required to pay as much on the balance of their bill at each billing cycle. Some of these bills will go uncollected, so the agency has some flexibility in attempting to collect the balance. The unpaid balance is a private matter, and not one that is prejudicial of certain groups at the time of the service agreement. On the negative side, this approach may scare away clients who may not be able to afford the full fee; they may be hesitant to commit to services even with knowledge of the nonaggressive collection procedures. They may seek services from an agency with a lower or sliding scale.

Some counselors are willing to charge lower fees but require full payment at the time of service. They may serve only a clientele that has ready access to funds to pay for services. This method avoids all of the work and expense of billing. Others use credit or debit card payments. Although a small fee is charged to the counselor for use of credit or debit cards, this method allows immediate guaranteed payment for services.

Regardless of the fee and billing procedure, it is important that counselors have a clearly articulated fee schedule and stick to the schedule. Varying fees and billing practices may be viewed as prejudicial and could be grounds for legitimate complaints against an agency or professional. Raising fees during counseling may prove uncomfortable for both the counselor and the client. Some counselors have a set fee for a particular client. If the client's case is terminated and then reopened, it is reopened at the current rate, even if that rate constitutes an increase over the previous rate. Once opened, the fee remains the same, no matter what changes occur in the fee schedule. Some professionals never raise a fee on a case once the client has initiated treatment—the fee always remains the same. This kind of policy helps to encourage future client contact with the professional. Other agencies or private practitioners raise fees regularly, even in the course of treatment of a client. Clients are (and should be) informed that rates are not permanent and may be increased during their treatment. No one fee-raising method is more ethical than another, but, certainly, clients should know the rules from the very beginning of counseling.

If arrangements are made about collections, such as hiring a collection agency or attorney to secure unpaid balances, these arrangements should be explained to clients when they initially agree to services (see the ACA and APA codes). Clients should agree to services with full knowledge of potential collection procedures by signing a written statement of the agreement. If collections or payments are made through a credit or debit card, it is wise to use an agency name that does not imply mental health services to avoid a potential breach of privacy. If the credit card company or bank receives a debit from "Anita's Counseling and Psychotherapy Service," the credit world knows that the client received such services. If the name of the agency is abbreviated in some way to disguise the service (e.g., Anita's Services, or Anita, Inc.), it is less likely that individuals will be able to identify the service provided.

Counselors can take some simple actions to prevent breach of client privacy. Mailed envelopes should list only the return address, without the agency name so that people picking up a client's mail (e.g., roommates or family members) do not know that there has been contact with a mental health service provider. Likewise, counselors should not leave detailed phone messages that imply counseling services on answering machines or with anyone other than the client. Leaving a name and return phone number is sufficient.

Fraudulent billing is another major issue. In many cases, medical insurance programs will not pay for certain types of counseling services unless they can be clearly defined as psychotherapy for a person diagnosed with a mental disorder. Counselors often provide services that technically do not meet the definition of psychotherapy in treatment of mental disorders. For example, marriage or family counseling is not technically medical psychotherapy. It is fraudulent billing practice to provide a service outside of the realm of medical psychotherapy and then to bill it as such. Clients may want services billed in a way that meets medical insurance standards to avoid paying out of pocket, but their consent in no way protects the counselor in cases of fraudulent billing. If marriage counseling is provided, marriage counseling should be billed, regardless of reimbursement issues. Clients should also know that when medical insurance is billed, it requires a medical (psychiatric) diagnosis. Counselors should not diagnose mental disorders unless "they are qualified and competent" to render such diagnoses and licensed to do so (Anderson, 1996, p. 75). Some clients prefer to avoid communicating such diagnoses to third-party payers, and they may request to make other payment arrangements.

Billing for services that were not provided or justified is another fraudulent practice. A psychologist was sued for and found guilty of Medicare fraud when it was learned he was billing for the intelligence testing of nursing home residents who suffered from diagnosed dementia (loss of intelligence). In most cases, the tests were never given, or only cursory procedures were used to document attempts to test the patients. The testing was found to be unnecessary and, in most cases, there was no record of actual test administration. This was a clear case of fraudulent practice.

Some mental health professionals have been found guilty of double billing—for example, billing a government agency and then billing a client or client's family in full for services already reimbursed by a third party.

Also there are instances where: (a) Billing for an individual session when the client is seen in group; and (b) Billing at a full credentialed rate for services rendered by students or a para-professional assistant. These are charges of fraud that are fairly common in the current managed care marketplace. Playing "get-rich schemes" at the expense of a third-party payer is a very dangerous game—such violations can result in felony convictions for insurance fraud, a loss of a license to practice, and/or censure from a professional organization.

Another issue of concern is submitting forms to a third-party provider (such as a managed care company) requesting therapy for a client and purposefully "overdiagnosing" the client to ensure payment or permission to treat the patient for an extended period of time. (See the related discussion of "upcoding" and "downcoding" in chapter 9.) The counselor purposefully uses a diagnosis that is more severe than diagnostically justified to ensure adequate insurance coverage for the anticipated treatments (Cummings, 1998). Cummings (1998) stated:

> With indemnity insurance and in times past, providers characteristically underdiagnosed ostensibly for the protection of their patients. The most innocuous reimbursable diagnosis was overly used, whereas schizophrenia was seldom evoked as in many states the patient could suffer such consequences as loss of a driver's license or ineligibility for life insurance. In contrast, the era of managed care has seen the mushrooming of the use of severe diagnoses. Forced on many occasions to demonstrate concepts of "medical necessity" or "life threatening," practitioners' exaggeration of findings on evaluation has become widespread. (p. 61)

Obviously, this is unacceptable activity. In addition to constituting insurance fraud, overdiagnosing can do harm to clients. Diagnoses may follow clients for a lifetime, and a false diagnosis may affect the client's future insurability and future relations with mental health professionals.

Missed sessions are another issue. Should clients be billed when they miss appointments without giving adequate notice to allow rescheduling? Woody (1989) stated: "Missed sessions are troubling for both the client and the practitioner. If a client fails to show up for an appointment, the client suffers from lack of treatment, and the practitioner suffers from lack of income" (p. 150). Most practitioners have a general rule about billing missed appointments, and whatever policy is established, it should be communicated clearly (on informed consent forms) and implemented consistently. Missed appointments are usually not upsetting to the practitioner who has other work to fill the time, but if the missed appointment is inconvenient and represents wasted time, it becomes problematic for the counselor. Legitimate emergencies that prevent attendance should be excused without penalty, and a policy about adequate advanced notice to cancel appointments should be clearly communicated to clients initiating treatment. Note that insurance companies do not pay for missed appointments—they pay only for services rendered, so bills for missed appointments go directly to the client.

Should counselors charge clients for phone contacts? Some charge one-tenth of an hour for every 6 minutes on the phone. Others do not charge for phone contacts unless they represent an extended therapeutic interaction. As with other billing issues, clients should know how they are being charged well in advance. A surprise on a bill is likely to incite already fragile clients and create a conflict situation. Phone contacts are typically not reimbursed by insurance carriers.

Counselors have at least two options in dealing with clients who do not pay their fees. First, the counselor has the right to terminate the counseling relationship. The ACA code states that termination is appropriate when clients do not pay fees charged. If, however, it is clear that clients cannot pay fees, the counselor has the option of serving the client "pro bono publico," for the public good, at no fee. The ACA code encourages such work. Counselors should know how much of their work is pro bono and if such an arrangement is acceptable to administrators and supervisors.

QUESTION FOR REFLECTION

You learn that one of your colleagues in a private agency is billing medical insurance for "medical psychotherapy" when, in fact, the counselor is providing career counseling services, including resume writing guidance. It is obvious that the individuals receiving the counselor's services are not seeking treatment for a mental disorder. What are your obligations in this situation as a professional counselor? Why is this conduct unethical? What specific course of action should you take?

AGREEMENTS WITH NONPROFESSIONAL STAFF MEMBERS

Most agencies and schools employ nonprofessional staff members, such as clerical and janitorial staff. All nonprofessional staff members (as well as other professional and paraprofessional staff) must be fully aware of the ethical obligations of professional counselors and must be fully informed of their specific obligations to ensure the ethical rights of clients. Both the ACA and APA ethics codes state that counselors are ethically responsible to guarantee that there is no breach of ethics by staff members under their direction. In-service (in agency or within school) ethics training with staff members is highly recommended. A formal written agreement between counselors and their staff members is also recommended; this assigns a formality and importance to matters of ethical sensitivity. A breach of ethics could, and in some cases should, lead to termination of an employee who knowingly breaks the rules. Staff members should be especially sensitive to the client's right to privacy and confidentiality. Use of temporary staff or temporary agency workers should be avoided—such workers may work at the counseling site for short periods and may be replaced prior to adequate ethics training.

ADVERTISING

It was once considered unprofessional for highly educated professionals to advertise or solicit for clients. Professional codes of ethics banned lawyers and doctors from advertising. Legal challenges to these ethics code edicts were successful, and today radio and TV advertisements for doctors, lawyers, health service providers, and mental health professionals are common. A 1987 survey of psychologists found that about one-fourth of the respondents advertised in newspapers and similar media (Pope, Tabachnick, & Keith-Spiegel, 1987).

Deception is the major issue related to advertising and soliciting clients. The ACA and APA codes caution practitioners and define deceptive advertising as unethical. Examples of deception include: (1) a master's-level, licensed professional counselor who earns a doctoral degree from a bogus degree program (or a degree in a field unrelated to counseling) and lists the doctorate as a professional qualification (Dattilio, 1989). A counselor who lists himself as a Ph.D. candidate or claims to have completed "Ph.D. studies," although not technically a misrepresentation, certainly is being deceptive—such status does not necessarily lead to attainment of the degree and may mislead the public. (3) A counselor who lists bogus, unrelated, or unfinished degrees as credentials is deceptive and is misrepresenting his legitimate (acceptable), professional counseling training.

Additionally, the ACA code requires that client testimonials be solicited only from clients who are not vulnerable in any way related to consent. Counselors should avoid making global statements related to the nature or success of treatment, such as "loving care," "your way to health and happiness"—counselors cannot guarantee that they will care in a loving way for *all* of their clients, nor should they guarantee that *all* clients will be "happy" once services are provided

(happiness may not be the acceptable outcome!). Trying to defend oneself against a client's claims that he or she did not feel happier after services, for example, could be a nightmare.

Cautions aside, and given the competitive nature of the health enterprise today, it may serve a counselor well to advertise. However, advertising should be prudent, tasteful, and free from global statements or guarantees that cannot be substantiated by professional literature or objective data.

If a counselor sells products in addition to providing services, such products should be advertised in a way that accurately depicts the product or service. It is quite legitimate for a counselor to sell relaxation audio- or videotapes to clients for use in the privacy of their homes. However, in many places a formal retail sales license is needed to sell products, and local laws must be examined to ensure there is nothing illegal with selling such products. Counselors should limit the sale of products to the purview of their professional license. Selling health aids for matters unrelated to mental health might be easily challenged by a client who is disenchanted by the product; such sales may constitute a potentially detrimental relationship. If a counselor sells vitamins or cleaning products as a sideline, selling such products to clients may infringe on the professional relationship. It is important to keep the role of the professional counselor clearly delineated.

Counselors employed in two or more settings should also avoid soliciting clients from one agency or setting of employment to another—for example, a counselor employed by a school should avoid soliciting clients for a private practice while in the role of a school counselor.

CREDENTIALS

For the professionally motivated individual, there is nothing more rewarding than earning a degree and being able to list degree initials after one's name. Once licensure status is earned, professionals can add additional letters after their names, such as L.P.C. for "licensed professional counselor." Professional certification by legitimate, professional certifying bodies offers a counselor another way of distinguishing himself or herself. The National Board of Certified Counselors (NBCC) and the Commission on Rehabilitation Counselor Certification (CRCC) allow individuals to list

NCC or CRC after their name to signify certification. It is common to see the initials M.A., L.P.C., N.C.C. after a counselor's name on correspondence, in case files, on letterhead, and on professional business cards. Counselors are proud to list such credentials. It is wise to list credentials in case file information to distinguish if services were provided by a counselor or other mental health professional, such as a psychiatric nurse, clinical psychologist, social worker, physician, or family therapist. In some cases, it is unnecessary to list all credentials—one does not have to present a resume with every letter of correspondence. A listing of basic credentials is sufficient. And in case files, it may be sufficient and prudent to list initials or titles associated with the professional license, for example "L.P.C.," or "Licensed Psychologist." Counselors must not misrepresent their credentials. Also, it is unacceptable for a counselor to state that one is licensed without providing information on what kind of license he or she holds. There should be no question as to whether a person is a licensed counselor, psychologist, social worker, nurse, family therapist, or physician.

Although professional memberships can be announced in correspondence, membership itself should not be held out as a credential, unless the association has a special designated membership level. For example, the American Association for Marriage and Family Therapy (AAMFT) has a "clinical member" category, which requires the member to have intense, approved supervision after receiving a degree. AAMFT "clinical membership" is a sought-after status and is a well-recognized credential.

Credentials in the mental health field are a dime a dozen. Literally anyone can set up a certification body and charge a fee for a fancy diploma. Use of such credentials to mislead the public about the competence or qualifications is highly dubious and reflects badly on the counselor and the profession (see Chapter 2). Such credentials may not stand the test of a court challenge in defense against incompetent practice or malpractice as a specialist. Generally, only credentials with linkages to legitimate professional organizations are valued in the mental health field. Beyond the NBCC and the CRCC, two examples of acceptable counseling credentials are those offered by (a) the National Academy of Certified Family Therapists (which has linkage to the ACA through its affiliate, the International Association for Marriage and Family Counseling), and (b) the "Certificate in Clinical Hypnosis" sponsored by the Ameri-

can Society of Clinical Hypnosis. Agency and school administrators should communicate which credentials are acceptable or valued and how, when, and where acceptable professional credentials are to be displayed or listed.

QUESTION FOR REFLECTION

A counselor lists on his business card that he is a certified hypnotherapist, but provides no further information. Is this unethical? If so, why?

MAINTENANCE OF RECORDS AND FILES

Offices sometimes become sloppy. It is not unusual to visit a professional counselor's office and to feel that it is "lived in" (to put it nicely). Although a professional office may feel like home to many, there are serious differences between professional and nonprofessional offices. Client records, unlike personal records, need to be protected. They should be filed in a safe place and locked away when not in use. Files should not be left out in the open, especially after work hours or when other clients are in close, visual contact.

It is standard procedure to destroy records a certain number of years after services have been terminated. Most licensure boards require that records be kept a certain period of time after services have been terminated for legal reasons (e.g., in case there is an ethics complaint). Records are generally kept for five to seven years after services have been terminated. Disposal of records is not as simple as just throwing them in the trash—records should be destroyed in a way that removes identification or by shredding. Old bills, office notes, and calendars should also be destroyed in a way that ensures privacy.

Counselors should also have policies about removing files from the office. Some agencies have strict policies that forbid removal of files from the office, which can be a dangerous practice—a file in a briefcase can be stolen, files may be left in an unsecure automobile, and a counselor's family members may have access to files in the home setting. Obviously, this is not good ethical practice. Counselors should have a compelling reason to remove a file to an unsecured environment.

COMMUNICATIONS WITH OTHER PROFESSIONALS

Communication with other professionals can take several forms. Communication occurs among the professionals within an agency and with professionals outside of the agency. Schools also have internal and external means of communications, primarily between counselors and teachers or administrators.

Clear agency or school guidelines should be established for intra- (within) agency/school communications, with the client's best interests at heart. Most agencies have general statements of confidentiality that allow for internal communications among professionals, such as counselors, psychologists, psychiatrists, and social workers on staff. Schools, however, may have policies that prevent the communication of sensitive counseling material to teachers or administrators without compelling educational or safety-related reasons. The prudent course of action is to keep confidential information as confidential as possible within a school or agency setting. Clients should never be the brunt of gossip in a teacher's lounge, nor should agency personnel know more than they need to know in regard to interactions with clients. However, there are cases that require cross-professional involvement—for example, between a psychiatrist and a counselor who are both involved with a client. Generally, clients should know when such interaction is necessary and the reasons for consultation. In most cases, special consent is not necessary for within-agency or school consultation; however, local and federal laws should be examined to assess if special obligations exist (see Chapters 13 and 18).

Communications with professionals outside of an agency or school are governed by rules of confidentiality and privacy. Formal consent should be obtained—confidentiality and privacy statements signed by the client at the outset of treatment should describe circumstances under which a counselor can communicate to other professionals in the best interests of the client (as in emergency situations). If ongoing formal consultation is requested, the counselor should have a formal agreement with the consultant allowing for such interaction—for example, a private practitioner might have an agreement with another private practitioner to discuss difficult cases. To ensure that professional feedback can occur without a breach of client rights, counselors can develop a consultant agreement that allows for detailed discussion of cases, perhaps without identifying information. Such agreements are in no way reflective of a supervisory or controlling relationship and simply allow for professional communication on challenging cases.

When a counselor makes a referral, he or she cannot receive remuneration for the referral. Such payment could compromise professional judgment, leading to referral to the remunerating professional for less than professional reasons. Counselors should refer to a list of qualified professionals rather than to one professional and allow clients to choose from the list on their own after researching their options. Counselors must consider the legal ramifications of referrals. Attorneys sometimes "shot-gun" lawsuits—broadly "shooting at" (suing) any involved professional. If a professional to whom a counselor referred a client does something wrong, the client's lawyer might sue the counselor as the referring agent.

QUESTION FOR REFLECTION

You are a professional school counselor employed in a secondary school. At lunch in the teachers' lounge, you overhear one of your counseling colleagues and a teacher discussing the family problems of a student. There is some laughter involved. What should you do?

DISAGREEMENTS WITH EMPLOYERS OR SUPERVISORS

Professional counselors sometimes have disagreements with employers, administrators, or supervisors. It is important to have a clear understanding of the role of the supervisor and the role of the supervised counselor. If the supervision is for professional licensure or certification, both parties should sign a formal supervision agreement (Remley & Herlihy, 2001). Such an agreement should spell out the responsibilities of both parties, the amount of time and the place where supervision is to take place, the nature of job duties covered by the supervision, the ethical obligations of the supervisor and supervised counselor, the nature of legal responsibility for work that is accomplished, the requirement of malpractice insurance and coverage on the supervisor's policy, an agreement on how the supervision can end (e.g., the circumstances and actions that can lead to a negative recommendation by the supervisor regarding licensure or certification), and the length of the proposed supervision. Failure to clarify details on such matters can lead to difficulties if there are disagreements. Supervised counselors should also have some understanding about what to do if they question the ethical judgment of their supervisors. An arbitration arrangement to address disagreement is one way to avoid conflicts—that is, if there is disagreement, an arbitrator acceptable to both parties is consulted to make a judgment on the acceptable course of action (Remley & Herlihy, 2001, offer a "Clinical Supervision Model Agreement" that serves as an excellent example of licensure supervision).

Conflicts with administrators sometimes are more problematic. If a noncounselor administrator establishes policy that conflicts with the conventional ethical wisdom of the profession, counselors have an obligation to educate the administrator. Administrative policies are sometimes crucial to the effectiveness of counseling—for example, an administrator may require that a number of clients too large to accomplish effective group counseling should be scheduled for group sessions. Counselors may be assigned a caseload that is too large to provide competent services; equipment and supplies may be out of date; facilities may be inadequate. A number of administrative issues can become problematic; counselors are obligated to address the problems with the people in charge. If changes are not made to ensure adequate, competent, and ethical services, a counselor should examine other employment options. However, the counselor's primary responsibility is to try to inspire changes within the organization according to both the ACA and APA ethics codes.

Counselors also have an obligation to prevent discrimination. If it appears that administrative policies are such that certain constituents are singled out, denied services, or treated unfairly, it is the counselor's obligation to address concerns with the administration. Both the ACA and the APA ethical codes have stipulations about nondiscrimination.

CHAPTER SUMMARY

Privacy issues should be utmost in the design of a professional office. Soundproofing, separate entry/exit doors, and maintaining privacy of client files are issues of importance. Offices should be organized to provide for the safety of clients and staff. In space-sharing arrangements, counselors must ensure the privacy of all client files and other case-relevant information. For-

mal, written ethics agreements between parties are recommended. Counselors must make provisions for individuals with disabilities: elevators in storied buildings, wheelchair accessible bathrooms, and accommodations for hearing or visually impaired clients. Offices that receive federal funds must be in compliance with accessibility standards.

Several systems are available for fee setting: (1) sliding fee scales; (2) flat fee, variable collection procedures; (3) low fee cash-only service, and (4) credit/debit card payments. Regardless of the fee and billing procedures, counselors must have a clearly articulated fee schedule and stick to the schedule. Clients must understand the procedures at initiation of treatment. Fraudulent billing is a major concern related to billing. Billing for services that were not provided or justified is fraudulent practice. Double billing can result in felony convictions for insurance fraud, a loss of license to practice, and censure from a professional organization. Overdiagnosing also constitutes insurance fraud and can do harm to clients.

All nonprofessional staff must be fully aware of their ethical obligations. Counselors are ethically responsible to guarantee no breach of ethics by staff members under their direction.

Counselors must avoid deception in advertising. Client testimonials should be solicited only from clients who are not vulnerable in any way related to consent. Counselors should avoid global statements they cannot guarantee. Counselors must not misrepresent their credentials. Use of credentials to mislead the public about competence or qualifications is highly dubious.

It is standard practice to destroy case records a certain number of years after services have been terminated, generally five to seven years. Records should be destroyed in a way that removes identification or by shredding.

Communication with other professionals can occur among the professionals within an agency and with professionals outside the agency. Clear guidelines should be established with the client's best interests at heart. Most agencies have general statements of confidentiality that allow for internal communications. Communications outside an agency or school are governed by rules of confidentiality and privacy.

It is important to have a clear understanding of the roles of the supervisor and the supervised counselor in case of disagreements. Agreements should spell out the responsibilities of both parties.

REFERENCES

Anderson, B. S. (1996). *The counselor and the law* (4th ed.). Alexandria, VA: American Counseling Association.

Association of State and Provincial Psychology Boards. (2001). *Ethics, law and avoiding liability in the practice of psychology.* Montgomery, AL: Author.

Cummings, N. A. (1998). Moral issues in managed mental health care. In R. F. Small & L. R. Barnhill (eds.). *Practicing in the new mental health marketplace: Ethical, legal and moral issues.* Washington, D.C.: American Psychological Association.

Dattilio, F. M. (1989). Fraudulent degrees: A threat to the mental health counseling field. *Journal of Mental Health Counseling, 11,* 151–154.

Gibson, W. T., & Pope, K. S. (1993). The ethics of counseling: A national survey of certified counselors. *Journal of Counseling and Development, 71,* 330–336.

Lien, C. (1993). The ethics of the sliding fee scale. *Journal of Mental Health Counseling, 15,* 334–341.

Pope, K. S., Tabachnick, B. G., & Keith-Spiegel, P. (1987). Ethics of practice: The beliefs and behaviors of psychologists as therapists. *American Psychologist, 42,* 993–1006.

Pope, K. S., & Vasquez, M. J. T. (1991). *Ethics in psychotherapy and counseling.* San Francisco: Jossey-Bass.

Remley, T. P., & Herlihy, B. (2001). Ethical, legal, and professional issues in counseling. Upper Saddle River, NJ: Merrill/Prentice Hall.

Woody, R. H. (1989). *Business success in mental health practice.* San Francisco, CA: Jossey-Bass.

PART IV

Ethical Challenges and Emerging Issues

CHAPTER 9

Ethical Issues in Health Care

Vilia M. Tarvydas
Barbara O'Rourke
Christine Malaski

Objectives

After reading this chapter, you should be able to:

- Discuss the health care issues that affect counseling practices and the resources that assist counselors in helping their clients face these issues.

- Explain the basic forms of managed health care and the ethical impact of managed health care on counselor practice in the areas of counselor competence, informed consent and confidentiality, fidelity, integrity, diagnosis, conflict of interest, and business relationships.

- Define the term "biomedical ethics" and summarize information from the bioethical literature that is relevant to counseling.

- Discuss the ethical aspects of the bioethical issues involved in genetics, hastened death (euthanasia, rational suicide), abortion, complementary and alternative medicine, HIV, fertility choices, cancer, and organ transplantation.

INTRODUCTION

In recent years, we have seen a trend in Westernized medicine toward a more holistic and comprehensive system of health care. This trend includes turning to types of care once considered alternative, as well as including family, community, and other aspects of an individual's life into health care plans. As this trajectory continues, counseling is seen as both healing art and science, and is becoming a more integral part of traditional health care. Concurrently, as the field of health care incorporates counseling as an important aspect of healing, counselors are integrating physical aspects of care into their practice. Counseling services now are acknowledged widely as being effective for clients who are experiencing certain types of physical problems.

Rehabilitation counselors, mental health counselors, and social workers have been educated to provide counseling service to people with acute and chronic health conditions and have been doing this type of work for years. In the precedent set by these disciplines, it is becoming more common to see counselors as part of a health care team in such a wide range of settings as family health agencies, rehabilitation facilities that assist in recovery from disabilities such as head or spinal injury, chemical dependency treatment centers, and pain clinics. Counselors in these settings provide supportive services like training in stress management, teaching coping skills, and coordinating the educational needs of young clients. In fact, major funding sources such as insurance companies and other third-party payer systems are demanding a more comprehensive, interdisciplinary approach to treatment. Thus, the practices of both medicine and counseling are shifting, and the requisite skills and abilities needed by all disciplines for sound practice are also expanding.

Mental health care is practiced increasingly within the context of medicine and biomedicine whether or not counselors practice directly in a medical or health care setting. All community-based counselors are likely to encounter clients who are facing health or medically related issues. School counselors see students who are considering abortion. Employment and rehabilitation counselors see people who are HIV-positive and struggling to deal with employment discrimination. Most counselors see people with mental disorders who are on medications and are using some type of complementary medical therapy. In the future, all will see the unknown impacts of genetic advances on the lives of the clients they serve.

MANAGED CARE

Health care reform continues to evolve in response to the escalating and devastating costs of health care. Cooper and Gottlieb (2000) presented a historical perspective of the emergence of the managed care movement, the evolution of managed mental health care, and the goals and key concepts involved in this health care reform. The types of service in managed care organizations (MCOs) typically take several forms. Organizations that participate in managed care include (a) health maintenance organizations **(HMOs),** which provide specified health services using a restricted group of providers at a fixed cost to the consumer; (b) preferred provider organizations **(PPOs),** which purchase health care from specific providers at a discounted rate; and (c) independent practice associations **(IPAs),** which allow consumers to choose independent practitioners, but retain a portion of the fees from providers who may be reimbursed either on a fee-for-service or capitated basis (Shore, 1996). The aim of managed care is twofold: (a) to limit the treatment to that required to return a client to a reasonable level of functioning as soon as possible, but not necessarily to deal with the underlying clinical illness; and (b) to address the secondary goal of prevention, on the theory that preventative care will reduce the overall cost of health care.

Reactions to managed care systems in the health care industry have been mixed. Strong ethical concerns and considerations have been generated in the area of mental health (Cooper & Gottlieb, 2000; Glosoff, Garcia, Herlihy, & Remley, 1999). Benefits for managed care consumers and counselors have been identified as (a) limited cost of services compared to traditional indemnity plans, (b) increased access to necessary mental health services, (c) no exclusions due to a pre-existing condition, (d) increased referral rate for some practitioners, and (e) establishment of quality control and monitoring of standards of practice (Lawless, Ginter, & Kelly, 1999). Disadvantages often noted include (a) a limited choice in health care providers, (b) an inability to consult a specialist directly, (c) a reduction in the variety of services available, (d) the potential for overuse of pharmacological interventions, (e) a limited treatment duration for some diagnoses, (f) the increased potential for overreliance on outpatient services, and (g) the use of a gatekeeping system. In the gatekeeper procedure, the managed care vendor often assigns the client to a care provider or dictates treatment options before their approval in an effort to control costs.

Nevertheless, managed care appears to be a reality that is here to stay. The questions then become, "What form will it take?" and "How will this form affect client care?" Hersch (1995) said, "It is time to move beyond our hurt, fear, and anger. It is time to become creative and adaptive by fully using the substantial repertoire of professional skills available" (p. 16) to assure quality client care. Counselors must be informed about managed care and involved in shaping the principles of managed care to provide sound, ethical care to clients. Despite whatever dissatisfaction, ambivalence, or resistance to managed mental health care that counselors may have, they may find it difficult to survive financially if they choose not to participate in such systems (Lawless, Ginter, & Kelly, 1999). This situation results from the fact that a majority of the U.S. population likely will obtain its future health care through some form of managed health care organization. Jensen, Morrisey, Gaffney, and Liston (1997) reported that in 1995, 73 percent of those receiving their health care through private health insurance did so through some type of managed care.

Elements of managed care continue to impact the ethical landscape of counseling. Cooper and Gottlieb (2000) cited several ethical issues in managed mental health care that must be addressed: (a) counselor competence, (b) informed consent and confidentiality, (c) fidelity, (d) conflict of interest, and (e) business relationships.

Counselor Competence

The obligation of counselor competence as mandated by the ACA and APA codes of ethics requires that counselors strive to maintain the highest level of professional services, and neither claim nor imply professional qualifications exceeding those they possess. Counseling practice in a managed care setting may present relevant questions regarding several aspects of a counselor's competence. One implication is that counselors must be trained adequately to appropriately select, diagnose, and treat clients in a managed care situation. The counselor must be able to identify who is appropriate for services, for what kind of treatment, and under what circumstances. Typically, managed care has resulted in more medical services, including mental health services, being rendered on an out-client or nonhospital basis. Moreover, brief, more cost-effective therapy modalities are the treatment of choice for numerous conditions within managed care situations.

With this context in mind, Haas and Cummings (1991) offered practice guidelines for out-client services. These authors said that practitioners must develop competency in the use of brief therapy and in their ability to screen the needs of prospective clients. They recommended that practitioners should be able to identify prospective clients who are appropriate for managed care treatment by using both exclusion and inclusion criteria. They offer a summary of criteria and examples from current literature (Figure 9–1).

Counselors who plan to practice in a managed care setting must demonstrate specific, requisite skills for being successful within that setting. Due to the advantages and disadvantages of managed care, counselors may be encouraged to provide services that are outside of their area of competency (Lawless, Ginter, & Kelly, 1999). Counselors should remember their individual professional codes of ethics and strive to uphold the ethical standards in provision of services. Moreover, counselors should be aware of specific skills that would assist them in facilitating success within a managed care environment, including effective communi-

Exclusion
1. Could not benefit from brief therapy, or requires other treatment modalities
   Examples: individuals with delirium, dementia, and active psychosis
2. Unable to attend to the process of verbal interaction
   Examples: clients with acute panic disorder and schizophreniform disorders
3. Possesses a characteriological style that precludes enduring the counseling work
   Examples: a history of repeated suicide attempts, entrenched alcoholism, and chronic obsessional phobic reactions
4. In sum, presents with chronic anger, psychopathy, organicity, or psychosis

Inclusion
1. Capacity to relate—at least one significant attachment
2. Psychologically minded
3. Motivated
4. Has adaptational strength
5. Presents with a clear-cut concern that has emerged at identifiable points in time

FIGURE 9–1. Criteria for Selection of Managed Care Outpatients
Source: From "Managed Outpatient Mental Health Plans: Clinical, Ethical, and Practical Guidelines for Participation" by L. J. Haas and N. A. Cummings, 1991, *Professional Psychology: Research and Practice, 22* (1). Copyright 1991 by the American Psychological Association. Adapted by permission.

cation and knowledge of business principles. Being business savvy is a definite asset to a counselor who wishes to practice in managed care. In addition, many managed care organizations encourage the use of brief therapy strategies. Counselors should learn these techniques for use with their clients in the managed care environment (Lawless, et al., 1999). However, not all clients may benefit from brief therapy approaches. Counselors must be able to evaluate clients critically to determine if brief services would be beneficial or if the client would be harmed more from brief services than if no therapy services were provided (Glosoff et al., 1999). Counselors must be aware of their own professional limitations and institute appropriate agency referrals for clients who require services outside of their professional competence.

When a managed care organization questions or challenges a counselor's decision-making process with regard to diagnosis and treatment, the counselor must

Counselors who work in a managed care environment should know:
1. The diagnostic categories within the *Diagnostic and Statistical Manual of Mental Disorders* (4th ed) (DSMIV)
2. The standards of professional practice for providing treatment of various clinical problems
3. Managed care terminology
4. The factors that impact client satisfaction with counseling and managed care services
5. The procedures for billing and reimbursement for services provided
6. The procedures to follow when a client's counselor is not available and the client requires services
7. How to balance the needs of the managed care organization in accessing confidential client medical records
8. How effective treatment plans develop
9. Recordkeeping procedures that are consistent with the counselor's area of professional expertise and fulfill the requirements of the managed care organization
10. How to obtain ongoing training to demonstrate continued competence in the counselor's area of expertise
11. Effective practice management strategies in the areas of billing, reporting, and basic accounting procedures
12. How to collect and maintain outcome and effectiveness data
13. Counseling philosophy to provide to potential clients and the managed care organization
14. How to work as a part of a team in a cooperative manner

FIGURE 9–2. Counselor Knowledge and Skills Needed in a Managed Care Environment

Source: Adapted from "Managed care: Ethical considerations for counselors" by H. L. Glosoff, J. Garcia, B. Herlihy, and T. P. Remley, 1999. *Counseling and Values, 44*(1). Copyright 1999 by the American Counseling Association, and from "Managed care: What mental health counselors need to know" by L. Lawless, E. J. Ginter, and K. R. Kelly, 1999. *Journal of Mental Health Counseling, 21*(1). Copyright 1999 by the American Mental Health Counseling Association. Adapted by permission.

be prepared to present empirical support as evidence of her clinical judgment. The counselor needs to present the information in language that can be easily understood and will be accepted by the managed care organization (Glosoff et al., 1999). Figure 9–2 lists the requisite knowledge and skills for competent counselors who practice in the managed care environment.

Counselor competence for short-term treatments requires that counselors must be prepared and able to focus on achievable, specific treatment goals, and to be active and more directive in conducting treatment. Short-term treatment should not be considered long-term therapy conducted in merely a more abbreviated time frame; it comprises a unique set of skills. Clinicians must be trained for this approach and provide only treatment that falls within their personal scopes of practice as determined by appropriate training and experience. They also must be fully informed and competent in facilitating appropriate client referrals.

Informed Consent and Confidentiality

Although information management is always of critical importance to the counselor, it is even more so within the context of managed care. Data tracking is crucial to both accessing and using the managed care system. Consequently, this necessary exchange of information presents problems and limitations for counselor-client confidentiality, especially given the increasing use of computerized data and facsimile exchanges of information. While accurate and full disclosure by both the client and the counselor is vital to the counseling process, disclosure must now occur in a climate where information can be used to withhold or dictate services. Recordkeeping is a formal process often dictated by managed care systems that threatens a client's autonomous rights by curtailing limits and decreasing an individual's freedom of choice. Counselors must provide their clients with comprehensive informed consent regarding limitations to confidentiality. Observers have noted that clients must become more assertive and carry greater responsibility for their own care under MCOs. The professional-client relationship requires more attention to maintain the necessary levels of trust needed to be effective under these more difficult conditions (Murphy, 1998). The potential limitations on a counselor's ability to retain confidentiality must be fully disclosed to the client before establishing a counseling relationship.

Due process is significant ethically in that it must include fully informed consent—for example, informed consent should include disclosure of all treatment alternatives that might be most beneficial to the client, regardless of cost or the payer's willingness to provide these services. Institutions must have an ethical grievance process that allows clients to challenge client care decisions in a timely and responsive manner. Patients must also be able to obtain assistance in resolving their problems at an earlier stage—for example, through the use of ombudsman and client assistance programs. There must be processes of appeal that address issues of discrimination and protect people who are disadvantaged within a context of client-centered care, wherein the client's preferences and values are important to the treatment outcome

Fidelity

Ethically, counselors must make themselves aware of the potential effects that a managed care situation may have on the counselor-client relationship and on their own ethical obligation to fidelity. They must minimize any detrimental effects of this care system on the obligation of fidelity to the best of their abilities. The managed care process could have a significant effect on the client's level of trust in the counselor–client relationship. If the client perceives the counselor is sharing private or negative information with insurers or employers through the managed care system, trust will be compromised. The principle of fidelity requires counselors to be concerned with issues of loyalty and faithfulness to the bonds created in this trusting relationship. Similarly, they must honor confidentiality and avoid harming their clients. Given the specific needs of each client, it would be useful and ethically sound for counselors to consider carefully the potential effects of varying forces and intrusions imposed by managed care upon aspects of their relationships with each client. For example, managed care might have an effect on counselors' loyalties and diagnostic and termination practices. If consumers are dissatisfied with the rate of reimbursement, the way in which their case is being reviewed, or their course of treatment, they must be advised of their rights and due process under the policies and procedures of their health care provider and the law in relation to the health care services they receive.

Conflicted Loyalties. The possibility exists that the professional counselor's loyalty could no longer be to the client or even to a professional's peers, but rather to the managers or systems in charge of prior authorization and utilization review of services. The philosophy of managed care demands awareness of limited resources, thereby expanding the counselor's moral role to include concerns about distribution of resources to groups or populations of individuals, as well as to individual clients. Traditionally, counselors have been held to the ethical responsibility of considering their clients' needs above those of others unless direct risk or harm to oth-

ers can be ascertained. Now mental health professionals are challenged to assume responsibility for population-based practice without losing concern for the individual.

This widening of ethical obligation to include more broad concerns about distributive justice for society is a revolutionary emphasis for counselors. Managed care has been recognized as involving at least two conflicting interests: the need for counselors (a) to balance their clients' needs with those of other clients in the managed system; and (b) to balance clients' needs with cost containment and financial resources. In managed care, this balance is usually mediated by an individual in a gatekeeping role, often called the **case manager.** Some authorities maintain that it is important that professionals recognize the overall responsibility for determining such weighty moral questions by challenging the broader community to address these issues through debate and formation of political and social policy. Counselors should participate in this policy debate both individually and through their professional organizations.

Several authors have written about the potential intrusion of the gatekeeper's function into the counselor's ethical analysis and have described the situation as if the managed care representative was present psychologically in the counseling session. Haas and Cummings (1991) offered the opinion that "the symbolic presence of the manager or third party intensifies the issues in vulnerable therapist-client pairs" (p. 49) and stands to erode the trusting relationship in counseling. Almost two decades ago, Pellegrino (1986) warned that "this [gatekeeper] role is morally dubious because it generates a conflict between the responsibility of the [caregiver] as a primary advocate of the client and as guardian of society's resources" (p. 23).

Counseling codes of ethics are clear in their stance that counselors' commitments to their clients come first. Sections in the APA and ACA codes of ethics, for example, protect the welfare of the consumer. However, interpretation of such consumer mandates has become more difficult in the context of managed care. As pressures mount on counselors, the profession will be called on to further clarify ethical standards and practices in managed care settings.

Integrity, Fraud, and Malpractice. The U.S. Justice Department has investigated managed care fraud in cases involving MCOs delaying their reports to Medicare regarding enrollment figures to obtain more capitation fees; embezzlement of capitation fees by MCO plans or subcontractors of the MCO; and specialists who receive "kickback" payments to keep referral rates low (Hallam, 1999). The government has developed new rules in the form of a voluntary compliance program. This program addresses such issues as the MCO's ability to enroll the healthiest individuals in the organization; use of physicians as marketing agents; MCO encouragement or initiation of disenrollment of clients from identified plans; quality of care including critical examination of underutilized services; and data collection and submission (Department of Health and Human Services, 2000; Hallam, 1999).

Diagnosis. Managed care has affected the very definition of mental illness. Counselors' moral and ethical responses to these changes are important, not only for the clients who sit in front of them, but also for all potential clients who may need their services in the future. The importance of diagnosis is heightened in the context of managed care, and labeling through diagnosis can be damaging to the clients. The stigma associated with diagnosis and the use of diagnosis to reduce managed care responsibilities to clients are but two examples of possible damaging effects of assigning a diagnosis to someone. Damage to clients may extend into their futures and include such effects as a decreased ability to obtain a job and insurance coverage, or to have the diagnosis used negatively in a custody hearing or other legal matters. Nevertheless, diagnosis generally has come to be accepted as a necessary process and presents counselors with a significant challenge. Wylie (1995) stated "therapists are increasingly caught in a three-way crunch between diagnostic accuracy (often complicated by ambiguous symptoms), confidentiality, and the power wielded by the insurer, usually around problem diagnoses that are stigmatized" (p. 32). Part of the challenge of appropriate diagnosis to counselors is to clarify the philosophical and moral systems they themselves hold regarding the use of a labeling system in mental health. They must address questions such as whether to use a less severe diagnosis to reduce the effect of labeling on a client. Conversely, they must examine if they have a tendency toward overreporting diagnosing clients' problems to help them qualify for services and to justify gaining reimbursability for services (Bilynsky & Vernaglia, 1998). The counselor is cautioned that such behavior could constitute insurance fraud and result in legal action.

Counselors need to be aware of the temptation to "upcode" or "downcode" a client diagnosis when working in a managed care environment (Cooper & Gottlieb, 2000). A counselor who **"upcodes"** a client diagnoses the client with a more serious or severe diagnosis than the client presents with in an attempt to obtain an increased number of counseling sessions from the managed care organization. A counselor who **"downcodes"** a client gives the client a less serious or severe diagnosis to obtain treatment for that client. For example, if a managed care company does not pay for services for a diagnosis of personality disorder, the counselor may omit reporting the condition and just report the condition. Both upcoding and downcoding are unethical and may be considered fraudulent (Cooper & Gottlieb, 2000).

The Health Care Finance Administration (HFCA), the United States Department of Justice (DOJ), the Office of Inspector General (OIG), and the Department of Health and Human Services (HHS) have become keenly aware of the use of upcoding for certain diagnoses as well as the improper discharge of clients only to readmit them in a very short period of time (Berenson, 1999; Department of Health and Human Services, 2000; Hallam, 1999). Practitioners who have felt limited due to reimbursement rates for a specific diagnosis have been identified as misdiagnosing a client and overdiagnosing or upcoding to obtain an increased number of sessions with the client, or the same amount of sessions, but more revenue due to the upcode. This latter practice is more questionable ethically—it appears practitioner self-interest is the primary motivation for this practice. Conversely, some practitioners have been observed as underdiagnosing clients to receive increased reimbursement and rewards from the MCO (Hallam, 1999). In a very stark sense, these pressures cause the counselor to struggle with the question of whose standards will establish the diagnosis—those of the professional or those of the MCO. Ethically, it is very clear that the responsibility for objective and honest professional diagnostic and treatment services rests with the counselor.

In defining *mental illness* as impaired functioning, the proponents of managed care have challenged the traditional definition and, subsequently, its traditional treatment goals. In some systems, this shift may deprive clients with certain diagnoses (such as personality disorder) of longer-term services. The managed care treatment model opts for minimal levels of acceptable function over maximizing the quality of life as its desired outcome. The *Diagnostic and Statistical Manual,* Fourth Edition (DSM–IV-TR, 2000) classification system is the required, primary diagnostic schema used by managed care corporations. This requirement has been accused of providing a mechanism for narrowing and constricting treatment and has been adopted as the official justification for denying "medical necessity"

(Wylie, 1995). Further, this system of diagnosis is incompatible with some orientations, such as systems theory and the psychosocial rehabilitation philosophy, which seeks to demedicalize or depathologize functional limitations and to focus on an asset-based model.

According to Kutchins and Kirk (1987), the original development of a diagnostic system in mental health was done for reasons of enhanced communication and not for economic purposes. However, the current thrust of the DSM system is fiduciary access. This means that payment of services often depends on the type of diagnosis according to this nomenclature. Moreover, to use this system of diagnosis accurately requires the evaluation and use of organic/physical information that is typically beyond the counselor's expertise. If these assumptions are true, diagnosis requires consultation or the collaborative effort of a physician or psychiatrist and a counselor when treating a client.

The DSM–IV-TR classification system's multiaxial approach was developed to facilitate this collaborative effort as a means to include the biological and psychosocial aspects of mental health. However, the reality in practice often results in an imbalance in the importance given to diagnoses placed under certain axes. For example, the use of V codes as "conditions that may be a focus of clinical attention" (DSM–IV-TR, 2000) is often not seen as significant for treatment and, therefore, is not reimbursable by managed care. This barrier to treatment may be applied to other diagnoses as well. Diagnoses that typically may not be reimbursable include adjustment disorders, personality disorders, and disorders that require long-term treatment such as post-traumatic stress disorder.

Even when the diagnosis itself is not in question, the current diagnostic system presents ethical challenges to counselors. For example, problems may arise concerning limitations of confidentiality and the ramifications of new technology with interconnecting computer data banks and Internet networking capabilities. Wylie (1995) asserted that "many diagnoses can still shadow a client's life like hounds from hell and much more efficiently in the cyberspace age than ever before" (p. 32). Clearly, counselors must work at all levels—personally and politically—to address these dilemmas. They also must know and understand their institutions' information management systems and policies so that they can best protect their clients' confidentiality and provide accurate informed consent.

Kutchins and Kirk (1987) offered counselors a list of suggestions to guide their use of the DSM classification system. A modified version of their list is provided in Figure 9–3.

- All diagnoses should be made with scrupulous regard for correct procedures. Know your boundaries of competence.
- Careful attention should be paid to organic conditions. Work in conjunction with a physician or carefully review all medical reports.
- A physician should be routinely consulted about the medical aspects of a diagnosis.
- Every diagnosis should be accurately reported to the client and to the insurer. Further, the client should be fully informed about the potential ramifications of using the diagnostic label before its use in formal documents.
- Patients should be advised, preferably in writing, that no diagnosis is meant to indicate a definitive judgment about any physical condition.
- Patients should be referred to physicians for the evaluation of any medical condition.

FIGURE 9–3. Procedures for Using DSM–IV System
Source: From "DSM–III–R and Social Work Malpractice" by H. Kutchins and S. Kirk, 1987, May, *Social Work.* Copyright 1987 by the National Association of Social Work. Adapted by permission.

Termination. Ethical guidelines for terminating a counselor-client relationship state that counselors should not abandon their client unless the client (a) no longer needs services, (b) is not benefiting from services, or (c) is being harmed by continued service. Responsible counselors inform their clients of these possibilities before counseling begins. Nevertheless, a potential conflict may arise when counseling services are no longer sanctioned by the client's managed care system and the financial assistance for the service is terminated. This problem is particularly pressing if a financial burden is potentially harmful to the client. The counselor must choose among several alternatives: (a) offer pro bono services, (b) provide alternatives that do not involve a financial burden (e.g., community or support groups), (c) negotiate referral, (d) challenge the managed care system, (e) offer continued services on a sliding-scale fee or variable collection arrangement until the client is stabilized, or (f) continue services at the present fee or a reduced fee to be paid directly by the client.

The counselor's advocacy on behalf of the client and the client's self-advocacy are paramount when such conflicts of interest arise. Proficiency in these advocacy roles requires educating clients to learn to advocate for themselves through skill-training interventions, as well as building the professionals' knowledge and skill base so they might become more proficient in systems advocacy skills. Problems of inappropriate or premature termination may occur more frequently under an increasingly prevalent managed care system, and they will continue to impose moral dilemmas for both counselors and their clients. In many codes of ethics, the professional's obligation to advocate for her clients with the MCO may not rise to the level of an enforceable ethical standard. However, some authorities on ethical issues in MCOs think that mental health professionals must become involved in both individual and systemic advocacy to improve the welfare of their clients, the public, and our professions (Acuff et al., 1999). In fact, the professional counselor must consider whether there may be a "duty to appeal" that would involve not just passively informing clients of their right to appeal adverse decisions within the MCO system, but rather to actively educate and support clients in appeals. From this more radical viewpoint, the counselor might initiate an appeal on behalf of the client when that approach is more effective or timely.

Revisions of current ethical codes will need to include guidelines for counseling practice that assist the counselor in allocating resources that facilitate client advocacy in these situations. The counseling profession and the governmental regulatory bodies must ensure that managed care techniques are implemented in a way that protects clients, the integrity of their relationship with their counselor, and the well-being of the profession itself.

Efforts to preserve the appropriate ethical role of the counselor include the development of appropriate procedures to reduce conflict in at least three ways: (a) developing practice guidelines that have been established at a higher policy-making level, (b) increasing the role of clients in the decision-making process, and (c) establishing a well-structured appeals process for clients who disagree with treatments or termination decisions.

Conflict of Interest and Business Relationships

In the managed care system, the counselor fulfills the role of the service provider as well as the managed care organization employee, even if the counselor is an independent practitioner. Working within a managed care environment places the counselor in the middle of potential competing interests (Cooper & Gootlieb, 2000). In this type of situation, the counselor is caught between advocating for the client who may require additional services and supporting the mission of the MCO to contain costs. In this ongoing situation, the practitioner has an ethical obligation to address conflict of interest issues with the client and the MCO to resolve the conflict.

Counselors must first clearly understand the difference between medical ethics and business ethics (Mariner, 1997). During their academic education, counselors are presented with information on professional ethics and medical ethics; however, they may have limited or no exposure to business ethics. Business ethics differ from medical ethics. Traditional medical ethics focus on the physician/patient relationship. However, in a managed care environment, these relationships are often much more complex. Managed care organizations do much more than provide medical care. They are an intricate blending of insurance, management, and health care delivery. The managed care organization does not provide the care per se; rather, health care professionals do (Mariner, 1997).

Counselors need to be mindful of the fact that the managed care organization is just that—an organization, not an individual or a profession with a history of professional ethics (Mariner, 1997; Taryvdas & Peterson, 1999). Therefore, ethical principles that are applied consistently to a variety of health care professionals are not applied easily to the managed care organization. Practitioners utilize evidence-based models of care. This differs from the managed care approach of utilizing actuarial models to examine health and illness.

To provide services in a managed care organization, counselors are typically required to sign a legally binding contract (Cooper & Gottlieb, 2000). These contracts may be filled with business and legal issues that are unfamiliar to the counselor. Counselors must read these documents with a critical eye and seek outside assistance in areas of uncertainty. Counselors are guided by professional ethical standards and need to make certain the managed care organization is aware of their ethical obligations. Should conflicts arise, counselors should take steps to resolve the dispute in a responsible and professional manner. Gag clauses, no-cause termination, utilization review, hold-harmless clauses, and indemnification clauses are all issues that the practitioner may have to deal with when working with a managed care organization. Counselors need to be aware of their professional rights and responsibilities in each of these situations (Cooper & Gottlieb, 2000).

Practitioner's Ethical Obligation to Self-Educate. Do you, as a counselor, understand the terms *capitation, utilization review, case rate, health maintenance organization, mixed model, management services organization,* and *independent practice association?* If not, you should consider updating your managed care language. Counselors are now required to have command of a new set of terms and acronyms such as PPO (preferred provider organization), PPA (preferred provider agreement), HMO (health maintenance organization), and UR (utilization review). With more frequency, clients are also presented with these terms and abbreviations and are often unaware of their meanings or their importance.

A study completed by the Center for Studying Healthcare System Change found that only 30 percent of health care consumers were able to correctly identify four basic health plan features of their managed care organization (Greiner, 2001). These four basic plan features include 1) whether consumers must choose from a provider network; 2) whether payment is provided for any of the cost out-of-network care; 3) whether the consumer must sign up with a primary care provider; and 4) whether referrals must be obtained for a referral for specialty care. These results indicate that many health care consumers lack a basic understanding of how their managed care plan can be utilized to their benefit. That deficit may have an impact on their ability to make informed health care decisions. Therefore, practitioners not only have an ethical responsibility to have a solid understanding of managed care practices themselves, but also have an obligation to educate and inform their clients of the complex information they need to know about the managed care organization. This information can assist clients in making effective decisions about cost and quality of care. If clients fail to effectively understand how their individual health plan can work to their benefit, their satisfaction and ability to independently access care can be compromised (Greiner, 2001).

Service providers should be able to describe basic managed care organization features, including (a) whether clients must choose from a provider network; (b) the plan's payment for out-of-network care; (c) the necessity of signing up with a primary care provider; and (d) whether or not a referral is necessary for specialty care (Greiner, 2001). Practitioners must be cautious not to facilitate further unjustified negativity on the part of their clients. This attitude only fuels the public backlash directed toward MCOs, which reflects decreased trust due to cost constraints, explicit rationing, and negative media coverage (Mechanic, 2001).

Practitioners should be able to evaluate managed care contracts effectively prior to entering a managed care agreement. Practitioners must determine if the financial or other mechanisms present within the managed care organization are consistent with their ethics and values of providing competent and compassionate care (Jecker, 1998). This includes providing care to clients in a manner that is not time-constrained. In addition, professionals should ensure that clients will not be denied clinically effective treatment services. If the organization indicates that payment will be on a capitated basis, professionals must determine if they will be able to provide quality care under these constraints.

Individuals who are considering practicing in a managed care environment may benefit from speaking with a colleague currently working in this environment. They may also benefit from review of the work of Cooper and Gottlieb (2000) and Acuff et al. (1999). These articles can provide the practitioner with a variety of situations that address informed consent, payment for services, approval/denial of services, and MCO involvement in treatment planning and implementation. Practitioners must be always mindful of their fiduciary relationship to their client.

BIOETHICAL ISSUES

The integration of health care services has created a new ethical landscape for all parties, including the counselor who participates in the health care system. Ethical, political, and social norms create a new complexity within this environment for counseling practice. Counselors who work in a health care setting are expected to operate within the prevailing biomedical model. All responsible counselors should be well informed about these far-reaching issues. Analysts of popular culture characterize the close of the 20th century as the "information" or "digital" age to acknowledge the profound effects of the vast pace of information generation and exchange on the evolution of society and culture. It seems clear that biomedical and health care advances—and, more importantly, the ethical challenges they pose—will be a profound force on contemporary society and culture during the first part of the 21st century. The ethical guidelines that have developed out of the traditions within the biomedical model are called **biomedical ethics.** (The decision-making climate in which this model is typically embedded was described in Chapter 6.)

According to Beauchamp and Childress (1994), biomedical ethics, a relatively young field, is a way of understanding complexity and examining moral life as it pertains to the biological sciences, medicine, and health care. Biomedical ethics applies general ethical theories for specific forms of conduct or moral judgment to these areas. Thus, this field is a type of practical or applied ethics.

The bioethical issues that most affect counselors include euthanasia, genetic testing, confidentiality of information, abortion, organ transplantation, and fertility choices. Bioethical issues will affect counselors with increased frequency in the future. To deal with these bioethical dilemmas, counselors should be aware of resources for assistance: bioethics centers, consultants, internal agency committees, and other professional colleagues with experience in bioethics.

The following sections consider current bioethical issues in the areas of genetics; euthanasia; complementary and alternative medicine; care of people who are HIV-positive; abortion; reproduction; and organ transplantation.

Genetics

Genetics is an area of science that presents serious ethical questions. Ongoing research in genetics provides new discoveries and challenges on virtually a daily basis. Although advances in genetics may have a positive impact on individuals and society in the future, genetics presently does not necessarily provide clear-cut answers, and it provides us with complex ethical questions (Dalzell, 2001).

Human Genome Project. The Human Genome Project was initially undertaken by the U.S. Department of Energy and the National Institutes of Health. These agencies worked in conjunction with private U.S. and international entities to identify all of the approximately 30,000 genes within human DNA (Human Genome Project [HGP], 2001). The initial draft sequence of the human genome was completed in 2000; the entire project is scheduled for completion by 2003 (Jegalian & Biesecker, 2000).

Genetics is the study of inherited traits, while **genomics** is the study of the entire set of human genes, the assembly of the gene sequence, gene expression, and the relationship between the different gene sequences (Larson, 2000). Researchers are studying normal and abnormal genes to identify the importance of individual genes and the consequences of genetic dysfunction (Jegalian & Biesecker, 2000). By decoding the human genome, researchers will have the ability to uncover the numerous mysteries of various diseases (Larson, 2000; Rieger, 2000).

The goals of the HGP also include storing this information on databases for access and retrieval; developing more effective treatment technologies; and addressing the ethical, legal, and social issues that arise as a result of the project (HGP, 2001). By un-

derstanding exactly how a disease develops, researchers can obtain information about interventions to prevent, reverse, or mitigate current health problems (Jegalian & Biesecker, 2000). However, identifying specific gene codes does not mean there will be a quick eradication to disease or disability. For example, researchers have known about the genetic defect that causes sickle cell anemia since the 1950s. Medications have been developed to treat the condition, but there continues to be no cure. Furthermore, genetic tests can determine genetic mutations present in individuals with cystic fibrosis and Huntington's disease; however, no cures exist for these deadly conditions. Some forms of predisposition to cancer also can be identified through genetic testing. Future researchers hope to be able to ascertain the genetic predisposition to all forms of cancer, heart disease, and diabetes, thus facilitating improved lifestyle changes in environment and diet that may impact disease process and progression (Rieger, 2000). The HGP is the first, large scientific project to address the ethical, legal, and social issues that may arise from the project (HGP, 2001). In addition to the potential benefits to individuals within society, business and industry are scrambling to obtain genome data for application development (HGP, 2001).

Genetic Testing and Counseling. The future of genomics and genetic testing necessitates that counselors become educated regarding current developments and be able to explain them to their clients (Larson, 2000). Counselors also need to be prepared to provide counseling services to survivors of individuals who have died as a result of unsuccessful gene repair (Bettelheim, 2000).

Genetic testing is a broad term that describes specific techniques that seek the presence of genetic mutations or altered gene proteins, which may indicate a genetic condition or a predisposition to disease (Rieger, 2000). In the past, genetic counseling was most often utilized with individuals interested in ascertaining genetic risks as they relate to reproduction. However, current genetic tests are utilized to ascertain predisposition to some forms of cancer as well as physical characteristics and behavioral traits that are within the range of normal human variation (Rieger, 2000; White, 1999). Despite these advances, genetic testing for cancer is not recommended at present because only 5 to 10 percent of cancer is inherited (Tufts University, 1998).

To assure that testing services are utilized in an appropriate fashion, comprehensive genetic counseling is

- Obtain an accurate family history and confirm diagnosis before testing.
- Provide information about the natural history of the condition and the purpose of the test.
- Discuss the predictive value of the test, the technical accuracy of the test, and the meaning of a positive or negative test.
- Explore options for approximation of risk without genetic testing.
- Explore the patient's motives for undergoing the test, the potential impact of testing on relatives, and the risk of passing a mutation on to children.
- Discuss the potential risk of psychosocial distress to the patient and family, even if no mutation is found.
- Explain the logistics of testing and fees involved for testing and counseling.
- Discuss issues involving confidentiality and the risk of unemployment and insurance discrimination.
- Describe the patient's medical options, the efficacy of available surveillance and prevention methods, and recommendations for screening if test results are negative.
- Provide a written summary of the content of the counseling session.
- Obtain informed consent for testing.
- Provide test results in person and offer follow-up support.

FIGURE 9–4.   Guidelines for Pretest Education, Informed Consent, and Post-test Counseling

Source: From "Genetic testing for disease susceptibility: Social, ethical and legal issues for family physicians" by M. T. White and F. Calliff-Daley, 1999, *American Family Physician, 60*(3). Copyright 1999 by the American Medical Association. Adapted by permission.

essential both before and after testing (White & CalliffDaley, 1999). White and Calliff-Daley (1999) have developed guidelines for pretest education, informed consent, and post-test counseling issues (see Figure 9–4).

Physicians, social workers, and nurses can provide genetic counseling (Parens & Asch, 1999). It is most often performed by master's-degree-level professionals with specific education in genetic principles and training in brief psychosocial counseling. One of the most important ethical practices in the area of genetic testing and counseling is providing individuals with informed consent to engage in genetic testing. Counselors also assist clients in reaching an informed decision about testing and explain how to utilize test results (Parens & Asch, 1999).

Counselors should be aware of the risks and benefits associated with genetic testing and be prepared to share this information with their clients. Risks associated with genetic testing include psychological stress, increased difficulty within family relationships, confidentiality and disclosure issues, and the potential for employment and insurance discrimination. Benefits of genetic testing include emotional relief and reassurance, increased knowledge that may impact future decisions, increased awareness that may impact high-risk behavior, and positive behavior changes (White & Calliff-Daley, 1999).

Each genetic decision is unique based upon individual responses to potential risk and uncertainty within the context of the client's personal values and specific circumstances. The consequences of genetic decisions do not typically impact one individual—rather, they may affect family members directly and society as a whole indirectly. Advances in the diagnosis and treatment of genetic disorders may change perceptions of what is considered a genetic disease or disability (White, 1999).

With all of these considerations in mind, the National Society of Genetic Counselors provides a code of ethics for counselors who intend to practice in this area. Counselors who are interested in knowing more about the code of ethics for genetic counselors are directed to examine the code online at: http://www.nsgc.org/about_code.asp. In addition, White and Calliff-Daley (1999) developed a set of guidelines for pretest education, informed consent, and post-test counseling.

Counselors who provide genetic counseling must understand the three components of the counseling process specific to this area: a comprehensive risk assessment, education, and psychosocial counseling (Jegalian & Biesecker, 2000). Counselors must have a clear understanding of the genetic foundation of the health problem to assist families in determining the risk that a disease will affect future generations (Jegalian & Biesecker, 2000). Upon completion of testing, counselors should provide services that focus on facilitating positive coping mechanisms and psychosocial adjustment within the family. They should also provide information about the disorder and help clients deal with the potential prognosis (Jegalian & Biesecker, 2000).

Genetic information has the ability to impact a client's sense of self and the most basic life decisions regarding career, marriage, and child-bearing (Oktay, 1998). Individuals who are provided with negative genetic testing results may experience guilt that is disproportionate to that experienced with other diseases.

They may apply religious or cultural interpretations to the information, such as viewing the disease as a curse on the family for some past transgression. Genetic counselors should assess their own values, use terms that are as value neutral as possible, provide unconditional support, understand current genetic information, articulate this information clearly to individuals and families, and assist clients in taking action that is consistent with their own values (Parens & Asch, 1999; White, 1999). These factors are essential. Many clients find it quite difficult to make these decisions due to the unfamiliar terminology and the difficulty of comprehending it under increased stress (White, 1999).

Confidentiality of Genetic Information.   One of the benefits of the Human Genome Project (HGP) may be increased awareness of risk factors that an individual can address to prevent disease or disability. However, this information has potential value to employers and insurance companies who may wish to use the information to predict future illness, associated health care costs, and an individual's ability to perform a job (Fuller et al., 1999). Family members and the courts may want access to genetic information in child custody cases. Thirty of the fifty states have current legislation to protect against potential insurance discrimination related to genetic information. Educational institutions may also want access to genetic information. Some individuals fear that genetic testing information may fuel a reemergence of the eugenics movement.

At present, genetic information has been used in discrimination against individuals in the areas of medical benefits and employment (Fuller et al., 1999). Current legislation attempts to protect genetic information by not having it placed in a client's regular medical record (Larson, 2000). In addition, the federal Privacy Act of 1974 provides safeguards for health, research, and other records that are in the possession of federal agencies. This statute protects individuals who have genetic testing at any federal agency. However, it does not cover testing by private entities. Even so, there have been instances in which appropriate disclosure without the consent of the individual was allowed (Fuller et al., 1999).

The Health Insurance Portability and Accountability Act of 1996 does not allow the categorization of a genetic predisposition as a pre-existing condition. The Act prevents insurance carriers from using these factors to deny or limit health care coverage for members of a group insurance plan. Further, it denies insurance carri-

ers the opportunity to charge different rates based on an individual's genetic information (Oktay, 1998). Genetic discrimination based on access to genetic information is wrong because individuals are unable to change their hereditary characteristics (Peters, 1996). States with specific state legislation that protects genetic information require written client consent for release of genetic test results. Legislation continues to be proposed and debated in Congress to prevent discrimination that results from genetic testing. However, lobbying efforts from the insurance industry, pharmaceutical manufacturers, and biotechnology companies often oppose such legislation (Oktay, 1998).

In 2000, former President Clinton signed an executive order that (a) prohibits federal employers from requesting genetic testing as a pre-employment requirement or as a method for obtaining benefits; (b) prohibits federal employers from using genetic information to classify employees in ways that may limit their professional advancement opportunities; and (c) provides privacy protections to genetic information used in medical treatment and research (HGPI, 2001). Furthermore, the Ethical, Legal and Social Implications (ELSI) subcommittee of the HGP has committed 5 percent of the subcommittee's annual budget directed toward the development and maintenance of ethical standards regarding genomic discoveries and information (HGP, 2001). Fuller et al. (1999) developed recommendations to protect privacy in genetics research (Figure 9–5).

Genetic Therapies.   **Gene therapy** is an approach used by researchers and medical professionals to prevent, treat, and cure disease processes through the alteration of an individual's genes. This technology is in its infancy and human clinical trials have been limited (Human Genome Project Information, 2001). Researchers have been unsuccessful in correcting disease and disability despite the work completed on the Human Genome Project (Parens & Asch, 1999). Gene repair, also known as *chimeraplasty*, is an evolving form of genetic therapy. Within the last 10 years, researchers have conducted clinical trials to treat genetic diseases through replacement of the faulty genes that cause the diseases. These trials have produced limited success in a few individuals (Ebersole, 2001). As of this writing, no researcher has attempted to utilize gene therapy to correct genetic flaws in a fetus. However, researchers predict success in this area soon (Parens & Asch, 1999).

The Federal Drug Administration and the National Institutes of Health are under fire from the U.S. Senate to

- Privacy protections for experimental research data in which health care is not delivered should exceed the protections established for medical records. Rules for third-party access to medical records should not be uniformly applied to experimental research data.
- Researchers should not place individually identifiable experimental research data not utilized in health care research in the medical record.
- Informed consent for research participation should include information about all potential disclosures of research information and the nature and magnitude of risks from such disclosures. Adequate measures to ensure compliance and punish violations should be in place.
- Current practices to protect confidentiality of experimental research data should be studied and best practices should be developed.
- Protections similar to Certificates of Confidentiality should be developed to protect research subjects from compelled disclosure of research results.
- Research participants should have access to experimental research data except when:
  a. The information includes information obtained under a promise of confidentiality, is about another person, and patient inspection would cause harm to another individual;
  b. Access to the information may reasonably be expected to endanger the life of physical safety of the research participant or anyone else;
  c. Access would break the "masking" of the study or otherwise significantly interfere with the conduct or results of the study; or
  d. The research results are of unproven clinical validity, and the institutional review board has judged that there is no benefit to the research subjects. In such circumstances, the informed consent must explicitly state that individual research results will not be shared.

FIGURE 9–5. Recommendations to Protect Privacy in Genetics Research

Source: From "Privacy in genetics research" by B. P. Fuller et al., 1999, *Science* (5432) *285,* 1359–1360. Copyright 1999 by The American Association for the Advancement of Science. Reprinted by permission.

provide adequate informed consent, especially concerning the serious side effects that have been experienced by patients in experimental clinical trials as a result of gene therapy over the last seven years (Bettelheim, 2000).

Counselors can anticipate being confronted with the following ethical questions in the area of gene therapy (Human Genome Project Information, 2001):

(a) What is "normal" and what constitutes a disability, and who is to make this decision? (b) What are diseases, or disabilities, and should they be prevented or cured? (c) How can we meet the financial needs of individuals who desire gene therapy, which are beyond what many individuals can afford? (d) Who should obtain these services and at what cost? (e) Does the search for a cure for specific disabilities for individuals who may be diagnosed in the future have a negative impact on those currently living with a disability?

QUESTION FOR REFLECTION

Counselors must consider their ethical responsibilities related to a new potential variant of the duty to warn. Imagine that a client has genetic testing for a specific condition, tests positive, and has siblings. The client does not wish to inform her siblings of the test results about the hereditary genetic condition and the fact that they are likely carriers of the condition. As a result, the siblings do not know that the condition can potentially be treated with medication. In such a scenario, the counselor must examine beneficence related to the possibility of breaching confidentiality (Leung, 2000). What actions should be taken?

Eugenics. **Eugenics** has been described as the use of a scientific strategy for orchestrating human evolution through methods of encouraging transmission of "desirable" traits and discouraging transmission of "undesirable" traits (Suzuki & Knudtson, 1990). The concept of eugenics dates back to the 1800s. This movement accelerated under the direction of Sir Francis Galton, a mathematician and the cousin of Charles Darwin, who began promoting the concept as early as the 1860s. Early proponents believed it was important to increase the number of people with desirable genetic traits through selective reproduction of individuals of high intelligence and moral character. Such a strategy was thought to reduce and possibly eliminate problems in the general population that were associated with low intelligence and moral character such as crime, alcoholism, and poverty (National Center for Genome Resources, 1997). By the late 1920s, 29 U.S. states had adopted legislation that forced sterilization on over 10,000 individuals who were identified as mentally retarded or alcoholic, or who possessed criminal tendencies. The interest in eugenics that was prevalent in the early half of the 20th century declined as a result of the horrific genocide and genetic engineering activities of the Nazis during World War II (National Reference Center for Bioethics Literature, 2001).

Scientists and clinicians hope that currrent and future advances in gene therapy and genetic counseling, screening, and testing will enable them to facilitate positive change in the lives of individuals. However, these great capabilities challenge our society to never repeat the destructive excesses of the eugenics movement. Such advances raise major moral and ethical questions related to changing human genes, performing genetic testing for a specific diagnosis when no cures exist, performing genetic testing to determine the presence of a disabling condition in utero for purposes of aborting such a "defective" fetus, and ethical and legal issues in the confidentiality of genetic information (National Reference Center for Bioethics Literature, 2001).

Hastened Death and Euthanasia

Euthanasia and other forms of hastened death are the most significant and polarizing social issues of our time (Albright & Hazler, 1995). **Hastened death** is a broad term that refers to any process by which people speed up the dying process, including suicide, rational suicide, euthanasia, and aid-in-dying (Werth & Holdwick, 2000). Historically, the first references to these practices occurred in the Hippocratic Oath (Emmanuel, 1994) and it has remained an issue with varying degrees of intensity since that time. Both the scholarly literature and codes of ethics in counseling have remained largely silent on these critical issues.

The term *euthanasia* is derived from two Greek words that mean "good death" (Beauchamp & Walters, 1989). Inadequate and often unclear definitions of euthanasia have been noted throughout the literature. This definitional problem has affected public perception of the issues surrounding euthanasia, as well as research and professional writing. This problem also has encumbered the resolution of the ethical and legal status of this important issue. Terms that describe euthanasia typically have been based on three criteria: (1) the basis of intention to die, (2) the nature of the critical action involved in effecting the death, and (3) the consent of the person requesting death. Qualifying terms have been used to distinguish these elements: *passive* or *indirect euthanasia* and *active euthanasia*. Either of these approaches can be classified as voluntary or involuntary. Emmanuel (1994) argued that while such definitional distinctions may be useful, the joining of each qualifier with the emotionally charged word *euthanasia* confuses moral judgment and distorts subsequent public and political debates. However, a clear definition is important to professional counseling research and scope of practice.

Passive euthanasia is the practice of withdrawing or withholding life-sustaining treatments. Legal rulings consistently support such practices under certain conditions. According to Emmanuel (1994), the medical literature demonstrates a rising consensus supporting the ethical appropriateness of such actions. For example, the ethical principle of double effect has evolved. **Double effect** is the idea that unacceptable consequences such as death are deemed acceptable under certain circumstances. This stance supports the use of medication for pain relief in terminal conditions, even if it shortens a person's life. Such a decision highlights the propensity toward beneficence over nonmaleficence as the guiding ethical principle in these circumstances. Another example of this concept is the common practice of do-not-resuscitate (DNR) orders for certain terminal clients. However, as Beauchamp and Childress (1994) pointed out, the debate is not over. These authors suggest that the distinctions between treatment and nontreatment are untenable and should be replaced by the distinction between obligatory and optional means of treatment. Such a conceptual framework would serve to offer a more adequate rationale for any given choice of action.

Beauchamp and Childress (1994) also considered the omission-commission distinctions regarding treatment. They concluded that the decision to stop treatment is often perceived as more momentous and consequential to the caregiver than the withholding of treatment. For example, the initiation of treatment can create expectations and imply responsibility on the part of the caregiver. However, Beauchamp and Childress (1994) argued that "paradoxically, the moral burden of proof often should be heavier when the decision is to withhold than when it is to withdraw treatments. In many cases, only after starting treatments will it be possible to make a proper diagnosis and prognosis" (p. 198). Either approach potentially can lead to the over- or undertreatment of clients. These authors suggested that such decisions should be based on the client's welfare and rights, which include a balanced consideration of the benefits and burdens of the treatment.

Advanced directives are health-related decisions obtained from a person before that person's loss of competence. The initiation of this legal process is based on ethical and legal considerations of individual autonomy. There are two types of advanced directives: "(1) **living wills**, which are specific substantive directives regarding medical procedures that should be provided or forgone in specific circumstances, and (2) **durable power of attorney (DPA)** for health care, or proxy directive" (Beauchamp & Childress, 1994, p. 242). The DPA allows individuals to select substitute decision makers who are empowered to make health care decisions on their behalf should they be incapacitated.

Active euthanasia or *mercy killing* or *assisted suicide,* is the intentional termination of life. Justifications for such actions are grounded in the principle of beneficence with regard to the person who delivers the lethal means, and in the principle of autonomy with regard to an individual's right to make the decision to end her life. Conversely, it has been argued that such acts are violations of nonmaleficence. Assisted suicide is legal in the state of Oregon as a result of the Oregon Death with Dignity Act and subsequent U.S. circuit court and Supreme Court rulings. The Netherlands has permitted assisted suicide for a number of years (Werth & Holdwick, 2000). At the same time, acts of suicide or attempted suicide have been decriminalized throughout most of the United States, creating a paradoxical situation in the minds of some persons.

The voluntary-versus-involuntary distinction is a means to further qualify the dying individual's degree of contribution to the decision. Voluntary status assumes that individuals elect and actively seek their own time and manner of death. Involuntary decisions are much more controversial because the individuals facing death have no active part in the decision making, due to being comatosed or otherwise incapacitated.

Ethical decisions regarding euthanasia and hastened death typically center on three key ethical principles: autonomy, beneficence, and nonmaleficence. Most discussions and writings in this area have been about the role of physicians or the role of a significant other. Either, or both, typically serve as the agent who delivers the means to death. However, counselors may be in a special position to understand the wants and needs of both the client and the client's family regarding this decision. Counselors are very likely to face issues of hastened death in their work. Surveys show that between one-fourth to one-third of nonpsychiatrist mental health professionals can expect to have at least one client die as a result of suicide during their careers (Rogers, Gueulette, Abbey-Hines, Carney, & Werth, 2001). Therefore, a counselor's contribution to a debate regarding the relevance of any guiding ethical principle to a client will be significant.

Many dying clients and their families face inadequate counseling, emotional support, and pain control. Counselors must address these inadequacies, along with the ethical issue of euthanasia. First, counselors must identify and reconcile their personal biases and values regarding related issues (e.g., death and quality of life with chronic or terminal illnesses) before working with clients and their families. Decisions about euthanasia more often are shaped by the personal values of the parties to this ethical and personal dilemma rather than by law. The recognition and reconciliation of issues of diversity—cultural, familial, and individual—are vital to sound ethical practice. This recognition requires an ongoing effort by counselors to better understand cultural and religious views of life and death that may be different from their own. For example, some Eastern religious traditions view death as a means to enter a blissful spiritual state. Counselors must be intimately familiar with the decision-making context of any individual facing such a decision. In all forms of hastened death, the counselor must make one very critical assessment—determining whether the client is clinically depressed or suffering from any other serious mental or cognitive disorder that may impair her judgment. Such disorders can seriously impair the client's ability to engage in rational decision making (Siegel, 1986). The counselor must ensure that the client's condition is evaluated properly, either directly by the counselor or by referral to a competent psychiatrist or psychologist. Counselors must clarify their own roles in providing assistance to clients and families as they consider euthanasia. Counselors' primary ethical charge is their obligation to respect the integrity and promote the welfare of the client. Understanding euthanasia and the arguments for and against it are important building blocks in a sound, ethical decision-making process in all areas of hastened considerations.

Arguments for Euthanasia. According to Beauchamp and Childress (1994) and Emmanuel (1994), four basic claims currently support euthanasia as a legitimate health care intervention. These arguments are based on (1) the principle of autonomy as an *a priori* principle; (2) the primacy of the principle of beneficence; (3) the assertion that passive euthanasia is an acceptable practice and that no real distinction between active and passive euthanasia exists; and (4) the argument is based on utility, which supports rules that promote the most favorable consequences for the largest number of people.

According to the first claim, the cultural context of the United States is based on individualism and self-determination; the rights of an individual are viewed as paramount. In this culture, these rights, including the right to die, clearly are supported by the ethical principle of autonomy. The essence of this right is a belief that all individuals must be given the opportunity to determine what is good and valuable in life. This determination includes the right to determine the time and manner of one's own death. Enactment of this

1. Requests should be made by a competent person on several occasions and in writing.
2. A thorough examination should be made to rule out or treat any prevailing psychological condition.
3. The act of assistance should be restricted to certified physicians who will not receive compensation for their work.
4. Careful documentation with reference to alternative treatments should be offered to the person.
5. All cases should be reported to an official body.

FIGURE 9–6.   Elements of Ethical Procedural Safeguards for Euthanasia

Source: From "Euthanasia: Historical, Ethical, and Empirical Perspectives" by E. J. Emmanuel, 1994, September 12, *Archives of Internal Medicine, 154.* Copyright 1994 by the American Medical Association. Reprinted by permission.

right rests on individual consent and assumes that obligations for action naturally follow this right. Put another way, rights form the justified basis of obligations.

Second, based on the duty to do good embedded in the principle of beneficence, euthanasia is seen as an acceptable way to end a life that would probably inflict more pain and suffering. In other words, euthanasia could be considered humane. This benevolent act has been sanctioned socially through the practice of refusing or not providing life-sustaining interventions. In fact, Brock (1992) claimed that such an opportunity may provide individuals with psychological insurance against anxiety over anticipated pain and suffering, and therefore is an integral part of a trusting relationship between a client and care providers. If this claim is accepted, euthanasia would not be considered separate from other alternatives of care. In fact, there has been discussion of broadening the claim of best interest to include the welfare of an individual's family, a controversial perspective.

The third argument proclaims that there is no distinction between active and passive euthanasia. An act and an omission are viewed as equivalent. Withholding life-sustaining care shares an equal intention of assisting in death. Arguably, there is no moral difference in the final results.

Finally, the utility argument suggests that rules should promote the greatest good. Proponents of this claim argue that bad consequences of euthanasia are remote and speculative. However, these proponents contend that tight procedures based on careful analysis and review will be necessary to prevent ill effects. Figure 9–6 presents safeguards for ethical euthanasia.

Arguments Against Euthanasia.   Six primary claims appear in the literature arguing against euthanasia as a sanctioned medical intervention. These arguments include (1) the overextension of the concept of autonomy, (2) the idea that legalization should not be promoted on the basis of beneficence, (3) the ethical distinction between active and passive euthanasia, (4) the potential to extend the practice to the noncompetent or nonconsenting, (5) the intrusion of the courts into the private realm, and (6) the potential for bias based on gender or disability.

John Stuart Mill (1910) warned that not all voluntary acts are justified by the principle of autonomy. Opponents of euthanasia use the analogy of voluntary slavery and argue that not all independent desires are justifiable. Further, they argue that satisfying preferences must not be confused with a legal right to autonomy. In other words, there can and should be boundaries of acceptable behavior. Consequently, withholding life-sustaining measures is clearly distinct from actively facilitating death.

Similarly, remote acts of beneficence that occur in rare cases of assisting the end of suffering do not justify the legalization of these acts in general. Opponents of euthanasia claim that traditional medical practice has not provided adequate treatment of pain and suffering. Therefore, the boundaries between acceptable and unacceptable conditions of pain and suffering have not been defined. In sum, an acceptable practice of euthanasia could undermine the pursuit of a health care goal of well-being.

In fact, some opponents say there is an ethical and true distinction between active and passive euthanasia based on the intentionality of the caregiver. Euthanasia could undermine the trust inherent in the healing relationship as well as the laborious provision of compassionate care. Potential healing might be supplanted by a view of killing as healing.

The potential exists for the natural and logical extension of arguments for euthanasia to include vulnerable and unprotected individuals such as incompetent, comatosed, or mentally deficient clients; children; and other disempowered people. This is known as the **slippery slope argument.** Beauchamp and Childress (1994) describe this effect as the "progressive erosion of moral restraints" (p. 231). They contend that a move in this permissive direction might be used as an argument to decrease the burden on a family or society, to eliminate individuals who have a perceived diminished quality of life based on a disability, and to consequently modify attitudes toward the respect for life.

The more direct political argument against legalizing practices of euthanasia parallels the abortion debates and warns against the intrusion of the courts into private matters of health and death. Such intrusions are deemed inevitable to ensure sound, procedural safeguards for such practices; therefore, they would be unavoidable if the practices of euthanasia were legalized.

Finally, there are serious concerns that hastened death may be a response the individual selects due to external influences, the expectations of others, or to being seen as a severely damaged or devalued person. Wolf (1996) cautioned that the debate regarding the use of euthanasia has been incomplete and the actual practice must not precede a more complete analysis. Before deciding to legitimize a euthanasia process, several salient variables must be examined. Gender is prominent among these factors. Wolf (1996) began this analysis and observed that women may request euthanasia at a higher rate than men. Women also seem to seek euthanasia for different reasons. These choices may be more related to the needs of others than relief from personal pain—an aspect of the valorization of women's propensity to self-sacrifice. Finally, Wolf questioned how the image of woman as the candidate for euthanasia may affect the public debate.

The public perception of persons with disabilities as a burden to society and the people around them has been a central concern of disability advocates and scholars for some time. Olkin (1999) reviewed "the burden literature" appearing since 1990 about people with disabilities and was struck by the volume of this work and the tendency to discuss the burden as attached to the person rather than the disability. This type of work and that of the popular media may play into prejudices and set the stage for making disabled individuals view themselves and their very existence as an overwhelming burden, thus influencing them to select euthanasia. Another potential danger is a growing perception that life with a disability is a worthless and negative existence, and a drain on limited resources, thus setting the stage for a climate that encourages severely disabled people to eliminate themselves. In such a cultural climate, parents who receive genetic tests that indicate their baby will have a serious disability may elect an abortion. While movement from such general concerns to charges of genocide—targeting persons with disabilities—may sound rather far-fetched, one need only read Friedlander's (1995) chilling and fascinating account of the evolution of the Nazi genocide, in which thousands of persons with disabilities were subjected to "euthanasia." It is important to

1. Keep current on the developing legal, social, and ethical information related to euthanasia.
2. Determine what culturally influenced moral theory, personal biases, and personal perspectives guide your practice. Continue to clarify personal beliefs and values.
3. Become adept at the skill of self-reflection. Assess your ethical decision-making process, understand it, and use it to deal consistently with issues.
4. Examine, understand, and reconcile institutional protocols, legal precedents, and liabilities.
5. Obtain differing professional perspectives.
6. Be knowledgeable about the potential course, prognosis, and all treatment alternatives related to a client's illness.
7. Be familiar with all contextual factors that may be influencing a client—e.g., who constitutes the client's support system and what are these individuals' perspectives?
8. Seek to understand clients by exploring their world.
9. Act as a resource person and empathic listener. Assist clients with psychic and physical pain. Provide support and maintain substantial autonomy.
10. Help clients understand the importance of various personal and formal documents associated with the end of life.
11. Be available to comfort significant others after a death has occurred.

FIGURE 9–7. Counselor Implications

Source: From "A Right to Die? Ethical Dilemmas of Euthanasia" by D. E. Albright and R. J. Hazler, 1995, *Counseling and Values, 39*. Copyright 1995 by the American Counseling Association. Reprinted by permission.

understand how such prejudices may develop into initially unthinkable results.

Implications for Counselors. Counselors may find themselves in a unique position of helping clients and their families during the decision-making process regarding euthanasia (Figure 9–7). Several authors have been particularly helpful in preparing counselors to engage in this process with clients (Albright & Hazler, 1995; Humphrey, 1991).

Rational Suicide

Much of the preceding discussion of euthanasia pertains to the area of rational suicide as well. In this form of contemplated death, the individual does not receive the means of death from the hands of another, but rather

Box 9.1   Criteria for Assessing Adequacy of Rational Suicide Decision

1. Has the person met the general requirements for receiving aid-in-dying (e.g., in Oregon: a diagnosis, by two physicians, of a terminal illness with a prognosis of 6 months or less)?

2. (a) Does the individual have the capacity to form reasoned decisions about his or her health care? (b) Has the person engaged in a sound decision-making process, considering all alternatives?

3. Is the person making the decision voluntarily or are there subtle or overt coercive pressures influencing the decision?

4. Is it possible to facilitate conversation among the suffering person and his or her significant others to make the dying process easier on all involved?

Source: J. L. Werth, & D. J. Holdwick. (2000). A primer on rational suicide and other forms of hastened death. *The Counseling Psychologist, 28,* 511–539.

ends her own life. More specifically, **rational suicide** is defined as "following a sound decision-making process, a person has decided, without being coerced by others, to end his or her life because of unbearable suffering associated with a terminal illness" (Werth & Holdwick, 2000, p. 513).

In their rulings on cases concerning physician-assisted suicide, the Ninth and Second Circuit Courts of Appeals ruled that laws prohibiting physician-assisted death were prohibited in the state of Washington (*Compassion in Dying v. Washington; Quill v. Vacco,* respectively). Those decisions were appealed to and ruled upon by the U.S. Supreme Court. At that time, ACA filed an *amicus curia* ("friend of the court") brief with the U.S. Supreme Court in conjunction with several other organizations. They took positions that spoke to the mental health issues involved in hastened death and supported the circuit court decisions (Werth, 1999). The U.S. Supreme Court eventually ruled that people who are terminally ill do not have a constitutional right to physician-assisted suicide, but that only the states could decide whether to allow such activities. For counselors, however, the ACA brief made an important statement—that clients who are terminally ill, mentally competent, and facing an imminent and inevitable death should be able "to choose the manner and hasten the timing of their death" (Brief of the WSPA et al., 1996, p. 2). Mental health professionals can play an important role in discussing this issue with people who are considering physician-assisted suicide. They can determine if the person has a mental disorder that would impair decision-making ability. Professionals can also determine if the person was unduly

pressured by others to make this decision, and if significant others were sufficiently involved in discussions leading up to the decision. These points closely parallel the necessary criteria for assessing if an individual is capable of making a decision concerning rational suicide (see Box 9.1).

In a survey of mental health counselors about their attitudes toward rational suicide, over 80 percent were moderately supportive of the idea that people can make decisions for themselves to undertake rational suicide as their best option (Rogers, Gueulette, Abbey-Hines, Carney, & Werth, 2001). This is a concern for the counseling profession because the ACA Code of Ethics and Standards of Practice does not provide sufficient guidance for counselors facing this type of client concern. It supports counselors' responsibility to respect the dignity, welfare, and autonomy of the client, yet seems to require counselors to violate confidentiality when disclosure is needed to protect the client from clear and imminent danger. Counselors must think carefully about what strategies and resources they would employ in such instances. Werth (1999) offers excellent guidelines for these considerations.

Complementary and Alternative Medicine

Natural phenomena began to be measured, understood, and subsequently controlled, in Galileo's time. Empirical science has now become the truth of Western civilization. According to Wilber (1988), this approach became a privileged way of knowing and created a chasm between science and other ways of knowing. Wilber (1988) argued that this gap has served to separate truth from meaning, and what we know about our bodies from whom we believe ourselves to be (our mind and spirit)—fracturing our holistic sense of self from our material body. In Western culture, this divide is exemplified in the current gap among traditional, institutionalized, and nontraditional health care.

Nowhere is this chasm more apparent than when a person is faced with making an important health care decision. In Western culture, science has long been the centerpiece of this type of decision making—the contemporary paradigm of truth. Over the last several decades, the privileged position of science as the exclusive truth in health care has been challenged by practices outside the biomedical realm. Such practices have been dubbed **complementary** (those that work with traditional medicine) and **alternative** (those used instead of traditional medicine). Complementary and alternative medicine **(CAM)** approaches are becoming more popular in health care, resulting in a marked shake-up in the health care world. Recent research has documented the tremendous growth in their use, including the results of a national survey that appeared in the *Journal of the American Medical Association*. The survey revealed that 4 out of 10 people (42%) use some form of CAM (Marcus, 1999). Some of the most frequently used CAMS are relaxation techniques, herbal medicine, massage, chiropractic, spiritual healing, megavitamin therapy, self-help, imagery, energy healing, homeopathy, hypnosis, biofeedback, and acupuncture (Eisenberg et al., 1998).

Proponents of biomedicine (practices based on empirical science) or traditional medical practice have responded to this challenge to biomedical dominance. For some observers, this debate between medicine and nontraditional practices takes the appearance of a full-scale cultural war. Patients are often faced with the dilemma of an either/or choice in health care services. Some practitioners from both sides of the debate have taken entrenched positions, demanding that their patients declare their loyalty and limit their access to other health care practices. Box 9.2 describes the emotionally painful and potentially psychologically damaging effects of such tensions in the life of one woman with a metastasized cancer and those who surround her.

Counselors can play a significant role in assisting individuals who are negotiating their health care choices in this current climate of uneasy acceptance of CAMs.

History of the Health Care Debate. In Western culture and particularly in the United States, biomedicine has political power and influence through legal practices and regulatory statutes. These powers secure the dominance of traditional health care to the exclusion of nonsanctioned practices. Practitioners of biomedicine historically criticize and thwart practices outside of traditional medicine's defined methods, calling more esoteric therapies "unconventional" and "unorthodox" at best and "irrational" and "dangerous" at worst (Cohen, 2000). Despite biomedicine's central position, there have been overwhelming gains in the number of people utilizing nonbiomedical practices, also known as **holistic care,** in the United States since the 1960s. The Landmark Healthcare Study showed that 42 percent of Americans now use complementary and alternative methods of health care (Eisenberg et al., 1998).

In 1992, the United States Congress created The Office for Study of Unconventional Medical Practices, which mandated the documentation of esoteric health care practices. This enactment resulted in a document entitled The Chantilly Report (NIH, 1994), which systematically categorized these practices. As the use of nontraditional health care practices continued to rise through the 1990s, the Office for Study eventually became designated the Office of Complementary and Alternative Medicine (CAM). This type of health care was granted full legitimacy when the National Center for Complementary and Alternative Medicine at the National Institutes of Health was formed in 1998. It now seems undeniable that the use of nontraditional medical practices is here to stay and their use is on the rise.

The *1999 United States Census Reports* documented that the United States has increased greatly in racial and cultural diversity. With this diverse population has come a wide range of cultural health care practices, further enhancing the tension between traditional and nontraditional health care practices. The clash of cultures and shift of paradigms are creating significant concerns for those who assist individuals in making health care choices. Questions are arising, such as: Who is effective? What is safe? How can my healers work together? Whom do I trust? To answer these and other questions, consumers must address and understand the relevant legal, ethical, and moral issues.

Legal Issues Related to CAMs. An increasing number of cases involving CAM practices are emerging in the court systems (Cohen, 2000; Studdert et al., 1998). As the legal system increasingly interfaces with health care in general, and CAM practices in particular, the landscape of healing practice is taking new shape.

One controversial part of the current health care landscape is the system of credentialing and sanctioning practitioners. Regulatory mechanisms such as certification and licensure can be an important avenue for

Box 9.2   A Counselor-in-Training Learns about Complementary and Alternative Medicine

Working on a hematology/oncology inpatient unit has its inspirational and heartbreaking moments. I feel the best part of my job is the patients with whom I have the privilege to work. Cancer in itself is a word that strikes many emotions. Working with cancer patients has presented me the opportunity to experience the hardest of emotions and learn the importance of assisting people facing a life threatening disease. Certainly I have learned the importance of patients having a positive relationship with the medical staff. At times I can see the looks of fear and discontentment among the medical staff. It scares me to think of how these reactions affect the care patients receive. Not very long ago I was confronted with a situation in which staff let their personal beliefs and attitudes interfere with the care a patient received.

With every admission, information is conveyed to the floor that helps us provide the best environment for a given patient. In this case we admitted a 40-year-old female with metastasized breast cancer who had a history of the condition for over a year. As noted on her admission orders she was to be seen for a first time evaluation of her cancer, which seemed odd given her year-long history. On arrival the patient was off to numerous diagnostic tests and I served as her floor liaison, escorting her about the hospital. I had been informed of the specifics of her case, which usually entailed only the diagnosis and reason for admission. Before I left the floor I got the impression that something was unique to this situation. As I inquired into the nurse's reaction to interviewing the patient, she revealed that the patient had been self-administering treatment for the past year. Nothing seemed odd about that until the nurse revealed the patient's occupation as a naturopathic healer. The immediate reactions of the staff were disbelief and criticism, for the patient's approach challenged every treatment principle practiced within our institution.

Walking into the room with a wheelchair, I confronted the fiancé of the patient. He diligently helped prepare the patient for her journey, lifting her by himself and putting her in the wheelchair. The patient could not stand or lift her legs without assistance. She displayed a flat affect and appeared physically and emotionally exhausted. The fiancé accompanied us to each test and along the way we conversed about the hospital as well as about their long, four-hour journey to the hospital. They remarked on the massive size of the hospital and how it was the first time they had been to the area. It was clear to me they both felt overwhelmed and out of place, which is a typical feeling of first-time patients I have encountered. The patient's family was four hours away and relying upon information conveyed through the fiancé. At the final test, the fiancé left to contact the patient's family to see about their safe arrival in town, and the two of us proceeded on to the diagnostic station.

As I waited for the completion of a test, the technician and I could not help but notice the unusually great number of doctors that were assembling about the diagnostic facility. It was hard not to be distracted by the gathering, for they were animatedly discussing the patient's case. The discussion was one of astonishment and skepticism. In their eyes, this patient had broken every principle by which they practiced. The comments were none too kind or sympathetic to the patient's condition. A consulting physician to the case conveyed his intention to confront the patient on the absurdity of her treatment approach and beliefs. It was clearly apparent to me that their skepticism would be conveyed to the patient. It was then that I left the situation to return to the floor, for my shift had just ended.

What followed was a clear display of unethical behavior by medical professionals. In fact, I left work that day shattered by the thought of the medical staff approaching the patient with the hostility and the disregard I had witnessed. On my return to work a few days later, the patient's situation was emotionally better because her family had visited and she continually received cards and words of encouragement from numerous supporters. The mocking never stopped, but her acceptance of medical treatment aided in decreasing her discomfort and increasing her quality of life. What kept this patient going through this whole ordeal was her supporters. Their strength and support showed me that she was not alone and it made quite an impression upon the staff.

continued

Box 9.2   A Counselor-in-Training Learns about Complementary and Alternative Medicine—*continued*

Personally, I may not have agreed with the patient's beliefs and alternative approach, but I felt that this opinion should not impede me from effectively assisting her at the current time. I feel she had already taken a big leap by coming to our institution and that our job was dependent upon establishing her need for consultation. In approaching this situation and others similar to it, I feel it is important to respect the wishes of the patients and become knowledgeable concerning their chosen approach as well as assist them in understanding the way in which I practice.

The use of complimentary and/or alternative treatment methods (CAMs) is a very hot topic in the medical and professional world. In my experience working within this hospital setting, medical professionals who endorse CAMs are typically given a cold shoulder by those who practice traditional treatment regiments or are working independently outside the hospital environment. CAMs present a challenge to the traditional medical community, threatening their typical practices. In their opinion, such practices put patients in jeopardy of the advancement for their cancer. Their major concern tends to be the lack of empirical data or evidence to support these types of treatments. However, many of these practices may be safe and very helpful to clients who use them to supplement, not substitute, for their traditional medical treatments. I feel that medical professionals are entitled to their opinions, yet when it comes to sharing that perspective, it must be done in such a way as to not threaten a patient's psychological and physical well being.

I think the most important bit of advice I can lend in relation to CAMs is to acknowledge their existence. Learn more about them so you can understand the consumer's perspective. I learn something new each day, especially at work. My awareness of this patient's situation helped me understand the right approach and information I needed to have in order to assist her effectively. If I had shut her out and mocked her beliefs, it would only add to her pain and discontent. Shutting out the use of CAMs is no way to handle the situation for it impedes the relationship, inviting stereotypes and bias to impede your judgment of what is best for your client's emotional and physical well being. It is important to handle the situation professionally, meaning that you are aware of your personal values and beliefs and able to appropriately confront clients without doing emotional harm. I think it is important to express your beliefs in a manner that is constructive and conducive to assisting individuals without degrading their beliefs. It is my hope that by doing so, the consumer may come to accept my approach.

Know where you stand on the use of CAMs. This understanding is the first step towards the awareness of your consumer's needs. It is imperative to keep an open mind and not let assumptions or judgments interfere with the care one provides to consumers utilizing CAMs. Imposing your values upon these individuals will, I feel, be met with resistance and will derail any attempt you may have in assisting them to meet their needs. Know who you are and know your limitations. This will help in the conveyance of your approach and contribute to its acceptance by your consumers.

—A Counselor-in-Training

a counselor in determining the legitimacy of a CAM practitioner to whom they may wish to refer a client. However, contemporary credentialing practices are creating some interdisciplinary tension among potential care providers. According to Cohen (2000), health care licensing laws are now being created to regulate CAM practices and are aimed at protecting the public. Such statutes ensure that only those who meet set criteria can legally practice; all others can be prosecuted. This seemingly beneficial move may serve to suppress other means of care, such as indigenous practices. Thus, the licensure system can be seen as creating a kind of paternalism that may fractionalize CAM and traditional medical practices, pitting one against another.

Medicine's legal claim to sole authority to provide healing services is being challenged for these very reasons. Numerous CAM practitioners are also becoming involved in the credentialing process. Cohen (2000) asserted that the desire to protect the public (do no harm) must be balanced against the wish to grant every opportunity for healing (autonomous choice of beneficial care). These are compelling philosophical arguments for a practicing counselor to consider.

Another important legal consideration in our evolving health care environment is the issue of professional liability. This is a particularly salient concern given the relative dearth of evidence on the efficacy and safety of many of the CAM approaches. Two specific examples of liability issues related to CAM practices that the current medical community is facing are referral liability and vicarious liability, including institutional liability. As the medical profession pioneers this legal frontier, counselors should remain apprised of these and other emerging issues as they relate to their own practice.

Referral liability is not a new issue but is one that is further complicated by the lack of coordination between CAM care and traditional medical practices. According to Studdert et al. (1998), an estimated 90 percent of patients using CAM care are not referred by their physician but are, instead, self-referred. A major reason for this lack of referral is the physician's concern about exposure to liability. This area has brought a complex set of concerns to bear on the physician's decision-making process (Studdert et al., 1998). The threat of liability lends substantial weight to the influence of medical paternalism. Physicians must choose between upholding the autonomous decision-making rights of their patients and protecting themselves against potential malpractice litigation.

The same complex dynamic can be extended to health care facilities in the form of **vicarious liability**— an organization's responsibility for the potential negligence of its employees' referrals. Studdert et al. (1998) noted that "hospitals and managed care organizations have a legal obligation to be diligent in selecting, retaining, and evaluating health care professionals; this same obligation will extend to their relationship with alternative medicine practitioners" (p. 1618). By and large, organizations tend to make more conservative choices, potentially sacrificing the rights of the individual to their choice of care options. Cohen (2000) asserted that the development of appropriate institutional protocols relating to CAM modalities includes creative, interdisciplinary rules and policies to govern these protocols.

A final and related legal concern that is relatively new to the courts is the area of third-party reimburse-

ment. Managed care typically seeks to minimize the use of specialists and expensive testing. For example, an insurance plan that offers to cover CAM services may determine that participants should be referred to a chiropractor rather than to an orthopedic surgeon, given certain predetermined indicators. Conversely, failure to refer to and use complementary modalities could constitute legal negligence. Health care in Western culture is, by and large, a capitalist adventure. The tension is real, and economic control is a major route through which a third party can provide self-protection. The actual cost of failure to include CAM care may be to the client in a diminished quality of care.

Ethical Issues Related to CAMs.   The principle of autonomy involves the right of any individual to exercise self-determination. In bioethics, this right refers to the ability to reject unwanted treatment and to make informed choices among treatment options. To exercise the right to self-determine, an individual must have sufficient and reliable information. This type of information traditionally has meant professional disclosure, provision of comprehensive information about any treatment, a state of voluntary choice, and a discernable competence on the part of the client to consent. Practitioners on both sides of the health care debate—both traditional and CAM—are faced with an increasing responsibility to provide opportunities for informed choice by addressing all relevant and available information about a condition and its documented treatments—traditional or otherwise. This information should include discussion of such factors as benefits, risks, consequences, and full disclosure of options of care. Practitioners are urged to share this information in a manner that precludes their own biases and facilitates their clients' informed choices.

The obligation to disclose comprehensive information and to assist an individual in making an informed and autonomous choice is a benchmark of a trusting relationship between practitioners and their clients. The need to maintain a strong working relationship represents the ethical principle of fidelity. When practitioners are not open to a dialogue with clients about viable alternatives under the guise of beneficent care, they create the potential for undetected harm. In fact, Clark (2000) stated that the current status quo is oftentimes, "don't ask and don't tell" (p. 455) by physicians, leading to medical paternalism. Conversely, well-meaning CAM advocates may be denying the role of traditional medicine that may be beneficial or even lifesaving for their clients.

Moral Issues Related to CAMs.   The creation of an atmosphere of dialogue and a sincere move to patient-centered care is essential for quality health care. Individuals must have sufficient and reliable information to make sound health care choices in an atmosphere that supports their personal goals, values, and beliefs.

This supportive atmosphere can be of particular concern for individuals with diverse backgrounds whose health care practices may be disparate from accepted health care practices. Issues of diversity can range from more obvious transcultural situations such as Aruvedic practices (Cohen, 2000) found among Indian cultures, to subcultural practices such as snake handling, which occurs among a population of Appalachian Christians (Covington, 1995). Conversely, adherence to traditional medicine can now be considered a radical approach.

Cancer and CAM Care. Because of cancer's lethal potential, the treatment of cancer patients has often been at the center of the debate between the use of traditional and nontraditional health care practices. Negotiating a diagnosis of cancer and the subsequent treatment stands as a touchstone for other health care decision-making practices. A cancer patient's decisions can literally mean the difference between life and death and/or between a life with a measure of quality versus a life bereft of meaning. According to Marwick (1998), "some 60% of the inquiries the OAM (Office of Alternative Medicine) receives deal with cancer. By far cancer is the largest single condition people ask about. National surveys show that half of cancer patients will use some kind of unconventional therapy" (OAM, p. 1554).

At a Symposium of the American Society of Clinical Oncology and the American Cancer Society in 1999, Dr. Wendy Harpham, an internal medicine physician and a cancer survivor, gave an address to a group of government and academic physicians who had joined to discuss the role of nontraditional approaches with cancer patients. In her address, Dr. Harpham attempted to personalize the current thinking about the use CAM cares in the treatment of cancer by telling her own story and owning her own biases for biomedicine while seriously examining nontraditional options. This account was later published in *CA, A Cancer Journal for Clinicians* (Harpham, 2001).

The summary of this article provides a fascinating snapshot of the prevailing attitudinal environment faced by this courageous individual: "Despite her scientific training and experience in medical practice, after being diagnosed with an indolent non-Hodgkin's lymphoma, [Dr. Harpham] was subjected to intense pressure about alternative therapies from well-meaning friends and relatives. While insulated

at first from these forces, disease recurrences and progression increased her vulnerability to the lure of seemingly gentler approaches. A data-driven study of alternative therapeutic methods, however, convinced [Dr. Harpham] that investigational strategies offered her a better chance of cure or improvement than unproven alternative methods. [Dr. Harpham] offers guidelines for physicians about what patients want, and emphasizes the importance of hope, caring, and information" (Harpham, 2001, p. 131). Dr. Harpham described the emotional and rational vicissitudes that were inherent in her decision-making process. From this experience, she was able to articulate six important factors for physicians (and other health care providers) to consider when helping patients make decisions about their health care. A modified version of these factors offers a good starting place for the development of a respectful approach integrating CAM and traditional health perspectives:

1. Patients want to get well. Establish your role as your patient's ally and advocate.
2. Patients want to avoid pain, distress, poverty, and uncertainty. Offer more than the cold statistics of conventional practices. Help the patient to access all resources to be well informed.
3. Patients want to enhance self-healing. Encourage these efforts. These may include providing information on exercise, nutrition, spirituality, etc.
4. Patients want to feel empowered. Encourage patient participation and active endeavors in their pursuits of health care.
5. Patients want the best possible treatment. Emphasize the strengths of the scientific method, acknowledge the limitations of this same method, and dedicate yourself to narrowing the gap between optimal and actual care.
6. Patients want hope (in fact, need hope). (Harpham, 2001, p. 135)

Dr. Harpham concluded that in the end, if physicians and those who share their biomedical worldview do not address the issue of CAM practices, they are, by their silence, unethically leaving their patients with an unbalanced input about treatment. Although her position represents one of known bias, her overarching goal is representative of sound moral, ethical, and legal practices—that is, the goal of safe, compassionate, and effective integration of health care practices.

Integrative care, which combines conventional and nonconventional therapies in a safe, effective, and appropriate way, is the answer to an on-going dilemma between conventionality and its opponents. Cohen (2000) stated that "while firm proponents and staunch opponents of CAM represent the poles of belief about the role, safety, and efficacy of such therapies, the term integrative health care, as just defined, expresses an achievable and desirable goal in the future of U.S. health care" (p. 3). Counselors must be prepared to address the difficulties of this integration while concurrently addressing the moral, ethical, and legal needs of their clients.

HIV and AIDS Care. The HIV/AIDS epidemic has presented counselors with new ethical decision-making dilemmas. This uncharted territory has required counselors to carefully examine and consider prudent action on unresolved ethical issues. Legal and professional norms of practice largely have remained undefined. These unresolved dilemmas are now embedded within a managed health care environment, rendering them even more complex. As counselors struggle to resolve these emerging ethical issues, they must have a working knowledge of the basic issues related to working with individuals touched by the HIV/AIDS epidemic.

Ryan and Rowe (1988) identified some predictable ethical dilemmas that counselors may encounter in providing services to people who are HIV-positive: (a) personal conflicts with clients' values and behaviors, (b) conflicts with colleagues whose personal biases or unresolved issues prevent them from serving clients appropriately, (c) concerns about a caregiver's right to know which clients are HIV-infected, (d) concerns about whether to reveal a client's positive status to sexual partners or partners sharing needles when the client refuses to inform others at risk, (e) conflicts with social service agencies that fail to provide appropriate training and supervision for caregivers or services for people who are HIV-positive, and (f) concerns about the increasing accountability of the counseling profession as an organization that should be advocating for people with HIV more effectively. Ryan and Rowe (1988) suggested two major areas of ethical concerns in working with people who have HIV: confidentiality and informed consent.

In general, counselors must provide the same, sound ethical practice to people who have HIV/AIDS that they provide to any other client. Specifically, they must strive to protect the privacy of their clients while promoting their welfare. Counselors who practice with HIV-positive clients must have an appropriate degree of practitioner competence. The counselor's competency must include a working knowledge of potential cultural or lifestyle differences; the HIV disease process (e.g., etiology, prognosis, and treatment); and an explicit degree of self-awareness with regard to the counselor's own values, assumptions, and fears. According to Melton (1988), the need to be educated in working with people who are HIV-positive is founded firmly upon the principle of beneficence. Beneficent practice also extends professional responsibilities to include client advocacy. Previous attempts at advocacy have extended the Rehabilitation Act of 1973 and the Americans with Disabilities Act to protect people who are HIV-positive as they would protect any other individuals with disabilities from undue discrimination.

Four major issues deal with confidentiality and the person who is HIV-positive: (a) the presence of a special relationship between client and counselor and the duty to treat, (b) assessment of the impending degree of dangerousness of the client, (c) the presence of an identifiable victim of client danger, and (d) the articulation of appropriate counselor actions in working with persons who are HIV-positive (Knapp & VandeCreek, 1990; Lamb, Clark, Drumheller, Frizzell, & Surrey, 1989; Morrison, 1989; Totten, Lamb, & Reeder, 1990).

Special Relationship and the Duty to Treat. The *Tarasoff* outcome (see Chapter 3) and other prevailing evidence support the conclusion that entering into a professional relationship is a sufficient condition for counselors to assume some responsibility for their clients. As a result, the counselor assumes some degree of responsibility for any third parties the counselor reasonably knows to be in danger from that client. The conclusions based on *Tarasoff* and related decisions suggest that confidentiality is valued highly in the special relationship between the counselor and the client; however, it is not bound as an absolute. Under certain circumstances, the counselor is bound ethically to protect a potential victim in the face of certain harm (Stanard & Hazler, 1995).

According to Melton (1988), most courts have considered the duties to third parties to be congruent with the *Tarasoff* logic. In this perspective, often referred to as the *duty to warn*, the counselor is charged with a duty to exercise reasonable care in warning a specific, intended third party who has been threatened by a client. *Tarasoff* limited the definition of "reasonable foreseeable harm" to include cases that involve a specific, identifiable victim. This threat must be weighed carefully against the harm that the client may incur by any breach of confidentiality. People who are HIV-positive are particularly vulnerable to any breach of confidentiality and face unique social and emotional threats because of the

1. Counselors who receive information from clients who may have a communicable disease known to be fatal must disclose information to relevant third parties if, and only if, the counselors have reason to believe that:
   a. There is medical evidence.
   b. The clients bear specific relation (e.g., sexual or shared needles) to specified third parties at high risk of contagion.
   c. The clients have not already informed the third parties nor are they likely to make such disclosures in a timely manner.
2. In cases wherein the above conditions are met, counselors' general obligation to third parties is defined by:
   a. Within the counseling context, before disclosure, counselors must make all reasonable efforts to educate the clients about the disease and to provide the clients with the support, understanding, encouragement, and opportunity to disclose the information to third parties on their own.
   b. The counselor must make third-party disclosure in a timely fashion.
   c. Before disclosure, counselors must inform clients of their intention.
   d. Counselors must disclose the information only to the parties at risk or to the legal guardian (in the case of minors).
   e. Counselors must limit the third-party disclosure to general medical information, in earnest, communicate to the third party a willingness to provide support in the form of counseling or to make an appropriate referral.

FIGURE 9–8. Limitations of Confidentiality

Source: From "Confidentiality, Counseling, and Clients Who Have AIDS: Ethical Foundations of a Model Rule" by E. D. Cohen, 1990, *Journal of Counseling and Development, 68,* 282–286. Copyright 1990 by the American Counseling Association. Reprinted by permission.

public's fear and anxiety of contagion. An intrusion of privacy should be no greater than necessary to exert reasonable care (Melton, 1988).

Figure 9–8 suggests guidelines for counselors who make decisions about limiting the degree of client confidentiality (Cohen, 1990). Ethical practice dictates that boundaries of confidentiality must be clear to the counselor and to the client before the counseling process begins.

Although there always have been implicit risks for health care providers in the course of providing their services, the deadliness of the HIV/AIDS epidemic has heightened the debate regarding the counselor's duty to treat. Justification for refusal to treat a client primarily has been based on the risk of contagion or on the presence of values conflicts between counselor and client (Morrison, 1989). Some counselors who elect not to treat people who are HIV-positive may do so because the issues clients bring to treatment constitute a values conflict that the counselor may view as insurmountable. Others may simply feel uncomfortable with people who have HIV—the lifestyle choices related to the types of people or the life issues related to the decision. While ethical codes of various disciplines suggest that counselors are obligated to respect clients and to protect the welfare of those seeking services, there is no clearly stated duty to treat undesirable or difficult clients. Refusal to treat a client is a moral, ethical, and legal decision and must be viewed from this perspective. People with HIV/AIDS are legally protected from discrimination based on their illness. While it may not be necessary for the counselor to assume an ethical responsibility to treat a person with HIV, the counselor is morally responsibile to reflect on the reasons for this decision. Moreover, the counselor has an ethical obligation to assist any individual seeking services in fully and respectfully obtaining appropriate referral services, even if this individual is not accepted as a client.

Assessment of Dangerousness. The prediction of dangerousness is considered to be significantly unreliable. The reasons for this high degree of unreliability are complex (Morrison, 1989). Certain behaviors, such as a history of violence or assaultive behavior, and the availability of weapons, have been shown to be related to future dangerousness, but have not proven to be directly predictive. Moreover, the dynamics of inherent dangerousness involved in the transmission of a fatal disease such as HIV/AIDS are substantively different from other assumed types of danger. Therefore, determining the degree of dangerousness of a client who is HIV-positive is a significantly difficult task.

Counselors must consider several important factors before concluding that a client who is HIV-positive is an inherent danger to another individual: (1) Counselors must acknowledge the limit of their own competence in the diagnosis and prognosis of HIV. (2) Counselors must obtain reliable medical proof that such a condition exists for a client and gather current, valid, and expert medical information regarding the course and transmission of the disease at varying stages and in relationship to this individual client's disease stage. (3) Counselors must establish the extent to which this particular client is engaging in high-risk behaviors. (4) Counselors must identify a victim of any dangerous behavior. (5) Counselors must assess the degree to which any strategies are being used by the client to reduce the degree of danger to a third party.

Historically, given the prognostic ambiguity in assessing a client's degree of dangerousness, mental health professionals tended to overpredict the degree of dangerousness—overprediction seemed a more prudent error than underprediction. According to most literature, the *Tarasoff* stance on the assessment of dangerousness has been upheld. However, counselors first must consider less intrusive means of diffusing any impending risk before violating the confidentiality and trusting relationship with their client. For example, including significant others in the counseling process or encouraging voluntary disclosure by the client to potential victims would protect others while not violating confidentiality.

Another important ethical consideration of dangerousness must not be overlooked. It is known that there is a substantially high risk of suicide among men with HIV/AIDS. In a study conducted by Marzuk et al. (1988), men with HIV were found to be about 36 times more likely to commit suicide than men in the general population. Ethical and legal responsibilities of counselors include preventive measures that range from persuasion to involuntary commitment. As discussed previously regarding euthanasia, the use of rationality in deciding to end one's life is central. For people with HIV, this rational process may become impaired due to the shock of hearing the diagnosis, a lack of accurate information about the disease, and the progressive cognitive changes that may accompany the disease process of HIV.

Identifiable Victim. According to legal rulings, a counselor is required to substantiate the presence of a specific, identified victim before breaching a client's confidentiality to warn a third party of danger. However, courts have extended the counselor's duty to protect unknown, but readily identifiable, others. For instance, a client may describe a specific person, such as a roommate, with whom the client shares an IV needle and not provide that person's name. With limited effort, the counselor may identify a specific, knowable person. However, a counselor cannot interrogate or independently investigate a client to obtain this information. The identification of a specific victim in impending danger comes solely from client disclosure.

According to Lamb et al. (1989), the issue of an identifiable victim has several implications for counselors who work with people who have HIV (Figure 9–9).

1. Become familiar and continually update medical information regarding HIV.
2. Be familiar with short- and long-term issues that may arise.
3. Be aware of one's own attitudes, biases, and prejudices as they relate to individuals with HIV.
4. Seek to inform and encourage all clients in high-risk groups to consider safe methods of having sex and using drugs.
5. Be prepared to refer clients to legal resources if warranted to protect their right to nondiscrimination.
6. Keep current regarding existing state and federal laws concerning the caregiver role in the spread of communicable diseases.
7. Articulate early in the therapeutic relationship the limitations of confidentiality, including the possible use of written formats to facilitate the informed consent process.
8. Determine mutual goals with the client as part of an ongoing assessment.
9. Remember that your principal duty is to your client.
10. Exercise your prerogative to refer or consult with other professionals as needed.
11. Maintain appropriate case notes that document confidentiality issues, understandings with your client, treatment goals and progress, and unusual events. Consider working notes separate from the formal client record.

FIGURE 9–9. General Counselor Implications for Working with People with AIDS

Source: From "Applying Tarasoff to AIDS-related Psychotherapy Issues" by D. H. Lamb, C. Clark, P. Drumheller, K. Frizzel, and L. Surrey, 1989, *Professional Psychology, 20.* Copyright 1989 by the American Psychological Association. Adapted by permission.

Appropriate Counselor Actions. As more counselors work with people who have HIV, informed, ethical practice must include thoughtful preparation for working with these clients. Counselors must consider and learn about the implications of HIV in all aspects of the counseling process, including prudent record-keeping procedures that protect the client's confidentiality, particularly in the context of managed care (Hughes & Friedman, 1994). Currently, membership in a high-risk group may be considered evidence for cancellation of a client's insurance benefits or may lead to the loss of a client's job. The client's record should contain all contacts with the client, a summation of the client's progress, documents that support informed consent, and all test data. Working notes should be kept separate from the client's record (Morrison, 1989).

Clearly, counselors must use all aspects of good ethical and clinical practice in serving people who have HIV.

Abortion. Counselors who work in a variety of environments, including school, rehabilitation, and marriage/family practice settings may be confronted with the issue of abortion during clinical practice. Abortion is a value-laden issue in society at large and also within the counseling setting. Without a massive shift in public opinion, abortion will remain one of the most divisive health care policy issues.

Because of the value-laden and emotional nature of the abortion issue, counselors must examine their own values and understand their clients' value systems (Wilcox, Robbennolt, & O'Keeffe, 1998). They must carefully analyze all relevant empirical research to assure that all involved parties in the debate appropriately characterize the scientific knowledge base. They should encourage health care policy and institutional policy that are based upon evidence rather than assumptions alone (Wilcox et al., 1998).

Counselors who consider providing services to individuals who are considering abortion must first examine the environment in which they are employed. Their agencies may have in place very specific procedures and guidelines as to whether the counselor can provide such counseling services, as well as the nature and direction of the services to be provided. Despite the fact that 70 percent of Americans feel that abortion should be legal in some form, there is a huge chasm regarding opinions about the circumstances under which it should be performed (Russo & Denious, 1998). Clearly, there is no simple answer.

Counselors may also find or seek employment in settings or agencies that provide counseling to clients considering alternatives to abortion. In those settings counseling focuses on such sensitive topics as: (a) garnering resources for young parents; (b) the prospect of single parenthood; or (c) the option of placing the child up for adoption. Counselors must be alert to the emotion-laden nature of such topics and pay special attention to the adjustment concerns of clients before and subsequent to the choices they make.

Some facilities provide counseling services for abortion only under specific circumstances (e.g., in cases of rape or incest). Others provide counseling at all times for any circumstance, and some refer clients to other appropriate counseling agencies. The public debate presently is divided into two sides: One camp addresses abortion as a right related to individual freedom, control, and equality for women. The other position views this action as a threat to morality and social cohesion (Russo & Denious, 1998).

Currently, some health care providers and advocates of women's health are concerned about the decrease in the number of physicians who perform abortions. This limited pool of providers has influenced the availability of such services (Henshaw, 1998). Counselors are also affected as clients seek advice on where they can obtain abortion services. At present, access is limited for women who are unable to pay, those living in nonurban areas, and those who are unwilling to face potential harassment at a large, urban clinic.

When a client makes the decision to have an abortion, she is protected, to a certain degree, by legislation that addresses the psychological and physical health risks of abortion and informed consent (Adler, Smith, & Tschann, 1998). Counselors who work with adolescents must be familiar with state regulations regarding parental consent. Many argue that parental consent legislation is in place because abortion carries with it a substantial risk and minors are incapable of making informed choices related to the risk.

Regardless of the client's age, it is the counselor's responsibility to address the client's competence to make the important decision about abortion and to provide meaningful informed consent (see Chapter 3). With adolescents and children, the counselor should focus on assessing competence to make an informed choice, whereas with adults the counselor must provide information to assure that the client is in a position to give informed consent and is making the decision of her free will (Koocher & DeMaso, 1990). The counselor is faced with a dilemma upon providing this information—there is no clear standard for determining when adolescents or adults have the capability of making an informed decision in this area (Adler, Smith, & Tschann, 1998).

Special Issues of Adolescents and Abortion. The issue of parental consent assumes the need to consult with a parent or guardian regarding an abortion decision. Zabin, Hirsch, Emerson, and Raymond (1992) found that 91 percent of adolescents did consult with a parent or other adult guardian after receiving a positive pregnancy test result. Another 4 percent of these adolescents discussed their pregnancy with an adult other than their parent(s) or older sibling. Many question the necessity of consent laws because it appears that a high percentage of minors consult with their parents voluntarily (Adler, Smith, & Tschann, 1998).

Counselors may encounter adolescents who fear telling their parents or adult guardians of their pregnancies, let alone their consideration of abortion. They may fear the potential response from their parents. This fear may also make them feel ill at ease in trying to obtain a judicial bypass of consent laws from the state. Counselors need to be aware that these adolescents may be at risk in several ways: (a) they may attempt to obtain an illegal abortion; (b) they may attempt to self-induce an abortion; and (c) they risk complications due to the delay of the abortion procedure because of the time it may take for the judicial bypass procedure. Some clients appear for counseling services because certain states allow parental consent to be waived if the adolescent has obtained professional counseling (Adler, Smith, & Tschann, 1998). At present, more research is needed in the area of adolescent competence and decision making.

Risks of Abortion.   Few studies show adverse effects to women who choose to have an abortion. However, adolescents have increased health risks, and many feel extra protection for adolescents is warranted (Adler, Smith, & Tschann, 1998).

Post-abortion emotional distress has been linked to psychological risk factors including psychological difficulties prior to the procedure, ambivalence about the decision, limited coping skills, and an inadequate social support system (Adler, Smith, & Tschann, 1998), regardless of age. Counselors must be aware of the best counseling approaches available and know when to refer potential clients for additional services.

Counselors who provide abortion services must be mindful of special issues that may emerge during abortion counseling: sexual abuse, assault, incest, multiple unintended pregnancies, religious reactions toward individuals who choose to have an abortion or are considering abortion, and special situations like selective abortion to increase the viability of remaining fetuses (Fisher, Castle, & Garrity, 1998). Unintended pregnancy is a unique crisis that is often approached differently than other life decisions (Adler, Smith, & Tschann, 1998).

Other Health Issues.   The diversity of complex medical and health issues that confront people in modern society is awe-inspiring. In the future, counselors will find their clients struggling with information and choices that are currently beyond our imagination. Professionals must be open to learning new perspectives that stimulate moral and ethical development.

Fertility Choices.   Counselors presently address fertility issues such as the reproductive rights of persons with disabilities, infertility, voluntarily sterilization, and

abortion. Counselors must prepare themselves to address future reproductive issues like cloning.

Although numerous individuals choose not to have children, many wish to bear children but cannot. These individuals may choose to undergo extensive and invasive testing and medical procedures (Daniluk, 1991). Upon receipt of a diagnosis, they may be faced with difficult decisions including which form of treatment to pursue—in-vitro fertilization, artificial insemination, or embryo transfers. Infertility can have a significant impact upon couples in the areas of sexual satisfaction and functioning, communication, and adjustment, and may cause emotional and psychological distress (Daniluk, 1991).

In providing treatment to infertile couples, counselors should facilitate the grieving process; identify where to relinquish and accept control; heal relationships; assess motivation for parenting; and explore options for parenting in the future (Daniluk, 1991). Research suggests that, on average, couples require 8 to 10 counseling sessions to accomplish these goals.

Organ Transplantation.   The United Network for Organ Sharing (UNOS) reported 22,854 organ transplants in 2000 (UNOS, 2001a). The number of single and multiorgan transplants increased 44 percent between 1990 and 1999 (UNOS, 2001b). In 2000, 5,605 transplant patients obtained organs from living donors (UNOS, 2001b). Living donors are anticipated to increase by 16.5 percent within one year—the largest increase ever reported by UNOS (2001a). These statistics have the potential to impact counselors, who could provide counseling services to both the transplant recipients and the living donors. As of 31 January, 1999, UNOS reported 72,110 individuals on the waiting list for transplant donation, and this number continues to rise (UNOS, 2001b). These individuals and their families may require and benefit from counseling services during the waiting process.

Many individuals say they are willing to donate their organs upon their death, but the number of people who actually donate organs is much smaller (Lauritzen, McClure, Smith, & Trew, 2001). This situation is further complicated by the difficulty in assessing the criteria that determine death. The variability of individual concepts of death also present limitations to organ transplantation. Counselors need to be prepared to address these issues.

An additional issue in counseling clients in this area is a common concern of many organ recipients (Lauritzen, et al., 2001). People who have had organ transplants may feel guilty if they do not have positive outcomes after transplantation. Many individuals describe a transplant recipient as someone who has "received the gift of life." Recipients may feel that they have failed to honor the "gift" that has been bestowed upon them (Lauritzen, et al., 2001).

CHAPTER SUMMARY

Organizations that participate in managed care include: (1) health maintenance organizations (HMOs), which provide specified health services using a restricted group of providers at a fixed cost to the consumer; (2) preferred provider organizations (PPOs), which purchase health care from specific providers at a discounted rate; and (3) independent practice associations (IPAs), which allow consumers to choose independent practitioners but retain a portion of the fees from providers who may be reimbursed either on a fee-for-service or capitated basis.

Counselors who practice in managed care settings must have effective communication skills; knowledge of business practices; knowledge and skills in providing competent counseling; knowledge of professional codes of ethics and ethical standards, including counselor competence, informed consent and confidentiality, integrity, conflict of interest, and business relationships.

Counselors confront a number of bioethical issues, including euthanasia, genetic testing, confidentiality, abortion, organ transplantation, HIV/AIDS, suicide, and fertility choices. Future scientific advances will continue to affect how counselors practice and treat clients. To effectively deal with these emerging issues, counselors must have a knowledge of biomedical ethics—understanding and examining moral life as it pertains to the biological sciences, medicine, and health care.

Complementary medical practices work with traditional medicine. Alternative medical practices are used instead of traditional medicine. CAM approaches are showing tremendous growth, and include relaxation techniques, herbal medicine, massage, chiropractic, spiritual healing, megavitamin therapy, self-help, imagery, energy healing, homeopathy, hypnosis, biofeedback, and acupuncture. CAM approaches are being used in cancer, HIV/AIDS, abortion, fertility, and organ transplantation therapies. Counselors must be prepared to address the legal, moral, and ethical issues that accompany these treatments.

REFERENCES

Acuff, C., Bennett, B. E., Bricklin, P. M., Canter, M. B., Knapp, S. J., & Moldawsky, S. (1999). Considerations for ethical practice in managed care. *Professional Psychology: Research and Practice, 30* (6), 563–575.

Adler, N. E., Smith, L. B., & Tschann, J. M. (1998). Abortion and adolescents. In L. J. Beckman & S. M. Harvey (Eds.), *The new civil war: The psychology, culture and politics of abortion* (pp. 285–286). Washington, D.C.: American Psychological Association.

Albright, D. E., & Hazler, R. J. (1995). A right to die? Ethical dilemmas of euthanasia. *Counseling and Values, 39,* 177–189.

American Psychiatric Association. (2000). *Diagnostic and statistical manual of mental disorders – IV – Text revision.* Washington, D.C.: Author.

Beauchamp, T., & Childress, W. (1994). *Principles of biomedical ethics* (5th ed.). Baltimore, MD: Johns Hopkins University Press.

Beauchamp, T., & Walters, L. (Eds.). (1989). *Euthanasia and the prolongation of life. Contemporary issues in bioethics* (3rd ed.). Belmont, CA: Wadsworth.

Berenson, R. A. (1999). Testimony on the balanced budget act's impact on fee-for-service medicare before the senate finance committee [On-line]. Available: http://www.hfca.gov/testimony/1999/feefro1.htm.

Bettelheim, A. (2000). Senators question adequacy of Federal Drug Administration, National Institute of Health protections for genetic therapy patients. *CQ Weekly, 58* (6), 250–252.

Bilynsky, N. S., & Vernaglia, E. R. (1998). The ethical practice of psychology in a managed case framework. *Psychotherapy, 35,* 54–68.

Brief of the Washington State Psychological Association; the American Counseling Association; the Association of Gay, Lesbian, and Bisexual Issues in Counseling; and the Coalition of Mental Health Professionals Supporting Individual Self-Determination in Decisions to Hasten Death. (1996, December). Filed with the Supreme Court of the United States, October 1996 term for *Washington v. Glucksberg* and *Vacco v. Quill.*

Brock, D. W. (1992). Voluntary active euthanasia. *Hastings Center Report, 22,* 10–22.

Clark, P. A. (2000). The ethics of alternative medicine therapies. *Journal of Public Health Policies, 21* (4), 447–467.

Cohen, E. D. (1990). Confidentiality, counseling, and clients who have AIDS: Ethical foundations of a model rule. *Journal of Counseling and Development, 68,* 282–286.

Cohen, M. H. (2000). *Beyond complementary medicine: Legal and ethical perspectives on health care and human revolution.* Ann Arbor, MI: The University of Michigan Press.

Compassion in Dying v. Washington, 79 F. 3d 790 (9th Cir. 1996).

Cooper, C. C., & Gottlieb, M. C. (2000). Ethical issues with managed care: Challenges facing counseling psychology. *The Counseling Psychologist, 28* (2), 179–237.

Covington, D. (1995). *Salvation on Sand Mountain: Snake handling and redemption in Southern Appalachia.* New York: Penguin Books.

Dalzell, M. D. (2001, May). Genetic medicine: Powerful opportunities for good and greed. *Managed Care,* 1–10.

Daniluk, J. C. (1991). Strategies for counseling infertile couples. *Journal of Counseling and Development, 69,* 317–320.

Department of Health and Human Services. (2000). Office of the inspector general compliance program for individual and small group physician practices. *Federal Register, 65* (194), 59434–59452.

Ebersole, R. S. (2001). Mending genes. *Current Science, 86* (10), 4–7.

Eisenberg, D. M., Davis, R. B., Ettner, S. L., Appel, S., Wilkey, S., Van Rompay, M., & Kessler, R. (1998). Trends in alternative medicine use in the United States 1990–1997: Results of a follow-up national survey. *Journal of the American Medical Association, 280* (18), 1569.

Emmanuel, E. J. (1994, September 12). Euthanasia: Historical, ethical, and empirical perspectives. *Archives of Internal Medicine, 154,* 1890–1901.

Fisher, B., Castle, M. A., & Garrity, J. M. (1998). A cognitive approach to patient-centered abortion care. In L. J. Beckman & S. M. Harvey (Eds*.), The new civil war: The psychology, culture and politics of abortion* (pp. 308–321). Washington, D.C.: American Psychological Association.

Friedlander, H. (1995). *The origins of the Nazi genocide: From euthanasia to the final solution.* Chapel Hill, NC: University of North Carolina.

Fuller, B. P., Kahn, M. J., Barr, P. A., Biesecker, L., Crowley, E., Garber, J., Mansoura, M. K., Murphy, P., Murray, J., Phillips, J., Rothenberg, K., Stopfer, J., Swergold, G., Weber, B., Collins, F. S., & Hudson, K. L. (1999). Privacy in genetics research. *Science, 285* (5432), 1359–1360.

Glosoff, H. L., Garcia, J., Herlihy, B., & Remley, T. P. (1999). Managed care: Ethical considerations for counselors. *Counseling & Values, 44* (1), 8–17.

Greiner, A. (2001). Only one-third of consumers correctly identify basic managed care plan features [On-line]. Available: http://www.hschange.org/content/297/?topic=topic06.

Haas, L. J., & Cummings, N. A. (1991). Managed outpatient mental health plans: Clinical, ethical, and practical guidelines for participation. *Professional Psychology: Research and Practice, 22* (1), 45–51.

Hallam, K. (1999). Sit up, take notice. *Modern Healthcare, 29* (25), 50.

Harpham, S. (2001). Alternative therapies for curing cancer: What do patients want? What do patients need? *CA, A Cancer Journal for Clinicians, 51* (2), 131–136.

Henshaw, S. K. (1998). Barriers to access to abortion services. In L. J. Beckman & S. M. Harvey (Eds.), *The new civil war: The psychology, culture and politics of abortion* (p. 61). Washington, D.C.: American Psychological Association.

Hersch, L. (1995). Adapting to health care reform and managed care: Three strategies for survival and growth. *Professional Psychology: Research and Practice, 26* (1), 16–26.

Hughes, R. B., & Friedman, A. L. (1994). AIDS-related ethical and legal issues for mental health professionals. *Journal of Mental Health Counseling, 16,* 445–458.

Human Genome Project Information. (2001). Gene therapy [On-line]. Available: http:// www.ornl.gov/hgmis/medicine/genetherapy.html [HGP]

Humphrey, D. (1991). *Final exit: The practicalities of self-deliverance and assisted suicide for the dying.* New York: Dell Publishing.

Jecker, N. S. (1998). Ethics in medicine: Managed care [On-line]. Available: http://eduserv.hscer.washington.edu/bioethics/topics/manag.html.

Jegalian, K., & Biesecker, L. (2000). The human genome project. *Exceptional Parent, 30* (3), 29–32.

Jensen, G., Morrisey, M. A., Gaffney, S., & Liston, D. K. (1997, January/February). The new dominance of managed care: Insurance trends in the 1990s. *Health Affairs, 16,* 125–136.

Knapp, S., & VandeCreek, L. (1990). Application of the duty to protect to HIV-positive clients. *Professional Psychology: Research and Practice, 21,* 161–166.

Koocher, G. P., & DeMaso, D. R. (1990). Children's competence to consent to medical procedures. *Pediatrician, 17,* 68–73.

Kutchins, H., & Kirk, S. (1987, May). DSM-III-R and social work malpractice. *Social Work,* 205–211.

Lamb, D. H., Clark, C., Drumheller, P., Frizzell, K., & Surrey, L. (1989). Applying Tarasoff to AIDS-related psychotherapy issues. *Professional Psychology: Research and Practice, 20,* 37–43.

Larson, L. (2000). Genomics. *Hospital & Health Networks, 74* (3), 76–81.

Lauritzen, P., McClure, M., Smith, M. L., & Trew, A. (2001, January/February). The gift of life and the common good. *Hasting Center Report,* 29–34.

Lawless, L., Ginter, E. J., & Kelly, K. R. (1999). Managed care: What mental health counselors need to know. *Journal of Mental Health Counseling, 21* (1), 50–66.

Leung, W. C. (2000). Results of genetic testing: When confidentiality conflicts with a duty to warn relatives. *British Medical Journal, 321* (7274), 1464–1467.

Marcus, C. (1999). Special report: Alternative medicine—the AMA reviews scientific evidence. *Clinical Reviews, 9* (2), 87–90.

Mariner, W. (1997). Business versus medical ethics: Conflicting standards for managed care. In J. W. Glaser & R. P. Hamel (Eds.), *Three realms of managed care* (pp. 92–111). Kansas City, MO: Sheed & Ward.

Marwick, C. (1998). Alterations are ahead at the OAM. *Journal of the American Medical Association, 280* (18), 1553–1554.

Marzuk, P. M., Tierney, H., Tardiff, K., Gross, E. M., Morgan, E. B., Hsu, M., & Mann, J. J. (1988). Increased risk of suicide in persons with AIDS. *Journal of the American Medical Association, 259,* 1333–1337.

Mechanic, D. (2001). The managed care backlash: Perceptions and rhetoric in health care policy and the potential for health care reform. *Milbank Quarterly, 79* (1), 14–18.

Melton, G. B. (1988). Ethical and legal issues in AIDS-related practice. *American Psychologist, 43,* 941–947.

Mill, J. S. (1910). Utilitarianism. In utilitarianism, or liberty, and representative government (pp. 1–60). London: J. M. Dent. & Sons (original work published 1863).

Morrison, C. F. (1989). AIDS: Ethical implications for psychological interventions. *Professional Psychology: Research and Practice, 20,* 166–171.

Murphy, M. J. (1998). Evolution of practice and values of professional psychology. In R. F. Small & L. R. Barnhill (Eds.), *Practicing in the new mental health marketplace: Ethical, legal, and moral issues* (pp. 37–52). Washington, D.C.: American Psychological Association.

National Center for Genome Resources. (1997). *Eugenics.* Retrieved July 11, 2001 from the Charles Sturt University Web site: http://www.csu.edu.au/learning/ncgr/gpi/odyssey/dolly-cloning/eugenics.html.

National Institutes of Health. (December, 1994). *Alternative medicine: Expanding medical horizons.* (A report to the National Institutes of Health on alternative medical systems and practices in the United States). NIH Publication 94–0666 [Chantilly Report].

National Reference Center for Bioethics Literature. (2001). *Scope note 28: Eugenics.* Retrieved July 11, 2001 from the Joseph and Rose Kennedy Institute of Ethics, Georgetown University Web site: http://www.georgetown.edu/research/nrcbl/scopenote/sn28.htm.

Oktay, J. S. (1998). Genetics cultural lag: What can social workers do to help? *Health and Social Work, 23* (4), 310–316.

Olkin, R. (1999). *What psychotherapists should know about disability.* New York: Guilford.

Parens, E., & Asch, A. (1999). The disability rights critique of prenatal testing:

Reflections and recommendations. *Special Supplement Hastings Center Report, 29* (5), S1–S22.

Pellegrino, E. D. (1986). Rationing health care: The ethics of medical gate keeping. *Journal of Contemporary Health, Law Policy, 2,* 23–45.

Peters, T. (1996). In search of the perfect child: Genetic testing and selective abortion. *Christian Century, 113* (31), 1034–1038.

Quill v. Vacco, 80F. 3d 716 (2d Cir. 1996).

Rieger, P. T. (2000). The gene genies. *American Journal of Nursing, 100* (10), 87–90.

Rogers, J. R., Gueulette, C. M., Abbey-Hines, J., Carney, J. V., & Werth, J. L. (2001). Rational suicide: An empirical investigation of counselor attitudes. *Journal of Counseling and Development, 79,* 365–372.

Russo, N. F., & Denious, J. E. (1998). Why is abortion such a controversial issue in the United States? In L. J. Beckman & S. M. Harvey (Eds.), *The new civil war: The psychology, culture and politics of abortion* (pp. 25–26). Washington, D.C.: American Psychological Association.

Ryan, C. C., & Rowe, M. J. (1988). AIDS: Legal and ethical issues. *Social Casework, 69,* 324–333.

Shore, M. (1996, January). Impact of managed care. *New England Journal of Medicine,* 116–118.

Siegel, K. (1986). Psycho-social aspects of rational suicide. *American Journal of Psychotherapy, 44,* 1053–1061.

Stanard, R., & Hazler, R. (1995). Legal and ethical implications of HIV and duty to warn for counselors: When does Tarasoff apply? *Journal of Counseling and Development, 73,* 397–400.

Studdert, D. M., Eisenberg, D. M., Miller, F. H., Curto, D. A., Daptchuk, T. J., and Brennan, T. A. (1998 November 11). Medical malpractice implications of alternative medicine. *Journal of the American Medical Association,* 280 (18), 1610–1616.

Suzuki, D., & Knudtson, P. (1990). *Genethics: The clash between new genetics and human values.* Cambridge, MA: Harvard University Press.

Tarvydas, V. M., & Peterson, D. B. (1999). Ethics in case management. In F. Chan & M. Leahy (Eds.), *Health care and disability: Care management* (pp. 317–354). Lake Zurich, IL: Vocational Consultants Press.

Totten, G., Lamb, G., & Reeder, G. D. (1990). Tarasoff and confidentiality in AIDS-related psychotherapy. *Professional Psychology: Research and Practice, 21,* 155–160.

Tufts University. (1998). When genetic testing might be appropriate. *Tufts University Health & Nutrition Letter, 16* (1), 8.

United Network for Organ Sharing (2001a). Living donation continues to increase and gains public attention [On-line]. Available: http://www.unos.org/newsroom/archive _story_20010608_living donation.htm.

United Network for Organ Sharing. (2001b). Overall transplant, survival and waiting list data [On-line]. Available: http://www.unos.org/data/anrpt00/ar00_datahigh_03.htm.

Werth, J. L. (1999). Mental health professionals and assisted death: Perceived ethical obligations and proposed guidelines for practice. *Ethics & Behavior,* 1, 159–163.

Werth, J. L., & Holdwick, D. J. (2000). A primer on rational suicide and other forms of hastened death. *The Counseling Psychologist, 28,* 511–539.

White, M. T. (1999). Making responsible decisions: An interpretive ethic for genetic decision making. *Hastings Center Report, 29* (1), 14–22.

White, M. T., & Calliff-Daley, F. (1999). Genetic testing for disease susceptibility: Social, ethical and legal issues for family physicians. *American Family Physician, 60* (3), 748–751.

Wilbur, K. (1988). *The marriage of sense and soul.* New York: Broadway Books.

Wilcox, B. L., Robbennolt, J. K., & O'Keeffe, J. E. (1998). In L. J. Beckman & S. M. Harvey (Eds.), *The new civil war: The psychology, culture and politics of abortion* (pp. 21–22). Washington, D.C.: American Psychological Association.

Wolf, S. (Ed.). (1996). Feminism and bioethics: *Beyond reproduction.* New York and Oxford, England: Oxford University Press.

Wylie, M. S. (1995, May/June). The power of DSM-IV: Diagnosing for dollars. *Networker,* 22–32.

Zabin, L. S., Hirsch, M. B., Emerson, M. R., & Raymond, E. (1992). To whom do inner-city minors talk about their pregnancies? Adolescents' communication with parents and parent surrogates. *Family Planning Perspectives, 24* , 148–154, 173.

CHAPTER 10

Ethics and Technology

David B. Peterson[1]

Objectives

■ ■ ■ ■ ■ ■ ■ ■ ■ ■

After reading this chapter, you should be able to:

- Provide an overview of technology as it is applied to counseling practice.
- Relate such technology to the ethical practice of counseling professionals in:
  - maintaining confidential records,
  - conducting confidential communication,
  - using technology to enhance counseling services,
  - using technology in place of direct counseling services,
  - using the Internet as a counseling service modality, and
  - conducting assessments to enhance counseling practice.
- Review ethical standards of practice relevant to the use of technology in counseling.
- Explore the use of technology in counselor education.

■ ■ ■ ■ ■ ■ ■ ■ ■ ■

INTRODUCTION

During the past 35 years, computer capabilities have dramatically increased while costs to implement such technology have decreased significantly (Ford, 1993; Sampson, 2000; Simons, 1985). Personal computers (PCs) have increased in sophistication, and PC-based programming languages are powerful and easy to use. These changes have increased the use of such technology in the counseling profession (Bloom & Walz, 2000; Colby, 1980; Ford, 1993; Levitan, Willis, & Vogelgesang, 1985; Sampson, 2000).

Computer-based applications for clinical situations in counseling-related professions began as early as the 1960s, with computer-based test interpretation (Butcher, 1987; Fowler, 1985). During the 1970s, researchers expanded computer-assisted testing capabilities to include administration, scoring, and interpretation of psychological

---

[1]The author wishes to express thanks to and acknowledge the conceptual and editorial contributions of Fong Chan, University of Wisconsin–Madison, and the editorial contributions of Gerry Murray, The University of Iowa, to the first edition of this chapter, as they continue to influence this iteration.

tests (Butcher, 1987). Computer-assisted assessments have increased in number throughout the 1980s and into the 21st century; and the use, assets, and limitations of such technologies have been well explored in the counseling literature (Bloom & Walz, 2000; Butcher, 1985, 1987; Eyde, 1987; Ford, 1993; Fowler, 1985; French, 1986; Matarazzo, 1985, 1986; Merrell, 1986; Sampson, 1990, 2000).

Computer-assisted therapy also originated in the 1960s, with much less success than computerized assessment applications (Colby, Gould, & Aronson, 1989; Colby, Watt, & Gilbert, 1966; Ford, 1993). Therapeutic applications received little further attention until the 1980s (Ford, 1993). Since then, various types of computer-assisted therapies have been used, including professional consultation programs, client therapeutic learning programs, and on-line therapy. Unlike computer-assisted assessment, little has been written on the ethical issues related to the use of computer-assisted therapy until recently (Bloom & Walz, 2000; Peterson, Murray, & Chan, 1998; Sampson, Kolodinsky, & Greeno, 1997).

As computer technology has become more affordable and desk and laptop computers have grown in number, tasks once dedicated to paper, typewriter, or pen have been transferred to more convenient computerized technologies. The advent of facsimile machines (faxes), computer modems for phone line communication, computer networks (e.g., the Internet), wireless satellite networks, and paperless technologies like personal assistants (PAs; e.g., Palm and Visor technology) have resulted in new forms of electronic media that the counseling profession uses with increasing frequency. As a result of these technological developments, the counseling profession has had little time to address the resulting ethical and professional issues (Bloom & Walz, 2000; Ford, 1993; Sampson, 2000; Sampson et al., 1997).

The ethical codes of practice and the literature associated with counseling and the allied health professions have been hard-pressed to keep pace with the dramatic changes in technology (Granello, 2000). Some ethical issues related to recent technological developments have been of concern to counselors and psychologists for many years. Other issues are unique to more recent technological developments. Several counseling-related organizations have addressed new standards of practice that will affect the standards and codes used today (APA, 1986, 1997; AERA, APA, & NCME, 1999; ACA, 1995, 1999; CRCC, 2001; NBCC, 2001).

It is essential for counseling professionals to remain current with efforts to develop and establish ethical standards and codes of conduct to protect and benefit their clients. Recent technological developments affect the practices and ethical decision-making processes of the counseling professional. As managed care continues to place new demands on the allied health professions, it is ethically essential that counseling-related professions explore the use of technology to facilitate ethical counseling practice (Bloom & Walz, 2000; Erdman & Foster, 1988; Sampson, 2000).

ETHICAL MANAGEMENT OF ELECTRONIC MEDIA

Ethical codes addressing the maintenance of client records, such as those established by the APA, mandate that psychologists maintain appropriate confidentiality in creating, storing, accessing, transferring, and disposing of all manner of records in their care. The American Counseling Association has a similar requirement—the ethical counseling professional must protect the client's right to confidentiality regardless of the type of electronic media.

All forms of electronic media used in counseling may contain sensitive material protected by client-therapist confidentiality and privileged communication. It is important that ethical counselors are aware of how the use of electronic media influences professional practice (Figure 10–1). Protocols need to be in place to ensure that electronic media will be accessible only to ethically appropriate parties. Electronic media storage systems may not be immediately understandable or visible to the counseling professional, and therefore ethical management of such data may be easily overlooked. Counseling professionals use a variety of types of electronic media, including personal computers, faxes, e-mail, and cellular phones.

---

1. Ethical codes require that the same safeguards be used for both printed and electronic media.
2. Electronic media may appear deceptively simple and safeguarded from unethical access. While privacy protocols are time-consuming and costly, they are essential to ethical data management.
3. Fax transmissions of ethically sensitive material must be carefully controlled.
4. E-mail should not be considered a confidential form of communication.
5. Discussion of confidential matters should not occur over cellular phones.

FIGURE 10–1. Reminders for Ethical Use of Electronic Media

Electronic Media on Personal Computers

Personal computer systems commonly used by counseling professionals are composed of hardware and software. Hardware consists of the electrical and mechanical devices of the computer system, including the central processing unit (CPU) of the computer (or the "brains" in the chassis of the computer), the monitor, the printer, and various peripheral (outside of the CPU) devices, such as a scanner. Hardware that stores electronic media includes (a) a hard disk drive, which is a sealed memory system located either within the chassis of the CPU or in a portable peripheral unit; (b) a floppy disk drive, with older 5¼-inch and more recent 3½-inch sized disks for reading from and writing information to a CPU; (c) compact disk drives with read-only-memory (CD-ROM), reading, recording, and overwriting capability (CD-RW), or single-record capability with longer archival life (CD-R); (d) ZIP and JAZ drives that are similar to floppy disk technology but store considerably more information; and (e) a server that has a large data storage drive for a network of computers. Electronic media can be safeguarded at the hardware level with a mechanical lock and key that prevent power from reaching the computer, thus maintaining confidentiality of the information within. Once turned on, such systems should not be left unattended unless protected at the software level.

Software includes the programs written for the CPU to perform various functions, or applications. Common computer applications used by counseling professionals include document production using word processing applications, financial and records management using spreadsheets, and record filing on databases. Word processors generate media formerly produced by typewriters and handwriting, such as case notes, letters, and test reports. Spreadsheets are used for numerical recordkeeping tasks like client billing and miscellaneous records. Databases are electronic "file cabinets" used to store and control large amounts of information, such as client mailing lists and community referral sources. Most recently, the development of software "suites" provides multiple functions in one software package. For example, *Therapist Helper* by Brand Software, Inc., is a suite of software that helps to manage lists of clients and referral resources, diagnostic codes, insurance billing transactions, reporting capabilities, managed care authorizations, and progress notes.

Documents created by a word processor, spreadsheet, or database application can be printed to create a hard copy and stored as files on memory systems. In addition to the need to control access to printed matter generated from computers, the data stored on hard disks, floppy disks, JAZ or ZIP disks, and CDs must be carefully controlled. Personnel with access to such data must be well trained regarding ethical management of electronic media. A 3½-inch floppy disk containing confidential information may be less obvious than a notebook-size chart containing paper copies of the same information. A small computer disk can store information equivalent to many client charts and is much easier to remove from an office than a rack full of confidential records. Paper records and electronic information must be locked in tamper-proof surroundings.

The storage of confidential material on a hard drive may be even less obvious to the counselor. All staff members within a counseling organization must be oriented to the appropriate ethical procedures for storage of client records and the related access protocols. For hard drives on PCs, security software is available that will allow access to certain files only if a person has an access code or password. People who are issued access codes must protect their codes from misuse. If a PC in a counseling organization does not require a security code to access confidential information, large amounts of data are at risk of being viewed by people who should not have access to such information.

Organizations that use a server for a network of computers, sometimes called a *local area network* (LAN), need to establish protocols that limit access only to ethically relevant parties. Servers can be accessed by personal computers with modems over telephone lines, dramatically increasing the audience potentially having access to the secured data. Computer systems management specialists who set up systems for business organizations must be made aware of the location of sensitive confidential material. They can design the system with the appropriate safeguards and security protocols to maintain confidentiality through security software that requires pass codes and the requisite employee training. LAN administrators routinely back up or duplicate LAN files as archives in the event of a hardware or software malfunction that results in the loss of data. If a PC user on the network has stored files on the server (e.g., word processor documents, spreadsheet files, database files, e-mail), the archived files may contain confidential material. Even though a given file may be deleted locally by a network user, there may be an archived copy stored somewhere, accessible to potentially inappropriate parties. Protocols must be established with LAN administrators regarding the archiving of potentially confidential information.

Unfortunately, counseling professionals may not be motivated to purchase adequate systems of protection due to ignorance or the presumed unlikelihood of unethical file disclosure. Establishing a secure computer system can be time-consuming and costly; nevertheless, confidential client information needs to be protected.

Faxes and E-mail

Fax machines allow the transmission of information either from paper or directly from a computer file. Generally, faxes are composed of printed matter, which can include any type of client information protected by client-therapist confidentiality. Counselors need to use caution when sending confidential information by fax. Many businesses have centrally located, public fax machines that are inappropriate for receiving confidential information. It is the counselor's responsibility to assure that confidential fax transmissions arrive in a secured environment. Faxes can be sent directly to a PC by fax/modem. The security precautions mentioned for electronic media storage apply to fax transmissions sent to PCs. A quick phone call to assess the situation before sending a confidential fax is appropriate to assure safe arrival of sensitive information. In the event that a destination PC or fax machine is not secure, the counselor should phone before transmitting documents to alert appropriate parties to intercept confidential information. Disclaimers placed on fax cover sheets are not sufficient protection against unscrupulous interception of confidential data.

Electronic mail, or e-mail, uses the Internet to send and receive messages among individuals or groups, simulating the sending and receiving of letters through the "mail." Confidential information on e-mail is vulnerable to interception by people other than the designated recipient; therefore, counselors must use caution when sending counseling-related information. Because of frequent use of e-mail by counselors, it is important to emphasize the ethical vulnerability of such communication.

Cellular Phones

While cellular phones are a tremendous convenience in today's frenetically paced society, they are neither secure nor private forms of communication. One need only use such technology in a major metropolitan area to discover the intrusion of unwelcome one- or two-way conversations. Discussion of confidential material should not occur over cellular phone networks.

COMPUTER-ASSISTED COUNSELING

Computer-assisted counseling exists in a variety of forms. Some programs function as therapeutic consultants (Goodman, Gingerich, & Shazer, 1989). The advent of the Internet and chat rooms has created the opportunity for direct, on-line communication between counselor and client (on-line counseling). Therapeutic software that is marketed to operate without therapist assistance is also available (Lawrence, 1986; Sampson, 1986a).

History

Computer-assisted therapy was first developed in the 1960s (Colby et al., 1966), but was relatively unsuccessful. Attempts to computerize psychotherapy were rejuvenated in the 1980s with the popularization of behavioral modes of therapy and the emphasis of bringing about change through education (Ford, 1993; Wagman, 1988). Early versions of counseling software that did not require counselor assistance included MORTON, which was based on cognitive behavior therapy and was designed primarily to treat mild forms of depression (Selmi, Klein, Greist, Johnson, & Harris, 1982). MORTON began with an educational component that addressed a cognitive model of depression with subsequent testing of the client's comprehension of the theory, feedback on a test of depression (Beck Depression Inventory), review of homework, and exercises to combat thoughts that perpetuate depression. The program offered response choices to the client, with limited free-responding. One experimental program, GURU, attempted to expand interactive conversation capabilities with the goal of increasing self-awareness (Colby, Colby, & Stoller, 1990).

More recently, virtual psychotherapy programs have been under development, such as *Avatars* (Duncan, 1997). This software depicts characterizations of the client via a computer image or graphic, with bubbles overhead to indicate ongoing dialogue. Another application, *Palace,* develops an "Intranet," or closed Internet system, allowing for virtual psychotherapy with a controlled audience (Duncan, 1997). Computer-assisted therapies have not gained a great audience to date (Granello, 2000). These applications require further research to evaluate their effectiveness as a counseling practice.

Career Counseling

Computerized career counseling has been evaluated by Kilvingham, Johnston, Hogan, and Mauer (1994). They concluded that clients who were highly motivated and goal directed benefited from the System for Interactive Guidance and Information-Plus (SIGI-PLUS). However, they determined that clients with less-clear goals and less motivation for independence did not benefit as much from the use of this program. Group or individual counseling was proposed as more appropriate in the latter case. In such a case, using computer career counseling software as an adjunct to individual and group counseling would be exemplary of good, ethical counseling practice.

Career counseling often involves a psychoeducational approach (information provision), which lends itself well to delivery through computer-assisted venues. A comprehensive review of research evaluating one of the most popular career guidance systems, DISCOVER, suggested that the computer-assisted format helped to increase self-efficacy and decision-making skills, increased planfulness, increased knowledge about specific occupations, and resulted in more targeted career goals (Taber & Luzzo, 1999). (For a comparison of 15 well-known computer-assisted guidance systems, see also Sampson et al. (1994), and for further information about the application of technology to career counseling, review the Web site of the Center for the Study of Technology in Counseling and Career Development at *www.career.fsu.edu/techcenter/.*)

Rehabilitation. As early as 1978, video games were used in the later phases of cognitive retraining for persons with a head injury. Cognitive retraining falls under the domain of therapy in a rehabilitation hospital setting. The novelty of the games made the monotonous, repetitive exercises that enhanced cognitive functioning more enjoyable (Caplan, 1987). A more sophisticated computerized testing application, the Computer Assisted Cognitive Retraining system (CACR), was developed in 1987 by the Brain Injury Rehabilitation Unit in Palo Alto, California. The CACR used various computer-driven exercises to enhance the individual's alertness, attention, concentration, fine-motor skills, memory, and certain language abilities (e.g., spelling, reading, and word finding). Performance scores were recorded by the computer and a graph indicated the client's progress.

Other Applications. A variety of theoretical orientations have been adapted to computer-assisted counseling, including behavioral, cognitive, educational, and psychodynamic approaches (Ford, 1993). Software has been developed to target AIDS education (Schinke & Orlandi, 1990; Schinke et al., 1989), the treatment of drug and alcohol abuse (Moncher et al., 1985), obesity (Burnett, Magel, Harrington, & Taylor, 1989; Burnett,

Taylor, & Agras, 1985; Taylor, Agras, Losch, Plante, & Burnett, 1991), personal distress (Wagman, 1980, 1988; Wagman & Kerber, 1980), sexual dysfunction (Binik, Servan-Schreiber, Freiwald, & Hall, 1988; Servan-Schreiber & Binik, 1989), smoking (Burling et al., 1989; Schneider, 1986; Schneider, Walter, & O'Donnell, 1990), and stress (Smith, 1987). Various clinical populations have benefited from computer-assisted counseling, including persons with depression (Selmi, Klein, Greist, Sorell, & Erdman, 1990), persons with phobia (Carr, Ghosh, & Marks, 1988; Salyer, 1997), people who are violent offenders (Ford & Vitelli, 1992), patients with burn pain (Salyer, 1997), and head trauma patients who need cognitive retraining (Niemann, Ruff, & Baser, 1990).

As computer technology continues to improve, so will the capabilities of computer-assisted therapy. The ethical implications of widespread use of such technology have not been adequately explored (Ford, 1993; Peterson, Murray, & Chan, 1998; Sampson et al., 1997). Research is needed to compare the outcomes of in vivo counseling and newly developed computer-assisted counseling, how they may be used together to affect change, and what factors of such technology contribute to effective therapy.

Computer-Assisted Counseling: Real Therapy?

Counselors with a psychodynamic or humanistic orientation may be most resistant to the use of computer-assisted counseling in lieu of individual face-to-face therapy (Ford, 1993). Many counselors do wonder—is computer-assisted counseling "real therapy"? The concepts of counseling and psychotherapy are so inclusive that further clarification of computer-assisted counseling is necessary before the point can be argued successfully. Grencavage and Norcross (1990) suggested that psychotherapies do have commonalities: (a) development of a therapeutic alliance, (b) opportunity for catharsis, (c) acquisition and practice of new behaviors, and (d) clients' positive expectations. The literature supports the contention that computer-assisted counseling can be used to practice new behaviors, test simulated situations, express feelings and emotions, receive feedback, develop insight, and learn how to better interact with others (Ford, 1993). Ford (1993) contended that if sharing a number of commonalities with recognized psychotherapy techniques is the criterion for determining the viability of computer-assisted psychotherapy, it can be argued strongly that such technology is, in fact, a form of psychotherapy.

Consumer Acceptance

Counselors have an ethical responsibility to use interventions that suit an individual client's needs. The acceptance of computer-assisted counseling interventions by the consumers of such services is a critical aspect of the overall ethical viability of such technology. History has shown that, for many consumers, acceptance of the technology is not an issue (Erdman, Klein, & Greist, 1985; French & Beaumont, 1987; Harrell, Honaker, Hetu, & Oberwager, 1987; Rozensky, Honor, Rasinski, Tovian, & Herz, 1986; Wyndowe, 1987). In fact, some consumers prefer technological alternatives over face-to-face interventions (Farrell, Camplair, & McCullough, 1987; Ford & Vitelli, 1992; Lukin, Dowd, Plake, & Kraft, 1985) with clients who express positive sentiments toward computer-assisted forms of counseling (Binik et al., 1988; Burda, Starkey, & Dominguez, 1991; Clarke & Schoech, 1984; Colby et al., 1989; Ford, 1988; Matthews, De Santi, Callahan, Koblenz-Sulcov, & Werden, 1987; McLemore & Fantuzzo, 1982; Servan-Schreiber & Binik, 1989).

Independent Use

The use of computer-assisted therapy independent from a therapist presents another ethical quandary. Many counselors are opposed to using such technology as a replacement for human therapists (Bloom & Walz, 2000; Colby et al., 1989; Davidson, 1985; Ford, 1988, 1993; Ford & Vitelli, 1992; Hartman, 1986a; Selmi et al., 1990). However, many such programs are designed so that at least moderately functioning clients do not need assistance with administration (Ford, 1993; Sampson, 1986a; Sampson & Krumboltz, 1991). One fact is clear: Counselors are necessary for the development and evaluation of effective computer-assisted counseling programs (Ford, 1993).

The ethical question facing counselors is, "How safe are these technologies for independent users?" There are certain benefits associated with making computer-assisted therapy available to independent users: "Cost, convenience, and privacy are just some of the advantages of self-help programs" (Ford, 1993, p. 391). "To the extent that it is possible to offer the public sound, effective programs that do not require professional intervention, it would be socially irresponsible to restrict unduly or to discourage psychologists from making such contributions" (Keith-Spiegel & Koocher, 1985, p. 217).

The criteria for determining whether a program should be used by someone who requires professional intervention remain a question. Due to the cost-effectiveness of computer-assisted therapy, help can be made available to people who otherwise could not afford therapy provided by a counselor (Colby, 1980, 1986; Davidson, 1985; Ford, 1993; Ford & Vitelli, 1992; Sampson & Krumboltz, 1991). However, making such technology available for those who may benefit from it also presents the potential for some to be harmed through its use.

Legal and ethical ramifications exist for improper use of computer-assisted therapy. Three probable malpractice complaints against counselors that may result from improper use of such technology are (a) negligent rendering of services, (b) negligence that leads to suicide, and (c) improper supervision of a disturbed client (Ford, 1993). As malpractice suits unfold, perhaps the necessary laws, codes, and standards will evolve. With respect to independent use, it seems best that computer-assisted counseling should be an adjunct to the relationship between counselor and client, so that harm to the client will be avoided through careful supervision.

Computer-Assisted Counseling Technology Validation

The ethical codes of the APA and the ACA require that software developers provide empirical evidence of the safety and effectiveness of computer-assisted assessment products before making any claims as to their effectiveness. This is not the case with computer-assisted therapy—there are no laws or ethical standards in place to require evidence of validity and reliability before developers can make claims in marketing their self-help software (Ford, 1993; Sampson et al., 1997). Given the precedent set by codes associated with computer-assisted assessment, software developers must demonstrate treatment effectiveness of their computer-assisted therapy empirically. Research can be done through experiments using the software with a sample of the target population and a peer review process. Standards to require this suggestion should become a priority for the counseling profession.

Another important point to address regarding program effectiveness is the credibility that is so easily extended by lay people toward information conveyed by computers (Hartman, 1986b; Sampson, 1986a). Ford (1993) proposed that it should be deemed unethical to capitalize on consumer naiveté as to the veracity of computer output. Appropriate training standards should be in place to assure the appropriate use of computer-assisted counseling (Figure 10–2).

1. Computer-assisted psychotherapy needs more evidence for validity and reliability. Potential applications and consumer acceptance argue for further development of this therapeutic modality.
2. It is unethical to capitalize on consumer naiveté as to the credibility or effectiveness of computer-assisted therapy.
3. Use of computer-assisted therapy software should be restricted to qualified professionals, much in the same way that testing materials are controlled by test publishers.

FIGURE 10–2.   Ideas for Reflection about Computer-Assisted Counseling

Access to Software

Companies that produce mental health software establish various levels of restricted access to therapeutic and testing software purchasers. However, there are few standards for access to such software, resulting historically in less-than-rigorous control over distribution (Ford, 1993). If software is designed for a client who should receive some type of therapy that is at least supervised by a clinician, the counseling profession must exercise some control over who has access to such software. Standards should be generated to make counseling-related software available only to qualified professionals, placing the liability for negligent use of the product on the practitioner (Ford, 1993; Schwitzgebel & Schwitzgebel, 1980).

Ethical Dilemmas in Computer-Assisted Counseling

There are at least four parties involved in computer-assisted counseling: (a) the client, (b) the counselor, (c) the software manufacturer, and (d) professional bodies such as the ACA, the APA, CRCC, and the NBCC. Responsibility for the ethical provision of electronic mental health services according to a specified set of standards is borne by the latter four parties at some level, and that responsibility must be given consideration by all participants involved.

The American Counseling Association (ACA) established a standard that addresses the use of computer technology in counseling. In summary, counselors have an obligation to assure that:

(1) the client is intellectually, emotionally, and physically capable of using the computer application; (2) the com-

puter application is appropriate for the needs of the client; (3) the client understands the purpose and operation of the computer applications; and (4) a follow-up of client use of a computer application is provided to correct possible misconceptions, discover inappropriate use, and assess subsequent needs.

These standards do not support the autonomous use of computer-assisted counseling by all clients, and acknowledge the potential for misunderstanding and the lack of contact between counselor and client inherent in such cases. The American Psychological Association has yet to publish standards or codes that specifically address computer-assisted therapy, but such efforts are under way (see the APA Ethics Statement in Appendix 10-A).

The use of computers to assist in the counseling process also introduces practical and financial ethical dilemmas. If a client is using a computer to assist with the therapeutic process, does this imply that services rendered are of a shorter duration than a face-to-face counseling modality? Counseling service providers must decide how to bill when computer applications are used as an adjunct to therapy. The client may ultimately save money because of less direct contact with the therapist. Conversely, if the therapist is maintaining ethical responsibility for the entire therapeutic process and chooses to closely monitor the use of computer technology, the difference in time used for therapy will merely be reappropriated to monitoring the technology introduced into therapy. The ethical codes and standards under development must address this financial issue.

Ford (1993) discussed the independent use of computer-assisted counseling services, specifically the legal issues that may arise out of litigation and legislation related to the electronic provision of counseling services. The lack of face-to-face monitoring of clients in computer-assisted telepsychology and cybercounseling sessions and issues related to *Tarasoff* liability (VandeCreek & Knapp, 1993) may result in malpractice lawsuits that shape legislative policy and ethical code development. Due to the nature of a fiduciary relationship established via electronic media, it is critical that counseling professionals using such technology remain aware of case law developments that affect practice. Legal issues ultimately may involve federal, state, and local legislation—and litigation. The literature that likely will be developed as a result of this new and technological enterprise will be of great importance to mental health professionals.

ON-LINE COUNSELING FORUMS

On-line forums of counseling can be found in the counseling research literature under a number of descriptors: psychotherapy in cyberspace (Stricker, 1996); counseling on the information highway (Sampson, Kolodinsky, & Greeno, 1997); behavioral telehealth (Nickelson, 1996); cybercounseling (Bloom & Walz, 2000; Duncan, 1997); telepsychology (Koocher & Morray, 2000); WebCounseling (NBCC, 2001); and, simply, counseling over the Internet. **On-line forums** of counseling represent one of the most recent technological developments in computer applications for the counseling profession (Bloom & Walz, 2000; Duncan, 1997; Sampson et al., 1997).

The Internet

The Internet is a product of computer networks originally used by the military to communicate with academics, government workers, and business people working on military projects (Sampson et al., 1997). This international network of computers allows for the interchange of messages, files, software, and communication among computer systems. Today's Internet has a number of features, including bulletin board systems (BBSs) and list servers that provide forums for the public exchange of text-based information by computer users.

BBSs are typically organized around a topic of interest; people can read a posting or add their own. An example of a counseling BBS may contain "posted messages on the content and process of counseling from participants who conduct discussions through these postings" (Sampson et al., 1997, pp. 203–204). Discussions can be moderated or unmoderated (Berge, 1994), allowing for controlled quality of discussion groups or potentially inappropriate information exchanges, respectively. Information on BBSs is not protected, so counselors must use caution to protect confidentiality when posting material. Encryption software uses an algorithm to re-sequence data codes to disguise data from parties who do not have the algorithm key. More research is needed to develop ways to prevent computer "hackers" (amateur software developers) from breaking such codes and accessing ethically sensitive material.

E-mail uses the Internet to send and receive messages. List servers are e-mail type software that provide easy, international dissemination of discussion lists and electronic journals (Sampson et al., 1997). Mental health professionals who use e-mail should recognize the ethical vulnerability of such communication— e-mail is vulnerable to interception by people other than the designated recipient.

Internet relay chat (IRC), or chat mode of Internet communication, allows two people to correspond in real time using a split screen—one side for each person (Duncan, 1997; Sampson et al., 1997). Computer conferencing allows groups of individuals to converse simultaneously through text, with one person potentially serving as moderator. In addition to the group counseling dynamic of such communication, the same limitations exist on the e-mail level of confidentiality. Chat rooms, a version of IRC with a little more privacy, are in frequent use. Although the audience is more limited in a chat room, the same ethical questions arise.

The World Wide Web (WWW) is composed of computer servers and graphical interfaces that are connected to the Internet. Together they provide an avenue of information exchange, including audio and visual material and text-based information. Individuals and organizations can establish and maintain a home page on the WWW, which is accessed on the Internet, to convey information about a specific person or organization. A Web site on the WWW comprises a home page with links, which are indicated by various graphical means. When activated (or "clicked" with a mouse), these links open up related home pages, Web sites, and multimedia files. The colloquialism "surfing the Net" implies searching for information on the WWW, which is connected via the Internet. Various software packages facilitate connection with the WWW and the associated home pages, Web sites, and links (e.g., Netscape or Microsoft Explorer).

Counseling Applications on the Internet

Bulletin board systems (BBSs) serve counselors as information resources, allowing access to specialized and current information regarding mental health issues (Marino, 1996). List servers and information databases (e.g. ERIC, PSYCHLIT) assist counselors in accessing diverse information quickly (Walz, 1996). However, the professional who accesses this information should treat such information with the same healthy skepticism as any printed material. Career counselors use the WWW, BBSs, and Web sites (Sampson et al., 1997), which provide job vacancy listings and even assistance in assembling resumés and submitting them to prospective employers (Allen, 1995; Boles, 1996; Jandt & Nemnich, 1995; Kennedy, 1995; Riley, Roehm, & Oserman, 1996; Woods & Ollis, 1996; Woods, Ollis, & Kaplan, 1996). Career counseling has also benefited from the use of video conferencing. After using the WWW to locate jobs and create and submit resumés, the interview between employer and prospective employee can occur in real time using on-line video interviewing technology (Bloom & Walz, 2000; Magnusen & Magnusen, 1995).

E-mail is used by consumers to access mental health professionals and to ask specific questions about diverse mental health issues (Hannon, 1996). The information exchange is similar to that in radio, print media, and television forums of advice-giving—the exchange is not in real time. A multitude of ethical concerns are associated with this type of counseling: misaddresses, the inability to see nonverbal behavior, increased opportunity for fraud, no guarantee of confidentiality, and limited use for clients without high verbal ability (Duncan, 1997).

The Information Highway: Future On-line Counseling. Sampson et al. (1997) predicted that the future information highway will be an integration of the Internet, multimedia-based PCs, cable TV networks, and wired and wireless telephone networks. The application potential of such an information highway is tremendous—enhancing existing technologies and creating uses not yet conceived. The information highway has become a reality for many citizens in the United States (Bloom & Walz, 2000; Gates, Myhrvold, & Rinearson, 1995). Many cable service carriers have combined efforts with telephone services, allowing access to the information highway through television cable networks.

Sampson et al. (1997), after providing a description of the future information highway, forecasted potential counseling applications on the information highway. They predicted that WWW home pages could be used for advertising on-line counseling services, provided that the methods used comply with standards set in place for advertising, public statements, and soliciting clients such as those of APA, ACA, CRCC, and NBCC. Multimedia presentation of counseling services has the potential to be quite creative and may allow for much more information dissemination than does a typical phone directory. With real-time video conferencing, clients can screen potential therapists before embarking on a therapeutic relationship. The counseling professional could potentially make suitability judgments as well. In the event that a referral is necessary, electronic media (e.g., e-mail) can be used to contact the referral sources and transfer associated records. However, counselors must use the appropriate encryption software to protect confidential information sent via e-mail.

Ultimately, the actual counseling sessions can occur in real time, using on-line computer technology on the information highway. The information highway allows "counselors to overcome problems of distance and time to offer opportunities for networking and interacting not otherwise available" (Walz, 1996, p. 417; see also Hufford, Glueckauf, & Webb, 1999). Orientation to counseling services can occur using computer-assisted instruction (Sampson, 1986a), freeing up on-line and counselor time and, subsequently, lessening client expense. The protocols necessary to protect such communication over the Internet, such as data encryption and video signal scrambling (as used for premium cable TV channels), need to be in place to guarantee confidential communication. Otherwise, such practice could be considered unethical.

Ethical Concerns with On-line Counseling

Direct, on-line counseling services are increasingly prevalent on the Internet (Bloom & Walz, 2000; Duncan, 1997; Sampson et al., 1997). A survey of the number of counseling-related home pages conducted between April 1996 and August 1996 revealed a potential annualized increase of 55 percent (Sampson et al., 1997). The same survey revealed charges ranging from a $15 fee for answering a question via e-mail to $65 per hour for a 60-minute chat session. Counselors offered services that ranged from single-treatment interventions to 35 specialty services. Credentials of practitioners varied, including Ph.D., M.D., M.A., and L.P.C. Some individuals who indicated degree credentials after their names did not indicate the disciplines in which they received their degrees, and many "counselors" did not indicate any credentials or training (Sampson et al., 1997). The ACA Code of Ethics requires that counselors identify their credentials in a manner that is not false, misleading, deceptive, or fraudulent. As codes and ethical standards are revised, specific guidelines for counseling activities over the Internet are being addressed.

The literature addressing ethics and counseling-related activity on the Internet is growing (Bloom & Walz, 2000; Duncan, 1997; Newman, 2001; Peterson, Murray, & Chan, 1998; Sampson et al., 1997). A survey by Sampson et al. (1997) of a sampling of the 3,764 counseling-related home pages identified in April 1996, revealed that there were at least 275 practitioners offering counseling services over the Internet. Such activity was projected to increase at a rate between 55 percent and 72 percent per year (Sampson et al., 1997).

Psychotherapy in cyberspace brings with it a number of ethical concerns, including (a) licensing

1. More research is needed to develop safeguards to confidentiality in venues of Internet-based counseling services.
2. Credentials vary for practitioners of Web-based counseling services, so the profession is obligated to educate the consumer as to the potential pitfalls of consuming services from unqualified practitioners (see also APA's "Commonsense in a 'Dot Com' World" at http://www.apa.org/practice/dotcom.html).
3. Counseling professionals must also assume responsibility for providing equal access to on-line counseling services in order to empower rather than disenfranchise consumers of Internet-based counseling services.

FIGURE 10–3. Thinking about Cybercounseling Ethical Obligations

criteria for such practice, (b) confidentiality issues, and (c) client safety issues (Stricker, 1996). People who offer counseling services over the Internet should use technological safeguards to protect confidentiality. Such assurances should be sought out before using such services. If the providers are not using appropriate security measures, such practice should be deemed unethical (Figure 10–3).

Security. A fully functional information highway needs a solid data security system, including means of safely transferring money (Duncan, 1997; Gates et al., 1995). Data encryption must become more sophisticated to keep pace with the increasing sophistication of people who illegally break such codes. As biometric technology (e.g., voiceprints or thumbprints) becomes more reliable and cost-effective, it will likely be used to control users at the receiving end of the information highway (Sampson et al., 1997).

Access to Services. Recent U.S. Department of Commerce (1999) data suggest that socioeconomic status (SES) plays an important role in access to Web-based services. Households with incomes of $75,000 and higher are 20 times more likely to have access to the Internet than those at the lowest income levels. Ethnicity also appears to play a part—Whites are more likely to have access to the Web from home than are people of color from any location. Finally, location of residence also plays a part in access to services: Americans living in rural areas are half as likely to have access to the Web as their urban counterparts, even at the lowest income levels. Socially responsible practitioners must make every effort to keep progressive technology in counsel-

ing equally accessible to all who need it, lest the technology itself becomes a vehicle of disenfranchisement rather than one of empowerment (see also Lee, 2000).

Cost to the Practitioner. While many users have free access to the Internet through organizations and educational institutions, enhanced technology for the information highway comes with a price. The counseling profession may be faced with cost-prohibitive factors of using such technology in some institutions. If the counseling profession becomes dependent on the free services currently available, and cannot shift the resources to continue accessing the information highway when costs increase, the people hurt by such a change may be the consumers of on-line counseling services. Counselors are ethically responsible to assess their ability to maintain consumer access to this technology as costs increase, or be prepared to provide reliable referral sources when on-line counseling services become too expensive for consumers.

While on-line technology removes some barriers of distance and time, the question remains whether counselors actually have the time and energy to accommodate the subsequent increase in client contact. The time constraints imposed by distance and circumstance allow counselors to process between client contacts, document interactions, and prepare for the next client. If counselors already have a full docket of clients, the remaining benefit of providing on-line counseling services is that of service availability to remotely located or individuals who are home-bound. It may be presumptuous to assume that on-line technology will result in more people served per counselor, given the necessary time to process and document counseling interactions.

For an up-to-date cyber overview of ongoing research, information from professionals on ethical dilemmas encountered on the Internet, and current updates on legal, technical, and practical aspects of Web counseling, point your Web browser to Cybertowers (Mahue, 1998) at *www.cybertowers.com*, or Psych Central (Grohol, 1998) at *www.grohol.com*.

ETHICS AND POLICY DEVELOPMENTS IN ON-LINE MENTAL HEALTH SERVICES

The Emergence of Telehealth

One of the greatest potentials in using the Internet to deliver mental health services is the ability to reach remote areas that were formerly without access to such services (Harris-Bowlsby, 2000). **Telehealth services,** or remote, electronic consultation between consumers and providers in the health care professions (e.g., via videoconferencing), have received increasing attention throughout the helping professions over the past decade.

Health care providers that participate in telehealth services are eligible for Medicare reimbursement in rural areas determined by the federal government to have a shortage of health professionals (e.g., North Dakota and Montana), with fee schedules remaining the same as those for regular office visits. In 1997, the states of California and Louisiana passed laws requiring private insurance carriers to provide reimbursement for such services. The Federal Communications Commission (FCC) provided grants for public, nonprofit entities wishing to develop their potential in these areas (see *www.fcc.gov/healthnet*).

In addition to the federal and state support for telehealth, a number of professional organizations have responded to the presence of Internet-based counseling services by developing policies and standards that can help guide counseling professionals through this new frontier. The trailblazer of this effort among counseling organizations is the National Board for Certified Counselors.

NBCC and CCE Efforts

In 1995, the National Board for Certified Counselors (NBCC) Board of Directors appointed a WebCounseling Task Force and, in cooperation with its affiliate, the Center for Credentialing and Education (CCE), created standards for the ethical practice of "WebCounseling" (NBCC, 2001; see Appendix 10-B). The Board of Directors of NBCC established and adopted a code in 1997 that was unique to W*ebCounseling* and *WebCounselors*. This group defined **WebCounseling** as "the practice of professional counseling and information delivery that occurs when client(s) and counselor are in separate or remote locations and utilize electronic means to communicate over the Internet." New standards were adopted by NBCC in 2001 and provide guidance for the currently termed area of Internet Counseling. In addition to the recommendation to adhere to the NBCC Code of Ethics (2001) pertaining to the practice of professional counseling, the following is a summary of NBCC's suggestions to guide the practice of Internet counseling:

1. Use code words or numbers to screen potential imposters and to correctly verify client identity.
2. Where parent/guardian consent are necessary, use similar technology to establish identity of consenting person.
3. Establish procedures for contacting Internet counselor when he or she is off-line.

4. Provide solutions in the event of technical failure (phone numbers, collect calls, time zone differences, response delays in e-mail correspondence).
5. Discuss the impact of the loss of visual cues where relevant and how to cope with misunderstandings.
6. Establish a counselor-on-call within the client's geographic region, as well as local crisis intervention hotline numbers.
7. Assist clients to identify free public access points to the Internet in their community to access counseling, assessment, information and instructional resources.
8. Make reasonable efforts to make the counselor's Web site accessible to clients with disabilities.
9. Consider the culture, language, time zone and other local conditions that may impact their clients.
10. Inform clients of encryption methods used to help insure confidentiality; clarify hazards of data that are not encrypted (e.g., unauthorized transmission or monitoring of records).
11. Inform clients how long treatment-related electronic data are preserved.
12. Follow appropriate procedures for release of confidential electronic information.
13. Review legal statutes (local, state, provincial, and national) and ethical codes as they pertain to Internet counseling and supervision; review codes and laws in the counselor's as well as client's home locations due to questions about jurisdiction; clarify local customs regarding age of consent, child abuse, and neglect reporting.
14. Provide links to Web sites of all relevant certification bodies and licensure boards to facilitate consumer protection.

NBCC's code provided an opportunity to consider possible difficulties in implementing telehealth treatment paradigms. However, some of the proposed solutions were unclear, ambiguous, and perhaps premature. For instance, the concept of "counselor-on-call" appears unclear or unwieldy and highlights the volatility of a distant counseling relationship. Notwithstanding the lack of conclusive research available on the types of presenting problems that are inappropriate for telehealth contexts, NBCC's list of presenting problems and the associated efforts to establish standards of practice in this emerging area were commendable, and were considered by other professional organizations embarking on similar missions. However, the ethical perils associated with **cybercounseling**—counseling on the Internet—are profound. Standards of practice in this area will continue to evolve.

ACA's Efforts

The American Counseling Association (ACA) built upon the work of the NBCC through its Ethics Committee. This group attempted to educate ACA's members of the risks associated with providing counseling services over the Internet (Hughs & Ruiz, 1998). ACA's Governing Council approved the Ethical Standards for Internet On-Line Counseling in October 1999 (see Appendix 10-C). ACA describes the Standards as guidelines that "establish appropriate standards for the use of electronic communications over the Internet to provide on-line counseling services, and should be used only in conjunction with the latest *ACA Code of Ethics and Standards of Practice*" (ACA, 1999). The standards are more detailed than those generated by the NBCC, and they appear to have benefited from NBCC's more general, yet trailblazing, efforts.

Additionally, ACA, in collaboration with the ERIC/Counseling & Student Services (ERIC/CASS) Clearinghouse, developed an edited text called *Cybercounseling and Cyberlearning: Strategies & Resources for the Millennium* (Bloom & Walz, 2000). This basic reference—or handbook of sorts—reviews the "state of the art" through 48 different contributors with expertise in the area. The editors describe the text as "a summing up that is a series of freestanding knowledge generalizations" (p. 405). Because of the newness of counseling cyberservices, it was difficult to produce a text that was not primarily speculation and opinion. The text contains some very useful Web resource directories, and some very enjoyable first-hand accounts of professionals engaging in cybercounseling and cyberlearning.

APA's Efforts

Since 1997, the American Psychological Association's (APA) Board of Professional Affairs (BPA) has allocated resources to consider the ethical implications of "telepsychology." In November 1997, BPA sponsored an institute on telehealth, where a broad range of stakeholder representatives (i.e., APA, federal government, private sector, and experts in the field) explored the rapidly developing realm of telehealth applications in psychology. BPA then appointed a Work Group on Professional Practice Issues in Telehealth to make recommendations for policy development. The group's position to date has been that the current ethical code adequately addresses the use of any innovative technology in psychological practice.

APA first issued a statement regarding "Psychotherapy by Telephone" in 1993. Subsequently, in 1995 and again in 1997, the Ethics Committee of the APA issued a statement that addressed services by telephone, teleconferencing, and the Internet (see Appendix 10-A). The statement suggested that the current APA ethics code sufficiently addresses the ethical cautions associated with emerging areas of practice (APA, November 1997).

However, Koocher and Morray (2000) suggested that professional ethical codes and guidelines do not go far enough—practitioners can avoid scrutiny by avoiding professional organizations that create enforceable standards, or by using unregulated titles or service descriptions to elude regulatory authorities. Many states have legislation that provides title-only provisions in credentialing legislation, so eluding authority is easy enough to achieve. State policies that address professional practice or function (rather than title only) will most likely be more effective in providing quality controls for ethical practice.

APA Practice Directorate staff also provided information regarding the unique needs of behavioral health consumers and practitioners through work groups that supported the federal Joint Working Group on Telemedicine (JWGT), an interagency work group deeply involved in federal administrative telehealth activity. APA's BPA appointed a Work Group on Professional Practice Issues in Telehealth to make recommendations for policy in this area. The group's work culminated in a set of 10 interdisciplinary principles for professional practice in telehealth (see Reed, McLaughlin, & Milholland, 2000). Additionally, APA's Division 31 sponsored, along with numerous division co-sponsors, a 1999 APA Telehealth Mini-convention that addressed "innovative practice and research opportunities" according to "top telehealth experts" (APAGS, Summer 1999). APA and its membership have made efforts to articulate and disseminate information regarding the emerging area of telepsychology, particularly as it applies to the broader area of telehealth and telemedicine.

The Executive Director for Practice at APA, Dr. Russ Newman, provided a recent statement on "on-line therapy" (March 2001). He described numerous inquiries to APA regarding the official position "for" or "against" on-line therapy. He wrote that this new technology is not a singular entity that argues for a singular position, and applauded the work of BPA's Work Group on Professional Practice Issues in Telehealth. He stated that the current state of affairs argues for practitioners to answer three questions: (1) under what conditions; (2) for what problems; and (3) with which interventions, "does the application of Internet technology facilitate the delivery of health care services?" (p. 56). Dr. Newman suggested that professionals evaluate "e-health sites" by visiting *www.helping.apa.org/dotcomsense*. "In the end" he concludes, "the profession must determine when the Internet is useful and when it is not" (p. 56). The Web site to which he referred also helps consumers of such services make good decisions about the consumption of Web-based counseling services.

NCDA's Efforts

The National Career Development Association (1997) contributed a set of standards for the helping profession's consumption as Web technology influences career-related endeavors (see *www.ncda.org/about/polnet.html*). The guidelines begin with suggestions for use of Internet delivery of career counseling and career planning services (see Appendix 10-D). The next section reviews the ethical use of the Internet for job posting and searching; the final section lists unacceptable counselor behaviors on the Internet and ends with a brief discussion of the need for research in the area of Web-assisted counseling and guidance.

Regulation of Telepsychology

According to Duncan (1997), 20 states developed legislation related to on-line counseling services by 1997. Koocher and Morray (2000) conducted a survey of State Attorneys General (AGs) regarding legal and regulatory issues related to the delivery of behavioral health services via electronic means (i.e., teleconference, Internet, and other electronic media). Questions included:

1. Which mental health professions are regulated by statute in your state: psychiatry, psychology, social work, marriage and family counseling, pastoral counseling, psychiatric nursing, rehabilitation counseling, and other fields?
2. Has your state enacted statutes regulating the practice of psychotherapy or counseling apart from the profession listed above?
3. Has your state enacted statutes regulating the practice of psychotherapy or counseling by means of telephone, Internet, or other electronic means?
4. Have any of the statutory mental health licensing authorities in your state adopted rules limiting or otherwise regulating the practice of psychotherapy or counseling by electronic means? If no, is such regulation contemplated?
5. Have any of the statutory mental health licensing authorities in your state brought charges against a li-

censed mental health practitioner for delivering psychotherapy or counseling by electronic means?
6. Does your state claim regulatory authority over mental health practitioners residing outside your state, who offer psychotherapy or counseling to residents of your state via telephone, Internet, or other electronic means? If no, do you contemplate seeking such authority? If yes, have you prosecuted such a case?
7. Has your office received complaints about psychotherapy or counseling services provided across state lines by electronic means?

AGs from 41 states and the District of Columbia replied. The survey suggested that, as of 1999, only 7 percent of states surveyed had enacted statutes addressing "telehealth" issues in the practice of psychotherapy or counseling by means just described. Additionally, 93 percent of the mental health licensing authorities had yet to adopt rules limiting or otherwise regulating such practice. Only 17 percent of those without policies in place contemplated future policy development in this area. This result may be explained by the fact that 85 percent of those surveyed indicated no charges had been brought against mental health professionals using telehealth modalities, with only 5 percent expressing the existence of such litigation. Clearly, case law review will continue to inform efforts to regulate practice in this innovative area.

Another interesting question addressed in the survey explored how states are handling practitioners who provide telehealth services across state jurisdictions. How will credentialing be addressed across jurisdictions? Is it possible for a practitioner to remain aware of all mandatory reporting laws as they vary across 51 jurisdictions (including the District of Columbia)? Under which state jurisdiction does the practitioner actually practice—his own or that of the recipient of services?

Although only 17 percent of those surveyed reported complaints about telehealth services provided across state lines, it appears that some states (particularly those with large rural areas that could benefit most from such services) have anticipated the emergence of such telepsychology practices. Forty-five percent of states surveyed claimed regulatory authority over mental health practitioners residing outside the state who offer mental health services to residents of that state, and 14 percent of those who responded described such policy development as pending. The financial implications for practitioners who need to be credentialed in multiple states to practice across jurisdictions could be profound, not to mention the bureaucratic burden presented to licensing boards. Some professions have begun to address the telehealth-across-jurisdictions dilemma (e.g., medicine), but counseling and psychology are behind in this regard (Nickelson, 1998). One notable exception is the Association of State and Provincial Psychology Boards (ASPPB), which established a credential of reciprocity that has experienced limited success in the United States.

While consumer complaints regarding telepsychology or behavioral telehealth practices are rare, it is clear that policymakers are considering this emerging technology and that increased regulatory activity in this regard is imminent. It is only a matter of time before malpractice lawsuits involving behavioral telehealth become significant events in case law. As one AG respondent explained, his psychology licensing board issued a public statement suggesting that those who provide psychotherapy services via the Internet should do so at their own risk (Koocher & Morray, 2000).

Given the lack of consensus that currently exists, Koocher and Morray (2000) offered the following recommendations with respect to telepsychology:

1. Before engaging in the remote delivery of mental health services via electronic means, practitioners should carefully assess their competence to offer the particular services and consider the limitations of efficacy and effectiveness that may be a function of remote delivery.
2. Practitioners should consult with their professional liability insurance carrier to ascertain whether the planned services will be covered. Ideally, a written confirmation from a representative of the carrier should be obtained.
3. Practitioners are advised to seek consultation from colleagues and to provide all clients with clear, written guidelines regarding planned emergency practices (e.g., suicide risk situations).
4. Because no uniform standards of practice exist at this time, thoughtful written plans that reflect careful consultation with colleagues may suffice to document thoughtful professionalism in the event of an adverse incident.
5. A careful statement on limitations of confidentiality should be developed and provided to clients at the start of the professional relationship. The statement should inform clients of the standard limitations (e.g., child abuse reporting mandates), any state-specific requirements, and cautions about privacy problems with broadcast conversations (e.g., overhead wireless phone conversations or captured Internet transmissions).
6. Clinicians should thoroughly inform clients of what they can expect in terms of services offered, unavailable services (e.g., emergency or psychopharmacology coverage), access to the practitioner, emergency coverage, and similar issues.
7. If third parties are billed for services offered via electronic means, practitioners must clearly indicate that fact on billing forms. If a third-party payer who is unsupportive of electronic service delivery is wrongly led to believe that services took place in vivo as opposed to on-line, fraud charges may ultimately be filed. (p. 505)

Another on-line activity affecting counselors is the use of on-line supervision and virtual practica, all of which fall under the umbrella of counselor education.

COMPUTER-ASSISTED ASSESSMENT

The application of computers to the area of assessment includes the ability to administer, score, and interpret most of the psychological assessment instruments and procedures that are used by clinicians—such as personality tests, cognitive tests, and structured interviews. Intelligence test scoring and interpretation applications were among the first commercially available programs for PCs and have been the primary focus of software developers (Honaker & Fowler, 1990). Recent development of the application of computerized cognitive and aptitude assessment includes (a) subtests of the Wechsler Adult Intelligence Scale-III (French & Beaumont, 1992; Psychological Corporation, 1997), (b) Air Force flight performance tests (Park & Lee, 1992), (c) the Wonderlic Personnel Test (Kennedy, Baltzley, Turnage, & Jones, 1989), (d) memory subtests from the Wechsler Memory Scale-III and the Benton Tests (Youngjohn, Larrabee, & Crook, 1991; WAIS-III SAWS, 1998), and (e) multidimensional assessment of elderly people (Stones & Kozma, 1989). At the beginning of the 1990s, computer programs involving personality assessment accounted for the largest single number of assessment software applications available—45 percent of all computerized assessment products (Honaker & Fowler, 1990). Such tests included the Minnesota Multiphasic Personality Inventory-2 (MMPI-2), the California Psychological Inventory (CPI), the Millon Clinical Multiaxial Inventory (MCMI), the 16 Personality Factor Test (16PF), the NEO Personality Inventory-Revised (NEO PI-R), and the Rorschach inkblot test. These tests continue to experience widespread use in their standard and computerized formats (Aiken, 2000; Hood & Johnson, 1997).

Benefits of Computer-Assisted Test Administration

One benefit of computerized test administration is rapid presentation of reliable and repetitive information, which can be taxing on both the client and the test administrator if administered orally (Argentero, 1989; Caplan, 1987). The storing and retrieval of test data can be simplified with computer applications, which allow the professional to attend to other important dynamics in the assessment and training process (Honaker & Fowler, 1990). Human error during data collection also can be minimized. Additionally, there is evidence of increased reliability in the scoring of intelligence tests administered in a computer format, which further increases the veracity of test results (Honaker & Fowler, 1990). However, the reliability of computer-assisted assessment relies on the competency of the administrator of the software. The administrator must understand the noncomputerized administration procedures of a given test and how these are influenced by computer technology (Drummond, 1996). A thorough understanding of an assessment tool (i.e., its development, validity, reliability, and theoretical framework) is essential before administration. Unfortunately, the ease of computer-assisted assessment is deceptive—this perception may encourage use by people who are not trained adequately in measurement and statistics or are operating outside a given area of competency, and may constitute unethical practice according to the codes established by the ACA, APA, and the NBCC.

Another benefit of the use of computer-administered assessment is the development of adaptive or tailored testing (Weiss, 1985; Wise & Plake, 1990). Computer technology allows the examinee's responses to determine which subsequent items are to be administered. The resultant number of items required generally is reduced by 50 percent, therefore reducing test time. For higher-ability examinees, boredom is avoided by offering more challenging items. Lower-ability examinees may avoid discouragement that can occur secondary to item difficulty. This provides for more equal and ethical test administration to examinees, regardless of ability level, thus optimizing a given person's performance (Wise & Plake, 1990).

The ethical administration of tests requires precision and consistency. Computerized administration of testing has the potential to improve precision and consistency, thus enhancing the ethical administration of tests. It is important that the counseling field continue to demonstrate the validity and reliability of computerized assessment tools and compare their performance with comparable and better-established, paper-and-pencil tests.

Limitations of Computerized Administration

The benefits of this reported ease of administration and data collection can be misleading. Accurate interpretation of test performance also requires careful observation of the examinee during the administration of any test. Computerized test administration may encourage less vigilance on the administrator's part, possibly resulting in the absence of important clinical data. Specifically, situational factors related to the individual during the testing process may be overlooked. Interpreting a test without taking into account those factors (e.g., environmental stimuli, distracters, arousal level of the client during the assessment process, and fluctuations in performance related to such factors) beyond the basic test scores generated by a computer program may result in the unethical use of test data. Thus, the data gathered are essentially incomplete and may not present a holistic view of the person (Maki, 1986).

Some domains of assessment do not transfer well to computerized assessment. One such area is neuropsychological testing. The stimulus-response complexity of many neuropsychological tests is difficult to duplicate with current computer technology. While computerized assessment has its place in the assessment process, it cannot replace the involvement of the professional. It can, however, serve as a useful adjunct to the assessment process (Binder & Thompson, 1994). Thus, the ethical use of computerized technology must be considered within the context of the discipline using such technology.

A social issue associated with computerized assessment is the limited access to such technology for people with socioeconomic limitations. In a publication addressing the ethical treatment of patients with brain injury, Ackerman and Banks (1990) highlighted the limitations that socioeconomic status of a consumer or providing institution can impose upon the availability of such technology. It is important that technology that improves outcomes in patient treatment is made available to all who need it, regardless of their ability to pay.

The use of computers to administer assessment instruments is not a replacement for the professional counselor. Counseling practice is essentially a human-to-human encounter that provides assistance to people in need of counseling interventions. The use of technology in assessment may facilitate such endeavors;

however, implementation of technology in the counseling process also requires careful monitoring and supervision by experienced professionals to promote sound ethical practice (see also Wall, 2000).

Computer-Generated Assessment Results and Reports

The use of PCs to assist in interpreting psychological test results is increasing and is known as *computer-based test interpretation* (CBTI). A great deal of controversy surrounds this area of technology. Programs have been developed to meet the demands of the counseling professional, including systems that schedule appointments, administer a battery of tests, perform statistical and data management functions, and produce results in the form of computer-generated reports. However, reliability and validity information for these integrated systems is limited. While the sophistication of modular-integrated systems of assessment is increasing, some serious ethical considerations remain.

When a counseling professional has access to computer-generated test results from given test data, there is potential for over-reliance on the computer to interpret the protocol. The computer is unable to incorporate qualitative data that are accessible to the counselor. Qualitative data can take exception to direct interpretation of the quantitative test data. Errors in data entry can also result in inaccurate test scores. Professionals who use such software are obligated ethically to carefully review the data entered. Computer-generated test reports must also be interpreted carefully to avoid unethical assessment practice. Such protocols generally request raw test data or data collected from a structured interview. The data are then incorporated into a template report that is adjusted, based on the data entered. The counseling professional must review the entire report for accuracy and correspondence to available test data. Individual test results do not always lend themselves to a predictable template interpretation. The professional must critically analyze the report content and edit and supplement the report accordingly. Computer-generated reports can be useful templates for producing reports but should not be provided to referral sources without careful scrutiny by the examiner.

Organizational pressures in today's mental health care settings from managed care and third-party payment sources may force many organizations to do more with less. Such pressure encourages the use of less-qualified technicians who are paid less to perform assessment procedures. Over-reliance on the ease of computer technology is of even greater concern when less-qualified

examiners are used in the assessment process. The temptation to take any information that a computer generates, be it data interpretation or a report, and accept it at face value is a reality with potentially serious consequences. Overconfidence in technology can overshadow reasonable interpretation of results. Technology can help make test administration, interpretation, and report generation a more efficient process. However, computerized assessment must be viewed in light of its assets and limitations.

Research Issues in Computerized Assessment

The update to the Standards for Educational and Psychological Testing (AERA, APA, & NCME, 1999) provides standards for the development of computer-administered tests, the use of computer-based testing in general, the use of computer-generated test interpretations, and the implementation of computer-adaptive testing.

The ethical appropriateness of using PCs to administer tests is being examined in research today. The APA (1986) Committee on Professional Standards, along with the Committee on Psychological Tests and Assessment, developed the *Guidelines for Computer-Based Tests and Interpretations*. The ethical codes of ACA and APA address the importance of ethical behavior regarding the application of any technology in the assessment of, and subsequent treatment of, clients.

Equivalence is a major issue addressed by the APA. The interchange of information between computer-based and conventional (paper-and-pencil) tests has been deemed allowable if (a) the rank orders of scores tested in alternative modes closely approximate each other, and (b) the means, dispersions, and shapes of the score distributions are approximately the same, or have been made approximately the same by rescaling the scores from the computer mode. The computerized version must be psychometrically similar to the paper-and-pencil version; thus, the term *equivalence*.

Scholars also are exploring the possibility that the exchange of people, paper, and pencil for computer technology changes how the examinee responds to evaluation. For example, personally sensitive issues appear to be easier to divulge to a computer program than to an actual therapist, which may increase the amount of data available to the counselor (Honaker & Fowler, 1990; Sampson, 2000). The psychological constructs tapped by clinical interviews and the traditional methods of testing may be different from those tapped when a computer is used for these same purposes. Because of these potential differences, norms generated by noncomputerized assessment tools may not generalize to the computer format.

To use a computer for ease of administration and then interpret the test by paper-and-pencil norms may not be ethical due to the potential error that can be introduced. More time is needed to establish appropriate norms for computerized test interpretation. Many computerized assessment instruments must be treated as experimental until further research clarifies the effect of the computer medium on the overall assessment process. Manuals that accompany any tests must be reviewed carefully to determine the appropriateness of the use of the instrument.

COMPUTER-ASSISTED COUNSELOR EDUCATION

On-line Supervision and Virtual Practica

Cyberspace, or the Internet, has been considered an alternative means of counselor supervision (Myrick & Sabella, 1995). Myrick and Sabella recommended the use of e-mail to share professional ideas and information with supervisees in remote and distant areas. Such technology also provides an opportunity for academic, organizational, or peer supervision. Myrick and Sabella (1995) also provided specific scenarios in which elementary school counselors were able to access timely assistance for complex cases, particularly when counselors were practicing in remote locations.

E-mail, or text-based supervision, has its limitations. Removing the one-to-one interaction between supervisor and supervisee limits the data to which supervisors may respond (e.g., body language or acceptance of constructive criticism). The development of satellite and computer technology that allows real-time video and audio interaction minimizes some limitations of text-based supervision. However, it is unclear how this technology compares with person-to-person supervision within the same space. The ethical issues identified in the on-line counseling section of this chapter also apply to on-line supervision and practica. Unless sufficient security protocols are in place, such activity could be considered unethical. Further research is needed regarding existing systems and protocols.

Distance Learning

Distance learning may be conceptualized as the use of technical equipment to guarantee consistent product quality in mass volumes, and use of technical media (e.g., television, radio, and satellite broadcasting) in place of in vivo teachers to broaden accessibility (Stewart, 1992). New technologies are being used to deliver pre-service and in-service training to counselors from various specialty areas (Davis & Yazak, 1995). Since the development of the British Open University in 1969, distance-learning programs have expanded worldwide. Distance learning is useful for persons in remote and rural areas, for learners who have limited mobility, and for professionals with busy schedules or economic limitations who wish to further their professional development through licensure and certification (Steele, 1993).

Advancement in technology is one factor that influences educators to consider distance learning (Davis & Yazak, 1995). Another compelling factor is the potential cost effectiveness of distance education in an era of increased college enrollment and decreasing government funding for higher education (Altekruse & Brew, 2000). The Internet connects millions of computers worldwide, allowing access to databases and library materials, and facilitating communication between instructors and students. HTML programming capabilities, CD-ROM technology, multimedia presentation of written material, and high-quality graphics have made learning through computer software a viable alternative or supplement to the traditional classroom experience (Bloom & Walz, 2000; Scriven, 1991; Sirkin, 1994).

Synchronous and Asynchronous Learning Paradigms

Two popular, Web-based distance learning paradigms include *synchronous* and *asynchronous* modalities. **Asynchronous** curriculum delivery can occur over the Web using software programs like Blackboard or Web CT; curricula are delivered through on-line files that are available continuously. Students can interact with the system on their own schedule. **Synchronous** delivery systems have a set time for on-line interaction, sometimes using streaming video to deliver on-line lectures to a prescheduled audience. There are also combinations of the two modalities that create a multi-modal interactive curriculum.

The U.S. Department of Education has supported efforts to further distance-learning initiatives. Four institutions have set the standard for delivering rehabilitation counseling education: (a) Utah State University offers a master's degree program composed of satellite broadcasts of videotaped modules, audio teleconferencing, and telephone support; (b) University of Northern Colorado, in cooperation with Mind Extension University (Bitter, Gregg, & Jackson, 1994), offers noncredit seminars, courses, and certificates via live telecasts, videotapes, computer bulletin boards, voice mail, phone support, and electronic meeting software; (c) San Diego State University offers credit courses to remote island groups in the Northern Pacific and several U.S. states via state-of-the-art methods designed to keep pace with evolving technologies (Davis & Yazak, 1995), and; (d) Virginia Commonwealth University offers graduate study at the master's and doctoral level as well as an advanced certificate in counseling (see *www.rehabcounseling.org*).

Ethical Concerns with Distance Learning

Distance learning brings several ethical concerns for counselor educators. Program integrity, continuity, and sophistication affect the quality of education that a given counselor receives. The available resources that facilitate a program's capacity to accomplish its objectives through distance learning must be considered case by case. It is erroneous to assume that an in vivo course of study will readily translate to a distance-learning format. An outcome research base is necessary to compare the difference between distance-learning programs and exemplary, traditional, university-based programs, and to examine the effectiveness of distance learning. Program accreditation standards can be developed from such data to ensure the integrity of counselor education programs.

In traditional university settings, courses can be evaluated through peer review. Course activity between teacher and student can be observed and evaluated by fellow professionals to provide developmental suggestions that enhance an instructor's pedagogy and, ultimately, the quality of the student's education. In a distance-learning setting, the interpersonal dynamic between instructor and student is different than a face-to-face experience. How this difference affects the learning process is not yet known, but it is clear this dynamic cannot be observed for distance learning in the same way it is in the traditional classroom setting. The dynamic difference between in vivo and remote education may also influence the student learning process. This dynamic has not been fully explored. Preliminary data suggest that modalities overall do not impact grades (Stocks & Freddolino, 1998). Students reported that the distance-education format provided a flexibility that was desirable, but it lacked the personal contact of in vivo formats (Keating & Hargitai, 1999). Methods to maintain in vivo, professional feedback that contributes to course quality and development within a distance learning context should be explored further.

Taped presentations of a distance-learning curriculum do not provide students the opportunity to ask questions and interact contemporaneously with instructors. It is unclear how this may affect the learning process. If a student is having difficulty grasping a concept in a real-time distance-learning presentation, the opportunity for one-to-one interaction for clarification is limited. The logistics of interacting with a classroom or an instructor remotely may inherently be more time-consuming than in a traditional classroom setting (e.g., timing of questions, coordinating multiple inquiries, and keeping the course moving in a timely manner). The difficulty associated with cueing an instructor in a remote setting may discourage active and lively class participation. Student-to-student interaction (e.g., breaking into small groups) is limited, although technologically possible. However, these situations introduce a number of factors that affect time, interpersonal interaction, and possibly the willingness to engage others. The effect of these limitations must be clarified before valid comparison of in vivo learning versus distance learning can be made.

If followup phone support is available to students, their ability to graphically clarify a concept is limited. People who are uncomfortable with phone communication are at a distinct disadvantage. The effect of video with phone interaction may alleviate some of this concern. Additionally, the expense of such communication may deter students from taking advantage of this assistance. The person-to-person conferences available to students on campus to assist with clarification of difficult material are not available to remote learners. Some courses may more readily lend themselves to remote presentation than others, again necessitating a case-by-case approach to the development of distance-learning curricula.

Some literature suggests that students and faculty generally prefer face-to-face interaction over distance learning (Bland, Morrison, & Ross, 1992). Some would say that simply accessing information in any technologically sophisticated fashion is inferior to an educational environment that includes two-way communication (Garrison, 1990; Law & Sissons, 1985). Most importantly, the personal development of students in counselor education is arguably as important as their professional and academic development. It is difficult for faculty to provide mentoring and role modeling of professional behavior without personal contact with students. All things considered, the development of distance-learning curricula should be carefully thought out.

Suggestions for Ethical Distance-Learning Curricula Development

Davis and Yazak (1995) suggest several areas of focus for the development of accreditation guidelines for distance-learning curricula. They modeled their suggestions after the Southern Association of Colleges and Schools' (Staff, 1993) areas of focus for program accreditation standards, which included mission, curriculum delivery, faculty, resources, student support, and evaluation.

Mission. Faculty should review the mission of their program and institution to consider the long-range strategic effect of distance learning on the fundamental philosophy of the institution and the existing curriculum. Issues such as regional accreditation (proposed catchment area of recruitment), potential student market, admission procedures, and program structure (e.g., time period of course acquisition that maintains program integrity) must be considered. Student skills of self-pacing, goal setting, and self-evaluation may require a greater emphasis in student recruitment. Without the local influence of professors or peers, student motivation becomes critical. Institutions that offer distance-learning curricula have an ethical responsibility to recruit candidates who will thrive in a distance-learning environment.

Curriculum Delivery. Establishing appropriate modes of information dissemination is crucial to the education process. Distance learning presents a number of factors that influence curriculum delivery. While it may be premature to rule out the viability of certain areas of curricula in distance learning, Eldredge, Gerard, and Smart (1994) suggested that instruction in the areas of counseling skills and testing evaluation "do not lend themselves well to distance education because of the individualized supervision required to assist full skill development" (p. 78). As Davis and Yazak (1995) recommended, "consideration of the characteristics of technical media in relation to the learning requirements of advanced and specialized curriculum is essential" (p. 297).

The presentation of information that is to be organized, generally understood, and memorized, such as historical and theoretical overviews, could perhaps be effectively accomplished through some of the distance-learning techniques already discussed (one-way audio-visual transmission, or videotaped curricula). However, course material that requires critical thinking, abstraction, active processing, and synthesis of information may require active instructor and student discussion that does not lend itself to some distance-learning formats (Davis & Yazak, 1995). Discussion of counseling scenarios and complex, ethical problem-solving skills that emerge from such experience could be jeopardized in such formats, which strongly questions the ethical appropriateness of using such approaches in counselor education. Clearly, more research is required to ethically present an entire advanced curriculum exclusively by distance-learning technology.

Faculty. Distance learning presents opportunities to instruct more nontraditional students in remote areas, which presents a new audience to many professional counselor educators. This opportunity may ultimately affect how existing curricula are presented to new audiences. Expertise in technology and troubleshooting are necessary to promote seamless and timely presentation of remote curricula (Davis-Bell, 1991; Fulmer, Hazzard, Jones, & Keene, 1992; Massoumian, 1989; Willis, 1992). "Distance learning faculty must be trained in how to plan lessons that must be precise, well-timed, and supported with high-quality visual aids" (Davis & Yazak, 1995). Courses in distance-learning technology and subsequent curriculum development may be necessary for counselor educators in training to facilitate proper use of such technology.

Two more issues need to be addressed with respect to faculty who are developing distance-learning material. First, faculty may share concerns with others who are creating computer-assisted counseling software. distance-learning curriculum development and counseling software development currently are not acknowledged by university administrators in the same spirit as are other quantitative research efforts, although they are equally time-consuming. Such efforts must be acknowledged effectively if such technology is to move forward. Second, guidelines for the protection of property rights of materials developed for distance-learning endeavors must be established. If a professor invests a great deal of time in curriculum development, the same ethical rights and restrictions placed on publications should be extended to distance-learning curricula.

Resources. Some distance-learning students, particularly those in remote locations, may not have access to the same resources that students have in a campus setting. Therefore, textbooks used in distance-learning courses should engage the students in active learning. Educators may choose texts with accompanying workbooks that encourage active processing of readings through exercises. Some courses may also require the use of a library or the Internet for in-depth study. If such resources are not available at a distance-learning site, and no alternatives exist (e.g., library networking, interlibrary loan services, or facsimile services), courses that require such resources may not be appropriate for a distance-learning curriculum.

Students benefit from speedy instructor feedback on assignments, such as quizzes, papers, and exams. In a distance-learning context, rapid turn-around of the student's work is likely to be confounded by proximity. Expedient methods of assignment exchanges are necessary for students to benefit from instructor feedback. In addition to using mail delivery systems and on-line computerized testing, faculty visits to distance classrooms are recommended whenever possible (Barker, 1986; Hodgson, 1986). However, travel to some remote areas may be cost-prohibitive, so the nature of the course must determine the optimal instructor feedback, and therefore dictate what types of courses will be worth offering through distance learning.

Student Support.   Professionals who recruit students to distance-learning programs are ethically responsible for assuring that the recruits have the coping skills necessary to thrive in such an environment. Pre-course counseling may help identify students who need remediation before embarking on such an endeavor. On-going tutoring services may also be required for students who have taken on more than they are capable of (Davis & Yazak, 1995; Hodgson, 1986).

Students in distance-learning programs need advice on career counseling, course selection, financial aid, registration, and practica/internship placement. Reasonable accommodations for persons with disabilities may also be an issue. Many program-accrediting bodies require a certain advisee-to-faculty ratio for programs to remain accredited. The Council on Rehabilitation Education (CORE) requires a ratio of less than 20:1 (Council on Rehabilitation Education, 2000). The recommended student-to-faculty ratio of the Council for Accreditation of Counseling and Related Education Programs (CACREP) is more rigorous—10:1 (CACREP, 1996). The impact of distance learning upon these requirements, given the temptation to use such technology to educate more students with the same number of faculty members, must be evaluated carefully.

Program Evaluation.   Evaluation of distance-learning effectiveness is an ethical responsibility of program developers and is a vital component of program accreditation (Davis & Yazak, 1995; Olcott, 1993). Fenwick (1992) described seven common indicators of quality for distance-learning curricula: (a) attrition rates, (b) work assignment response rates, (c) student course evaluations, (d) quality of the learning package, (e) the learning process, (f) degree of freedom of pace and method, and (g) the level of student independence. Formal feedback from students is even more critical for distance-learning programs because students have comparatively less contact with program faculty (Davis & Yazak, 1995). Audio conferencing, phone communication, and e-mail communication can facilitate frequent feedback to distance-learning program developers. The ethical concerns that apply to the electronic media are relevant to distance learning as well. For a recent discussion of faculty perceptions of the pros and cons of developing and delivering an on-line course, see Altekruse and Brew (2000), Peterson (2000), and Daniels, Tyler, and Christie (2000).

Computer-Assisted Instruction

Computer-assisted instruction (CAI) uses tutorials to present concepts and examples of instructional tasks. Some program applications can measure performance and present feedback to the learner, while other simulations require the learner to use constructs in an applied situation to solve problems (Sampson & Krumboltz, 1991). Like computerized technology in assessment and counseling, CAI has experienced more widespread use as affordability has improved. While the business world has used CAI extensively, the counseling field has not used it to its fullest potential (Granello, 2000; Lambert, 1988; Sampson & Krumboltz, 1991). Computerized-assessment and career-counseling software programs have experienced the widest use by, and the greatest financial investment from, large software developers. The financial limitations of individual developers have resulted in restricted development and marketing of CAI software in counseling.

The academic community, particularly those academicians in programs of education, is an excellent resource for CAI development. However, academic institutions traditionally have failed to recognize software development as viable scholarly activity that applies toward promotion and tenure, much like textbook writing (depending upon the tenure-granting institution). This situation inherently limits software development efforts by faculty members, who typically have much to do with limited time and resources.

While counseling and CAI may be conceptualized as distinct, separate activities, it is also possible to see similarities between them. The definition of CAI in counseling offered by Sampson and Krumboltz (1991) is similar to that of Grencavage and Norcross (1990), who described the commonalities among psychotherapies in computer-assisted counseling. Many of the ethical issues of computer-assisted counseling also apply to CAI in counseling. Additionally, the ethical obligations that educators have to use sound theory and peer review processes in curriculum development and instruction are important to consider in the proliferation of CAI in counseling. For further discussion of computer-assisted instruction in counselor education and supervision, see Granello (2000, pp. 8–11).

"TECHNOCENTERED" AND "TECHNOANXIOUS"

Harris-Bowlsbey (2000), an early pioneer in the development of computer-based, career planning systems, suggested that many warm and caring counselors with enterprising and artistic proclivities may find embracing cybertechnology as foreign and uncomfortable. Counselors' reactions to technology span a continuum from acceptance to anxiety. Brod (1984) dichotomized people's reactions to technology as **technocentered** (comfortable with computer technology) and **technoanxious** (fearful and avoiding computerization of the profession). Counselors' resistance to computerization of various counseling tasks could be explained in part by technoanxiety (Ford, 1993). The benefits to technological advances are numerous and substantial. The best way to assure the appropriate implementation of progress, both ethically and in addressing people with technoanxiety, is through preservice and in-service training of counseling professionals (ACES, 1999; Ford, 1993; Hammer & Hile, 1985; Meier & Geiger, 1986).

Not all resistance to the computerization of counseling is related to anxiety. There are many ethical concerns associated with the implementation of new technology, so the use of computers and related technology in the counseling field must be carried out carefully after appropriate research. In addition, standards should be set to assure its continued safe use. The very nature of computerization—its objectivity and relationship to quantifiable data—also brings limitations to situations that require abstract problem solving and clinical judgment. Computerization may restrict the exchange of questions and answers, emphasizing concrete data at the expense of less-quantifiable phenomena (Murphy & Pardeck, 1988). Counselors-in-training must be aware of these limitations before embarking on their own professional practice.

ETHICAL USE OF SOFTWARE

Software **pirating,** or the illegal copying and use of software, is a blatant breach of ethics. The sharing of software between professionals can be considered doing a co-worker a favor. Clearly, the motivation is to save several hundred dollars in acquiring a piece of software. However, the unethical reproduction and transfer of computer software results in both increased cost to the consumer and loss of revenue for the author of the product. Because unauthorized reproduction of software is illegal, the ethical integrity of counselors who engage in this behavior is called into question. Software pirating can easily go undetected, increasing the responsibility of counselors to practice the ethical use of electronic media autonomously.

CHAPTER SUMMARY

Technology plays an important role in counseling-related professions. All forms of electronic media used in counseling may contain sensitive material protected by client-therapist confidentiality and privileged communication. Ethical codes that address maintenance of client records mandate that counselors maintain appropriate confidentiality in creating, storing, accessing, transferring, and disposing of all client records.

Counseling professionals use a variety of types of electronic media, including personal computers, faxes, e-mail, and cellular phones. Protocols must be in place to ensure that all types of media are accessible only to ethically appropriate parties.

Computer-assisted counseling exists in a variety of forms, including therapeutic software, on-line counseling, career counseling, rehabilitation software, and behavioral, cognitive, educational, and psychodynamic approaches. Software has been developed to target AIDS education, drug and alcohol abuse, obesity, personal distress, sexual dysfunction, smoking, and stress.

On-line counseling forums represent a recent technological development in computer applications. These forums use the Internet, BBSs, and list servers for the public exchange of text-based information. List servers and information databases assist counselors in accessing diverse information quickly. Ethical concerns with on-line counseling include security, access to services, and cost.

Telehealth services are remote electronic consultations between consumers and health care provider, often in remote or rural areas that have a shortage of health professionals.

The application of computers to the area of assessment includes the ability to administer, score, and interpret psychological assessment instruments. Computer-assisted assessment has the benefits of rapid presentation of information and increased reliability in test scoring. However, test administrators may have less vigilance and may overlook situational factors during testing. Some domains of assessment do not transfer well to computerized assessment.

Computer-assisted counselor education included on-line supervision and virtual practica, distance learning, and synchronous and asynchronous curriculum delivery. Computer-assisted instruction uses tutorials to present concepts and instructional tasks.

REFERENCES

Ackerman, R. J., & Banks, M. E. (1990). Computers and the ethical treatment of brain-injured patients. *Social Science Computer Review, 8*(1), 83–95.

Aiken, L. R. (2000). *Psychological testing and assessment* (10th ed.). Boston: Allyn & Bacon.

Allen, C. (1995). job.search @ internet. *Journal of Career Planning & Employment, 55*(3), 53–55.

Altekruse, M. K., & Brew, L. (2000). Using the web for distance learning. In J. W. Bloom & G. R. Walz, (Eds.), *Cybercounseling and cyberlearning: Strategies and resources for the millennium* (pp. 129–141). Alexandria, VA: American Counseling Association.

American Counseling Association. (1999). *Ethical standards for Internet on-line counseling*. Available at *www.counseling.org*.

American Educational Research Association, American Psychological Association, & National Council on Measurement in Education. (1999). *Standards for educational and psychological testing*. Washington, D.C.: American Educational Research Association.

American Psychological Association. (1986). *Guidelines for computer-based tests and interpretations*. Washington, D.C.: Author.

American Psychological Association. (1997, November 5). *Services by telephone, teleconferencing, and Internet: A statement by the ethics committee of the American Psychological Association*. Available at *http://www.apa.org.ethics/stmnt01.html*.

American Psychological Association of Graduate Students. (1999). *Newsletter of APAGS: 1999 APA Telehealth Mini-Convention*. Available at *http://www.apa.org/apags/sum99/4.html*.

Argentero, P. (1989). Computerized psychological testing: An annotated bibliography. *Bollettino di Psicologia Applicata, 190,* 21–38.

Association for Counselor Education and Supervision. (1999). *Recommended technical competencies for counselor education students*. Alexandria, VA: Author.

Barker, K. (1986). Dilemmas at a distance. *Assessment and Evaluation in Higher Education, 11,* 219–230.

Berge, Z. L. (1994). Electronic discussion groups. *Communication Education, 43,* 102–111.

Binder, L. M., & Thompson, L. L. (1994). The ethics code and neuropsychological assessment practices. *Archives of Clinical Neuropsychology, 10,* 27–46.

Binik, Y. M., Servan-Schreiber, D., Freiwald, S., & Hall, K. S. (1988). Intelligent computer-based assessment and psychotherapy: An expert system for sexual dysfunction. *The Journal of Nervous and Mental Disease, 176,* 387–400.

Bitter, J., Gregg, J., & Jackson, W. (1994). Leadership training by distance. *Journal of Rehabilitation Administration, 18,* 81–86.

Bland, K., Morrison, G. R., & Ross, S. M. (1992). *Student attitudes toward learning link: A distance education project*. Paper presented at the annual meeting of the Mid-South Educational Research Association, Knoxville, TN.

Bloom, J. W., & Walz, G. R. (Eds.). (2000). *Cybercounseling and cyberlearning: Strategies and resources for the millennium*. Alexandria, VA: American Counseling Association.

Boles, R. N. (1996, March). The Internet and the job hunt. *Career Planning and Adult Development Network Newsletter, 18*(3), 1–4.

Brod, C. (1984). *Technostress: The human cost of the computer revolution*. Don Mills, Ontario, Canada: Addison-Wesley.

Burda, P. C., Starkey, T. W., & Dominguez, F. (1991). Computer-administered treatment of psychiatric inpatients. *Computers in Human Behavior, 7,* 1–5.

Burling, T. A., Marotta, J., Gonzalez, R., Moltzen, J. O., Eng, A. M., Schmidt, G. A., Welch, R. L., Ziff, D. C., & Reilly, P. M. (1989). Computerized smoking cessation program for the worksite: Treatment outcome and feasibility. *Journal of Consulting and Clinical Psychology, 57,* 619–622.

Burnett, K. F., Magel, P. M., Harrington, S., & Taylor, C. B. (1989). Computer-assisted behavioral health counseling for high school students. *Journal of Counseling Psychology, 36,* 63–67.

Burnett, K. F., Taylor, C. B., & Agras, W. S. (1985). Ambulatory computer-assisted therapy for obesity: A new frontier for behavior therapy. *Journal of Consulting and Clinical Psychology, 53,* 698–703.

Butcher, J. N. (Ed.). (1985). Perspectives on computerized psychological assessment [Special issue]. *Journal of Consulting and Clinical Psychology, 53,* 745–838.

Butcher, J. N. (1987). The use of computers in psychological assessment: An overview of practices and issues. In J. N. Butcher (Ed.), *Computerized psychological assessment: A practitioner's guide* (pp. 3–14). New York: Basic Books.

Caplan, B. (1987). *Rehabilitation psychology desk reference*. Rockville, MD: Aspen.

Carr, A. C., Ghosh, A., & Marks, I. M. (1988). Computer-supervised exposure treatment for phobias. *Canadian Journal of Psychiatry, 33,* 112–117.

Clarke, B., & Schoech, D. (1984). A computer-assisted game for adolescents: Initial development and comments. In M. D. Schwartz (Ed.), *Using computers in clinical practice: Psychotherapy and mental health applications* (pp. 335–353). New York: Hayworth.

Colby, K. M. (1980). Computer psychotherapists. In J. B. Sidorski, J. H. Johnson, & T. A. Williams (Eds.), *Technology in mental health care delivery systems* (pp. 109–117). Norwood, NJ: Ablex.

Colby, K. M. (1986). Ethics of computer-assisted psychotherapy. *Psychiatric Annals, 16,* 414–415.

Colby, K. M., Colby, P. M., & Stoller, R. J. (1990). Dialogues in natural language with GURU, a psychological inference engine. *Philosophical Psychology, 3,* 171–186.

Colby, K. M., Gould, R. L., & Aronson, G. (1989). Some pros and cons of computer-assisted psychotherapy. *The Journal of Nervous and Mental Disease, 177,* 105–108.

Colby, K. M., Watt, J. B., & Gilbert, J. P. (1966). A computer method of psychotherapy: Preliminary communication. *The Journal of Nervous and Mental Disease, 142,* 148–152.

Commission on Rehabilitation Counselor Certification (June, 2001). *Code of professional ethics for Certified Rehabilitation Counselors and CRCC guidelines and procedures for processing complaints.* Rolling Meadows, IL: Author.

Council for Accreditation of Counseling and Related Education Programs. (1996). *CACREP accreditation standards and procedures manual* (Rev. ed.). Alexandria, VA: Author.

Council on Rehabilitation Education. (2000). *Re-accreditation manual for rehabilitation counselor education programs.* Rolling Meadows, IL: Author.

Daniels, H. M., Tyler, J. M., & Christie, B. S. (2000). On-line instruction in counselor education: Possibilities, implications, & guidelines. In J. W. Bloom & G. R. Walz (Eds.), *Cybercounseling and cyberlearning: Strategies and resources for the millennium* (pp. 303–317). Alexandria, VA: American Counseling Association.

Davidson, R. S. (1985). Applications of computer technology to learning therapy. *Journal of Organizational Behavior Management, 6,* 155–168.

Davis, A., & Yazak, D. (1995). Implementation and accreditation issues in the development of distance learning programs. *Rehabilitation Education, 9,* 293–307.

Davis-Bell, J. (1991). Distance learning: New technology and new potential. *Legislative Reports, 16*(6), 1–10.

Drummond, R. J. (1996). *Appraisal procedures for counselors and helping professionals.* Upper Saddle River, NJ: Prentice-Hall.

Duncan, D. M. (1997). *Counseling over the Internet: Ethical and legal considerations.* Presentation at the American Counseling Association's 1997 World Conference, Orlando, FL.

Eldredge, G., Gerard, G., & Smart, J. (1994). A distance education model for rehabilitation counseling. *Journal of Rehabilitation Administration, 18,* 75–79.

Erdman, H. P., & Foster, S. W. (1988). Ethical issues in the use of computer-based assessment. In J. W. Murphy & J. T. Pardeck (Eds.), *Technology and human service delivery: Challenges and a critical perspective* (pp. 71–87). New York: Haworth.

Erdman, H. P., Klein, M. H., & Greist, J. H. (1985). Direct patient computer interviewing. *Journal of Consulting and Clinical Psychology, 53,* 760–773.

Eyde, L. D. (Ed.). (1987). Computerized psychological testing [Special issue]. *Applied Psychology: An International Review, 36,* 223–235.

Farrell, A. D., Camplair, P. S., & McCullough, L. (1987). Identification of target complaints by computer interview: Evaluation of the computerized assessment system for psychotherapy evaluation and research. *Journal of Consulting and Clinical Psychology, 55,* 691–700.

Fenwick, J. (1992). *A question of quality.* Paper presented at the International Council for Distance Education 16th World Conference, Bangkok, Thailand.

Ford, B. D. (1988). *An ongoing computerized adjunct to psychotherapy program: Two years plus in a two years minus correctional center.* Paper presented at Counseling as Education Conference, Lakehead University, Thunder Bay, Ontario, Canada.

Ford, B. D. (1993). Ethical and professional issues in computer-assisted therapy. *Computers in Human Behavior, 9,* 387–400.

Ford, B. D., & Vitelli, R. (1992). Inmate attitudes towards computerized clinical interventions. *Computers in Human Behavior, 8,* 223–230.

Fowler, R. D. (1985). Landmarks in computer-assisted psychological assessment. *Journal of Consulting and Clinical Psychology, 53,* 748–759.

French, C. F. (1986). Microcomputers and psychometric assessment. *British Journal of Guidance and Counseling, 14,* 33–45.

French, C. C., & Beaumont, J. G. (1987). The reaction of psychiatric patients to computerized assessment. *British Journal of Clinical Psychology, 26,* 267–278.

French, C., & Beaumont, J. G. (1992). Microcomputer version of a digit span test in clinical use. *Interacting with Computers, 4,* 163–178.

Fulmer, J., Hazzard, M., Jones, S., & Keene, K. (1992). Distance learning: An innovative approach to nursing education. *Journal of Professional Nursing, 8,* 289–294.

Garrison, D. R. (1990). An analysis and evaluation of audio teleconferencing to facilitate education at a distance. *The American Journal of Distance Education, 4*(3), 13–24.

Gates, W., Myhrvold, N., and Rinearson, P. (1995). *The road ahead.* New York: Viking.

Goodman, H., Gingerich, W. J., & Shazer, S. (1989). BRIEFER: An expert system for clinical practice. *Computers in Human Services, 5,* 53–68.

Granello, P. F. (2000). Historical context: The relationship of computer technologies and counseling. In J. W. Bloom & G. R. Walz (Eds.), *Cybercounseling and cyberlearning: Strategies and resources for the millennium* (pp. 3–15). Alexandria, VA: American Counseling Association.

Grencavage, L. M., & Norcross, J. C. (1990). Where are the commonalities among the therapeutic common factors? *Professional Psychology: Research and Practice, 21,* 372–378.

Grohol, J. M. (1998). The state of mental health on-line. [On-line]. Available: *http://mental help.net/phi/phi31b.htm.*

Hammer, A. L., & Hile, M. G. (1985). Factors in clinicians' resistance to automation in mental health. *Computers in Human Services, 1,* 1–23.

Hannon, K. (1996, May 13). Upset? Try cybertherapy. *U.S. News & World Report, 81,* 83.

Harrell, T. H., Honaker, L. M., Hetu, M., & Oberwager, J. (1987). Computerized versus traditional administration of the multidimensional aptitude battery-verbal scale: An examination of reliability and validity. *Computers in Human Behavior, 3,* 129–137.

Harris-Bowlsbey, J. (2000). The Internet: Blessing or bane for the counseling profession? In J. W. Bloom & G. R. Walz (Eds.), *Cybercounseling and cyberlearning: Strategies and resources for the millennium* (pp. 39–49). Alexandria, VA: American Counseling Association.

Hartman, D. E. (1986a). Artificial intelligence or artificial psychologist? Conceptual issues in clinical microcomputer use. *Professional Psychology: Research and Practice, 17,* 528–534.

Hartman, D. E. (1986b). On the use of clinical psychology software: Practical, legal, and ethical concerns. *Professional Psychology: Research and Practice, 17,* 462–465.

Hodgson, V. E. (1986). The interrelationship between support and learning materials. *Programmed Learning and Educational Technology, 23,* 56–61.

Honaker, L. M., & Fowler, R. D. (1990). Computer-assisted psychological assessment. In G. Goldstein & M. Hersen (Eds.), *Handbook of psychological assessment* (2nd ed.). Elmsford, NY: Pergamon Press.

Hood, A. B., & Johnson, R. W. (1997). *Assessment in counseling: A guide to the use of psychological assessment procedures* (2nd ed.). Alexandria, VA: American Counseling Association.

Hufford, B. J., Glucckauf, R. L., & Webb, P. M. (1999). Home-based, interactive videoconferencing for adolescents with epilepsy and their families. *Rehabilitation Psychology, 44,* 176–193.

Hughs, A. L., & Ruiz, N. J. (1998, April). Ethics in counseling: Cyberspace and the counseling practice. *Counseling Today*, pp. 16, 22.

Jandt, F. E., & Nemnich, M. B. (1995). *Using the Internet in your job search*. Indianapolis, IN: JIST Works, Inc.

Keating, A. B., & Hargitai, J. (1999). *The wired professor*. New York: New York University Press.

Keith-Spiegel, P., & Koocher, G. P. (1985). *Ethics in psychology*. New York: Random House.

Kennedy, J. L. (1995). *Hook up, get hired! The Internet job search revolution*. New York: Wiley.

Kennedy, R., Baltzley, D., Turnage, J., & Jones, M. (1989). Factor analysis and predictive validity of microcomputer-based tests. *Perceptual and Motor Skills, 69,* 1059–1074.

Kilvingham, Jr., F. M., Johnston, J. A., Hogan, R. S., & Mauer, E. (1994). Who benefits from computerized career counseling? *Journal of Counseling and Development, 72,* 289–292.

Koocher, G. P., & Morray, E. (2000). Regulation in telepsychology: A survey of State Attorneys General. *Professional Psychology: Research and Practice, 31,* 503–508.

Lambert, M. (1988). Computers in counselor education: Four years after a special issue. *Counselor Education and Supervision, 28,* 100–109.

Law, M., & Sissons, L. (1985). The challenge of distance education. *New Directions for Continuing Education, 26,* 43–54.

Lawrence, G. H. (1986). Using computers for the treatment of psychological problems. *Computers in Human Behavior, 2,* 43–62.

Lee, C. C. (2000). Cybercounseling and empowerment: Bridging the digital divide. In J. W. Bloom & G. R. Walz (Eds.), *Cybercounseling and cyberlearning: Strategies and resources for the millennium* (pp. 85–93). Alexandria, VA: American Counseling Association.

Levitan, K. B., Willis, E. A., & Vogelgesang, J. (1985). Microcomputers and the individual practitioner: A review of the literature in psychology and psychiatry. *Computers in Human Services, 1,* 65–84.

Lukin, M. E., Dowd, T., Plake, B. S., & Kraft, R. G. (1985). Comparing computerized versus traditional psychological assessment. *Computers in Human Behavior, 1,* 49–58.

Magnusen, K. O., & Magnusen, O. C. (1995). On the leading edge of video interviewing. *Journal of Career Planning & Employment, 55*(4), 45–47.

Mahue, 1998. Cybertowers [On-line]. Available *www.cybertowers.com*

Maki, D. (1986). Foundations of applied rehabilitation counseling. In T. Riggar, D. Maki, & A. Wolf (Eds.), *Applied rehabilitation counseling* (pp. 3–11). New York: Springer.

Marino, T. W. (1996, January). Counselors in cyberspace debate whether client discussions are ethical. *Counseling Today,* 8.

Massoumian, B. (1989). Successful teaching via two-way interactive video. *Tech Trends, 34*(2), 16–19.

Matarazzo, J. D. (1985). Clinical psychological test interpretations by computer: Hardware outpaces software. *Computers in Human Behavior, 1,* 235–253.

Matarazzo, J. D. (1986). Computerized clinical psychological test interpretation: Unvalidated plus all mean and no sigma. *American Psychologist, 41,* 14–25.

Matthews, T. J., De Santi, S. M., Callahan, D., Koblenz-Sulcov, C. J., & Werden, J. L. (1987). The microcomputer as an agent of intervention with psychiatric patients: Preliminary studies. *Computers in Human Behavior, 3,* 37–47.

McLemore, C. W., & Fantuzzo, J. W. (1982). CARE: Bridging the gap between clinicians and computers. *Professional Psychology, 13,* 501–510.

Meier, S. T., & Geiger, S. M. (1986). Implications of computer-assisted testing and assessment for professional practice and training. *Measurement and Evaluation in Counseling and Development, 19,* 29–34.

Moncher, M. S., Parms, C. A., Orlandi, M. A., Schinke, S. P., Miller, S. O., Palleja, J., & Schinke, M. B. (1985). Microcomputer-based approaches for preventing drug and alcohol abuse among adolescents from ethnic-racial minority backgrounds. *Computers in Human Behavior, 5,* 79–93.

Murphy, J. W., & Pardeck, J. T. (1988). Dehumanization, computers and clinical practice. *Journal of Social Behavior and Personality, 3,* 107–116.

Myrick, R., & Sabella, R. (1995). Cyberspace: A new place for counselor supervision. *Elementary School Guidance and Counseling, 30* (1), 35–44.

National Board of Certified Counselors (1997a). *Code of ethics.* Charlotte, NC: Author.

National Board of Certified Counselors (2001). *Standards for the ethical practice of InternetCounseling* [Online]. Available: *http://www.nbcc.org/ethics/webethics.htm.*

National Career Development Association. (1997). Guidelines for the use of the Internet for provision of career information and planning services. Columbus, OH: Author.

Newman, R. (2001, March). Professional point: Not a question of 'for' or 'against.' *APA Monitor, 32,* (3), 56.

Nickelson, D. W. (1996). Telehealth and the evolving health care system: Strategic opportunities for professional psychology. *Professional Psychology: Research and Practice, 29,* 527–535.

Niemann, H., Ruff, R. M., & Baser, C. A. (1990). Computer-assisted attention retraining in head-injured individuals: A controlled efficacy study of an outpatient program. *Journal of Consulting and Clinical Psychology, 58,* 811–817.

Olcott, Jr., D. (1993). Access to learning: Integrating telecommunications instruction in university extended degree programs. *The Journal of Higher Education, 41,* 16–24.

Park, K., & Lee, S. (1992). A computer aided aptitude test for predicting flight performance of trainees. *Human Factors, 34,* 189–204.

Peterson, D. B., Murray, G., & Chan, F. (1998). Ethics and technology. In R. R. Cottone & V. M. Tarvydas, *Ethical and professional issues in counseling* (pp. 196–235). New York: Prentice-Hall.

Peterson, M. (2000). Electronic delivery of career development university courses. In J. W. Bloom & G. R. Walz (Eds.), *Cybercounseling and cyberlearning: Strategies and resources for the millennium* (pp. 143–159). Alexandria, VA: American Counseling Association.

Psychological Corporation. (1997). *Scoring assistant for the Weschler Scales-adult (SAWS-A)* [Computer Software]. San Antonio: Author.

Reed, G. M., McLaughlin, C. J., & Milholland, K. (2000). Ten interdisciplinary principles for professional practice in telehealth: Implications for psychology. *Professional Psychology: Research and Practice, 31,* 170–178.

Riley, M., Roehm, F., & Oserman, S. (1996). *The guide to Internet job searching.* Lincolnwood, IL: VGM Career Books.

Rozensky, R. H., Honor, L. F., Rasinski, K., Tovian, S. M., & Herz, G. I. (1986). Paper-pencil versus computer-administered MMPI's: A comparison of patient's attitudes. *Computers in Human Behavior, 2,* 111–116.

Salyer, S. (1997, July). The dawn of 'virtual therapy.' *USA Weekend,* 18–20.

Sampson, J. P., Jr. (1986a). The use of computer-assisted instruction in support of psychotherapeutic processes. *Computers in Human Behavior, 2,* 1–19.

Sampson, J. P., Jr. (1990). Computer-assisted testing and the goals of counseling psychology. *The Counseling Psychologist, 18,* 227–239.

Sampson, J. P., Jr. (1998). Potential problems and ethical concerns. In J. Harris-

Bowlsbey, M. Riley-Kikel, & J. P. Sampson, Jr. (Eds.), *The Internet: A tool for career planning* (pp. 31–37). Columbus, OH: National Career Development Association.

Sampson, J. P., Jr. (2000). Computer applications. In C. E. Watkins, Jr. & V. L. Campbell (Eds.), *Testing and assessment in counseling practice* (2nd ed.) (pp. 517–544). Hillside, NJ: Lawrence Erlbaum.

Sampson, J. P., Jr., Kolodinsky, R. W., & Greeno, B. P. (1997). Counseling on the information highway: Future possibilities and potential problems. *Journal of Counseling & Development, 75,* 203–212.

Sampson, J. P., Jr., & Krumboltz, J. D. (1991). Computer-assisted instruction: A missing link in counseling. *Journal of Counseling and Development, 69,* 395–397.

Sampson, J. P., Jr., Reardon, R. C., Wilde, C. K., Norris, D. S., Peterson, G. W., Strausberger, S. J., Garis, J. W., Lenz, J. G., & Saunders, D. E. (1994). Comparison of the assessment components of 15 computer-assisted career guidance systems. In J. T. Kapes, M. Moran-Mastie, & E. A. Whitfield (Eds.), *A counselor's guide to career assessment instruments* (pp. 373–379). Alexandria, VA: National Career Development Association.

Schinke, S. P., & Orlandi, M. A. (1990). Skills-based, interactive computer interventions to prevent HIV infection among African-American and Hispanic adolescents. *Computers in Human Behavior, 6,* 235–246.

Schinke, S. P., Orlandi, M. A., Gordon, A. N., Weston, R. E., Moncher, M. S., & Parms, C. A. (1989). AIDS prevention via computer-based intervention. *Computers in Human Services, 5,* 147–156.

Schneider, S. J. (1986). Trial of an on-line behavioral smoking cessation program. *Computers in Human Behavior, 2,* 277–286.

Schneider, S. J., Walter, R., & O'Donnell, R. (1990). Computerized communication as a medium for behavioral smoking cessation treatment: Controlled evaluation. *Computers in Human Behavior, 6,* 141–151.

Schwitzgebel, R. L., & Schwitzgebel, R. K. (1980). *Law and psychological practice.* Toronto: Wiley.

Scriven, B. (1991). Distance education and open learning: Implications for professional development and retraining. *Distance Education, 12,* 297–305.

Selmi, P. M., Klein, M. H., Greist, J. H., Johnson, J. H., & Harris, W. G. (1982). An investigation of computer-assisted cognitive-behavior therapy in the treatment of depression.

Behavior Research Methods and Instrumentation, 14, 181–185.

Selmi, P. M., Klein, M. H., Greist, J. H., Sorell, S. P., & Erdman, H. P. (1990). Computer-administered cognitive-behavioral therapy for depression. *American Journal of Psychiatry, 147,* 51–56.

Servan-Schreiber, C., & Binik, Y. M. (1989). Extending the intelligent tutoring system paradigm: Sex therapy as intelligent tutoring. *Computers in Human Behavior, 5,* 241–259.

Simons, G. (1985). *Silicon shock.* New York: Basil Blackwell.

Sirkin, J. (1994). Learning at a distance. *On Campus, 14*(3), 7–10.

Smith, J. J. (1987). The effectiveness of computerized self-help stress coping program with adult males. *Computers in Human Services, 2,* 37–49.

Staff. (1993). *Evaluation consideration for distance learning activities.* Decatur, GA: Southern Association of Colleges and Schools.

Steele, R. L. (1993). Distance learning delivery systems: Instructional options. *Media and Methods, 29*(4), 14.

Stewart, D. (1992). *Student support systems in distance education.* Paper presented at the world conference of the International Council for Distance Education, Bangkok, Thailand.

Stocks, T. J., & Freddolino, P. P. (1998). Evaluation of a World-Wide Web: Overview and basic design principles. *Educational Technology, 37*(3), 7–15.

Stones, M., & Kozma, A. (1989). Multidimensional assessment of the elderly via a microcomputer: The SENOTS program and battery. *Psychology and Aging, 4,* 113–118.

Stricker, G. (1996). Psychotherapy in cyberspace. *Ethics and behavior, 6*(2), 169, 175–177.

Taber, B. J., & Luzzo, D. A. (1999). *A comprehensive review of research evaluating the effectiveness of DISCOVER in promoting career development* (ACT Research Report 99.3). Iowa City, IA: ACT.

Taylor, C. B., Agras, W. S., Losch, M., Plante, T. G., & Burnett, K. (1991). Improving the effectiveness of computer-assisted weight loss. *Behavior Therapy, 22,* 229–236.

U.S. Department of Commerce, National Telecommunications and Information Administration. (1999). *Falling through the net: Defining the digital divide.* Washington, D.C.: U.S. Government Printing Office.

VandeCreek, L., & Knapp, S. (1993). *Tarasoff and beyond: Legal and clinical considerations in the treatment of life-endangering*

patients (Rev. ed.). Sarasota, FL: Professional Resource Press.

Wagman, M. (1980). PLATO DCS: An interactive computer system for personal counseling. *Journal of Counseling Psychology, 27,* 16–30.

Wagman, M. (1988). *Computer psychotherapy systems.* New York: Gordon and Breach Science Publishers.

Wagman, M., & Kerber, K. W. (1980). PLATO DCS, an interactive computer system for personal counseling: Further development and evaluation. *Journal of Counseling Psychology, 27,* 31–39.

Wall, J. E. (2000). Technology-delivered assessment: Power, problems, and promise. In J. W. Bloom & G. R. Walz (Eds.), *Cybercounseling and cyberlearning: Strategies and resources for the millennium* (pp. 237–251). Alexandria, VA: American Counseling Association.

Walz, G. R. (1996). Using the I-Way for career development. In R. Feller & G. Walz (Eds.), *Optimizing life transitions in turbulent times: Exploring work, learning and careers* (pp. 415–427). Greensboro, NC: University of North Carolina, ERIC Clearinghouse on Counseling and Student Services.

Weiss, D. J. (1985). Adaptive testing by computer. *Journal of Consulting and Clinical Psychology, 53,* 774–789.

Willis, B. (1992). From a distance. *Educational Technology, 32*(6), 35–37.

Wise, S., & Plake, B. S. (1990). Computerized testing in higher education. *Measurement and Evaluation in Counseling and Development, 23,* 3–10.

Woods, J. F., & Ollis, H. (1996). Labor market, job information proliferates on-line. *Workforce Journal, 5*(1), 32–44.

Woods, J. F., Ollis, H., & Kaplan, R. (1996). *To spin a web: Job, career, and labor market on the Internet* (Occasional Paper No. 8). Washington, D.C.: National Occupational Information Coordinating Committee.

Wyndowe, J. (1987). The Microcomputerized Diagnostic Interview Schedule: Clinical use in an out-patient setting. *Canadian Journal of Psychiatry, 32,* 93–99.

Youngjohn, J., Larrabee, G., & Crook, T. (1991). First-Last Names and the Grocery List Selective Reminding Test: Two computerized measures of everyday verbal learning. *Archives of Clinical Neuropsychology, 6,* 287–300.

APPENDIX 10-A

APA Statement on Services by Telephone, Teleconferencing, and Internet

A statement by the Ethics Committee of the American Psychological Association

The American Psychological Association's Ethics Committee issued the following statement on November 5, 1997, based on its 1995 statement on the same topic.

The Ethics Committee can only address the relevance of and enforce the "Ethical Principles of Psychologists and Code of Conduct" and cannot say whether there may be other APA Guidelines that might provide guidance. The Ethics Code is not specific with regard to telephone therapy or teleconferencing or any electronically provided services as such and has no rules prohibiting such services. Complaints regarding such matters would be addressed on a case-by-case basis.

Delivery of services by such media as telephone, teleconferencing and Internet is a rapidly evolving area. This will be the subject of APA task forces and will be considered in future revision of the Ethics Code. Until such time as a more definitive judgment is available, the Ethics Committee recommends that psychologists follow Standard 1.04c, Boundaries of Competence, which indicates that:

"In those emerging areas in which generally recognized standards for preparatory training do not yet exist, psychologists nevertheless take reasonable steps to ensure the competence of their work and to protect patients, clients, students, research participants, and others from harm."

Other relevant standards include Assessment (Standards 2.01–2.10), Therapy (4.01–4.09, especially 4.01 Structuring the Relationship and 4.02 Informed Consent to Therapy), and Confidentiality (5.01–5.11). Within the General Standards section, standards with particular relevance are 1.03, Professional and Scientific Relationship; 1.04 (a, b, and c), Boundaries of Competence; 1.06, Basis for Scientific and Professional Judgments; 1.07a, Describing the Nature and Results of Psychological Services; 1.14, Avoiding Harm; and 1.25, Fees and Financial Arrangements. Standards under Advertising, particularly 3.01–3.03 are also relevant.

Psychologists considering such services must review the characteristics of the services, the service delivery method, and the provisions for confidentiality. Psychologists must then consider the relevant ethical standards and other requirements, such as licensure board rules.

APPENDIX 10-B

The Practice of Internet Counseling

National Board for Certified Counselors, Inc. and Center for Credentialing and Education, Inc. (Adopted November 3, 2001)

This document contains a statement of principles for guiding the evolving practice of Internet counseling. In order to provide a context for these principles, the following definition of Internet counseling, which is one element of technology-assisted distance counseling, is provided. The Internet counseling standards follow the definitions presented below.

A TAXONOMY FOR DEFINING FACE-TO-FACE AND TECHNOLOGY-ASSISTED DISTANCE COUNSELING

The delivery of technology-assisted distance counseling continues to grow and evolve. Technology assistance in the form of computer-assisted assessment, computer-assisted informa-

tion systems, and telephone counseling has been available and widely used for some time. The rapid development and use of the Internet to deliver information and foster communication has resulted in the creation of new forms of counseling. Developments have occurred so rapidly that it is difficult to communicate a common understanding of these new forms of counseling practice.

The purpose of this document is to create standard definitions of technology-assisted distance counseling that can be easily updated in response to evolutions in technology and practice. A definition of traditional face-to-face counseling is also presented to show similarities and differences with respect to various applications of technology in counseling. A taxonomy of forms of counseling is also presented to further clarify how technology relates to counseling practice.

NATURE OF COUNSELING

Counseling is the application of mental health, psychological, or human development principles, through cognitive, affective, behavioral or systemic intervention strategies, that address wellness, personal growth, or career development, as well as pathology.

Depending on the needs of the client and the availability of services, counseling may range from a few brief interactions in a short period of time, to numerous interactions over an extended period of time. Brief interventions, such as classroom discussions, workshop presentations, or assistance in using assessment, information, or instructional resources, may be sufficient to meet individual needs. Or, these brief interventions may lead to longer-term counseling interventions for individuals with more substantial needs. Counseling may be delivered by a single counselor, two counselors working collaboratively, or a single counselor with brief assistance from another counselor who has specialized expertise that is needed by the client.

FORMS OF COUNSELING

Counseling can be delivered in a variety of forms that share the definition presented above. Forms of counseling differ with respect to participants, delivery location, communication medium, and interaction process. Counseling *participants* can be individuals, couples, or groups. The *location* for counseling delivery can be face-to-face or at a distance with the assistance of technology. The *communication medium* for counseling can be what is read from text, what is heard from audio, or what is seen and heard in person or from video. The *interaction process* for counseling can be synchronous or asynchronous. Synchronous interaction occurs with little or no gap in time between the responses of the counselor and the client. Asynchronous interaction occurs with a gap in time between the responses of the counselor and the client.

The selection of a specific form of counseling is based on the needs and preferences of the client within the range of services available. Distance counseling supplements face-to-face counseling by providing increased access to counseling on the basis of necessity or convenience. Barriers, such as being a long distance from counseling services, geographic separation of a couple, or limited physical mobility as a result of having a disability, can make it necessary to provide counseling at a distance. Options, such as scheduling counseling sessions outside of traditional service delivery hours or delivering counseling services at a place of residence or employment, can make it more convenient to provide counseling at a distance.

A Taxonomy of Forms of Counseling Practice. Table 1 presents a taxonomy of currently available forms of counseling practice. This schema is intended to show the relationships among counseling forms.

TABLE 1 A Taxonomy of Face-to-Face and Technology-Assisted Distance Counseling

Counseling

- Face-to-Face Counseling
- Individual Counseling
- Couple Counseling
- Group Counseling
- Technology-Assisted Distance Counseling
- Telecounseling
- Telephone-Based Individual Counseling
- Telephone-Based Couple Counseling
- Telephone-Based Group Counseling
- Internet Counseling
- E-Mail-Based Individual Counseling
- Chat-Based Individual Counseling
- Chat-Based Couple Counseling
- Chat-Based Group Counseling
- Video-Based Individual Counseling
- Video-Based Couple Counseling
- Video-Based Group Counseling

DEFINITIONS

Counseling is the application of mental health, psychological, or human development principles, through cognitive, affective, behavioral or systemic intervention strategies, that address wellness, personal growth, or career development, as well as pathology.

Face-to-face counseling for individuals, couples, and groups involves synchronous interaction between and among counselors and clients using what is seen and heard in person to communicate.

Technology-assisted distance counseling for individuals, couples, and groups involves the use of the telephone or the computer to enable counselors and clients to communicate at a distance when circumstances make this approach necessary or convenient.

Telecounseling involves synchronous distance interaction among counselors and clients using one-to-one or conferencing features of the telephone to communicate.

Telephone-based individual counseling involves synchronous distance interaction between a counselor and a client using what is heard via audio to communicate.

Telephone-based couple counseling involves synchronous distance interaction among a counselor or counselors and a couple using what is heard via audio to communicate.

Telephone-based group counseling involves synchronous distance interaction among counselors and clients using what is heard via audio to communicate.

Internet counseling involves asynchronous and synchronous distance interaction among counselors and clients using e-mail, chat, and videoconferencing features of the Internet to communicate.

E-mail-based individual Internet counseling involves asynchronous distance interaction between counselor and client using what is read via text to communicate.

Chat-based individual Internet counseling involves synchronous distance interaction between counselor and client using what is read via text to communicate.

Chat-based couple Internet counseling involves synchronous distance interaction among a counselor or counselors and a couple using what is read via text to communicate.

Chat-based group Internet counseling involves synchronous distance interaction among counselors and clients using what is read via text to communicate.

Video-based individual Internet counseling involves synchronous distance interaction between counselor and client using what is seen and heard via video to communicate.

Video-based couple Internet counseling involves synchronous distance interaction among a counselor or counselors and a couple using what is seen and heard via video to communicate.

Video-based group Internet counseling involves synchronous distance interaction among counselors and clients using what is seen and heard via video to communicate.

STANDARDS FOR THE ETHICAL PRACTICE OF INTERNET COUNSELING

These standards govern the practice of Internet counseling and are intended for use by counselors, clients, the public, counselor educators, and organizations that examine and deliver Internet counseling. These standards are intended to address *practices* that are unique to Internet counseling and Internet counselors and do not duplicate principles found in traditional codes of ethics.

These Internet counseling standards of practice are based upon the principles of ethical practice embodied in the NBCC Code of Ethics. Therefore, these standards should be used in conjunction with the most recent version of the NBCC ethical code. Related content in the NBCC Code are indicated in parentheses after each standard.

Recognizing that significant new technology emerges continuously, these standards should be reviewed frequently. It is also recognized that Internet counseling ethics cases should be reviewed in light of delivery systems existing at the moment rather than at the time the standards were adopted.

In addition to following the NBCC® Code of Ethics pertaining to the practice of professional counseling, Internet counselors shall observe the following standards of practice:

Internet Counseling Relationship

1. In situations where it is difficult to verify the identity of the Internet client, steps are taken to address impostor concerns, such as by using code words or numbers. (Refer to B.8)
2. Internet counselors determine if a client is a minor and therefore in need of parental/guardian consent. When parent/guardian consent is required to provide Internet counseling to minors, the identity of the consenting person is verified. (Refer to B.8)
3. As part of the counseling orientation process, the Internet counselor explains to clients the procedures for contacting the Internet counselor when he or she is off-line and, in the case of asynchronous counseling, how often e-mail messages will be checked by the Internet counselor. (Refer to B.8)
4. As part of the counseling orientation process, the Internet counselor explains to clients the possibility of technology failure and discusses alternative modes of communication, if that failure occurs. (Refer to B.8)
5. As part of the counseling orientation process, the Internet counselor explains to clients how to cope with potential misunderstandings when visual cues do not exist. (Refer to B.8)
6. As a part of the counseling orientation process, the Internet counselor collaborates with the Internet client to identify an appropriately trained professional who can provide local assistance, including crisis intervention, if needed. The Internet counselor and Internet client should also collaborate to determine the local crisis hotline telephone number and the local emergency telephone number. (Refer to B.4)
7. The Internet counselor has an obligation, when appropriate, to make clients aware of free public access points to the Internet within the community for accessing Internet counseling or Web-based assessment, information, and instructional resources. (Refer to B.1)
8. Within the limits of readily available technology, Internet counselors have an obligation to make their Web site a barrier-free environment to clients with disabilities. (Refer to B.1)
9. Internet counselors are aware that some clients may communicate in different languages, live in different time zones, and have unique cultural perspectives. Internet counselors are also aware that local conditions and events may impact the client. (Refer to A.12)

Confidentiality in Internet Counseling

10. The Internet counselor informs Internet clients of encryption methods being used to help insure the security of client/counselor/supervisor communications. (Refer to B.5)

Encryption methods should be used whenever possible. If encryption is not made available to clients, clients must be informed of the potential hazards of unsecured communication on the Internet. Hazards may include unauthorized monitoring of transmissions and/or records of Internet counseling sessions.

11. The Internet counselor informs Internet clients if, how, and how long session data are being preserved. (Refer to B.6)

Session data may include Internet counselor/Internet client e-mail, test results, audio/video session recordings, session notes, and counselor/supervisor communications. The likelihood of electronic sessions being preserved is greater because of the ease and decreased costs involved in recording. Thus, its potential use in supervision, research, and legal proceedings increases.

12. Internet counselors follow appropriate procedures regarding the release of information for sharing Internet client information with other electronic sources. (Refer to B.5)

Because of the relative ease with which e-mail messages can be forwarded to formal and casual referral sources, Internet counselors must work to insure the confidentiality of the Internet counseling relationship.

Legal Considerations, Licensure, and Certification

13. Internet counselors review pertinent legal and ethical codes for guidance on the practice of Internet counseling and supervision. (Refer to A.13)

Local, state, provincial, and national statutes as well as codes of professional membership organizations, professional certifying bodies, and state or provincial licensing boards need to be reviewed. Also, as varying state rules and opinions exist on questions pertaining to whether Internet counseling takes place in the Internet counselor's location or the Internet client's location, it is important to review codes in the counselor's home jurisdiction as well as the client's. Internet counselors also consider carefully local customs regarding age of consent and child abuse reporting, and liability insurance policies need to be reviewed to determine if the practice of Internet counseling is a covered activity.

14. The Internet counselor's Web site provides links to Web sites of all appropriate certification bodies and licensure boards to facilitate consumer protection. (Refer to B.1)

APPENDIX 10-C

Ethical Standards for Internet On-line Counseling

Approved by the ACA Governing Council, October 1999

These guidelines establish appropriate standards for the use of electronic communications over the Internet to provide on-line counseling services, and should be used only in conjunction with the latest *ACA Code of Ethics & Standards of Practice*.

CONFIDENTIALITY

a. **Privacy Information.** Professional counselors ensure that clients are provided sufficient information to adequately address and explain the limitations of (i) computer technology in the counseling process in general and (ii) the difficulties of ensuring complete client confidentiality of information transmitted through electronic communications over the Internet through on-line counseling. (See A.12.a., B.1.a., B.1.g.)

1. **SECURED SITES:** To mitigate the risk of potential breaches of confidentiality, professional counselors

provide one-on-one on-line counseling only through "secure" Web sites or e-mail communications applications which use appropriate encryption technology designed to protect the transmission of confidential information from access by unauthorized third parties.

2. **NON-SECURED SITES:** To mitigate the risk of potential breaches of confidentiality, professional counselors provide only general information from "non-secure" Web sites or e-mail communications applications.

3. **GENERAL INFORMATION:** Professional counselors may provide general information from either "secure" or "non-secure" Web sites, or through e-mail communications. General information includes non-client-specific, topical information on matters of general interest to the professional counselor's clients as a whole, third-party resource and referral information, addresses and phone numbers, and the like. Additionally, professional counselors using either "secure" or "non-secure" Web sites may provide "hot links" to third-party Web sites such as licensure boards, certification bodies, and other

resource information providers. Professional counselors investigate and continually update the content, accuracy and appropriateness for the client of material contained in any "hot links" to third-party Web sites.

4. **LIMITS OF CONFIDENTIALITY:** Professional counselors inform clients of the limitations of confidentiality and identify foreseeable situations in which confidentiality must be breached in light of the law in both the state in which the client is located and the state in which the professional counselor is licensed.

b. **Informational Notices.**

1. **SECURITY OF PROFESSIONAL COUNSELOR'S SITE:** Professional counselors provide a readily visible notice that (i) information transmitted over a Web site or e-mail server may not be secure; (ii) whether or not the professional counselor's site is secure; (iii) whether the information transmitted between the professional counselor and the client during on-line counseling will be encrypted; and (iv) whether the client will need special software to access and transmit confidential information and, if so, whether the professional counselor provides the software as part of the on-line counseling services. The notice should be viewable from all Web site and e-mail locations from which the client may send information. (See B.1.g.)

2. **PROFESSIONAL COUNSELOR IDENTIFICATION:** Professional counselors provide a readily visible notice advising clients of the identities of all professional counselor(s) who will have access to the information transmitted by the client and, in the event that more than one professional counselor has access to the Web site or e-mail system, the manner, if any, in which the client may direct information to a particular professional counselor. Professional counselors inform clients if any or all of the sessions are supervised. Clients are also informed if and how the supervisor preserves session transcripts. Professional counselors provide background information on all professional counselor(s) and supervisor(s) with access to the on-line communications, including education, licensing and certification, and practice area information. (See B.l.g.)

3. **CLIENT IDENTIFICATION:** Professional counselors identify clients, verify identities of clients, and obtain alternative methods of contacting clients in emergency situations.

c. **Client Waiver.** Professional counselors require clients to execute client waiver agreements stating that the client (i) acknowledges the limitations inherent in ensuring client confidentiality of information transmitted through on-line counseling and (ii) agrees to waive the client's privilege of confidentiality with respect to any confidential information transmitted through on-line counseling that may be accessed by any third party without autho-

rization of the client and despite the reasonable efforts of the professional counselor to arrange a secure on-line environment. Professional counselors refer clients to more traditional methods of counseling and do not provide on-line counseling services if the client is unable or unwilling to consent to the client waiver. (See B.1.b.)

d. **Records of Electronic Communications.** Professional counselors maintain appropriate procedures for ensuring the safety and confidentiality of client information acquired through electronic communications, including but not limited to encryption software; proprietary on-site file servers with fire walls; saving on-line or e-mail communications to the hard drive or file server computer systems; creating regular tape or diskette back-up copies; creating hard-copies of all electronic communications; and the like. Clients are informed about the length of time for, and method of, preserving session transcripts. Professional counselors warn clients of the possibility or frequency of technology failures and time delays in transmitting and receiving information. (See B.4.a., B.4.b.)

e. **Electronic Transfer of Client Information.** Professional counselors electronically transfer client confidential information to authorized third-party recipients only when (i) both the professional counselor and the authorized recipient have "secure" transfer and acceptance communication capabilities, (ii) the recipient is able to effectively protect the confidentiality of the client confidential information to be transferred, and (iii) the informed written consent of the client, acknowledging the limits of confidentiality, has been obtained. (See B.4.e., B.6.a., B.6.b.)

ESTABLISHING THE ON-LINE COUNSELING RELATIONSHIP

a. **The Appropriateness of On-Line Counseling.** Professional counselors develop an appropriate in-take procedure for potential clients to determine whether on-line counseling is appropriate for the needs of the client. Professional counselors warn potential clients that on-line counseling services may not be appropriate in certain situations and, to the extent possible, informs the client of specific limitations, potential risks, and/or potential benefits relevant to the client's anticipated use of on-line counseling services. Professional counselors ensure that clients are intellectually, emotionally, and physically capable of using the on-line counseling services, and of understanding the potential risks and/or limitations of such services. (See A.3.a., A.3.b.)

b. **Counseling Plans.** Professional counselors develop individual on-line counseling plans that are consistent with both the client's individual circumstances and the limitations of on-line counseling. Professional counselors shall specifically take into account the limitations, if any, on the use of any or all of the following in on-line counseling: initial client appraisal, diagnosis, and assessment methods employed by the professional counselor. Professional counselors who determine that on-line counseling is inappropriate for the client should avoid entering into or immediately terminate the on-line counseling relationship and encourage the client to continue the counseling relationship through an appropriate alternative method of counseling. (See A.11.b., A.11.c.)

c. **Continuing Coverage.**   Professional counselors provide clients with a schedule of times during which the on-line counseling services will be available, including reasonable anticipated response times, and provide clients with an alternate means of contacting the professional counselor at other times, including in the event of emergencies. Professional counselors obtain from, and provide clients with, alternative means of communication, such as telephone numbers or pager numbers, for back-up purposes in the event the on-line counseling service is unavailable for any reason. Professional counselors provide clients with the name of at least one other professional counselor who will be able to respond to the client in the event the professional counselor is unable to do so for any extended period of time. (See A.11.a.)

d. **Boundaries of Competence.**   Professional counselors provide on-line counseling services only in practice areas within their expertise and do not provide on-line counsel-

ing services to clients located in states in which professional counselors are not licensed. (See C.2.a., C.2.b.)

e. **Minor or Incompetent Clients.**   Professional counselors must verify that clients are above the age of minority, are competent to enter into the counseling relationship with a professional counselor, and are able to give informed consent. In the event clients are minor children, incompetent, or incapable of giving informed consent, professional counselors must obtain the written consent of the legal guardian or other authorized legal representative of the client prior to commencing on-line counseling services to the client.

LEGAL CONSIDERATIONS

Professional counselors confirm that their liability insurance provides coverage for on-line counseling services, and that the provision of such services is not prohibited by or otherwise violating any applicable (i) state or local statutes, rules, regulations, or ordinances; (ii) codes of professional membership organizations and certifying boards; and/or (iii) codes of state licensing boards.

Professional counselors seek appropriate legal and technical assistance in the development and implementation of their on-line counseling services.

Available at ACA's Web site, *www.counseling.org.*

APPENDIX 10-D

NCDA Guidelines for the Use of the Internet for Provision of Career Information and Planning Services

Approved by the NCDA Board of Directors, October 1997

Developed by members of the NCDA Ethics Committee: Dr. David Caulum, Don Doerr, Dr. Pat Howland, Dr. Spencer Niles, Dr. Ray Palmer, Dr. Richard Pyle (Chair), Dr. David Reile, Dr. James Sampson, and Dr. Don Schutt

INTRODUCTION

Based on readily available capabilities at the time of this writing, the Internet could be used in four ways for the purpose of providing career counseling and/or career planning services to clients. These are:

1. To deliver information about occupations, including their descriptions, employment outlook, skills re-

quirements, estimated salary, etc. through text, still images, graphics, and/or video. In this event, the standards for information development and presentation are the same as those for print materials and audiovisual materials as stated in NCDA's documents on these matters.

2. To provide online searches of occupational databases for the purpose of identifying feasible occupational alternatives. In this event, the standards developed by NCDA and the Association of Computer-based Systems for Career Information (ACSCI) apply.

3. To deliver interactive career counseling and career planning services. This use assumes that clients, either as individuals or as part of a group, have intentionally

placed themselves in direct communication with a professional career counselor. Standards for use of the Internet for these purposes are addressed in this document.

4. To provide searches through large databases of job openings for the purpose of identifying those that the user may pursue. Guidelines for this application are included in this document.

GUIDELINES FOR USE OF THE INTERNET FOR DELIVERY OF CAREER COUNSELING AND CAREER PLANNING SERVICES

"Career planning services" are differentiated from "career counseling" services. Career planning services include an active provision of information designed to help a client with a specific need, such as review of a resumé; assistance in networking strategies; identification of occupations based on interests, skills, or prior work experience; support in the job-seeking process; and assessment by means of online inventories of interest, abilities, and/or work-related values. Although "Career Counseling" may include the provision of the above services, the use of the term implies a deeper level of involvement with the client, based on the establishment of a professional counseling relationship and the potential for dealing with career development concerns well beyond those included in career planning.

Multiple means of online provision of career planning or career counseling services currently exist, the most common of which are e-mail, newsgroups, bulletin boards, chat rooms, and Web sites offering a wide variety of services. Telephone or audiovisual linkages supported by the Internet exist in their infancy, and will likely grow in potential as the technology improves and the costs decline.

1. **Qualifications of Developer or Provider.** Web sites and other services designed to assist clients with career planning should be developed with content input from professional career counselors. The service should clearly state the qualifications and credentials of the developers not only in the content area of professional career counseling, but also in the development of interactive online services.

2. **Access and Understanding of Environment.** The counselor has an obligation to be aware of free public access points to the Internet within the member's community, so that a lack of financial resources does not create a significant barrier to clients accessing counseling services or information, assessment or instructional resources over the internet.

   The counselor has an obligation to be as aware as possible of local conditions, cultures, and events that may impact the client.

3. **Content of Career Counseling and Planning Services on the Internet.** The content of a Web site or other service offering career information or planning services should be reviewed for the appropriateness of content offered in this medium. Some kinds of content have been extensively tested for online delivery due to the long existence of computer-based career information and guidance systems. This includes searching of databases by relevant search variables; display of occupational information; development of a resumé; assessment of interests, abilities, and work-related values and linkage of these to occupational titles; instruction about occupational classification systems; relationship of school majors to occupational choices; and the completion of forms such as a financial needs assessment questionnaire or a job application.

   When a Web site offers a service which has not previously been extensively tested (such as computer-based career guidance and information systems), this service should be carefully scrutinized to determine whether it lends itself to the Internet. The Web site should clearly state the kinds of client concerns that the counselor judges to be inappropriate for counseling over the Internet, or beyond the skills of the counselor.

4. **Appropriateness of Client for Receipt of Services via the Internet.** The counselor has an ethical and professional responsibility to assure that the client who is requesting service can profit from it in this mode. Appropriate screening includes the following:
   a. A clear statement by clients of their career planning or career counseling needs.
   b. An analysis by the counselor of whether meeting those needs via Internet exchange is appropriate and of whether this particular client can benefit from counseling services provided in this mode. A judgment about the latter should be made by means of a telephone or videophone teleconference designed to specify the client's expectations, how the client has sought to meet these through other modes, and whether or not the client appears to be able to process information through an Internet medium.

5. **Appropriate Support to the Client.** The counselor who is providing services to a client via the Internet has ethical responsibility for the following:
   a. Periodic monitoring of the client's progress via telephone or videophone teleconference.
   b. Identification by the counselor of a qualified career counselor in the client's geographic area should referral become necessary. If this is not possible, the web counselor using traditional referral sources to identify an appropriate practitioner, should assist the client in the selection of a counselor.

c. Appropriate discussion with the client about referral to face-to-face service should the counselor determine that little or no progress is being made toward the client's goals.

6. **Clarity of Contract with the Client.**   The counselor should define several items in writing to the client in a document that can be downloaded from the Internet or faxed to the client. This document should include at least the following items:

a. The counselor's credentials in the field.

b. The agreed-upon goals of the career counseling or career planning Internet interchange.

c. The agreed-upon cost of the services and how this will be billed.

d. Where and how clients can report any counselor behavior which they consider to be unethical.

e. Statement about the degree of security of the Internet and confidentiality of data transmitted on the Internet and about any special conditions related to the client's personal information (such as potential transmission of client records to a supervisor for quality-control purposes, or the collection of data for research purposes).

f. A statement of the nature of client information electronically stored by the counselor, including the length of time that data will be maintained before being destroyed.

g. A statement about the need for privacy when the client is communicating with the counselor, e.g., that client communication with the counselor is not limited by having others observe or hear interactions between the counselor and client.

h. If the service includes career, educational, or employment information, the counselor is responsible for making the client aware of the typical circumstances where individuals need counseling support in order to effectively use the information.

7. **Inclusion of Linkages to Other Web sites.**   If a career information or counseling Web site includes links to other Web sites, the professional who creates this linkage is responsible for assuring that the services to which his or hers are linked also meet these guidelines.

8. **Use of Assessment.**   If the career planning or career counseling service is to include online inventories or tests and their interpretation, the following conditions should apply:

a. The assessments must have been tested in computer delivery mode to assure that their psychometric properties are the same in this mode of delivery as in print form; or the client must be informed that they have not yet been tested in this same mode of delivery.

b. The counselor must abide by the same ethical guidelines as if he or she were administering and interpreting these same inventories or tests in face-to-face mode and/or in print form.

c. Every effort must be exerted to protect the confidentiality of the user's results.

d. If there is any evidence that the client does not understand the results, as evidenced by e-mail or telephone interchanges, the counselor must refer the client to a qualified career counselor in his or her geographic area.

e. The assessments must have been validated for self-help use if no counseling support is provided, or that appropriate counseling intervention is provided before and after completion of the assessment resource if the resource has not been validated for self-help use.

PROFESSIONAL AND ETHICAL GUIDELINES RELATED TO THE USE OF THE INTERNET FOR JOB POSTING AND SEARCHING

1. The posting must represent a valid job opening for which those searching on the Internet have an opportunity to apply.

2. Job postings must be removed from the Internet database within 48 hours of the time that the announced position is filled.

3. Names, addresses, resumés, and other information that may be gained about individuals should not be used for any purposes other than provision of further information about job openings.

UNACCEPTABLE COUNSELOR BEHAVIORS ON THE INTERNET

1. Use of a false e-mail identity when interacting with clients and/or other professionals. When acting in a professional capacity on the Internet, a counselor has a duty to identify him/herself honestly.

2. Accepting a client who will not identify him/herself and be willing to arrange for phone conversation as well as online interchange.

3. "Sharking" or monitoring chat rooms and bulletin board services, and offering career planning and related services when no request has been made for services. This includes sending out mass unsolicited e-mails. Counselors may advertise their services but must do so observing proper "netiquette" and standards of professional conduct.

NEED FOR RESEARCH AND REVIEW

Since the use of the Internet is new for the delivery of career planning and counseling services, it is mandatory that the career counseling profession gain experience with this medium and evaluate its effectiveness through targeted research. The capabilities of Internet delivery of services will expand rapidly as the use of sound and video becomes more feasible. These early guidelines will need constant monitoring and revision as research data become available and additional capabilities become cost-feasible.

CHAPTER 11

Ethics and Multiculturalism

Tarrell Awe Agahe Portman

Objectives

■ ■ ■ ■ ■ ■ ■ ■ ■ ■

After reading this chapter, you should be able to:

- Discuss the historical scope and importance of multiculturalism in the field of counseling.
- Define multiculturalism and multicultural concepts in counseling.
- Identify critical professional and ethical issues specific to multiculturalism.
- Explain the specific codes of ethics that address multicultural and diversity issues.

■ ■ ■ ■ ■ ■ ■ ■ ■ ■

INTRODUCTION

"All counseling, and, in fact, all communications are inherently and unavoidably multicultural" (Pedersen, 2001, p. 18). Pedersen made a similar statement in 1987, which used the term *cross-cultural counseling*. His view has served as the essence of most multicultural dialogue for the past 20 years. **Cross-cultural counseling** is defined as "counseling between individuals from different cultural backgrounds" (Gladding, 2001, p. 34) and has evolved into the term **multicultural counseling,** which is defined as a helping relationship involving two or more individuals with differing socially constructed worldviews (Gladding, 2001; Helms & Cook, 1999). The development of multicultural counseling began with attention to counseling services provided by counselors from predominantly majority power cultural groups to oppressed ethnic minority clientele. Since this one-sided beginning, multicultural counseling has evolved into attention on "multicultured" counselors providing services to "multicultured" clientele. For this reason, multiculturalism, with all its various components, is critical in the larger counseling framework, not as a specialty area of the profession but as an integral element of all human interaction. Indeed, as an essential element for professional inclusion, multiculturalism must be addressed in professional codes of ethics.

Box 11.1 Questions for Reflection

Take a moment to write down four of your personal fears. Who would you turn to for help facing each of these fears? How might you choose to handle each situation? Now consider four of your friends who are from different cultural backgrounds than your own. To whom might each of your friends turn in the same situations? How might they handle each situation? What are the similarities and differences? After completing the initial task, contemplate how easy or difficult the task was for you. Did you have difficulty selecting friends from culturally different backgrounds? What did you learn about yourself? How will your awareness from this activity transfer to working with clients?

EVOLUTION OF MULTICULTURALISM

Brief Historical Overview

Multiculturalism has evolved from the initial consideration of **culture,** defined as ethnicity and race in testing and assessment procedures, to the intermediate consideration of therapeutic concerns regarding White counselors working with minority clients. Currently, the concept of **multiculturalism** involves inclusion of all cultures and diverse groups. This evolution began as an ember in the 1950s, addressing issues regarding the significance of culture in the "administration of standard tests" (Jackson, 1995, p. 8). The multicultural fire was fueled by the civil rights movement of the 1960s, which focused attention on how counselors could counsel minority clients who were culturally different, and the neglect of minority issues in counselor preparation programs (Jackson, 1995). Multicultural attention began to blaze during the 1970s with more attention to multicultural scholarship, a shift toward inclusion of nonethnic cultural groups, and the creation of a division in the American Counseling Association specifically for non-White concerns (currently the Association for Multicultural Counseling and Development, AMCD) (Jackson, 1995). The 1980s and early 1990s consisted of a controlled fire with a focus on multicultural counseling as a specialty area in the field of counseling (Jackson, 1995). By the late 1990s, the flames began to smolder with a few flares of multicultural controversies. Pedersen (2001) described the impact of these controversies on multiculturalism: "The paradigm shift in psychology resulting from these controversies has positioned multiculturalism as a 'fourth force' dimension of psychology and counseling in a historically unique perspective" (p. 18). Thus, multiculturalism began to be represented as the "fourth force" in counseling, holding equal significance with

behaviorism, psychodynamism, and humanism as explanations of human behavior (Essandoh, 1996; Pedersen, 2001). Accordingly, a multicultural perspective is seen as "central to the psychodynamic definitions of the conscious, the reinforcing contingencies of behaviorism, and the personal/meaningful comprehension of humanism" (Pedersen, 2001, p. 18).

In the first decade of the 21st century, counselors are witnessing a paradigm rising from the ashes of multiculturalism within the counseling profession. The import of this paradigm is represented through the following commentary by Pedersen (2001):

> One clear indication that multiculturalism is introducing a permanent paradigm shift and not merely a passing fad in counseling is the strength of the multicultural controversies in the field of counseling. By "paradigm shift" I refer to changes in the underlying assumptions about psychology [and counseling] moving from a monocultural to a multicultural basis with profound implications for how psychology [and counseling] is applied in direct service. (p. 15)

Pedersen (2001) provides a framework of 12 positive advantage statements from his earlier work in support of the multicultural paradigm:

1. Recognizing that all behavior is learned and displayed in a cultural context makes possible accurate assessment, meaningful understanding and appropriate interventions relative to that cultural context. Interpreting behavior out of context is likely to result in misattribution.
2. People who express similar positive expectations or values through different culturally learned behaviors share the "common ground" that allows them to disagree in their behaviors while sharing the same ultimate positive goal. Not everyone who

smiles at you is your friend and not everyone who shouts at you is your enemy.

3. Recognizing the thousands of "culture teachers," each of us has internalized from the friends, enemies, relatives, heroes, heroines and fantasies helps us understand and identify the sources of our individual identity. As we encounter problems we are likely to imagine how one or another influential figure we knew might act in a similar situation.

4. Just as a healthy eco-system requires a diversity in the gene pool so a healthy society requires a diversity of cultural perspectives for its psychological health. By considering many different perspectives in problem solving we are less likely to overlook the right answer.

5. Recognizing our natural tendency to encapsulate ourselves, cultural diversity protects us from imposing our self-reference criteria inappropriately by challenging our assumptions. We have been taught to "do unto others as you would have them do unto you," imposing our own wants and needs on others.

6. Contact with different cultures provides opportunities to rehearse adaptive functioning skills that will help us survive in the diversified global village of the future. By learning to work with those different from ourselves we already know we can develop the facility for working with future cultures that we do not yet know.

7. Social justice and moral development require the contrasting cultural perspectives of multiculturalism to prevent any one dominant group from holding the standards of justice hostage. Every social system that has imposed the exclusive will of the dominant culture as the measure of just and moral behavior has ended up being condemned by history.

8. By looking at both similarities and differences at the same time according to the "quantum metaphor," it becomes possible to identify nonlinear alternatives to rigidly absolutist thinking. It is not just the content of our thinking but the very process of thinking itself which can become culturally encapsulated.

9. We are able to continue our learning curve to match the rapid social changes around us by understanding all education as examples of culture shock. We know we have learned something new when we experience a sense of surprise, making education metaphorically similar to a journey.

10. Spiritual completeness requires that we complement our own understanding of Ultimate Reality with the different understandings others have to increase our spiritual completeness. The well known metaphor that all trails lead to the top of the mountain may indeed apply to our sense of spiritual understanding.

11. The untried political alternative of cultural pluralism provides the only alternative to absolutism on the one hand and anarchy on the other. Our survival in the future will depend on our ability to work with persons who are different from ourselves without sacrificing integrity while at the same time finding common ground.

12. A culture-centered [multicultural] perspective will strengthen the relevance and applicability of psychology by more adequately reflecting the complex and dynamic reality in which we all live. The multicultural perspective resembles the fourth dimension in time as it complements our understanding of three-dimensional space. (pp. 19–20)

These 12 support statements provide a basis for change within the professional counseling organization "meta-worldview" that consists of the collective worldviews of the membership.

Multicultural Terminology

To understand multiculturalism, counselors must have a working understanding of the terminology shifts that have occurred. Terms such as *cross-cultural counseling* and *multicultural counseling* have evolved and may be used interchangeably by some authors, but the terms are different. Multicultural counseling may be viewed as the process of professional interaction within a helping relationship. On the other hand, multiculturalism characterizes an individual's or an organization's underlying beliefs, attitudes, and values that are employed for the formulation of attributions of others. **Attributions** are inferences or characteristics assigned to an individual through a "process people use to assign cause and effect to behavior" (Nairne, 1997, p. 592). The assignments of attributions help counselors to explain their own behavior and the experiences of others (Portman, 2001). Perceptions of race, ethnicity, and culture influence the attributions that counselors assign to clients.

The terms *race, ethnicity,* and *culture* have often been used interchangeably (LaFromboise, Foster, & James, 1996). **Race** is an anthropological classification based on physical appearance that some authorities believe should be eliminated from any scholarly discussion on multiculturalism (Gladding, 2001; LaFromboise et al., 1996). **Ethnicity** describes peoples who "share a common origin and a unique social and cultural heritage"

Box 11.2   Questions for Reflection

Consider the following list. Rank each item in the order of importance to you. What factors influenced your rankings? Choose one item and consider what life experiences may have helped in constructing your worldview. Why might someone else have a different ranking from your own? How might the aspirational ethical views of a counselor be influenced by socially constructed worldviews?

1. A sense of belonging to an organized church or temple
2. A respect for older adults and elders
3. A need to be a good representative of your family and community
4. A strong desire to be viewed as independent and self-sufficient
5. A desire to honor others through gift giving

(Gladding, 2001, p. 45). The term *culture* accurately articulates the current mindset in the counseling profession. Culture is a psychological construct that is a socially learned set of constructs encompassing "affective styles and values regarding personal control, communication, familial patterns, and societal norms" (Betancourt & Lopez, 1993, p. 631). Similarly, Gladding (2001) defined culture as "the shared values, beliefs, expectations, worldviews, symbols, and appropriate behaviors of a group that provide its members with norms, plans, and rules for social living" (p. 34). Differences in such definitions of culture tend to be based on theoretical orientation or internalized value systems. Both definitions agree that culture is the product of social construction to some degree. Each population group has different ways of learning cultural norms and values. Cultural norms may vary both between groups and within groups.

The term **minority** has often been used to describe any identifiable group with differential power and a history of mistreatment (Atkinson & Hackett, 1988; Gladding, 2001; LaFromboise et al., 1996). In earlier literature, the term *minority* referred to ethnic minority groups in the United States (i.e., African American, American Indian, Asian American, and Hispanic). This terminology has changed to include terms such as *visible racial ethnic groups* and *people of color* (Helms & Cook, 1999). Minority, however, is a mathematical concept. Given the current socio-demographic changes in many communities, traditional minority groups may be the numerical majority, so the term *oppressed populations* may be substituted. However, counselors are reminded that many White ethnic groups were oppressed (i.e., Irish Americans, Polish Americans, Italian Americans, Jews).

Some terminology represents outdated and possibly harmful concepts. Language such as **culturally disadvantaged** and **cultural deficit** was utilized in counselor training programs a few decades ago and may still linger in the minds of counselors and in the archival literature. Currently, these terms are not even listed in *The Counseling Dictionary: Concise Definitions of Frequently Used Terms* (Gladding, 2001). The terms *culturally disadvantaged* and *deficit* may cause harm by establishing a psychological assignment of attributions to oppressed group members that inhibits their perceived ability to excel or compete with dominant culture group members. Counselors who embrace a deficit model of interacting with oppressed clients may, in fact, lower their expectations of these clients at the risk of hindering client growth or terminating prematurely. Counselors must recognize these concepts to advocate for their clients. Case Scenario 11-1 provides an example of a cultural deficit frame of reference.

CASE SCENARIO 11-1

The Counseling Relationship—Client Welfare—Career and Employment Needs

Eduardo is a 38-year-old, self-employed construction worker who has his own roofing crew. He is concerned that he will not be able to continue in his current employment as he ages. He is seeking the help of a career counselor for exploration of possible occupational changes. The counselor explores various skilled labor positions with Eduardo. Eduardo attempts to explain that he has been managing his own roofing business for 18 years, but the counselor ignores his business skills and instead focuses on Eduardo's construction knowledge. Eduardo has the opportunity to purchase an established recycling business with a lucrative clientele and would like to explore his potential skills as a business owner. Without assessing Eduardo's managerial skills, the counselor encourages

Eduardo to stay with labor occupations in which other Latinos have been successful. Is the counselor violating any ethical codes by attributing less ability to Eduardo?

YES.   The counselor is mandated by ethical codes to work with Eduardo to consider his overall abilities, vocational limitations, physical restrictions, general temperament, interests and aptitude patterns, social skills, education, general qualifications, and other relevant characteristics and needs. The counselor made assumptions based on Eduardo being a Latino and concluded that Eduardo was not capable of being successful running his own business. The counselor curtailed exploration of Eduardo's potential based on a cultural deficit perspective.

Counselors must be aware of the linguistic changes within the multicultural literature so as not to misinterpret an author's intended meaning. However, some multicultural terms have remained consistent throughout the literature. One such term is **cultural encapsulation.** Cultural encapsulation was coined by Gilbert Wrenn (1962) and refers to a tendency for people to treat others relative to their own cultural perspective, disregarding important cultural differences. The concept of cultural encapsulation becomes extremely important when examining professional ethical codes and standards due to the process of assigning attributions to clients in determining appropriate treatment or service delivery. If counselors are culturally encapsulated, they view the experiences of their clients through their own socially constructed experiences and perspectives—potentially misattributing client intent and motive. Such professional issues play a significant role in ethical decision making concerning multiculturalism in counseling. Professional counselors must consider their own cultural perspectives, as well as those of their client population. These professional issues hold great significance for the advancement of multiculturalism in counseling.

PROFESSIONAL ISSUES OF SIGNIFICANCE TO MULTICULTURALISM

Professional issues of significance regarding multicultural issues in counseling can be divided into two categories: external and internal factors. External factors are identified as issues that require mandated attention by federal or state governments and influence the sociopolitical structure of American society. Internal factors may include major contributions to the advancement of multiculturalism, or issues that may constitute controversies among professional counselors.

External Factors

One of the most challenging political issues to affect multiculturalism in recent years is the change in procedure in the 2000 census conducted by the U.S. Census Bureau. Counseling professionals acknowledged the changing demographic characteristics of the American population long before the 2000 census data were available (Bradt, 1997; Byington, Fischer, Walker, & Freeman, 1997; Pedersen, 1997; Sue, 1996). However, now that the census data are available, the analysis is confounding. Political decisions made by the U.S. Census Bureau changed the manner in which race was reported by the 2000 census. Two changes actually occurred: First, participants were able to select one or more race categories. Second, all respondents were asked if they were of Hispanic or Latino origin. The U.S. government distinguishes between racial groups and Hispanic origin groups. According to the U.S. Census Bureau, "Hispanics may be of any race. The terms 'Hispanic' and 'Latino' are used interchangeably" (Grieco & Cassidy, 2001). Therefore, the numerical information is nondiscrete or overlapping in many instances. Counselors must consider the relevance of these changes for the profession—the relevance of any census information for counselors is a matter of preparation to serve possible clientele. Given that counselors are ethically mandated to practice only within the bounds of their competence, they must be proactive in gaining multicultural awareness, knowledge, and skills. Proactive preparation requires being fully informed of potential multicultural client groups. The 2000 census provides such information for counselors.

The Census 2000 data on race provide only descriptive information. Changes in data collection procedures that allowed participants to identify by selecting one or more race categories negate comparison to previous census collections (Grieco & Cassidy, 2001). On the one hand, the change limits using census data to predict population trends. Yet, on the other hand, the descriptive information for multiracial classifications is invaluable for counseling professionals. The census information for all racial groups provides more explicit information that is directly relevant to the counseling profession through the identification of potential multicultural client populations.

Over 281 million people participated in the 2000 census, and 98 percent identified themselves in the "one race only" categories: White, Black or African American, American Indian and Alaska Native, Asian, Native Hawaiian and Other Pacific Islander, and some other race. Three-quarters (75%) of the total group identified themselves as White. The remaining "one race" categories were reported as Black or African American (12%), Asian (4%), American Indian or Alaska Native (0.9%), Native Hawaiian and Other Pacific Islander (0.1%), and some other race (5.5%). The majority of respondents in the "some other race" category were of Hispanic origin (97%)—not considered a standard Office of Management and Budget (OMB) race category (Grieco & Cassidy, 2001). These population figures are relevant for counseling professionals because they provide an overview of general clientele possibilities. The need to consider each of these recognized racial groups as potential clients holds relevance for counselor preparation programs for inclusion in the curriculum.

Yet, the most relevant findings for counselors may be in the clear identification of respondents in the "two or more races" category. The reporting of multiple racial identification categories in the 2000 census is a major contribution to multiculturalism. Over 6 million people, or 2.4 percent of the population, identified themselves as being multiracial (Grieco & Cassidy, 2001). These multiracial categories provide much needed insight for the profession concerning implications for future research. The percentages of people in each multiracial classification are noted in Table 11–1. These five categories listed in Table 11–1 account for 75 percent of all people who identified themselves as multiracial. Census participants selected a combination of two racial identities predominantly over multiracial options. Therefore, counselors must increase their multicultural competence specifically with biracial populations to practice within their boundaries of

competence. Counselors must be aware both in practice and in research that attention must be given to biracial individuals' concerns.

Members of the counseling profession must not overlook the importance of the U.S. government descriptions of racial and ethnic groups. The U.S. Office of Management and Budget has designated the five "one race" categories (White, Black or African American, American Indian and Alaska Native, Asian, Native Hawaiian and Other Pacific Islander) and the four biracial categories (White/American Indian and Alaska Native, White/Asian, White/Black or African American, and Black or African American/American Indian or Alaska Native) for civil rights monitoring and enforcement (Grieco & Cassidy, 2001).

The exclusion of Latino populations as a racial category in the 2000 census is a professional advocacy issue of relevance to counselors. Attention to this social justice concern may prevent unfair treatment of Latino populations in the future. Therefore, the exclusion of a Hispanic/Latino classification as a racial category needs to be monitored for social advocacy in the counseling profession.

Counselors have an ethical responsibility for multicultural awareness to develop their social advocacy skills and to ensure the welfare of multicultural clients. They must foster active, participatory awareness for informed decision making and to promote client welfare. Overall, the majority of external factors may be beyond the control of counselors, but internal factors are open to change within the profession.

Internal Factors

Internal factors are conditions found within the counseling profession that influence multicultural delivery of services. These conditions may promote or impede counselors from fully embracing a multicultural perspective. Four internal factors have been selected to represent current conditions found within the counseling profession: (1) inclusion versus exclusion of population groups, (2) cultural encapsulation, (3) inadequate ethical standards, and (4) training issues.

Inclusion versus Exclusion of Population Groups. Multiculturalism embraces members of ethnic and diverse populations. The inclusion or exclusion of specific population groups is a major internal factor that affects the counseling profession. The question is, "Whom does the profession include under the umbrella of multiculturalism?"

TABLE 11–1 Census 2000 Respondents Identifying in the Two or More Race Category

Category	Percentage
White/American Indian and Alaska Native	15.9%
White/Asian	12.7%
White/Black or African American	11.5%
Black or African American/American Indian and Alaska Native	2.7%
White/some other race	32.3%

Source: From E. M. Grieco and R. C. Cassidy. (2001). Overview of race and Hispanic origin: Census brief 2000. (Issue Brief No. CZKBe/OH). Washington, D.C.: U.S. Department of Commerce.

A controversy does exist within the counseling profession related to the inclusion of diverse viewpoints. This controversy is represented in the following excerpt:

> There are those who would like to define culture broadly to include race, ethnicity, class, affectional orientation, religion, sex, age, and so forth. As such, multicultural counseling would include not only racial and ethnic minorities, but also women, gays and lesbians, and other special populations. There are those who prefer to limit the discussion of multicultural counseling to what has been referred to as "Visible Racial Ethnic Minority Groups"—African Americans, American Indians, Asian Americans, and Hispanics and Latinos. Those who hold this point of view acknowledge that to some extent all counseling is cross-cultural, but the term can be defined so broadly that it dilutes the focus on racial and ethnic concerns (a primary one being racism) and allows counseling professionals to avoid and omit dealing with the four major groups in our society. (Sue, Arredondo, & McDavis, 1992, pp. 477–478)

This debate is well documented in the literature (Gladding, 2001; Pedersen, 2001; Sue et al., 1992).

Practicing counselors can be affected either overtly or covertly by this controversy as they begin to gain multicultural competence. Overt influences can occur through professional literature or training programs that embrace an exclusionary view of multiculturalisms, which only considers ethnicity as a criterion. Covert influences can occur through exposure to professional growth opportunities wherein facilitators do not provide a disclaimer regarding their views of inclusion or exclusion of specific groups. Counselors should be aware of the multicultural theoretical continuum that has dichotomous endpoints. A multicultural theoretical continuum presented by Stone (1997) has endpoints ranging from inclusion of only the four major American ethic groups to inclusion of all diverse groups (i.e., people with disabilities, sexual orientation, religion). Counselors must be knowledgeable consumers when presented with multicultural knowledge and resource materials so they can properly interpret and transfer their knowledge to the appropriate clientele. Proponents on both sides of the controversy have valid points. However, ethical codes are relevant for every client, not just a few. Counselors must apply the ethical codes in all circumstances regardless of their underlying theoretical beliefs on who is to be included in multicultural dialogues based on the degree of historical oppression, prejudice, or discrimination faced by their clients' ancestors. Whatever the outcome of this debate

among counseling professionals, the reality of the circumstances supported by the 2000 U.S. census is that clients from diverse "ethnographic, demographic, status and affiliational" (Pedersen, 2001, p. 17) backgrounds will present themselves to counselors for services.

Cultural Encapsulation. The concept of cultural encapsulation is not new to the counseling profession as an internal factor. In this view, the counselor embraces and imposes only one set of assumptions that are based on dominant cultural values as being universal, disregarding any cultural variations or influences that may impact client progress (Pedersen, 2001; Wrenn, 1962).

Forty years after Wrenn (1962) coined the term, cultural encapsulation continues to be evident, as described by the following passage:

> The Basic Behavioral Science Task Force of the National Advisory Mental Health Council (1996) in their national plan for behavioral science research identified areas where cultural encapsulation continues to be evident in mental health services. First, anthropological and cross-cultural research has demonstrated that cultural beliefs influence diagnosis and treatment. Second, diagnosis of mental illness differs across cultures. Third, individuals express symptoms differently in each cultural context. Fourth, culturally biased variations in diagnosis follow the diagnostic categories relevant to the majority population. Fifth, most providers come from majority cultures while most clients come from minority cultures. (Pedersen, 2001, p. 17)

Cultural encapsulation also continues to impact research and training programs (Lonner & Ibrahim, 1996; Paniagua, 1994; Ponterotto, 1988). Even ethical standards are viewed as being culturally encapsulated in dominant culture values (LaFromboise et al., 1996; Pedersen, 1995).

Cultural encapsulation, as an internal factor, may be the most predominant deterrent to the implementation of multiculturalism within the profession. Just as racism can be intentional or unintentional, so too can cultural encapsulation. Yet, even if it is unintentional, the direct delivery of counseling services can be affected (Pedersen, 2001; Ridley, 1995)—for an example, treating all people the same regardless of cultural background or the multicultural concept of color blindness (Case Scenario 11-2).

CASE SCENARIO 11-2

The Counseling Relationship—Positive Growth and Development

A 38-year-old female counselor (Irish American, fourth generation) is providing counseling services to Betsy, a

34-year-old female client (Asian American, first generation). Betsy is an only child and resides with her aging parents. Betsy is self-referred. Her presenting issue is difficulty with decision making related to her career as a teacher. Betsy is considering a career change to cosmetology but knows this will upset her parents, who take great pride that their daughter is an American teacher. The counselor encourages Betsy to explore her options in cosmetology. However, the counselor expresses a concern that Betsy's difficulty in making decisions is related to her lack of autonomy from her parents. The counselor begins to explore alternative living arrangements that will help Betsy develop independence. Should the counselor encourage independence and growth that, in the counselor's view, is fostering the client's interest and welfare?

NO.   Although the ACA ethics code clearly indicates a counseling relationship involves the counselor encouraging "client growth and development in ways that foster the client's interest and welfare," in a multicultural situation this code is in direct contradiction with the code on "respecting differences." This counselor did not stop and actively pursue information about the client's cultural belief system related to family. The counselor also may have been imposing a dominant worldview upon the client, which embraces independence and autonomy from family that may not be shared in an Asian American worldview. The counselor needs to explore her own values and beliefs related to family and the possibility of being culturally encapsulated in dominant cultural values. Culturally competent counselors must be aware of their own biases that may unconsciously enter the counseling relationship.

Inadequate Ethical Standards.   Unclear or inadequate inclusion of the language of multiculturalism in professional organization ethical codes and standards of practice requires immediate attention (Bradt, 1997; Pedersen, 1997, 2001). In fact, many assert a serious discrepancy exists between the cultural contexts in which the ethical codes and standards are being applied and the cultural context in which the codes were created (Ivey, 1987; LaFromboise et al., 1996; Pedersen, 1997). This discrepancy is evident in patterns of systematic cultural bias in the ACA ethics code. As Sue et al. (1992) stated, "Too often, lip service is given to multicultural concerns, without the commitment to translate them into ethical standards and see that they become part of the accreditation criteria" (p. 480).

A limited pattern consisting of three primary concerns has emerged from the literature on the inclusion of multiculturalism in current codes. Several conclusions can be reached from this analysis:

1. Current codes of ethics do not include specific language related to multiculturalism, except superficially. Therefore, the import of counselor inclusion of multicultural concerns is diminished (Bradt, 1997; Pedersen, 1997, 2001; Sue et al., 1992).
2. Codes provide implicit direction related to multiculturalism, which leads practitioners to determine their own interpretations of multicultural competence (Ponterotto & Casas, 1991). Explicit guidelines are not available to practitioners nor to legal authorities determining ethical conduct related to multiculturalism.
3. The codes themselves are framed from a majority worldview stemming primarily from an individualistic perspective (Pedersen, 2001).

Currently, the ACA Ethics Committee is examining the ACA Code of Ethics for its "multicultural content and sensitivity" with the intent of revising the existing code (ACA Web site—*http://www.counseling.org/urgent/special11159.html*). The ACA Ethics Committee has begun this task by soliciting input from the ACA membership.

Training Issues.   After the civil rights movement, counselor training programs were openly criticized for not providing students with the opportunity to learn how to work with multicultural clientele (Jackson, 1995). In fact, the July 1973 American Psychological Association's conference at Vail, Colorado, provided the impetus for addressing ethical behavior in multicultural counseling through a resolution that suggested that counselors who are not trained or competent to provide services to culturally diverse clients but do so are behaving unethically (Korman, 1974; Pedersen & Marsella, 1982).

The attention from this scholarly dialogue led to the inclusion of multicultural training standards by accreditation bodies such as APA, CACREP, and CORE, and eventually to the creation of multicultural competency guidelines through ACA and AMCD. Accrediting standards require multicultural training. Recent research has demonstrated the effectiveness of training in enhancing multicultural competence (Byington et al., 1997). Many training programs only offer one course in multicultural counseling. Others may offer none at all, choosing to opt for an infusion of multicultural issues into the curriculum. It may be both necessary to offer a specific course as well as infuse multicultural content into the curriculum to provide trained, culturally competent counselors to the field. However, accrediting boards recognize few programs, and the programs that are unaccredited are not required to follow the accreditation criterion. Therefore, the significance of ethical codes becomes more important in ensuring the welfare of multicultural clients.

ISSUES OF SIGNIFICANCE TO MULTICULTURALISM

Ethics

Multicultural professional interaction is becoming pervasive; however, ethical codes and standards of practice may not be adequately inclusive of multiculturalism. The implicit nature of the current ethical codes creates an atmosphere of implied choice and lack of commitment by professional organizations to multiculturalism as a mandated area of concern for counselors (Pedersen, 1997). In essence, implied ethical standards are not enforceable in grievance processes, which limits the profession's ability to protect consumers from being harmed by incompetent multicultural practices. Yet, until the codes are revised, the current standards serve as guidelines in counselors' professional training and service delivery to all clients.

A closer examination of the codes and standards is necessary to increase counselor awareness of multicultural responsibilities. So, how does a practitioner begin to align implied ethical guidelines with multicultural service delivery?

First, basic ethics need to be revisited so that a discussion of basic, ethical decision making can occur (Herlihy & Corey, 1996). Basic, ethical decision making requires reexamination of the distinction between the concepts of mandatory and aspirational ethics. Herlihy and Corey (1996) distinguished between mandatory ethics, meaning to function according to minimum legal standards, and aspirational ethics, meaning to function at a higher standard in accordance with the spirit behind the literal meaning of the code. By ascribing to aspirational ethical standards in multicultural counseling, counselors identify fundamental values while recognizing that different cultures may express those values through their own culturally learned behaviors. The expression of learned cultural behaviors surfaces as the basic foundation of multiculturalism. The basic premise involves respecting different cultural worldviews. Accepting a diversity of worldviews and opinions leads to a quandary in ethical decision making—how can a profession mandate respecting diversity and yet clearly establish enforceable behavioral

codes of conduct that respect every diverse opinion? Thus, the dilemma of multiculturalism and ethics exists in both mandatory and aspirational ethics. When does the organizational worldview take precedence over the individual practitioner's worldview?

The circular loop created in multicultural ethics may be best served through a discussion on principle and virtue ethics. Jordan and Meara (1990) distinguished between principle and virtue ethics. Principle ethics focuses on rational, objective, universal, and impartial principles mandating actions and choices. Virtue ethics focuses on the counselor's motives, intentions, character, and ethical consciousness. Virtue ethics recognizes the need to interpret principles differently in each cultural context. This complexity in ethical consideration is compounded by the intricacy of cultural worldviews, which may place different levels of importance on the hierarchy of mandatory, aspirational, principle, and virtue ethics. Therefore, clear statements regarding multicultural context and professional responsibility must emerge within future ethical codes. Ponterotto and Casas (1991) highlighted four philosophical premises necessary to translate ethical theory: (1) altruism, (2) responsibility, (3) justice, and (4) caring. These premises assist counselors in making "more purposive and intentional" ethical decisions in multicultural settings (Pedersen, 1995, p. 37).

Pedersen and Marsella (1982) called for "responsible disobedience" of ethical guidelines in multicultural situations that require adherence to the underlying ethical principles represented by specific ethical guidelines at the expense of respect for cultural diversity.

Helms and Cook (1999) actually acknowledged they had instituted responsible disobedience in varying from current ethical standards in multicultural counseling situations. Their statement is presented here as an indication of how counselors must justify reconciling their professional judgments and values with the existing codes of ethics. Helms and Cook (1999) stated:

> Some readers may have already reported us to their professional ethics boards for some of the therapeutic practices that we have recommended thus far. However, although we may have straddled the ethical boundaries a bit, we do not believe that we have actually crossed any of them. Perhaps our most distressing recommendation for traditionally trained psychologists is our suggestion that having contact with clients outside of therapy is appropriate. Some of them may argue that such behavior constitutes multiple relationships with clients. The other place therapists sometimes have trouble with our therapy approach is our recommendation that therapists

practice fluid terminations when necessary for the client's benefit . . . Our approach merely attempts to ensure that the client does not feel abandoned. (p. 195)

Helms and Cook (1999) conducted a deliberate analysis of the ethical codes related to potentially detrimental relationships and respecting diversity. This example of processing ethical codes related to multiculturalism proves a valuable method of self-regulation needed in the profession. Counselors must be cautious in their execution of responsible disobedience or the ethical codes will become diluted and nonfunctioning. Counselors must make a professional decision when one ethical guideline aligns against another. The most efficient outcome will be a congruent set of ethical standards.

Ethical Standards

Strong (1986) as cited in Sue et al. defined a multicultural organization as "one which is genuinely committed to diverse representation of its membership; is sensitive to maintaining an open, supportive, and responsive environment; is working toward and purposefully including elements of diverse cultures in its ongoing operations; and one which is authentic in its response to issues confronting it" (p. 7). Organizational systems reflect their collective members' values, attitudes, and beliefs. These factors cycle between the organizational governing principles and the actual behavior and practice of the membership. Thus, change or cyclical movement may occur when the membership begins to express dissatisfaction with current standards or policies. Indeed, this may be ongoing or enmeshed in a paradigmatic shift within the counseling profession—such as that now occurring with multiculturalism in counseling.

The ACA Code of Ethics and Standards of Practice[1] approved by the governing council in April 1995 was a historic move toward inclusion of multicultural statements. Sections on respecting diversity, public responsibility, and relationships with other professionals clearly articulate the language of nondiscrimination and sexual harassment, and respecting cultural differences in an inclusive manner. However, some authors point out there is room for improvement. Pedersen (1995) and Sue (1996) are probably the strongest proponents for multicultural consideration in ethical codes of the counseling profession. Weaknesses exist in both the APA and the ACA ethical guidelines, according to Pedersen (1995). He noted that the ethical codes "lack explicit philosophical principles, assume a dominant culture perspective, and generally minimize or trivialize

the role of culture in ethical decision making" (Pedersen, 1995, p. 42).

Pedersen (1995, 1997, 2001) called for organizational change in the area of ethics for the counseling profession. His insight serves as an impetus for change. Pedersen stated that the ACA ethical standards contain a fundamental notion that "what is good for the counselor is good for everyone" (p. 46). This stance forces clients to be at the professional whim of their counselors. According to Pedersen, the ethical codes show a discriminatory bias similar to cultural encapsulation, accompanied by a one-dimensional application of the codes to cultural concerns and an absolute standard for right and wrong (Pedersen, 1995). The "one size fits all" perspective is unacceptable according to the 1995 ACA and 1992 APA codes of ethics, as can be read in both preambles.

CASE SCENARIO 11-3

Research Responsibilities—Use of Human Subjects
A counselor educator joins a student in researching developmental issues of African American children. The researchers have determined that a convenience sampling of children living in a low-income housing unit with a resident population that is 98 percent African American would be a good source for research participants. The counselor educator contacts the social worker who works with the residents to set up a time to present the study. The social worker informs the researchers that a mandatory meeting has already been scheduled to discuss housing regulations and the research study could be presented at that time. Should the researchers agree to this mandatory meeting?

NO. There are multiple considerations with this scenario. First, research participation should always be voluntary. Second, a convenience sampling that narrows the participant pool to one small segment of a population is not representative of the general population of African American children. Therefore, the researchers need to consider expanding the research sample to be more rep-

---

[1]The ethical standards and code comparisons discussed here are meant to accentuate the strengths and weaknesses in ethics codes in general even though the 1995 American Counseling Association (ACA) and the 1992 American Psychological Association (APA) codes are discussed to illustrate specific issues. This is not an exhaustive overview of these standards, but merely a general analysis of these codes. It is a useful exercise since these are historic documents that represent the first major attempts by these organizations to infuse multicultural content into their codes. Even as revised codes may be enacted in the future, the same concerns will be relevant to evaluating the multicultural sensitivity of these new documents.

resentative so as not to add misinformation or overgeneralize findings that may encourage further stereotyping of a cultural group.

Counselors must reexamine the ethical codes and standards of practice by viewing each guideline through the new lenses of multiculturalism. Examples of ethical codes and standards that require re-examination fall within five major areas of concern: (1) implicit cultural bias, (2) cultural encapsulation, (3) favoritism toward the dominant culture, (4) issues of professional self-regulation, and (5) a lack of measurable multicultural accountability (LaFromboise, 1996; Pedersen, 1995; Sue, 1996).

Implicit Cultural Bias. Implicit cultural bias in the 1995 ACA Code of Ethics is represented in the preamble and sections on client welfare, dual relationships, confidentiality, and evaluation and assessment. The preamble states: "Association members recognize diversity in our society and embrace a cross-cultural approach in support of the worth, dignity, potential, and uniqueness of each individual" (p. 1). This statement implies an individualistic perspective over a collectivistic worldview (Pedersen, 1995). Under client welfare concerning a discourse on counseling plans, counselors are to respect the client's "freedom of choice." The implication of freedom based on individual choice leans heavily toward an individualistic cultural perspective (Pedersen, 1995). Many collectivistic cultural worldviews base personal choice on the potential consequences experienced by cultural or familial group. The sections on dual relationships also ignore the relational values often present in collectivistic cultures (Pedersen, 1995; Sue, 1996). The code sections on confidentiality and evaluation, assessment, and interpretation contain generic, well-meaning statements concerning client rights. However, multicultural consideration is only implied and attention to collectivistic cultural differences is not explicit (Pedersen, 1995).

Cultural Encapsulation. Cultural encapsulation permeates the 1995 ACA Code of Ethics and standards. A few examples can be found in sections on nondiscrimination, cultural sensitivity, and research and publication. On the one hand, the nondiscrimination section contains the necessary aspirational statement requesting counselors to respect diversity by attacking discrimination based on an inclusive population multicultural perspective. Yet, on the other hand, this same section does not acknowledge that the counselor needs to appreciate that there may be "simultaneous cultural affiliations" such as in a combination of identities that suffer from discrimination (Pedersen, 1997, p. 25). An example would be a fundamental Protestant man who is African American and gay. Counselors must acknowledge the potential for multiple oppression and discrimination of such a client. Counselors must also be aware that their own biases may be confounded in situations wherein clients hold simultaneous cultural affiliations. A similar situation related to counselor roles may occur. The ethical code section on potentially detrimental relationships asserts, "If it becomes apparent that counselors may be called upon to perform potentially conflicting roles, they clarify, adjust or withdraw from roles appropriately" (ACA, p. 3). In multicultural situations in a collectivistic culture or possibly in geographically diverse situations, roles may overlap and "role diffusion" may be unavoidable (Pedersen, 1997, p. 25). A clear, behaviorally specific statement that outlines expectations could provide much needed guidance in the area of potentially detrimental relationships and collectivistic cultural situations.

Favoritism Toward Dominant Cultural Worldviews. Favoritism toward a dominant worldview is prevalent within the ACA Code of Ethics, as illustrated in sections relating to personal needs and values of counselors, bartering, and boundaries of professional competence. Counselors' self-awareness concerning their worldview (i.e., values, attitudes, beliefs, and behavior) and its potential effects on diverse clients, as indicated under the section of personal needs and values, provides an example of favoritism toward the dominant culture (Pedersen, 1997). Three factors affect the intent of this ethical code: (1) a low level of cultural self-awareness among counselors, (2) an inability of counselors with low cultural self-awareness to realize their limitations, and (3) counseling practice being heavily weighted in culturally encapsulated values (Pedersen, 1997; Ridley, 1995).

Bartering is discouraged in the ethical codes. The discouragement of bartering favors a monetary economic system based on dominant culture, which may hold different meanings for clients based on their status or cultural background (Pedersen, 1997). An implied consent is integrated into the code making bartering a possibility when the relationship is not exploitive. This again places the responsibility on the counselor to make the determination. However, this guideline may be one example of clear, measurable behavioral guidelines related to counselors participating in a bartering relationship: client request, nonexploitive relationship, clear written contract, and accepted practice in the community. Counselors would benefit if other guidelines held such content.

Issues of Professional Self-Regulation. Professional self-regulation allows counselors the opportunity to monitor their own multicultural behaviors. This may encourage counselors to continue unintentional racism, discrimination, and imposition of their own worldviews when working with clients. Both the 1995 ACA and 1992 APA codes of ethics assume counselors will be self-regulatory. An examination of several APA codes helps to clarify these issues. One of the general principles is the respect for people's rights and dignity. This principle challenges APA membership to respect client rights in multiple areas and to self-regulate by not knowingly engaging in "unfair discriminatory practices" (APA). The use of the word "unknowingly" provides a loophole for unintentional racism, discrimination, and imposition of the counselor's worldview. This principle may even appear incongruent with the APA standards on boundaries of competence. However, the boundaries of competence standards contain no language directly related to multicultural competence. Other ethical standards such as those on human differences, nondiscrimination, harassment, and multiple relationships are implied, but are associated with multiculturalism and contain multicultural language for self-regulatory purposes. Thus, counselors must examine implied meanings instead of applying actual guidelines to specific multicultural cases or personal practice.

The APA endorsed guidelines for provision of psychological services to ethnic, linguistic, and culturally diverse populations (APA, 1993; see Appendix 11-A). These guidelines provide a solid foundation for APA members in multicultural awareness and competence; however, they are a separate set of guidelines from the ethical code and therefore appear to be aspirational in nature.

CASE SCENARIO 11-4

Professional Responsibility—Nondiscrimination

Sarah is a school counselor at an affluent elementary school. She has been conducting small groups successfully for five years. Parents have been willing to give permission for their children to participate in the groups and often keep Sarah informed of their children's developmental needs. Recently, a group foster home was established within the school district's boundary area. One child from the foster home was selected to participate in a fifth-grade friendship group. A parent called to complain about her child being in a group with "one of those poor kids" and asked that the child from the foster home be removed from her daughter's group. The counselor requested an appointment with the parent to discuss the issue face to face. The parent agreed. At the meeting, the counselor explained her ethical obligation concerning nondiscrimination as a public and professional responsibility. The counselor listened to the parent's complaints. Did the counselor behave in an ethical manner?

YES. The school counselor must serve the needs of every child in her building in a manner that is nondiscriminatory. Socioeconomic status is a diversity issue that is often overlooked. The counselor listened to the concerns of the parent without imposing her beliefs on the parent and stated professional responsibility. The parent maintained the right to refuse services by requesting her child be removed from the group. However, the counselor may have an ethical responsibility to be an advocate for the children in the foster home if this parent's attitude is a reflection of the community at large.

Another critique of current ethical codes is the need for specific behaviorally observable statements of competencies or practices that give clear guidance and are enforceable by ethics boards. In 1982, Pedersen and Marsella brought attention to the ethical dilemma in multicultural counseling service delivery. Almost 20 years later, the counseling profession is beginning to reassess ethics related to multiculturalism. This movement appears to be emerging from within the membership. In 1992, AMCD, a division of ACA, published Multicultural Counseling Competencies and Standards as a means of providing guidance for counseling professionals (see Appendix 11-B). These multicultural competencies clearly indicate a positive move in the profession. However, professional members of divisional groups of ACA continue to present the need to add explicit statements in ethical codes and standards of practice related to multiculturalism (Burn, 1992; McGinn, Flowers, & Rubin, 1993; Tarvydas & Cottone, 2000). A clear mandate is presented in the 1995 ACA Code of Ethics that: "Counselors practice only within the boundaries of their competence, based on their education, training, supervised experience, state and national professional credentials, and appropriate professional experience. Counselors will demonstrate a commitment to gain knowledge, personal awareness, sensitivity, and skills pertinent to working with a diverse client population" (ACA, 1995, p. 7). This is a positive statement and possibly the strongest multicultural statement in the entire code. However, ACA as an organization must demonstrate a commitment to multiculturalism to its membership (Sue et al., 1992). This commitment to multiculturalism can be shown in multiple ways: (1) A clear articulation of specific, measurable, behavioral statements of competencies or practices in the ethical codes that provide well-structured guidance to counseling practitioners; (2) The enforcement of multicultural aspects of the codes of ethics in a manner that indicates a solid commitment to multiculturalism by the ethics boards; and (3) A strong statement denouncing cultural encapsulation as an accepted practice among counseling professionals prominently presented in the preamble and throughout ethical standards.

CHAPTER SUMMARY

Multicultural counseling must be grounded in the underlying premise of multiculturalism. It is the ethical responsibility of counselors to provide services to all clients either individually or in groups in a competent manner sensitive to the multiple cultural perspectives of those clients and in a manner that is not biased by the counselor's own multiple cultural perspectives. This ethical responsibility also is assumed by the larger professional organizations of ACA, APA, and their divisions. These professional organizations must articulate to their memberships that multiculturalism is a necessary assessment criterion for determining client treatment or interventions.

Historically, multiculturalism has been viewed as a separate specialty area in the field of counseling. However, the current multicultural movement appears to be elevating multiculturalism to an equal dimensional status with the movements of behaviorism, psychodynamics, and humanism. This professional stance provides impetus for the increased importance of multiculturalism in the lives of clients and counselors.

The lack of a mutually agreed-upon definition for multiculturalism is a major hindrance to the counseling profession. It is critical for codes of ethics and standards of practice to be explicit in their articulation of multicultural issues so that both mandatory and aspirational ethics may be applied. Given the current revisiting of the ACA and APA ethics codes in relation to multicultural integration, the future may hold more inclusive guidelines for the counseling profession. Multiculturalism in counseling is a separate level of discourse, and scholarly research is needed on this topic within the counseling profession.

REFERENCES

American Psychological Association. (1993). Guidelines for providers of psychological services to ethnic, linguistic, and culturally diverse populations. *American Psychologist, 48,* 45–48.

Atkinson, D. R., & Hackett, G. (1988). *Counseling non-ethnic American minorities.* Springfield, IL: Charles C. Thomas.

Betancourt, H., & Lopez, S. R. (1993). The study of culture, ethnicity, and race in American psychology. *American Psychologist, 48,* 629–637.

Bradt, J. (1997). Ethical issues in multicultural counseling: Implications for the field of music therapy. *Arts in Psychotherapy, 24* (2), 137–143.

Burn, D. (1992). Ethical implications in cross-cultural counseling and training. *Journal of Counseling & Development, 70,* 578–583.

Byington, K., Fischer, J., Walker, L., & Freeman, E. (1997). Evaluating the effectiveness of a multicultural counseling ethics and assessment training. *Journal of Applied Rehabilitation Counseling, 28* (4), 15–19.

Essandoh, P. K. (1996). Multicultural counseling as the "fourth force": A call to arms. *Counseling Psychologist, 24,* 126–137.

Gladding, S. T. (2001). *The counseling dictionary: Concise definitions of frequently used terms.* Upper Saddle River, NJ: Merrill-Prentice Hall.

Grieco, E. M., & Cassidy, R. C. (2001, March). *Overview of race and Hispanic origin: Census Brief 2000* (Issue Brief No. C2KBR/01-1). Retrieved May 29, 2001 from the U.S. Census Bureau via GPO Access *www.census.gov/population/www/ cen2000/briefs. html.* Washington, D.C.: U.S. Department of Commerce.

Guidelines for provision of psychological services to ethnic, linguistic and culturally diverse populations. (1990, August). Retrieved December 18, 2001, from http://www.apa.org/pi/guide.html.

Helms, J. E., & Cook, D. A. (1999). *Using race and culture in counseling and psychotherapy.* Needham Heights, MA: Allyn & Bacon.

Herlihy, B., & Corey, G. (Eds.). (1996). *ACA ethical standards casebook.* Alexandria, VA: American Counseling Association.

Ivey, A. E. (1987). The multicultural practice of therapy: Ethics, empathy, and dialectics. *Journal of Social and Clinical Psychology, 5* (2), 195–204.

Jackson, M. L. (1995). Multicultural counseling: Historical perspectives. In J. G. Ponterotto, J. M. Casas, L. A. Suzuki, & C. M. Alexander (Eds.), *Handbook of multicultural counseling* (pp. 3–16). Thousand Oaks, CA: Sage.

Jordan, A., & Meara, N. (1990). Ethics and the professional practice of psychologists: The role of virtue and principles. *Professional Psychology: Research and Practice 21* (2), 107–114.

Korman, M. (1974). National conference on levels and patterns of professional training in psychology: Major themes. *American Psychologist, 29,* 441–449.

LaFromboise, T. D., Foster, S., & James, A. (1996). Ethics in multicultural counseling. In P. B. Pedersen, J. G. Draguns, W. J. Lonner, & J. E. Trimble (Eds.), *Counseling Across Cultures* (pp. 47–72). Thousand Oaks, CA: Sage.

Lonner, W., & Ibrahim, F. (1996). Appraisal and assessment in cross-cultural counseling. In P. Petersen & J. Draguns (Eds.), *Counseling across cultures* (pp. 293–322). Thousand Oaks, CA: Sage.

McGinn, F., Flowers, C., & Rubin, S. E. (1993). In quest of an explicit multicultural emphasis in ethical standards for rehabilitation counselors. *Rehabilitation Education, 7* (4), 261–268.

Multicultural competencies. (1991, April). Retrieved December 18, 2001, from *http:// www.counseling.org/multi_diversity/ competencies.htm*

Nairne, J. S. (1997). *Psychology: The adaptive mind*. Pacific Grove, CA: Brooks Cole.

Paniagua, F. (1994). *Assessing and treating culturally diverse clients: A practical guide*. Thousand Oaks, CA: Sage.

Pedersen, P. B. (1995). Culture-centered ethical guidelines for counselors. In J. G. Ponterotto, J. M. Casas, L. A. Suzuki, & C. M. Alexander (Eds.), *Handbook of multicultural counseling* (pp. 34–49). Thousand Oaks, CA: Sage.

Pedersen, P. B. (1997). The cultural context of the American Counseling Association Code of Ethics. *Journal of Counseling & Development, 76*, 23–28.

Pedersen, P. B. (2001). Multiculturalism and the paradigm shift in counseling: Controversies and alternative futures. *Canadian Journal of Counseling, 35* (1), 15–25.

Pedersen, P. B., & Marsella, A. J. (1982). The ethical crisis for cross-cultural counseling

and therapy. *Professional Psychology, 13*, 492–500.

Ponterotto, J., & Casas, J. (1991). *Handbook of racial/ethnic minority counseling research*. Springfield: Charles C. Thomas.

Portman, T. (2001). Sex role attributions of American-Indian women. *Journal of Mental Health Counseling, 23*, 72–84.

Ridley, C. (1995). *Overcoming unintentional racism in counseling and therapy: A practitioner's guide to intentional intervention*. Thousand Oaks, CA: Sage.

Stone, G. (1997). Multiculturalism as a context for supervision: Perspectives, limitations, and implications. In D. Pope-Davis & H. Coleman (Eds.), *Multicultural competencies: Assessment, education and training, and supervision*. Thousand Oaks, CA: Sage.

Strong, L. (1986). Race relations for personal and organizational effectiveness. Unpublished manuscript.

Sue, D. W. (1996). Ethical issues in multicultural counseling. In B. Herlihy & G. Corey (Eds.), *ACA ethical standards casebook* (pp. 193–204). Alexandria, VA: American Counseling Association.

Sue, D. W., Arredondo, P., & McDavis, R. J. (1992). Multicultural counseling competencies and standards: A call to the profession. *Journal of Counseling & Development, 70*, 477–486.

Tarvydas, V. M., & Cottone, R. R. (2000). The code of ethics for professional rehabilitation counselors: What we have and what we need. *Rehabilitation Counseling Bulletin, 43*, 188–196.

Wrenn, G. C. (1962). The culturally encapsulated counselor. *Harvard Educational Review, 32*, 444–449.

APPENDIX 11-A

Guidelines for Provision of Services to Ethnic, Linguistic, and Culturally Diverse Populations

To view the APA guidelines for this topic, please see the following Web site:

> http://www.apa.org/pi/guide.html

APPENDIX 11-B

Multicultural Competencies

To view the multicultural competencies for this topic, please see the following Web site:

> http://www.counseling.org/multi_diversity/
> competencies.htm

PART V

Ethical Practice within Counseling Specialties

CHAPTER 12

Couple and Family Counseling[1]

Objectives

■ ■ ■ ■ ■ ■ ■ ■ ■ ■

After reading this chapter, you should be able to:

- Discuss the major issues in couple and family counseling, including professional identification, licensure, and certification.
- Explain the crucial ethical concerns that arise in the practice of couple and family counseling.
- Compare the applicable ethical codes in couple and family counseling.

■ ■ ■ ■ ■ ■ ■ ■ ■ ■

INTRODUCTION

Couple and family counseling is developing and growing as a counseling specialty. It is also recognized by some individuals as a profession separate from the larger profession of "counseling." "Marriage and family therapy," represented by the professional organization known as the American Association for Marriage and Family Therapy (AAMFT), has its own training standards, accreditation of graduate programs, and licensure. However, many counselor licensure statutes allow for the practice of marriage and family "counseling" within the purview of the general counseling license. The American Counseling Association (ACA) has taken the position that couple, marriage, and family "counseling" is a specialty area within the larger counseling profession. Therefore, couple and family counseling is unique— it is viewed by some as a separate profession *and* by others as a counseling specialty (Gladding, Remley, & Huber, 2001). This dual professional identity has its pros and cons. On the negative side, competing professional associations seek members from an overlapping pool of mental health professionals. Credentials sponsored by the associations also compete, and rivalry and debate exist over the legitimacy of the two professions. On the positive side, two groups are seeking to legitimize the practice of couple and family counseling (or therapy), and two groups are lobbying for such services to be included in health care and other service provider programs. Regardless, the dual professional identity is confusing, and beginning students in counsel-

---

[1]The term "couple" refers to all loving partnerships, including premarital and married couples.

Box 12.1 Exploring the Codes

How do the standards in the American Association of Marriage and Family Therapy (AAMFT, 2001) ethics code on the issue of "dual" or "multiple relationships" compare to the standards on potentially detrimental relationships discussed in Chapter 3? (See appendix 12-B.)

Does the ethics code of the International Association for Marriage and Family Counseling (IAMFC, 1993) address training standards? (See appendix 12-A.)

Which code is more thorough and comprehensive—the IAMFC or AAMFT ethics code?

What guidance is given to AAMFT "Clinical Members" in using that designation in advertising by the AAMFT (2001) ethics code?

ing are asked to suspend judgment on which professional association (the AAMFT or the ACA) is right or wrong in the debate over professional identity until a thorough study of the matter is undertaken.

DEFINING THE SPECIALTY, SETTING, AND CLIENTS

The specialty of couple and family counseling has found a home in the International Association for Marriage and Family Counseling (IAMFC), an affiliate of the American Counseling Association (ACA). The IAMFC became a recognized affiliate of the ACA in 1989, and it soon became one of the fastest-growing affiliates in the ACA. At present, it is one of the largest affiliate groups of the ACA. In cooperation with several other family therapy organizations, the IAMFC was successful in helping to sponsor the National Academy for Certified Family Therapists (NACFT), a freestanding certification body that identifies qualified family counselors. Counselors who wish to affiliate with other counselors in the area of couple and family counseling can congregate through a professional organization (affiliated with the ACA) and seek certification as recognized and qualified family counselors through the NACFT.

There are other organizations that seek to represent couple and family therapists. The AAMFT is the largest and most visible. Its membership is composed of individuals who may have educational backgrounds in counseling, social work, medicine, or specifically in marriage and family therapy. In the past, the AAMFT has been an interdisciplinary interest and certifying group. More recently, the AAMFT has sought to carve a niche for a separate profession in the name of "marriage and family therapy." The AAMFT is a recognized leader in advocating for the practice of marriage and family therapy—a

visible reminder of the interdisciplinary roots of the professional specialty of couple and family counseling.

Generally, couple and family counselors work in settings that provide services to couples or families, such as family service agencies, clinics, counseling centers, private practices, hospitals, and other general mental health service settings. Unless couple and family counselors are trained in the more general counseling field as a mental health practitioner, they limit their practices to work with couples or families (or in some cases to individuals with serious relationship problems). It is unusual for couple and family counselors to provide individual counseling as a service of preference. The reason they choose to work with couples or families is primarily theoretical—couple and family counselors are directed, to a large degree, by social systems theory, or what has been also identified as systemic-relational theory (Cottone, 1992; Gladding, 2002). Systemic-relational theory is a set of assumptions about the nature of mental health problems. Problems are defined as deriving from relationships, which are viewed as real and assessable processes between people. It is what happens *between* people that is of interest to the couple and family counselor trained in systemic-relational theory.

The clients of couple and family counselors are couples or families with identified problems of a relational nature. Even if the problem is not identified as relational, the couple and family counselor will probably conceptualize the problem as such. Even in cases of identified patients—individuals viewed as "problems" that need to be fixed—the couple and family counselor will probably redefine the concern as the interpersonal pattern of interaction in which problematic behavior manifests itself. Even when couple and family counselors see individuals in treatment, they most usually focus the counseling on relationship concerns.

ISSUES OF SIGNIFICANCE TO THE SPECIALTY

Professional Differentiation

The ACA is composed of affiliate organizations representing groups such as rehabilitation counselors, school counselors, mental health counselors, group counselors, and others. The IAMFC is the only ACA affiliate that specifically addresses concerns of couples, marriages, or families. Couple and family counseling is unique among the counseling specialties represented by the ACA. It is the only specialty with theorists and counselors subscribing to a form of treatment that does not focus attention on the individual. Instead, relationships are the targets of couple and family counseling.

Ethical Issues

Confidentiality and Privileged Communication. Confidentiality, as an anti-gossip guarantee, is designed to prevent revelation of privately communicated information to other individuals. In the classic one-client and one-counselor relationship, confidentiality is a simple issue of counselor responsibility. Counselors are bound by their ethical codes or legal ethical standards (e.g., ethical standards in licensure statutes) to maintain the information communicated in counseling sessions in confidence—that is, in a way that does not share information with others unless there are extenuating circumstances in which confidentiality would not stand (recognized exemptions). Couple or family counseling, however, presents complications. First, such counseling almost always involves more than one person as a client. Couple and family counselors, by philosophy, often treat relationship "systems" as the unit or target of intervention. Often, therefore, two or more people overhear what other individuals communicate in a session. In this sense, there is no one-to-one confidential relationship.

Most ethical codes and licensure statutes were designed primarily for one-to-one counseling relationships. However, the AAMFT Code of Ethics does address the issue of more than one person being the unit of treatment. The AAMFT Code of Ethics (2001) states:

> Marriage and family therapists have unique confidentiality concerns because the client in a therapeutic relationship may be more than one person. Therapists respect and guard confidences of each individual client (Section 2).

Further, the code states:

> When providing couple, family, or group treatment, the therapist does not disclose information outside the treatment context without a written authorization from each individual competent to execute a waiver. In the context of couple, family or group treatment, the therapist may not reveal any individual's confidences to others in the client unit without the prior written permission of that individual (Section 2.2).

Essentially *all* legally responsible parties in couple or family therapy are required formally to release the information before it can be communicated to other individuals. But not all ethics codes or licensure standards are as clear as the AAFMT Code of Ethics on this issue. It is especially important for licensed professionals to examine their licensure statutes and any ethical references in those statutes. First, the statutes must be examined to ensure that provision of standard services to couples or families is clearly within the purview of the practice of the profession, meaning that the scope of professional practice must clearly reference couples, marriages, relationships, systems, or family work. Second, if couple or family counseling is referenced in the legal definition of professional practice, ethical standards should then be examined in light of the definition of professional practice. Is a confidential relationship described in the statute's ethical guidelines? Does confidentiality extend to relationships beyond the one-on-one counseling relationship? These questions must be addressed in an examination of relevant ethical standards.

Regardless, unique circumstances in couple and family counseling still exist that are worth noting in any discussion of confidentiality and privileged communication. For example, even in a situation wherein legal confidentiality exists by statute for communications made within the context of relationship treatment, certain information may be allowed to be communicated to a therapist in private by one member of a family or couple in treatment. In fact, Margolin (1982) stated: "Some therapists, in fact, arrange for sessions with individual family members to actively encourage the sharing of 'secrets' to better understand what is occurring in the family" (p. 791). When one member of a couple or family privately reveals a secret to the counselor (in treatment), the counselor is faced with deciding whether that privately communicated information is confidential in a one-to-one sense. Can that information be communicated subsequently in the context of relationship treatment? What if one member of a couple communicates that he is involved in a secret, extramarital sexual relationship? Obviously this information is crucial to marital counseling, but if it is communicated in a formal counseling setting with no other parties present, it is considered confidential. It is ethically compromising for a counselor to continue relationship counseling with such information (essentially counseling in a way that does not acknowledge the infidelity). Margolin (1982) believed that therapists have several options in such a situation: The therapist can choose (a) to keep the secret, (b) to reveal the secret, or (c) to reveal the secret in certain circumstances. But, importantly, it is crucial that counselors communicate their policy on such matters *before counseling is initiated.* Margolin (1982) stated, "The most difficult predicament for the therapist would be if she or he failed to convey a policy on confidentiality" (p. 792). The same is true for any communication made by one individual in private to a counselor when that party is involved in relationship treatment with the counselor. Secrets, such as physical or sexual abuse, child molestation, sexual orientation, infection with a sexually transmitted disease, or drug involvement, often are revealed to counselors, and counselors must be prepared to reiterate their policy on confidentiality (with legal exceptions noted) and to follow whatever policy has been communicated and agreed to by the involved parties.

However, there is the additional problem that some secrets may involve illegal activity. For example, adultery is considered a punishable crime in some states. If the counselor keeps a secret of illegal adultery from a spouse, it is possible (although highly unlikely) that the counselor could be charged by the spouse with criminal conspiracy or "alienation of affection" (Cottone, Mannis, & Lewis, 1996; Margolin, 1982). Some argue (Cottone et al., 1996) that counselors must not condone illegal activity by keeping secrets. Counselors are most ethically and legally safe when they maintain a policy that such secrets will be openly discussed in counseling sessions with all involved parties present (or the counselor can choose to reveal in circumstances wherein there is potential significant personal, physical, or emotional harm to unknowing partners or family members).

Privileged communication, like confidentiality, is more complicated in the context of couple and family counseling. Privileged communication is referenced in statutes most typically as related to one-to-one communication. In other words, communications made by one person in private to a counselor are considered safe from revelation in a legal proceeding, unless there are legal exceptions or the client waives the privilege. But what about cases in which several people are involved in counseling? As with confidentiality, the way the statute is written is critical to interpreting this legal standard. If the statute provides for privileged communication, it must be examined as to whether the privilege extends to all people in a session, or whether it is limited to one-on-one communications made to a counselor. Also, state case law (judgments in past relevant legal cases) is crucial in determining the extent of coverage of privileged communication. Unfortunately, legal standards are often unclear and many states lack definitive case law. Consequently, counselors must act conservatively. Margolin (1982) stated: "Lacking definitive legislation on these issues … family therapists cannot comfortably assume that existing privilege statutes protect the communications that occur during family therapy" (p. 794). Clients should know the risks of communicating secrets in circumstances in which there is no clear confidentiality or privileged communication.

Informed Consent.   Vesper and Brock (1991) stated: "The doctrine of *informed consent* was originally designed to require physicians and surgeons to explain medical procedures to patients and to warn them of any risks or dangers that could result from treatment. The intent of the doctrine was to permit the patient to make an intelligent, informed choice as to whether to undergo the proposed treatment or procedure" (p. 50). As with medical patients, clients of counselors have the right to consent to treatment or to refuse treatment (Caudill, 1998). Discussions of informed consent are often juxtaposed with discussions of the issue of client competency, which usually refers to clients' abilities to understand and to make judgments or decisions in their best interests. Clients judged to be competent to make decisions in their best interests have a right to be fully informed about the nature of treatments, the professional's qualifications and experience performing procedures or treatments, the risks and benefits of treatment, and alternative treatments (Caudill, 1998). Generally speaking, children are considered not competent to make such decisions; parents or guardians must be consulted when a child is involved. Also, when counselors treat people who have disabilities, the elderly, or those legally defined as not competent to make such decisions, they must consult a guardian for approval before initiating treatment. In couple and family counseling, it is accepted procedure to have adult participants (or otherwise competent individuals) sign a statement of "consent to treatment" once treatment issues have been addressed. However, compromising situations exist. One or more competent parties in the family may refuse to sign the consent form; in such a case, family treatment with all family members present cannot proceed. In effect, the legal and ethical autonomy of the individual overrides that of the majority of the family members. One person's hesitance can lead to a decision to abandon certain types of relationship counseling. Counselors, therefore, should encourage and seek the informed consent of all competent adult participants in couple and family counseling.

Potentially Detrimental Counselor-Client Interactions or Relationships.   The historical issue of "dual" or "multiple" relationships (e.g., a counselor and client establishing a relationship outside of counseling, whether sexual or nonsexual) in couple and family counseling has aroused some debate in the field (e.g., AAMFT, 1993; Ryder & Hepworth, 1990). The reason for the debate probably centers on marriage and family counseling's underlying philosophical position that relationships have great potential in the process of aiding others. Social systems theory posits that relationships are the primary cause of disturbance in individuals and also can affect a positive change in observed behavior, as defined within a specified cultural context. In effect, establishing healthy relationships with clients is basic to the systemic-relational framework. The question of potentially detrimental relationships, then, is an important one. Certain relationships outside of the counseling relationship can be viewed as very helpful to clients.

Obviously, certain types of relationships can be harmful. But should all relationships outside of counseling be considered harmful or potentially harmful? It has been argued (Ryder & Hepworth, 1990; Tomm, 1993) that a closer examination of the issue is warranted because a blanket ban on relationships outside of counseling may prevent the development of some healthy interactions between a counselor and client. For example, Ryder and Hepworth (1990) suggested that the AAMFT rule to avoid dual relationships, which was expanded to nonsexual and apparently nonromantic relationships in 1988, was undesirable. They argued that such a rule masked a complex issue that should be addressed by students in marriage and family therapy. They took the position that it is more important that dual relationship issues be viewed as complex, and they believed the issues of exploitation and power were the crucial concerns. In effect, they argued against a blanket ban on all dual relationships while arguing in favor of a "serious emphasis" in training and supervision programs on the assessment of complex relationship issues.

As a result of the Ryder and Hepworth (1990) article, and a response by Karl Tomm (1993), a highly recognized marriage and family therapy theorist, a 1993 AAMFT Conference plenary session was held on the topic, entitled "Dual Relationships: Sex, Power, and Exploitation" (AAMFT, 1993). The plenary allowed for an airing of concerns in a forum where differences of opinion could be and were expressed in a public way. Participants included Ingeborg Haug, Karl Tomm, Linda Terry, and Katharine Wexler. Interestingly, several of the presenters described personal experiences in which they were in violation of the proscription to avoid dual relationships. Tomm described situations wherein he was in violation of the code. He stated:

> When I reviewed the draft of the 1991 code, I realized I was in violation of dual relationship provisions in all three sections—clinical, teaching, and research areas. Clinically, I had colleagues who were in therapy with me—friends I had seen in therapy. In terms of teaching, there were some students and trainees who asked to see me in therapy. I did see them during some important crises they were going through. In the research area, I just completed writing a paper with a couple that I was seeing in therapy and whom I'm still seeing from time-to-time, and part of this paper was to distinguish the therapeutic moments of our work together—this was obviously a dual relationship.[2]

Tomm, after consulting colleagues and even the involved parties, came to the conclusion that he had done nothing harmful, and that perhaps the code proscriptions to avoid such relationships were in error. Likewise, Linda Terry described situations in which she was involved in friendship relationships with her clinical supervisor and a university trainee. She argued that those friendships brought about "desirable possibilities that would not have been happening without the multiple role relationships." She concluded: "Dual relationships can be growth enhancing at times." Katharine Wexler described several cases of accidental dual relationships—one that proved to be beneficial as described by a client. The presenters essentially provided case examples in which relationships other than the initial professional relationship proved to be harmless or even beneficial to the client/trainee.

There were some persuasive arguments made against a blanket ban on counselor-client or counselor-trainee relationships subsequent to the initial contracted relationship. Tomm made the case that exploitation was

---

[2]Page numbers are unavailable for the 1993 AAMFT plenary—quotes were transcribed from an audiotape.

clearly the issue. He argued against a linear, causal view of dual relationships and in favor of exploration of "what it is, in fact, that does enhance the possibilities of exploitation and injuries." He proposed that the focus should be on generating "a greater sense of inner responsibility and respect," and how counselors can relate to "clients on the basis of that responsibility and respect." Linda Terry, focusing primarily on the circumstances faced by women and minorities, argued that "continuity and loyalty" in counselor-client relationships are critical, and she pointed out cases in which therapists must go out of their way to communicate these messages. She stated:

> Standards should define ethical responsibilities of therapists to manage interpersonal boundaries with respect for multi-contextual influences. Our system underpinnings describe that interpersonal boundaries are managed in terms of the balance of hierarchy and reciprocity, proximity and distance, stability and change, and interpersonal stage.

She essentially made the case for "culturally responsive care" and posed that dual or multiple roles in such circumstances should be viewed as positive.

On the other side of the argument, Ingeborg Haug, speaking as the chair of the AAMFT ethics committee, made a compelling presentation about problems of potentially detrimental relationships. She stated that "two-thirds of all complaints against our members alleged dual relationships in various forms including sexual." That is a staggering percentage. She argued that "multiple relationships give rise to multiple agendas." Further, she stated that therapists "naively fail to realize there are multiple realities and that our clients' perceptions and experiences can be very different from the therapists'." She described the road from nonsexual, dual relationships to sexual, dual relationships as a "slippery slope," and quoted statistics that showed that "a clear relationship between nonsexual and sexual dual relationships does exist."

The plenary presentations made it clear that counselor-client and counselor-trainee relationships subsequent to the initial contracted relationship are complex. Where there are multiple roles, there are multiple meanings. Some relationships can be entered with ideal intentions; others can be, or can evolve into, detrimental interactions. The question is, "How does a profession, based on a systemic-relational worldview, maximize the beneficial effects of counselor-client and counselor-trainee interactions without risking harm to clients or trainees?"

The issue of dual relationships, which can be viewed as straightforward by many, actually presents a dilemma for those who value relationships as elements in facilitating the emotional health of clients or the professional development of trainees.

The recent revision of the AAMFT Code of Ethics (2001) may have actually created less clarity, unfortunately. Although the new code appropriately bans outright sexual intimacy with clients in a separate standard (Section 1.4), it deletes a provision requiring avoidance of multiple roles, opting for a statement that banned only those multiple roles that have the potential "to impair professional judgment or increase the risk of exploitation" (Section 1.3). The new standard appears to put the burden on the client to prove that the counselor's intent was to exploit, or that the counselor was in some way impaired. The standards to avoid potentially detrimental counselor-client interactions or relationships (as described in Chapter 3) are more clear and less equivocal; also, certain (limited) potentially beneficial interactions or relationships are acceptable, so long as clear forethought and written documentation are involved and no harm is done to clients.

According to the IAMFC ethical code, dual relationships with current or former clients or their families are considered unethical.

Responsibility.   The issue of responsibility to clients, which seems uncomplicated when only one client is being seen in individual treatment, becomes a concern when more than one person is in the counselor's office. Margolin (1982) stated:

> The dilemma with multiple clients is that in some situations an intervention that serves one person's best interests may be counter-therapeutic to another. Indeed, the very reason that families tend to seek therapy is because they have conflicting goals and interests. (p. 789)

Couple and family counselors are in a unique counseling circumstance in which competing interests may enter into therapeutic decision making, if, in fact, the individuals in treatment are viewed as clients to be served. Fortunately, systemic-relational theory provides guidance in supporting the contention that the system of relationships is the focus of treatment. This theoretical focus allows the therapist the flexibility to define the system itself, or the relationship of significance, to be the target of treatment. Allegiance, therefore, can be given to the system or the relationships. Margolin described this as relationship advocacy. She stated, "The family therapist then becomes an advocate of the family system and avoids becoming an agent of any one family member" (p. 789). Of course, there are circumstances in which advocating for the system or relationships must be abandoned, such as in cases of child abuse or neglect, or situations in which one party is endangered by the threats or actions of another member in the family. In such situations, relationship advocacy must be abandoned to protect the endangered party (Margolin, 1982). For the vast majority of cases, however, relationship advocacy is a legitimate position. Counselors simply define the *couple* or the *family* as the unit to which they are responsible and focus their activities on doing what is right for the relationship or the family as a whole. Relationship advocacy is one option of the couple and family counselor that is not available to counselors who provide individual treatment. It is a difference of ethical significance that is theoretically and practically unique to systemic-relational practice.

Values.   Huber (1994) stated: "Values are a core component of any professional endeavor and are particularly critical to the professional practice of marriage and family therapy" (p. 225). Values are beliefs about what is desirable. They may be highly individual or they may be shared within a social context. Couple and family counseling poses value dilemmas that are not usually encountered in other types of counseling. For example, a counselor's view of divorce is significant to the tone of marital therapy. Some counselors do all that is possible to guide clients away from consideration of divorce. Other counselors may openly discuss divorce as an option, even early in counseling. Of course, it is implicit in marriage counseling that the marriage is valued. Both the IAMFC and AAMFT ethical codes place value on the well-being or welfare of the family. But to what degree is the individual practitioner bound to a strict, value-driven practice? On the issue of divorce, for example, the AAMFT code specifically states that decisions on marital status are the responsibility of the client (Section 1.8). This appears to give the practitioner latitude in recommending that couples discuss privately their desires related to separation or divorce as options, but it appears also to prevent a practitioner from stating, unconditionally, that a person or couple should seek divorce or separation. Value issues are involved, and beyond the directives of the code, a counselor's values may be highly relevant to what actually occurs in counseling. For example, according to some religions, such as the Roman Catholic religion, divorce is not accepted because marriage is viewed as a sacrament. A Roman Catholic practitioner counseling a Roman Catholic couple may undertake therapy with this overriding religious value di-

recting the options for the couple. Certain values—religious and otherwise—enter into couple and family counseling practice that may only be tangentially or incompletely addressed by a code of ethics. Also, certain value issues relevant to couple and family counseling may not be relevant in other specialties of counseling, and ethical codes covering general practice (e.g., the APA and ACA codes) may not adequately address the value issues at the heart of couple and family counseling.

Other value issues typically encountered by couple and family counselors include judgments about extramarital affairs (sexual or otherwise), sex roles, parenting roles, division of labor in the marital relationship, multicultural or mixed cultural relations, marital sexuality, birth control, involvement with the extended family, decision making and control of resources, and others.

Most textbooks on professional ethics in the human services (e.g., Corey, Corey & Callanan, 1998; Huber, 1994) direct practitioners to assess their values through a process of values clarification and to be alert to circumstances in practice that may activate a value judgment. In situations in which it is apparent that the values of the counselor may be in conflict with those of the couple or family in treatment, the counselor must decide if counseling can be undertaken in a way that is consistent with the family values or whether referral to another counselor is appropriate.

Counselor Competence.   Given that the specialty of couple and family counseling is founded on a theoretical framework that is philosophically quite distinct from the foundations of individual psychotherapy (Cottone, 1992), it is imperative that couple and family counselors have special training and supervision in systemic-relational treatment. Both the AAMFT and the National Academy of Certified Family Therapists have set standards for professional marriage and family counselors. The standards are specific in defining the need for a thorough understanding of relationship theory. The standards are also quite demanding regarding adequate supervision: Those who aspire to be specialists in couple and family counseling must obtain supervision under the direction of qualified supervisors. In fact, the AAMFT certifies individuals as "approved supervisors" for the oversight of clinicians in training. It is not enough for a counselor to receive a general counseling degree and then begin seeing couples or families in practice; they must complete adequate coursework or supervision specifically in couple or family counseling.

Because procedures and techniques in couple and family counseling vary dramatically from procedures and techniques in individual counseling, practitioners should have more than a cursory understanding of specialty approaches. There is a unique literature in the field of couple and family counseling that may be complementary to, or even incompatible with, good clinical practice in individual counseling. For example, a counselor who treats an individual might be trained to be empathic and acknowledging of the client's perspective. A couple's counselor might be viewed as taking sides if the counselor is overly empathic or acknowledging of one person's perspective, unless the counselor conveys an attitude of neutrality. Family counseling techniques are also designed to facilitate interaction between participants and require an active style of counseling to prevent the counselor from losing control of the process, which can occur easily when there are several active counseling participants. All in all, the practice of couple and family counseling is different to the degree that some practices of individual counseling do not easily or competently apply.

Competency also requires that counselors use up-to-date theory and technique. The practice of couple counseling is being affected significantly by the works of Gottman (e.g., Gottman, 1994), who has done well-controlled empirical research related to marriage success and failure. Some classic myths of marriage have been uncovered by his work. For example, for years it has been believed that similarity of opinions is beneficial to a marriage. Gottman's response is as follows:

> In my research, where I actually observed couples hashing out disagreements and then tracked them down years later to check on how stable their marriages were, I found that couples who initially had complaints about each other's attitudes were among the most stable marriages as the years went on. My research shows that much more important than having compatible views is how couples work out their differences. In fact, occasional discontent, especially during a marriage's early years, seems to be good for the union in the long run. (pp. 23–24)

Couples and family counselors, like all counselors, must ensure that they are current on the literature and applying valid theory and technique.

CODE COMPARISONS

Two ethical codes apply to counselors in the specialty of couple and family counseling. The first is the American Association for Marriage and Family Therapy Code of Ethics (AAMFT, 2001); the second is the Ethical Code for the International Association of Marriage and Family Counselors (IAMFC, 1993). The IAMFC is an affiliate organization of the larger ACA; therefore, members of the IAMFC are bound by the more general ACA code, but are directed by the IAMFC code as an aspirational guide. The IAMFC and AAMFT codes are reprinted at the end of this chapter in the chapter appendices.

Generally, both codes promote the welfare of families and individuals. This is different from more general codes of ethics, which often focus on the individual a one-on-one or group counseling context. Both codes, for example, provide for confidentiality of communications made in counseling/therapy. They also require that all competent parties involved in counseling sign a waiver of confidentiality before any information can be released to a third party. Both codes address issues of competence, recognizing that practitioners should not diagnose or treat problems outside the scope of their professional training and supervision, which in this case relates directly to relationship treatment. Both codes recognize ethical concerns related to supervision of students, employees, or supervisees.

The 2001 AAMFT Code of Ethics appears to give equivocal guidance on multiple relationship issues that can be potentially confusing to practitioners—there is no outright provision to avoid such relationships. The IAMFC code, on the other hand, is unequivocal—dual relationships with current or former clients or family members are banned.

There are other differences in the codes. The IAMFC code has a section specifically dealing with assessment, which reflects the counseling profession's scope of practice, including use of educational and psychological testing devices. AAMFT members may not have training in psychological or counseling assessment. The AAMFT code has a section on advertising and specifically addresses the use of the AAMFT "Clinical Member" designation, which is recognized nationally as a professional credential. Whereas the AAMFT code addresses "financial arrangements" specifically, the IAMFC code addresses "private practice" in general.

The codes have other similarities and differences, and readers are directed to the codes themselves to analyze their contents. Regardless, the professional specialty of couple and family counseling requires knowledge of how treating relationships compounds ethical issues in clinical practice.

ISSUES OF DIVERSITY

Given that couple and family counseling is founded on systemic-relational theory, both positive and negative implications exist from a multicultural perspective.

Systemic-relational theory offers a perspective of cause and effect that relieves the individual of blame. Accordingly, it is the system of relationships that is considered causative of what can be observed to be a problem. For example, if there is a misbehaving child in a family, the family dynamics and patterns of interactions would be analyzed and the child's behavior would be interpreted within the context of the family system. The "cause" of the child's problem would not be identified as being within the individual psychology or learning of the child; rather the family system's patterns of interactions would be implicated. When a relationship is considered problematic, neither individual in the relationship is culpable—blame is placed on the larger relationship pattern. Further, the relationship problem would be interpreted within an encompassing system of relationships within which the problem is imbedded. For example, a couple's concern might be interpreted as a lack of fit between two family systems interacting through the marital relationship. The influences of family relationships currently and historically would be analyzed in assessing the nature of the problem and a means to solution.

Feminist theorists have attacked this cause-and-effect perspective (Bograd, 1984). In the case of physical abuse of a spouse (95% of victims being females), to blame the relationship and relational dynamics is, to some degree, to implicate the victim in the abuse (as a part of the sick relationship). Feminist theorists view the position that a perpetrator is not culpable as indefensible. The concerns raised by feminist theorists are even more salient when child abuse is the issue. Can a 3-year-old child be viewed in any way as dynamically "causative" of his or her sexual abuse? To somehow relieve the blame of a child abuser is essentially a double victimization of the child. Several theorists (Cottone, 1992; Cottone & Greenwell, 1992; Dell, 1989) have attempted to accommodate this critique of systemic-relational theory by modifying the theory to account for linear causal processes—processes wherein one individual, in a power position, has straightforward causal influence. The person in power can then be blamed in abusive circumstances.

On the positive side, revision of systemic-relational theory has led to a position that within certain contexts, cause can be viewed as either circular and relational or linear and individual (Cottone & Greenwell, 1992). Systemic-relational theorists are embracing theoretical developments in psychology and biology, which have adopted a position that *realities* are defined and constructed socially. Such theoretical developments have come forward under the rubric of "social constructivism," "social constructionism," "contextualism," and "post-modernism" (Cottone, 1992; Gergen, 1985; Hoffman, 1988). Accordingly, a social consensus can be developed around a circumstance, such as abuse, that an individual is culpable (Cottone & McConaghy, 1998). In such circumstances, individual treatment along with relational treatments would be indicated. In this sense, a relational definition of a problem can lead to implication and treatment of an individual.

Additionally, advances in systemic-relational theory allow for an understanding of cultural difference as they arise from socially constructed "realities." When reality is viewed as socially constructed—that is, arising from a consensus in a group—it is then possible to conceive of competing, but equally legitimate, realities (Maturana, 1978). No cultural group or cultural norm can be viewed as better or more valid than any other. Each cultural norm derives from a reality established in the context of social relations within cultural boundaries. Before such advances, systemic-relational theorists depended on theories that defined what was considered right or acceptable in families. For example, Minuchin (1974), a preeminent family therapist, theoretically defined hierarchy in families as important to what is viewed as healthy family organization. Likewise, other theorists defined what they believed to be healthy family organizations or interactional patterns. Currently, counselors are not bound by absolute conceptions of mental health within a family relational framework; rather, they can accommodate cultural diversity in their techniques and approaches to family systems because no one family norm exists.

CHAPTER SUMMARY

The practice of couple and family counseling is unique among the counseling specialties. It is primarily based on a philosophical position that values relationships as being crucial to mental health and observable behavioral difficulties. This philosophical position allows for unique ethical considerations, including concerns over multicultural issues. It also allows for unique solutions to ethical concerns, which would otherwise not be forthcoming from other counseling specialties.

Couple and family counseling is founded on theory that has evolved to be culturally relevant and acknowledges cultural differences.

REFERENCES

American Association for Marriage and Family Therapy. (1991). *AAMFT Code of Ethics*. Washington, DC: Author.

American Association for Marriage and Family Therapy. (1993). *AAMFT luncheon plenary on "Dual relationships: Sex, power, and exploitation."* Audiotape cassette recording published through the AAMFT Resource Link, Norcross, GA (Call: 1-800-241-7785).

American Association for Marriage and Family Therapists. (2001). *AAMFT Code of Ethics*. Washington, D.C.: Author.

Bograd, M. (1984). Family systems approaches to wife battering: A feminist critique. *American Journal of Orthopsychiatry, 54,* 558–568.

Caudill, O. B. (1998, February/March). The hidden issue of informed consent. *Family Therapy News,* 7.

Corey, G., Corey, M. S., & Callanan, P. (1998). *Issues and ethics in the helping professions* (5th ed.). Pacific Grove, CA: Brooks/Cole.

Cottone, R. R. (1992). *Theories and paradigms of counseling and psychotherapy.* Needham Heights, MA: Allyn & Bacon.

Cottone, R. R., & Greenwell, R. J. (1992). Beyond linearity and circularity: Deconstructing social systems theory. *Journal of Marital and Family Therapy, 18,* 167–177.

Cottone, R. R., Mannis, J., & Lewis, T. (1996). Uncovering secret extramarital affairs in marriage counseling. *The Family Journal, 4,* 109–115.

Cottone, R. R., & McConaghy, J. S. (1998). The systemic view of violence: An ethical perspective. *Family Process, 37,* 51–63.

Dell, P. F. (1989). Violence and the systemic view: The problem of power. *Family Process, 28,* 1–14.

Gergen, K. J. (1985). The social constructionist movement in modern psychology. *American Psychologist, 40,* 266–275.

Gladding, S. T. (2002). *Family therapy: History, theory, and practice* (3rd ed). Upper Saddle River, NJ: Merrill/Prentice Hall.

Gladding, S. T., Remley, T. P., & Huber, C. H. (2001). *Ethical, legal, and professional issues in the practice of marriage and family therapy* (3rd ed.). Upper Saddle River, NJ: Merrill/Prentice Hall.

Gottman, J. (1994). *Why marriages succeed or fail.* New York: Fireside.

Hoffman, L. (1988). A constructivist position for family therapy. *The Irish Journal of Psychology, 9,* 110–129.

Huber, C. H. (1994). *Ethical, legal, and professional issues in the practice of marriage and family therapy.* Upper Saddle River, NJ: Merrill/Prentice Hall.

International Association of Marriage and Family Counseling. (1993). Ethical code for the International Association of Marriage and Family Counselors. *The Family Journal: Counseling and Therapy for Couples and Families, 1,* 73–77.

Margolin, G. (1982). Ethical and legal considerations in marital and family therapy. *American Psychologist, 37,* 788–801.

Maturana, H. R. (1978). Biology of language: The epistemology of reality. In G. A. Miller & E. Lenneberg (Eds.), *Psychology and biology of language and thought* (pp. 27–63). New York: Academic Press.

Minuchin, S. (1974). *Families and family therapy.* Cambridge, MA: Harvard University Press.

Ryder, R., & Hepworth, J. (1990). AAMFT ethical code: "Dual relationships." *Journal of Marital and Family Therapy, 16,* 127–132.

Tomm, K. (1993). *AAMFT luncheon plenary on "Dual relationships: Sex, power, and exploitation."* Audiotape cassette recording published through the AAMFT Resource Link, Norcross, GA (Call: 1-800-241-7785).

Vesper, J. H., & Brock, G. (1991). *Ethics, legalities, and professional practice issues in marriage and family therapy.* Needham Heights, MA: Allyn & Bacon.

APPENDIX 12-A

Ethical Code for the International Association of Marriage and Family Counselors

PREAMBLE

The IAMFC (The International Association of Marriage and Family Counselors) is an organization dedicated to advancing the practice, training, and research of marriage and family counselors. Members may specialize in areas such as: premarital counseling, intergenerational counseling, separation and divorce counseling, relocation counseling, custody assessment and implementation, single parenting, stepfamilies, nontraditional family and marriage life-styles, healthy and dysfunctional family systems, multicultural marriage and family concerns, displaced and homeless families, interfaith and interracial families, and dual career couples. In conducting their professional activities, members commit themselves to protect and advocate for the healthy growth and development of the family as a whole, even as they conscientiously recognize the integrity and diversity of each family and family member's unique needs, situations, status,

and condition. The IAMFC member recognizes that the relationship between the provider and consumer of services is characterized as an egalitarian process emphasizing co-participation, co-equality, co-authority, co-responsibility, and client empowerment.

This code of ethics promulgates a framework for ethical practice by IAMFC members and is divided into eight sections: client well-being, confidentiality, competence, assessment, private practice, research and publications, supervision, and media and public statements. The ideas presented within these eight areas are meant to supplement the ethical standards of the American Counseling Association (ACA), formerly the American Association for Counseling and Development (AACD), and all members should know and keep to the standards of our parent organization. Although an ethical code cannot anticipate every possible situation or dilemma, the IAMFC ethical guidelines can aid members in ensuring the welfare and dignity of the couples and families they have contact with, as well as assisting in the implementation of the Hippocratic mandate for healers: Do no harm.

SECTION I: CLIENT WELL-BEING

a. Members demonstrate a caring, empathic, respectful, fair, and active concern for family well-being. They promote client safety, security, and place-of-belonging in family, community, and society. Due to the risk involved, members should not use intrusive interventions without a sound theoretical rationale and having thoroughly thought through the potential ramifications to the family and its members.

b. Members recognize that each family is unique. They respect the diversity of personal attributes and do not stereotype or force families into prescribed attitudes, roles, or behaviors.

c. Members respect the autonomy of the families that they work with. They do not make decisions that rightfully belong to family members.

d. Members respect cultural diversity. They do not discriminate on the basis of race, sex, disability, religion, age, sexual orientation, cultural background, national origin, marital status, or political affiliation.

e. Members strive for an egalitarian relationship with clients by openly and conscientiously sharing information, opinions, perceptions, processes of decision making, strategies of problem solving, and understanding of human behavior.

f. Members pursue a just relationship that acknowledges, respects, and informs clients of their rights, obligations, and expectations as a consumer of services, as well as the rights, obligations, and expectations of the provider(s) of service. Members inform clients (in writing if feasible) about the goals and purpose of the counseling, the qualifications of the counselor(s), the scope and limits of confidentiality, potential risks and benefits associated with the counseling process and with specific counseling techniques, reasonable expectations for the outcomes and duration of counseling, costs of services, and appropriate alternatives to counseling.

g. Members strive for a humanistic relationship that assists clients to develop a philosophy of meaning, purpose, and direction of life and living that promotes a positive regard of self, of family, of different and diverse others, and of the importance of humane concern for the community, nation, and the world at large.

h. Members promote primary prevention. They pursue the development of clients' cognitive, moral, social, emotional, spiritual, physical, educational, and career needs, as well as parenting, marriage, and family living skills, in order to prevent future problems.

i. Members have an obligation to determine and inform all persons involved who their primary client is—i.e., is the counselor's primary obligation to the individual, the family, a third party, or an institution? When there is a conflict of interest between the needs of the client and counselor's employing institution, the member works to clarify his or her commitment to all parties. Members recognize that the acceptance of employment implies that they are in agreement with the agency's policies and practices, and so monitor their place of employment to make sure that the environment is conducive to the positive growth and development of clients. If, after utilizing appropriate institutional channels for change, the member finds that the agency is not working toward the well-being of clients, the member has an obligation to terminate his or her institutional affiliation.

j. Members do not harass, exploit, coerce, engage in dual relationships, or have sexual contact with any current or former client or family member to whom they have provided professional services.

k. Members have an obligation to withdraw from a counseling relationship if the continuation of services is not in the best interest of the client or would result in a violation of ethical standards. If a client feels that the counseling relationship is no longer productive, the member has an obligation to assist in finding alternative services.

l. Members maintain accurate and up-to-date records. They make all file information available to clients unless the sharing of such information would be damaging to the status, goals, growth, or development of the client.

m. Members have the responsibility to confront unethical behavior conducted by other counselors. The first step should be to discuss the violation directly with the counselor. If the problem continues, the member should first use procedures established by the employing institution and then those of the IAMFC. Members may wish to also contact any appropriate licensure or certification board. Members may contact the IAMFC executive director, president, executive board members, or chair of the ethics committee at any time for consultation on remedying ethical violations.

SECTION II: CONFIDENTIALITY

a. Clients have the right to expect that information shared with the counselor will not be disclosed to others and, in the absence of any law to the contrary, the communications between clients and marriage and family counselors should be viewed as privileged. The fact that a contact was made with a counselor is to be considered just as confidential as the information shared during that contact. Information obtained from a client can only be disclosed to a third party under the following conditions.

1. The client consents to disclosure by a signed waiver. The client must fully understand the nature of the disclosure (i.e., give informed consent), and only information described in the waiver may be disclosed. If more than one person is receiving counseling, each individual who is legally competent to execute a waiver must sign.

2. The client has placed him- or herself or someone else in clear and imminent danger.

3. The law mandates disclosure.
4. The counselor is a defendant in a civil, criminal, or disciplinary action arising from professional activity.
5. The counselor needs to discuss a case for consultation or education purposes. These discussions should not reveal the identity of the client or any other unnecessary aspects of the case and should only be done with fellow counseling professionals who subscribe to the IAMFC ethical code. The consulting professional counselor has an obligation to keep all shared information confidential.

b. All clients must be informed of the nature and limitations of confidentiality. They must also be informed of who may have access to their counseling records, as well as any information that may be released to other agencies or professionals for insurance reimbursement. These disclosures should be made both orally and in writing whenever feasible.

c. All client records should be stored in a way that ensures confidentiality. Written records should be kept in a locked drawer or cabinet and computerized record systems should use appropriate passwords and safeguards to prevent unauthorized entry.

d. Clients must be informed if sessions are to be recorded on audio- or videotape and sign a consent form for doing so. When more than one person is receiving counseling, all persons who are legally competent must give informed consent in writing for the recording.

e. Unless alternate arrangements have been agreed upon by all participants, statements made by a family member to the counselor during an individual counseling or consultation contact are to be treated as confidential and are not disclosed to other family members without the individual's permission. If a client's refusal to share information from individual contacts interferes with the agreed upon goals of counseling, the counselor may have to terminate treatment and refer the clients to another counselor.

SECTION III: COMPETENCE

a. Members have the responsibility to develop and maintain basic skills in marriage and family counseling through graduate work, supervision, and peer review. An outline of these skills is provided by the Council for Accreditation of Counseling and Related Educational Programs (CACREP) *Environmental and Specialty Standards for Marriage and Family Counseling/Therapy.* The minimal level of training shall be considered a master's degree in a helping profession.

b. Members recognize the need for keeping current with new developments in the field of marriage and family counseling. They pursue continuing education in forms such as books, journals, classes, workshops, conferences, and conventions.

c. Members accurately represent their education, areas of expertise, training, and experience.

d. Members do not attempt to diagnose or treat problems beyond the scope of their abilities and training.

e. Members do not undertake any professional activity in which their personal problems might adversely affect their performance. Instead, they focus their energies on obtaining appropriate professional assistance to help them resolve the problem.

f. Members do not engage in actions that violate the moral or legal standards of their community.

SECTION IV: ASSESSMENT

a. Members utilize assessment procedures to promote the best interests and well-being of the client in clarifying concerns, establishing treatment goals, evaluating therapeutic progress, and promoting objective decision making.

b. Clients have the right to know the results, interpretation, and conclusions drawn from assessment interviews and instruments, as well as how this information will be used.

c. Members utilize assessment methods that are reliable, valid, and germane to the goals of the client. When using computer-assisted scoring, members obtain empirical evidence for the reliability and validity of the methods and procedures used.

d. Members do not use inventories and tests that have outdated test items or normative data.

e. Members do not use assessment methods that are outside the scope of their qualifications, training, or statutory limitations. Members using tests or inventories have a thorough understanding of measurement concepts.

f. Members read the manual before using a published instrument. They become knowledgeable about the purpose of the instrument and relevant psychometric and normative data.

g. Members conducting custody evaluations recognize the potential impact that their reports can have on family members. As such, they are committed to a thorough assessment of both parents. Therefore, custody recommendations should not be made on the basis of information from only one parent. Members only use instruments that have demonstrated validity in custody evaluations and do not make recommendations based solely on test and inventory scores.

h. Members strive to maintain the guidelines in the *Standards for Educational and Psychological Testing,* written in collaboration by the American Educational Research Association, American Psychological Association, and National Council on Measurement in Evaluation, as well as the *Code of Fair Testing Practices,* published by the Joint Committee on Testing Practices.

SECTION V: PRIVATE PRACTICE

a. Members assist the profession and community by facilitating, whenever feasible, the availability of counseling services in private settings.

b. Due to the independent nature of their work, members in private practice recognize that they have a special obligation to act ethically and responsibly, keep up to date through continuing education, arrange consultation and supervision, and practice within the scope of their training and applicable laws.

c. Members in private practice provide a portion of their services at little or no cost as a service to the community. They also provide referral services for clients who will not be seen pro bono and who are unable to afford private services.

d. Members only enter into partnerships in which each member adheres to the ethical standards of their profession.

e. Members should not charge a fee for offering or accepting referrals.

SECTION VI: RESEARCH AND PUBLICATIONS

a. Members shall be fully responsible for their choice of research topics and the methods used for investigation, analysis, and reporting. They must be particularly careful that findings do not appear misleading, that the research is planned to allow for the inclusion of alternative hypotheses, and that provision is made for discussion of the limitations of the study.

b. Members safeguard the privacy of their research participants. Data about an individual participant are not released unless the individual is informed about the exact nature of the information to be released and gives written permission for doing so.

c. Members safeguard the safety of their research participants. Members receive approval from, and follow guidelines of, any institutional research committee. Prospective participants are informed, in writing, about any potential danger associated with a study and are notified that they can withdraw at any time.

d. Members make their original data available to other researchers.

e. Members only take credit for research in which they made a substantial contribution, and give credit to all such contributors. Authors are listed from greatest to least amount of contribution.

f. Members do not plagiarize. Ideas or data that did not originate with the author(s) and are not common knowledge are clearly credited to the original source.

g. Members are aware of their obligation to be a role model for graduate students and other future researchers and so act in accordance with the highest standards possible while engaged in research.

SECTION VII: SUPERVISION

a. Members who provide supervision acquire and maintain skills pertaining to the supervision process. They are able to demonstrate for supervisees the application of counseling theory and process to client issues. Supervisors are knowledgeable about different methods and conceptual approaches to supervision.

b. Members who provide supervision respect the inherent imbalance of power in the supervisory relationship. They do not use their potentially influential positions to exploit students, supervisees, or employees. Supervisors do not ask supervisees to engage in behaviors not directly related to the supervision process, and they clearly separate supervision and evaluation. Supervisors also avoid dual relationships that might impair their professional judgment or increase the possibility of exploitation. Sexual intimacy with students or supervisees is prohibited.

c. Members who provide supervision are responsible for both the promotion of supervisee learning and development and the advancement of marriage and family counseling. Supervisors recruit students into professional organizations, educate students about professional ethics and standards, provide service to professional organizations, strive to educate new professionals, and work to improve professional practices.

d. Members who provide supervision have the responsibility to inform students of the specific expectations surrounding skill building, knowledge acquisition, and the development of competencies. Members also provide ongoing and timely feedback to their supervisees.

e. Members who provide supervision are responsible for protecting the rights and well-being of their supervisees' clients. They monitor their supervisees' counseling on an ongoing basis, and create procedures to protect the confidentiality of clients whose sessions have been electronically recorded.

f. Members who provide supervision strive to reach and maintain the guidelines provided in the *Standards for Counseling Supervisors* published by the ACA Governing Council (cf. *Journal of Counseling & Development,* 1990, Vol. 69, pp. 30–32).

g. Members who are counselor educators encourage their programs to reach and maintain the guidelines provided in the CACREP *Environmental and Specialty Standards for Marriage and Family Counseling/Therapy.*

SECTION VIII: MEDIA AND PUBLIC STATEMENTS

a. Members accurately and objectively represent their professional qualifications, skills, and functions to the public. Membership in a professional organization is not to be used to suggest competency.

b. Members have the responsibility to provide information to the public that enhances marriage and family life. Such statements should be based on sound, scientifically acceptable theories, techniques, and approaches. Due to the inability to complete a comprehensive assessment and provide follow-up, members should not give specific advice to an individual through the media.

c. The announcement or advertisement of professional services should focus on objective information that allows the client to make an informed decision. Providing information such as highest relevant academic degree earned, licenses or certifications, office hours, types of services offered, fee structure, and languages spoken can help clients decide whether the advertised services are appropriate for their needs. Members advertising a specialty within marriage and family counseling should provide evidence of training, education, and/or supervision in the area of specialization. Advertisements about workshops or seminars should contain a description of the audience for which the program is intended. Due to their subjective nature, statements either from clients or from the counselor about the uniqueness,

effectiveness, or efficiency of services should be avoided. Announcements and advertisements should never contain false, misleading, or fraudulent statements.

d. Members promoting psychology tapes, books, or other products for commercial sale make every effort to ensure that announcements and advertisements are presented in a professional and factual manner.

Reader's Note: Mary Allison, R. P. Ascano, Edward Beck, Stuart Bonnington, Joseph Hannon, David Kaplan (chair), Patrick McGrath, Judith Palais, Martin Ritchie, and Judy Ritterman are members of the IAMFC ethics committee who formulated the IAMFC Code of Ethics.

Reprinted from *The Family Journal: Counseling and Therapy* for *Couples and Families,* Vol. 1, January 1993 (pp. 73–77). Reprinted by permission.

APPENDIX 12-B

AAMFT® Code of Ethics

PREAMBLE

The Board of Directors of the American Association for Marriage and Family Therapy (AAMFT) hereby promulgates, pursuant to Article 2, Section 2.013 of the Association's Bylaws, the Revised AAMFT Code of Ethics, effective July 1, 2001.

The AAMFT strives to honor the public trust in marriage and family therapists by setting standards for ethical practice as described in this Code. The ethical standards define professional expectations and are enforced by the AAMFT Ethics Committee. The absence of an explicit reference to a specific behavior or situation in the Code does not mean that the behavior is ethical or unethical. The standards are not exhaustive. Marriage and family therapists who are uncertain about the ethics of a particular course of action are encouraged to seek counsel from consultants, attorneys, supervisors, colleagues, or other appropriate authorities.

Both law and ethics govern the practice of marriage and family therapy. When making decisions regarding professional behavior, marriage and family therapists must consider the AAMFT Code of Ethics and applicable laws and regulations. If the AAMFT Code of Ethics prescribes a standard higher than that required by law, marriage and family therapists must meet the higher standard of the AAMFT Code of Ethics. Marriage and family therapists comply with the mandates of law, but make known their commitment to the AAMFT Code of Ethics and take steps to resolve the conflict in a responsible manner. The AAMFT supports legal mandates for reporting of alleged unethical conduct.

The AAMFT Code of Ethics is binding on Members of AAMFT in all membership categories, AAMFT-Approved Supervisors, and applicants for membership and the Approved Supervisor designation (hereafter, AAMFT Member). AAMFT

members have an obligation to be familiar with the AAMFT Code of Ethics and its application to their professional services. Lack of awareness or misunderstanding of an ethical standard is not a defense to a charge of unethical conduct.

The process for filing, investigating, and resolving complaints of unethical conduct is described in the current Procedures for Handling Ethical Matters of the AAMFT Ethics Committee. Persons accused are considered innocent by the Ethics Committee until proven guilty, except as otherwise provided, and are entitled to due process. If an AAMFT Member resigns in anticipation of, or during the course of, an ethics investigation, the Ethics Committee will complete its investigation. Any publication of action taken by the Association will include the fact that the Member attempted to resign during the investigation.

PRINCIPLE I: RESPONSIBILITY TO CLIENTS

Marriage and family therapists advance the welfare of families and individuals. They respect the rights of those persons seeking their assistance, and make reasonable efforts to ensure that their services are used appropriately.

1.1 Marriage and family therapists provide professional assistance to persons without discrimination on the basis of race, age, ethnicity, socioeconomic status, disability, gender, health status, religion, national origin, or sexual orientation.

1.2 Marriage and family therapists obtain appropriate informed consent to therapy or related procedures as early as feasible in the therapeutic relationship, and use language that is reasonably understandable to clients.

The content of informed consent may vary depending upon the client and treatment plan; however, informed consent generally necessitates that the client: (a) has the capacity to consent; (b) has been adequately informed of significant information concerning treatment processes and procedures; (c) has been adequately informed of potential risks and benefits of treatments for which generally recognized standards do not yet exist; (d) has freely and without undue influence expressed consent; and (e) has provided consent that is appropriately documented. When persons, due to age or mental status, are legally incapable of giving informed consent, marriage and family therapists obtain informed permission from a legally authorized person, if such substitute consent is legally permissible.

1.3 Marriage and family therapists are aware of their influential positions with respect to clients, and they avoid exploiting the trust and dependency of such persons. Therapists, therefore, make every effort to avoid conditions and multiple relationships with clients that could impair professional judgment or increase the risk of exploitation. Such relationships include, but are not limited to, business or close personal relationships with a client or the client's immediate family. When the risk of impairment or exploitation exists due to conditions or multiple roles, therapists take appropriate precautions.

1.4 Sexual intimacy with clients is prohibited.

1.5 Sexual intimacy with former clients is likely to be harmful and is therefore prohibited for two years following the termination of therapy or last professional contact. In an effort to avoid exploiting the trust and dependency of clients, marriage and family therapists should not engage in sexual intimacy with former clients after the two years following termination or last professional contact. Should therapists engage in sexual intimacy with former clients following two years after termination or last professional contact, the burden shifts to the therapist to demonstrate that there has been no exploitation or injury to the former client or to the client's immediate family.

1.6 Marriage and family therapists comply with applicable laws regarding the reporting of alleged unethical conduct.

1.7 Marriage and family therapists do not use their professional relationships with clients to further their own interests.

1.8 Marriage and family therapists respect the rights of clients to make decisions and help them to understand the consequences of these decisions. Therapists clearly advise the clients that they have the responsibility to make decisions regarding relationships such as cohabitation, marriage, divorce, separation, reconciliation, custody, and visitation.

1.9 Marriage and family therapists continue therapeutic relationships only so long as it is reasonably clear that clients are benefiting from the relationship.

1.10 Marriage and family therapists assist persons in obtaining other therapeutic services if the therapist is unable or unwilling, for appropriate reasons, to provide professional help.

1.11 Marriage and family therapists do not abandon or neglect clients in treatment without making reasonable arrangements for the continuation of such treatment.

1.12 Marriage and family therapists obtain written informed consent from clients before videotaping, audio recording, or permitting third-party observation.

1.13 Marriage and family therapists, upon agreeing to provide services to a person or entity at the request of a third party, clarify, to the extent feasible and at the outset of the service, the nature of the relationship with each party and the limits of confidentiality.

PRINCIPLE II: CONFIDENTIALITY

Marriage and family therapists have unique confidentiality concerns because the client in a therapeutic relationship may be more than one person. Therapists respect and guard the confidences of each individual client.

2.1 Marriage and family therapists disclose to clients and other interested parties, as early as feasible in their professional contacts, the nature of confidentiality and possible limitations of the clients' right to confidentiality. Therapists review with clients the circumstances where confidential information may be requested and where disclosure of confidential information may be legally required. Circumstances may necessitate repeated disclosures.

2.2 Marriage and family therapists do not disclose client confidences except by written authorization or waiver, or where mandated or permitted by law. Verbal authorization will not be sufficient except in emergency situations, unless prohibited by law. When providing couple, family or group treatment, the therapist does not disclose information outside the treatment context without a written authorization from each individual competent to execute a waiver. In the context of couple, family or group treatment, the therapist may not reveal any individual's confidences to others in the client unit without the prior written permission of that individual.

2.3 Marriage and family therapists use client and/or clinical materials in teaching, writing, consulting, research, and public presentations only if a written waiver has been obtained in accordance with Subprinciple 2.2, or when appropriate steps have been taken to protect client identity and confidentiality.

2.4 Marriage and family therapists store, safeguard, and dispose of client records in ways that maintain confidentiality and in accord with applicable laws and professional standards.

2.5 Subsequent to the therapist moving from the area, closing the practice, or upon the death of the therapist, a marriage and family therapist arranges for the storage, transfer, or disposal of client records in ways that maintain confidentiality and safeguard the welfare of clients.

2.6   Marriage and family therapists, when consulting with colleagues or referral sources, do not share confidential information that could reasonably lead to the identification of a client, research participant, supervisee, or other person with whom they have a confidential relationship unless they have obtained the prior written consent of the client, research participant, supervisee, or other person with whom they have a confidential relationship. Information may be shared only to the extent necessary to achieve the purposes of the consultation.

PRINCIPLE III: PROFESSIONAL COMPETENCE AND INTEGRITY

Marriage and family therapists maintain high standards of professional competence and integrity.

3.1   Marriage and family therapists pursue knowledge of new developments and maintain competence in marriage and family therapy through education, training, or supervised experience.

3.2   Marriage and family therapists maintain adequate knowledge of and adhere to applicable laws, ethics, and professional standards.

3.3   Marriage and family therapists seek appropriate professional assistance for their personal problems or conflicts that may impair work performance or clinical judgment.

3.4   Marriage and family therapists do not provide services that create a conflict of interest that may impair work performance or clinical judgment.

3.5   Marriage and family therapists, as presenters, teachers, supervisors, consultants and researchers, are dedicated to high standards of scholarship, present accurate information, and disclose potential conflicts of interest.

3.6   Marriage and family therapists maintain accurate and adequate clinical and financial records.

3.7   While developing new skills in specialty areas, marriage and family therapists take steps to ensure the competence of their work and to protect clients from possible harm. Marriage and family therapists practice in specialty areas new to them only after appropriate education, training, or supervised experience.

3.8   Marriage and family therapists do not engage in sexual or other forms of harassment of clients, students, trainees, supervisees, employees, colleagues, or research subjects.

3.9   Marriage and family therapists do not engage in the exploitation of clients, students, trainees, supervisees, employees, colleagues, or research subjects.

3.10   Marriage and family therapists do not give to or receive from clients (a) gifts of substantial value or (b) gifts that impair the integrity or efficacy of the therapeutic relationship.

3.11   Marriage and family therapists do not diagnose, treat, or advise on problems outside the recognized boundaries of their competencies.

3.12   Marriage and family therapists make efforts to prevent the distortion or misuse of their clinical and research findings.

3.13   Marriage and family therapists, because of their ability to influence and alter the lives of others, exercise special care when making public their professional recommendations and opinions through testimony or other public statements.

3.14   To avoid a conflict of interest, marriage and family therapists who treat minors or adults involved in custody or visitation actions may not also perform forensic evaluations for custody, residence, or visitation of the minor. The marriage and family therapist who treats the minor may provide the court or mental health professional performing the evaluation with information about the minor from the marriage and family therapist's perspective as a treating marriage and family therapist, so long as the marriage and family therapist does not violate confidentiality.

3.15   Marriage and family therapists are in violation of this Code and subject to termination of membership or other appropriate action if they: (a) are convicted of any felony; (b) are convicted of a misdemeanor related to their qualifications or functions; (c) engage in conduct which could lead to conviction of a felony, or a misdemeanor related to their qualifications or functions; (d) are expelled from or disciplined by other professional organizations; (e) have their licenses or certificates suspended or revoked or are otherwise disciplined by regulatory bodies; (f) continue to practice marriage and family therapy while no longer competent to do so because they are impaired by physical or mental causes or the abuse of alcohol or other substances; or (g) fail to cooperate with the Association at any point from the inception of an ethical complaint through the completion of all proceedings regarding that complaint.

PRINCIPLE IV: RESPONSIBILITY TO STUDENTS AND SUPERVISEES

Marriage and family therapists do not exploit the trust and dependency of students and supervisees.

4.1   Marriage and family therapists are aware of their influential positions with respect to students and supervisees, and they avoid exploiting the trust and dependency of such persons. Therapists, therefore, make every effort to avoid conditions and multiple relationships that could impair professional objectivity or increase the risk of exploitation. When the risk of impairment or exploitation exists due to conditions or multiple roles, therapists take appropriate precautions.

4.2   Marriage and family therapists do not provide therapy to current students or supervisees.

4.3 Marriage and family therapists do not engage in sexual intimacy with students or supervisees during the evaluative or training relationship between the therapist and student or supervisee. Should a supervisor engage in sexual activity with a former supervisee, the burden of proof shifts to the supervisor to demonstrate that there has been no exploitation or injury to the supervisee.

4.4 Marriage and family therapists do not permit students or supervisees to perform or to hold themselves out as competent to perform professional services beyond their training, level of experience, and competence.

4.5 Marriage and family therapists take reasonable measures to ensure that services provided by supervisees are professional.

4.6 Marriage and family therapists avoid accepting as supervisees or students those individuals with whom a prior or existing relationship could compromise the therapist's objectivity. When such situations cannot be avoided, therapists take appropriate precautions to maintain objectivity. Examples of such relationships include, but are not limited to, those individuals with whom the therapist has a current or prior sexual, close personal, immediate familial, or therapeutic relationship.

4.7 Marriage and family therapists do not disclose supervisee confidences except by written authorization or waiver, or when mandated or permitted by law. In educational or training settings where there are multiple supervisors, disclosures are permitted only to other professional colleagues, administrators, or employers who share responsibility for training of the supervisee. Verbal authorization will not be sufficient except in emergency situations, unless prohibited by law.

PRINCIPLE V: RESPONSIBILITY TO RESEARCH PARTICIPANTS

Investigators respect the dignity and protect the welfare of research participants, and are aware of applicable laws and regulations and professional standards governing the conduct of research.

5.1 Investigators are responsible for making careful examinations of ethical acceptability in planning studies. To the extent that services to research participants may be compromised by participation in research, investigators seek the ethical advice of qualified professionals not directly involved in the investigation and observe safeguards to protect the rights of research participants.

5.2 Investigators requesting participant involvement in research inform participants of the aspects of the research that might reasonably be expected to influence willingness to participate. Investigators are especially sensitive to the possibility of diminished consent when participants are also receiving clinical services, or have impairments which limit understanding and/or communication, or when participants are children.

5.3 Investigators respect each participant's freedom to decline participation in or to withdraw from a research study at any time. This obligation requires special thought and consideration when investigators or other members of the research team are in positions of authority or influence over participants. Marriage and family therapists, therefore, make every effort to avoid multiple relationships with research participants that could impair professional judgment or increase the risk of exploitation.

5.4 Information obtained about a research participant during the course of an investigation is confidential unless there is a waiver previously obtained in writing. When the possibility exists that others, including family members, may obtain access to such information, this possibility, together with the plan for protecting confidentiality, is explained as part of the procedure for obtaining informed consent.

PRINCIPLE VI: RESPONSIBILITY TO THE PROFESSION

Marriage and family therapists respect the rights and responsibilities of professional colleagues and participate in activities that advance the goals of the profession.

6.1 Marriage and family therapists remain accountable to the standards of the profession when acting as members or employees of organizations. If the mandates of an organization with which a marriage and family therapist is affiliated, through employment, contract or otherwise, conflict with the AAMFT Code of Ethics, marriage and family therapists make known to the organization their commitment to the AAMFT Code of Ethics and attempt to resolve the conflict in a way that allows the fullest adherence to the Code of Ethics.

6.2 Marriage and family therapists assign publication credit to those who have contributed to a publication in proportion to their contributions and in accordance with customary professional publication practices.

6.3 Marriage and family therapists do not accept or require authorship credit for a publication based on research from a student's program, unless the therapist made a substantial contribution beyond being a faculty advisor or research committee member. Coauthorship on a student thesis, dissertation, or project should be determined in accordance with principles of fairness and justice.

6.4 Marriage and family therapists who are the authors of books or other materials that are published or distributed do not plagiarize or fail to cite persons to whom credit for original ideas or work is due.

6.5 Marriage and family therapists who are the authors of books or other materials published or distributed by an organization take reasonable precautions to ensure that the organization promotes and advertises the materials accurately and factually.

6.6 Marriage and family therapists participate in activities that contribute to a better community and society, including devoting a portion of their professional activity to services for which there is little or no financial return.

6.7   Marriage and family therapists are concerned with developing laws and regulations pertaining to marriage and family therapy that serve the public interest, and with altering such laws and regulations that are not in the public interest.

6.8   Marriage and family therapists encourage public participation in the design and delivery of professional services and in the regulation of practitioners.

PRINCIPLE VII: FINANCIAL ARRANGEMENTS

Marriage and family therapists make financial arrangements with clients, third-party payors, and supervisees that are reasonably understandable and conform to accepted professional practices.

7.1   Marriage and family therapists do not offer or accept kickbacks, rebates, bonuses, or other remuneration for referrals; fee-for-service arrangements are not prohibited.

7.2   Prior to entering into the therapeutic or supervisory relationship, marriage and family therapists clearly disclose and explain to clients and supervisees: (a) all financial arrangements and fees related to professional services, including charges for canceled or missed appointments; (b) the use of collection agencies or legal measures for nonpayment; and (c) the procedure for obtaining payment from the client, to the extent allowed by law, if payment is denied by the third-party payor. Once services have begun therapists provide reasonable notice of any changes in fees or other charges.

7.3   Marriage and family therapists give reasonable notice to clients with unpaid balances of their intent to seek collection by agency or legal recourse. When such action is taken, therapists will not disclose clinical information.

7.4   Marriage and family therapists represent facts truthfully to clients, third-party payors, and supervisees regarding services rendered.

7.5   Marriage and family therapists ordinarily refrain from accepting goods and services from clients in return for services rendered. Bartering for professional services may be conducted only if: (a) the supervisee or client requests it, (b) the relationship is not exploitative, (c) the professional relationship is not distorted, and (d) a clear written contract is established.

7.6   Marriage and family therapists may not withhold records under their immediate control that are requested and needed for a client's treatment solely because payment has not been received for past services, except as otherwise provided by law.

PRINCIPLE VIII: ADVERTISING

Marriage and family therapists engage in appropriate informational activities, including those that enable the public, referral sources, or others to choose professional services on an informed basis.

8.1   Marriage and family therapists accurately represent their competencies, education, training, and experience relevant to their practice of marriage and family therapy.

8.2   Marriage and family therapists ensure that advertisements and publications in any media (such as directories, announcements, business cards, newspapers, radio, television, Internet, and facsimiles) convey information that is necessary for the public to make an appropriate selection of professional services. Information could include: (a) office information, such as name, address, telephone number, credit card acceptability, fees, languages spoken, and office hours; (b) qualifying clinical degree (see subprinciple 8.5); (c) other earned degrees (see subprinciple 8.5) and state or provincial licensures and/or certifications; (d) AAMFT clinical member status; and (e) description of practice.

8.3   Marriage and family therapists do not use names that could mislead the public concerning the identity, responsibility, source, and status of those practicing under that name, and do not hold themselves out as being partners or associates of a firm if they are not.

8.4   Marriage and family therapists do not use any professional identification (such as a business card, office sign, letterhead, Internet, or telephone or association directory listing) if it includes a statement or claim that is false, fraudulent, misleading, or deceptive.

8.5   In representing their educational qualifications, marriage and family therapists list and claim as evidence only those earned degrees: (a) from institutions accredited by regional accreditation sources recognized by the United States Department of Education, (b) from institutions recognized by states or provinces that license or certify marriage and family therapists, or (c) from equivalent foreign institutions.

8.6   Marriage and family therapists correct, wherever possible, false, misleading, or inaccurate information and representations made by others concerning the therapist's qualifications, services, or products.

8.7   Marriage and family therapists make certain that the qualifications of their employees or supervisees are represented in a manner that is not false, misleading, or deceptive.

8.8   Marriage and family therapists do not represent themselves as providing specialized services unless they have the appropriate education, training, or supervised experience.

Violations of this Code should be brought in writing to the attention of: AAMFT Ethics Committee, 1133 15th Street, NW, Suite 300, Washington, D.C. 20005-2710. *Effective July 1, 2001.* (telephone 202/452-0109) (email: *ethics@aamft.org*).

CHAPTER 13

School Counseling

Donna A. Henderson

Objectives
■ ■ ■ ■ ■ ■ ■ ■ ■ ■

After reading this chapter, you should be able to:

- Discuss the scope of a school counseling practice.
- Describe the clients of school counselors.
- Identify critical professional and ethical issues specific to school counseling.
- Discuss the *Ethical Standards for School Counselors*.
- Explain the multicultural and diversity issues specific to school counseling.

■ ■ ■ ■ ■ ■ ■ ■ ■ ■

INTRODUCTION

Educational institutions in the United States are microcosms that reflect the diversity of demographic, economic, and social variables in our nation. That combination provides school counselors, as much as any other counseling specialty, with the opportunity to serve a wide variety of clients. The varied roles of school counselors, the range of services they provide to students and adults in the educational setting, the dynamic and diverse population with whom they work, and the stimulating settings that schools create, all contribute to the complexity of school counseling. This complexity breeds challenging situations that often require immediate action. All of these demanding circumstances necessitate that school counselors know both the ethical implications and the legal consequences of any action they choose.

DEFINING THE SPECIALTY, SETTING, AND CLIENTS

School counseling has evolved as a profession within the past 100 years. In the early 1900s, Jesse Davis established a program in the public schools of Grand Rapids, Michigan. The program was a forerunner of school counseling—a preventative education program to teach character development to students. About the same time, Frank Parsons was building another program in Boston. The focus of that effort was vocational guidance aimed at growth and prevention—helping young people make thoughtful career decisions. From these foundations emerged the steadily growing

---

Box 13.1   Exploring the Codes (see the ACA and APA codes in the book appendices and the school counselor's code in Appendix 13-A).

1. What are the limits of a school counselor's responsibility in working with peer helper programs?
2. To what groups does a school counselor have ethical responsibilities?
3. What are some of school counselors' responsibilities to themselves?
4. In what areas do legal and ethical concerns differ?
5. Which federal laws establish procedures for safeguarding student records?

---

profession of school counseling. Later, the National Defense Education Act of 1958 provided federal funds for upgrading school counseling programs and for training school counselors. This impetus expanded the numbers and increased the quality of school counselors who have continued to advance the profession and its significance in U.S. schools.

A school counseling program is a critical part of the educational enterprise. The American School Counselor Association endorses a developmental, comprehensive approach to school counseling programs that promotes and enhances student learning. ASCA's (1997) position statement describes the programs as systematic, sequential, clearly defined, and accountable. These programs are designed around three interrelated areas of student development: academic development, career development, and personal-social development. *Sharing the Vision: The National Standards for School Counseling Programs* (Campbell & Dahir, 1997) provided guidelines for the content and delivery of school counseling programs and outlined the desired learning outcomes relative to these three areas of student development at each grade level. *Academic development* includes the skills, attitudes, and knowledge related to learning throughout life. *Career development* is defined as the foundation of skills, attitudes, and knowledge that enable students to make a successful transition from school into a career. *Personal/social development* relates to the skills, attitudes, and knowledge that help people understand and respect self and others, obtain effective interpersonal skills, understand and practice safety and survival skills, and become contributing members of society. These guidelines provide school counselors with a foundation to organize, implement, and coordinate school counseling programs with the goal of providing "all students with life success skills" (ASCA, 1997).

Farrell (1998) reports that 20 states and the District of Columbia mandate counseling services in schools. School counselors practice in elementary, middle/junior high, and secondary school settings. They work with all students in their schools, including those with special needs. Their role statement (ASCA, 1999h) suggests that school counselors should focus on providing direct services in their schools, using the following four interventions:

1. *Counseling*—working with individuals and in small groups to help them resolve or cope with their problems and concerns;
2. *Large group guidance*—working collaboratively with teachers to design and implement a planned, developmental program of guidance activities that foster student development;
3. *Consultation*—building partnerships with teachers, administrators, parents, and others to devise and implement strategies to help students do well in schools; and
4. *Coordination*—leading the organization, managing and evaluating the program assisting parents in finding needed services for their children, and serving as a liaison to the community.

The school counselor's functions vary across communities as a result of the views of parents, the school board or policy-setting body, the school administration, the teachers, and student needs. Therefore, school counselors may not always be able to define their day-to-day jobs as they wish. For example, some counselors are hired only to do career counseling or individual counseling or to handle scheduling and administrative duties. Furthermore, some school districts restrict personal counseling to only helping students make career decisions, and other districts choose to do without developmental programs in classrooms.

The clients of school counselors also vary according to individual job descriptions. Counselors have their school children as their primary clients, but also work with parents, teachers, and administrators in a consultant role. Counselors who facilitate parenting groups have parents of school children as clients. Some counselors serve as a referral source for teachers and other adults; those adults are the clients of that referral interview. Thus, the variation in school counseling reflects the numerous clients served by the counselor.

Each of the fifty states requires that school counselors be licensed, certified, endorsed, or credentialed in some manner. The requirements for those designations vary significantly from state to state. The qualifications for each state credential are summarized in *A Guide to State Laws and Regulations on Professional School Counseling* (Farrell, 1998). Most often, these standards are defined by the individual state departments of education and adhere to the process followed by teachers in being certified or licensed. In 1995, ASCA resolved that the designation "Professional School Counselor" be used as the title for individuals who engage in the practice of school counseling, provide the services listed previously, have specialized training in school counseling at a minimum master's-degree level, meet state certification standards, and abide by the laws in the states where they are employed. School counselors who meet requirements for the National Certified Counselor (NCC) credential become eligible to seek a national credential, National Certified School Counselor, by completing specialized courses and experiences that are specific to school counseling (Paisley & Borders, 1995).

In 1984, the American School Counselor Association (ASCA) approved the *Ethical Standards for School Counselors* as a document for guiding school counselors through the complicated issues of their job (ASCA, 1998). The most current revision of the standards occurred on June 25, 1998.

As stated in the *Ethical Standards for School Counselors* (ASCA, 1998), school counselors have responsibilities to each group they serve as well as to themselves. These standards are reprinted in Appendix 13-A at the end of this chapter. Huey (1986) noted that ethical standards are only guidelines and seldom provide concrete answers; each situation must be judged in context. The standards of ASCA are most specific to school counselors and deserve diligent study by practicing counselors.

ETHICAL ISSUES OF SIGNIFICANCE TO THE SPECIALTY

Responsibilities to Students

Focus. The primary ethical obligation of the school counselor is to students and their educational, career, emotional, and behavioral needs. Counselors must respect each person as a unique individual. They should refrain from imposing their own personal orientations on the values, plans, decisions, or beliefs of students. School counselors must maintain their knowledge of laws, regulations, or policies that relate to their work and protect the rights of students (ASCA, 1998).

In the summary of tips to school counselors, the Ethics Committee of the American School Counselor Association (1999–2001) identified these related points:

■ Act in the best interests of the clients at all times. Act in good faith and in the absence of malice.
■ Increase awareness of personal values, attitudes, and beliefs; refer when personal characteristics hinder effectiveness. (p. 1)

Counseling Process. Ethical standards stipulate that school counselors inform students about the purposes, goals, techniques, and rules of procedure for counseling in a written disclosure statement. The student should also be informed about the meaning and limits of confidentiality, privileged communication, authoritative restraints, and the possibility that the counselor may want to consult with other professionals. This explanation should occur at or before a counseling relationship begins. This requirement, called *informed consent,* is also discussed in Chapters 3 and 4. The Ethics Committee of ASCA (1999–2001) has also identified the critical necessity of informing clients of potential limitations of the counseling relationship.

Muro and Kottman (1995) suggested that a written disclosure statement to clients makes the process of informed consent more concrete for students. The language should be simple and appropriate for schoolchildren. Kaplan (2001) lists desirable sections that could be included in the disclosure statement and/or brochure:

■ Theoretical framework and treatment approach that the counselor typically uses with clients;
■ Confidentiality definition and limits such as clear danger of harm to self or others, reporting child

abuse, maltreatment and/or neglect; school rules that conflict with confidentiality such as having to report knowledge of alcohol, drugs, or smoking in school;
- The counselor's educational background and training, including degrees and work experiences;
- Rules about appointments such as how to contact the counselor, how often students may see the counselor, guidelines for getting out of class, possibilities for before- or after-school sessions; and
- Acknowledgement by the student's signature that the statement has been read and understood.

Where required by law, parents must sign consent forms prior to initiation of counseling. The ethical standards state that a counselor must safeguard information received in a counseling relationship according to both legal and ethical standards as well as written policies. Counselors can reveal such information to others only with the consent of the parents and the student and in accordance with professional obligations. Hammond and Gantt (1998) remind counselors that art may also be considered communication and probably requires the same type of protection. Counselors may ask the court not to require the release of confidential information if the disclosure may lead to potential harm to the counselee. Counselee's records and personal data are similarly protected. Student information stored in computers should receive the same protective care.

When the condition of the student indicates the presence of a clear and imminent danger to the student or to others, the counselor is responsible for informing authorities and parents or guardians. Additionally, the revision of the standards states that school counselors may reveal information to an identifiable third party who may be at a high risk of contracting a communicable and fatal disease as a result of a relationship with the counselee. That disclosure comes only after the counselor has determined that the third party has not already been informed and that the counselee is not going to tell the third party in the immediate future.

When confidentiality is broken, the counselor should inform the student of that action. School counselors should disclose confidential information only after careful deliberation and, if possible, after consultation with other professionals (see Isaacs, 1997, and Isaacs and Stone, 1999).

Plans.   School counselors and counselees should mutually develop counseling plans that are consistent with the abilities and circumstances of both. Plans should be reviewed regularly. The ASCA Ethics Committee (1999–2001) stated, "Be able to fully explain why you do what you do. A theoretical rationale should undergird counseling strategies and interventions" (p. 1). Providing information allows counselors to help their clients become active partners in the counseling process. As well as being an ethical obligation, involving clients in planning the intervention builds their autonomy and demonstrates the counselor's respect for them (Corey, Corey, & Callanan, 1998).

Huey (1986) cautioned that "counselors who work with children need to be particularly careful not to promote acceptance of the counselor's values as the 'right' ones" (p. 321). ASCA ethical standards state that counselors should refrain from imposing their own personal orientations about values, plans, decisions, or beliefs on students and must be careful never to direct a student's decision based on the counselor's ideas of right and wrong. However, situations may arise in which a counselor may choose to express personal values. In such situations, the counselor may explain that these beliefs were established after thought and exploration and may not be right for all people (Huey, 1986). If personal values are so strong that a counselor cannot be effective in a relationship, the counselor should refer the student to another professional for help. The role of values in counseling is complex (see Chapters 5 and 6).

During the course of a counseling relationship, or in other circumstances, the school counselor may refer the counselee to outside resources. Counselors must know about available resources and facilitate the referral transition to minimize interruption of services. Salo and Shumate (1993) stated that the list of referrals should include medical and legal services as well as resources for other mental health services, social service agencies, and others.

The ethical standards also state that professionals must keep and secure records necessary for providing counseling services. James and DeVaney (1995) stated that school counselors' personal notes should contain factual, concrete, and behaviorally oriented language. Those notes should be kept in a location where privacy can be ensured. If requested to submit the notes by the court, the counselor should consult with an attorney to see if the documents are protected.

Group Work.   School counselors who work with groups have ethical considerations specific to that intervention. The *Ethical Guidelines for Group Counselors* (Association for Specialists in Group Work,

1989), Rapin and Keel's (1998) *Best Practice Guidelines,* and the ASCA ethical standards provide direction for school counselors who work with groups. These standards stress the importance of screening potential group members, attending to the safety and growth of group members, and establishing a norm of confidentiality (see Chapter 16 for a discussion of ethical issues in group counseling).

Terres and Larrabee (1985) and Corey, Corey, Callanan, and Russell (1988) emphasized the possibility for ethical dilemmas in the planning and implementation of groups in schools. At the planning stage, school counselors must determine their competence as group leaders of the specific type of group they will be facilitating. Counselors need to determine the appropriateness of the group experience for the specific children and the appropriateness of the specific child to the group and to the group experience. Ritchie and Huss (2000) outline special considerations in recruiting and screening students for group counseling in schools. Student and parent rights, as well as internal and external constraints of the school setting, also must be considered in planning group counseling in schools. To implement groups, counselors should provide information about the purpose of the group, the leader's qualifications, and other facts about the group process both to the participating students and to their parents. These experts suggest discussing the importance of confidentiality initially and at each meeting. School counselors should recognize they can only guarantee that they personally will abide by the standard of confidentiality in group counseling, but should stress to the group members the importance of keeping private the information shared in the group. Group sessions can occur after provisions for space, privacy, participant factors, and session length and duration are determined, with all decisions informed by the developmental stages of the students who are involved. The guidelines provided by Terres and Larrabee (1985) are helpful to school counselors who conduct group counseling.

Potentially Detrimental Relationships. Whenever a counselor interacts with a client in more than one capacity, potentially detrimental relationships can occur (Fisher & Hennessy, 1994). The ethical standards (ASCA, 1998) state that counselors must avoid these relationships if possible. Corey, Corey, and Callanan (1998) stated that in these situations, incompatible roles have the potential for drastically decreasing the effectiveness of the professional relationship. According to the ethical standards, potentially detrimental relationships to be avoided include counseling relatives, close friends, or associates. If a counselor finds it impossible to avoid conflicting relationships, he or she must be active in eliminating or reducing the potential for harm in those relationships by using the safeguards of informed consent, consultation, supervision, and documentation.

Potentially detrimental relationships vary from those that are potentially very harmful to those with little potential for harm. Counselors in such a relationship are always obligated to reduce the potential for harm. Counselors need to monitor the relationship closely, gauging the benefits of counseling with the risks of impaired judgment or exploitation of the student client. Counselors should also continually evaluate the effectiveness of their counseling and refer the student to another counselor if possible (Fisher & Hennessy, 1994). Counselors should seek consultation or supervision, use informed consent, and document carefully to reduce the potential for harm inherent in potentially detrimental relationships (Muro & Kottman, 1995). Sexual relationships with student clients are prohibited in the ethical standards of all mental health organizations and are illegal in many states (Kitchener & Harding, 1990).

In determining what action to take in ethical dilemmas presented by potentially detrimental relationships, school counselors should follow these steps:

■ Identify the primary client (in most cases, the students in school).
■ Identify the ethical issues or dilemma involved.
■ Consult the necessary codes and experts.
■ Think carefully before acting.

Using the ethical decision-making model presented in Chapter 6 may also help school counselors make responsible and ethical choices. Herlihy and Corey (1992) noted that the harm to clients is derived from the practitioner who exploits the relationship rather than from the duality itself.

Testing. The ASCA Code of Ethics requires that counselors adhere to all professional standards in choosing, giving, and interpreting assessment measures. Counselors must be cautious with instruments that have norm groups different from the population with which the measurement is being used. Counselors who use computer testing programs should receive specific training in those assessment techniques. Sampson and Pyle

(1988) suggest that counselors must ensure the accuracy and proper functioning of the computer programs they use. Counselors must ensure the confidentiality of the student data generated in computer testing. Counselors should monitor for the possibility of scoring errors that may be difficult to determine in computer-based testing applications. Overcoming the inadequacies of the generalized test interpretations that accompany the test results is an important counselor obligation, as is the need for followup with the computer user.

A counselor is obligated to explain clearly the nature, purposes, and results of assessment instruments to students. Counselors must not misuse results and interpretations and should attempt to prevent others from doing so. Talbutt (1983b) presented practical recommendations for school counselors and testing in schools. She suggested reviewing school policy to become knowledgeable about the counselor's responsibilities related to testing. According to Talbutt, counselors should follow all regulations and guidelines from state and local boards of education, abide by professional guidelines, keep abreast of current testing information, and be diligent in selecting and interpreting testing instruments.

Computers.   Two examples of expanded counseling services to students include computer applications and peer helper programs. The ethical standards specify that the counselor is responsible for explaining the benefits and limitations of computer applications. The use of computers in counseling should be determined by an assessment of the appropriateness of the use of the computer for the student's needs, the student's understanding of the application, and followup counseling assistance. All groups should have equal access to computer applications that are unbiased by discriminatory information and values.

ASCA's (2000) position statement on student safety on the Internet suggests that school counselors can provide Internet guidelines to parents and to school personnel. The National Center for Missing and Exploited Children has prepared a document that can be disseminated for that purpose (Net Smartz Workshop, <http://www.missingkids.org>).

The ethical standards related to using computers in counseling services are enhanced by guidelines offered by Sampson and Pyle (1988), Childers (1988), and Sampson, Kolodinski, and Greeno (1997). These authors discuss ways of safeguarding stored data by maintaining security procedures, restricting content and access, preserving anonymity when possible, and limiting the time period of storage. If a counselor is using computer ap-

plications with a client, the counselor should provide guidelines that include informed consent and release forms specific to computer use. These authors identify potential problems and provide safeguards as solutions. Additional discussions of ethical issues involved in computer use can be found in Chapter 10.

The ethical standards also clarify the responsibilities of school counselors who coordinate peer helper groups. The pertinent standard states that counselors are responsible for the welfare of students in peer programs under their direction. ASCA (1999g) identifies the school counselor's role in determining the needs of the school population and for implementing a peer helping program to help meet those needs. Welfel (1998) stated that peer helpers must be chosen carefully, trained well, and supervised closely. The National Peer Helpers Association (2001) Code of Ethics includes the following points:

- A philosophy that upholds the effectiveness of peer helping;
- Commitment to an individual's right to dignity, self-development, and self-direction;
- Guidelines for excellence in program development and implementation; and
- Promotion of realistic expectations of the program.

Responsibilities to Parents

The difficulties of ethical practice often emerge when school counselors try to balance the responsibilities to students with those to parents or guardians. Counselors must determine how to maintain confidentiality for a student and provide information to parents. The ASCA (1998) ethical standards stipulate the following counselor obligations to parents:

- To respect the inherent rights and responsibilities of all parents for their children;
- To establish a cooperative relationship with parents, maintaining the confidentiality of their communications with the counselor; and
- To recognize legal and local guidelines when helping parents with family difficulties that interfere with students' effectiveness and welfare.

In some cases, counselors need a clear understanding of the meaning of custody and the legal issues that affect noncustodial parents and their access to information about their child. Wilcoxon and Magnuson (1999) present definitions and other considerations for school counselors serving noncustodial parents. For example, these authors encourage school counselors to assist schools in developing guidelines that promote family involvement rather than focusing only on the custodial parent. They recommend that school counselors anticipate difficulties caused by the marital decree and design policies and procedures that are not only sensitive to the family but also prevent difficulties in the school setting.

Parents and Confidentiality. The responsibilities of the school counselor related to parents and confidentiality are as follows:

- To inform parents about the role of the school counselor, emphasizing the importance of confidentiality in that role
- To give parents "accurate, comprehensive, and relevant information in an objective and caring manner, as appropriate and consistent with ethical responsibilities to the counselee" (ASCA, 1998, p. 3)
- To make reasonable efforts to honor the wishes of parents and guardians about information concerning the counselee. (ASCA, 1998)

Balancing the responsibilities to students and to parents presents counselors with ethical dilemmas that often have to be decided case by case. Consultation with another counselor and supervision may be helpful in making those decisions. Welfel (1998) noted that parents are often reassured when they learn that counselors have no intention of working beyond the limits of their competence, that counselors will make reasonable efforts to honor the parents' requests, and that counselors will be respectful of family values. She suggested a brochure or handbook to distribute this information. The ASCA Ethics Committee calls for counselors to "encourage family involvement, where possible, when working with minors in sensitive areas which might be controversial" (p. 1). Stromberg and colleagues (1993) stated the general rule is that a parent is entitled to general information from the counselor about the child's progress in counseling. School counselors may satisfy parents' requests for information with short updates on the child's progress. Corey, Corey, and Callanan (1998) recognized that school counselors must be discrete in the kind and extent of information revealed to parents or guardians.

ASCA's (1999f) position statement on parental consent for services suggests that written information about the school counseling program must be provided to parents. Parents can thereby gain a better understanding of the counseling relationship, and the trust among the counselor, the counselee, and the parents will increase. School counselors must obtain parental permission for counseling services if required by local law or policy.

Responsibilities to Colleagues and Professional Associates

School counselors have an obligation to establish and maintain a professional relationship with the faculty, staff, and administration. Those relationships help maximize the potential of the school counseling program. School counselors must carefully define the parameters of their professional role by informing colleagues about guidelines regarding confidentiality, public and private information, and consultation. Corey, Corey, and Callanan (1998) stated the importance of talking to everyone about matters of confidentiality. Freeman (2000) suggests that ethical counselors maintain open communication lines and provide school personnel with information they need to provide services to students. That exchange of information occurs within the framework of confidentiality and privileged communication guidelines.

Counselors should also be active in cooperating and collaborating with community agencies, organizations, and individuals in the best interests of students and, therefore, establish a network to be used in referring students and their families. Muro and Kottman (1995) suggested providing at least three referral sources. When school counselors do refer students to other professionals, the counselors must provide information that is accurate, objective, and concise in order to assist. If a counselee is being seen by another mental health professional, the school counselor should ask the counselee and parents where necessary for permission to talk to the other professional. The school counselor and mental health professional should develop agreements to prevent confusion and conflict for the counselee.

Responsibilities to School and Community

School counselors have obligations to the school program and to the community as well as to faculty, staff, and administration. The ethical standards (ASCA, 1998) stipulate those obligations as follows:

- Counselors protect the educational program from anything that is not in the best interests of the students.
- While honoring confidentiality, counselors report to the appropriate authorities any potentially disruptive or damaging conditions that may threaten the school's mission, personnel, and/or property.
- Counselors clearly define their role and functions and report conditions that may impede the effectiveness of the program and services.
- School counselors only accept employment for which they are qualified and recommend only qualified, competent people for counseling positions.
- The school counselor helps develop a positive school environment, an educational program to meet students' needs, and an evaluation process for the counseling program, services, and personnel. The information from the evaluation process is used for planning programs and services.

Huey (1986) stated, "Counselors should adhere to local school policies, whether determined by the principal or the board of education, to the extent possible without compromising their primary responsibility to the client" (p. 321). When conflicts exist between loyalty to the student client and to the employer, Huey suggested a resolution that protects the rights of the student. Counselors may actively try to change existing policies that cause the conflicts.

The Ethics Committee of ASCA (1999–2001) provided this tip for school counselors: "Follow written job descriptions. Be sure what you are doing is defined as an appropriate function in your work setting" (p. 1).

The dilemma of parents' rights in educational control is an ongoing controversy. Parents may continue to challenge the content and activities of school counseling programs. Kaplan (1997) reviewed the current status of parents' rights and lists ways for counselors to prevent and to respond to parental concerns. Kaplan (1996) also suggested that bringing parents into the program might prevent problems as well as heighten their sensitivity. Including parents on an advisory committee would be one way school counselors could provide an opportunity for this involvement.

ASCA's (1999b) position statement on censorship verifies the profession's endorsement of the following activities as part of a counselor's role:

- Teaching civic values for effective citizenship;
- Developing critical thinking and problem-solving skills;

- Promoting an environment of trust and positive interactions; and
- Advocating services for all student needs.

The statement recommends that counselors offer a comprehensive collection of materials that are chosen according to the basic written selection criterion of the school district.

Responsibilities to Self

School counselors also have obligations to themselves and to their ability to accomplish their duties, including operating within the boundaries of their individual professional competence and being aware of their personal strengths and limitations. Counselors who monitor their own psychological health, participate in continuing education, and stay current with literature in the profession maintain competence in the school counseling setting. Carroll, Schneider, and Wesley (1985) identified formal education, professional training, and supervised experience as the criteria that define competence.

Varhely and Cowles (1991) discussed the counselor's responsibility to engage in self-examination continually. These authors outlined a process for this self-scrutiny. The first step is recognizing that one's personal beliefs, values, and needs may bias behavior in ways that are beyond one's consciousness. As counselors increase their awareness of the impact of their personal worldviews, their thoughtful, ongoing exploration of self is the next step. These two processes lead the counselor to become more aware of cues that may imply a conflict between personal issues and professional responsibilities. By constantly examining their own values, counselors become sensitive to whether they are unconsciously influencing students.

School counselors should monitor their personal performance and effectiveness, always avoiding any inadequacy in professional services or any potential harm to students. Counselors must be aware of their own biases and personal characteristics and their potential effects on students. School counselors must have specific training to ensure they provide appropriate and effective services to people who have differences related to age, gender, race, religion, sexual orientation, and socioeconomic and ethnic backgrounds. Hobson and Kanitz (1996) considered multicultural counseling as an ethical issue for school counselors and challenge school counselors to assess their level of multicultural competence and seek training opportunities to overcome any deficiencies. Continuing education and personal growth are professional obligations of school counselors. Several tips from the Ethics Committee of ASCA (1999–2001) address these responsibilities:

- Function within the boundaries of personal competence. Be aware of personal skill levels and limitations.
- Consult with other professionals. Have a readily accessible support network of professionals.
- Stay up-to-date with laws and current court rulings.
- Actively attempt to understand the diverse cultural backgrounds of the clients with whom you work. (pp. 1–2)

Responsibilities to the Profession

School counselors have obligations to the profession that include maintaining professionally appropriate conduct, participating in advancing knowledge in the field of counseling, and belonging to professional organizations. School counselors should not use their position to recruit or to gain clients or to receive personal gains. The ASCA standards emphasize that school counselors must abide by ethical standards of the profession as well as other official policy statements and relevant legal mandates.

The Ethics Committee of ASCA (1999–2001) emphasizes these points:

- Read and adhere to the ethical standards of your profession. Keep copies of the ethical standards on hand, review them periodically, and act accordingly.
- Join appropriate professional associations. Read association publications and participate in professional development opportunities. (p. 2)

LEGAL ISSUES OF SIGNIFICANCE TO THE SPECIALTY

A consideration of the ethical standards for school counselors would be incomplete without discussing the legal standards that affect school counselors' responsibilities, including confidentiality; exceptions to confidentiality, including the duty to warn and reporting child abuse; the Family Educational Rights and Privacy Act; and the Education for All Handicapped Children Act.

Confidentiality

Confidentiality, the assurance to the client that what is said in a counseling relationship will not be revealed, is an ethical responsibility of counselors in all settings. School counselors have unique challenges in trying to honor that obligation because they work with minors. Remley and Herlihy (2001) noted that legal and ethical requirements seldom conflict, but an exception occurs in counseling minor clients.

Privileged Communication. Children have an ethical right to privacy and confidentiality. Remley (1985) noted that in the legal structure of the United States, children have some of the protections granted to adults; however, in many ways the protection of children's rights depends on interpretations made by their parents, guardians, or the courts. The legal status pertinent to the discussion of confidentiality is privileged communication, which means that a client is protected from confidential communications being disclosed in a legal proceeding.

Isaacs (1997), Isaacs and Stone (1999), and Glosoff, Herlihy, and Spence (2000) offered a review of privileged communication. Herlihy and Sheeley (1987) and Sheeley and Herlihy (1987) summarize their survey of the provision of privileged communication to the clients of school counselors.

In approximately 20 states, students in schools are granted the legal right of privileged communication when talking with a school counselor (Taylor & Adelman, 1989). The restrictions that are placed on the privileged communication vary among the states. School counselors must know whether privilege is granted and examine the limits that exist in the statute.

The level of privilege to which a minor is entitled is a complicated legal determination (Waldo & Malley, 1992) that school counselors must investigate in the state in which they are employed. Additionally, a recent decision by the U.S. Supreme Court in *Jaffee v. Redmond* has possible implications about privileged communication for all counselors, according to Remley, Herlihy, and Herlihy (1997). In that decision, the Supreme Court ruled that the communications between a master's-level social worker and her client were privileged communication under the Federal Rules of Evidence. The social worker was referred to as "therapist" or "psychotherapist" in the decision and the activities were referred to as "counseling sessions," "counseling," or "psychotherapy." According to Remley, Herlihy, and Herlihy, the decision is important for establishing a precedent in an official federal court that provides protection to communications between therapists and their patients. School counselors need to remain informed about how the implications from that decision may extend to minors and to the school setting.

ASCA Position Statement on Confidentiality. Regardless of whether privilege has been mandated to protect student communications with counselors, confidentiality within that relationship is imperative. The position statement on the school counselor and confidentiality ASCA (1999d) details the obligations of a school counselor for establishing and maintaining confidentiality in schools and places no age limitation on who is entitled to a confidential relationship. The position paper contains definitions and limitations pertinent to school counselors' practice and should be reviewed carefully. One significant point in the statement is that counselors have a responsibility to protect the privacy of information received from students, parents, and teachers. A critical phrase that is repeated throughout the position statement is "confidentiality must not be abridged by the counselor except where there is clear and present danger to the student and/or other persons" (p. 1).

Employer Policy and Expectations. Tompkins and Mehring (1993) discussed considerations of privilege and confidentiality, and stated that the third consideration of student-counselor privacy is the policy and expectation of the employer. Counselors are specialized members of the school community who receive requests from teachers, school administration or staff, and others concerned with the educational enterprise. They must respect, and presumably follow, dictates from the school principal and superintendent (Remley, 1993). Because teachers and administrators are able to reveal all that a child says to them, it is often difficult for these individuals to understand why school counselors should not do so as well.

CASE SCENARIO 13-1

Responding to the Policies of the School and Maintaining Confidentiality

An elementary school counselor is attending an integrated team meeting with administrators, teachers, and a school psychologist about a student, Joey, a third grader who is increasingly withdrawn in the classroom. Joey is not completing his work and is not participating in any classroom activities. The counselor has been working with the child, whose single-parent mother has been diagnosed with an inoperable brain tumor. During the school team meeting, the principal asked the counselor to explain what has been happening to Joey. Should the counselor provide this information to the principal and the team?

NO. The counselor should maintain the confidentiality of Joey's communication and simply respond that Joey has

been encountering some stressful situations and the effects are obviously being expressed in the classroom. The counselor should continue by saying that perhaps, together, she and the school team could determine strategies to help Joey become more engaged in class.

The competing demands of maintaining confidentiality for the student and some employer policies further complicate the counselor's responsibilities. Before accepting employment, counselors should clarify the policy and expectations of the school.

Options for Counselors in Matters Related to Confidentiality.   Several options have been proposed to help school counselors in matters related to confidentiality. Remley and Herlihy (2001) identified some pertinent facts about children and confidentiality:

- Younger children do not have an understanding of the concepts of confidentiality or privacy and are probably not as concerned about confidentiality as the counselor is. Huey (1996) supports that statement.
- On the other hand, preadolescents and adolescents may have a higher desire for privacy. That concern relates to their confusion about identity and other developmental changes.
- Some children at all ages may not be concerned at all about privacy. Counselors should not automatically assume that minors do not want their parents or guardians to know what they are discussing.
- Some children may confide in an adult, thinking that adult will act as an intermediary to resolve their concern.
- Children's limited reasoning capacity may interfere with their ability to make decisions that are in their best interests.

Tompkins and Mehring (1993) and Davis and Ritchie (1993) suggest that counselors:

1. Stay informed about the law and written policy in the area of the practice.
2. Operate within the ethical code of the professional organization.
3. Review expectations and policy before employment is accepted.
4. Operate within their personal limits of expertise.
5. Keep the best interest of the children their predominant concern.

By providing informed consent for the child and for the parent when dealing with sensitive issues or before engaging in long-term counseling, the counselor should establish a climate of confidentiality. Remley (1985) stated that counselors fulfill their confidentiality responsibilities by informing the child before consulting with anyone about the child's problem, involving the child in the decision-making process, and keeping the child informed. The guidelines provided by Zingaro (1983) included some specifics helpful to the practice of school counseling. He suggested that when it is in the best interest of the child for a significant adult to have information, the counselor may respond by telling the adult how he can help the child rather than revealing specific information disclosed by the child. Taylor and Adelman (1989) suggested that counselors should focus on establishing a relationship in which youngsters take the lead in sharing information when appropriate. Those authors provided guidelines for enhancing clients' motivation and choice to resolve their problems by confiding in other adults. Strein and Hershenson (1991) offered suggestions for using a "need-to-know" basis as an alternative guideline to confidentiality when counselors work in situations that are not one-to-one relationships, a common occurrence in schools.

When a parent or guardian demands to know the content of counseling sessions and the counselee strongly resists this disclosure, school counselors may find the following steps suggested by Remley and Herlihy (2001) useful:

1. Discuss the situation fully with the minor and see if the minor will disclose the content of the sessions to the adult. If not,
2. Work to persuade the adult that the child's best interests would not be served by disclosing the information. Telling the adult about the counseling relationship and assuring the adult that information would been revealed if the child were in danger may be helpful. If not,
3. Schedule a joint session with the adult and the minor and assume the role of the mediator. If the conflict has not been resolved yet, choose one of the following;
   a. Inform the child ahead of time and then disclose the content of the sessions to the adult. Remember that the adult may have legal rights to the information.
   b. Refuse to disclose the information. Inform your direct supervisor before doing this and remember that the adult may have legal rights to the information.

CASE SCENARIO 13-2

Sharing Information on a "Need-to-Know" Basis
How would you respond to this request?

Teacher: *What is going on with Jamie? She has asked to go to your office twice in the last two days and she is so testy lately. Every time I speak to her directly, she rolls her eyes and huffs. I hate to stop her from coming to see you, but of course I cannot let her take advantage of my good nature and continue to see you unless I know she has a legitimate reason.*

Should you provide the teacher with the specific circumstances that are creating Jamie's difficulty?

NO. You should phrase your response in such a way that protects Jamie's confidentiality yet tells the teacher some specific actions she can take to assist Jamie. An example of such a response follows.

Counselor: *I know how well you get along with your students and how interested you are in helping them. Jamie does need time with me right now and I appreciate you letting her come to talk with me when you feel you can. What seems like her frustration with you is probably a result of other concerns. She should be better in time. In the meantime, you might talk with her and arrange a signal to let her know when her reactions are inappropriate so you can have less tense interactions. I remember when you tried that last year with Juan—things went much better for both of you.*

Varhely and Cowles (1991) suggested that an overlooked dilemma in conflicts over confidentiality involves the counselor's personal beliefs, experiences, and values. Counselors must strive to determine their personal beliefs about the rights and responsibilities of children, their needs for belonging and a sense of adequacy, and their personal value system. Without a continual process to develop self-awareness in these areas, counselors may further complicate the difficulties inherent in maintaining confidentiality in school settings. Case Scenario 13-3 illustrates a situation in which a counselor's values might shape how a situation is treated.

CASE SCENARIO 13-3

The Influence of Personal Values and Beliefs on Professional Decisions

You are a school counselor on your way home after a long day. A teacher walks you to your car in the school parking lot and starts a discussion about a student you both know. How would you respond?

Eighth-grade teacher to school counselor: Thank goodness I got a chance to see you. You need to do something about that Duvoe child. Danny is in my class and I can't do anything with him! He's so unkempt; his hair is falling over his shoulders! I told him the second day of class that he needed a haircut, but it's as if he is defying me. Now he doesn't even tie it back. It falls all over his face. I can't even see his eyes when I look at him! He should be made to cut his hair and to look me in the eye when I'm talking to him.

Danny's teacher is asking the school counselor to "do something" because his hair is long. Is that a problem in which a counselor should be involved?

NO. While Danny does not appear to be behaving in a manner that indicates he has a personal problem, it is the counselor's responsibility to provide support and assistance to teachers who may be struggling to meet the needs of diverse students. You should attempt to better understand the situation and demonstrate your support to this teacher in a manner that will not encourage undue imposition of either the teacher's or the counselor's values upon Danny. One response might be the following: "You are concerned about Danny's appearance but I'm not sure I understand how Danny's long hair is a problem." Counselors need to be responsive to teachers to be considered a part of the learning team; however, acting on the teacher's request may not be in line with the values of a counselor who believes in allowing students to be individuals.

Exceptions to Confidentiality

Some exceptions to confidentiality relate to protecting children from harm—the duty to warn and reporting child abuse. School counselors should be aware that, as with privileged communication, the statutes that determine a counselor's liability in situations of duty to warn and of reporting child abuse are mandated by the state in which the counselor is practicing. Counselors must do a careful review of legislative updates and judicial opinions in their states to make informed decisions (Hopkins & Anderson, 1990).

Duty to Warn and Protect. Counselors must determine actions to take in the delicate balance between confidentiality and the duty to warn others on a case-by-case basis (Sheeley & Herlihy, 1989). They may be vulnerable to a lawsuit if they breach confidentiality. However, if counselors could have prevented an incident, they may be sued if a student client is injured, injures someone else, or commits suicide. Counselors should make the decision between breaching confiden-

tiality and warning others with diligence and careful judgment. The first step is to be fully informed about state laws and court decisions. Legal mandates and statutes are continually interpreted and revised; keeping abreast of the laws and decisions is an ongoing process.

If the school district does not have a policy on confidentiality and its limitations, school counselors should work actively to develop one. That local policy should be adequately disclosed to all students and to all parents.

Sheeley and Herlihy (1989) and Remley and Sparkman (1993) have additional suggestions for school counselors who work with students who may be suicidal. Their suggestions are useful in establishing policy and procedures for this difficult situation:

1. Be able to recognize the warning signs of students with suicidal potential.
2. Have an established plan for dealing with the crisis.
3. Have referral sources for crisis situations.
4. Develop the skills to help students and families if a student threatens suicide.
5. Take action if it is determined that a student is at risk of harming himself or herself.
6. Consider actions that are the least intrusive steps, but that will nevertheless ensure the safety of the person who is suicidal.
7. Consult with colleagues in determining risk as well as the appropriate action to take.
8. Inform school administrators and parents when counselors have determined that a student client is at risk of attempting suicide.
9. If these adults are reluctant to become involved, school counselors have an ethical responsibility to do all they can do to prevent the suicide.

Box 13.2 discusses a court decision in a case involving a student suicide. This decision has strong implications for school counselors to warn parents of the suicidal intentions of students. Eating disorders, substance abuse, reckless sexual behavior, cult membership, criminal activity, and other dangerous activities may also be viewed as instances of harm to self. School counselors should question the degree to which such behaviors constitute a student's potential for harm to self that might necessitate breaching confidentiality.

Coll (1995) and Sealander, Schwiebert, Oren, and Weekley (1999) discussed the legal and ethical concerns about confidentiality in substance abuse prevention programs. Their review and guidelines may

---

Box 13.2   Duty to Warn of Suicide Intent (see the ACA and APA codes in the book appendices and the school counselor's code in Appendix 13-A).

Friends of a middle school student, Nicole, reported to school counselors that she intended to kill herself. The counselors questioned Nicole and she denied making suicidal statements. The counselors did not inform school officials or Nicole's parents. Nicole died in a suicide pact with another student, and her parents sued. On appeal of the original verdict that favored the school personnel, the question of the counselor's duty to warn the parents was considered. The court found "a special relationship sufficient to create a duty of care when an adolescent in a school setting expresses an intention to commit suicide and the counselor becomes aware of such intention" (Fisher & Sorenson, 1996).

---

provide additional insights. Federal guidelines (42 U.S.C. 290 dd-3 and ee-3; 42 CFR Part 2) govern the circumstances of disclosure of the records of people who are receiving treatment for substance abuse or who are participating in prevention or referral activities. Generally, the confidentiality of the records is protected. Exceptions are made for medical emergencies, child abuse or neglect, or the endangering of a third party. These are considered situations in which the benefits produced or the harms prevented justify overriding confidentiality. Even in these cases, only information pertinent to the current problem should be revealed. The federal regulations about minors in substance abuse treatment, prevention, or referral programs permit notification of parents unless state laws restrict requiring or prohibiting notice.

Another situation that may call for breaching confidentiality is when a student client indicates harm to others. The *Tarasoff* decision was a call for reasonable action by a therapist to protect third parties. In a discussion of this legal duty, Gehring (1982) reviewed and analyzed the court's interpretations of the decision. More recently, Waldo and Malley (1992) concluded that this duty to protect requires several actions on the part of a therapist—not only the duty to warn an intended victim. They explain the four criteria used to assess what might be expected of school counselors in a decision involving the duty to protect:

■ Special relationship to the dangerous person or to the potential victim;
■ The presence of a clear threat and the imminence of danger;
■ The ability to identify potential victim(s); and
■ Reasonable care when making decisions.

According to these authors, courts have defined the following obligations of school counselors in such cases:

(a) to assemble necessary background information, (b) to confer with a psychiatrist when consultation is needed, and (c) to keep careful records. Seeking professional legal advice is a suggestion but not an obligation. The actions that school counselors may take to protect a person at risk are (a) making referrals by notifying the parents of the student client, (b) notifying a probation officer, (c) notifying the police, (d) designating someone to inform the intended victim, (e) warning the potential victim, (f) detaining the client, and (g) seeking voluntary or involuntary commitment. Counselors may choose one or more of these possibilities (Waldo & Malley, 1992).

Assessing the dangerousness of the situation is difficult. Gross and Robinson (1987) and Thompson and Rudolph (2000) discussed case studies with guidelines and procedures for each situation. Counselors may find these useful practice scenarios.

CASE SCENARIO 13-4

Assessing Dangerousness

As a school counselor, you have been conducting a small group for children whose parents are recently divorced. A 13-year-old from that group, Eleanor, has told a friend that she cannot stand her life with her mother and the live-in boyfriend at home any more. Her mother's boyfriend is "impossible," no one is paying any attention to her, and her father refuses to intervene. Eleanor has said that she isn't sure how she is going to do it but she's going to end the lives of the people who are making her feel so miserable so that she can go live with her father. Eleanor's friend has told you about these threats. Should you intervene?

YES.   You should assess the dangerousness of the situation before determining how to work with Eleanor to resolve the situation. Determine if Eleanor has a specific plan and the plausibility of the plan, whether she has the means to carry out the plan and how accessible those means are, and how pervasive these thoughts are to her. If you determine the threat is credible, you should tell

Eleanor that you must report the situation to her parents and possibly to the police. Make the reports and document the actions. Consultation with another professional is advisable. Proceed simultaneously with other actions that are directed at supporting Eleanor in resolving her difficult situation; for example, arrange an agreement with Eleanor for individual counseling to consider alternative actions, arrange a meeting (with Eleanor's permission) with all the parties to work on acceptable solutions to the home situation, or refer Eleanor to another professional for more intensive counseling.

Counselors also deal with two sensitive dilemmas that involve youth sexuality—counseling minors about birth control or abortion and counseling students with AIDS. McWhirter, McWhirter, McWhirter, and McWhirter (1998) and Gustafson and McNamara (1987) discussed the difficulties in determining whether to tell parents about the sexual activity of a minor, especially in relation to seeking birth control or abortion information. State laws that mandate reporting, or protect counselors from such reports, are as varied as other laws. In some states, minors can discuss sexually transmitted diseases or pregnancy prevention or cessation with counselors without the legal requirement of parents' notification (Stadler, 1989). Other states mandate notification. Counselors should remain informed about the legal issues, consult with colleagues, and be deliberate about their decisions.

Talbutt (1983a) reviewed court cases related to abortions. She noted legal and ethical issues in school employees providing abortion information and concluded that counselors should be familiar with their school district's policy and know the laws and current court rulings that have implications for abortion counseling. Urging minors to discuss plans with parents may be both a legal mandate and a counseling goal. Talbutt noted the need for counselors to establish procedures before taking a crisis approach. The procedure should include family members and local referral agencies.

Likewise, Lynch (1993) provided a thoughtful discussion of the process of counseling someone with AIDS in which counselors balance confidentiality concerns with the duty to protect. Her overview is for those who work in college counseling centers, but the dilemmas she recognizes are applicable to other school settings. Both her article and the position statement *The School Counselor and AIDS* (ASCA, 1999a) promote positive health education, familiarity with current resources, and prudent adherence to the primary role of counselors. McWhirter et al. (1998) suggested that

counselors notify state public health agencies of possible communicable or reportable diseases after determining measures to protect confidentiality. Those authors proposed that such disclosure protects the third person and the client's confidentiality and demonstrates the counselor's measures to prevent harm. Current ASCA ethical standards advise counselors to inform a third party who is at risk for contracting a communicable disease if that person has not already been notified of the danger.

The dilemmas associated with school counselors, their counselees, and issues of confidentiality provoke much discussion. Isaacs (1999) summarized the factors that affect the choices made by counselors to breach confidentiality and suggested the following:

■ Determine in advance the kinds of behaviors and issues that might warrant breach.
■ Establish a network of peers.
■ Determine alternative actions to breaching confidentiality.

Reporting Child Abuse.   All states require some type of reporting of suspected cases of child abuse. As with other state mandates, the specifics of the laws vary from state to state. Counselors should understand the requirements of the laws in their states and the procedures in their districts. Laws are being revised constantly and must be monitored by school counselors. Sandberg, Crabbs, and Crabbs (1988) provided responses to frequently asked questions about legal issues in child abuse.

The Professional School Counselor and Child Abuse and Neglect Prevention is an ASCA (1999c) position statement that outlines various counselor responsibilities beyond the reporting of child abuse. This statement includes a useful set of definitions and examples of the signs of abuse and neglect.

According to the ASCA position statement (1999c), **abuse** is the infliction by other than accidental means of physical harm upon the body of a child, continual psychological damage, or denial of emotional needs. Some signs and examples of child abuse cited in this statement are the following:

■ Extensive bruises or patterns of bruises
■ Burns or burn patterns
■ Lacerations, welts, or abrasions
■ Injuries inconsistent with information offered
■ Sexual abuse

■ Emotional disturbances caused by continuous friction in the home, marital discord, or mentally ill parents
■ Cruel treatment

The ASCA position statement defines **neglect** as the failure to provide necessary food, care, clothing, shelter, supervision, or medical attention for a child. According to this statement, children who suffer from neglect include those who are:

■ Malnourished, ill-clad, dirty, without proper sleeping arrangements, lacking in appropriate health care
■ Unattended, lacking adequate supervision
■ Ill and lacking essential medical attention
■ Irregularly and illegally absent from school
■ Exploited and overworked
■ Lacking essential psychological/emotional nurturance
■ Abandoned

This position statement defines **corporal punishment** as an act of physical force upon a student for the purpose of punishing the student. The definition does not cover any reasonable force used by a school employee in self-defense, in defense of someone else, or to restrain a disruptive student.

Counselors are encouraged to implement activities to educate and to support other school personnel involved in protecting children from abuse and neglect. They are also charged with providing ongoing services to the children and/or the family in the crisis or to refer them to an appropriate agency. Providing child abuse/neglect prevention programs is also among counselors' duties (Minard, 1993). Remley and Fry (1993) identified the multiple roles of the counselor in reporting child abuse: informant, counselor to the victim or perpetrator, employee, liaison, court witness, and counselor to the family. Clearly, the potential for role conflict, as well as the burden of being a resource for so many people, makes this area a difficult one for school counselors. Counselors must have the qualities of awareness, knowledge, commitment, and effective communication skills to face the process of reporting and preventing child abuse and neglect (Howell-Nigrelli, 1988).

Case Scenario 13-5

Reporting Suspected Cases of Child Abuse
You are a school counselor who has just met with a student referred to you by her classroom teacher. Based on that session, you arranged an appointment that same morning with your school principal. The meeting leaves

you conflicted:

School Counselor: *Mr. B., I need to report this case of suspected abuse to the state reporting agency. Angela Adams has a series of welts on her back that look like the mark of a belt. In addition, she has a large bruise, just darkening, on her shoulder. Her teacher brought her to see me due to these marks, and Angela said she and her dad got into a fight last weekend. She said that her brother looks worse than she does because, "Dad really beat him up."*

Principal: *Angela Adams? This is surprising. I met her mom at open house this year, and she and her husband have helped out on several school and community projects. I really doubt that this could be the right story. Angela can be very obstinate, you know. I had her in my office twice last year for not following teacher directives. I think we should wait on this and see if anything further happens. I know the Adams's neighbors. I'll ask if they ever hear anything.*

Have you discharged your responsibility to report this suspected child abuse by leaving matters in the principal's hands?

NO. You have both a legal mandate to report suspected abuse and a personal belief that the incident should be reported. If others in the school system do not agree, you should carefully consider the dilemma and be prepared to convince others of your position.

The addition of corporal punishment to this position statement acknowledges that the abuse of children may also occur at school. This ASCA position statement states that school counselors should not support the use of corporal punishment as a disciplinary tool.

Another issue of abuse that is not addressed clearly in the ethical standards is psychological maltreatment in the schools, either by educators or students' peers. Although ASCA provides no position statement and no ethical standards are available, counselors need to monitor the emerging literature about bullying and psychologically abusive teachers (Neese, 1989).

Student Records

Sealander et al. (1999) reviewed the laws that uphold the privacy of student information. The Family Educational Rights and Privacy Act (FERPA) establishes parameters on accessing and disclosing student records. The Drug Abuse Office and Treatment Act (1976) protects the drug and alcohol treatment records of students in any institution that receives federal assistance. The Individuals with Disabilities Education Act further stipulates the care of the records of students in special education. The American Counseling Association (1998) has compiled a helpful resource that also clarifies federal law on student records.

Family Educational Rights and Privacy Act (FERPA). In November 1974, the Family Educational Rights and Privacy Act (FERPA), or the Buckley Amendment, became law. The intent of this federal mandate was to provide parents and eligible students (older than age 18) the right to inspect school records and to protect the dissemination of educational records. The Act is reprinted in Appendix 13-B at the end of this chapter. Federal funds may be withheld from school districts that do not adhere to the policies of allowing parents access to records and denying access without parental permission. All U.S. school districts develop a records policy statement and procedures for access and protection to explain how the regulations are implemented. The U.S. Department of Education at 600 Independence, SW, Washington, D.C. 20202-4605 provides a model policy entitled *Student Records Policies and Procedures for the Alpha School District.* However, the model lacks specific guidelines for counselors. Walker and Larrabee (1985) and Fisher and Sorenson (1996) presented the following useful information on the application of FERPA guidelines:

■ Parents or eligible students should be informed of their rights under this act. This right is extended to custodial and noncustodial parents, unless a court order restrains the access of the noncustodial parent.
■ Information about types of educational records that exist and the procedures for accessing those records is disseminated. The content of educational records may include academic progress, test scores, identification data, home background, health information, educational history, anecdotal remarks, case summaries, and recommendations.
■ Parents or eligible students may review educational records, request changes, pursue a hearing if the change is disallowed, and add personal statements as explanations, if necessary.
■ Personally identifiable information is not released without prior written consent of a parent or an eligible student.
■ Parents and eligible students are allowed to see the school's record of disclosure.
■ Records made by educators that remain in the sole possession of the maker and therefore are not accessible or revealed to any other individual are not subject to disclosure under this act (Fisher & Soren-

son, 1996). This indicates that private notes do not have to be revealed under this federal act.

School counselors who have administrative responsibility for the educational records of children should comply with local policy, state law, and the Buckley Amendment. Remley (1990) discussed whether counselors have a legal or ethical obligation to keep counseling records and the content of the records. He described circumstances in which personnel may be obligated to disclose counseling records and outlined procedures for maintaining, transferring, and discarding counseling records.

The Education for all Handicapped Children Act (PL 94-142). The Education for all Handicapped Children Act is Public Law 94-142. In 1990, that Act was amended by PL 101-476 and renamed the Individuals with Disabilities Education Act. The Act was revised in 1997. This law guarantees a free and appropriate education in the least restrictive environment possible to all students regardless of the nature and degree of their handicapping conditions. While the law does not refer to school counselors specifically, they are involved in offering many services to students with handicapping conditions and may be included in the Individual Education Plan (IEP) for students with exceptionalities. School counselors need to be aware of federal guidelines that apply. Henderson (2001) has compiled a helpful overview of the Individuals with Disabilities Education Act and Section 504 of the Rehabilitation Act of 1973. These federal laws provide educators with specifics about the eligibility for services, responsibilities, funding, due process, and evaluation/placement procedures.

CODE COMPARISONS

Kaczmarek (2000) discussed ethical and legal complexities in working with minors. She lists references to minors in the ethical codes of the American Psychological Association, the American Association for Marriage and Family Therapy, the American Counseling Association, and the American School Counselor Association. Her review highlights three issues: (1) Counselors need to have professional competence to work with children and adolescents and must demonstrate their knowledge of age-related differences that influence the counseling process. (2) The challenges of confidentiality and the boundaries need to be established with the counselee, parent, and counselor. (3) Informed consent is of the utmost importance. The significance of the three concerns—competence, confidentiality, and informed consent—is evident by their presence in all of the listed ethical codes.

School counselors should abide by the codes of ethics of the American Counseling Association, the National Board of Certified Counselors, the National Peer Helpers Association, the Association for Specialists in Group Work, and the more specific Ethical Standards for School Counselors. The mechanisms for aspirational and mandatory enforcements of ethical standards are described in Chapter 1. Counselors are subject only to the enforcement of the ethical codes of those organizations of which they are members or of those credentials they hold, even though they should aspire to the ethical standards endorsed by these organizations. The Ethical Standards for School Counselors differ from the others by clearly delineating specific responsibilities of school counselors to students, parents, colleagues and professional associations, schools and communities, self, and the profession. These responsibilities derive from four basic tenets of the counseling process:

- Each person has the right to receive respect and dignity as a unique human being and to counseling services without prejudice as to person, character, belief, or practice.
- Each person has the right to self-direction and self-development.
- Each person has the right of choice and the responsibility for decisions reached.
- Each person has the right to privacy and, thereby, the right to expect the counselor-client relationship to comply with all laws, policies, and ethical standards pertaining to confidentiality (ASCA, 1998).

The specificity of the standards can assist counselors in two important ways: (1) School counselors can prepare themselves to be ethical practitioners. For example, school counselors who inform parents of the counselor role and emphasize the nature of the confidential relationship between the counselor and the student guard the confidentiality of the student while according parents the same privilege. (2) School counselors can educate individuals who have no knowledge

about guidelines by providing a reference document. Members of a school board, principals, parent organizations, and others directly involved with schools will benefit by reading the guidelines provided by a national professional organization.

ISSUES OF DIVERSITY

ASCA's (1999e) position statement on cross/multicultural counseling encourages school counselors to work within the school setting to increase sensitivity of students, parents, and staff to cultural diversity and to increase awareness of culturally diverse populations. School counselors should also consult with school personnel to identify barriers in attitudes and policies that may inhibit students' learning process. ASCA suggests that counselors use strategies, activities, and resources in schools, through community outreach, and within the school districts. Counselors should be advocates for sexual harassment victims in schools (McFarland & Dupuis, 2001; Stone, 2000), not only providing a safe place for victims but also working with school officials to adopt a plan of action to eliminate the harassment.

CHAPTER SUMMARY

School counselors make significant contributions to the educational and personal development of students (Borders & Drury, 1992; Whiston & Sexton, 1998). However, while implementing a counseling program, school counselors may encounter multiple dilemmas in providing services to students, parents, and teachers. The ethical standards of the American School Counselor Association outline the responsibilities of counselors to the groups with whom they work. Counselors must know the guidelines and the local, state, and federal laws and procedures; seek consultation; and stay informed of changes to make decisions ethically. By being fully informed, counselors will be prepared in situations that demand careful judgment to protect the best interest of the child.

REFERENCES

American Counseling Association. (1998). *Professional counselor's guide to federal law on student records.* Alexandria, VA: Author.

American School Counselor Association (ASCA). (1997). *ASCA Position Statement: The professional school counselor and comprehensive school counseling* *programs* (Rev. ed.). Alexandria, VA: Author.

American School Counselor Association (ASCA). (1998). *Ethical standards for school counselors* (Rev. ed.). Alexandria, VA: Author.

American School Counselor Association (ASCA). (1999a). *ASCA position statement: The professional school counselor and acquired immune deficiency syndrome (AIDS)* (Rev. ed.). Alexandria, VA: Author.

American School Counselor Association (ASCA). (1999b). *ASCA position statement: The professional school counselor and censorship* (Rev. ed.). Alexandria, VA: Author.

American School Counselor Association (ASCA). (1999c). *ASCA position statement: The professional school counselor and child abuse and neglect prevention* (Rev. ed.). Alexandria, VA: Author.

American School Counselor Association (ASCA). (1999d). *ASCA position statement: The professional school counselor and confidentiality* (Rev. ed.). Alexandria, VA: Author.

American School Counselor Association (ASCA). (1999e). *ASCA position statement: The professional school counselor and cross/multicultural counseling* (Rev. ed.). Alexandria, VA: Author.

American School Counselor Association (ASCA). (1999f). *ASCA position statement: The professional school counselor and parent consent for services.* Alexandria, VA: Author.

American School Counselor Association (ASCA). (1999g). *ASCA position statement: The professional school counselor and peer helping* (Rev. ed.). Alexandria, VA: Author.

American School Counselor Association (ASCA). (1999h). *The role of the professional school counselor.* Alexandria, VA: Author.

American School Counselor Association (ASCA). (2000). *ASCA position statement: The professional school counselor and student safety on the Internet.* Alexandria, VA: Author.

Association for Specialists in Group Work. (1989). *Ethical guidelines for group counselors.* Alexandria, VA: Author.

Borders, L., & Drury, S. (1992). Comprehensive school counseling programs: A review for policy makers and practitioners. *Journal of Counseling and Development, 70,* 487–498.

Campbell, C., & Dahir, C. (1997). *Sharing the vision: The national standards for school counseling programs.* Alexandria, VA: American School Counselor Association.

Carroll, M. A., Schneider, H. G., & Wesley, G. R. (1985). *Ethics in the practice of psychology.* Upper Saddle River, NJ: Prentice-Hall.

Childers, J. H., Jr. (1988). The counselor's use of microcomputers: Problems and ethical issues. In W. C. Huey & T. P. Remley, Jr. (Eds.), *Ethical and legal issues in school counseling* (pp. 262–270). Alexandria, VA: American School Counselor Association.

Coll, K. M. (1995). Legal challenges in secondary prevention programming for students with substance abuse problems. *The School Counselor, 43,* 35–41.

Corey, G., Corey, M. S., & Callanan, P. (1998). *Issues and ethics in the helping professions* (5th ed.). Pacific Grove, CA: Brooks/Cole.

Corey, G., Corey, M. S., Callanan, P., & Russell, J. M. (1988). Ethical considerations in using group techniques. In W. C. Huey & T. P. Remley, Jr. (Eds.), *Ethical and legal issues in school counseling* (pp. 211–222). Alexandria, VA: American School Counselor Association.

Davis, T., & Ritchie, M. (1993). Confidentiality and the school counselor: A challenge for the 1990s. *The School Counselor, 41,* 23–30.

Ethics Committee of the American School Counselor Association (1999–2001). Ethical issues: Tips for school counselors. http://www.schoolcounselor.org/ethics/ethicaltips.htm (Retrieved 07/05/2001).

Farrell, P. (1998). *A guide to state laws and regulations on professional school counseling.* Alexandria, VA: American Counseling Association.

Fisher, C. B., & Hennessy, J. (1994). Ethical issues. In J. L. Ronch, W. Van Ornum, & N. C. Stilwel (Eds.), *The counseling sourcebook: A practical reference on contemporary issues* (pp. 175–185). New York: Crossroad.

Fischer, L., & Sorenson, G. P. (1996). *School law for counselors, psychologists, and social workers* (3rd ed.). White Plains, NY: Longman.

Freeman, S. J. (2000). *Ethics: An introduction to philosophy and practice.* Boston: Wadsworth.

Gehring, D. D. (1982). The counselor's "duty to warn." *The Personnel and Guidance Journal, 61,* 208–210.

Glosoff, H. L., Herlihy, B., & Spence, E. B. (2000). Privileged communication in the counselor-client relationship. *Journal of Counseling and Development, 78,* 454–462.

Gross, D. R., & Robinson, S. E. (1987). Ethics, violence, and counseling: Hear no evil, see no evil, speak no evil? *Journal of Counseling and Development, 65,* 340–344.

Gustafson, K. E., & McNamara, J. R. (1987). Confidentiality with minor clients: Issues and guidelines for therapists. *Professional Psychology: Research and Practice, 18,* 503–508.

Hammond, L. C., & Gantt, L. (1998). Using art in counseling: Ethical considerations. *Journal of Counseling and Development, 76,* 271–276.

Henderson, K. (2001, March). An overview of ADA, IDEA, and Section 504: Update 2001. http://ericec.org/digests/e606.html (retrieved 7/16/2001).

Herlihy, B., & Corey, G. (1992). *Dual relationships in counseling.* Alexandria, VA: American Association for Counseling and Development.

Herlihy, B., & Sheeley, V. L. (1987). Privileged communication in selected helping professions: A comparison among statutes. *Journal of Counseling and Development, 65,* 479–483.

Hobson, S. M., & Kanitz, H. M. (1996). Multicultural counseling: An ethical issue for school counselors. *The School Counselor, 43,* 245–255.

Hopkins, B. R., & Anderson, B. S. (1990). *The counselor and the law.* Alexandria, VA: American Association for Counseling and Development.

Howell-Nigrelli, J. (1988). Shared responsibility for reporting child abuse cases: A reaction to Spiegel. *Elementary School Guidance and Counseling, 22,* 289–290.

Huey, W. C. (1986). Ethical concerns in school counseling. *Journal of Counseling and Development, 64,* 321–322.

Huey, W. C. (1996). Counseling minor clients. In B. Herlihy & G. Corey (Eds.), *ACA ethical standards casebook* (5th ed.). Alexandria, VA: American Counseling Association.

Isaacs, M. L. (1997). The duty to warn and protect: *Tarasoff* and the elementary school counselor. *Elementary School Guidance and Counseling, 31* (4), 326–342.

Isaacs, M. L. (1999). School counselors and confidentiality: Factors affecting professional choices. *Professional School Counseling, 99* (2), 258–267.

Isaacs, M. L., & Stone, C. (1999). School counselors and confidentiality: Factors affecting professional choices. *Professional School Counseling, 2* (4), 258–266.

James, S. H., & DeVaney, S. B. (1995). Preparing to testify: The school counselor as court witness. *School Counselor, 43* (2), 97–103.

Kaczmarek, P. (2000). Ethical and legal complexities inherent in professional roles with child and adolescent clients. *Counseling and Human Development, 33,* 1–15.

Kaplan, D. M. (2001). Developing an informed consent brochure for secondary students. http://www.schoolcounselor.org/ethics/informed.htm (retrieved 07/05/2001).

Kaplan, L. S. (1996). Outrageous or legitimate concerns: What some parents are saying about school counseling. *The School Counselor, 43,* 165–170.

Kaplan, L. S. (1997). Parents' rights: Are school counselors at risk? *The School Counselor, 44,* 334–343.

Kitchener, K. S., & Harding, S. S. (1990). Dual role relationships. In B. Herlihy and L. Golden (Eds.), *Ethical standards casebook* (4th ed., pp. 145–148). Alexandria, VA: American Association for Counseling and Development.

Lynch, S. K. (1993). AIDS: Balancing confidentiality and the duty to protect. *Journal of College Student Development, 34,* 148–153.

McFarland, W. P., & Dupuis, M. (2001). The legal duty to protect gay and lesbian students from violence in school. *Professional School Counseling, 4* (3), 171–179.

McWhirter, J. J., McWhirter, B. T., McWhirter, A. M., & McWhirter, E. H. (1998). *At-risk youth: A comprehensive response* (2nd ed.). Pacific Grove, CA: Brooks/Cole.

Minard, S. M. (1993). The school counselor's role in confronting child sexual abuse. *The School Counselor, 41,* 9–15.

Muro, J. J., & Kottman, T. (1995). *Guidance and counseling in the elementary and middle schools: A practical approach.* Madison, WI: Brown & Benchmark.

National Peer Helpers Association. (2001). Programmatic standards. http://www.peerhelping.org/standards (retrieved 07/10/2001).

Neese, L. A. (1989). Psychological maltreatment in schools: Emerging issues for counselors. *Elementary School Guidance and Counseling, 23,* 194–200.

Paisley, P. O., & Borders, L. D. (1995). School counseling: An evolving specialty. *Journal of Counseling and Development, 74,* 150–153.

Rapin, L., & Keel, L. (1998). *Association for specialists in group work best practice guidelines.* http://asgw.educ.kent.edu/best.htm.

Remley, T. P., Jr. (1985). The law and ethical practices in elementary and middle schools. *Elementary School Guidance and Counseling, 19,* 181–189.

Remley, T. P., Jr. (1990). Counseling records: Legal and ethical issues. In B. Herlihy & L. Golden (Eds.), *AACD ethical standards casebook* (4th ed., pp. 162–169). Alexandria, VA: American Association for Counseling and Development.

Remley, T. P., Jr. (1993). What responsibilities do I have for student counseling records? *The American Counselor, 2* (4), 32–33.

Remley, T. P., Jr., & Fry, L. J. (1993). Reporting suspected child abuse: Conflicting roles for the counselor. *The School Counselor, 40,* 253–259.

Remley, T. P., Jr., & Herlihy, B. (2001). *Ethical, legal, and professional issues in counseling.* Upper Saddle River, NJ: Merrill.

Remley, T. P., Jr., Herlihy, B., & Herlihy, S. B. (1997). The U.S. Supreme Court decision in *Jaffee v. Redmond:* Implications for counselors. *Journal of Counseling and Development, 75,* 213–218.

Remley, T. P., Jr., & Sparkman, L. B. (1993). Student suicides: The counselor's limited legal liability. *The School Counselor, 40,* 164–169.

Ritchie, M. H., & Huss, S. N. (2000). Recruitment and screening of minors for group counseling. *Journal for Specialists in Group Work, 25* (2), 146–156.

Salo, M. M., & Shumate, S. G. (1993). *The ACA legal series: Vol. 4. Counseling minor clients.* Alexandria, VA: American Counseling Association.

Sampson, J. P., Jr., Kolodinski, R. W., & Greeno, B. P. (1997). Counseling on the information highway: Future possibilities and potential problems. *Journal of Counseling and Development, 75,* 203–212.

Sampson, J. P., Jr., & Pyle, K. R. (1988). Ethical issues involved with the use of computer-assisted counseling, testing, and guidance systems. In W. C. Huey and T. P. Remley, Jr. (Eds.), *Ethical and legal issues in school counseling* (pp. 249–261). Alexandria, VA: American School Counselor Association.

Sandberg, D. N., Crabbs, S. K., & Crabbs, M. A. (1988). Legal issues in child abuse: Questions and answers for counselors. *Elementary School Guidance and Counseling, 22,* 268–274.

Sealander, K. A., Schwiebert, V. L., Oren, T. A., & Weekley, J. L. (1999). Confidentiality and the law. *Professional School Counseling, 3* (2), 122–127.

Sheeley, V. L., & Herlihy, B. (1987). Privileged communication in school counseling: Status update. *The School Counselor, 34,* 268–272.

Sheeley, V. L., & Herlihy, B. (1989). Counseling suicidal teens: A duty to warn and protect. *The School Counselor, 37,* 89–97.

Stadler, H. A. (1989). Balancing ethical responsibilities: Reporting child abuse and neglect. *The Counseling Psychologist, 17,* 102–110.

Stone, C. B. (2000). Advocacy for sexual harassment victims: Legal support and ethical aspects. *Professional School Counseling 4* (1), 23–30.

Strein, W., & Hershenson, D. B. (1991). Confidentiality in nondyadic counseling situations. *Journal of Counseling and Development, 69,* 312–316.

Stromberg, C., and his colleagues in the law firm of Hogan & Harson of Washington, D.C. (1993, April). Privacy, confidentiality and privilege. *The Psychologist's Legal Update.* Washington, D.C.: National Register of Health Service Providers in Psychology. As Cited in G. Corey, M. S. Corey, & P. Callanan. (1998). *Issues and ethics in the helping professions* (5th ed.). Pacific Grove, CA: Brooks/Cole.

Talbutt, L. C. (1983a). Current legal trends regarding abortions for minors: A dilemma for counselors. *The School Counselor, 31,* 120–124.

Talbutt, L. C. (1983b). The counselor and testing: Some legal concerns. *The School Counselor, 30,* 245–250.

Taylor, L., & Adelman, H. (1989). Reframing the confidentiality dilemma to work in children's best interests. *Professional Psychology Research and Practice, 20,* 79–83.

Terres, C. K., & Larrabee, M. J. (1985). Ethical issues and group work with children. *Elementary School Guidance and Counseling, 19,* 190–197.

Thompson, C. L., & Rudolph, L. B. (2000). *Counseling children* (5th ed.). Pacific Grove, CA: Brooks/Cole.

Tompkins, L., & Mehring, T. (1993). Client privacy and the school counselor: Privilege, ethics, and employer policies. *The School Counselor, 40,* 335–342.

Varhely, S. C., & Cowles, J. (1991). Counselor self-awareness and client confidentiality: A relationship revisited. *Elementary School Guidance and Counseling, 25,* 269–276.

Waldo, S. L., & Malley, P. (1992). *Tarasoff* and its progeny: Implications for the school counselor. *The School Counselor, 40,* 46–54.

Walker, M. M., & Larrabee, M. J. (1985). Ethics and school records. *Elementary School Guidance and Counseling, 19,* 210–216.

Welfel, E. R. (1998). *Ethics in counseling and psychotherapy: Standards, research, and emerging issues.* Pacific Grove, CA: Brooks/Cole.

Whitson, S. C., & Sexton, T. L. (1998). A review of school counseling outcome research: Implications for practice. *Journal of Counseling and Development, 76,* 412–426.

Wilcoxon, S. A., & Magnuson, S. (1999). Considerations for school counselors serving noncustodial parents: Premises and suggestions. *Professional School Counseling, 2* (4), 275–280.

Zingaro, J. C. (1983). Confidentiality: To tell or not to tell. *Elementary School Guidance and Counseling, 17,* 261–267.

APPENDIX 13-A

American School Counselor Association Ethical Standards for School Counselors

PREAMBLE

The American School Counselor Association (ASCA) is a professional organization whose members have a unique and distinctive preparation, grounded in the behavioral sciences, with training in counseling skills adapted to the school setting. The school counselor assists in the growth and development of each individual and uses his/her specialized skills to ensure that the rights of the counselee are properly protected within the structure of the school program. School counselors subscribe to the following basic tenets of the counseling process from which professional responsibilities are derived:

1. Each person has the right to respect and dignity as a unique human being and to counseling services without prejudice as to person, character, belief or practice.
2. Each person has the right to self direction and self development.
3. Each person has the right of choice and the responsibility for decisions reached.
4. Each person has the right to privacy and thereby the right to expect the counselor-client relationship to comply with all laws, policies, and ethical standards pertaining to confidentiality.

In this document, the American School Counselor Association has specified the principles of ethical behavior necessary to maintain and regulate the high standards of integrity and leadership among its members. The Association recognizes the basic commitment of its members to the *Ethical Standards* of its parent organization, the American Association for Counseling and Development (AACD), and nothing in this document shall be construed to supplant that code. *The Ethical Standards for School Counselors* was developed to complement the AACD standards by clarifying the nature of ethical responsibilities for present and future counselors in the school setting. The purposes of this document are to:

1. Serve as a guide for the ethical practice of all professional school counselors regardless of level, area, population served, or membership in this Association.
2. Provide benchmarks for both self-appraisal and peer evaluations regarding counselor responsibilities to students, parents, colleagues and professional associates, school and community, self, and the counseling profession.
3. Inform those served by the school counselor of acceptable counselor practices and expected professional deportment.

Source: Reprinted from American School Counselor Association *Ethical Standards for School Counselors.* Reprinted with permission.

A. RESPONSIBILITIES TO STUDENTS

The School Counselor

1. Has a primary obligation and loyalty to the student, who is to be treated with respect as a unique individual, whether assisted individually or in a group setting.
2. Is concerned with the total needs of the student (educational, vocational, personal and social) and encourages the maximum growth and development of each counselee.
3. Informs the counselee of the purposes, goals, techniques and rules of procedure under which she/he may receive counseling assistance at or before the time when the counseling relationship is entered. Prior notice includes confidentiality issues such as the possible necessity for consulting with other professionals, privileged communication, and legal or authoritative restraints. The meaning and limits of confidentiality are clearly defined to counselees.
4. Refrains from consciously encouraging the counselee's acceptance of values, lifestyles, plans, decisions, and beliefs that represent only the counselor's personal orientation.
5. Is responsible for keeping abreast of laws relating to students and strives to ensure that the rights of students are adequately provided for and protected.
6. Avoids dual relationships which might impair his/her objectivity and/or increase the risk of harm to the client (e.g., counseling one's family members, close friends or associates). If a dual relationship is unavoidable, the counselor is responsible for taking action to eliminate or reduce the potential for harm. Such safeguards might include informed consent, consultation, supervision and documentation.
7. Makes appropriate referrals when professional assistance can no longer be adequately provided to the counselee. Appropriate referral requires knowledge of available resources.
8. Protects the confidentiality of students' records and releases personal data only according to prescribed laws and school policies. Student information maintained through electronic data storage methods is treated with the same care as traditional student records.
9. Protects the confidentiality of information received in the counseling relationship as specified by law and ethical standards. Such information is only to be revealed to others with the informed consent of the counselee and consistent with the obligations of the counselor as a professional person.

In a group setting, the counselor sets a norm of confidentiality and stresses its importance, yet clearly states that confidentiality in group counseling cannot be guaranteed.

10. Informs the appropriate authorities when the counselee's condition indicates a clear and imminent danger to the counselee or others. This is to be done after careful deliberation and, where possible, after consultation with other professionals. The counselor informs the counselee of actions to be taken so as to minimize confusion and clarify expectations.

11. Screens prospective group members and maintains an awareness of participants' compatibility throughout the life of the group, especially when the group emphasis is on self disclosure and self-understating. The counselor takes reasonable precautions to protect members from physical and/or psychological harm resulting from interaction within the group.

12. Provides explanations of the nature, purposes, and results of tests in language that is understandable to the client(s).

13. Adheres to relevant standards regarding selection, administration, and interpretation of assessment techniques. The counselor recognizes that computer-based testing programs require specific training in administration, scoring and interpretation which may differ from that required in more traditional assessments.

14. Promotes the benefits of appropriate computer applications and clarifies the limitations of computer technology. The counselor ensures that (1) computer applications are appropriate for the individual needs of the counselee, (2) the counselee understands how to use the applications, and (3) follow-up counseling assistance is provided. Members of underrepresented groups are assured of equal access to computer technologies and the absence of discriminatory information and values within computer applications.

15. Has unique ethical responsibilities in working with peer programs. In general, the school counselor is responsible for the welfare of students participating in peer programs under her/his direction. School counselors who function in training and supervisory capacities are referred to the preparation and supervision standards of professional counselor associations.

B. RESPONSIBILITIES TO PARENTS

The School Counselor

1. Respects the inherent rights and responsibilities of parents for their children and endeavors to establish a cooperative relationship with parents to facilitate the maximum development of the counselee.

2. Informs parents of the counselor's role, with emphasis on the confidential nature of the counseling relationship between the counselor and counselee.

3. Provides parents with accurate, comprehensive and relevant information in an objective and caring manner, as appropriate and consistent with ethical responsibilities to the counselee.

4. Treats information received from parents in a confidential and appropriate manner.

5. Shares information about a counselee only with those persons properly authorized to receive such information.

6. Adheres to laws and local guidelines when assisting parents experiencing family difficulties which interfere with the counselee's effectiveness and welfare.

7. Is sensitive to changes in the family and recognizes that all parents, custodial and noncustodial, are vested with certain rights and responsibilities for the welfare of their children by virtue of their position and according to law.

C. RESPONSIBILITIES TO COLLEAGUES AND PROFESSIONAL ASSOCIATES

The School Counselor

1. Establishes and maintains a cooperative relationship with faculty, staff and administration to facilitate the provision of optimal guidance and counseling programs and services.

2. Promotes awareness and adherence to appropriate guidelines regarding confidentiality, the distinction between public and private information and staff consultation.

3. Treats colleagues with respect, courtesy, fairness and good faith. The qualifications, views and findings of colleagues are represented accurately and fairly to enhance the image of competent professionals.

4. Provides professional personnel with accurate, objective, concise and meaningful data necessary to adequately evaluate counsel and assist the counselee.

5. Is aware of and fully utilizes related professions and organizations to whom the counselee may be referred.

D. RESPONSIBILITIES TO THE SCHOOL AND COMMUNITY

The School Counselor

1. Supports and protects the educational program against any infringement not in the best interest of students.

2. Informs appropriate officials of conditions that may be potentially disruptive or damaging to the school's mission, personnel and property.

3. Delineates and promotes the counselor's role and function in meeting the needs of those served. The counselor will notify appropriate school officials of conditions

which may limit or curtail their effectiveness in providing programs and services.

4. Assists in the development of: (1) curricular and environmental conditions appropriate for the school and community, (2) educational procedures and programs to meet student needs, and (3) a systematic evaluation process for guidance and counseling programs, services and personnel. The counselor is guided by findings of the evaluation data in planning programs and services.

5. Actively cooperates and collaborates with agencies, organizations, and individuals in the school and community in the best interest of counselees and without regard to personal regard or remuneration.

E. RESPONSIBILITIES TO SELF

The School Counselor

1. Functions within the boundaries of individual professional competence and accepts responsibility for the consequences of his/her actions.

2. Is aware of the potential effects of her/his own personal characteristics on services to clients.

3. Monitors personal functioning and effectiveness and refrains from any activity likely to lead to inadequate professional services or harm to a client.

4. Recognizes that differences in clients relating to age, gender, race, religion, sexual orientation, socioeconomic and ethnic backgrounds may require specific training to ensure competent services.

5. Strives through personal initiative to maintain professional competence and keeps abreast of innovations and trends in the profession. Professional and personal growth is continuous and ongoing throughout the counselor's career.

F. RESPONSIBILITIES TO THE PROFESSION

The School Counselor

1. Conducts herself/himself in such a manner as to bring credit to self and the profession.

2. Conducts appropriate research and reports findings in a manner consistent with acceptable educational and psychological research practices. When using client data for research, statistical or program planning purposes, the counselor ensures protections of the identity of the individual client(s).

3. Actively participates in local, state and national associations which foster the development and improvement of school counseling.

4. Adheres to ethical standards of the profession, other official policy statements pertaining to counseling, and relevant statutes established by federal, state and local governments.

5. Clearly distinguishes between statements and actions made as a private individual and as a representative of the school counseling profession.

6. Contributes to the development of the profession through the sharing of skills, ideas and expertise with colleagues.

G. MAINTENANCE OF STANDARDS

Ethical behavior among professional school counselors, association members and nonmembers, is expected at all times. When there exists serious doubt as to the ethical behavior of colleagues, or if counselors are forced to work in situations or abide by policies which do not reflect the standards as outlined in these *Ethical Standards for School Counselors or the AACD Ethical Standards,* the counselor is obligated to take appropriate action to rectify the condition. The following procedure may serve as a guide.

1. If feasible, the counselor should consult with a professional colleague to confidentially discuss the nature of the complaint to see if she/he views the situation as an ethical violation.

2. Whenever possible, the counselor should directly approach the colleague whose behavior is in question to discuss the complaint and seek resolution.

3. If resolution is not forthcoming at the personal level, the counselor shall utilize the channels established within the school and/or school district. This may include both informal and formal procedures.

4. If the matter still remains unresolved, referral for review and appropriate action should be made to the Ethics Committees in the following sequence:

   • local counselor association
   • state counselor association
   • national counselor association

5. The ASCA Ethics Committee functions in an educative and consultative capacity and does not adjudicate complaints of ethical misconduct. Therefore, at the national level, complaints should be submitted in writing to the AACD Ethics Committee for review and appropriate action. The procedure for submitting complaints may be obtained by writing the AACD Ethics Committee, c/o The Executive Director, American Association for Counseling and Development, 5999 Stevenson Avenue, Alexandria, VA 22304.

H. RESOURCES

School counselors are responsible for being aware of, and acting in accord with, the standards and positions of the counseling profession as represented in official documents such as those listed below.

Code of Ethics (1989). National Board for Certified Counselors. Alexandria, VA

Code of Ethics for Peer Helping Professionals (1989). National Peer Helpers Association. Glendale, CA

Ethical Guidelines for Group Counselors (1989). Association for Specialists in Group Work. Alexandria, VA

Ethical Standards (1988). American Association for Counseling and Development. Alexandria, VA

Position Statement: The School Counselor and Confidentiality (1986). American School Counselor Association. Alexandria, VA

Position Statement: The School Counselor and Peer Facilitation (1984). American School Counselor Association. Alexandria, VA

Position Statement: The School Counselor and Student Rights (1982). American School Counselor Association. Alexandria, VA

Ethical Standards for School Counselors was adopted by the ASCA Delegate Assembly, March 19, 1984. This revision was approved by the ASCA Delegate Assembly, March 27, 1992.

APPENDIX 13-B

Family Educational Rights and Privacy Act of 1974 (FERPA)
Public Law 93-380

Sec. 513.(a) Part C of the General Education Provisions Act is further amended by adding at the end thereof the following new section:

PROTECTION OF THE RIGHTS AND PRIVACY OF PARENTS AND STUDENTS

Sec. 438.(a)(1) No funds shall be made available under any applicable program to any State or local educational agency, any institution of higher education, any community college, any school, any agency offering a preschool program, or any other educational institution which has a policy of denying, or which effectively prevents, the parents of students attending any school of such agency, or attending such institution of higher education, community college, school, preschool, or other educational institution, the right to inspect and review any and all official records, files, and data directly related to their children, including all material that is incorporated into each student's cumulative record folder, and intended for school use or to be available to parties outside the school or school system, and specifically including, but not necessarily limited to identifying data, academic work completed, level of achievement (grades, standardized achievement test scores), attendance data, scores on standardized intelligence, aptitude, and psychological tests, interest inventory results, health data, family background information, teacher or counselor ratings of serious or recurrent behavior patterns. Where such records or data include information on more than one student, the parents of any student shall be entitled to receive, or be informed of, that part of such record or data as pertains to their child. Each recipient shall establish appropriate procedures for the granting of a request by parents for access to their child's school records within a reasonable period of time, but in no case more than forty-five days after the request has been made.

(2) Parents shall have an opportunity for a hearing to challenge the content of their child's school records, to insure that the records are not inaccurate, misleading, or otherwise in violation of the privacy or other rights of students, and to provide an opportunity for the correction or deletion of any such inaccurate, misleading, or otherwise inappropriate data contained therein.

(b)(1) No funds shall be made available under any applicable program to any State or local educational agency, any institution of higher education, any community college, any school, any agency offering a preschool program, or any other educational institution which has a policy of permitting the release of personally identifiable records or files (or personal information contained therein) of students without the written consent of their parents to any individual, agency, or organization, other than to the following—

(A) other school officials, including teachers within the educational institution or local educational agency who have legitimate educational interests;

(B) officials of other schools or school systems in which the student intends to enroll, upon condition that the student's parents be notified of the transfer, receive a copy of the record if desired, and have an opportunity for a hearing to challenge the content of the record;

(C) authorized representatives of (i) the Comptroller General of the United States, (ii) the Secretary, (iii) an administrative head of an educational agency (as defined in section 409 of this Act), or (iv) State educational authorities, under the conditions set forth in paragraph (3) of this subsection; and

(D) in connection with a student's application for, or receipt of, financial aid.

(2) No funds shall be made available under any applicable program to any State or local educational agency, any institution of higher education, any community college, any school, agency offering a preschool program, or any other educational institution which has a policy of practice of furnishing, in any form, any personally identifiable information, contained in personal school records, to any persons other than those listed in subsection (b)(1) unless—

(A) there is written consent from the student's parents specifying records to be released, the reasons for such release, and to whom, and with a copy of the records to be released to the student's parents and the student if desired by the parents, or

(B) such information is furnished in compliance with judicial order, or pursuant to any lawfully issued subpoena, upon condition that parents and the student are notified of all such orders or subpoenas in advance of the compliance therewith by the educational institution or agency:

(3) Nothing contained in this section shall preclude authorized representatives of (A) the Comptroller General of the United States, (B) the Secretary, (C) an administrative head of an educational agency or (D) State educational authorities from having access to student or other records which may be necessary in connection with the audit and evaluation of Federally-supported education programs, or in connection with the enforcement of the Federal legal requirements which relate to such programs: *Provided* that, except when collection of personally identifiable data is specifically authorized by Federal law, any data collected by such officials with respect to individual students shall not include information (including social security numbers) which would permit the personal identification of such students or their parents after the data so obtained has been collected.

(4)(A) With respect to subsections (c)(1) and (c)(2) and (c)(3), all persons, agencies, or organizations desiring access to the records of a student shall be required to sign a written form which shall be kept permanently with the file of the student, but only for inspection by the parents or student, indicating specifically the legitimate educational or other interest that each person, agency, or organization has in seeking this information. Such form shall be available to parents and to the school official responsible for record maintenance as a means of auditing the operation of the system.

(B) With respect to this subsection, personal information shall only be transferred to a third party on the condition that such party will not permit any other party to have access to such information without the written consent of the parents of the student.

(C) The Secretary shall adopt appropriate regulations to protect the rights of privacy of students and their families in connection with any surveys or data-gathering activities conducted, assisted, or authorized by the Secretary or an administrative head of an education agency. Regulations established under this subsection shall include provisions controlling the use, dissemination, and protection of such data. No survey or data-gathering activities shall be conducted by the Secretary, or an administrative head of an education agency under an applicable program, unless such activities are authorized by law.

(D) For the purpose of this section, whenever a student has attained eighteen years of age, or is attending an institution of postsecondary education the permission or consent required of and the rights accorded to the parents of the student shall thereafter be required of and accorded to the student.

(E) No funds shall be made available under any applicable program unless the recipient of such funds informs the parents of students, or the students, if they are eighteen years of age or older, or are attending an institution of postsecondary education, of the rights accorded them by this section.

(F) The Secretary, or an administrative head of an education agency, shall take appropriate actions to enforce provisions of this section and to deal with violations of this section, according to the provisions of this Act, except that action to terminate assistance may be taken only if the Secretary finds that there has been a failure to comply with the provisions of this section, and he has determined that compliance cannot be secured by voluntary means.

(G) The Secretary shall establish or designate an office and review board within the Department of Health, Education, and Welfare for the purpose of investigating, processing, reviewing, and adjusting violations of the provisions of this section and complaints which may be filed concerning alleged violations of this section, according to the procedures contained in sections 434 and 437 of this Act.

(b)(1)(i) The provisions of this section shall become effective ninety days after the date of enactment of section 438 of the General Education Provisions Act.

(2)(i) This section may be cited as the "Family Educational Rights and Privacy Act of 1974."

PROTECTION OF PUPIL RIGHTS

Sec. 514.(a) Part C of the General Education Provisions Act is further amended by adding after section 438 the following new section:

Protection of Pupil Rights

Sec. 439. All instructional material, including teacher's manuals, films, tapes, or other supplementary instructional material which will be used in connection with any research or experimentation program or project shall be available for inspection by the parents or guardians of the children engaged in such program or project. For the purpose of this section "research or experimentation program or project" means any program or project in any applicable program designed to explore or develop new or unproven teaching methods or techniques.

(b) The amendment made by subsection (a) shall be effective upon enactment of this Act.

CHAPTER 14

Mental Health Counseling and Assessment

Objectives

■ ■ ■ ■ ■ ■ ■ ■ ■ ■ ■

After reading this chapter, you should be able to:

- Define the specialty of mental health counseling.
- Differentiate the roles and functions of practitioners of mental health counseling from those of practitioners of other counseling specialties.
- Explain the political issues of importance to mental health counselors.
- Discuss the ethical issues specific to the practice of mental health counseling.
- Outline professional credentialing and licensure matters.
- Review the assessment issues related to mental health counseling.

■ ■ ■ ■ ■ ■ ■ ■ ■ ■

INTRODUCTION

Mental health counseling, once a fledgling specialty struggling to develop an identity, has become a dominating force in defining how the overall profession of counseling presents itself in the mental health service arena. Mental health counseling is to counseling what clinical psychology has become to psychology. As a specialty, mental health counseling has begun to flex its own muscles politically, separate from the larger, more inclusive field of counseling. The political activity of counselors affiliated with specialty interests has its good and bad points. For example, it can be argued that mental health counseling is the "tail" that is wagging the larger profession of counseling "dog," meaning the larger profession has begun to follow the specialty's lead, perhaps reluctantly. Mental health counselors, as represented by the American Mental Health Counseling Association (AMHCA), have organized to the extent they are making demands on the organization that represents counseling as a whole—the ACA. In 1996, there was even a concerted effort by a constituency of AMHCA to disaffiliate from the ACA. At that point, the ACA Governing Council voted to revoke the AMHCA charter (affiliation) if AMHCA failed to comply with ACA by-laws (Governing Council, 1996). Later, under a major reorganization of the ACA, AMHCA, along with a number of other ACA affiliates (including the American Rehabilitation Counseling Association and the American School Counseling Association) was allowed to solicit freestanding members (members not affiliated with the

ACA) and to establish its own governing administration separate from the ACA. The ACA reorganization was a political move to appease certain counseling specialties (with specific political and economic agendas) without jeopardizing the overarching allegiance to the counseling profession as a whole. Although AMHCA members need not be ACA members, they may choose to be members of the ACA as part and parcel of their AMHCA affiliation. ACA members, through ACA channels, may choose to affiliate with and pay dues to AMHCA. These members maintain ACA organizational affiliation, but at the cost of a separate administrative and membership arrangement. This also allows AMHCA to speak for itself on matters of legislation and lobbying.

Beyond influencing the larger profession of counseling, mental health counselors also influence mental health services nationally through efforts to ensure that mental health counselors and their services are available to individuals served by government and private health service providers. Mental health counselors, both through AMHCA and the ACA, have become outspoken advocates for the benefits of counseling; both groups have lobbied for the inclusion of counseling in laws that oversee health service provision. For example, the AMHCA Public Policy and Legislation Committee published its 2000–2001 federal legislative agenda and listed the following issues: (a) gain Medicare reimbursement for mental health counselors; (b) eliminate discriminatory physician referral and supervision requirements under CHAMPUS/TRICARE (two military medical insurance programs); (c) ensure that mental health counselors are reimbursed by plans participating in the Federal Employee Health Benefits Program; (d) support legislation protecting patient rights regarding access to treatment and confidentiality; and (e) support legislation to name mental health counselors as independent providers in military family service centers.

At about the same time that mental health counseling spread its wings and took flight, it encountered the "wind shear" of managed care. With the growth of managed care, mental health counselors, like other (competing) mental health professionals, are challenged to provide services under the scrutiny of a managing agency. This is a significant change from the days when mental health professionals just billed their standard fee to an insurance program (for reimbursement that was almost guaranteed). Today, mental health professionals must be on a managed care company's provider list (meeting the company's standards) before most insurance payments are allowed, and re-

ferrals are often made through a "case manager." The case manager defines the number of sessions of psychotherapy to be provided within the financial constraints of the managed care contract. A **managed care contract** is an agreement between the managed care company and the provider of counseling services (usually a counselor in independent practice or an agency providing counseling services). The contract usually defines the type of services that can be provided, the amount of money to be paid for provided services, and other limitations of services. Counselors must agree to abide by the managed care company's contract or they risk being left off the panel and not receiving referrals. If a client self-refers and the counselor is not on the managed care panel overseeing the client's benefits, no services are reimbursed by the insurer. Because it has become competitive to be accepted by a managed care company as a provider, the fees for services under managed care are often less than those traditionally billed for services to insurance companies or to individuals paying on their own. In effect, managed care has changed the rules of reimbursement for health services.

Regardless, mental health counseling may be well positioned to take a leading role in the mental health enterprise of the future, even with managed care. With managed care's overarching goal of cost containment, the services of master's-degree-trained mental health counselors may be preferable (by cost) to services provided by more expensive doctoral-trained mental health practitioners (e.g., psychologists and psychiatrists). However, as with any service oversight mechanism, there will be limits as to the nature and extent of services to be provided.

DEFINING THE SPECIALTY, SETTING, AND CLIENTS

Mental health counselors usually work in clinical settings (state, private, or nonprofit clinics, hospitals, and other health service agencies) and in private practice. In the early years of AMHCA, the membership was employed primarily in community mental health centers; however, by the mid 1980s there was a shift to private practice as the predominant employment setting (Hershenson & Power, 1987). Mental health counselors and rehabilitation counselors who specialize in psychiatric rehabilitation also are hired by managed care companies to be case managers, overseeing services provided by their colleagues in the field.

Box 14.1   Exploring the Codes

What section of the American Mental Health Counseling Association (AMHCA, 2000) Code of Ethics (see Appendix 14-A) addresses the use of tests in assessment of clients?

According to the AMHCA ethics code, can a counselor terminate services to a client for nonpayment of fees? What actions should be taken to ensure there is no abandonment of clients in this circumstance?

What should a mental health counselor do if his or her client is being treated by another mental health professional, according to the AMHCA ethics code?

Does the Responsibility of Users of Standardized Tests, RUST (American Counseling Association, 1989) (see Appendix 14-B) address adequately issues of test selection, especially related to reliability, validity, applicability, and norming?

Mental health counselors primarily assess and treat individuals with mental disorders, with an emphasis on promoting healthy development and on coping rather than on "cure" (Hershenson & Power, 1987). Most services are provided to individuals who meet criteria for a diagnosis or diagnoses according to the *Diagnostic and Statistical Manual of Mental Disorders, Fourth Edition (DSM-IV),* published by the American Psychiatric Association (1994). The *DSM-IV* provides a detailed listing of mental disorders classified by larger groupings of disorders, such as mood disorders, anxiety disorders, and schizophrenia and other psychotic disorders. In addition, each disorder is described by its characteristic behaviors, and behavior-specific criteria are listed for a diagnosis to be met. Statistical data are provided on the prevalence of disorders, along with a complete description of associated features, cultural- and age-related factors, the course of the disorder, and predisposing factors. Guidance also is provided for **differential diagnosis,** the process wherein one disorder is considered over another disorder with similar diagnostic signs, symptoms, or course. Mental health counseling is considered the specialty of counseling most suited, by educational and supervised training standards, to serve individuals with mental disorders. However, there is a subtle distinction related to the definition of mental health counseling compared with other "clinical" mental health professions (e.g., clinical psychology; clinical social work). Hershenson and Power (1987) stated:

As its name implies, mental health counseling does not seek to cure illness (implicit in the terms *psychiatric* and *clinical* in the names of … most of the other mental health fields), but rather seeks to promote healthy development and coping. It works with both the client and the environment, building on existing strengths wherever possible and using scientifically evaluated methods. (p. 5)

The focus of treatment in the mental health specialty is the developing individual with the mental disorder, not the mental disorder itself. According to Hershenson and Power (1987), the role of the mental health counselor includes (a) prevention of problems, (b) facilitation of healthy growth, (c) remediation of maladaption, (d) rehabilitation, and (e) enhancing and improving the quality of life.

The issues of diagnosis and treatment of mental disorders have been controversial for the field of counseling as a whole. However, in general, the role of the professional counselor is being expanded to include diagnosis and treatment of mental disorders. Leaders in the field are beginning to recognize the necessity of clearly defining diagnosis and treatment as part of the role and function of the professional counselor. In a monograph on "The Role and Function of the Professional Counselor in the 21st Century," Altekruse, Harris, and Brandt (2000) stated:

The role of the professionally competent counselor of the 21st century is proposed to be a continued focus on the preventative/developmental model with an added emphasis on diagnosis and treatment strategies. The professionally competent counselor of the future needs the knowledge and skills to work with clients in their respected developmental stages and to provide strategies and approaches that help prevent mental illness. This counselor has the ability and skills to diagnose and treat. (p. 25)

The reality of practice in mental health counseling is such that counselors need to be able to view the client from a developmental, nondiagnostic standpoint (focusing on building strengths) while functioning within a system that supports the diagnosis and treatment of individuals according to psychiatric standards (e.g., the *DSM-IV*). Adequate training of mental health counselors in the practices of diagnosis and treatment is necessary (Altekruse & Sexton, 1995).

To a large degree, the types of clients encountered by the mental health counselor vary by setting. For example, a counselor working in a state, county, or city acute care facility will probably be faced with seriously disturbed individuals who lack resources to obtain medical benefits coverage through private insurers. On the other hand, a counselor working in a private clinic in a rich community primarily may treat clients with adjustment concerns to everyday living situations. However, mental health counselors must be prepared to serve the full range of mental disorders and to deal with situations involving serious psychopathology. Clients may suffer from mild symptoms of anxiety or depression, or they may be severely disabled by a mental condition such as chronic schizophrenia.

Assessment or diagnostic procedures may be undertaken to provide a clear evaluation of the individual's concerns and the effect of the mental disorder on the individual's daily activities. **Assessment** is the process of evaluating a client against a normative standard—a set of criteria for classification—in diagnosis, planning, or treatment. Along this line, mental health counselors may assess clients through a diagnostic interview, which typically involves a detailed history of the individual's symptoms, stressors, and family background. Additionally, a mental status examination may be performed. A **mental status examination** is a structured interview designed to provide a controlled, interpersonal setting for the emergence and observation of symptoms and signs of mental disorders (Cottone, 1992). Treatment usually involves individual psychotherapy, but mental health counselors may also be involved in group treatment. They may choose to specialize further, by focusing on children, adolescents, or adults. They may specialize in working with clients who have one mental disorder (e.g., panic disorder) or one type of mental disorder (e.g., anxiety disorders). Treatment may vary according to the disorder. Regardless, in contrast to psychiatry or clinical psychology, the mental health counselor's emphasis should be on building strengths, facilitating healthy growth, preventing future problems, and rehabilitating the client.

Mental health counselors often work side-by-side with other mental health professionals in their settings. For example, in a hospital setting, a psychiatrist and social worker may often be assigned to a client, and treatment may follow the dictates of a team decision. Most typically, mental health counselors work with psychiatric nurses, social workers, rehabilitation counselors, psychologists, and psychiatrists. The professional who leads in team decision-making is often defined by the rules of the employing organization. Regardless, the mental health counselor works primarily from an "asset-oriented" model rather than from an "illness-oriented" model (Hershenson & Power, 1987), focusing on building the strengths of the individual rather than simply ameliorating symptoms or deficiencies.

At present, AMHCA is the organization that best represents the interests of the mental health counselor. Since its inception, it has been an advocate for the specialty and has facilitated the development of specialty designation through the National Board of Certified Counselors (NBCC). Currently, NBCC offers a specialty designation in mental health counseling. To be certified, NBCC requires that the candidate must meet the general requirements for certification as a National Certified Counselor (NCC), which is a generic credential. In addition, candidates for the Clinical Mental Health Counselor certificate must complete 60 semester hours of graduate training (the NCC requires only an acceptable master's degree, but does not specify a number of semester hours). Graduate courses are required in areas such as theories of counseling, psychopathology or abnormal psychology, ethics, social and cultural foundations, and group counseling. Three thousand hours of post-master's-supervised experience is required under a supervisor acceptable to the board. In effect, the standards for the Clinical Mental Health Counselor certificate are among the highest in the counseling profession.

As with all members of the ACA, mental health counselors are directed by the ACA's Responsibilities of Users of Standardized Tests (RUST), originally drafted in 1978 but revised in 1987 in cooperation with the Association for Assessment in Counseling, an affiliate of the ACA. The RUST spells out specific guidelines of test use decisions, the qualification requirements for those who administer tests, test selection, test administration, scoring, and interpretation. Guidance is also given for communicating test results. The AMHCA Code of Ethics also give detailed guidance on test selection, administration, and interpretation.

Box 14.2　Questions for Reflection

What is the best way to ensure that licensed professional counselors are well-prepared, competitive, competent, and ethical mental health practitioners? Should graduate program admissions standards be strict? Is it better to have graduated from a program that requires more graduate semester credit hours? Is more supervision during or after graduate training necessary? Should degree programs require stringent entrance or exit examinations? Should licensure standards remain the same or be modified in some way? Consider licensure requirements in your state or a state that is geographically near your state. How do these standards compare to those of other mental health professions? Are the requirements adequate to ensure the health and safety of clients with serious mental disorders who are treated by licensed professional counselors?

ISSUES OF SIGNIFICANCE TO THE SPECIALTY

Professional Differentiation

Mental health counseling has identified itself as the "health" specialty of counseling specialties. Although other specialties in counseling also are involved with medical concerns (e.g., rehabilitation counseling), mental health counseling focuses on the provision of services to prevent and to facilitate healthy development and growth of individuals diagnosed with mental disorders. Mental health counselors focus on building the strengths of people with problems; the focus is on the development of the individual beyond deficiency (Hershenson & Power, 1987). Unique ethical concerns arise due to the medical nature of the settings within which mental health counselors work and due to the nature of the work itself. Like rehabilitation counselors, mental health counselors must be prepared to work with individuals with severe disabilities in need of urgent care.

A major professional issue for the mental health counselor is the inconsistency between specialty training and training required by most states for licensure to do the full range of mental health services. The Council for Accreditation of Counseling and Related Educational Programs (CACREP), the professional accreditation body for graduate counseling programs, requires that mental health counseling programs must be 60-semester-hour degree programs. The degree program prepares graduates to sit for the specialty examination in mental health counseling—the National Clinical Mental Health Counseling Exam (NCMHCE). However, over 50 percent of the states that license counselors for independent practice require only 48 (or less) semester hours for graduate degrees (see Altekruse, 2001). The examination used by all but six

states for licensure is the more general National Counselor Examination (NCE), which does not focus on mental health specialty practice. There are major license portability (reciprocity across states) issues. Even mental health counselors who graduate from CACREP-accredited mental health counseling degree programs and pass the competitive NCMHCE may have problems getting licensed in certain states (where, for example, the NCE is required). The portability issue is a major concern for mental health counselors who are mobile or wish to be licensed by several states; it is also an important matter for the profession as a whole (Altekruse, 2001). The American Counseling Association's "Model Licensing Law" requires 60-semester-hour degree programs, which is in line with CACREP training in mental health counseling. If more states adopt the ACA model, revising their statutes to be in sync with the professional association's standards, the norm could become the 60-hour degree program.

A related issue is the presentation or advertisement of fraudulent or unaccredited degrees by mental health counselors. Because the profession is a master's-level licensure profession, and master's-level licensed counselors often compete with doctoral-trained professionals in psychology and medicine, there is the potential for presentation or advertisement of fraudulent or unaccredited doctoral degrees. This is a concern that received attention dating back to the 1980s. Dattilio (1989) stated: "What is particularly upsetting is that one of the primary choices of media focus is the mental health field, which appears to have become one of the largest victims of individuals holding 'bogus degrees' " (p. 152). Dattilio further stated: "Most of us would be shocked to see the statistics on those in education, research, and most particularly the clinical practice of counseling and psychotherapy who hold phony or questionable degrees" (p. 152). Several state licensure

---

Box 14.3   Questions for Reflection

What do you believe will happen in the area of professional credentialing in counseling? Will the 60-hour degree program requirement prevail in licensure standards? Will the more focused mental health counseling examination (the NCMHCE) become the standard examination for practice (versus the NCE)?

---

boards have established rules that licensed professional counselors may not represent their training at the doctoral-degree level unless the doctoral degree is clearly a counseling-relevant degree and is earned from an acceptably accredited college or university. Presenting a bogus or unaccredited doctoral degree as a legitimate credential may be a breach of the AMHCA Code of Ethics, Principle 13, "Public Statements," which requires "accurate" and objective representation of credentials. (See the AMHCA Code of Ethics in Appendix 14-A at the end of this chapter.)

Ethical Issues

Privacy.   Privacy issues in mental health counseling are complicated by the presence of a third paying party, usually an insurance company, sometimes through a managed care overseer or through government or other agencies that fund services. Occasionally, clients pay for counseling out of their own pockets, but not as often as in some specialties of counseling in which clients are sometimes willing to pay for services separate from medical insurance (e.g., marriage counseling). Privacy relates to the "freedom of individuals to choose for themselves the time and the circumstances under which and the extent to which their beliefs, behavior, and opinions are to be shared or withheld from others" (Spiegel, 1979, p. 251). Privacy is an ethical principle that makes private (a) the fact that a person has sought counseling, and (b) what is communicated in counseling. The client has control over how the information will be used. Privacy and confidentiality, although different concepts, are related; they both involve the right of the client regarding information or behaviors that are shared with a counselor. Whereas privacy issues relate to a constitutional right (Huber, 1994), confidentiality issues address the specific counseling context. Privacy issues extend to such areas as (a) discrete scheduling of sessions to prevent clients from encountering other clients in waiting rooms, (b) billing and administration of case records, (c) use of client information over computers or

phone lines or through testing services, and (d) other activities that do not necessarily relate to information provided in counseling sessions. Confidentiality is generally understood to deal with the content of counseling sessions. Huber (1994) stated: "These [privacy] questions are particularly important when insurance companies and other third-party payers attempt to gain access to therapy information about clients or when therapists are bound by law and/or professional codes of ethics to break confidentiality" (p. 23). Ethically sensitive counselors do their best to ensure that information about clients is considered private.

In a noteworthy recent development, the U.S. Department of Health and Human Services (DHHS) issued a major rule related to privacy of individual patient records. The rule, effective 14 April 2001, "generally gives patients the right to see their records (although not psychotherapy notes), to receive notice of how their records may be disclosed, and to have an accounting of their records that have been released to parties beyond the treating provider" ("New Patient Records Privacy Rule," 2001, p. 1). An article in the *Practitioner Update* of the American Psychological Association stated:

> Separate patient authorization is required for the release of psychotherapy notes—in addition to consent the patient gives to disclose his or her other records—to parties beyond the treating provider. Psychotherapy notes are the only type of record given heightened privacy protection under this rule. Importantly, a health plan or provider may not make treatment, payment, enrollment or eligibility for benefits conditional on a patient's authorization to release psychotherapy notes. ("New Patient Records Privacy Rule," 2001, p. 1)

All agencies that receive federal funding may not, by law, release confidential psychotherapy notes, unless there is separate signed client permission to do so. Further, the rule covers material from a private counseling session or a group, joint, or family counseling session. "'Psychotherapy notes' excludes medication prescription and monitoring, counseling session start and stop times, the modalities and frequencies of treatment furnished, results of clinical tests, and any summary of the following items: diagnosis, functional status, the treatment plan, symptoms, prognosis, and progress to date" ("New Patient Records Privacy Rule," 2001, p. 1). The new privacy rules have direct relevance to the related concept of confidentiality.

Confidentiality and Privileged Communication.
Mental health counselors, more so than any other type of counselor (except rehabilitation counselors), counsel adult clients who are not competent to make judgments about such issues as money management, treatment compliance, or privacy issues. It may be too easy for the unethical practitioner to get the permission of a mentally disturbed individual to share information with other individuals, or even to share the information in legal proceedings. One of the most prevalent traits of individuals with mental disorders listed in the *DSM-IV* is the presence of poor judgment. Clients who have limitations of judgment or ability must be given special treatment as related to the confidentiality issue because they may release information inadvertently to serve a counselor's agenda rather than their own needs. Ethical counselors ensure that every effort is made to explain fully the relevant issues so clients can make fully informed decisions.

Confidentiality is akin to an anti-gossip guarantee. Counselors must be alert to the need to keep information learned in counseling as private as legally possible. Because individuals with mental disorders often manifest behaviors that are odd or unusual, their behaviors make for interesting general conversation. At more than one social gathering, counselors have been overheard entertaining others by talking about the strange behaviors of their clients. Such behavior shows poor respect for individuals in serious personal situations and poor regard for the profession, which allows counselors the privilege of serving people in need. No matter how seriously disturbed a client's behavior may be, it is incumbent on the counselor to respect the individual and to maintain the privacy of client information.

Pietrofesa, Pietrofesa, and Pietrofesa (1990) described the mental health counselor's responsibility related to the "duty to warn" endangered parties. They stated, "It is clear that ethically and legally the mental health counselor is required to protect an identifiable victim of a client from harm" (p. 135). They provided "steps" to be taken when there is potential danger to a client. Costa and Altekruse (1994) also provided guidelines for mental health counselors when duty to warn is

an issue. Their duty-to-warn guidelines included (a) get informed consent, (b) plan ahead through consultation, (c) develop contingency plans, (d) obtain professional liability insurance, (e) be selective about clients, (f) involve the client, (g) obtain a detailed history, (h) document in writing, and (i) implement procedure to warn. Further, they provided vignettes of potential dilemmas in working with families and analyses of the circumstances according to three conditions related to duty to warn: a special relationship, a prediction of harmful conduct, and a forseeable victim. Duty-to-warn situations may arise in mental health counseling because many of the served clients experience acute symptoms of a serious nature that may affect their judgment. In cases of imminent danger, a breach of confidentiality is acceptable.

As described in Chapter 3, privileged communication relates to revelation of confidential information in legal proceedings. As with many specialties of counseling, mental health counselors may be called upon to testify at legal proceedings. It is important that mental health counselors know the laws that relate to privileged communication in their states.

The AMHCA Code of Ethics (2000) gives detailed guidance on the matter of confidentiality. The code specifically addresses 14 separate but relevant issues under the heading of confidentiality. The confidentiality "principle" (as it is defined in the AMHCA Code of Ethics) is broad and makes specific reference to such issues as taping (recording) sessions, dealing with minors, working with families, group work, and record keeping (both standard and electronic).

Informed Consent.   In a recent actual case, a young woman (diagnosed with a reading disorder, depression, and borderline intelligence), unwittingly had her children taken away when she signed a form presented to her by a family services agency caseworker. The caseworker had full knowledge of the person's limitations and inability to read and did not inform the woman of the contents of the form fully, even when the woman asked for an explanation. The children later were returned after much legal maneuvering, when it was learned that the client signed a paper she could not read and that was not thoroughly explained to her.

Mental health counselors must be sure that their clients have the capability to consent to treatment. Handelsman, Kemper, Kesson-Craig, McLain, and Johnsrud (1986) found that the readability of consent forms for therapy was difficult—equivalent to an academically oriented periodical. At this level, few clients

Box 14.4   Recognizing Signs and Taking Action in Cases of Potential Suicide

Recent statistics published by the American Association of Suicidology (AAS) document the staggering toll of suicide in the United States. In 1999, 29,199 individuals committed suicide—the equivalent of one person dying every 18 minutes due to suicide. In 1999, suicide was the 11th ranking cause of death in the U.S., and the 3rd ranking cause of death among youth (ages 15–24). Counselors need to be especially alert to the warning signs of suicide, as listed by the AAS. A person may be suicidal if he or she:

- Talks about committing suicide.
- Has trouble eating or sleeping.
- Experiences drastic changes in behavior.
- Withdraws from friends and/or social activities.
- Loses interest in hobbies, work, school, etc.
- Prepares for death by making out a will and final arrangements.
- Gives away prized possessions.
- Has attempted suicide before.
- Takes unnecessary risks.
- Has had recent severe losses.
- Is preoccupied with death and dying.
- Loses interest in personal appearance.
- Increases use of alcohol or drugs.

If someone appears to be threatening suicide, the AAS recommends that you:

- Be direct. Talk openly and matter-of-factly about suicide.
- Be willing to listen. Allow expressions of feelings. Accept the feelings.
- Be non judgmental. Don't debate whether suicide is right or wrong.
- Be available, and show interest and support.
- Don't dare him or her to commit suicide.
- Don't act shocked.
- Don't be sworn to secrecy.
- Offer hope that alternatives are available, but do not offer glib reassurance.
- Take action to remove means, such as guns or stockpiled pills.
- Get help from persons or agencies specializing in crisis intervention or suicide prevention.

Source: American Association for Suicidology, 4201 Connecticut Ave., NW (Suite 408), Washington, D.C. 20008; phone: (202) 237-2280; Web site: www.suicidology.org.

---

of even average intelligence can understand a consent document fully. Clients who are emotionally disabled may not be in a state of mind to fully comprehend their rights related to accepting or refusing treatment. Handelsman (2001) outlined general "themes" for "accurate and effective informed consent," and his work provides an excellent context for understanding the process approach to informed consent. He stated,

"Think of informed consent as a process rather than an event" (p. 6). A process view of informed consent is welcomed, especially with clients whose capability is in question.

The ACA and APA codes of ethics give guidance on this issue of informed consent. Further, the consent from a legally authorized person is sought for those who are legally incapable of giving informed consent;

yet it is a standard that the incapable person is still consulted and informed of the actions to be taken by the therapist, and that person's "assent" is still sought (**assent** implies agreement) (see the APA ethics code). The AMHCA Code of Ethics (2000) states that "In the event that a client is a minor or possesses disabilities that would prohibit informed consent, the mental health counselor acts in the client's best interest" (Principle 1J). These guidelines generally relate to individuals diagnosed as mentally retarded, organically impaired, or seriously emotionally disturbed. It also applies to individuals under adult age as defined in the legal jurisdiction of practice.

Detrimental Counselor-Client Relationships.   The AMHCA Code of Ethics (2000) specifically states under a principle titled "Welfare of the Consumer" under the subheading of "Dual Relationships": "Mental health counselors make every effort to avoid dual relationships with clients that could impair professional judgement or increase the risk of harm. Examples of such relationships may include, but are not limited to: familial, social, financial, business, or close personal relationships with the clients" (Principle 1, section F). In section G under the same principle, the code states, "Sexual relationships with clients are strictly prohibited. Mental health counselors do not counsel persons with whom they have had a previous sexual relationship" (Principle 1, section G). Sexual intimacies with former clients are banned for two years subsequent to termination of services, with professional scrutiny (for exploitation) of such relations as a qualifying factor.

The term "dual relationship" is unclear, and the term is not implicitly a negative term, as the standard implies. The AMHCA 2000 standard does not differentiate between professional and nonprofessional "dual" relationships, and they should be separated for clarity. The ban on sexual relationships with former clients for two years appears to be too short a period, and the provision for scrutiny of relationships initiated two years subsequent to treatment appears to allow for equivocation, which becomes problematic when enforcement is an issue. A five-year ban on relationships with former clients appears justified and is less equivocal. The standard gives no guidance for potentially beneficial interactions with clients outside of treatment, whereas the standards discussed in Chapter 3 provide guidance in this area.

Responsibility.   The AMHCA (2000) Code of Ethics states that the "primary responsibility of the mental health counselor is to respect the dignity and integrity of the client. Client growth and development are encouraged in ways that foster the client's interests and promote welfare" (Principle 1, Section A1).

Professional obligation should always start with the client. This is especially true for the mental health counselor, who may be working with individuals who are vulnerable to the whims of others or to agencies involved in the client's treatment. What should a mental health counselor do if a request for additional services is denied by a managed care organization, when such a denial is to the detriment of the patient or even endangers the patient or other parties? Obviously, the mental health counselor's primary obligation is to the patient. The counselor should make an effort to inform the managed care organization that actions to deny services may, in fact, endanger individuals or be to the detriment of a patient. The counselor should inform the managed care organization in an appropriate and professional manner, and, if necessary, provide and seek written documentation of correspondence with the managed care organization. It is imperative that counselors not accede to the insurance company's decisions when serious issues of client survival or welfare are imminent. If unsuccessful in appealing what may appear to be an unwise decision to discontinue treatment by an insurer (managed or not), the counselor must consider treating the client **pro bono publico**—for the public good (without a fee or for a minimal fee). Principle 1, Section M of the AMHCA (2000) Code of Ethics states: "Mental health counselors contribute to society by devoting a portion of their professional activity to services for which there is little or no financial return." Regardless, the counselor must be prepared to take the appeal to higher authorities if it is believed that a client has been treated unjustly. Mental health counselors must never confuse their primary responsibility to patients with secondary obligations to paying parties or employers.

Values.   Value issues enter into mental health counseling when counselors must make a judgment or take an action that may conflict with their personal values. What should a counselor do when confronted with a patient who confesses to repeatedly and seriously sexually abusing children? Treating such an individual may be abhorrent to the counselor, who might prefer to assist and counsel the victims of abuse. Treating abusers or perpetrators may clash with the counselor's most basic values related to children: How can a counselor view perpetrators in a way that allows for fair and competent treatment if their actions are seriously objectionable? Counselors continually must assess their personal values and make appropriate judgements about their own limitations. If counselors find that working with a particular patient or a type of patient is objectionable, they must assess whether they can serve the client competently and objectively. Obviously, referring the client to another counselor or therapist who specializes in counseling such problems is recommended. But, in some cases, for example, in sparsely populated areas without available mental health alternatives, counselors may have to make judgments to serve clients that they otherwise would refuse to treat. In such cases, counselors are obliged to inform patients of their concerns or feelings, and counseling should proceed only under the full and informed consent of the patients. Many issues may arise in counseling that produce value conflicts (see Chapter 5). In such cases, counselors must be prepared to address the concerns professionally and ethically. Some of the more common value issues that arise in mental health counseling involve (a) abuse of children or defenseless/dependent individuals, (b) pregnancy issues (e.g., abortion), (c) current, recent, or past illegal actions by a patient, (d) sexuality concerns or deviant sexual practices, and (e) alcohol or drug abuse.

Counselor Competence. Counselor competence involves (a) the quality of the provided service, and (b) the boundaries or scope of professional activity. The AMHCA Code of Ethics (AMHCA, 2000) provides a detailed section outlining the principle of "competence." High standards are to be maintained, according to the code. Principle 7 of the code, "Competence," reads as follows:

> The maintenance of high standards of professional competence is a responsibility shared by all mental health counselors in the best interests of the public and the profession. Mental health counselors recognize the boundaries of their particular competencies and the limitation of their expertise. Mental health counselors only provide those services and use only those techniques for which they are qualified by education, training or experience. Mental health counselors maintain knowledge of relevant scientific and professional information related to the services they render, and they recognize the need for on-going education. (Principle 7)

Consider the standard of "competence" in light of a recent news report by the Reuters News Service (2001) about two Colorado therapists who were convicted of "reckless child abuse resulting in death" of a 10-year-old client. The therapists were using a "rebirthing" technique to treat a "reactive attachment disorder." The client was bound in a sheet and told to fight her way out so she could be "reborn" to her adoptive mother. The Reuters (2001) article stated: "The girl begged for

air and screamed for mercy after she was bound head-to-toe in a flannel sheet during a discredited psychotherapy procedure called rebirthing." Further, the article stated, "the girl begged for air and screamed that she was dying only to have her pleas met with sarcasm from the therapists." She lost consciousness during the procedure and died the next day. The state of Colorado has now banned this sort of treatment. The two therapists were convicted and each was sentenced to 16 years in prison. Obviously, clients should not be physically endangered by a therapeutic technique. Counselors must ensure that the techniques they use have sound empirical and theoretical foundations (based on theory that has stood the test of refereed review in the best counseling journals). The procedure in the Colorado case was dangerous, and it also raises the issue of competency—was this procedure a sound technique and was application of this technique within the scope of the therapists' practice?

Use of new, untested, or controversial techniques is always unwise. It is best to delay use of untested techniques until research supports the technique. The use of "paradoxical technique" is a good example. In this procedure, the counselor directs a client to do something illogical, such as "prescribing the symptom," to produce a resistance reaction wherein the client resists being symptomatic. Sexton, Montgomery, Goff, and Nugent (1993) stated:

> The use of paradox is a complicated matter and the debate concerning its use is likely to continue. However, consideration of the ethical treatment and the legal issues associated with paradox can help guide the mental health counselor. For example, given the current status of the research, the current enthusiasm for paradoxical therapeutic procedures is not altogether justified. Although there is strong anecdotal evidence, and some controlled experimental evidence of treatment effectiveness, additional well-controlled research is needed to substantiate proponents' claims. At this time, it seems that results of empirical research most clearly support the use of paradox with sleep-onset insomnia and some anxiety disorders. The effects of paradox with other types of concerns, such as family problems, appear to be [sic] less clearly documented empirical support. Furthermore, there appears to be little knowledge of either possible inadvertent effects or of issues such as treatment acceptability. (pp. 271–272)

When counselors are put in the position of having to defend the choice of a professional technique or procedure, they are wise to have chosen techniques that are based on sound empirical grounds.

On more general issues related to the scope of professional practice, there are continual "turf battles" over the extent of services to be provided by counselors and other mental health providers. Such a battle raged in Ohio in 1996, when the state attorney general offered a legal opinion allowing licensed professional or clinical counselors to use the term *psychological* to "describe their work of testing and evaluating people for mental and emotional disorders" ("Ohio," 1996, p. 9). The opinion was opposed by the Ohio Board of Psychology and the Ohio Psychological and School Psychologist Associations. In essence, counselors, by the opinion of the leading law enforcement agency of the state, were told they could use a term that had been associated historically only with the practice of psychology. Some viewed this opinion as a major challenge to psychology in Ohio. Typically, battles over scope of practice of mental health counselors involve the issues of testing, diagnosis, and the use of the term *psychotherapy*. Counselors are required by licensure laws to practice within the limits of their defined competence and training and consistent with definitions of practice within licensure statutes.

ASSESSMENT

To a large degree, issues of assessment pervade many of the ethical issues addressed in the previous sections. However, the RUST standards (ACA, 1989) should be consulted for detailed guidelines on assessment matters. (The RUST standards are listed in Appendix 14-B at the end of this chapter). The RUST standards (section III, Qualifications of Test Users) state:

> While all professional counselors and personnel workers should have formal training in psychological and educational measurement and testing, this training does not necessarily make one an expert and even an expert does not have all the knowledge and skills appropriate to some particular situations or instruments. Questions of user qualifications should always be addressed when testing is being considered.... Lack of proper qualifications can lead to errors and subsequent harm to clients. Each professional is responsible for making judgements on this in each situation and cannot leave that responsibility either to clients or to others in authority. It is incumbent upon the individual test user to obtain appropriate training or arrange for proper supervision and assistance when engaging in testing.

The RUST qualifications for test users depend on four factors: (a) purposes of testing, (b) characteristics of tests, (c) settings and conditions of test use, and (d) roles of test selectors. The test selected should be based on the purpose of testing, the validity of instruments (how well a test measures what it purports to measure), and other technical standards related to test quality (e.g., reliability—how consistently a test measures what it purports to measure). The test should be administered in a way that will produce a valid and accurate assessment of the individual. Test scoring should be done in a standardized way against proper norms, if applicable. Interpretation should be according to guidelines in test manuals and as objective as possible. Safeguards should be taken to ensure a client's privacy and to prevent misuse of the test data.

The AMHCA (2000) Code of Ethics provides detailed guidance on "Utilization of Assessment Techniques" (Principle 4). This ethical category has been expanded in the most recent version of the AMHCA ethics code. It includes three distinct subcategories: (a) test selection, (b) test administration, and (c) test interpretation. The guidance under these categories appears to be comprehensive and consistent with RUST standards.

CODE COMPARISONS

The AMHCA (2000) Code of Ethics (see Appendix 14-A at the end of this chapter) is a vast improvement over the prior (1987) AMHCA ethics code. The prior code was less comprehensive and, at the time, was an aspirational and supplemental code (enforcement was left up to the ACA according to the enforceable ACA Code of Ethics and Standards of Practice). Unfortunately, the 2000 version of the AMHCA ethics code is also aspirational and nonenforceable, and because AMHCA members do not have to affiliate with the ACA (thereby not being bound by the mandatory and enforceable ACA ethics code), there is no professionally binding ethical standard for AMHCA members who do not affiliate with the ACA. The last "principle" of the AMHCA Code of Ethics reads: "Neither the American Mental Health Counselors Association, its Board of Directors, nor its National Committee on Ethics investigate or adjudicate ethical complaints. In the event a member has his or her license suspended or revoked by an appropriate state licensure board, the AMHCA Board of Directors may then act in accordance with AMHCA's National By-Laws to suspend or revoke his or her membership." The decision of the AMHCA Board of Directors to defer enforcement of its code to the decisions of state licensure boards and ethical codes and standards referenced in licensure statutes renders the AMHCA code of ethics impotent. The lack of enforcement by the AMHCA appears to be a negative byproduct of AMHCA administrative separation from the ACA.

Regardless, the RUST standards provide specialized guidance on issues of tests and measurement that are not addressed adequately in the ACA, AMHCA, or APA codes. Additional standards related to testing are also published by the APA, including the "Standards for Educational and Psychological Tests" and the "Code for Fair Testing Practices in Education."

ISSUES OF DIVERSITY

The issue of deviance or maladjustment is one of the most predominant multicultural issues in mental health counseling. Axelson (1993) described the "cultural model" of *maladjustment* as defining:

> A normal person as one who is in harmony with self and environment. The definition emphasizes conformity with the cultural requirements, mores, and injunctions of the community. Thus, normality tends to be equated with what is conventional and abnormality with what is viewed as antisocial conduct and/or different behavior. (p. 275)

This view of maladjustment is in contrast to the American Psychiatric Association's (1994) definition in the *Diagnostic and Statistical Manual of Mental Disorders, Fourth Edition (DSM-IV)*. The *DSM-IV* defines a mental disorder as:

> A clinically significant behavioral or psychological syndrome or pattern that occurs in an individual and that is associated with present distress (e.g., a painful symptom) or disability (e.g., impairment in one or more important areas of functioning) or with a significantly increased risk of suffering death, pain, disability, or an important loss of freedom. In addition, this syndrome or pattern must not be merely an expectable and culturally sanctioned response to a particular event, for example, the death of a loved one. Whatever its original cause, it must currently be considered a manifestation of a behavioral, psychological, or biological dysfunction in the individual. Neither deviant behavior (e.g., political, religious, or sexual) nor conflicts that are primarily between the individual and society are mental disorders unless the deviance or conflict is a symptom of a dysfunction in the individual, as described above. (pp. xxi–xxii)

The cultural definition of maladjustment takes into consideration cultural variation, whereas the *DSM-IV* definition plays down, minimizes, or subsumes cultural factors by focusing on disorders "in the individual."

For the mental health counselor working in a context that requires diagnosis of mental disorders according to *DSM-IV* criteria, cultural sensitivity may produce discomfort with standardized procedures. This occurs because the culturally sensitive counselor recognizes that mental disorders may not be equally prevalent across cultural contexts. Should inner-city ghetto inhabitants be diagnosed as "antisocial personality disorders" because they act out of the norm to survive in a difficult environment? Should bulimia or anorexia be interpreted outside of a cultural context that promotes unnaturally thin standards of body weight and attractiveness?

Issues of diversity also are predominant when objective tests are used. Because minorities are usually outnumbered in norm bases, it can be argued that tests, no matter how broadly normed, cannot reflect cultural differences accurately in the development of abilities, interests, aptitudes, or achievement. Although some tests are more culturally sensitive than others, it is imperative that test data are not interpreted out of social or cultural context.

The greatest challenge to culturally sensitive mental health counselors is to view clients in context, and to dispute labels that require an internalistic or broadly normative view of mental disorder. As Sue (1996) stated:

> If we believe that many problems reside outside the person (prejudice and discrimination) and not within (person-blame), ethical practice dictates that professionals develop alternative helping roles that are aimed at *system intervention*. The traditional counseling role has been primarily confined to a one-to-one, remediation-oriented, in-the-office form of help, but recognition that problems may reside in the social system dictates use of nontraditional roles. These roles may include adviser, advocate, consultant, change agent, facilitator of indigenous support systems, and facilitator of indigenous healing systems. Most counselor education programs do not train us in these roles, yet they are some of the most effective in multicultural helping. (p. 196)

Whether problems should be viewed as internal or external to individuals is a challenge that may best be met by the profession as a whole. Certainly, counselors should be alert to the pressure to view disorders or measured characteristics according to "clinical" standards at the expense of clients acting to survive in difficult or unusual cultural contexts. The emphasis on client assets and the development of potential that rests at the base of the mental "health" counselor's philosophy may be an asset when addressing issues of diversity.

CHAPTER SUMMARY

Mental health counseling has taken a lead in the mental health field and represents a health specialty in counseling. Through specialty certification by means of the NBCC and through development of a specialized code of ethics, mental health counselors have established themselves as a viable and identifiable specialty. Although the pressures of managed care may affect the practice of mental health counseling, the specialty may also be positioned well to interface with the managed care system. Mental health counselors may find jobs in managed care companies as case managers and service providers. Because mental health counselors, like social workers, are primarily master's-level-trained men-tal health professionals, they may suit the needs of managed care's cost containment efforts by undercut-ting the rates and salaries of doctoral-level-trained professionals (such as psychologists and psychiatrists). Mental health counseling may be situated ideally to survive the managed care movement in the mental health field. Yet, the field, which has defined itself as a "health" specialty, must also deal with the issue that mental health may be a culturally relative issue, and not just a matter of diagnosing and treating individual deviance.

There are ethical and professional issues unique to mental health practice. The professional identity of the mental health counselor is developing alongside other counseling specialties. Mental health counselors have carved a niche that positions them well to provide services to individuals with diagnosed mental disorders. The developmental model, which lies at the root of mental health counseling practice, may serve the specialty well as the mental health enterprise transitions in the 21st century.

REFERENCES

Altekruse, M. K. (2001). *Counselor portability.* Power point presentation as chair of the American Counseling Association Professionalization Committee. (Available from Dr. Altekruse at UNT, P.O. Box 311337, Denton, TX 76203-1337).

Altekruse, M. K., Harris, H. L., & Brandt, M. A. (2000). *The role of the professional counselor in the 21st century.* Unpublished manuscript.

Altekruse, M. K., & Sexton, T. L. (Eds.). (1995). *Mental health counseling in the 90's: A research report for training and practice* (1st ed.). Tampa, FL: The National Commission for Mental Health Counseling.

American Counseling Association (in cooperation with the Association for Assessment in Counseling). (1989). *Responsibilities of users of standardized tests.* Alexandria, VA: Author.

American Mental Health Counseling Association. (1987). *Code of ethics of the American Mental Health Counselors Association.* Alexandria, VA: Author.

American Mental Health Counseling Association. (2000). *AMHCA code of ethics.* Alexandria, VA: Author.

American Psychiatric Association. (1994). *Diagnostic and statistical manual of mental disorders* (4th ed.). Washington, D.C.: Author.

Axelson, J. A. (1993). *Counseling and development in a multicultural society.* Pacific Grove, CA: Brooks/Cole.

Costa, L., & Altekruse, M. (1994). Duty-to-warn guidelines for mental health counselors. *Journal of Counseling and Development, 72,* 346–350.

Cottone, R. R. (1992). *Theories and paradigms of counseling and psychotherapy.* Needham Heights, MA: Allyn & Bacon.

Dattilio, F. M. (1989). Fraudulent degrees: A threat to the mental health counseling field. *Journal of Mental Health Counseling, 11,* 151–154.

Governing Council. (1996, August). *Counseling Today,* p. 1.

Handelsman, M. M. (2001). Accurate and effective informed consent. In E. Welfel & E. Ingersoll (Eds.), *The mental health desk reference: A sourcebook for counselor and therapists.* New York: Wiley.

Handelsman, M. M., Kemper, M. B., Kesson-Craig, P., McLain, J., & Johnsrud, C. (1986). Use, content, and readability of written informed consent forms for treatment. *Professional Psychology: Research and Practice, 17,* 514–518.

Hershenson, D. B., & Power, P. W. (1987). *Mental health counseling: Theory and practice.* New York: Pergamon.

Huber, C. H. (1994). *Ethical, legal, and professional issues in the practice of mar-riage and family therapy* (2nd ed.). Upper Saddle River, NJ: Merrill/Prentice Hall.

New Patient Records Privacy Rule. (2001). New patient records privacy rule takes effect. *Practitioner Update, 9*(1), 1.

Ohio A-G legal opinion allows counselors to call testing and evaluations 'psychological.' (1996, July/August). *The National Psychologist,* p. 9.

Pietrofesa, J., Pietrofesa, C., & Pietrofesa, J. D. (1990). The mental health counselor and "duty to warn." *Journal of Mental Health Counseling, 12,* 129–137.

Reuters News Service. (2001). *Two therapists get 16 years each in death of girl.* Published in the St. Louis Post Dispatch.

Sexton, T. L., Montgomery, D., Goff, K., & Nugent, W. (1993). Ethical, therapeutic, and legal considerations in the use of paradoxical techniques: The emerging debate. *Journal of Mental Health Counseling, 15,* 260–277.

Spiegel, S. B. (1979). Separate principles for counselors of women: A new form of sexism. *The Counseling Psychologist, 8*(1), 49–50.

Sue, D. W. (1996). Ethical issues in multicultural counseling. In B. Herlihy & G. Corey (Eds.), *Ethical standards casebook* (5th ed.). Alexandria, VA: American Counseling Association.

APPENDIX 14-A

American Mental Health Counselors Association Code of Ethics

PREAMBLE

Mental health counselors believe in the dignity and worth of the individual. They are committed to increasing knowledge of human behavior and understanding of themselves and others. While pursuing these endeavors, they make every reasonable effort to protect the welfare of those who seek their services, or of any subject that may be the object of study. They use their skills only for purposes consistent with these values and do not knowingly permit their misuse by others. While demanding for themselves freedom of inquiry and community, mental health counselors accept the responsibility this freedom confers: competence, objectivity in the application of skills, and concern for the best interest of clients, colleagues, and society in general. In the pursuit of these ideals, mental health counselors subscribe to the principles listed throughout this appendix.

CLINICAL ISSUES

Principle 1. Welfare of the Consumer

A. **Primary Responsibility**

1. The primary responsibility of the mental health counselor is to respect the dignity and integrity of the client. Client growth and development are encouraged in ways that foster the client's interest and promote welfare.
2. Mental health counselors are aware of their influential position with respect to their clients, and avoid exploiting the trust and fostering dependency of their clients.
3. Mental health counselors fully inform consumers as to the purpose and nature of any evaluation, treatment, education or training procedure and they fully acknowledge that the consumer has the freedom of choice with regard to participation.

B. **Counseling Plans**

Mental health counselors and their clients work jointly in devising integrated, individual counseling plans that offer reasonable promise of success and are consistent with the abilities and circumstances of the client. Counselors and clients regularly review counseling plans to ensure their continued viability and effectiveness, respecting the client's freedom of choice.

C. **Freedom of Choice**

Mental health counselors offer clients the freedom to choose whether to enter into a counseling relationship and determine which professionals will provide the counseling. Restrictions that limit clients' choices are fully explained.

D. **Clients Served by Others**

1. If a client is receiving services from another mental health professional or counselor, the mental health counselor secures consent from the client, informs that professional of the arrangement, and develops a clear agreement to avoid confusion and conflicts for the client.
2. Mental health counselors are aware of the intimacy and responsibilities inherent in the counseling relationship. They maintain respect for the client and avoid actions that seek to meet their personal needs at the expense of the client. Mental health counselors are aware of their own values, attitudes, beliefs and behaviors, and how these apply in a diverse society. They avoid imposing their values on the consumer.

E. **Diversity**

1. Mental health counselors do not condone or engage in any discrimination based on age, color, culture, disability, ethnic group, gender, race, religion, sexual orientation, marital status or socioeconomic status.
2. Mental health counselors will actively attempt to understand the diverse cultural backgrounds of the clients with whom they work. This includes learning how the counselor's own cultural/ethical/racial/religious identity impacts his or her own values and beliefs about the counseling process. When there is a conflict between the client's goals, identity and/or values and those of the mental health counselor, a referral to an appropriate colleague must be arranged.

F. **Dual Relationships**

Mental health counselors are aware of their influential position with respect to their clients and avoid exploiting the trust and fostering dependency of the client.

1. Mental health counselors make every effort to avoid dual relationships with clients that could impair professional judgement or increase the risk of harm. Examples of such relationships may include, but are not limited to: familial, social, financial, business, or close personal relationships with the clients.
2. Mental health counselors do not accept as clients individuals with whom they are involved in an administrative, supervisory, and evaluative nature. When acting as supervisors, trainers, or employers, mental health counselors accord recipients informed choice, confidentiality and protection from physical and mental harm.
3. When a dual relationship cannot be avoided, counselors take appropriate professional precautions such as informed consent, consultation, supervision and documentation to ensure that judgement is not impaired and no exploitation has occurred.

G. **Sexual Relationships**

Sexual relationships with clients are strictly prohibited. Mental health counselors do not counsel persons with whom they have had a previous sexual relationship.

H. Former Clients

Counselors do not engage in sexual intimacies with former clients within a minimum of two years after terminating the counseling relationship. The mental health counselor has the responsibility to examine and document thoroughly that such relations did not have an exploitative nature based on factors such as duration of counseling, amount of time since counseling, termination circumstances, the client's personal history and mental status, adverse impact on the client, and actions by the counselor suggesting a plan to initiate a sexual relationship with the client after termination.

I. Multiple Clients

When mental health counselors agree to provide counseling services to two or more persons who have a relationship (such as husband and wife, or parents and children), counselors clarify at the outset which person or persons are clients, and the nature of the relationship they will have with each involved person. If it becomes apparent that counselors may be called upon to perform potentially conflicting roles, they clarify, adjust, or withdraw from roles appropriately.

J. Informed Consent

Mental health counselors are responsible for making their services readily accessible to clients in a manner that facilitates the clients' abilities to make an informed choice when selecting a provider. This responsibility includes a clear description of what the client can expect in the way of tests, reports, billing, therapeutic regime and schedules, and the use of the mental health counselor's statement of professional disclosure. In the event that a client is a minor or possesses disabilities that would prohibit informed consent, the mental health counselor acts in the client's best interest.

K. Conflict of Interest

Mental health counselors are aware of possible conflicts of interests that may involve the organization in which they are employed and their client. When conflicts occur, mental health counselors clarify the nature of the conflict and inform all parties of the nature and direction of their loyalties and responsibilities, and keep all parties informed of their commitments.

L. Fees and Bartering

1. Mental health counselors clearly explain to clients, prior to entering the counseling relationship, all financial arrangements related to professional services, including the use of collection agencies or legal measures for nonpayment.

2. In establishing fees for professional counseling services, mental health counselors consider the financial status of their clients and locality. In the event that the payment of the mental health counselor's usual fees would create undue hardship for the client, assistance is provided in attempting to find comparable services at an acceptable cost.

3. Mental health counselors ordinarily refrain from accepting goods or services from clients in return for counseling service because such arrangements create inherent potential for conflicts, exploitation and distortion of the professional relationship. Participation in bartering is only used when there is no exploitation, if the client requests it, if a clear written contract is established, and if such an arrangement is an accepted practice among professionals in the community.

M. Pro Bono Service

Mental health counselors contribute to society by devoting a portion of their professional activity to services for which there is little or no financial return.

N. Consulting

Mental health counselors may choose to consult with any other professionally competent person about a client. In choosing a consultant, the mental health counselor should avoid placing the consultant in a conflict of interest situation that would preclude the consultant from being a proper party to the mental health counselor's effort to help the client.

O. Group Work

1. Mental health counselors screen prospective group counseling/therapy participants. Every effort is made to select members whose needs and goals are compatible with goals of the group, who will not impede the group process, and whose well being will not be jeopardized by the group experience.

2. In the group setting, mental health counselors take reasonable precautions to protect clients from physical and psychological harm or trauma.

3. When the client is engaged in short term group treatment/training programs, i.e. marathons and other encounter type or growth groups, the members ensure that there is professional assistance available during and following the group experience.

P. Termination and Referral

Mental health counselors do not abandon or neglect their clients in counseling. Assistance is given in making appropriate arrangements for the continuation of treatment, when necessary, during interruptions such as vacation and following termination.

Q. Inability to Assist Clients

If the mental health counselor determines that their services are not beneficial to the client, they avoid entering or terminate immediately a counseling relationship. Mental health counselors are knowledgeable about referral sources and appropriate referrals are made. If clients decline the suggested referral, mental health counselors discontinue the relationship.

R. Appropriate Termination

Mental health counselors terminate a counseling relationship, securing a client's agreement when possible, when it is reasonably clear that the client is no longer benefiting, when services are no longer required, when counseling no longer serves the needs and interests of the client, when clients do not pay fees charged, or when agency or institution limits do not allow provision of further counseling services.

Principle 2. Clients' Rights

The following apply to all consumers of mental health services, including both in- and out-patients and all state, county, local, and private care mental health facilities, as well as clients of mental health practitioners in private practice.

The client has the right:

a. to be treated with dignity, consideration and respect at all times;
b. to expect quality service provided by concerned, trained, professional and competent staff;
c. to expect complete confidentiality within the limits of the law, and to be informed about the legal exceptions to confidentiality; and to expect that no information will be released without the client's knowledge and written consent;
d. to a clear working contract in which business items, such as time of sessions, payment plans/fees, absences, access, emergency procedures, and third-party reimbursement procedures are discussed;
e. to a clear statement of the purposes, goals, techniques, rules of procedure and limitations, as well as the potential dangers of the services to be performed, and all other information related to or likely to affect the ongoing mental health counseling relationship;
f. to appropriate information regarding the mental health counselor's education, training, skills, license and practice limitations and to request and receive referrals to other clinicians when appropriate;
g. to full, knowledgeable, and responsible participation in the ongoing treatment plan to the maximum extent feasible;
h. to obtain information about their case record and to have this information explained clearly and directly;
i. to request information and/or consultation regarding the conduct and progress of their therapy;
j. to refuse any recommended services and to be advised of the consequences of this action;
k. to a safe environment free of emotional, physical and sexual abuse;
l. to a client grievance procedure, including requests for consultation and/or mediation; and to file a complaint with the mental health counselor's supervisor, and/or the appropriate credentialing body; and
m. to a clearly defined ending process, and to discontinue therapy at any time.

Principle 3. Confidentiality

Mental health counselors have a primary obligation to safeguard information about individuals obtained in the course of practice, teaching, or research. Personal information is communicated to others only with the person's written consent or in those circumstances where there is clear and imminent danger to the client, to others or to society. Disclosure of counseling information is restricted to what is necessary, relevant and verifiable.

a. At the outset of any counseling relationship, mental health counselors make their clients aware of their rights in regard to the confidential nature of the counseling relationship. They fully disclose the limits of, or exceptions to, confidentiality, and/or the existence of privileged communication, if any.
b. All materials in the official record shall be shared with the client, who shall have the right to decide what information may be shared with anyone beyond the immediate provider of service and be informed of the implications of the materials to be shared.
c. Confidentiality belongs to the clients. They may direct the mental health counselor, in writing, to release information to others. The release of information without the consent of the client may only take place under the most extreme circumstances. The protection of life, as in the case of suicidal or homicidal clients, exceeds the requirements of confidentiality. The protection of a child, an elderly person, or a person not competent to care for themselves from physical or sexual abuse or neglect requires that a report be made to a legally constituted authority. The mental health counselor complies with all state and federal statutes concerning mandated reporting of suicidality, homicidality, child abuse, incompetent person abuse and elder abuse. The protection of the public or another individual from a contagious condition known to be fatal also requires action that may include reporting the willful infection of another with the condition.

The mental health counselor (or staff member) does not release information by request unless accompanied by a specific release of information or a valid court order. Mental health counselors will comply with the order of a court to release information but they will inform the client of the receipt of such an order. A subpoena is insufficient to release information. In such a case, the counselor must inform his client of the situation and, if the client refuses release, coordinate between the client's attorney and the requesting attorney so as to protect client confidentiality and one's own legal welfare.

In the case of all of the above exceptions to confidentiality, the mental health counselor will release only such information as is necessary to accomplish the action required by the exception.
d. The anonymity of clients served in public and other agencies is preserved, if at all possible, by withholding names and personal identifying data. If external conditions require reporting such information, the client shall be so informed.
e. Information received in confidence by one agency or person shall not be forwarded to another person or agency without the client's written permission.

f. Service providers have the responsibility to ensure the accuracy and to indicate the validity of data shared with their parties.

g. Case reports presented in classes, professional meetings, or publications shall be so disguised that no identification is possible unless the client or responsible authority has read the report and agreed in writing to its presentation or publication.

h. Counseling reports and records are maintained under conditions of security, and provisions are made for their destruction when they have outlived their usefulness. Mental health counselors ensure that all persons in his or her employ, volunteers, and community aides maintain privacy and confidentiality.

i. Mental health counselors who ask that an individual reveal personal information in the course of interviewing, testing or evaluation, or who allow such information to be divulged, do so only after making certain that the person or authorized representative is fully aware of the purposes of the interview, testing or evaluation, and of the ways in which the information will be used.

j. Sessions with clients may be taped or otherwise recorded only with their written permission or the written permission of a responsible guardian. Even with a guardian's written consent, one should not record a session against the expressed wishes of a client. Such tapes shall be destroyed when they have outlived their usefulness.

k. Where a child or adolescent is the primary client, or the client is not competent to give consent, the interests of the minor or the incompetent client shall be paramount. Where appropriate, a parent(s) or guardian(s) may be included in the counseling process. The mental health counselor must still take measures to safeguard the client's confidentiality.

l. In work with families, the rights of each family member should be safeguarded. The provider of service also has the responsibility to discuss the contents of the record with the parent and/or child, as appropriate, and to keep separate those parts, which should remain the property of each family member.

m. In work with groups, the rights of each group member should be safeguarded. The provider of service also has the responsibility to discuss the need for each member to respect the confidentiality of each other member of the group. He must also remind the group of the limits on and risk to confidentiality inherent in the group process.

n. When using a computer to store confidential information, mental health counselors take measures to control access to such information. When such information has outlived its usefulness, it should be deleted from the system.

Principle 4. Utilization of Assessment Techniques

A. Test Selection

1. In choosing a particular test, mental health counselors should ascertain that there is sufficient evidence in the test manual of its applicability in measuring a certain trait or construct. The manual should fully describe the development of the test, the rationale, and data pertaining to item selection and test construction. The manual should explicitly state the purposes and applications for which the test is intended, and provide reliability and validity data about the test. The manual should furthermore identify the qualifications necessary to properly administer and interpret the test.

2. In selecting a particular combination of tests, mental health counselors need to be able to justify the logic of those choices.

3. Mental health counselors should employ only those tests for which they judge themselves competent by training, education, or experience. In familiarizing themselves with new tests, counselors thoroughly read the manual and seek workshops, supervision, or other forms of training.

4. Mental health counselors avoid using outdated or obsolete tests, and strive to remain current regarding test publication and revision.

5. Tests selected for individual testing must be appropriate for that individual in that appropriate norms exist for variables such as age, gender, and race. The test form must fit the client. If the test must be used in the absence of available information regarding the above subsamples, the limitations of generalizability should be duly noted.

B. Test Administration

1. Mental health counselors should faithfully follow instructions for administration of a test in order to ensure standardization. Failure to consistently follow test instructions will result in test error and incorrect estimates of the trait or behavior being measured.

2. Tests should only be employed in appropriate professional settings or as recommended by instructors or supervisors for training purposes. It is best to avoid giving tests to relatives, close friends or business associates, in that doing so constructs a dual professional/personal relationship, which is to be avoided.

3. Mental health counselors should provide the test taker with appropriate information regarding the reason for assessment, the approximate length of time required, and to whom the report will be distributed. Issues of confidentiality must be addressed, and the client must be given the opportunity to ask questions of the examiner prior to beginning the procedure.

4. Care should be taken to provide an appropriate assessment environment in regard to temperature, privacy, comfort, and freedom from distractions.

5. Information should be solicited regarding any possible handicaps, such as problems with visual or auditory acuity, limitations of hand/eye coordination, illness, or other factors. If the disabilities cannot be accommodated effectively, the test may need to be postponed or the limitations of applicability of the test results noted in the test report.

6. Professionals who supervise others should ensure that their trainees have sufficient knowledge and experience before utilizing the tests for clinical purposes.

7. Mental health counselors must be able to document appropriate education, training, and experience in areas of assessment they perform.

C. Test Interpretation

1. Interpretation of test or test battery results should be based on multiple sources of convergent data and an understanding of the tests' foundations and limits.

2. Mental health counselors must be careful not to make conclusions unless empirical evidence is present to justify the statement. If such evidence is lacking, one should not make diagnostic or prognostic formulations.

3. Interpretation of test results should take into account the many qualitative influences on test-taking behavior, such as health, energy, motivation, and the like. Description and analysis of alternative explanations should be provided with the interpretations.

4. One should not make firm conclusions in the absence of published information that establishes a satisfactory degree of test validity, particularly predictive validity.

5. Multicultural factors must be considered in test interpretation and diagnosis, and formulation of prognosis and treatment recommendations.

6. Mental health counselors should avoid biased or incorrect interpretation by assuring that the test norms reference the population taking the test.

7. Mental health counselors are responsible for evaluating the quality of computer software interpretations of test data. Mental health counselors should obtain information regarding validity of computerized test interpretation before utilizing such an approach.

8. Supervisors should ensure that their supervisees have had adequate training in interpretation before entrusting them to evaluate tests in a semi-autonomous fashion.

9. Any individual or organization offering test scoring or interpretation services must be able to demonstrate that their programs are based on sufficient and appropriate research to establish the validity of the programs and procedures used in arriving at interpretations. The public offering of an automated test interpretation service will be considered a professional-to-professional consultation. The formal responsibility of the consul-

tant is to the consultee, but his or her ultimate and overriding responsibility is to the client.

10. Mental health counselors who have the responsibility for making decisions about clients or policies based on test results should have a thorough understanding of counseling theory, assessment techniques, and test research.

11. Mental health counselors do not represent computerized test interpretations as their own and clearly designate such computerized results.

D. Test Reporting

1. Mental health counselors should write reports in a clear fashion, avoiding excessive jargon or clinical terms that are likely to confuse the lay reader.

2. Mental health counselors should strive to provide test results in as positive and nonjudgmental manner as possible.

3. Mindful that one's report reflects on the reputation of oneself and one's profession, reports are carefully proofread so as to be free of spelling, style, and grammatical errors as much as is possible.

4. Clients should be clearly informed about who will be allowed to review the report and, in the absence of a valid court order, must sign appropriate releases of information permitting such release. Mental health counselors must not release the report or findings in the absence of the aforementioned releases or order.

5. Mental health counselors are responsible for ensuring the confidentiality and security of test reports, test data, and test materials.

6. Mental health counselors must offer the client the opportunity to receive feedback about the test results, interpretations, and the range of error for such data.

7. Transmissions of test data or test reports by fax or e-mail must be accomplished in a secure manner, with guarantees that the receiving device is capable of providing a confidential transmission only to the party who has been permitted to receive the document.

8. Mental health counselors should train their staff to respect the confidentiality of test reports in the context of typing, filing, or mailing them.

9. Mental health counselors (or staff members) do not release a psychological evaluation by request unless accompanied by a specific release of information or a valid court order. A subpoena is insufficient to release a report. In such a case, the counselor must inform his/her client of the situation and, if the client refuses release, coordinate between the client's attorney and the requesting attorney so as to protect client confidentiality and one's own legal welfare.

Principle 5. Pursuit of Research Activities

Mental health counselors who conduct research must do so with regard to ethical principles. The decision to undertake research should rest upon a considered judgement by the individual counselor about how best to contribute to counseling and to human welfare. Mental health counselors carry out their investigations with respect for the people who participate and with concern for their dignity and welfare.

1. The ethical researcher seeks advice from other professionals if any plan of research suggests a deviation from any ethical principle of research with human subjects. Such deviation must still protect the dignity and welfare of the client and places on the researcher a special burden to act in the subject's interest.

2. The ethical researcher is open and honest in the relationship with research participants.
   a. The ethical researcher informs the participant of all features of the research that might be expected to influence willingness to participate and explains to the participant all other aspects about which the participant inquires.
   b. Where scientific or human values justify delaying or withholding information, the investigator acquires a special responsibility to assure that there are no damaging consequences for the participants.
   c. Following the collection of the data, the ethical researcher must provide the participant with a full clarification of the nature of the study to remove any misconceptions that may have arisen.
   d. As soon as possible, the participant is to be informed of the reasons for concealment or deception that are part of the methodological requirements of a study.
   e. Such misinformation must be minimized and full disclosure must be made at the conclusion of all research studies.
   f. The ethical researcher understands that failure to make full disclosure to a research participant gives added emphasis to the researcher's abiding responsibility to protect the welfare and dignity of the participant.

3. The ethical researcher protects participants from physical and mental discomfort, harm and danger. If the risks of such consequences exist, the investigator is required to inform the participant of that fact, secure consent before proceeding, and take all possible measures to minimize the distress.

4. The ethical researcher instructs research participants that they are free to withdraw their consent from participation at any time.

5. The ethical researcher understands that information obtained about research participants during the course of an investigation is confidential. When the possibility exists that others may obtain access to such information, the participant must be made aware of the possibility and the plans for protecting confidentiality as a part of the procedure for obtaining informed consent.

6. The ethical researcher gives sponsoring agencies, host institutions, and publication channels the same respect and opportunity for informed consent that they accord to individual research participants.

7. The ethical researcher is aware of his or her obligation to future research workers and ensures that host institutions are given feedback information and proper acknowledgement.

Principle 6. Consulting

A. Mental health counselors acting as consultants must have a high degree of self-awareness of their own values, knowledge, skills and needs in entering a helping relationship that involves human and/or organizational change. The focus of the consulting relationship should be on the issues to be resolved and not on the personal characteristics of those presenting the consulting issues.

B. Mental health counselors should develop an understanding of the problem presented by the client and should secure an agreement with the consultation client, specifying the terms and nature of the consulting relationship.

C. Mental health counselors must be reasonably certain that they and their clients have the competencies and resources necessary to follow the consultation plan.

D. Mental health counselors should encourage adaptability and growth toward self-direction. Mental health counselors should avoid becoming a decision-maker or substitute for the client.

E. When announcing consultant availability for services, mental health counselors conscientiously adhere to professional standards.

F. Mental health counselors keep all proprietary information confidential.

G. Mental health counselors avoid conflicts of interest in selecting consultation clients.

PROFESSIONAL ISSUES

Principle 7. Competence

The maintenance of high standards of professional competence is a responsibility shared by all mental health counselors in the best interests of the public and the profession. Mental health counselors recognize the boundaries of their particular competencies and the limitations of their expertise. Mental health counselors only provide those services and use only those techniques for which they are qualified by education, techniques or experience. Mental health counselors maintain knowledge of relevant scientific and professional information related to the services they render, and they recognize the need for on-going education.

a. Mental health counselors accurately represent their competence, education, training and experience.

b. As teaching professionals, mental health counselors perform their duties based on careful preparation in order that their instruction is accurate, up to date and educational.

c. Mental health counselors recognize the need for continued education and training in the area of cultural diversity and competency. Mental health counselors are open to new procedures and sensitive to the diversity of varying populations and changes in expectations and values over time.

d. Mental health counselors and practitioners recognize that their effectiveness depends in part upon their ability to maintain sound and healthy interpersonal relationships. They are aware that any unhealthy activity would compromise sound professional judgement and competency. In the event that personal problems arise and are affecting professional services, they will seek competent professional assistance to determine whether they should limit, suspend or terminate services to their clients.

e. Mental health counselors have a responsibility both to the individual who is served and to the institution within which the service is performed to maintain high standards of professional conduct. Mental health counselors strive to maintain the highest level of professional services offered to the agency, organization or institution in providing the highest caliber of professional services. The acceptance of employment in an institution implies that the mental health counselor is in substantial agreement with the general policies and principles of the institution. If, despite concerted efforts, the member cannot reach an agreement with the employer as to acceptable standards of conduct that allows for changes in institutional policy conducive to the positive growth and development of counselors, then terminating the affiliation should be seriously considered.

f. Ethical behavior among professional associates, mental health counselors and non-mental health counselors is expected at all times. When information is possessed that raises serious doubts as to the ethical behavior of professional colleagues, whether association members or not, the mental health counselor is obligated to take action to attempt to rectify such a condition. Such action shall utilize the institution's channels first and then utilize procedures established by the state licensure board.

g. Mental health counselors are aware of the intimacy of the counseling relationship, maintain a healthy respect for the integrity of the client, and avoid engaging in activities that seek to meet the mental health counselor's personal needs at the expense of the client. Through awareness of the negative impact of both racial and sexual stereotyping and discrimination, the member strives to ensure the individual rights and personal dignity of the client in the counseling relationship.

Principle 8. Professional Relationships

Mental health counselors act with due regard for the needs and feelings of their colleagues in counseling and other professions. Mental health counselors respect the prerogatives and obligations of the institutions or organizations with which they associate.

a. Mental health counselors understand how related professions complement their work and make full use of other professional, technical, and administrative resources that best serve the interests of consumers. The absence of formal relationships with other professional workers does not relieve mental health counselors from the responsibility of securing for their clients the best possible professional services; indeed, this circumstance presents a challenge to the professional competence of mental health counselors, requiring special sensitivity to problems outside their areas of training, and foresight, diligence, and tact in obtaining the professional assistance needed by clients.

b. Mental health counselors know and take into account the traditions and practices of other professional groups with which they work and cooperate fully with members of such groups when research, services and other functions are shared, or in working for the benefit of public welfare.

c. Mental health counselors treat professional colleagues with the same dignity and respect afforded to clients. Professional discourse should be free of personal attacks.

d. Mental health counselors strive to provide positive conditions for those they employ and to spell out clearly the conditions of such employment. They encourage their employees to engage in activities that facilitate their further professional development.

e. Mental health counselors respect the viability, reputation, and proprietary rights of organizations that they serve. Mental health counselors show due regard for the interest of their present or perspective employers. In those instances where they are critical of policies, they attempt to effect change by constructive action within the organization.

f. In pursuit of research, mental health counselors are to give sponsoring agencies, host institutions, and publication channels the same respect and opportunity for giving informed consent that they accord to individual research participants. They are aware of their obligation to future research workers and ensure that host institutions are given feedback information and proper acknowledgement.

g. Credit is assigned to those who have contributed to a publication, in proportion to their contribution.

h. Mental health counselors do not accept or offer referral fees from other professionals.

i. When mental health counselors violate ethical standards, mental health counselors who know firsthand of such activities should, if possible, attempt to rectify the situation. Failing an informal solution, mental health counselors should bring such unethical activities to the attention of the appropriate state licensure board committee on ethics and professional conduct. Only after all professional alternatives have been utilized will mental health counselors begin legal action for resolution.

Principle 9. Supervisee, Student and Employee Relationships

Mental health counselors have an ethical concern for the integrity and welfare of supervisees, students, and employees. They maintain these relationships on a professional and confidential basis. They recognize the influential position they have with regard to both current and former supervisees, students and employees. They avoid exploiting their trust and dependency.

A. Mental health counselors do not engage in ongoing counseling relationships with current supervisees, students and employees.

B. All forms of sexual behavior with supervisees, students and employees are unethical. Further, mental health counselors do not engage in sexual or other harassment of supervisees, students, employees or colleagues.

C. Mental health counselor supervisors advise their supervisees, students and employees against offering or engaging in or holding themselves out as competent to engage in professional services beyond their training, level of experience and competence.

D. Mental health counselors make every effort to avoid dual relationships with supervisees, students and employees that could impair their judgement or increase the risk of personal or financial exploitation. When a dual relationship can not be avoided, mental health counselors take appropriate professional precautions to make sure that judgement is not impaired. Examples of such dual relationships include, but are not limited to, a supervisee who receives supervision as a benefit of employment, or a student in a small college where the only available counselor on campus is an instructor.

E. Mental health counselors do not disclose supervisee confidences except:
   1. To prevent clear and eminent danger to a person or persons.
   2. As mandated by law.
      a. As in mandated child or senior abuse reporting.
      b. Where the counselor is a defendant in a civil, criminal or disciplinary action.
      c. Educational or training settings where only other professionals who will share responsibility for the training of the supervisee are present.
      d. Where there is a waiver of confidentiality obtained in writing prior to such a release of information.

F. Supervisees must make their clients aware in their informed consent statement that they are under supervision and they must provide their clients with the name and credentials of their supervisor.

G. Mental health counselors require their supervisees, students and employees to adhere to the Code of Ethics. Students and supervisees have the same obligations to clients as those required of mental health counselors.

Principle 10. Moral and Legal Standards

Mental health counselors recognize that they have a moral, legal and ethical responsibility to the community and to the general public. Mental health counselors should be aware of the prevailing community standards and the impact of professional standards on the community.

a. To protect students, mental health counselors/teachers will be aware of diverse backgrounds of students and will see that material is treated objectively and fairly to reflect the multicultural community in which they live.

b. Providers of counseling services conform to the statutes relating to such services as established by their state and its regulating professional board(s).

c. As employees, mental health counselors refuse to participate in an employer's practices that are inconsistent with the moral and legal standards established by federal or state legislation regarding the treatment of employees. In particular and for example, mental health counselors will not condone practices that result in illegal or otherwise unjustified discrimination on the basis of race, sex, religion or national origin in hiring, promotion or training.

d. In providing counseling services to clients, mental health counselors avoid any action that will violate or diminish the legal and civil rights of clients or of others that may be affected by the action.

e. Sexual conduct, not limited to sexual intercourse, between mental health counselors and clients is specifically in violation of this Code of Ethics. This does not, however, prohibit the use of explicit instructional aids including films and videotapes. Such use is within excepted practices of trained and competent sex therapists.

Principle 11. Professional Responsibility

In their commitment to the understanding of human behavior, mental health counselors value objectivity and integrity, and in providing services they maintain the highest standards. They accept responsibility for the consequences of their work and make every effort to ensure that their services are used appropriately.

a. Mental health counselors accept ultimate responsibility for selecting appropriate areas for investigation and the methods relevant to minimize the possibility that their finding will be misleading. They provide thorough discussion of the limitations of their data and alternative hypotheses, especially where their work touches on social policy or might be misconstrued to the detriment of specific age, sex, ethnic, socioeconomic, or other social categories. In publishing reports of their work, they never discard observations that may modify the interpretation of results. Mental health counselors take credit only for the work they have actually done. In pursuing research, mental health counselors ascertain that their efforts will not lead to changes in individuals or organizations unless such changes are part of the agreement at the time of obtaining informed consent. Mental health counselors clarify in advance the expectations for sharing and utilizing research data. They avoid dual relationships that may limit objectivity, whether theoretical, political, or monetary, so that interference with data, subjects, and milieu is kept to a minimum.

b. As employees of an institution or agency, mental health counselors have the responsibility to remain alert to institutional pressures that may distort reports of counseling findings or use them in ways counter to the promotion of human welfare.

c. When serving as members of governmental or other organizational bodies, mental health counselors remain accountable as individuals to the Code of Ethics of the American Mental Health Counselors Association.

d. As teachers, mental health counselors recognize their primary obligation to help others acquire knowledge and skill. They maintain high standards of scholarship and objectivity by presenting counseling information fully and accurately, and by giving appropriate recognition to alternative viewpoints.

e. As practitioners, mental health counselors know that they bear a heavy social responsibility because their recommendations and professional actions may alter the lives of others. They therefore remained fully cognizant of their impact and alert to personal, social, organizational, financial or political situations or pressures that might lead to the misuse of their influence.

f. Mental health counselors provide reasonable and timely feedback to employees, trainees, supervisors, students, clients, and others whose work they may evaluate.

Principle 12. Private Practice

a. A mental health counselor should assist, where permitted by legislation or judicial decision, the profession in fulfilling its duty to make counseling services available in private settings.

b. In advertising services as a private practitioner, mental health counselors should advertise the services in such a manner so as to accurately inform the public as to services, expertise, profession, and techniques of counseling in a professional manner. Mental health counselors who assume an executive leadership role in the organization shall not permit their name to be used in professional notices during periods when not actively engaged in the private practice of counseling. Mental health counselors advertise the following: highest relevant degree, type and level of certification or license, and type and/or description of services or other relevant information. Such information should not contain false, inaccurate, misleading, partial, out of context, descriptive material or statements.

c. Mental health counselors may join in partnership/ corporation with other mental health counselors and/or other professionals provided that each mental health counselor of the partnership or corporation makes clear his/her separate specialties, buying name in compliance with the regulations of the locality.

d. Mental health counselors have an obligation to withdraw from an employment relationship or a counseling relationship if it is believed that employment will result in violation of the Code of Ethics, if their mental capacity or physical condition renders it difficult to carry out an effective professional relationship, or if the mental health counselor is discharged by the client because the counseling relationship is no longer productive for the client.

e. Mental health counselors should adhere and support the regulations for private practice in the locality where the services are offered.

f. Mental health counselors refrain from attempts to utilize one's institutional affiliation to recruit clients for one's private practice. Mental health counselors are to refrain from offering their services in the private sector when they are employed by an institution in which this is prohibited by stated policy that reflects conditions of employment.

Principle 13. Public Statements

Mental health counselors in their professional roles may be expected or required to make public statements providing counseling information or professional opinions, or supply information about the availability of counseling products and services. In making such statements, mental health counselors take into full account the limits and uncertainties of present counseling knowledge and techniques. They represent, as accurately and objectively as possible, their professional qualifications, expertise, affiliations, and functions, as well as those of the institutions or organizations with which the statements may be associated. All public statements, announcements of services, and promotional activities should serve the purpose of providing sufficient information to aid the consumer public in making informed judgements and choices on matters that concern it. When announcing professional counseling services, mental health counselors may describe or explain those services offered but may not evaluate as to their quality or uniqueness and do not allow for testimonials by implication. All public statements should be otherwise consistent with this Code of Ethics.

Principle 14. Internet On-Line Counseling

Mental health counselors engaged in delivery of services that involve the telephone, teleconferencing, and the Internet in which these areas are generally recognized. Standards for preparatory training do not yet exist. Mental health counselors take responsible steps to ensure the competence of their work and protect patients, clients, students, research participants and others from harm.

A. **Confidentiality**

Mental health counselors ensure that clients are provided sufficient information to adequately address and explain the limitations of computer technology in the counseling process in general and the difficulties of ensuring complete client confidentiality of information transmitted through electronic communications over the Internet through on-line counseling. Professional counselors inform clients of the limitations of confidentiality and identify foreseeable situations in which confidentiality must be breached in light of the law in both the state in which the client is located and the state in which the professional counselor is licensed. Mental health counselors shall become aware of the means for reporting and protecting suicidal clients in their locale. Mental health counselors shall become aware of the means for reporting homicidal clients in the client's jurisdiction.

B. **Mental Health Counselor Identification**

Mental health counselors provide a readily visible notice advising clients of the identities of all professional counselor(s) who will have access to the information transmitted by the client. Mental health counselors provide background information on all professional communications, including education, licensing and certification, and practice information.

C. **Client Identification**

Professional counselors identify clients, verify identities of clients, and obtain alternative methods of contacting clients in emergency situations.

D. **Client Waiver**

Mental health counselors require clients to execute client waiver agreements stating that the client acknowledges the limitations inherent in ensuring client confidentiality of information transmitted through on-line counseling and acknowledge the limitations that are inherent in a counseling process that is not provided face-to-face. Limited training in the area of on-line counseling must be explained and the client's informed consent must be secured.

E. **Electronic Transfer of Client Information**

Mental health counselors electronically transfer client confidential information to authorized third-party recipients only when both the professional counselor and the authorized recipient have "secure" transfer and acceptance communication capabilities; the recipient is able to effectively protect the confidentiality of the client's confidential information to be transferred; and the informed written consent of the client, acknowledging the limits of confidentiality, has been obtained.

F. **Establishing the On-Line Counseling Relationship**

1. **Appropriateness of On-line Counseling**

Mental health counselors develop an appropriate intake procedure for potential clients to determine whether on-line counseling is appropriate for the needs of the client. Mental health counselors warn potential clients that on-line counseling services may not be appropriate in certain situations and, to the extent possible, inform the client of specific limitations, potential risks, and/or potential benefits relevant to the client's anticipated use of on-line counseling services. Mental health counselors ensure that clients are intellectually, emotionally, and physically capable of using on-line counseling services, and of understanding the potential risks and/or limitations of such services.

2. **Counseling Plans**

Mental health counselors develop individual on-line counseling plans that are consistent with both the client's individual circumstances and the limitations of on-line counseling. Mental health counselors who determine that on-line counseling is inappropriate for the client should avoid entering into or immediately terminate the on-line counseling relationship and encourage the client to continue the counseling relationship through a traditional alternative method of counseling.

3. **Boundaries of Competence**

Mental health counselors provide on-line counseling services only in practice areas within their expertise. Mental health counselors do not provide services to clients in states where doing so would violate local licensure laws or regulations.

G. **Legal Considerations**

Mental health counselors confirm that the provision of on-line services are not prohibited by or otherwise violate any applicable state or local statutes, rules, regulations or ordinances, codes of professional membership organizations and certifying boards, and/or codes of state licensing boards.

Principle 15. Resolution of Ethical Problems

Neither the American Mental Health Counselors Association, its Board of Directors, nor its National Committee on Ethics investigate or adjudicate ethical complaints. In the event a member has his or her license suspended or revoked by an appropriate state licensure board, the AMHCA Board of Directors may then act in accordance with AMHCA's National By-Laws to suspend or revoke his or her membership.

Any member so suspended may apply for reinstatement upon the reinstatement of his or her licensure.

Source: Revised 2000. Reprinted with permission of the American Mental Health Association.

APPENDIX 14-B

Responsibilities of Users of Standardized Tests

I. INTRODUCTION

Background

At the 1976 AACD (then APGA) Convention, the Board of Directors requested the development of a statement on the responsible use of standardized tests to promote proper test use, reflecting the advantages of assessment along with concerns about negative effects, and to help its members employ safeguards against misuse of tests. A committee representing all AACD Divisions and Regions spent two years studying the issues and developed a statement, published in the October, 1978, issue of *Guidepost*, titled "Responsibilities of Users of Standardized Tests." The Association for Measurement and Evaluation in Counseling and Development was charged with maintaining ongoing review of the so-called RUST Statement. The present statement has grown out of that review.

Target Audience

The statement is intended to address the needs of the members of AACD and its Divisions, Branches, and Regions, including counselors and other human service workers. Although it may interest test developers, teachers, administrators, parents, the press, or the general public, it is not specifically designed for these audiences.

Organization and Focus

The statement is organized into eight sections: Introduction, Test Decisions, Qualifications of Test Users, Test Selection, Test Administration, Test Scoring, Test Interpretation, and Communicating Test Results. Basic to the statement is the assumption that test data are merely numbers and that guidelines can help to promote their constructive use. The statement specifies general principles and activities which constitute responsible practice. These are grouped around similar issues and are indexed for ease of reference.

II. TEST DECISIONS

Decisions should be based on data. In general, test data improve the quality of decisions. However, deciding whether or not to test creates the possibility of three kinds of errors. First, a decision not to test can result in misjudgements that stem from inadequate or subjective data. Second, tests may produce data which could improve accuracy in decisions affecting the client, but which are not used in counseling. Third, tests may be misused. The responsible practitioner will determine, in advance, the purpose for administering a given test, considering protections and benefits for the client, practitioner, and agency.

A. Define purposes for testing by developing specific objectives and limits for the use of test data in relation to the particular assessment purpose:
   1. Placement: If the purpose is selection or placement, the test user should understand the programs or institutions into which the client may be placed and be able to judge the consequences of inclusion or exclusion decisions for the client.
   2. Prediction: If the purpose is prediction, the test user should understand the need for predictive data as well as possible negative consequences (e.g., stereotyping).
   3. Description: If the purpose is diagnosis or description, the test user should understand the general domain being measured and be able to identify those aspects which are adequately measured and those which are not.
   4. Growth: If the purpose is to examine growth or change, the test user should understand the practical and theoretical difficulties associated with such measurement.
   5. Program Evaluation: If the purpose of assessment is the evaluation of an agency's programs, the test user should be aware of the various information needs for the evaluation and of the limitations of each instrument used to assess those needs, as well as how the evaluation will be used.
B. Determine Information Needs and Assessment Needs:
   1. Determine whether testing is intended to assess individuals, groups, or both.
   2. Identify the particular individual and/or group to be tested with regard to the agency's purposes and capabilities.
   3. Determine the limitations to testing created by an individual's age; racial, sexual, ethnic, and cultural background; or other characteristics.
   4. Avoid unnecessary testing by identifying decisions which can be made with existing information.
   5. Assess the consequences for clients of deciding either to test or not to test.
   6. Limit data gathering to the variables that are needed for the particular purpose.
   7. Cross-validate test data using other available information whenever possible.

III. QUALIFICATIONS OF TEST USERS

While all professional counselors and personnel workers should have formal training in psychological and educational measurement and testing, this training does not necessarily make one an expert and even an expert does not have all the knowledge and skills appropriate to some particular situations or instruments. Questions of user qualifications should always be addressed when testing is being considered.

Lack of proper qualifications can lead to errors and subsequent harm to clients. Each professional is responsible for making judgements on this in each situation and cannot leave that responsibility either to clients or to others in authority. It is incumbent upon the individual test user to obtain appropriate training or arrange for proper supervision and assistance when engaged in testing. Qualifications for test users depend on four factors:

A. Purposes of Testing: Technically proper testing for ill-understood purposes may constitute misuse. Because the purposes of testing dictate how the results are used, qualifications of test users are needed beyond general testing competencies to interpret and apply data.
B. Characteristics of Tests: Understanding the nature and limitations of each instrument used is needed by test users.
C. Settings and Conditions of Test Use: Assessment of the quality and relevance of test user knowledge and skill to the situation is needed before deciding to test or to participate in a testing program.
D. Roles of Test Selectors, Administrators, Scorers and Interpreters: Test users must be engaged in only those testing activities for which their training and experience qualify them.

IV. TEST SELECTION

The selection of tests should be guided by information obtained from a careful analysis of the characteristics of the population to be tested; the knowledge, skills, abilities or attitudes to be assessed; the purposes for testing; and the eventual use and interpretation of the test scores. Use of tests should also be guided by criteria for technical quality recommended by measurement professionals (i.e., the APA/AERA/NCME "Standards for Educational and Psychological Tests" and the APA/AERA/NCME/AACD/ASHA "Code of Fair Testing Practices in Education").

A. Relate Validity to Usage:
  1. Determine the validity of a test (whether the test measures what is meant to be measured) through evidence of the constructs used in developing the test, the correlation of the test performance with other appraisals of the characteristics being measured, and/or the predictions of specified behaviors from the test performance.
  2. Determine whether a test is congruent with the users' definition of the characteristics of human performance to be appraised.
  3. Use tests for selection purposes only when they show predictive validity for the specific tasks or competencies needed in an educational or employment expe-

rience and when they maintain legal and ethical prescriptions for non-discriminatory practices in program selection, employment, or placement.
B. Use Appropriate Tests:
  1. Document tests as appropriate for the characteristics of the population to be tested.
  2. Only use tests within the level of skills of administration and interpretation possessed by the practitioner.
  3. Use tests consistent with local needs:
    a. Give attention to how the test is designed to handle variation of motivation, working speed, language facility, and experiential background among persons taking it; bias in response to its content; and effects of guessing in response to its questions.
    b. Determine whether a common test or different tests are required for accurate measurement of groups with special characteristics.
      i. Recognize that the use of different tests for cultural, ethnic and racial groups may constitute ineffective means for making corrections for differences.
      ii. Determine whether persons or groups that use different languages should be tested in either or both languages and, in some instances, tested first for bilingualism or language dominance.
C. Consider Technical Characteristics:
  1. Select only tests that have documented evidence of reliability or consistency.
  2. Select only tests that have adequate documented evidence of the effectiveness of the measure for the purpose to be served and justification of the inferences based on the results.
  3. Scrutinize standardization and norming procedures for relevance to the local population and use of the data.
  4. Use separate norms for men and women or other subgroups when empirical evidence indicates they are appropriate.
  5. Determine the degree of technical quality demanded of a test on the basis of the nature of the decisions to be made.
  6. Include ease and accuracy of the procedures for scoring, summarizing, and communicating test performance among the criteria for selecting a test.
  7. Consider practical constraints of cost, conditions, and time for testing as secondary test selection criteria.
D. Employ User Participation in Test Selection: Actively involve everyone who will be using the assessments (administering, scoring, summarizing, interpreting, making decisions) as appropriate in the selection of tests so that they are congruent with local purposes, conditions, and uses.

V. TEST ADMINISTRATION

Test administration includes procedures to ensure that the test is used in the manner specified by the test developers and that the individuals being tested are working within conditions which maximize opportunity for optimum, comparable performance.

A. Provide Proper Orientation:
   1. Inform testing candidates, parents, and institutions or agencies in the community as appropriate about the testing procedures. The orientation should make the test meaningful for the individual or group being tested, and should include the purposes of the test, the kinds of tasks it involves, how it is administered and how the scores will be reported and used.
   2. Provide persons being tested sufficient practice experiences prior to the test.
   3. Prior to testing, check all test takers' ability to record their responses adequately (e.g., in the use of machine-scorable answer sheets).
   4. Provide periodic training by qualified personnel for test administrators within agencies or institutions using tests.
   5. Review test materials and administration sites and procedures prior to the time for testing to ensure standardized conditions and appropriate response to any irregularities which may occur.
B. Use Qualified Test Administrators:
   1. Acquire any training required to administer the test.
   2. Ensure that individuals taking self-administered or self-scored instruments have the necessary understanding and competencies.
C. Provide Appropriate Testing Conditions:
   1. Ensure that the testing environment (seating, work surfaces, lighting, heating, freedom from distractions, etc.) and psychological climate are conducive to the best possible performance of the test-takers.
   2. Carefully observe, record, and attach to the test record any deviation from prescribed test administration procedure.
   3. Use a systematic and objective procedure for observing and recording environmental, health, or emotional factors, or other elements which may invalidate test performance. This record should be attached to the test scores of the persons tested.
   4. Use sufficiently trained personnel to provide uniform conditions and to observe the conduct of the examinees when large groups of individuals are tested.
D. Give Proper Directions:
   1. Present each test in the manner prescribed in the test manual to ensure that it is fair to each test taker.
   2. Administer standardized tests with the verbatim instructions, exact sequence and timing, and identical materials that were used in the test standardization.
   3. Demonstrate verbal clarity, calmness, empathy for the examinees, and impartiality toward all being tested. Because taking a test may be a new and frightening experience or stimulate anxiety or frustration for some individuals, the examinees should attempt each task

with positive application of their skills and knowledge and the expectation that they will do their best.
E. Coordinate Professional Collaboration: In settings where skill and knowledge is pooled and responsibility shared, consider the qualifications of the testing team as a whole as more important than those of individuals. However, coordination and consistency of responsibilities with expertise must be maintained.

VI. TEST SCORING

Accurate measurement of human performance necessitates adequate procedures for scoring the responses of examinees. These procedures must be audited as necessary to ensure consistency and accuracy of application.

A. Consider Accuracy and Interpretability: Select a test scoring process that maximizes accuracy and interpretability.
B. Rescore Samples: Routinely rescore samples of examinee responses to monitor the accuracy of the scoring process.
C. Screen Test Results: Screen reports of test results using personnel competent to recognize unreasonable or impossible scores.
D. Verify Scores and Norms: Verify the accuracy of computation of raw scores and conversion to normative scales prior to release of such information to examinees or users of test results.
E. Communicate Deviations: Report as part of the official record any deviation from normal conditions and examinee behaviors.
F. Label Results: Clearly label the date of test administration along with the scores.

VII. TEST INTERPRETATION

Test interpretation encompasses all the ways that meaning is assigned to the scores. Proper interpretation requires knowledge about the test which can be obtained by studying its manual and other materials along with current research literature with respect to its use; no one should undertake the interpretation of scores on any test without such study.

A. Consider Reliability: Reliability is important because it is a prerequisite to validity and because the degree to which a score may vary due to measurement error is an important factor in its interpretation.
   1. Estimate test stability using a reliability (or other appropriate) coefficient.
   2. Use the standard error of measurement to estimate the amount of variation due to random error in individual scores and to evaluate the precision of cut scores in selection decisions.
   3. Consider, in relationship to the uses being made of the scores, variance components attributed to error in the reliability index.

4. Evaluate reliability estimates with regard to factors that may have artificially raised or lowered them (e.g., test speededness, biases in population sampling).
5. Distinguish indices of objectivity (i.e., scorer reliability) from test reliability.

B. Consider Validity: Proper test interpretation requires knowledge of the validity evidence available for the intended use of the test. Its validity for other uses is not relevant. Indeed, use of a measure for a purpose for which it was not designed may constitute misuse. The nature of the validity evidence required for a test depends upon its use.

1. Use for Placement: Predictive validity is the usual basis for valid placement.
   a. Obtain adequate information about the programs or institutions in which the client may be placed to judge the consequences of such placement.
   b. Use all available evidence to infer the validity of an individual's score. A single test score should not be the sole basis for a placement or selection recommendation. Other items of information about an individual (e.g., teacher report, counselor opinion) frequently improve the likelihood that proper judgments and decisions will be made.
   c. Consider validity for each alternative (i.e., each placement option) when interpreting test scores and other evidence.
   d. Examine the possibility that a client's group membership (socioeconomic status, gender, subculture, etc.) may affect test performance and, consequently, validity.
   e. Estimate the probability of favorable outcomes for each possible placement before making recommendations.
   f. Consider the possibility that outcomes favorable from an institutional point of view may differ from those that are favorable from the individual's point of view.

2. Use for Prediction: The relationship of the test scores to an independently developed criterion measure is the basis for predictive validity.
   a. Consider the reliability and validity of the criterion measure(s) used.
   b. Consider the validity of a measure in the context of other predictors available (i.e., does the test make a valid contribution to prediction beyond that provided by other measures).
   c. Use cross validation to judge the validity of prediction processes.
   d. Consider the effects of labeling, stereotyping, and prejudging people (e.g., self-fulfilling prophecies that may result from labeling are usually undesirable).
   e. If a statistically valid predictor lacks both construct and content validity, analyze the mechanism by which it operates to determine whether or not its predictive validity is spurious.

3. Use for Description: Comprehensiveness of information is fundamental to effective description, since no set of test scores completely describes an individual.
   a. Clearly identify the domain assessed by any measure and the adequacy of the content sampling procedures used in developing items.
   b. Clarify the dimensions being measured when multiple scores from a battery or inventory are used for description.
      i. Examine the content and/or construct validity of each score separately.
      ii. Consider the relative importance of each of the separate elements for interpretation.
      iii. Give appropriate weights to reflect the variabilities (e.g., standard deviations) and relationships (e.g., correlations) of scores which are to be combined.
   c. Distinguish characteristics that can be validated only empirically and those for which content specifications exist.

4. Use for Assessment of Growth: Assessment of growth or change requires valid tests as well as a valid procedure for combining them.
   a. Specifically evaluate the reliability of differences between scores as measures of change.
   b. Establish the validities of the measures used to establish change in relation to one another as well as individually.
   c. Consider comparability of intervals in scales used to assess change.
      i. Evaluate derived or extrapolated scores (e.g., grade equivalents) for possible different meanings at different score levels.
      ii. Consider problems in interpretation and comparability of tests (e.g. floor or ceiling effects, content changes from level to level, poor articulation in multilevel tests, lack of comparability of alternate forms, inadequacy of score-equating across forms, and differences in administration and timing of tests from that of their norming).
   d. Assess potential for undesirable correlations of difference scores with the measures entering into their calculations (e.g., regression toward the mean).
   e. Recognize the potential lack of comparability between norms for differences derived from norms and norms for differences derived from differences (i.e., mathematically derived norms for differences are not necessarily equivalent to norms based on distributions of actual differences).

5. Use for Program Evaluation: Assessments of group differences (between groups or within groups over time) are based on research designs which to varying degrees admit competing interpretations of the results.

a. Use procedures in the evaluation which ensure that no factors other than those being studied have major influence on the results (i.e., internal validity).

b. Use statistical procedures which are appropriate and have all assumptions met by the data being analyzed.

c. Evaluate the generalizability (external validity) of the results for different individuals, settings, tests, and variables.

C. Scores, Norms, and Related Technical Features: The result of scoring a test or subtest is usually a number called a raw score which by itself is not interpretable. Additional steps are needed to translate the number directly into either a verbal description (e.g., pass or fail) or into a derived score (e.g., a standard score). Less than full understanding of these procedures is likely to produce errors in interpretation and ultimately in counseling or other uses.

1. Examine appropriate test materials (e.g., manuals, handbooks, users' guides, and technical reports) to identify the descriptions or derived scores produced and their unique characteristics.

a. Know the operational procedures for translating raw scores into descriptions or derived scores.

b. Know specific psychological or educational concepts or theories before interpreting the scores of tests based on them.

c. Consider differential validity along with equating error when different tests, different test forms, or scores on the same test administered at different times are compared.

2. Clarify arbitrary standards used in interpretation (e.g., mastery or nonmastery for criterion-referenced tests).

a. Recognize that when a score is interpreted based on a proportion score (e.g., percent correct), its elements are being given arbitrary weights.

b. Recognize that the difficulty of a fixed standard (e.g., 80 percent right) varies widely and thus does not have the same meaning for different content areas and for different assessment methods.

c. Report the number (or percentage) of items right in addition to the interpretation when it will help others understand the quality of the examinee's performance.

3. Employ derived scores based on norms which fit the needs of the current use of the test.

a. Evaluate whether available norm groups are appropriate as part of the process of interpreting the scores of clients.

i. Use norms for the group to which the client belongs.

ii. Recognize that derived scores based on different norm groups may not be comparable.

iii. Use local norms and derived scores based on them whenever possible.

b. Choose a score based on its intended use.

i. Consider relative standing scores (e.g., percentile ranks) for comparison of individuals to the norm or reference group.

ii. Consider standard or scaled scores whenever means and variances or other arithmetic operations are appropriate.

iii. When using a statistical technique, use the test's derived score which best meets the assumptions of the analysis.

D. Administration and Scoring Variation: Stated criteria for score interpretations assume standard procedures for administering and scoring the test. Departures from standard conditions and procedures modify and often invalidate these criteria.

1. Evaluate unusual circumstances peculiar to the administration and scoring of the test.

a. Examine reports from administrators, proctors, and scorers concerning irregularities or unusual conditions (e.g., excessive anxiety) for possible effects on test performance.

b. Consider potential effects of examiner-examinee differences in ethnic and cultural background, attitudes, and values based on available relevant research.

c. Consider any reports of examinee behavior indicating the responses were made on some basis other than that intended.

d. Consider differences among clients in their reaction to instructions about guessing and scoring.

2. Evaluate scoring irregularities (e.g., machine scoring errors) and bias and judgement effects when subjective elements enter into scoring.

VIII. COMMUNICATING TEST RESULTS

The responsible counselor or other practitioner reports test data with a concern for the individual's need for information and the purposes of the information. There must also be protection of the right of the person tested to be informed about how the results will be used and what safeguards exist to prevent misuse (right to information) and about who will have access to the results (right to privacy).

A. Decisions About Individuals: Where test data are used to enhance decisions about an individual, the practitioner's responsibilities include:

1. Limitations on Communication:

a. Inform the examinee of possible actions that may be taken by any person or agency who will be using the results.

b. Limit access to users specifically authorized by the law or by the client.

    c. Obtain the consent of the examinee before using test results for any purpose other than those advanced prior to testing.

2. Practitioner Communication Skills:
   a. Develop the ability to interpret test results accurately before attempting to communicate them.
   b. Develop appropriate communication skills, particularly with respect to concepts that are commonly misunderstood by the intended audience, before attempting to explain test results to clients, the public, or other recipients of the information.

3. Communication of Limitations of the Assessment:
   a. Inform persons receiving test information that scores are not perfectly accurate and indicate the degree of inaccuracy in some way, such as by reporting score intervals.
   b. Inform persons receiving test information of any circumstances that could have affected the validity or reliability of the results.
   c. Inform persons receiving test information of any factors necessary to understand potential sources of bias for a given test result.
   d. Communicate clearly that test data represent just one source of information and should rarely, if ever, be used alone for decision making.

4. Communication of Client Rights:
   a. Provide test takers or their parents or guardians with information about any rights they may have to obtain test copies and/or their completed answer sheets, to retake tests, to have tests rescored, or to cancel test scores.
   b. Inform test takers or their parents or guardians about how long the test scores will remain on file along with the persons to whom, and circumstances under which, they may be released.
   c. Describe the procedures test takers or their parents or guardians may use to register complaints or have problems resolved.

B. Decisions About Groups: Where standardized test data are being used to describe groups for the purpose of evaluation, the practitioner's responsibilities include:

1. Background Information:
   a. Identify the purposes for which the reported data are appropriate.
   b. Include additional information (e.g., population characteristics) if it can improve accuracy of understanding.

2. Averages and Norms:
   a. Clarify the amount of meaning that can be attached to differences between groups (e.g., statistical significance should not be taken as a judgement of importance).
   b. Qualify norms based on their appropriateness for the group being tested.

3. Use obsolescence schedules so that stored data are systematically relocated to historical files or destroyed.

4. Process data used for research or program evaluation to assure individual anonymity (e.g., released only in aggregated form).

5. Political Usage:
   a. Emphasize that test data should be used only for the test's stated purposes.
   b. Public release of test information provides data for many purposes. Take steps to minimize those which may be adverse to the interests of those tested.

6. Agency Policies:
   a. Advocate agency test-reporting policies designed to benefit the groups being measured.
   b. Advocate the establishment of procedures for periodic review of test use.

IX. EXTENSIONS OF THESE PRINCIPLES

This statement is intended to address current and emerging problems and concerns that are generic to all AACD divisions, branches, and regions by formulating principles that are specific enough to serve as a template for more closely focused statements addressed to specific situations. Individual divisions, branches, and regions are encouraged to elaborate upon this statement to reflect principles, procedures, and examples appropriate to their members.

Source: Reprinted by permission of the American Counseling Association, 1987.

This revision of the 1978 RUST Statement was prepared by a standing committee of AMECD chaired by William D. Schafer. Participating in the revision were Esther E. Diamond, Charles G. Eberly, Patricia B. Elmore, Jo-Ida C. Hansen, William A. Mehrens, Jane E. Myers, Larry Rawlins, and Alan G. Robertson.

Additional copies of the RUST Statement may be obtained from the American Association for Counseling and Development, 5999 Stevenson Avenue, Alexandria, VA 22304. Single copies are free.

CHAPTER 15

Career Counseling

Mark Pope
Vilia M. Tarvydas

Objectives

■ ■ ■ ■ ■ ■ ■ ■ ■ ■ ■

After reading this chapter, you should be able to:

- Define the specialty of career counseling.
- Differentiate the roles and functions of practitioners of career counseling from those of practitioners of other counseling specialties.
- Address political issues of importance to career counselors.
- Explain the ethical issues specific to the practice of career counseling.
- Outline professional credentialing and licensure matters for career counselors.
- Review the assessment issues of career counseling.

■ ■ ■ ■ ■ ■ ■ ■ ■ ■

INTRODUCTION

The birth and subsequent development of career counseling in the United States occurred during times of major societal change (Brewer, 1942; Pope, 2000a). Career counseling, which was called "vocational guidance," was born in the United States in the latter part of the 19th century out of societal upheaval, transition, and change. This new profession was described by historians as a "progressive social reform movement aimed at eradicating poverty and substandard living conditions spawned by the rapid industrialization and consequent migration of people to major urban centers at the turn of the 20th century" (Whiteley, 1984, p. 2). Pope (2000a) characterized this time thusly:

> The societal upheaval giving birth to career counseling was characterized by the loss of jobs in the agricultural sector, increasing demands for workers in heavy industry, the loss of "permanent" jobs on the family farm to new emerging technologies such as tractors, the increasing urbanization of the USA, and the concomitant calls for services to meet this internal migration pattern, all in order to retool for the new industrial economy. Returning veterans from World War I and those displaced by their return also heightened the need for career counseling. (p. 234)

Career counseling evolved out of the resulting needs to understand the world of work, how to best prepare individuals to enter it, and how to find a suitable match between the demands of the workplace and the skills and needs of individuals within it. Whether those requiring guidance and counseling were students, adults with industrial injuries, or veterans, the need to understand the individual and how that person's individual needs and skills could be used to find a satisfying and satisfactory match with vocational opportunities became a powerful impetus to career counseling.

Over the last 85 years since the founding of organized counseling, there has been significant social and political support for studying the world of work and training professionals to help people make vocational choices and adjust to problems of vocational placement. Career counseling received important legislative support for the emergence and continued growth of information and methods in the field. A description of these federal laws is provided by Pope (2000a) and integrates over 30 separate pieces of federal legislation in the fields of school guidance (e.g., Elementary and Secondary Education Act, 1969), vocational education (Vocational Education Act, 1963 and its Amendments to this Act in 1968 and 1976), workforce development (Manpower Development and Training Act, 1962), employment services (Economic Opportunity Act, 1964), vocational rehabilitation (Vocational Rehabilitation Administration Budget, 1965), social security (Social Security Act, 1967, which created the Work Incentive Program), international trade (Omnibus Trade and Competitiveness Act, 1988), and welfare (Welfare to Work Act, 1997). The evolution of career counseling has been influenced greatly by social and cultural forces affecting the work lives of Americans and the legislation and programs created as a result of these forces.

Frank Parsons (1909) is credited with defining practice in the field of career or vocational guidance through the development of the theoretical model that underlies the trait and factor approaches. These trait and factor theoretical approaches have permeated the development of career counseling (Isaacson & Brown, 2000; Salomone, 1996; Zunker, 1994). This model of career counseling identifies three core factors in vocational choice: (a) a clear self-understanding; (b) a knowledge of occupations; and (c) the ability to understand relationships between the self and information about occupations.

The traditional focus of career counseling has been on helping individuals successfully enter the world of work. This theoretical underpinning is shared with counseling psychology, a specialty within psychology, that is represented in the American Psychological Association by Division 17 (Counseling Psychology). Counseling psychology had an early and significant influence on the evolution of vocational counseling and psychology (Whiteley, 1984). Historically, professionals in these areas have done extensive vocational counseling, and their most frequent employment settings are in educational settings such as colleges and universities. In the evolution of counseling psychology's research base and the training model that has guided its curriculum, many scholarly and practice interventions have been added that enhance the skills and knowledge available to all career counselors.

It has long been recognized that many clients of career counselors cannot make vocational decisions as a result of personal or psychological problems for which they may need counseling before they can successfully deal with the vocational issues facing them. More recently, career counseling has increasingly taken a total life-role perspective to understand the place of work within the overall context of people's lives (Brown & Brooks, 1991; Hansen, 1997; Super, 1974). This holistic focus primarily has been pursued through the development of various career/life planning approaches. Career/life perspectives emphasize a wide range of factors that influence career choice including needs related to work, family, home, and leisure.

There is an ongoing tension in career counseling concerning the relationship between personal and career counseling (Pope, Cheng, & Leong, 1998). Of course, the degree of focus for all practitioners depends on the needs of their clients, the institutional mission within which they practice, and their individual professional scopes of competency. Salomone (1996) provided a description of the areas of personal and career counseling that clarifies the relationships among these areas of professional practice. **Personal counseling** involves professionals who help clients "understand, accept, and resolve their problems" by using "basic counseling techniques so that their clients can lead more satisfying, well-adjusted lives." In contrast, "**career counseling** focuses on a certain realm of the counselee's life—the world of work" (Salomone, 1996, p. 368). It is incorrect to say that career counseling is distinct from personal counseling, because a counselor may assist the client personally as part of the vocational counseling process. It could be said that "it is impossible to do career counseling without simultaneously doing personal counseling" (Salomone, 1996, p. 369).

Box 15.1   Exploring the Codes

What section of the NCDA Ethical Standards (see Appendix 15-A at the end of this chapter) addresses the use of tests in assessment of clients?

What should a career counselor do if her client is being treated by another mental health professional, according to the NCDA Ethical Standards?

What section of the NCDA Ethical Standards refers to the use of technology in career counseling?

What must career counselors do if they disagree with the general policies and principles of the institution paying them for their services, according to the NCDA Ethical Standards?

What are the responsibilities of career counselors who counsel individuals from a different culture, according to the NCDA Ethical Standards?

DEFINING THE SPECIALTY, SETTING, AND CLIENTS

As a counseling specialty, career counseling has two structural characteristics important to understanding its organization and professional positioning. First, career counseling was key to establishing the earliest professional organizational structures for the entire counseling movement. Second, career counseling has always taken the lead in establishing standards for the profession.

Specialty

The National Career Development Association (NCDA), the primary organization that represents career counseling and development professionals, is the oldest counseling organization in the world and has been defining the profession, its ethics, and standards for almost 90 years. The group's ethical standards are reprinted in Appendix 15-A along with four documents that provide standards for occupational materials. NCDA was established in 1913 as the National Vocational Guidance Association (NVGA), and was a founding division of APGA (now ACA) in 1952 (Engels, 1994; Pope, 2000a).

NCDA/NVGA had always taken the lead in establishing standards for the profession: (1) standards for the practice of vocational guidance, (2) standards for occupational materials, (3) standards for the training of counselors, and (4) standards for vocational counseling agencies (Norris, 1954a, b). In 1982, as a result of the emergence of the private practice career counselor and under heavy pressure from within the profession, NVGA initiated a specific credential for career coun-

seling professionals. The National Certified Career Counselor (NCCC) credential included substantial academic and experiential requirements along with an examination (National Career Counselor Examination). As a precursor to that credential, NVGA promulgated Vocational/Career Counseling Competencies in 1982, which were developed as a "list of competencies necessary for counselors to perform the task of career/vocational guidance and counseling" (NVGA, 1982, p. 1). The competencies were preceded by the American Vocational Association-NVGA Position Paper on Career Development (1973), the American Personnel and Guidance Association (APGA, now ACA) Position Paper on Career Guidance (1975), the Association for Counselor Education and Supervision (ACES) Position Paper on Counselor Preparation for Career Development (1976), the AIR Report on Competencies Needed for Planning, Supporting, Implementing, Operating, and Evaluating Career Guidance Programs (1979), and the APGA Career Education Project (1980) (Pope, 2000a). Pope (2000a) reported that NVGA then established the National Council for Credentialing Career Counselors in 1983. Using the list of competencies, this independent credentialing body developed the National Career Counselor Examination, which was first administered at the 1984 American Association for Counseling and Development (AACD, now ACA) Convention in Houston, Texas. Also in 1984, a letter of intent to affiliate was filed with the new National Board for Certified Counselors (NBCC). The National Certified Career Counselor credential became the first specialty certification area for NBCC.

To hold an NBCC specialty certification, the professional counselor must first attain certification as a

Box 15.2   Questions for Reflection

What do you believe is the professional role of career management professionals, career coaches, and career development facilitators? Should they be part of the career counseling profession or should they develop their own professional organizations?

National Certified Counselor (NCC), the more general level of counseling certification. Although at the time, over 800 people held the NCCC specialty credential through NBCC (Engels, Minor, Sampson, & Splete, 1995), in 1999 NBCC officially "retired" the NCCC credential (along with the National Certified Gerontological Counselor [NCGC]). This was done to strengthen the NBCC general practice credential in counseling (NCC) and to to begin the process of dismantling its specialty credentialing programs. NCDA then moved quickly to re-establish the NCCC and renamed it the Master Career Counselor (MCC) in 2000 (Pope, 2000b).

Another credentialing issue was the development of the Career Development Facilitator (CDF) occupation by NCDA and the National Occupational Information Coordinating Committee (NOICC). In the 1980s and 1990s, there was an influx of paraprofessionals into the career development field. Some came as career technicians out of California's school systems; some came as consultants to business and industry through outplacement consulting firms and were hired to provide employment counseling to employees about to be fired. Many of these individuals who were providing career services had little, if any, training in career counseling and yet were providing career development services to corporate clients who were paying large sums of money for their services. NCDA decided to bring those people into the profession rather than ostracize them.

NCDA, as one of the founding divisions of ACA, had previously fought a long battle within ACA to maintain "Development" in the NCDA name. Some in NCDA wanted to change the name to the National Career Counseling Association. They also wanted to keep noncounselors outside of the profession. The leadership of NCDA at that time (Ken Hoyt, Jane Goodman, Michael Shanasarian, Mark Pope, and Nancy Schlossberg) was determined not to allow this to happen and to broaden the membership base of the profession by including noncounseling career development professionals as full voting members.

Settings

Career counseling has several types of constituencies that both enrich the practice of career counseling and allow the career counseling professional association to define its organizational base easily. It sometimes has been unclear whether career counseling constitutes a specialty unto itself, or whether it is a specialized or advanced practice area within a number of other professional counseling groups. Even NCDA has noted in its career counseling competencies document (Engels, 1994) that its standards provide guidelines for people interested in a variety of career development occupations, not simply career counseling (Box 15.2). These standards state that career counselors should be trained at the master's level or higher with a specialty in career counseling. They further defined 10 competency areas that constitute minimum training for career counseling specialists. Counseling professional groups that might consider themselves to have a specialized background in career counseling, depending on their individual programs of preparation and practice, might include school counselors, counseling psychologists, college counselors, private practice counselors, employment counselors, and rehabilitation counselors.

As the level of professionalization in career counseling has increased, NCDA has strongly promulgated its standards for career counseling, and cautioned that it must be differentiated from other career services such as job placement specialists, outplacement consultants, career management professionals, career coaches, and employment agents. Members of the latter occupational groups often provide quite limited or specific career services, rather than working more broadly to place career concerns within a comprehensive approach to increase client career- and self-awareness and development (Engels, 1994). Often the clients for these groups are employers rather than employees or prospective employees. NCDA has acknowledged, however, the following career development specialties and set minimum training and competence standards for each:

a. Career counseling (private and public settings);
b. Human resource, career development, and employee assistance specialists (in-house organizational setting, external HR/DC/EAP firms);
c. Career and employment search consultants (private setting);
d. Cooperative education instructors (educational setting);
e. Employment agents (private setting);
f. Outplacement consultants;
g. Job placement specialists (public setting); and
h. School counselors, community college and college counselors, and counselors in postsecondary technical institutes (Engels, 1994).

Clearly, career counselors may practice in a variety of settings that demand proficiency in the core career counseling knowledge and skill areas. The 11 minimum competency areas required by NCDA (1994) are:

1. Career development theory
2. Individual and group counseling skills
3. Individual/group assessment
4. Information/resources
5. Program promotion, management, and implementation
6. Coaching, consultation, and performance improvement
7. Diverse populations
8. Supervision
9. Ethical/legal issues
10. Research/evaluation
11. Technology

While many organizations may relate to the specialized practice of career counseling, the core organization that most clearly represents this area is NCDA with its specialty certification (the MCC).

In some instances, the career counseling service is not rendered to an individual, but to a corporation or some other organization, often through a consulting relationship. These and other innovative aspects of career counseling make the professional and ethical demands on this group ever more challenging.

Due to a traditional emphasis on holistic practice, career counselors in private practice are beginning to see themselves as part of a total health team. The composition of the team is dictated by the nature of the treatment setting and needs of the clients. Whether the team is in-house or is physically dispersed, career counselors find themselves frequently working in a collaborative team framework. Thus, it is apparent that career counselors are involved in wide-ranging spheres of professional counseling practice and might affect the lives of more members of our society than better-known mental health professionals such as clinical psychologists and social workers.

Clients

The practice of career counseling involves a diverse group of clients. When reflecting on the need for career counseling, Crites (1981) remarked that the need for it is even greater than the need for psychotherapy. This observation was proven in a series of Gallup polls that were co-sponsored by NCDA and the National Occupational Information Coordinating Committee (NOICC)—an agency of the federal government established to coordinate career information among all the various producers and users of such information. These first-ever surveys of the attitudes and beliefs of the American workforce regarding career development were accomplished through grants from NOICC. NCDA commissioned the Gallup Organization to conduct three national surveys in 1989, 1992, and 1994, with a fourth survey funded for 2000. These survey results were published as books and received much national attention, including being cited by federal legislators on the floor of the U.S. Congress. Each national survey covered a topic for which there was little national data published and provided important data on general population attitudes toward work and careers, attitudes of ethnic and racial minorities in the United States on work and careers, and attitudes of the U.S. general population toward how schools were preparing them for work realities and the school-to-job transition (Brown & Minor, 1989, 1992; Hoyt & Lester, 1995).

These surveys documented a tremendous need for career counseling and development services throughout all segments of our society (Pope, 2000a). Economic and political changes—nationally and globally—are creating monumental and rapid changes in business and industry that complicate career choice and career-life development. These elements challenge career counselors to provide career services to an extremely diverse population.

Traditionally, career counselors worked most often in a variety of organizational settings with students who were preparing themselves for a career choice and adults who were entering or re-entering the workforce. Career counseling is most often provided in primary and secondary schools, postsecondary institutions (e.g., college counseling or career placement centers), one-stop career centers, employment service settings (both public and private), vocational rehabilitation settings (both public and private), organizations that serve their own employees (e.g., employee assistance or outplacement programs), and private practice career counseling (Engels, 1994). Thus, the material on ethical issues in school counseling or rehabilitation counseling may also be of particular interest to many career counselors. Within all of these contexts, an increasingly diverse clientele wishes to address its career decisions and career-life planning issues. In addition to the more traditional clients, groups such as middle school and elementary school students, retirees, people whose career development has suffered because of bias or stereotyping, or people who wish to advance in their careers are also seeking career counseling services (Engels, 1994).

ISSUES OF SIGNIFICANCE TO THE SPECIALTY

Because of its long professional history, career counseling has well-developed credentialing and accreditation processes. There are several requirements for establishing a profession: developing professional com-

petencies, accrediting institutions to train new professionals, and credentialing individuals who meet these certain minimum requisites.

Career Counseling Competencies

The National Career Development Association, as a precursor to the development of the NCCC credential, developed the Vocational/Career Counseling Competencies in 1982 (Box 15.3). These were developed as a "list of competencies necessary for counselors to perform the task of career/vocational guidance and counseling" (NVGA, 1982, p. 1). Career counselors need these competencies to provide the professional services expected by the public (Engels, 1994).

Accreditation

The Council for the Accreditation of Counseling and Related Educational Programs (CACREP) is the accrediting body for all professional counseling programs. NCDA has had a member on the CACREP Board of Directors from its founding. Until 2000, career counseling was considered a specialization under the community counseling curriculum and received accreditation as a specialization of community counseling. In the new 2001 CACREP Standards, career counseling has taken

---

Box 15.3 NCDA Career Counseling Competencies and Performance Indicators (NCDA, 1994)

CAREER DEVELOPMENT THEORY

Theory base and knowledge considered essential for professionals engaging in career counseling and development. Demonstration of knowledge of:

1. Counseling theories and associated techniques.
2. Theories and models of career development.
3. Individual differences related to gender, sexual orientation, race, ethnicity, and physical and mental capacities.
4. Theoretical models for career development and associated counseling and information-delivery techniques and resources.
5. Human growth and development throughout the life span.
6. Role relationships which facilitate life-work planning.
7. Information, techniques, and models related to career planning and placement.

INDIVIDUAL AND GROUP COUNSELING SKILLS

Individual and group counseling competencies considered essential to effective career counseling. Demonstration of ability to:

1. Establish and maintain productive personal relationships with individuals.
2. Establish and maintain a productive group climate.
3. Collaborate with clients in identifying personal goals.
4. Identify and select techniques appropriate to client or group goals and client needs, psychological states, and developmental tasks.
5. Identify and understand clients' personal characteristics related to career.
6. Identify and understand social contextual conditions affecting clients' careers.
7. Identify and understand familial, subcultural and cultural structures and functions as they are related to clients' careers.
8. Identify and understand clients' career decision-making processes.
9. Identify and understand clients' attitudes toward work and workers.
10. Identify and understand clients' biases toward work and workers based on gender, race, and cultural stereotypes.
11. Challenge and encourage clients to take action to prepare for and initiate role transitions by:
    - locating sources of relevant information and experience,
    - obtaining and interpreting information and experiences, and acquiring skills needed to make role transitions.
12. Assist the client to acquire a set of employability and job search skills.
13. Support and challenge clients to examine life-work roles, including the balance of work, leisure, family, and community in their careers.

INDIVIDUAL/GROUP ASSESSMENT

Individual/group assessment skills considered essential for professionals engaging in career counseling. Demonstration of ability to:

1. Assess personal characteristics such as aptitude, achievement, interests, values, and personality traits.
2. Assess leisure interests, learning style, life roles, self-concept, career maturity, vocational identity, career indecision, work environment preference (e.g., work satisfaction), and other related life style/development issues.
3. Assess conditions of the work environment (such as tasks, expectations, norms, and qualities of the physical and social settings).
4. Evaluate and select valid and reliable instruments appropriate to the client's gender, sexual orientation, race, ethnicity, and physical and mental capacities.
5. Use computer-delivered assessment measures effectively and appropriately.
6. Select assessment techniques appropriate for group administration and those appropriate for individual administration.
7. Administer, score, and report findings from career assessment instruments appropriately.
8. Interpret data from assessment instruments and present the results to clients and to others.
9. Assist the client and others designated by the client to interpret data from assessment instruments.
10. Write an accurate report of assessment results.

continued

INFORMATION/RESOURCES

Information/resource base and knowledge essential for professionals engaging in career counseling. Demonstration of knowledge of:

1. Education, training, and employment trends; labor market information and resources that provide information about job tasks, functions, salaries, requirements, and future outlooks related to broad occupational fields and individual occupations.
2. Resources and skills that clients utilize in life-work planning and management.
3. Community/professional resources available to assist clients in career planning, including job search.
4. Changing roles of women and men and the implications that this has for education, family, and leisure.
5. Methods of good use of computer-based career information delivery systems (CIDS) and computer-assisted career guidance systems (CACGS) to assist with career planning.

PROGRAM PROMOTION, MANAGEMENT, AND IMPLEMENTATION

Knowledge and skills necessary to develop, plan, implement, and manage comprehensive career development programs in a variety of settings. Demonstration of knowledge of:

1. Designs that can be used in the organization of career development programs.
2. Needs assessment and evaluation techniques and practices.
3. Organizational theories, including diagnosis, behavior, planning, organizational communication, and management useful in implementing and administering career development programs.
4. Methods of forecasting, budgeting, planning, costing, policy analysis, resource allocation, and quality control.
5. Leadership theories and approaches for evaluation and feedback, organizational change, decision-making, and conflict resolution.
6. Professional standards and criteria for career development programs.
7. Societal trends and state and federal legislation that influence the development and implementation of career development programs.

Demonstration of ability to:

8. Implement individual and group programs in career development for specified populations.
9. Train others about the appropriate use of computer-based systems for career information and planning.
10. Plan, organize, and manage a comprehensive career resource center.
11. Implement career development programs in collaboration with others.
12. Identify and evaluate staff competencies.
13. Mount a marketing and public relations campaign on behalf of career development activities and services.

COACHING, CONSULTATION, AND PERFORMANCE IMPROVEMENT

Knowledge and skills considered essential in relating to individuals and organizations that impact the career counseling and development process. Demonstration of ability to:

1. Use consultation theories, strategies, and models.
2. Establish and maintain a productive consultative relationship with people who can influence a client's career.
3. Help the general public and legislators to understand the importance of career counseling, career development, and life-work planning.
4. Impact public policy as it relates to career development and workforce plan.
5. Analyze future organizational needs and current level of employee skills and develop performance improvement training.
6. Mentor and coach employees.

DIVERSE POPULATIONS

Knowledge and skills considered essential in relating to diverse populations that impact career counseling and development processes. Demonstration of ability to:

1. Identify development models and multicultural counseling competencies.
2. Identify developmental needs unique to various diverse populations, including those of different gender, sexual orientation, ethnic group, race, and physical or mental capacity.
3. Define career development programs to accommodate needs unique to various diverse populations.
4. Find appropriate methods or resources to communicate with limited-English-proficient individuals.
5. Identify alternative approaches to meet career planning needs for individuals of various diverse populations.
6. Identify community resources and establish linkages to assist clients with specific needs.
7. Assist other staff members, professionals, and community members in understanding the unique needs/characteristics of diverse populations with regard to career exploration, employment expectations, and economic/social issues.
8. Advocate for the career development and employment of diverse populations.
9. Design and deliver career development programs and materials to hard-to-reach populations.

SUPERVISION

Knowledge and skills considered essential in critically evaluating counselor or career development facilitator performance, maintaining and improving professional skills. Demonstration of ability to:

1. Recognize own limitations as a career counselor and to seek supervision or refer clients when appropriate.
2. Utilize supervision on a regular basis to maintain and improve counselor skills.

continued

3. Consult with supervisors and colleagues regarding client and counseling issues and issues related to one's own professional development as a career counselor.
4. Utilize supervision models and theories.
5. Provide effective supervision to career counselors and career development facilitators at different levels of experience.
6. Provide effective supervision to career development facilitators at different levels of experience by:
   - knowledge of their roles, competencies, and ethical standards,
   - determining their competence in each of the areas included in their certification,
   - further training them in competencies, including interpretation of assessment instruments,
   - monitoring and mentoring their activities in support of the professional career counselor; and scheduling regular consultations for the purpose of reviewing their activities.

ETHICAL/LEGAL ISSUES

Information base and knowledge essential for the ethical and legal practice of career counseling. Demonstration of knowledge of:

1. Adherence to ethical codes and standards relevant to the profession of career counseling (e.g., NBCC, NCDA, and ACA).
2. Current ethical and legal issues which affect the practice of career counseling with all populations.
3. Current ethical/legal issues with regard to the use of computer-assisted career guidance systems.
4. Ethical standards relating to consultation issues.
5. State and federal statutes relating to client confidentiality.

RESEARCH/EVALUATION

Knowledge and skills considered essential in understanding and conducting research and evaluation in career counseling and development. Demonstration of ability to:

1. Write a research proposal.
2. Use types of research and research designs appropriate to career counseling and development research.
3. Convey research findings related to the effectiveness of career counseling programs.
4. Design, conduct, and use the results of evaluation programs.
5. Design evaluation programs which take into account the needs of various diverse populations, including persons of both genders, differing sexual orientations, different ethnic and racial backgrounds, and differing physical and mental capacities.
6. Apply appropriate statistical procedures to career development research.

TECHNOLOGY

Knowledge and skills considered essential in using technology to assist individuals with career planning. Demonstration of knowledge of:

1. Various computer-based guidance and information systems as well as services available on the Internet.
2. Standards by which such systems and services are evaluated (e.g. NCDA and ACSCI).
3. Ways in which to use computer-based systems and Internet services to assist individuals with career planning that are consistent with ethical standards.
4. Characteristics of clients which make them profit more or less from use of technology-driven systems.
5. Methods to evaluate and select a system to meet local needs.

its place with the other fully recognized counseling specialties such as school counseling and mental health counseling.

There is a movement in the CACREP Board of Directors to only accredit counseling programs that require 60 units for graduation. Representatives of NCDA to the CACREP Board have consistently fought for the accreditation of counseling programs at 48 semester units rather than the 60-semester-unit minimums required by the mental health counseling and marriage and family counseling specialties.

National Credentialing

NCDA has now replaced the NCCC with an MCC credential and added a Master Career Development Professional (MCDP) for Career Development Facilitators (CDF). A Fellow membership category was added to honor persons who have made outstanding contributions to the profession (Box 15.4).

State Credentialing

Under the political pressure of organized professional career counselors, states have also begun to take a look at methods of credentialing career counselors. Both New Jersey and Arkansas have identified career counseling as a specialty under their licensing laws for professional counseling. Another way of approaching this credentialing is the establishment of a "registry," or list of individuals, who have voluntarily submitted their credentials to an independent board that makes a decision on their inclusion. California career counselors established such a career counselor registry as a part of their drive toward career counselor licensing in the 1990s (Porter, 2001).

Professional Differentiation

Career counseling has a broad area of practice and a diverse practitioner base, yet has clearly identified standards for what constitutes appropriate professional practice. NCDA, a division of ACA, is the organization most closely aligned with career counseling. NCDA has strongly promulgated training standards for the MCC that include: (a) a graduate degree in counseling or in a related professional field from a regionally accredited higher education institution, (b) graduate-level coursework pertinent to the practice of career counseling and related specialties, and (c) supervised counseling experience that includes career counseling (Engels, 1994).

Standards

NCDA has developed specific standards for the computer delivery of career guidance and information systems along with guidelines for the evaluation of printed career information, videos, and software. The Career Information Review Service (CIRS), an NCDA committee, uses these guidelines to annually evaluate career materials. Reviews are also published in various ways by NCDA, including in the *Career Development Quarterly* (NCDA journal), in *Career Developments* (NCDA newsletter), and on the Internet at the NCDA Web site (http://ncda.org). These guidelines can be found at http://ncda.org. NCDA is currently developing its own "seal of approval" for materials judged by CIRS reviewers to meet the guidelines.

The use of various computer-based career guidance and information systems to deliver career counseling services as well as the use of the Internet in such delivery are some of the most important issues confronting

Box 15.4 Special Issue: Credentialing

The National Certified Career Counseling (NCCC) credential offered by NBCC was officially "retired" by NBCC in 1999. Individual career counselors who were holders of the NCCC were allowed to continue to use that certification, but no continuing education requirements or fees were required.

NCDA immediately established a Task Force on Credentialing Career Services Providers composed of Mark Pope (Chair), A. Dean Porter, Judith Grutter, Frank Karpati, and Norma Zuber. This Task Force studied this issue through a survey of NCCC and NCDA members, through hearings at the NCDA Global Conferences in Portland (1999) and Pittsburgh (2000), and through study of how other professional associations were handling credentialing issues. Recommendations were presented to the NCDA Board of Directors and Delegate Assembly to establish three new membership categories—the Master Career Counselor, the Master Career Development Professional, and the Fellow.

Each of these membership categories were recommended in response to important constituencies within NCDA. The Master Career Counselor credential was recommended to replace the NCCC for private practice career counselors. The Master Career Development Professional was added in response to the growing numbers of Career Development Facilitators (CDFs) who were joining NCDA. CDFs are a paraprofessional occupation developed by NCDA and NOICC to meet the needs of noncounselor career services providers. The Fellow was recommended as a result of the desire to recognize larger numbers of individuals who made significant contributions to the career development profession. While the "NCDA Eminent Career Award" could be awarded to only one person per year, the Fellow could be awarded to more than one person and provides important recognition of the contributions of these professionals.

This comprehensive reform of how career services providers were to be credentialed was fully agreed to in 2000 and implemented in 2001 by NCDA. Both the MCC and MCDP are considered credentials and are certified by NCDA as such.

MASTER CAREER COUNSELOR

The term "Master Career Counselor" designates a person who has met high standards of practice in the career counseling profession, similar to the American Association of Marriage and Family Therapists (AAMFT) "clinical member" and American Board for Professional Psychology (ABPP) "diplomate." The MCC is a special membership category as defined in the NCDA Bylaws and only members of NCDA can be granted and maintain this special status. NCDA confers this title on career counseling practitioners who have met certain standards. Anyone who is both a career counseling practitioner and a member of NCDA is eligible to receive such a status if they meet those standards.

The requirements for the Master Career Counselor credential are substantially the same as its predecessor—the NCCC—with the exception that there is no requirement to take the National Career Counselor Examination. The MCC requirements include:

1. Minimum of a master's degree in counseling or psychology or a related program from a graduate program in a regionally accredited college or university;

2. Graduate coursework in career information, career theories, and career assessment;

3. Graduate-level supervised practicum, internship, or field experience in career counseling;

4. Two years of professional career counseling practice experience subsequent to the master's degree, with at least 50 percent of the time devoted to career counseling activities (2000 hours);

5. Three letters of recommendation from other Master Career Counselors, NCCCs, RPCCs, or ABVEs;

6. NCDA membership for no less than one year;

7. NCDA membership when Master Career Counselor status is conferred and continued membership to maintain this credential;

8. A majority professional career focus on the practice of career counseling;

9. Agreement to abide by the ethical standards of NCDA; and

10. Approval by the Board of Directors.

FELLOW

The term "Fellow" has a long-standing usage within academic societies. A "Fellow" is a person of professional distinction within an academic institution or society. The status of "Fellow" is conferred to recognize outstanding and substantial contributions in science, teaching and training, practice, service, policy development, and political action. Few people get elected to this prestigious position—it is considered an honor.

The requirements for Fellow status are:

a. Minimum of a master's degree in counseling or a related field;

b. Membership in NCDA for no less than one year;

c. Five years of professional experience subsequent to the master's degree in the field of career counseling and development;

d. Major and significant impact on career development theory or practice as demonstrated by national and/or international recognition;

e. Work in a sustained program of professional contributions within the field of career counseling and development such as (1) technique, instrument, or intervention; (2) theoretical model or concept; or (3) significant synthesis of theory and practice;

f. Strong and sustained leadership in the career counseling and development profession;

g. Education and training, practice, or research in career counseling and development;

h. Age and stage of career are not major criteria, but it is assumed that the nominee has a sustained commitment to career counseling and development through research, theory, practice, or leadership;

i. Membership in NCDA when Fellow status is conferred and continued membership to maintain status;

j. Nomination by three other Fellows, but, upon recommendation of the Board of Directors, the requirement may be waived for individual cases;

k. Recommendation by Brain Trust; and

l. Approval by the Board of Directors.

To qualify as a Fellow in NCDA, the person must make a significant and distinctive contribution to career counseling and development in one or more of the following areas:

a. Professional practice: development of innovations to practice, advancing career counseling and development as a field of practice; development of a reputation as a recognized authority in an area of intervention; documented evidence of sustained and distinguished service delivery in the practice of career counseling and development; should be licensed or certified appropriately for practice and have spent a majority of professional time in service delivery over an extended period of time;

b. Scientific achievement: programmatic research and/or theory development that makes a substantial and distinctive contribution to career counseling and development;

continued

c. Leadership and governance: demonstrated leadership and governance contributions that have an impact beyond the local level; leadership in advocacy for and advancement of career counseling and development as a field of practice; participation and leadership in activities supportive of goals of NCDA, such as outstanding participation and leadership in associations relevant to NCDA (e.g., service on committees relating to the practice of counseling in general);

d. Teaching and training: development of innovative curricula and teaching/supervision practices; development of instructional materials for special populations; leadership in professional organizations directly related to the teaching, training, and supervision function; special awards and recognitions by regional and national groups for sustained and significant contribution to the preparation of career counselors or other career development professionals;

e. Recognition of excellence: involves evidence of having received national or international recognition from one's colleagues for contribution to career counseling and development as a profession; examples might include selection as an officer in a national or international career or vocational group or organization, serving as an editor for a scholarly journal that is widely respected in career counseling and development, recognition by a national or international career or vocational organization that is based on peer-review or other examination process, beyond what is typically expected of NCDA members.

In summary, a Fellow describes a person: (a) whose national and/or international contributions to career counseling and development are considered significant beyond those expected of the successful career counseling and development professional; and (b) whose creative leadership (e.g., major conceptual or theoretical models, instruments, techniques, interventions) as attested to by others, is worthy or deserving of one of the highest and most prestigious honors that can be accorded by the National Career Development Association.

MASTER CAREER DEVELOPMENT PROFESSIONAL

The Master Career Development Professional (MCDP) was added to designate a noncounseling career development practitioner who met certain criteria. It designates a person who has met high standards of practice in the career development facilitator profession. The MCDP is a special membership category as defined in the NCDA Bylaws and only members of NCDA can be granted and maintain this special status. NCDA confers this title on those individuals who are career development practitioners and have met certain standards. Anyone who is both a career counseling practitioner and a member of NCDA is eligible to receive such a status if he meets those standards.

The requirements for Master Career Development Professional credential include:

1. Minimum of a master's degree from a graduate program in a regionally accredited college or university;

2. Two years of professional career development practice experience subsequent to the master's degree, with at least 50 percent of the time devoted to career development activities (2000 hours);

3. Three letters of recommendation;

4. NCDA membership for no less than one year;

5. NCDA membership when MCDP status is conferred and continued membership to maintain this credential;

6. A majority professional career focus on the practice of career development;

7. Agreement to abide by the ethical standards of NCDA; and

8. Approval by the Board of Directors.

professional career counseling. NCDA has been a leader in the development of standards for such delivery and published the "NCDA Guidelines for the Use of the Internet for Provision of Career Information and Planning Services" in October 1997. These guidelines can be found at http://ncda.org. These guidelines were developed by the NCDA Ethics Committee—David Caulum, Don Doerr, Pat Howland, Spencer Niles, Ray Palmer, Richard Pyle (Chair), David Reile, James Sampson, and Don Schutt. Issues raised by the NCDA Ethics Committee included standards by which such systems and services are evaluated; ways in which to use computer-based systems and Internet services to assist individuals with career planning that are consistent with ethical standards; characteristics of clients that make them profit more or less from use of technology-driven systems; and methods to evaluate and select a system to meet local needs.

ETHICAL ISSUES

Confidentiality and Privileged Communication

Any number of complications can arise for career counselors with regard to confidentiality and privilege. As with all professional counselors, the trust engendered by the assurance of confidentiality is the most critical element of the counseling relationship. Confidentiality is the ethical obligation that counselors should not disclose material that clients reveal during the counseling relationship. Privilege is the client's legal or statutory right to protect confidences shared within the counseling relationship from being revealed in a legal proceeding.

Several newer areas of practice—such as vocational or forensic expert practices—require that career counselors take particular care in observing requirements to guard client confidentiality. They must clearly address confidentiality limitations with all of the individuals involved. The NCDA Ethical Standards provide a rule that embodies well-accepted advice in such situations.

There are many instances of clients having misunderstood the nature of the services provided by a career counselor. Clients may think that information they provided to the professional will be held in confidence, only to be shocked and angered later to discover that it is included in a report or deposition that resulted in a negative outcome for them, such as a loss of benefits. Such anecdotal reports are unfortunate illustrations of a need for greater care in observing the informed consent procedures regarding confidentiality limitations. The client must be informed clearly when the counselor is employed by a third party. Clients must be helped to understand fully how that relationship will influence any information given to the client, or how services provided to the client will be limited or changed.

Another potentially devastating and costly misunderstanding on the part of career counselors is the uncritical assumption that privileged communication extends to their practices. Because privileged communication is granted only through statute and legal precedent, the types of professionals covered by this privilege vary by jurisdiction (Cottone, Pullen, & Wilson, 1983). Thus, possessing a national certification, such as MCC or NCCC, does not entitle one to legal privilege for therapeutic communications in and of itself. Career counselors must research the nature of the laws governing the granting of privilege in their own areas of practice and in their geographic location.

Generally, privileged communication is extended only to licensed professionals. The recent *Jaffee v. Redmond* ruling by the U.S. Supreme Court underscored this position (see Chapter 4 for more specific information about privileged communication). It is unclear how many career counselors hold licensure in their states of residence. It is almost certain, however, that a great number of them must be in practice without state licensure and the benefit of privileged communication protections for their clients. It is imperative that both the counselors and the clients in these relationships are aware of this.

Many career counselors in educational institutions perform their work within a multi- or interdisciplinary team context. Such an arrangement is often considered the intervention of choice, but it does present the counselor with additional factors for consideration of confidentiality. Different team members have varying levels of training and understanding of this ethical obligation, and may have a legitimate desire and need to know information the counselor may have about the client. While, generally, it is acknowledged that professionals may have an appropriate need to communicate information to other people involved in the client's care, the client must be informed clearly and fully of this common limitation to confidentiality at the outset of counseling. Indeed, it is a common and sensible practice to obtain suitable written release of information regarding this and other limitations to confidentiality in a written consent to treatment document (see Chapter 4), as well as discussing this practice with the client. The client should be informed of when, how, to whom, to what extent, and what type of information will be shared with others. This process must be done in such a way as to avoid coercion of clients or the implication that they will not be served if they do not grant blanket permission.

Even when consent is obtained, the career counselor must be circumspect about revealing information to others. The counselor must determine the appropriateness of the disclosure before providing information by asking, "Is it likely that the information that I am about to share with my team member(s) will substantially enhance that person's work with the client?" (Strein & Hershenson, 1991, p. 313). The same analysis should be applied to decisions about including material in case records that will be viewed by these individuals. Strein and Hershenson (1991) provided additional benchmark concepts to be considered when fostering confidentiality within a team context. Their recommendations include taking steps to (a) articulate the specific rules the treatment team will follow regarding confidentiality, (b) reinforce the obligation of confidentiality with the team in any circumstance in which it appears that a team member may not realize the confidentiality of the information, and (c) inform the client before material will be shared with members of the team.

Career counselors also should be aware of other important limitations to confidentiality because it would not be unusual to have a number of clients with issues that could limit confidentiality. Examples might include people with psychiatric or addictions disabilities, HIV/AIDS, and clients with correctional histories who might become dangerous to themselves or others. Clients of career counselors may be involved in group treatment or counseling for purposes ranging from job-seeking skills and support groups to more traditional psychotherapeutic adjustment counseling groups. Counselors must inform their clients of confidentiality limitations (although the norm of confidentiality is set, confidentiality cannot be guaranteed in a group context). They must also inform clients that the courts generally do not uphold privilege for therapeutic communication in a group setting. It is imperative that the counselor become skilled and comfortable in providing informed consent opportunities to clients, for it is never possible to anticipate when these issues might arise with any client. Career counselors working in certain specialized settings also must become knowledgeable about specific additional state or federal laws that apply to confidentiality and privilege in those settings. Examples include the access to records of minors by their parents as required by the federal Family and Educational Rights and Privacy Act (FERPA), and the laws extending stricter confidentiality to those in treat-

ment in any addictions treatment facility that receives federal funding.

Informed Consent

Informed consent ensures that clients are given sufficient information regarding the treatment or services in which they will be involved in a manner the clients can understand. The intent is to be sure that clients have a sufficient understanding of the circumstances so they can exercise their autonomy and make informed choices. The three required elements of informed consent are (a) capacity, (b) comprehension, and (c) voluntariness (see Chapter 4).

Career counselors may find themselves in situations wherein they are employed by a company to provide outplacement services for an employee who has been fired. If the fired employee has not been fully informed of the limits of confidentiality (e.g., if the employee tells the career counselor she stole money from the company), the counselor is not allowed to inform the employer of this illegal activity.

Career counselors who work in school settings may participate in the development of the Individual Educational Plan (IEP) as part of the requirement of providing educational services to students with disabilities. Some clients may not have developed decision-making skills, or they may have a limited base of life experiences or other cognitive or psychological limitations. The determination of when a client is legally or ethically competent to provide informed consent is a critical consideration for career counselors and depends on the laws of the state. If a client appears to be under the influence of a drug, the counselor must think carefully about whether informed consent is possible, or whether other measures are needed. The counselor might need to wait until the person is in a better position to provide consent.

Some clients may have a legal guardian who may need to be involved in the informed consent process. A **legal guardian** is a person who is appointed by the court to make decisions regarding an individual's person or property. This concept presumes the client is incompetent to make these decisions (Anderson & Fearey, 1989). The legal guardian must always consent to services for the client.

Potentially Detrimental Counselor-Client Relationships

Potentially detrimental counselor-client relationships are an important and common issue for counselors working in all areas of the profession. Career counselors are no exception, and the NCDA Ethical Standards prohibit engaging in such relationships (see Chapter 3). The core issues that make these relationships so potentially dangerous to client and counselor are the power differential between the two parties and a potential loss of objectivity on the part of the counselor. The effects of such relationships may range from harmful to positive or no appreciable effect. However, due to the potential for harm, the counselor should avoid these overlapping roles whenever possible. NCDA strictly prohibits sexual intimacy with current clients because of the strong potential for serious harm to the client in such relationships.

Herlihy and Corey (1992) provided five specific safeguards to assist counselors in managing these potentially detrimental counselor-client relationships:

1. Informed consent: The counselor should fully inform the client of all possible risks involved, the limitations of the relationships, and the safeguards in place.
2. Ongoing discussions: The counselor should have periodic discussions with all the parties involved in the relationships to identify and work through any conflicts or concerns that develop.
3. Consultation: If the counselor does proceed with the potentially detrimental relationship, an ongoing consultation with a colleague should be in place so that all aspects of the situation will be evaluated to guard against overlooking a problem.
4. Supervision: If the situation involves a high risk for harm, more continuous supervision may be warranted.
5. Documentation: Counselors should document all aspects of the potentially detrimental relationship and issues that arise within the process, including the techniques used to manage the situation.

A major issue in career counseling concerns the emergence of issues that could be described loosely as contiguous professional or nonprofessional relationships—issues that involve conflicts of interest for the counselor. In these situations, counselors provide services that involve a group or team of professionals affiliated with the same client. If one team member has a monetary or business interest in a certain outcome for the client's case, such as an attorney in litigation or a managed care case manager paid through capitation, there may be potential for danger to the client if the counselor begins a noncollegial type of relationship with the first team member. If there is only a professional relationship between the counselor

and the other professional, there is no unusual conflict for the counselor in protecting the client's interests. If, however, the counselor is the other professional's lover or business partner, there could be considerable negative pressure exerted on the counselor. Even the appearance of such undue influence is ethically troublesome. Because career counselors pursue various private practice options, the possibilities for business and personal concerns creating multiple and conflicting loyalties is an increasing danger. Consultants and vocational experts are often well-known to the hiring organization or professional. This increases the potential for conflicts of interest. Counselors must evaluate such circumstances carefully before entering into or continuing a professional service relationship (Newman, 1993), even if they do not provide direct counseling services.

Responsibility

The NCDA Ethical Standards clearly assert that the primary responsibility of the counselor is to the client. It is clear, however, that there are secondary responsibilities to other parties in counseling. Career counseling has a long history of practicing primarily within agency or institutional settings. This fact is embodied by standards that enjoin career counselors to respect the rights and responsibilities they owe to their employing agencies and the need to try to resolve disputes with them through constructive, internal processes. NCDA elaborates about the nature of that obligation by stating:

> The acceptance of employment in an institution implies that the career counselor is in agreement with the general policies and principles of the institution.... If, despite concerted efforts, the career counselor cannot reach agreement with the employer as to acceptable standards of conduct that allow for changes in institutional policy that are conducive to the positive growth and development of clients, then terminating the affiliation should be seriously considered. (NCDA, 1991, p.26)

If the ethical values of the institution are in conflict with a counselor's professional ethics, she must seriously consider resigning.

All areas of counseling must address issues of counselor stereotyping and treatment system bias and how they affect clients' rights as counseling attempts to better serve an increasingly multicultural and diverse population of clients (Sue, 1996). Sue (1996) stated:

> If we believe that many problems reside outside the person (prejudice and discrimination) and not within

(person-blame), ethical practice dictates that professionals develop alternative helping roles that are aimed at system intervention. (p. 196)

This belief—that the context in which an individual functions may be part of the problem—is central to all multicultural counseling.

Values

Any number of value issues could be addressed in the area of career counseling. The richness and complexity of values and the valuing process and how they influence counseling were explored in Chapter 5. At this point, one overriding value of concern might be overlooked for its obviousness—work! The central importance that American society places on work is pervasive and strong. We assume that not only must we all value work, but we also must share similar preferences and interpretations regarding what constitutes meaningful and valuable work. Career counseling originated in answer to the powerful societal approbation of this valued role in our culture and the need to give others more effective access to this all-defining status. It is at the very core of the entire vocational counseling process for career counselors to examine the work-related meanings, needs, and interests of their clients and to help them find their niche in this world of work.

Counselors must understand that societal attitudes toward work can affect them in both positive and negative ways as they serve their clients (Gatens-Robinson & Rubin, 1995). Counselors, their agencies, and clients receive support for their career counseling activities as long as the outcomes of the process result in productive or visible economic contributions through work. If a career counselor's client achieves great financial success through dealing drugs or illegally trading stocks, the work of that counselor will not be considered professionally appropriate. If the work obtained by clients is not considered by society (or even counselors themselves) to be valuable, those who find alternative or nonremunerative activities or those who cannot be competitive in the employment market may be devalued. A variety of counseling ethical dilemmas may ensue from our uncritical assumption of values regarding work. Counselors may choose not to work with more difficult vocational clients if the agency only rewards particular types of placements or closures. Counselors may not react positively to clients who choose to work in the home as caregivers to children or elders, or who work only part time to pursue avocational interests. They may pressure clients to take jobs they are not suited for, or are

even harmed by, to appear successful. What reactions do vocational counselors have to clients who choose to work in the hidden job market, not reporting income or bartering for payment? These forms of activity may be the only ones preferred or realistically available to the client due to barriers to employment. Counselors may be tremendously conflicted by working with such issues in vocational counseling. These tensions are likely only to increase as changes in the nature of employment and business and industrial structures continue in the 21st century. In addition to the other value issues that confront all counselors, they will be required to lead the professions in interpreting and supporting work-related values in collaboration with their clients.

Counselor Competence

Competence issues occur in the work of all counselors on an ongoing basis. Counselors must develop and practice an approach to quality control in their work that assures quality and the safety of services they provide to their clients. Counselors must also work within the legal and ethical boundaries of their scopes of practice. Career counselors monitor competence in at least two specific areas of contemporary practice: (a) the integration of a mental health counseling or diagnostic focus with their usual practices, and (b) competence around assessment services.

CASE SCENARIO 15-1

The Case of Ms Diagnosis

Shelby Diagnosis was the daughter of a prominent banker in a small town in the Midwest. She was referred by her family physician to Carerra Decisiones, M.Ed., LPC, NCCC for career counseling. Counselor Decisiones did a diagnostic interview with Ms Diagnosis and reported to the family physician that Ms Diagnosis was very "clinically depressed" and "had to be treated for that before career counseling would be effective." Ms Diagnosis stated that she would only go to Counselor Decisiones for treatment of her depression. Counselor Decisiones has a degree that is regionally accredited by the Western Association of Schools and Colleges and CACREP in community counseling with a specialization in career counseling. Counselor Decisiones proceeds to treat Ms Diagnosis for depression and, when those symptoms are under control, commences counseling for the career problems for which Ms Diagnosis had originally been referred. Did Counselor Decisiones do anything that might be considered unethical?

NO. As a licensed professional counselor, Counselor Decisiones was operating well within her scope of practice.

Her university and her program were also both appropriately accredited. It might appear as if the counselor had competence only in career counseling, but she has the appropriate accreditations and licenses. Further, the fact that she graduated from a CACREP-accredited program means she met competencies in counseling individuals for personal concerns. Finally, assessment is also a core competency of all CACREP-accredited programs.

The managed care treatment paradigm has grown tremendously through health care reform efforts and the forceful advocacy of the American Mental Health Counselors Association (AMHCA) for mental health specialization as the core clinical counseling specialization. Both of these forces require all counselors to reevaluate the role of diagnosis and clinical models of practice in their work.

The career counseling tradition is significant in that it is a counseling model that is highly focused on developmental counseling traditions and interventions. Thus, it is at odds with any model based on psychopathological interpretations. Niles and Pate (1989) described the distinction between career counseling and mental health counseling as artificial. They saw the fields as needing to be integrated because mental health and work concerns are inextricably linked in the human experiences brought to counseling. As a result of this reasoning, they made a case for examining how the competence and educational standards of both groups need to be enhanced. They viewed the lack of past career counseling competence standards (knowledge and skill) in standards related to treatment of mental and emotional disorders as distressing. If adding diagnostic and treatment planning competencies will be required of career counselors in the future, this will occasion a re-design of training standards in the field to ensure that practitioners meet minimum levels of knowledge and skill in this complex area. Of course, individual practitioners may reach these levels of capability through their individualized programs of specialized professional experience and preparation. (See the discussion of the ethical considerations in diagnosis in Chapter 8—career counselors are likely to be required to know more about this process in the future.)

The second area of specialized emphasis on counselor competence is assessment and testing. Career counselors spend substantial portions of their time in performing these functions. The use of various vocational assessment devices has been integral to the development of the trait and factor model of career counseling that is at the core of this specialized area.

Assessment and testing are primary tools to gain information to be used by client and counselor alike in the career counseling processes (Hood & Johnson, 1991). As such, these tools have tremendous potential for both assistance and harm to clients. Blackwell et al. (1994) distinguished between testing and assessment. **Testing** is the use of a specific tool to gather information or measure some individual quality or characteristic, such as career interest patterns or aptitudes or educational achievement. **Assessment** refers to the process that involves the coordinated planning of information collection and evaluation to address a client's counseling concern or problem. The assessment function requires a higher level of professional training for proper service (Blackwell et al., 1994).

Career counselors are often involved in using career assessment inventories with clients. Career counselors use inventories developed to measure career interest patterns, personality, values, career beliefs, work environment, aptitude, achievement, salience, career maturity, and career obstacles. Career counselors who have been trained to use such inventories for personnel selection must always ensure that the examinee's welfare, explicit prior understanding, and agreement determine who will receive the test results. Further, if such results are to be used in research and publication, each of the elements of informed consent must be met.

The issue of who has sufficient knowledge and training to administer the different types and levels of tests properly is critical in counselor competence. Tests vary greatly in the complexity of administration and interpretation required for appropriate usage. At one extreme are tests such as the individually administered intelligence tests, the Weschler intelligence tests. At the other extreme are simple tests of vocational skills, including typing or language skills like spelling. Copious work has been done to develop competence standards for the qualifications required of test users and other standards for educational and psychological tests. These standards primarily have exerted an influence in controlling the qualifications of test users. Many of the major test distributors require a statement of qualifications by the purchasers of tests. This statement embodies qualifications developed by the Test User Qualifications Group in consultation with test developers (Hood & Johnson, 1991). The Test User Qualifications Group is composed of a number of the professional associations whose members perform assessment and testing services, including ACA and APA. Counselors should review and seek to conform to these qualification requirements for any and all tests that they utilize in their practices. The NCDA Ethical Standards have specific and detailed requirements concerning the ethical obligations of their members in observing the competence standards set for use of these instruments and techniques.

Recent controversies are raging around the attempts of psychology to restrict the ability of nonpsychologists to administer various testing instruments, and they demonstrate the tremendously important role of user competence standards. In recent years, several psychology boards have taken a variety of legal actions to restrict other helping professionals from using various tests. States where actions have been taken include California, Georgia, Indiana, Louisiana, and Ohio (Marino, 1996). While this effort is not yet national, there is a disturbing increase in these actions. As a result, various concerned professional groups formed a coalition to develop strategies to deal with this threat to professional autonomy in scope of practice. The group, the Fair Access Coalition on Testing (FACT), is said to represent more than 500,000 professionals (Marino, 1996). The concerns of career counselors have been represented by the leaders of NCDA in the activities of FACT. While the issues may be resolved in the future, the importance of preserving this essential function of the counselor's role in practice is clear. Career counselors always have worked closely with vocational testing and other types of assessment. The ethical obligations of career counselors should be affirmed by all counselors as they work to preserve this aspect of their services to clients.

CODE COMPARISONS

In terms of ethical standards, NCDA indicates that career counselors are expected to follow the ethical guidelines of the organizations pertinent to them, including NCDA, NBCC, ACA, and APA as well as the laws, such as the Code of Federal Regulations, Title 45, Subtitle A, Part 46; Family Educational Rights and Privacy Act (Buckley Amendment to P. L. 93-380 of the Laws of 1974); and all current federal regulations and various state privacy statutes (NCDA, 1991). The NCDA ethical standards were developed by NBCC and adopted with only minor revision by NCDA. Because NCDA is a division of ACA, its members also are subject to discipline through that body; however, over 1000 members of NCDA have chosen recently to not be dual members with ACA (Pennington, D., 2001, June 25, personal communication). The NCDA Ethics Committee and Professional Standards Committee

have yet to issue guidelines for how to handle such ethics complaints.

ISSUES OF DIVERSITY

Cultural issues are addressed in various parts of the NCDA Ethical Standards. Any time there is a cultural dissimilarity between career counselor and client, the counselor must exercise care in the ensuing interactions (Pope, 1995a, b; Sue, Arredondo, & McDavis, 1992).

Individual versus Collectivist Cultures

One of the most important models to emerge from the multicultural counseling literature over the past 25 years is that of Asante's Afrocentric (collectivist) versus Eurocentric (individualist) model (Asante, 1987). In a collectivist culture, almost all important decisions in a person's life involve both family and community. Clients from collectivistic cultures rarely make career decisions without both family and community consultation (Leong, 1992; Pope, 1999; Pope & Chung, 2000; Pope, Cheng, & Leong, 1998).

Pope (1999) reported that when clients first present for career counseling, it is important that counselors assess how much involvement of both extended family and community is needed by the client in her decision-making process. All or selected family and community members may attend each of the group sessions or only selected sessions, depending on the strength of collectivist ideals in the family. Prior to family attendance, it is especially important that the counselor discuss with the client the roles of each family and community member to identify the most important person in the group decision-making process. This person will need the most information and most deference when the client is ready to choose an occupation.

The difficulty in this situation is in sharing information and identifying who is the client. When offering extended family career counseling as developed by Pope (1999), informing all family members, getting agreement, and maintaining the agreement are the keys to effective career counseling.

Assessment

Hartung et al. (1998) addressed the issue of the appropriate use of career assessment instruments with culturally diverse populations. Career assessment instruments should only be used on populations for whom they have been previously normed. Use of these inventories with individuals who are not included in the normative studies is inappropriate.

Pope (1992) identified inappropriate use of assessment with gay and lesbian clients, which included fear of identification/exposure of sexual orientation, especially in the highly sensitive personnel selection area; bias and prejudice (heterosexism) of the counselor; appropriate interpretation based on identification of client response set; issues of sex-role and "sexual orientation" stereotyping (male "feeling" types and female "thinking" types); and, generally, the appropriate interpretation of psychological tests with a gay male or lesbian client.

Gay and Lesbian Clients

Career counseling with gay and lesbian clients has become a regular topic in the journals of the profession (Pope, 1995a, b, 1996). The refusal by certain career counselors to provide services to gay and lesbian clients on the basis of the counselor's religious beliefs is a topic that is discussed in the ethics and career counseling classes of the profession. The NCDA Ethical Standards state:

> Section A.11—NCDA members avoid bringing their personal or professional issues into the counseling relationship. Through an awareness of the impact of stereotyping and discrimination (e.g., biases based on age, disability, ethnicity, gender, race, religion, or sexual preference), career counselors guard the individual rights and personal dignity of the client in the counseling relationship. (NCDA, 1991)

Gay and lesbian individuals are often the targets of the prejudices of a culture represented by those whose religious beliefs state that homosexual behavior is a sin.

The refusal of professionals who hold such beliefs to provide quality career counseling services to gay and lesbian clients is troubling. In recent years, NCDA, ACA, and APA have been supportive of the rights of gay and lesbian clients to receive ethical and supportive counseling care by all mental health professionals.

CHAPTER SUMMARY

The focus of career counseling has been on helping individuals successfully enter the world of work. Career counselors increasingly take a total life-role perspective that includes factors related to work, family, home, and leisure.

Personal counseling involves professionals who help clients understand and resolve their problems using basic counseling techniques so clients can lead well-adjusted lives. Career counseling focuses on the work realm of a counselee's life. Counselors can assist clients personally as part of the vocational counseling process.

The National Career Development Association (NCDA) is the primary organization that represents career counseling and development professionals. This group defines the profession, its ethics, and standards. Career counselors practice in a variety of settings and render services to diverse individuals, corporations, and organizations.

Career counselors must take particular care in observing requirements to guard client confidentiality, privileged communication, and informed consent, and avoid potentially detrimental counselor-client relationships. Career counselors also must have sufficient knowledge and training to assess clients and administer tests.

REFERENCES

Anderson, T. P., & Fearey, M. S. (1989). Legal guardianship in traumatic brain injury rehabilitation: Ethical implications. *Journal of Head Trauma Rehabilitation, 4,* 57–64.

Asante, M. K. (1987). *The Afrocentric idea.* Philadelphia: Temple University Press.

Blackwell, T. L., Martin, W. E., & Scalia, V. A. (1994). *Ethics in rehabilitation.* Athens, GA: Elliott & Fitzpatrick.

Brewer, J. M. (1942). *History of vocational guidance.* New York: Harper.

Brown, D., & Brooks, L. (1991). *Career counseling techniques.* Boston: Allyn & Bacon.

Brown, D., & Minor, C. W. (Eds.). (1989). *Planning for and working in America: Report of a national survey.* Alexandria, VA: National Career Development Association.

Brown, D., & Minor, C. W. (Eds.). (1992). *Career needs in a diverse workforce: Implications of the NCDA Gallup survey.* Alexandria, VA: National Career Development Association.

Cottone, R. R., Pullen, J. R., & Wilson, W. C. (1983). Counselor licensure, confidentiality, and privileged communication: Implications for private practice in rehabilitation. *Journal of Applied Rehabilitation, 14,* 6–8.

Crites, J. O. (1981). *Career counseling: Models, methods, and materials.* New York: McGraw-Hill.

Engels, D. W. (Ed.). (1994). *The professional practice of career counseling and consultation: A resource document* (2nd ed.). Alexandria, VA: National Career Development Association.

Engels, D. W., Minor, C. W., Sampson, J. P., Jr., & Splete, H. H. (1995). Career counseling specialty: History, development, and prospect. *Journal of Counseling & Development, 37,* 134–138.

Gatens-Robinson, E., & Rubin, S. E. (1995). Societal values and ethical commitments that influence rehabilitation service delivery behavior. In S. E. Rubin & R. T. Roessler (Eds.), *Foundations of the vocational rehabilitation process* (pp. 157–174). Austin, TX: Pro-Ed.

Hansen, L. S. (1997). *Integrated life planning*. San Francisco: Jossey-Bass.

Hartung, P. J., Vandiver, B. J., Leong, F. T. L., Pope, M., Niles, S. G., & Farrow, B. (1998). Appraising cultural identity in Career-Development Asessment and Counseling. *Career Development Quarterly, 46,* 276–293.

Herlihy, B., & Corey, G. (1992). *Dual relationships in counseling*. Alexandria, VA: American Counseling Association.

Hood, A. B., & Johnson, R. W. (1991). *Assessment in counseling: A guide to the use of psychological assessment procedures*. Alexandria, VA: American Counseling Association.

Hoyt, K. B., & Lester, J. N. (1995). *Learning to work: The NCDA Gallup Survey*. Alexandria, VA: National Cancer Development Association.

Isaacson, L. E., & Brown, D. (2000). *Career information, career counseling, and career development* (7th ed.). Boston: Allyn & Bacon.

Leong, F. T. L. (1992). Guidelines for minimizing premature termination among Asian American clients in group counseling. *Journal for Specialists in Group Work, 17,* 218–228.

Marino, T. W. (1996, November). Fair Access Coalition on Testing holds meeting in Washington, D.C. *Counseling Today, 13,* 19.

National Career Development Association (1991). *Ethical Standards (revised)*. Alexandria, VA: NCDA.

National Vocational Guidance Association (1982). *Vocational/Career Counseling Competencies*. Alexandria, VA: NVGA.

Newman, J. L. (1993). Ethical issues in consultation. *Journal of Counseling & Development, 72,* 148–156.

Niles, S. G., & Pate, R. H., Jr. (1989). Competency and training issues related to the integration of career counseling and mental health counseling. *Journal of Career Development, 16,* 63–71.

Norris, W. (1954a). Highlights in the history of the National Vocational Guidance Association. *Personnel and Guidance Journal, 33*(4), 205–208.

Norris, W. (1954b). *The history and development of the National Vocational Guidance Association*. Unpublished doctoral dissertation, George Washington University, Washington, D.C.

Parsons, F. (1909). *Choosing an occupation*. Boston: Houghton Mifflin.

Pope, M. (1992). Bias in the interpretation of psychological tests. In S. Dworkin & F. Gutierrez (Eds.), *Counseling gay men and lesbians: Journey to the end of the rainbow* (pp. 277–291). Alexandria, VA: American Counseling Association.

Pope, M. (1995a). Career interventions for gay and lesbian clients: A synopsis of practice knowledge and research needs. *Career Development Quarterly 44*(2), 191–203.

Pope, M. (1995b). The "salad bowl" is big enough for us all: An argument for the inclusion of lesbians and gays in any definition of multiculturalism. *Journal of Counseling & Development, 73*(3), 301–304.

Pope, M. (1996). Gay and lesbian career counseling: Special career counseling issues. *Journal of Gay and Lesbian Social Services, 4*(4), 91–105.

Pope, M. (1999). Applications of group career counseling techniques in Asian cultures. *Journal for Multicultural Counseling and Development, 27*(1), 18–30.

Pope, M. (2000a). A brief history of career counseling in the USA. *Career Development Quarterly, 48*(3), 194–211.

Pope, M. (2000b, Summer). Report on the survey on recognition of career providers. *Career Developments, 4,* 11.

Pope, M., & Chung, Y. B. (2000). From bakla to tongzhi: Counseling and psychotherapy issues for gay and lesbian Asian and Pacific Islander Americans. In D. S. Sandhu (Ed.), *Asian and Pacific Islander Americans: Issues and concerns for counseling and psychotherapy*. Commack, NY: Nova Science Publishers.

Pope, M., Cheng, W. D., & Leong, F. T. L. (1998). The case of Chou: The inextricability of career to personal/social issues. *Journal of Career Development, 25*(1), 53–64.

Porter, A.D. (2001, Aug–Sep). Counselor licensure: Why now? *CACD Compass,* p. 8.

Salomone, P. R. (1996). Career counseling and job placement: Theory and practice. In E. M. Szymanski & R. M. Parker (Eds.), *Work and disability: Issues and strategies in career development and job placement* (pp. 365–420). Austin, TX: Pro-Ed.

Strein, W., & Hershenson, D. (1991). Confidentiality in nondyadic counseling situations. *Journal of Counseling & Development, 69,* 312–316.

Sue, D. W. (1996). Ethical issues in multicultural counseling. In B. Herlihy & G. Corey (Eds.), *ACA Ethical standards casebook* (pp. 193–204). Alexandria, VA: American Counseling Association.

Sue, D. W., Arredondo, P., & McDavis, R. (1992). Multicultural counseling competencies and standards: A call to this profession. *Journal of Multicultural Counseling and Development, 20,* 64–88.

Super, D. E. (1974). The broader context of career development and vocational guidance: American trends in world perspective. In E. L. Herr (Ed.), *Vocational guidance and human development* (pp. 63–79). Washington, D.C.: Houghton-Mifflin.

Whiteley, J. M. (1984). *Counseling psychology: A historical perspective*. Schenectady, NY: Character Research Press.

Zunker, V. G. (1994). *Career counseling: Applied concepts of life planning*. Pacific Grove, CA: Brooks/Cole.

APPENDIX 15-A

National Career Development Association Ethical Standards (Revised 1991)

These Ethical Standards were developed by the National Board for Certified Counselors (NBCC), an independent, voluntary, not-for-profit organization incorporated in 1982. Titled "Code of Ethics" by NBCC and last amended in February 1987, the Ethical Standards were adopted by the National Career Development Association (NCDA) Board of Directors in 1987 and revised in 1991, with minor changes in wording (e.g., the addition of specific references to NCDA members).

PREAMBLE

NCDA is an educational, scientific, and professional organization dedicated to the enhancement of the worth, dignity, potential, and uniqueness of each individual and, thus, to the service of society. This code of ethics enables the NCDA to clarify the nature of ethical responsibilities for present and future professional career counselors.

SECTION A: GENERAL

1. NCDA members influence the development of the profession by continuous efforts to improve professional practices, services, and research. Professional growth is continuous through the career counselor's career and is exemplified by the development of a philosophy that explains why and how a career counselor functions in the helping relationship. Career counselors must gather data on their effectiveness and be guided by their findings.

2. NCDA members have a responsibility to the clients they are serving and to the institutions within which the services are being performed. Career counselors also strive to assist the respective agency, organization, or institution in providing the highest caliber of professional services. The acceptance of employment in an institution implies that the career counselor is in agreement with the general policies and principles of the institution. Therefore, the professional activities of the career counselor are in accord with the objectives of the institution. If, despite concerted efforts, the career counselor cannot reach agreement with the employer as to acceptable standards of conduct that allow for changes in institutional policy that are conducive to the positive growth and development of clients, then terminating the affiliation should be seriously considered.

3. Ethical behavior among professional associates (e.g., career counselors) must be expected at all times. When accessible information raises doubt as to the ethical behavior of professional colleagues, the NCDA member must take action to attempt to rectify this condition. Such action uses the respective institution's channels first and then uses procedures established by the American Counseling Association, of which NCDA is a division.

4. NCDA members neither claim nor imply professional qualifications which exceed those possessed, and are responsible for correcting any misrepresentation of these qualifications by others.

5. NCDA members must refuse a private fee or other remuneration for consultation or counseling with persons who are entitled to their services through the career counselor's employing institution or agency. The policies of some agencies may make explicit provisions for staff members to engage in private practice with agency clients. However, should agency clients desire private counseling or consulting services, they must be apprised of other options available to them. Career counselors must not divert to their private practices, legitimate clients in their primary agencies or of the institutions with which they are affiliated.

6. In establishing fees for professional counseling services, NCDA members must consider the financial status of clients and the respective locality. In the event that the established fee status is inappropriate for the client, assistance must be provided in finding comparable services of acceptable cost.

7. NCDA members seek only those positions in the delivery of professional services for which they are professionally qualified.

8. NCDA members recognize their limitations and provide services or only use techniques for which they are qualified by training and/or experience. Career counselors recognize the need, and seek continuing education, to assure competent services.

9. NCDA members are aware of the intimacy in the counseling relationship, maintain respect for the client, and avoid engaging in activities that seek to meet their personal needs at the expense of the client.

10. NCDA members do not condone or engage in sexual harassment which is defined as deliberate or repeated comments, gestures, or physical contacts of a sexual nature.

11. NCDA members avoid bringing their personal or professional issues into the counseling relationship. Through an awareness of the impact of stereotyping and discrimination (e.g., biases based on age, disability, ethnicity, gender, race, religion, or sexual preference), career counselors guard the individual rights and personal dignity of the client in the counseling relationship.

12. NCDA members are accountable at all times for their behavior. They must be aware that all actions and behaviors of a counselor reflect on professional integrity and, when inappropriate, can damage the public trust in the counseling profession. To protect public confidence in the counseling profession, career counselors avoid public behavior that is clearly in violation of accepted moral and legal standards.

13. NCDA members have a social responsibility because their recommendations and professional actions may alter the lives of others. Career counselors remain fully cognizant of their impact and are alert to personal, social, organizational, financial, or political situations or pressures which might lead to misuse of their influence.

14. Products or services provided by NCDA members by means of classroom instruction, public lectures, demonstrations, written articles, radio or television programs, or other types of media must meet the criteria cited in Sections A through F of these Ethical Standards.

SECTION B: COUNSELING RELATIONSHIP

1. The primary obligation of NCDA members is to respect the integrity and promote the welfare of the client, regardless of whether the client is assisted individually or in a group relationship. In a group setting, the career counselor is also responsible for taking reasonable precautions to protect individuals from physical and/or psychological trauma resulting from interaction within the group.

2. The counseling relationship and information resulting from it remains confidential, consistent with the legal obligations of the NCDA member. In a group counseling setting, the career counselor sets a norm of confidentiality regarding all group participants' disclosures.

3. NCDA members know and take into account the traditions and practices of other professional groups with whom they work, and they cooperate fully with such groups. If a person is receiving similar services from another professional, career counselors do not offer their own services directly to such a person. If a career counselor is contacted by a person who is already receiving similar services from another professional, the career counselor carefully considers that professional relationship and proceeds with caution and sensitivity to the therapeutic issues as well as the client's welfare. Career counselors discuss these issues with clients so as to minimize the risk of confusion and conflict.

4. When a client's condition indicates that there is a clear and imminent danger to the client or others, the NCDA member must take reasonable personal action or inform responsible authorities. Consultation with other professionals must be used where possible. The assumption of responsibility for the client's behavior must be taken only after careful deliberation, and the client must be involved in the resumption of responsibility as quickly as possible.

5. Records of the counseling relationship, including interview notes, test data, correspondence, audio or visual tape recordings, electronic data storage, and other documents are to be considered professional information for use in counseling. They should not be considered a part of the records of the institution or agency in which the NCDA member is employed unless specified by state statute or regulation. Revelation to others of counseling material must occur only upon the expressed consent of the client; career counselors must make provisions for maintaining confidentiality in the storage and disposal of records. Career counselors providing information to the public or to subordinates, peers, or supervisors have a responsibility to ensure that the content is general; unidentified client information should be accurate and unbiased, and should consist of objective, factual data.

6. NCDA members must ensure that data maintained in electronic storage are secure. The data must be limited to information that is appropriate and necessary for the services being provided and accessible only to appropriate staff members involved in the provision of services by using the best computer security methods available. Career counselors must also ensure that electronically stored data are destroyed when the information is no longer of value in providing services.

7. Data derived from a counseling relationship for use in counselor training or research shall be confined to content that can be disguised to ensure full protection of the identity of the subject/client and shall be obtained with informed consent.

8. NCDA members must inform clients, before or at the time the counseling relationship commences, of the purposes, goals, techniques, rules and procedures, and limitations that may affect the relationship.

9. All methods of treatment by NCDA members must be clearly indicated to prospective recipients and safety precautions must be taken in their use.

10. NCDA members who have an administrative, supervisory, and/or evaluative relationship with individuals seeking counseling services must not serve as the counselor and should refer the individuals to other professionals. Exceptions are made only in instances where an individual's situation warrants counseling intervention and another alternative is unavailable. Dual relationships with clients that might impair the career counselor's objectivity and professional judgment must be avoided and/or the counseling relationship terminated through referral to another competent professional.

11. When NCDA members determine an inability to be of professional assistance to a potential or existing client, they must, respectively, not initiate the counseling relationship or immediately terminate the relationship. In either event, the career counselor must suggest appropriate alternatives. Career counselors must be knowledgeable about referral resources so that a satisfactory referral can be initiated. In the event that the client declines a suggested referral, the career counselor is not obligated to continue the relationship.

12. NCDA members may choose to consult with any other professionally competent person about a client and must notify clients of this right. Career counselors must avoid placing a consultant in a conflict-of-interest situation that would preclude the consultant's being a proper party to the career counselor's efforts to help the client.

13. NCDA members who counsel clients from cultures different from their own must gain knowledge, personal awareness, and sensitivity pertinent to the client populations served and must incorporate culturally relevant techniques into their practice.

14. When NCDA members engage in intensive counseling with a client, the client's counseling needs should be

assessed. When needs exist outside the counselor's expertise, appropriate referrals should be made.

15. NCDA members must screen prospective group counseling participants, especially when the emphasis is on self-understanding and growth through self-disclosure. Career counselors must maintain an awareness of each group participant's welfare throughout the group process.

16. When electronic data and systems are used as a component of counseling services, NCDA members must ensure that the computer application, and any information it contains, are appropriate for the respective needs of clients and is nondiscriminatory. Career counselors must ensure that they themselves have acquired a facilitation level of knowledge with any system they use including hands-on application, search experience, and understanding of the uses of all aspects of the computer-based system. In selecting and/or maintaining computer-based systems that contain career information, career counselors must ensure that the systems provide current, accurate, and locally relevant information. Career counselors must also ensure that clients are intellectually, emotionally, and physically compatible with the use of the computer application and understand its purpose and operation. Client use of a computer application must be evaluated to correct possible problems and assess subsequent needs.

17. NCDA members who develop self-help, stand-alone computer software for use by the general public must first ensure that it is initially designed to function in a stand-alone manner, as opposed to modifying software that was originally designed to require support from a counselor. Secondly, the software must include program statements that provide the user with intended outcomes, suggestions for using the software, descriptions of inappropriately used applications, and descriptions of when and how counseling services might be beneficial. Finally, the manual must include the qualifications of the developer, the development process, validation data, and operating procedures.

SECTION C: MEASUREMENT AND EVALUATION

1. NCDA members must provide specific orientation or information to an examinee prior to and following the administration of assessment instruments or techniques so that the results may be placed in proper perspective with other relevant factors. The purpose of testing and the explicit use of the results must be made known to an examinee prior to testing.

2. In selecting assessment instruments or techniques for use in a given situation or with a particular client, NCDA members must evaluate carefully the instrument's specific theoretical bases and characteristics, validity, relia-bility, and appropriateness. Career counselors are professionally responsible for using unvalidated information with special care.

3. When making statements to the public about assessment instruments or techniques, NCDA members must provide accurate information and avoid false claims or misconceptions concerning the meaning of psychometric terms. Special efforts are often required to avoid unwarranted connotations of terms such as IQ and grade-equivalent scores.

4. Because many types of assessment techniques exist, NCDA members must recognize the limits of their competence and perform only those functions for which they have received appropriate training.

5. NCDA members must note when tests are not administered under standard conditions or when unusual behavior or irregularities occur during a testing session and the results must be designated as invalid or of questionable validity. Unsupervised or inadequately supervised assessments, such as mail-in tests, are considered unethical. However, the use of standardized instruments that are designed to be self-administered and self-scored, such as interest inventories, is appropriate.

6. Because prior coaching or dissemination of test materials can invalidate test results, NCDA members are professionally obligated to maintain test security. In addition, conditions that produce most favorable test results must be made known to an examinee (e.g., penalty for guessing).

7. NCDA members must consider psychometric limitations when selecting and using an instrument, and must be cognizant of the limitations when interpreting the results. When tests are used to classify clients, career counselors must ensure that periodic review and/or retesting are conducted to prevent client stereotyping.

8. An examinee's welfare, explicit prior understanding, and agreement are the factors used when determining who receives the test results. NCDA members must see that appropriate interpretation accompanies any release of individual or group test data (e.g., limitations of instrument and norms).

9. NCDA members must ensure that computer-generated assessment administration and scoring programs function properly, thereby providing clients with accurate assessment results.

10. NCDA members who are responsible for making decisions based on assessment results must have appropriate training and skills in educational and psychological measurement including validation criteria, test research, and guidelines for test development and use.

11. NCDA members must be cautious when interpreting the results of instruments that possess insufficient technical data, and must explicitly state to examinees the specific purposes for the use of such instruments.

12. NCDA members must proceed with caution when attempting to evaluate and interpret performances of

minority group members or other persons who are not represented in the norm group on which the instrument was standardized.

13. NCDA members who develop computer-based interpretations to support the assessment process must ensure that the validity of the interpretations is established prior to the commercial distribution of the computer application.

14. NCDA members recognize that test results may become obsolete, and avoid the misuse of obsolete data.

15. NCDA members must avoid the appropriation, reproduction, or modification of published tests or parts thereof without acknowledgment and permission from the publisher.

SECTION D: RESEARCH AND PUBLICATION

1. NCDA members will adhere to relevant guidelines on research with human subjects. These include:
   a. Code of Federal Regulations, Title 45, Subtitle A, Part 46, as currently issued.
   b. American Psychological Association. (1982). *Ethical principles in the conduct of research with human participants*. Washington, D.C.: Author.
   c. American Psychological Association. (1981). Research with human participants. *American Psychologist, 36,* 633–638.
   d. Family Educational Rights and Privacy Act. (Buckley Amendment to P. L. 93-380 of the Laws of 1974).
   e. Current federal regulations and various state privacy acts.

2. In planning research activities involving human subjects, NCDA members must be aware of and responsive to all pertinent ethical principles and ensure that the research problem, design, and execution are in full compliance with the principles.

3. The ultimate responsibility for ethical research lies with the principal researcher, although others involved in research activities are ethically obligated and responsible for their own actions.

4. NCDA members who conduct research with human subjects are responsible for the subjects' welfare throughout the experiment and must take all reasonable precautions to avoid causing injurious psychological, physical, or social effects on their subjects.

5. NCDA members who conduct research must abide by the following basic elements of informed consent:
   a. a fair explanation of the procedures to be followed, including an identification of those which are experimental.
   b. a description of the attendant discomforts and risks.
   c. a description of the benefits to be expected.
   d. a disclosure of appropriate alternative procedures that would be advantageous for subjects.
   e. an offer to answer any inquiries concerning the procedures.
   f. an instruction that subjects are free to withdraw their consent and to discontinue participation in the project or activity at any time.

6. When reporting research results, explicit mention must be made of all the variables and conditions known to the NCDA member that may have affected the outcome of the study or the interpretation of the data.

7. NCDA members who conduct and report research investigations must do so in a manner that minimizes the possibility that the results will be misleading.

8. NCDA members are obligated to make available sufficient original research data to qualified others who may wish to replicate the study.

9. NCDA members who supply data, aid in the research of another person, report research results, or make original data available, must take due care to disguise the identity of respective subjects in the absence of specific authorization from the subject to do otherwise.

10. When conducting and reporting research, NCDA members must be familiar with, and give recognition to, previous work on the topic, must observe all copyright laws, and must follow the principles of giving full credit to those to whom credit is due.

11. NCDA members must give due credit through joint authorship, acknowledgment, footnote statements, or other appropriate means to those who have contributed significantly to the research and/or publication, in accordance with such contributions.

12. NCDA members should communicate to others the results of any research judged to be of professional value. Results that reflect unfavorably on institutions, programs, services, or vested interests must not be withheld.

13. NCDA members who agree to cooperate with another individual in research and/or publication incur an obligation to cooperate as promised in terms of punctuality of performance and with full regard to the completeness and accuracy of the information required.

14. NCDA members must not submit the same manuscript, or one essentially similar in content, for simultaneous publication consideration by two or more journals. In addition, manuscripts that are published in whole or substantial part in another journal or published work should not be submitted for publication without acknowledgment and permission from the previous publication.

SECTION E: CONSULTING

Consultation refers to a voluntary relationship between a professional helper and help-needing individual, group, or social unit in which the consultant is providing help to the client(s) in defining and solving a work-related problem or potential work-related problem with a client or client system.

1. NCDA members acting as consultants must have a high degree of self-awareness of their own values, knowledge, skills, limitations, and needs in entering a helping relationship that involves human and/or organizational change. The focus of the consulting relationship must be on the issues to be resolved and not on the person(s) presenting the problem.
2. In the consulting relationship, the NCDA member and client must understand and agree upon the problem definition, subsequent goals, and predicted consequences of interventions selected.
3. NCDA members must be reasonably certain that they, or the organization represented, have the necessary competencies and resources for giving the kind of help that is needed or that may develop later, and that appropriate referral resources are available to the consultant.
4. NCDA members in a consulting relationship must encourage and cultivate client adaptability and growth toward self-direction. NCDA members must maintain this role consistently and not become decision makers for clients or create a future dependency.
5. NCDA members conscientiously adhere to the NCDA Ethical Standards when announcing consultant availability for services.

SECTION F: PRIVATE PRACTICE

1. NCDA members should assist the profession by facilitating the availability of counseling services in private as well as public settings.
2. In advertising services as private practitioners, NCDA members must advertise in a manner that accurately informs the public of the professional services, expertise, and counseling techniques available.
3. NCDA members who assume an executive leadership role in a private practice organization do not permit their names to be used in professional notices during periods of time when they are not actively engaged in the private practice of counseling.

4. NCDA members may list their highest relevant degree, type, and level of certification and/or license, address, telephone number, office hours, type and/or description of services, and other relevant information. Listed information must not contain false, inaccurate, misleading, partial, out-of-context, or otherwise deceptive material or statements.
5. NCDA members who are involved in partnership or corporation with other professionals must, in compliance with the regulations of the locality, clearly specify the separate specialties of each member of the partnership or corporation.
6. NCDA members have an obligation to withdraw from a private-practice counseling relationship if it violates the NCDA Ethical Standards, if the mental or physical condition of the NCDA member renders it difficult to carry out an effective professional relationship, or if the counseling relationship is no longer productive for the client.

PROCEDURES FOR PROCESSING ETHICAL COMPLAINTS

As a division of the American Counseling Association (ACA), the National Career Development Association (NCDA) adheres to the guidelines and procedures for processing ethical complaints and the disciplinary sanctions adopted by ACA. A complaint against an NCDA member may be filed by any individual or group of individuals ("complainant"), whether or not the complainant is a member of NCDA. Action will not be taken on anonymous complaints.

For specifics on how to file ethical complaints and a description of the guidelines and procedures for processing complaints, contact:

ACA Ethics Committee
c/o Executive Director
American Counseling Association
5999 Stevenson Avenue
Alexandria, VA 22304
Telephone: 1-800-347-6647

APPENDIX 15-B

NCDA Guidelines for Career Information

Guidelines for the Preparation and Evaluation of Career and Occupational Information Literature

http://ncda.org

Overview
Definition of Terms

General Guidelines
    Dating and Revisions
    Credits
    Accuracy of Information

OVERVIEW

These guidelines are designed to be used by both the publishers and the consumers of career and occupational information literature. Because career and occupational literature is often an individual's initial (and sometimes only) exposure to a specific occupation or occupational field, it is very important that this information be accurately and comprehensively conveyed to the user. The guidelines represent the National Career Development Association's (NCDA) views of what constitutes good career and occupational literature. The Association encourages the use of these guidelines by publishers to ensure quality control in their publications and by those who select and use career and occupational literature to ensure maximum value from their purchases.

Helping individuals obtain, evaluate, and use career and occupational information is within the scope of NCDA's mission to facilitate the career development of individuals. The revision of these Guidelines is one of the services provided by NCDA to encourage the development of accurate and reliable information by publishers, and the informed use of this information by consumers and clients.

The nature of career information has changed considerably in its content and its delivery since NCDA was founded in 1913, as the National Vocational Guidance Association. However, the need for career and vocational information as an important consideration in career planning has remained constant. As recently as 1989, 65% of the adults who participated in the NCDA Gallup Survey indicated that if they could plan their work lives again, they would try to get more information about career choices and options.

In addition to their evaluative use locally, these guidelines also form the basis for the ratings of current career and occupational literature by the Career Information Review Service of NCDA. These ratings appear in *The Career Development Quarterly* to assist professionals in their selection of quality career and occupational information literature.

DEFINITION OF TERMS

The first step in any evaluation process is to determine that all parties concerned are using terms that communicate the same meaning to all. To address this issue of clarity, the following guidelines have been designed to be used for occupational literature and for career literature. The content and purpose of these two types of literature are closely related but differ in some important aspects. Therefore, the terms occupation, occupational field, career, and career progression have been used in these guidelines to refer to the specific type of information being discussed. Occupation refers to a specific job, usually indicated by a job title and/or number. Occupational field refers to a group or cluster of related occupations, often but not necessarily requiring similar skills, knowledge, and abilities and sharing similar working conditions. Career is a more encompassing term that includes, but is not limited to, the series of occupations one might expect to hold in the course of his or her working history. Career progression refers to the series of occupations that might be held during one's work history, each involving increasing levels of decision making, responsibility, status, and compensation.

GENERAL GUIDELINES

This section discusses items related to the general preparation and presentation of career and occupational literature.

1. Dating and Revisions.   The date of publication should be clearly indicated. Because of rapid changes in employment outlook and earnings, material should be revised at least every three to four years to stay current and accurate. This is particularly important in highly technical and skilled occupations and less a factor in unskilled or semiskilled occupations.
2. Credits.   Credits should include (a) publisher, (b) consultants, (c) sponsor, and (d) sources of any statistical data. Photographs and original artwork should be accompanied by the name of the photographer/artist, photographic outfit, and copyright mark (if any).
3. Accuracy of Information.   Information should be accurate and free from distortion caused by self-serving bias, sex stereotyping, or dated resources. Whenever possible, resources over five years old should be avoided. Information should be secured from and/or reviewed by knowledgeable sources within the occupation, the occupational field, or career research. Reviewers should be selected to reflect different viewpoints germane to an occupation (e.g., business and labor) and be trained in the evaluation process. Reviewers must not use the literature to promote their own concerns or viewpoints. Data such as earnings and employment projections should be based on current, reliable, and comprehensive research.
4. Format.   The information should be conveyed in a clear, concise, and interesting manner. Although infor-

mation from the Content Guidelines should appear in all publications, publishers are encouraged to vary the manner of presentation for the sake of stimulation and appeal. A standard style and format for grammar should be adopted and utilized throughout the document.

5. Vocabulary.   The vocabulary of the information should be appropriate to the target group. Career and occupational information is used by people of varying ages and abilities. Information designed for a specific age range or for any other clearly identifiable group should be clearly identified as such. Information designed for broader use should be comprehensible to younger persons but suitable in style for adults. Technical terminology or jargon should be either fully explained or avoided. The use of nonsexist language is essential.

6. Use of Information.   The intended purpose, the target audience, and the potential use of the information should be clearly identified in the introduction to the material. Reviews should specify the intended audience, such as elementary schools, middle/junior high schools, high schools, vocational schools, community college, colleges/universities, employment/training programs, rehabilitation agencies, correctional agencies, libraries, or specify other audiences. Persons often do not have the opportunity to thoroughly review materials until after the materials have been purchased. The authors and publishers should help potential purchasers determine whether the materials present useful information.

7. Bias and Stereotyping.   Care should be taken in all publications to eliminate bias and stereotyping against persons with a disability, or based on gender, race, social status, ethnicity, age, or religion. Job title and information should be bias-free. Particular care should be taken to ensure the use of gender-free language. If graphics are used, people of different races, ages, sexes, and physical abilities should be portrayed at various occupational levels. Where applicable, data, information, or resources relevant to equal opportunity for women, minorities, or persons with a disability should be included.

8. Graphics.   Graphic displays, when used, should enhance the value of the narrative information. Pictures should be current and portray individuals engaged in activities primary to the occupation or unique to it. Again, the importance of portraying individuals of different sexes, races, ages, and physical abilities in a variety of roles cannot be overemphasized.

CONTENT GUIDELINES

This section discusses guideline items that deal with the content of information on occupations and/or occupational fields. Reviews of nonoccupational materials will rely primarily on the previously discussed criteria.

1. Duties and Nature of the Work.   The career and occupational literature should describe in a clear and interesting fashion: (a) the purpose of the work, (b) the activities of the worker, (c) the skills, knowledge, interests, and abilities necessary to perform the work, and (d) any specializations commonly practiced in the occupation. Literature that describes occupational fields should also include: (a) the overall function and importance of the field, (b) the variety of occupations available, (c) the common skills, knowledge, interests, and abilities shared by members of the field or industry, and (d) contrasts among the various occupations represented in the field.

2. Work Setting and Conditions.   The portrayal of the work setting and conditions should include a description of the physical and mental activities and the work environment. Where applicable, the information should include the full range of possible settings in which the work may be performed. The range of typical physical and mental activities should be described. Environmental characteristics should include the physical surroundings, the psychological environment, and the social environment. In addition to these characteristics, other conditions related to the performance of the work, such as time requirements or travel requirements, should be described.

Aspects of the work that might be regarded as undesirable are as crucial to realistic decision making as those that are generally considered desirable; therefore, care should be taken to make descriptions as comprehensive as possible. Because different individuals may view a given work condition as either positive or negative, the descriptions should be free of the author's bias and present a balanced picture. The variety and similarity of settings should be discussed. Specific geographic locations related to employment in the occupational field should be included.

3. Preparation Required.   The preparation required for entrance into the occupation, or into various levels of an occupation, should be clearly stated. The length and type of training required and the skills, knowledge, abilities, and interests of successful students or trainees should be indicated. Typical methods of financial support during training should be included. Alternative means of obtaining the necessary preparation or experience should be stated where applicable. Readers should be informed of any preferred employer selection criteria over and above minimal preparation requirements. In literature that describes a range of occupations in a career progression, the various levels of preparation required for employment in each successive occupation should also be highlighted.

4. Special Requirements or Considerations.   Bonafide physical requirements that are necessary for entrance into a particular occupation should be included. Only bonafide occupational qualifications should be

addressed. Consideration should be given to addressing job accommodations that can and are legally required to open opportunity to all the members of our society.

Licenses, certifications, or memberships in unions or professional societies may also be required for some occupations. These requirements should be indicated and the process necessary for achieving any of these requirements should be described.

Personal criteria: The listing of qualities desired of any worker (e.g., honesty, dependability) is not particularly valuable to individuals attempting to differentiate various career possibilities. On occasion it may be useful and appropriate to consider personal criteria, if available, regarding unique skills, knowledge, mental and physical abilities, and interests. The basis for the information should be clearly identified.

Social and psychological factors: Participation in an occupation has important effects on the lifestyle of the individual (and his or her family), and these effects should receive appropriate consideration in the presentation of information. When these factors are determined to be appropriate to the use of the material, the source of the information presented on social and psychological factors should be clearly identified.

5. Methods of Entry. The variety of means for typical entry into the occupation should be indicated, as well as any preferred avenues for entry. Alternative approaches should be described where applicable—particularly for those occupations where experience can be substituted for education and other formal preparation or where education can be substituted for work experience.

6. Earnings and Other Benefits. Current data on entry wages, average earnings, and the typical range of earnings in the occupation should be presented. In addition, variations in average earnings by geographic region should be reported if available. Fringe benefits have become an increasingly important aspect of total compensation, and ample coverage of both typical benefits and those that are unique to the occupation or occupational field should be given.

7. Usual Advancement Possibilities. The typical and alternative career progressions related to the occupational field should be presented. The supplementary skills, knowledge, and abilities necessary for advancement and the alternative means for acquiring them should be indicated. Issues such as the role of job change, availability of training, and seniority should be discussed as they pertain to advancement in the particular occupational field.

8. Employment Outlook. Statements concerning the employment outlook should be realistic and include both the short-range and the long-range outlook for the occupation and occupational field. Mention of the past record of the occupation may be useful in completing its outlook picture. A broad range of factors that may have an impact on the employment outlook, including economic, demographic, technological, geographic, social, and political factors, should be considered. Current U.S. Department of Labor or other expert research should be consulted. Realism is essential, but readers should not be discouraged from entering highly competitive fields if they have the ability, interest, and motivation to succeed.

9. Opportunities for Experience and Exploration. Literature should list opportunities for part-time and summer employment; opportunities for internships, apprenticeships, and cooperative work programs; and opportunities for volunteer work. Pertinent clubs and organizations, as well as school-related activities and programs, should be described. Publishers are encouraged to give sufficient attention to this heading because these career-related possibilities can be acted on immediately and thus have high motivational value.

10. Related Occupations. Occupations that share similar requirements on aptitudes, interest patterns, or work environments with the occupation under consideration should be listed. In addition to its value in early exploration, this information is particularly useful to adults considering lateral occupational changes.

11. Sources of Additional Information. Reference should be made to additional sources of information such as professional or trade organizations and associations, specific books or pamphlets, journals or trade publications, audiovisual materials, and literature available from public agencies. For students, the assistance of school guidance counselors or college career counselors is recommended.

CAREER AND OCCUPATIONAL LITERATURE REVIEWER'S RATING FORM—1991

This 1991 edition of the guidelines is a revision of the guidelines for career and occupational literature previously published by NCDA/NVGA. This revision was prepared under the direction of Jennifer B. Wilson, Ph.D., University of Wisconsin-La Crosse, La Crosse, Wisconsin (Chairperson of the CIRS Subcommittee on Print Materials), with the assistance of the Career Information Review Service Committee, chaired by Roger Lambert, Ph.D., University of Wisconsin-Madison. The guidelines were approved by the NCDA Board of Directors April, 1991.

APPENDIX 15-C

NCDA Guidelines for Videos

Guidelines for the Preparation and Evaluation of Video Career Media

http://ncda.org

Overview
Content
Production Considerations
User's Guide
Bias-Free Presentation
NCDA Video Production and Review
Service Evaluation Form

OVERVIEW

These guidelines are designed to assist those who select and use career-related video media. They will also assist producers in creating quality materials to meet the needs and standards of the career development field.

High-quality videos accomplish specific purposes with particular audiences. Producers must not only design materials to accomplish particular ends, but must assume the responsibility for conveying information regarding the effective use of such materials.

These guidelines are geared to a particular point of view because of the user-audience orientation of the majority of guideline readers. The emphasis on content, instructional design, bias, and quality of information is considered more relevant to the concerns of NCDA members. Individuals using these guidelines must determine the extent to which videos meet the criteria. (No judgement should be made regarding the effectiveness of any materials in serving purposes other than those related to career development.)

Each criterion is designed to focus attention on standards that would discriminate between a video that is considered excellent versus one that is considered fair. Such criteria should guide users in the selection and appropriate use of videos as well as prove useful to producers who are concerned about designing highly marketable products.

CONTENT

This section deals with the objectives, concepts, and information portrayed in the video. It directs attention to the impact of the video on the audience. The specific criteria assess what may be learned (content) as well as the instructional design (process).

1. Early Presentation of Intent. The purpose of the video must be obvious to the viewer within the first quarter of the presentation. Explicit or implicit presentation of the purpose early in the video prepares the audience for the learning tasks involved and increases the effectiveness of the video as a motivational and learning tool. Deviations from this practice are acceptable providing they are a part of a rational instructional design. In such instances, the instructional design should be clearly explained in the user's guide.

2. Integrity of Title. The title must accurately reflect the content or purpose of the video, but creativity for the sake of audience motivation or in the name of poetic license is not ruled out. In no case, however, should the title be misleading in terms of audience anticipation or to influence potential purchasers.

3. Free of Extraneous (Noncareer Related) Material. The video must adhere to an organized development of the content required in order to fulfill adequately the stated objectives. The relationship of the content to the objectives must be clearly stated in the user's guide and video packaging, and should be obvious when viewing the video.

   The costs involved with videos may induce both producer and purchaser to favor videos that attempt to accomplish too much for too many. Materials must effectively deal with a manageable number of objectives for specified audiences. The video that addresses a limited number of objectives adequately is usually more desirable than one that overwhelms the audience with content and a multitude of purposes. A video directed toward a specific audience is an ideal vehicle for developing content and eliciting responses that are appropriate to the abilities and interests of that audience. The differences among audiences are too significant to be sacrificed in the name of false economy.

4. Accurate and Adequate Presentation of Concepts and Information. Concepts must be portrayed and illustrated within the video in a manner appropriate for the comprehension level of the intended audience(s). Terminology referring to basic career development concepts must be defined in the user's guide whenever there is a possibility of ambiguity.

   Occupational information must be accurate, comprehensive, and current. Occupations and occupation groups must be portrayed in a manner that makes the video a reliable source of current information. Videos with the primary mission of conveying occupational information should include the following details:

Work performed
Work settings
Potential personal rewards
Entry requirements and advancement possibilities
Related occupations and career alternatives
Credential requirements and union/professional affiliations
Personal qualifications
Occupational outlook in terms of short-range and long-range conditions

Factors underlying trends and changes must be identified when possible to help interpret facts as they might exist at the time of viewing. Information that is more than two years old must be considered questionable. Most videos require revision every two years in order to update information presented. It is suggested that videos be revised/updated or retrieved if they contain information more than three years old.

Information should be balanced in terms of the advantages and disadvantages of the career alternatives. Although the purpose of the video or those of the producer or distributor may preclude a totally unbiased presentation, sufficient objectivity is required to ensure credibility and accuracy of information.

5. Stimulates Transition from Passive to Active Response. The video must motivate the audience toward some appropriate, overt behavioral response. The content and manner in which it is presented must help the transition from passive viewing to discussion, follow-up activities, or other responses to provide the active involvement that is essential for optimal learning.

PRODUCTION CONSIDERATIONS

This section deals with technical matters as they contribute to or detract from the video as an effective instructional tool. The specific items are intended to identify those characteristics that may be shortcomings in technical quality. Artistic judgements and aesthetic taste are left to the discretion of the producer.

1. Credits. Because credits serve more than just a utilitarian function in career guidance videos, the following information must appear in the screen credits to help the user and the audience identify the viewpoint and assess the reliability of the information presented in the video.

    Date of production or revision. The date of production or release of the revision must appear in the credits to inform the viewer of the currency of the information presented. Although marketing considerations may cause producers to ignore this standard, career guidance videos must provide the viewer with this important date.

    Name of producer or distributor, sponsor, contributor, and sources of funds. This information not only helps the user distinguish between videos with similar titles or contents, but it provides important reference information when the guides and other materials are separated from the videos. This information may also establish a point of view or identify a potential bias that should be considered by the audience.

    Name, title, and credentials of consultants. This information often gives credence to the production in the eyes of the audience. Although the listing must be brief, this portion of the credits should do more than just exhibit a name that conveys no meaning to the intended audience. The information may also be a reference for the user when materials accompanying the video are unavailable.

2. Picture Quality. The visual portion of the video must be viewed in terms of focus, clarity, color accuracy, contrast, and color balance. Individual frames and visual sequences should be free of any characteristics that detract from the intended message and impact of the video.

3. Sound Quality. The audio portion of the video must be viewed in terms of clarity, volume, pace, and narrative music mix. Voices should use appropriate diction and dynamics and should feature distinctive qualities when recognition of more than one voice is required of the audience. Voices should also match the individuals pictured. Music and sound effects should contribute to the meaning and message of the video. The total effect of the sound should be free of any characteristics that detract from the intended message and impact of the video.

4. Length. The length of the video should be weighed in balance with the content, intended audience, other technical considerations, and entertainment or aesthetic value.

5. Packaging. The packaging should be designed to assure maximum security of the materials and facilitate their identification and use. Color and labeling should expedite identification for storage, retrieval, and delivery. The video's general purpose, specific behavioral objectives, intended audience(s), and running time in minutes must be stated within the packaging.

USER'S GUIDE

The user's guide is an important part of any instructional package. It is a reference document and a source of information to guide potential users in selecting and using videos effectively. The user's guide must identify the audience and purpose of the video and how to use it most effectively. It must also provide instructions and suggestions to help use the video effectively.

1. Credits. Credits must be comprehensive and complete in order to serve their reference function satisfactorily. The following information should be included:

Date of production/revision. The date of production or release must be stated in the guide to inform the user of the recency of the information contained in the video. Revisions must be noted and the original titles and production dates included.

Name and address of producer and distributor, sponsor, contributor, and source of funds. This is basic identification data. Not all of this information may be available or appropriate. Such information, however, as sponsors, contributors, and sources of funds may alert the user to possible points of view or bias that may exist in the video. These data may also suggest possible sources of additional materials or information.

Name, title, and credentials of consultant. A competent professional staff is required to produce quality career guidance materials. Producers often supplement their professional staff with qualified consultants, who have had an active involvement in the production of videos and materials to meet the standards and needs of the field. The user should know of these efforts, or their lack, as a factor to consider when examining the reliability and efficacy of the video. The credentials of consultants or appropriate staff members should be explicit in terms of field of endeavor and areas of professional expertise and specialization.

2. Purposes, Objectives, and Audience(s). The general purpose and the specific behavioral objectives of the video must be stated in the user's guide. Such statements must also identify the audience(s) toward which the video is directed.

   Objectives must be concise and stated in terms that enable the user and the audience to envision the learning tasks, address those tasks, and assess the degree to which they are accomplished. Terminology referring to basic career development concepts must be defined when there is a possibility of ambiguity.

3. Synopsis. The synopsis must convey an accurate description of the content of the video and the teaching strategy used to accomplish the stated purpose. It must include the running time in minutes. It is recommended that the guide also include additional aids such as full or partial scripts, frame reproductions or descriptions, and suggested stop-and-discuss points in order to assist the user in planning for effective use of the video.

4. Verifiable Results of Field Testing. Reputable producers must use some kind of evaluation procedures to determine the effectiveness of their materials. Although the state of the art precludes a statement of minimum standards for field testing and evaluation at this time, the user must have information regarding results obtained when the video was used with audiences similar to the target audience(s) identified in the guide.

5. Discussion, Activities, and Resources. Specific suggestions must be provided to assist the user in moving the audience from passive viewing to active involvement that is relevant to the purposes of the videos and the developmental level of the intended audience(s).

Discussion questions should help the user focus on the important issues and concepts presented in the video. Suggested questions should generate reflective and inferential thinking rather than simple recall. The interests and abilities of the intended audience(s) must be considered. Suggested activities must serve some useful purpose in terms of the career development of the audience. Activities should function as opportunities for follow-up action suggested in the video or to seek answers to questions raised in the video.

A bibliography of related sources of information, a list of resources available to further the purposes of the video, and other such references must be provided to help the user amplify the impact of the video.

BIAS-FREE PRESENTATION

This section addresses itself explicitly to the responsibilities of the video producers to produce bias-free materials. Videos must go beyond tokenism and conventional role stereotyping and provide real examples of the world of work. A video lacking a progressive social orientation would also be deficient in objectivity and accuracy of information. The criteria in the section, however, are considered of fundamental importance and worthy of independent consideration when evaluating videos to be used for career guidance.

1. Free of Sex/Age Role Stereotyping. Occupational role stereotyping must be avoided. Individuals at all ages and of both sexes should be equitably portrayed at employment levels ranging from training to executive positions. The term "equitable" is used to connote fairness and justice rather than some statistically determined division.

2. Free of Ethnic/Race/Religious/Physical Impairment Stereotyping. American society is multiracial and multiethnic and must be represented as such in career guidance videos. Care must be taken to avoid ethnic stereotyping and materials should be free of stereotyping based on physical impairment. Representatives from all ethnic groups as well as all individuals qualified to do a job, regardless of handicapping condition, should be portrayed at all levels of employment. Religion is not an appropriate topic in career guidance videos except as an area of employment for certain occupations.

3. Free of Value Purposes, Social Class Bias, and Self-Serving or Promotional Purposes. The videos must present information objectively and not imply a particular value orientation or social class bias. Explicit or implicit value judgements must not be evident regarding any work ethic. The video must be devoid of self-serving purposes and must not overtly promote a particular occupation, career field, business, or industry without due representation of both the positive and the negative factors involved.

NCDA Video Production and Review Service Evaluation Form

Video Title:
Date Released:
Sale Price: $_____
Rental Price: $_____

Producer:
Street Address:
City: State: Zip:

Distributor:
Street Address:
City: State: Zip:

SETTING/POPULATION(S):

_____ Elementary Schools
_____ Middle or Junior High Schools
_____ High Schools
_____ Vocational Schools
_____ Two-Year Colleges
_____ Four-Year Colleges or Universities
_____ Other

RATING SCALE:

5 = Outstanding, 4 = Good, 3 = Satisfactory, 2 = Poor,
1 = Unsatisfactory, 0 = Does not apply

Content:
5 4 3 2 1 0   Early presentation of intent
5 4 3 2 1 0   Integrity of title
5 4 3 2 1 0   Free of extraneous (noncareer related) material
5 4 3 2 1 0   Accurate and adequate presentation of concepts/information
5 4 3 2 1 0   Stimulates transition from passive to active response
Total points for content = _____

Production Considerations:
5 4 3 2 1 0   Credits
5 4 3 2 1 0   Picture Quality
5 4 3 2 1 0   Sound Quality
5 4 3 2 1 0   Length
5 4 3 2 1 0   Packaging
Total points for production considerations = _____

User's Guide:
5 4 3 2 1 0   Credits
5 4 3 2 1 0   Purpose, objectives, and audience
5 4 3 2 1 0   Synopsis
5 4 3 2 1 0   Verifiable results of field testing
5 4 3 2 1 0   Discussion, activities, and resources
Total points for user's guide = _____

Bias-Free Presentation:
5 4 3 2 1 0   Free of sex/age role stereotyping
5 4 3 2 1 0   Free of ethnic/race/religious/physical impairment stereotyping
5 4 3 2 1 0   Free of value purposes, social class bias, and self-serving or promotional purposes
Total points for bias-free presentation = _____

TOTAL POINTS ALL AREAS = _____

75–90 = Outstanding, 59–74 = Good,
42–58 = Satisfactory, 25–41 = Poor,
0–24 = Unsatisfactory

Synopsis (Give summary of content without judgement):

Critical Comments (Give strengths or weaknesses of content, production considerations, user's guide, bias-free presentation):

Comments (Recommendations and suggestions for the producers/authors; if there is a discrepancy between the total score and your evaluation, please document your evaluation decision):

Reviewed by: _____.

Date: _____.

Source: The 1992 edition of the Guidelines for the Preparation and Evaluation of Video Career Media was prepared under the direction of Rich Feller, Ph.D., Colorado State University, Fort Collins, CO (chairperson of the CIRS Subcommittee on Video Review Guidelines), with the assistance of the Career Information Review Service Committee, chaired by Charles Mollerup, Idaho SOICC, Boise, ID. The committee wishes to thank Roger Lambert and Paul Downes for the initial leadership in this effort. The Guidelines were approved by the NCDA Board of Directors January, 1992.

APPENDIX 15-D

Career Software Review Guidelines

INTRODUCTION

The National Career Development Association (NCDA) has a long history of evaluating career materials. The Association's career information reviews have for years helped counselors and career center coordinators select from available career information books and pamphlets.

In the last decade, several professional groups have developed evaluation criteria for career software. As computers came into use to help individuals access career information, the United States Department of Labor and then the National Occupational Information Coordinating Committee provided start-up grants so individual states could implement systems of career information. State system operators formed the Association of Computer-Based Systems for Career Information (ACSCI) and adopted standards for the operation of such systems, publishing them periodically since 1980. In 1985, ACSCI also published guidelines for the effective use of computer-based systems for career information.

Several states conducted or commissioned evaluations before adopting a system for state operation, and several individuals and research centers have published guidelines for system selection or guides to available career information delivery software. In 1988, the American Association for Counseling and Development published a comprehensive guide to counseling software.

Several educational organizations, including the International Society for Technology in Education, publish guides to instructional software and guidelines for evaluation of instructional software.

The existing standards provided ample precedence for these NCDA guidelines. All of them help clarify important issues regarding career development software while equipping professionals to choose software appropriate for their counseling practices or their school's or agency's service needs. The purpose here is not to compile all of the good guidelines or to supersede well-established software standards and evaluations, but to reinforce them with NCDA's efforts.

These NCDA guidelines apply to software that individuals use in planning their own careers. Because the computer is an information tool and its major use in career development is for information delivery, the guidelines are specific about the content, orientation, and coverage of occupational and educational information. The computer is not just an information storage and retrieval device, however, nor is career planning based solely on facts about work and schooling. Computers are also used to organize information about the individual and to aid decision making. Criteria for the evaluation of those career development programs are also included in the guidelines. By selecting the applicable criteria, a reviewer can evaluate special purpose programs as well as comprehensive career information systems.

Useful software rarely consists only of computer programs and data. User guides, coordinator manuals, evaluation reports, and implementation strategies are all valuable and are covered by the guidelines.

Many career software programs have companion publications or refer users to other information sources. Similarly, software developers are beginning to add other visual and electronic media to their career programs. Therefore, these software review guidelines rely on and are designed to complement two other sets of NCDA guidelines—those for print and those for media.

These guidelines are written for use by NCDA members and others in selecting and using career software. They can also be useful to NCDA in reviewing career software and to developers in producing career planning software.

The guidelines have two parts: (a) a format for describing the software and (b) criteria for evaluating the program. These two parts can be used separately or together, depending on the purposes of the user.

References

Association of Computer-Based Systems for Career Information. (1982). *Handbook of standards for computer-based career information systems.* Eugene, OR: ACSCI Clearinghouse.

Association of Computer-Based Systems for Career Information. (1985). *Guidelines for the use of computer-based career information and guidance systems.* Eugene, OR: ACSCI Clearinghouse.

Herlihy, B., & Golden, L. (1990). *Ethical standards casebook.* Alexandria, VA: American Association for Counseling and Development.

National Career Development Association Career Information Review Service. (1987). *Instructions for CIRS committee—career information review service.* Alexandria, VA: Author.

Northwest Regional Educational Laboratory. (1988). *Evaluator's guide for microcomputer-based instructional packages.* Eugene, OR: International Society for Technology in Education (formerly International Council for Computers in Education).

Walz, G., & Bleuer, J. (1990). *Counseling software guide: A resource for the guidance and human development professions.* Alexandria, VA: American Association for Counseling and Development.

The 1991 edition of the Career Software Review Guidelines was prepared under the direction of Bruce McKinlay, Ph.D., University of Oregon, Eugene, Oregon (chairperson of the CIRS Subcommittee on Software Resources), with the assistance of the Career Information Review Service Committee, chaired by Roger Lambert, Ph.D., University of Wisconsin-Madison. The Guidelines were approved by the NCDA Board of Directors April, 1991.

Software Description Form
Software Evaluation Criteria

Software Description
Title:
Developer:
Version:
Hardware Requirements:

Topics:

User Materials Provided:

Applicable to the Following Career Development Activities:

_____ Career Awareness
_____ Career Growth
_____ Career Exploration
_____ Career Change
_____ Skill & Knowledge Development
_____ Other
_____ Career Decision Making

Applicable in:

_____ Instruction
_____ Counseling
_____ Job Search
_____ Human Resource Development

Appropriate for Settings such as:

_____ Elementary Schools
_____ Middle & Junior High Schools
_____ High Schools
_____ Vocational Schools
_____ Community & Junior Colleges

_____ Colleges & Universities
_____ Job & Training Programs
_____ Rehabilitation Agencies
_____ Counseling Agencies
_____ Correctional Institutions
_____ Job Placement Services
_____ Personnel Offices
_____ The Workplace
_____ Libraries & Resource Centers

Cost:
Software for:
    Single-User Computer $_____
    Networked or Time-Shared Computer $_____

Consumable Materials: $_____ per _____

Licensing provisions for multi-user installations (networks, computer labs, etc.)

Field tested data are available:

_____ On Request
_____ With the Program
_____ Not Available

Objectives:

_____ Stated by Developer
_____ Inferred

Prerequisites for successful use:

_____ Stated by Developer
_____ Inferred

Content and Structure:

Potential Uses:

Description prepared by: _____ Date: _____

SOFTWARE EVALUATION CRITERIA

You can evaluate five aspects of a program with these criteria categories:

    information in the program,
    career development process,
    user interaction,
    technical aspects of the software and materials, and
    support services.

There are few software programs, even comprehensive career information systems, to which you would apply all 67 of the criteria listed. You will need to omit the criteria that are not appropriate to the type of program you are evaluating.

Some of the criteria are standards of quality that any career development software program should meet. These include such standards as nondiscriminatory language, current and valid information, user control of decision making, program reliability, and availability of technical assistance. Use these important standards of quality to rate every program.

Other criteria (e.g., inclusion of test results or appropriateness for small group use) are features which may not be important for a particular type of program. Do not rate items that are not applicable to the kind of product you are evaluating; cross out their rating scales instead.

If you are rating one program and doing it yourself, you can select criteria and do the rating at the same time. However, if you are comparing several programs, or if several people are doing independent ratings, you first need to make several copies of the rating form. In that case, cross out the criteria that are not applicable, then make copies of the rating form.

For each applicable criterion, rate the program:

5 = Outstanding, 4 = Good, 3 = Satisfactory, 2 = Poor, 1 = Unsatisfactory

After you have finished rating the program, you can construct a summary score for it. If you want a summary score,

sum the points assigned and divide the total points by the number of items rated, omitting the items you decided were not applicable. Use the overall numeric score only as a guide. If an essential criterion is rated unsatisfactory, you may decide to reject the program even if some of its features are attractive.

INFORMATION IN THE PROGRAM

These information criteria cover the following aspects of the program: relevance to the audience, appropriate language, organization of the information, and information quality.

Outstanding ⇔ Unsatisfactory

Criterion					
1. The information is clear, concise, and informative to the intended audience	5	4	3	2	1
2. The language is nondiscriminatory. Content is free from race, ethnic, gender, age, and other stereotypes	5	4	3	2	1
3. The content is free from spelling and grammatical errors	5	4	3	2	1
4. All subjects are covered in a comprehensive manner. For example, information about all types of occupations is presented. It covers 90% of total employment in the area where the program is being used. Or, if the information applies specifically to one field of training, it covers all relevant instructional programs	5	4	3	2	1
5. The information for each topic encourages comparisons among schools or occupations	5	4	3	2	1
6. Occupational information covers standard occupational categories, duties, abilities, skills, working conditions, equipment, earnings, employment, outlook, training, and methods of entry. It identifies related occupations	5	4	3	2	1
7. Information about educational programs covers program objectives, specialties, degrees conferred, sample courses, and schools offering the program	5	4	3	2	1
8. Information about schools includes general information, admissions, programs of study, housing, costs, financial aid, and student service	5	4	3	2	1
9. The program lists only schools that meet basic licensing requirements. It reports accreditation by recognized organizations	5	4	3	2	1
10. The information is based on empirical data that are current and valid	5	4	3	2	1
11. Updated information is distributed promptly, at least yearly	5	4	3	2	1
12. In a personal search questionnaire, there is a clear, empirical relationship between characteristics of the user and those of the occupations, schools, or other activities being sorted	5	4	3	2	1
13. In a program using off-line or computer-administered assessment instruments, those instruments conform to accepted standards of validity and reliability	5	4	3	2	1
14. Advice is clearly distinguished from factual information. The sources of advice are identified	5	4	3	2	1
15. Statements made in one component are consistent with those made in other components of the program	5	4	3	2	1
16. If the program produces only lists of titles, it effectively refers users to specific sources of accurate information	5	4	3	2	1
17. Published information sources are readily available, for example, in local career information centers	5	4	3	2	1
18. To supplement objective information, the program suggests interviewing individuals about their personal career histories, including how they feel about their schools or jobs	5	4	3	2	1

CAREER DEVELOPMENT PROCESS

These criteria evaluate the compatibility of the program with important career development principles.

	Outstanding ⇔ Unsatisfactory				
19. The program motivates individuals to develop their own career plans	5	4	3	2	1
20. The program fosters self-knowledge relevant to work and learning	5	4	3	2	1
21. The program helps individuals to integrate and develop their values, interests, abilities, skills, and goals	5	4	3	2	1
22. Using the program broadens an individual's awareness of current options for employment and education	5	4	3	2	1
23. If there is a search process, it broadens the outlook of individuals regardless of their race, ethnic group, gender, or age	5	4	3	2	1
24. The program supports informed decision making by helping individuals generate ideas, obtain necessary information, and evaluate alternatives in responsible and personally relevant ways	5	4	3	2	1
25. The program encourages the user to get appropriate counseling and advice in making long-term decisions	5	4	3	2	1
26. Using the program integrates planning with previous experiences	5	4	3	2	1
27. The user, not the program, controls the decision making	5	4	3	2	1
28. The structure of the program demonstrates that career planning is a developmental, lifelong process	5	4	3	2	1
29. The program is appropriate for individual use	5	4	3	2	1
30. The program is appropriate for small-group use	5	4	3	2	1
31. The program can be a useful resource in a counseling program	5	4	3	2	1
32. The program provides information that can be useful in instruction	5	4	3	2	1
33. The program can be a useful resource in a job search program	5	4	3	2	1
34. Using the program contributes to a person's career development	5	4	3	2	1

USER INTERACTION

These criteria cover the user's interaction with the program, the objectives and features of the program, and your analysis of it.

	Outstanding ⇔ Unsatisfactory				
35. The purpose of the program is well defined and clearly explained to the user	5	4	3	2	1
36. The organization is clear, logical, and effective, making it easy for the intended audience to understand	5	4	3	2	1
37. The language in the program and in the user's guide is clear to the intended audience	5	4	3	2	1
38. User materials are easy to use, appealing to users, and readily available	5	4	3	2	1
39. Prerequisites are identified and instruction is provided in the software or in the user guides so individuals can run the program and understand its results	5	4	3	2	1
40. The individual has the choice of going directly to desired information or using a structured search to identify relevant topics	5	4	3	2	1
41. The individual can operate the program independently, creating his or her own sequence of presentation and review	5	4	3	2	1
42. The program acknowledges input. Feedback on user responses is employed effectively	5	4	3	2	1
43. Invalid commands are handled constructively. The program tolerates variations in command formats (e.g., upper or lower case, extra spaces, etc.)	5	4	3	2	1

	Outstanding ⇔ Unsatisfactory				
44. Individuals can easily start and exit the program. It is easy to back up, change answers, and give commands	5	4	3	2	1
45. If there are "help" and "hint" messages, they are easy to access	5	4	3	2	1
46. If the program contains tests of knowledge or skill, it reports which items were missed and which were correct	5	4	3	2	1
47. The program is attractive and interesting. It motivates users to continue using the program and exploring career options	5	4	3	2	1
48. The program is demonstrably effective with the intended audience, including people of varying abilities and experiences	5	4	3	2	1
49. The program can be used by various cultural groups	5	4	3	2	1
50. The program achieves its purpose	5	4	3	2	1

TECHNICAL ASPECTS OF THE SOFTWARE AND MATERIALS

These criteria cover aspects of the computer hardware and programs.

	Outstanding ⇔ Unsatisfactory				
51. The system uses standard equipment that is reliable, widely available, and applicable to a variety of uses	5	4	3	2	1
52. Computer capabilities such as graphics, color, or sound are used for appropriate instructional reasons	5	4	3	2	1
53. If the program requires special equipment, the requirements are minimal and clearly stated by the developer	5	4	3	2	1
54. The program is reliable in normal use. Software is bug free	5	4	3	2	1
55. The program provides a copy or summary of its basic information to the user for future reference	5	4	3	2	1
56. Printouts are clear and well organized. The printouts are dated	5	4	3	2	1
57. Updates can be loaded easily into the system	5	4	3	2	1
58. If any processing in the program is based on assessment scores, course grades, or other client records, the program explains to the user how the records are being used	5	4	3	2	1
59. If the program uses client records, it does not restrict an individual in exploring any of the information in the program	5	4	3	2	1
60. If the program creates a permanent record for a user, that record is secure and confidential. There is provision for erasing the record when the information is no longer valuable in providing services	5	4	3	2	1

SUPPORT

These criteria cover aspects of support for professionals who implement the program: written materials, staff training, service, and cost.

	Outstanding ⇔ Unsatisfactory				
61. The site coordinator's manual explains the content and process for updating information	5	4	3	2	1
62. Print or computer materials explain the content and effective use of the program to local site coordinators	5	4	3	2	1
63. Training on appropriate and effective use of the program is provided	5	4	3	2	1

	Outstanding ⇔ Unsatisfactory				
64. There is a system of communication between user sites and the system developer which may include newsletters, telephone assistance, and annual evaluations	5	4	3	2	1
65. On-site technical assistance is available for effective program use	5	4	3	2	1
66. Evaluations of the program's effectiveness are available to site coordinators	5	4	3	2	1
67. The cost per user makes it feasible to serve most clients who can benefit from the program	5	4	3	2	1

SUMMARY COMMENTS

Major Strengths:

Major Weaknesses:

Other Comments:

Evaluation prepared by: _____ Date: _____

APPENDIX 15-E

Guidelines for the Internet

NCDA Guidelines for the Use of the Internet for Provision of Career Information and Planning Services Approved by the NCDA Board of Directors, October 1997

http://ncda.org

Developed by members of the NCDA Ethics Committee:
Dr. David Caulum, Don Doerr, Dr. Pat Howland, Dr. Spencer Niles, Dr. Ray Palmer, Dr. Richard Pyle (Chair), Dr. David Reile, Dr. James Sampson, and Dr. Don Schutt

Introduction
Guidelines for Use of the Internet for Delivery of Career Counseling and Career Planning Services
Professional and Ethical Guidelines Related to the Use of the Internet for Job Posting and Searching
Unacceptable Counselor Behaviors on the Internet
Need for Research and Review

INTRODUCTION

Based on readily-available capabilities at the time of this writing, the Internet could be used in four ways for the purpose of providing career counseling and/or career planning services to clients. These are:

1. To deliver information about occupations, including their descriptions, employment outlook, skills requirements, estimated salary, etc. through text, still images, graphics, and/or video. In this event, the standards for information development and presentation are the same as those for print materials and audiovisual materials as stated in NCDA's documents on these matters.

2. To provide online searches of occupational databases for the purpose of identifying feasible occupational alternatives. In this event, the standards developed by NCDA and the Association of Computer-based Systems for Career Information (ACSCI) apply.

3. To deliver interactive career counseling and career planning services. This use assumes that clients, either as individuals or as part of a group, have intentionally placed themselves in direct communication with a professional career counselor. Standards for use of the Internet for these purposes are addressed in this document.

4. To provide searches through large databases of job openings for the purpose of identifying those that the user may pursue. Guidelines for this application are included in this document.

Guidelines for Use of the Internet for Delivery of Career Counseling and Career Planning Services

"Career planning" services are differentiated from "career counseling" services. Career planning services include an active provision of information designed to help a client with a specific need, such as review of a resume; assistance in networking strategies; identification of occupations based on interests, skills, or prior work experience; support in the job-seeking process; and assessment by means of online inventories of interest, abilities, and/or work-related values. Although "career counseling" may include the provision of the above services, the use of the term implies a deeper level of involvement with the client, based on the establishment of a professional counseling relationship and the potential for dealing with career development concerns well beyond those included in career planning.

Multiple means of online provision of career planning or career counseling services currently exist, the most common of which are e-mail, newsgroups, bulletin boards, chat rooms, and Web sites offering a wide variety of services. Telephone or audiovisual linkages supported by the Internet exist in their infancy, and will likely grow in potential as the technology improves and the costs decline.

1. Qualifications of Developer or Provider

   Web sites and other services designed to assist clients with career planning should be developed with content input from professional career counselors. The service should clearly state the qualifications and credentials of the developers not only in the content area of professional career counseling, but also in the development of interactive online services.

2. Access and Understanding of Environment

   The counselor has an obligation to be aware of free public access points to the Internet within the member's community, so that a lack of financial resources does not create a significant barrier to clients accessing counseling services or information, assessment, or instructional resources over the Internet.

   The counselor has an obligation to be as aware as possible of local conditions, cultures, and events that may impact the client.

3. Content of Career Counseling and Planning Services on the Internet

   The content of a Web site or other service offering career information or planning services should be reviewed for the appropriateness of content offered in this medium. Some kinds of content have been extensively tested for online delivery due to the long existence of computer-based career information and guidance systems. This includes searching of databases by relevant search variables; display of occupational information; development of a resumé; assessment of interests, abilities, and work-related values and linkage of these to occupational titles; instruction about occupational classification systems; relationship of school majors to occupational choices; and the completion of forms such as a financial needs assessment questionnaire or a job application.

   When a Web site offers a service which has not previously been extensively tested (such as computer-based career guidance and information systems), this service should be carefully scrutinized to determine whether it lends itself to the Internet. The Web site should clearly state the kinds of client concerns that the counselor judges to be inappropriate for counseling over the Internet, or beyond the skills of the counselor.

4. Appropriateness of Client for Receipt of Services via the Internet

   The counselor has an ethical and professional responsibility to assure that the client who is requesting service can profit from it in this mode. Appropriate screening includes the following:

   a. A clear statement by clients of their career planning or career counseling needs.

   b. An analysis by the counselor of whether meeting those needs via Internet exchange is appropriate and of whether this particular client can benefit from counseling services provided in this mode. A judgement about the latter should be made by means of a telephone or videophone teleconference designed to specify the client's expectations, how the client has sought to meet these through other modes, and whether or not the client appears to be able to process information through an Internet medium.

5. Appropriate Support to the Client

   The counselor who is providing services to a client via the Internet has ethical responsibility for the following:

   a. Periodic monitoring of the client's progress via telephone or videophone teleconference.

b. Identification by the counselor of a qualified career counselor in the client's geographic area should referral become necessary. If this is not possible, the web counselor using traditional referral sources to identify an appropriate practitioner should assist the client in the selection of a counselor.

c. Appropriate discussion with the client about referral to face-to-face service should the counselor determine that little or no progress is being made toward the client's goals.

6. Clarity of Contract with the Client

The counselor should define several items in writing to the client in a document that can be downloaded from the Internet or faxed to the client. This document should include at least the following items:

a. The counselor's credentials in the field.

b. The agreed-upon goals of the career counseling or career planning Internet interchange.

c. The agreed-upon cost of the services and how this will be billed.

d. Where and how clients can report any counselor behavior which they consider to be unethical.

e. Statement about the degree of security of the Internet and confidentiality of data transmitted on the Internet and about any special conditions related to the client's personal information (such as potential transmission of client records to a supervisor for quality-control purposes, or the collection of data for research purposes).

f. A statement of the nature of client information electronically stored by the counselor, including the length of time that data will be maintained before being destroyed.

g. A statement about the need for privacy when the client is communicating with the counselor, e.g., that client communication with the counselor is not limited by having others observe or hear interactions between the counselor and client.

h. If the service includes career, educational, or employment information, the counselor is responsible for making the client aware of the typical circumstances where individuals need counseling support in order to effectively use the information.

7. Inclusion of Linkages to Other Web sites

If a career information or counseling Web site includes links to other Web sites, the professional who creates this linkage is responsible for assuring that the services to which his or hers are linked also meet these guidelines.

8. Use of Assessment

If the career planning or career counseling service is to include online inventories or tests and their interpretation, the following conditions should apply:

a. The assessments must have been tested in computer delivery mode to assure that their psychometric properties are the same in this mode of delivery as in print form; or the client must be informed that they have not yet been tested in this same mode of delivery.

b. The counselor must abide by the same ethical guidelines as if he or she were administering and interpreting these same inventories or tests in face-to-face mode and/or in print form.

c. Every effort must be exerted to protect the confidentiality of the user's results.

d. If there is any evidence that the client does not understand the results, as evidenced by e-mail or telephone interchanges, the counselor must refer the client to a qualified career counselor in his or her geographic area.

e. The assessments must have been validated for self-help use if no counseling support is provided, or that appropriate counseling intervention is provided before and after completion of the assessment resource if the resource has not been validated for self-help use.

PROFESSIONAL AND ETHICAL GUIDELINES RELATED TO THE USE OF THE INTERNET FOR JOB POSTING AND SEARCHING

1. The posting must represent a valid job opening for which those searching on the Internet have an opportunity to apply.

2. Job postings must be removed from the Internet database within 48 hours of the time that the announced position is filled.

3. Names, addresses, resumés, and other information that may be gained about individuals should not be used for any purposes other than provision of further information about job openings.

UNACCEPTABLE COUNSELOR BEHAVIORS ON THE INTERNET

1. Use of a false e-mail identity when interacting with clients and/or other professionals. When acting in a professional capacity on the Internet, a counselor has a duty to identify him/herself honestly.

2. Accepting a client who will not identify him/herself and be willing to arrange for phone conversation as well as online interchange.

3. "Sharking" or monitoring chat rooms and bulletin board services, and offering career planning and related services when no request has been made for services. This includes sending out mass, unsolicited e-mails. Counselors may advertise their services but must do so observing proper "netiquette" and standards of professional conduct.

NEED FOR RESEARCH AND REVIEW

Since the use of the Internet is new for the delivery of career planning and counseling services, it is mandatory that the career counseling profession gain experience with this medium and evaluate its effectiveness through targeted research. The capabilities of Internet delivery of services will expand rapidly as the use of sound and video becomes more feasi-

ble. These early guidelines will need constant monitoring and revision as research data become available and additional capabilities become cost-feasible.

NCDA opposes discrimination against any individual on the basis of race, ethnicity, gender, sexual orientation, age, mental/physical disability, or creed.

Source: Revised by the NCDA Board of Directors, April 1994.

CHAPTER 16

Group Counseling

Objectives
■ ■ ■ ■ ■ ■ ■ ■ ■ ■ ■

After reading this chapter, you should be able to:

- Explain the complexities of group counseling and discuss how those complexities translate to ethical dilemmas.
- Summarize professional identity, training, and credentialing issues in group counseling.
- Summarize crucial ethical issues in group counseling.
- Provide an overview of multicultural issues in group counseling practice.

■ ■ ■ ■ ■ ■ ■ ■ ■ ■ ■

INTRODUCTION

Group counseling raises some interesting ethical dilemmas because treatment involves more than one client. In addition, the clients are usually unrelated (nonfamily members). Ethical issues such as confidentiality, privileged communication, and privacy are crucial concerns in group counseling.

Group counseling is a popular style of counseling. Corey and Corey (1997) stated:

> Group therapy originated in response to a shortage during World War II of personnel trained to provide individual therapy. At first, the group therapist assumed a traditional therapeutic role, frequently working with a small number of clients with a common problem. Gradually, leaders began to experiment with different roles and various approaches. Over time, practitioners discovered that the group setting offered unique therapeutic possibilities. Exchanges among the members of a therapy group are viewed as instrumental in bringing about change. This interaction provides support, caring, confrontation, and other qualities not found in individual therapy. Within the group context, members are able to practice new social skills and apply some of their new knowledge. (p. 11)

Beyond therapeutic benefits, group counseling has economic benefits for clients—both financial and time-related. Group counseling is usually much less expensive than individual counseling; fees for one hour of treatment may be one-fourth or one-fifth the standard fee for individual therapy. In addition, counselors can treat as many as 8 to 10 people at one time. With constraints of limited government resources, and

---

Box 16.1   Exploring the Code

What section (or sections) of the ACA ethics code addresses group counseling?
What is the relationship between the ACA ethics code and the ASGW "Best Practice Guidelines"? (See Appendix 16-A at the end of this chapter.)

---

under the veil of managed care, group counseling and
psychotherapy may have an expanded role in the mental health service enterprise.

Although some people view group counseling as
a mode of treatment, others view group counseling as
a separate counseling specialty, requiring specialized
training and supervision.

DEFINING THE SPECIALTY, SETTINGS, AND CLIENTS

Group counseling occurs in a variety of settings: private counseling practices, clinics, college counseling
centers, chemical dependency treatment programs,
hospitals, schools, and just about any counseling context where there is enough physical space (for three or
more individuals) and a pool of available clients.
Group counseling usually occurs in a room with chairs
arranged in a circular fashion, but the variety of group
types and configurations of groupings are unlimited.
Some counselors allow clients to sit on the floor or they
may recline. Group decision-making about how counseling is to be accomplished is common, usually with
a defined theme or topic as central to the group task.
However, some groups are highly structured and may
imitate a classroom-like atmosphere. The directiveness
(focus on a specific topic or goal) of groups varies
widely, along with the purpose of the group. For example, a group addressing issues of teen drug use may
involve open, facilitated discussion, may be educational, or may involve some combination of discussion
and didactic activities. A group addressing recovery
from trauma may involve open discussion so that individuals can vent their feelings in a supportive environment. There are also differences around the makeup of
the group—groups may be organized by such factors
such as gender, age, common experiences, conditions
of individuals (e.g., physical or mental disorders), or
interests. They may be composed of individuals, couples, families, or other groups. The nature of groups

varies widely, and the subsequent dynamics of a group
vary according to its nature, makeup, and purpose.

At the current time, there is no recognized certifying body for group specialists established under the
auspices or direction of the American Psychological
Association (APA) or the American Counseling Association (ACA). There is, however, a member organization
of the ACA, the Association for Specialists in Group
Work (ASGW), which has a "Best Practice" document
specifically written for group work practice. Members
of the ASGW must also be members of the ACA, so
they are bound to the mandatory ethical guidelines of
the ACA ethics code (which, in sections, specifically
addresses group work). The APA has a division (Division 49, Group Psychology and Group Psychotherapy)
that serves as a formal organization for psychologists
interested in the study and practice of group counseling. Accordingly, group counseling is a specialty that
does not meet formal specialty criteria that involve the
credentialing of individuals through a formal specialty
board and through specialty designation at the level of
training. In essence, group counseling represents a
specialized mode of treatment.

Group counseling is distinct in treating several
clients at the same time. This distinct treatment modality leads to interesting ethical dilemmas, some of which
are not adequately addressed by codes of ethics that
focus primarily on individual treatment. The ASGW
(1998a) "Best Practice Guidelines," is a useful document that gives added guidance to counselors who use
group methods.

ISSUES OF SIGNIFICANCE TO THE SPECIALTY

Professional Differentiation

Group counseling does not meet the typical criteria for
a formal specialty of counseling, even though the
ASGW uses the term "specialists" in its title. Group

counseling should be considered a specialized mode of treatment. Whereas specialties such as school counseling or rehabilitation counseling imply a type of setting (schools or rehabilitation agencies, respectively) and a type of client (students or individuals with disabilities, respectively), group counseling has no such boundaries. It can be used with many types of clients in many types of settings. Regardless, it is imperative that counselors who use this mode of treatment seek supervision and training in group procedures and processes. Even specialized training for certain types of groups is warranted because there are so many variations among groups themselves. Group types range from the "encounter groups" of the 1960s and 1970s, which emphasized personal growth (Rogers, 1970), to a plethora of applications developed since World War II, such as psychodrama groups, behavior therapy groups, Gestalt therapy groups (see Gazda's [1975] classic text). Generally, individuals who have credentials in a type of therapy (e.g., Gestalt, Rational-Emotive), who hold credentials in addressing a type of concern (e.g., chemical dependency, sexual dysfunction), and who are trained and experienced in group procedures can supervise group counseling.

To confuse matters more, the ASGW (2000) "Professional Standards for the Training of Group Workers" defines four "specializations" in group work, requiring different training beyond receipt of a master's degree (consistent with standards of the Council on Accreditation of Counseling and Related Educational Program, CACREP, 1994). The specializations are: (a) Task and Work Group Facilitation; (b) Psychoeducational Group Leadership; (c) Group Counseling; and (d) Group Psychotherapy. ASGW recommends at least one course in group procedures plus 10 to 20 hours of experience in groups as "core" training. In addition, "specialization" coursework and experience is defined in the "Professional Standards for Training of Group Workers" (ASGW, 2000). For example, under the specialization of "Group Counseling," coursework includes, but is not limited to, human development, health promotion, and theory and practice of group counseling. The experience requirement is 45 clock hours of supervised practice conducting a counseling group appropriate to the age and clientele of the group leader's specialty area (e.g., school, rehabilitation, mental health).

Related to ethical issues, the Professional Standards (ASGW, 2000) document states: "All graduates of specialization training will understand and demonstrate consistent effort to comply with principles of ethical, best practice, and diversity-competent practice of

group work consistent with the program's declared specialization area(s)" (Section III G). The ASGW (1998a) also provides a "Best Practice Guideline" document that gives guidance of an ethical nature (see Appendix 16-A).

Group work is a complex area of counseling practice, and although it does not meet criteria for a classic "specialty" in counseling, it certainly is a specialized mode of treatment that requires focused training through coursework and experience.

Ethical Issues

Confidentiality and Privileged Communication.

Complex ethical circumstances arise in groups that do not arise in other counseling situations. In a recently publicized case in a Midwestern state, a member of an Alcoholics Anonymous group confessed to his group that he had committed murder. The revelation was reported in the newspapers, apparently leaked by other group members. The authorities subsequently investigated the individual who made the revelation. Questions of group counseling confidentiality were raised, and the consensus of the mental health community was that there was no confidentiality except as was voluntarily agreed to by the members of the group.

In the absence of a licensed professional, no protection can be given legally to the information provided in a group. But even in the presence of a licensed professional whose clients are afforded legal confidentiality and privileged communication, the presence of other individuals in a group (nonprofessionals) compromises confidentiality—other group members are not required by law to keep information private or secret. In an article addressing confidentiality in a support group for individuals with Acquired Immune Deficiency Syndrome (AIDS), Posey (1988) described some circumstances unique to group treatment:

> In our group, discussions of confidentiality have been triggered by people dropping in, one member identifying another at a bar, issues of how or whether to leave telephone messages, and how to respond to a member's family and friends at the hospital. Initially, a member distributed names and telephone numbers of the group members but recalled them when members expressed discomfort. Once, a news reporter appeared at a meeting and wanted to sit in, and he guaranteed that identities would be protected. The group agreed to discuss his interest but would not allow him to attend the meeting. (p 226)

Unusual, and sometimes unpredictable, issues of confidentiality arise in group settings. This is partly because nonprofessional group members may reveal information communicated in a group at their discretion, judgment, or in some cases, misjudgment. The ASGW "Best Practice" document specifically states: "Group workers have the responsibility to inform all group participants of the need for confidentiality, potential consequences of breaching confidentiality and that legal privilege does not apply to group discussions (unless provided by state statute)" (Section A7).

Group counselors must stress the importance of confidentiality and set a norm of confidentiality regarding all group disclosures. The importance of maintaining confidentiality should be emphasized before the group begins and at various times throughout the group sessions. Participants should also know that confidentiality cannot be guaranteed.

It is important for clients to know that although counselors will act to protect the right to confidentiality of clients, counselors cannot enforce a ban on gossip among other members of the group or between members of the group and outsiders.

Confidentiality is also complicated in groups when other individuals have access to records. For example, if a group of minors is being counseled, the parents of the minors technically have the right to information about the nature and content of counseling (unless there is a legal exemption to parental consent or oversight). Parents even have legal access to case file information. Revelation of group counseling case file information to parents of one or more members of a group (such as a group counseling case note) that references other individuals in the group essentially breaches the confidentiality of the other group members, unless those other group members' parents allow for such revelation.

Group counselors have a special responsibility to ensure that case notes for group counseling are written for each individual in the group. Further, information about other group members should be deleted or omitted from the case files of the group member for whom the case notes are written. This situation is complicated further by federal law. The federal Family Education Rights and Privacy Act of 1974 (FERPA), which covers all educational institutions that receive federal funding from preschool through university graduate training, clearly states:

> The parents of students [have] the right to inspect and review any and all official records, files, and data directly related to their children, including all material that is incorporated into each student's cumulative record

folder.... Where such records or data include information on more than one student, the parents of any student shall be entitled to receive or be informed of, that part of such record or data as pertains to their child. (Section 438.[a] [1])

Counselors must ensure that records for each client are kept separate and that group case notes do not reference other individuals specifically. In effect, counselors in educational settings must document group counseling case files carefully in light of a legal standard that allows parents full access to such information, even if a parent's child is referenced in another client's case notes.

Regardless of the specific situation in which an issue of confidentiality arises, the counselor must inform each group participant of the limits of confidentiality before that individual consents to treatment (Gregory & McConnell, 1986). The APA and ACA codes and the ASGW (1998a) "Best Practice Guidelines" all agree that the limits of confidentiality must be discussed with clients. Initiation of groups should not occur until all members of the group are privy to and informed of the limits of confidentiality, and clients should be made to acknowledge such awareness (e.g., by signing a statement of understanding).

Standard exemptions to confidentiality apply in group counseling just as in individual counseling (see Chapter 3). Depending on the state law that applies, counselors must typically breach confidentiality in situations in which there is (a) suspected or substantiated child abuse or neglect, (b) evidence or suspicion that a client intends to do harm to an individual or society (e.g., through an illegal act), (c) a request by a parent or legal guardian, (d) client permission to reveal, (e) the need to confer with other involved professionals, and (f) in other cases covered by law or specific ethical standard.

In an interesting study of confidentiality dilemmas in group psychotherapy, Roback and Purdon (1992) examined how group psychotherapists reported handling serious confidentiality issues. They stated:

> The overall findings of this exploratory study suggest that when confronted with a patient disclosure involving psycholegal issues (criminal behavior, threatened harm to others, potential danger to a child, or past physical abuse of an adolescent), experienced group psychotherapists are highly unlikely to deal with the situation totally within the group context. Rather, they attempt to deal with such incidents by adding private, individual therapy sessions for the patient. However, rarely do they take the incident entirely out of the group context. Realistically, there are groups that are too volatile to manage

inflammable patient disclosures such as intended homicide, and patients who are too disturbed (e.g., the agitated paranoid) to be defused within the group context. Competent patient care requires the therapist to be sufficiently flexible to discriminate when the group process will be inadequate for a given situation. (p. 6)

Further, they found that male and female therapists acted differently: "Male group therapists report being more likely to attempt to neutralize patient threats in the group context alone, whereas their female counterparts are more likely to deal with such incidents by augmenting the patient's group sessions with private individual sessions" (p. 6). Beyond ethical considerations, group counseling process issues arise in such conflicts.

The issue of privileged communication, too, is complicated in group treatment circumstances. Privileged communication prevents the revelation of confidential information in a legal proceeding. A counselor cannot be forced to testify on a client's case if the privilege stands—the client owns the privilege. But privileged communication, historically, has been accorded most usually in one-to-one communication circumstances. It may not apply to circumstances in which other individuals are present in counseling. Unless group counseling is specifically addressed in laws that provide for privileged communication, it is probably wise to assume that group communications will not be considered privileged, and counselors may be required to testify. On the other hand, if group counseling is referenced in the law that provides for privileged communication, counselors may proceed with the intent to hold information that is communicated in group contexts as privileged. However, even in those cases in which group counseling is referenced in laws providing the privilege, there may be no definitive standard as to whether clients will be protected from revelation of private information in a legal proceeding unless there is clear case law in the legal jurisdiction within which the counselor practices. In such cases, clients should know that there is a possibility that information may be vulnerable to revelation in a legal context, although the counselor will make every effort to prevent such revelation. Counselors should study state statutes and case law carefully.

Some statutes provide for privilege under certain circumstances. Many state licensure statutes allow for privileged communication on civil, not criminal, cases only. Most states allow for revelation of suspected or substantiated child abuse or neglect, and state statutes that cover such matters may override any privileged communication provided to clients of counselors. In group settings where such matters are commonly dis-

cussed, clients should have prior knowledge of the limits on their privilege.

Individuals who seek group therapy often are involved in individual therapy as well. This occurs in both private practice and in institutional settings. There should be clear guidelines for the sharing of group information among agency employees in institutional settings. Codes of ethics typically require that when there is a relationship between professionals, there should be a formal agreement regarding issues of confidentiality. When a group counselor consults with a client's individual counselor (with the client's permission), the group counselor should be assured that the information communicated will be held in confidence and protected from revelation to outsiders.

Certainly, there are ethical concerns related to the contiguous professional relationship if a counselor is performing both individual and group treatment (for a nongroup matter) with one client (see Glass, 1998). Counselors must be cautious in this circumstance to prevent contamination of group treatment with information from the individual treatment. Counselors should avoid seeing clients in both the group facilitator and individual counselor roles. Concerns also arise if a client participates in individual treatment with another mental health professional. Glass (1998) said:

Confidentiality questions about what information is to be shared by the two therapists need to be worked out. There is also a danger that the patient will use the individual sessions to drain off affect elicited in the group instead of dealing with it in the group. Using different individual and group therapists will be most productive if the patient consents to allow both therapists to communicate freely with one another throughout the course of treatment. Otherwise the danger is great that the two therapists may find themselves working at cross purposes. (p. 110)

Glass recommended "only one form of treatment at a time" (p. 110) to prevent the ethical dilemmas that arise.

Informed Consent. In establishing groups, counselors must play a special role that extends beyond the informed consent of clients agreeing to group treatment. Of course, as with any type of counseling, clients have the right to consent to treatment or to refuse treatment. However, it is also true that an individual can be misplaced in a group that is not consistent with the client's interests or concerns. Obviously, the counselor is obligated ethically to screen clients in or out of groups to ensure appropriate placement. Both the ACA code and the ASGW guidelines emphasize the importance of screening prospective group members. Corey, Williams, and Moline (1995) stated:

> The purpose of screening is twofold: (a) to determine if an individual is compatible for a particular group and (b) for the person to determine if the group is compatible with his or her personal goals. If both the leader and the prospective member are in agreement with respect to the appropriateness of the group for the member, there is a basis for forming what is likely to become a working group. Proper screening and orientation can occur only if the group counselor is clear about the purpose of the group and is able to provide persons with adequate information prior to joining a group. (p. 164)

Methods of screening include individual interviewing, a group interview with prospective group members, an interview done by a team of leaders, or screening through written questionnaires. Care must be given to prevent a serious misplacement, such as putting a victim of sexual abuse in a group of sexual perpetrators, or placing an abstinent drug abuser in a group that abuses substances. Even more subtle misplacement may occur, and the counselor must be alert to the possible consequences of misplacement and must act to prevent problems by careful group assignment. When it is obvious that a misplacement has occurred, procedures should be in place to provide a formal means for an individual to terminate services in a way that is not harmful to any group participant. Termination procedures should be discussed with members of a group before a group begins. Members should know they may leave the group at any time, but there may be repercussions for premature withdrawal from the group (especially in cases of mandatory treatment). A "trial period" after which members can formally exit the group of their own volition is highly recommended. Certainly, clients should be informed of their obligation to alert the group leader and other group members of their concerns or intentions regarding group attendance.

Coercion is not acceptable; a client's rights have been breached if undue group pressure comes to bear on that client's decision to remain in or participate in group activities. Corey, Williams, and Moline (1995) stated: "Some degree of group pressure is inevitable, and it is even therapeutic in many instances. It is essential for group leaders to differentiate between 'destructive pressure' and 'therapeutic pressure.' People may need a certain degree of pressure to aid them in breaking through their usual forms of resistance" (p. 166). Aside from what can be considered "therapeutic pressure," counselors must protect clients from coercion, physical threats, undue pressure, and intimidation.

Ideally, individual clients should screen the group before committing to attend sessions. Counselors have an obligation to provide prospective members with enough information about the group so that they can make fully informed decisions about group attendance. This includes information about the counselor's credentials and background, procedures or rules of the group, the purpose of the group, counselor expectations regarding client behavior, and the rights, responsibilities, and risks of group membership (ASGW, 1998a).

Detrimental Counselor-Client Relationships.   As with any type of counseling, potentially detrimental counselor-client relationships are to be avoided. Group counseling presents some different ethical configurations, however. Although it would be unethical for a counselor to establish a romantic relationship with a group member, can group members establish romantic or other dual relationships among themselves? The counselor must discourage such activity. The outdated ASGW (1989) code stated that "Group counselors discuss with group members the potential detrimental effects of group members engaging in intimate inter-member relationships outside of the group" (section 9f), but current standards make no such statement. The current "Best Practice Guidelines" (ASGW, 1998a) require only that informed consent statements address "implications of out-of-group contact or involvement among members" (Section A.7.). Counselors should discourage potentially detrimental relationships among group members because of their possible negative effects on the group process and possible negative personal outcomes. Obviously, if a member of a group is privy to outside information about another member or is intimately involved with another member, revelations of information that otherwise would be considered private may be made. There is also the potential for covert coalitions among members of a group, which could result in **scapegoating** another member—a process wherein one member of a group is placed in an "odd person out" position or is treated by others as a deviant, thereby receiving negative messages from some other members of the group. Scapegoating has been implicated in producing an unhealthy social context, or a two (or more) against-one scenario (Hoffman, 1981). However, the activities of group members outside of the group cannot be enforced by a group leader, and certainly, a group leader cannot be held responsible for extra-group entanglements. In this regard, counselors can minimize risks by using a contract for treatment that addresses relationships and other issues. Corey et al. (1995) stated: "One way to minimize psychological risks in groups is to use a contract in which leaders specify what their responsibilities are and members specify their commitment to the group by declaring what they are willing to do. If members and leaders operate under a contract that clarifies expectations, there is less chance for members to be exploited or damaged by a group experience" (p. 172). There is great potential benefit through group treatment, but there are added risks.

Some authors (e.g., Brittain & Merriam, 1988) caution counselors against leading two related types of groups—for example, one group of clients and another group of "significant others" to the first group. A counselor should not lead a group of survivors of child sexual abuse and also lead a group of significant others to survivors of child sexual abuse. In such cases, the objectivity of the counselor may be jeopardized (Brittain & Merriam, 1988).

Responsibility.   Group leaders have a dual responsibility to individual members of the group and to the group itself. The responsibility to the group does not supersede responsibility to individual members of the group. For example, if a counselor recognizes that one member of a group is being scapegoated and believes that the client's continued participation in the group could be detrimental to his or her mental health, the counselor is obligated to protect the individual participant, even if it means that the group membership and process might be negatively affected. Counselors should be equitable in their treatment to all members, and they are directed by the ACA code to protect the welfare of their clients. Implicit in such directives is recognition that when there are conflicts between the needs of the group and the needs of an individual member who is potentially traumatized by the group, the counselor must protect the individual. The group counselor should not abdicate his responsibility for the group, but must clearly take action to protect the individual.

The counselor's responsibility to the individual group member is critical when the force of the group can have negative consequences. Glass (1998) said:

> Recognizing that powerful forces are generated in groups, and that the leader has only partial control over what occurs, the group therapist faces a complex set of responsibilities. Not only must he or she act ethically, but moreover also create an ethical climate in the group. Some leaders may respond to this challenge by becoming overly controlling and authoritarian in an attempt to insure that the group functions in an appropriate fashion. Unfortunately this undermines the very element which is the group's strength, namely, its collective influence for therapeutic benefit. Conversely, the laissez faire leader

who simply encourages the group to "do its own thing" without guidance or direction may be courting disaster. Such leaders often are reluctant to interfere with the functioning of the group out of a belief that groups are inherently wise, offer only good advice, and bring to bear pressures on their members that are ultimately for the individual's own good. Such a leadership approach often results in chaos, where the group never gels into an effective entity, or in harming members through coercive patterns that may emerge in the group. (pp. 99–100)

A group leader must be watchful of serious, personal challenges to a group member that may have detrimental effects (Glass, 1998). Leader responsibility and the ability to intervene at critical moments of potential harm are important aspects of group facilitation.

When a client ends affiliation with a group, the counselor should follow the formal "termination" procedures that were established and communicated before the client consented to group treatment. The counselor should make an appropriate referral so the client can receive continued treatment, if necessary.

There are cases, however, in which the needs of the individual and the needs of the group are not in serious conflict yet still require attention. For example, if a group member in a cancer support group raises concerns over disciplining a misbehaving child, the group leader must weigh the needs of the individual against the needs of the group. To focus on the issue of a misbehaving child, which may be tangential to the group purpose, would be a disservice to other group members. In such a case, the counselor would be wise to refer the member to an appropriate treatment source for the child-rearing concern. In this case, neither the individual client nor the group as a whole is placed in a position of lesser priority. Of course, the counselor must ensure that the focus of the group was clearly stated initially so that referral for such a concern does not seem out of the ordinary.

Ethical codes alone are not enough to ensure responsible group counselors. Kotter (1982) suggested self-monitoring related to personal responsibility as important to group leadership. Gregory and McConnell (1986) stated:

> The notion of equal treatment of all group members is often more myth than reality. Therapists like mere human beings are more attracted to some persons than others. Despite efforts to equalize interactions, therapists are prone to give more time, attention, and to be more responsive to group members whom they find personally reinforcing. (p. 60)

Counselors must recognize their own limits and ensure that they do not inadvertently scapegoat members of the group. Counselors, therefore, have a responsibility to self-monitor throughout the group process and to take appropriate corrective action if serious biases reveal themselves.

Values.   Biases and values may affect the group leader and the group process. Corey, Corey, and Callanan (1993) stated:

> Group counselors are sometimes timid about making their values known, lest they influence the direction that the members are likely to take. Practitioners are not value-neutral, however, for the interventions they use are based on values. What is critical is an awareness of how values operate and influence strategies. (p. 346)

Obviously, a group counselor should not be put in a position of leading a group of clients whose behavior is abhorrent or unacceptable to the counselor. A counselor who is a right-to-life (anti-abortion) advocate who works in a hospital setting or mental health center should not be required against his will by agency or other directives to counsel a group of individuals who have had abortions. A counselor who feels uncomfortable addressing issues of sexuality should not be made to direct a group in which sexual concerns are frequently and appropriately raised. However, there are circumstances in which a counselor may have a value conflict, unrelated to the group purpose, with one or more members of a group. In such cases, the counselor is obligated to address such value differences. The ASGW guidelines state that "Group workers assess their values, beliefs and theoretical orientation and how these impact upon the group, particularly when working with diverse and multicultural populations" (Section A.3.). When values conflict, the professional should disclose the conflict and assess the implications of the value conflict and disclosure for the group process.

When value conflicts arise that may affect the group process, the counselor must decide to either proceed or to modify the nature, focus, composition, or leadership of the group.

Counselor Competence.   Counselor competence relates to two issues: (a) the quality of provided services, and (b) the boundaries or scope of professional activity. This text takes the position that individual counselors must be trained and appropriately credentialed (e.g., licensed) professionals—a somewhat con-

troversial position. A number of self-help groups are led by peers, nonprofessionals, or paraprofessionals (individuals trained usually to the level of a bachelor's degree). Some of the best examples of these are 12-step groups such as Alcoholics Anonymous, Narcotics Anonymous, and Overeaters Anonymous. Some facilities also have paraprofessionals leading groups; this is common in the field of rehabilitation wherein individuals with bachelor's degrees serve as group educators/counselors for individuals needing guidance on job procurement, social skills, money management, or grooming. It can be argued that there is no need to have a highly trained counselor directing such groups when nonprofessionals and paraprofessionals are able to provide quality services. However, such a response does not take into account issues of ethics other than the obligation to provide quality services. When a professional counselor or psychologist is involved, the client is guaranteed some legal protection (depending on the laws and statutes in the legal jurisdiction). In states where there are licensure statutes with ethical standards, an unlicensed provider or paraprofessional does not accord the group member legal or professional confidentiality (or in some cases, privileged communication). Clients have no recourse if they suspect a breach of privacy or malpractice, unless they sue the agency that directs the nonlicensed provider. Having a professional lead a group is some protection to group members. Attending a group with a nonprofessional group leader puts clients at added risk if there is dissatisfaction with the group or the group leader. When clients seek any service for a fee, they are always wise to learn the credentials of the provider and to address protection or limits under the law.

Is a professional's appropriate licensure as a counselor or psychologist an acceptable standard for group counseling practice? Licensure in and of itself is no guarantee that a counselor has been adequately trained and experienced in leading groups. Even though group counseling has been defined as a "mode of treatment" (not meeting other criteria for a specialty designation), group counseling still qualifies as a technically sophisticated mode of treatment requiring special training. General credentials are not enough to provide the group leader adequate background in group processes and ethical standards. This is the position of the ASGW (2000). Qualified counselors who plan to lead groups should have a formal graduate course in group procedures/processes and supervision in providing group services through practica, internships, and post-graduate training, following the ASGW (2000)

"Professional Standards for the Training of Group Workers." This ensures that the counselor has adequate knowledge and experience directing groups. This position is consistent with the position of the Council for Accreditation of Counseling and Related Educational Programs (CACREP, 2001), which requires accredited graduate programs in counseling to include training in "group work." CACREP (2001) requires study of group topics such as (a) group dynamics, (b) group leadership, (c) theories of group counseling, (d) methods of group counseling, (e) approaches used in such group types as task, psychoeducational, and therapy groups, (f) professional preparation standards for group leaders, and (g) ethical considerations. Additionally, the CACREP clinical training standards (e.g., practicum and internship training as part of the degree program) require development of individual counseling and group work skills under supervision. Subsequent to receipt of the degree, ethical counselors who plan to provide group services must seek supervision of his or her group work activity.

CODE COMPARISONS

The ASGW is an affiliate organization of the ACA. The ASGW "Best Practice Guidelines" are aspirational guides—that is, without a mechanism for adherence and in addition to the ACA ethics code. The ACA code is a mandatory code of ethics for all ACA members (including ASGW members). In fact, the introduction of the ASGW "Best Practice Guidelines" states (see Appendix 16-A):

> The Association for Specialists in Group Work recognizes the commitment of its members to the [ethics code] of its parent organization, the American Counseling Association, and nothing in this document shall be construed to supplant that code. These Best Practice Guidelines are intended to clarify the application of the ACA [ethics code] to the field of group work by defining group workers' responsibility and scope of practice involving those activities, strategies and interventions that are consistent and current with effective and appropriate professional ethical and community standards. (Preface)

The ASGW guidelines focus on activities of counselors involved in counseling individuals in group contexts and are required reading for counselors involved in group treatment. The guidelines address issues only addressed in a cursory fashion in more general codes and give specific guidance to the practitioner.

ISSUES OF DIVERSITY

In what many consider a milestone publication on the topic of multicultural counseling, Sue, Arrendondo, and McDavis (1992) outlined the need for counselors to have a multicultural perspective and presented cross-cultural competencies and standards. Building on the work of Sue and Sue (1990), Sue et al. (1992) described the culturally competent counselor as:

> First ... one who is actively in the process of becoming aware of his or her own assumptions about human behavior, values, biases, preconceived notions, personal limitations, and so forth .... Second ... one who actively attempts to understand the worldview of his or her culturally different client without negative judgments. ... Third ... one who is in the process of actively developing and practicing appropriate, relevant, and sensitive intervention strategies and skills in working with his or her culturally different clients. (p. 481)

It is crucial for the group counselor to be culturally sensitive, not only to direct his or her own actions, but to observe any cross-cultural differences among group members that may affect or potentially affect the group process (Glass, 1998).

The ASGW has developed "Principles for Diversity—Competent Group Workers" (1998b), a document that outlines definitions related to cultural difference and "principles" related to self-awareness, awareness of group members' worldviews, and diversity-appropriate intervention strategies. This document reflects the Association's commitment to multicultural sensitivity in group counseling practice. The conclusion of the document reads as follows:

> This document is the "starting point" for group workers as we become increasingly aware, knowledgeable, and skillful in facilitating groups whose memberships represent the diversity of our society. It is not intended to be a "how to" document. It is written as a call to action and/or a guideline and represents ASGW's commitment to moving forward with an agenda for addressing and understanding the needs of the populations we serve.

Differences on issues of value arise because "difference" is a fact of a multicultural and diverse society. Accordingly, counselors must be alert to how differences manifest themselves in interactions, and they must ensure that actions are neither discriminatory nor disenfranchising of individuals or groups of individuals. Especially in screening group members for participation in groups, counselors must not simply "screen out" individuals due to differences of culture, race, religion, or sexual orientation, unless failing to do so would be a serious detriment to another group member or members. In fact, counselors are wise to ensure that there is variation among group members along factors of diversity; in this way the counselor may facilitate an acquaintance or acceptance of difference. As biases reveal themselves, trained and culturally sensitive counselors should address them. Sue et al. (1992) stated, as related to counselor interventions: "When they [counselors] sense that their helping style is limited and potentially inappropriate, they can anticipate and ameliorate its negative impact" (p. 483).

On issues of gender, DeChant (1996) and her contributors made some compelling presentations on the nuances of working with women in group contexts in a thought-provoking text entitled *Women and Group Psychotherapy*. They explored topics such as sex role issues in mixed-gender groups, gender-linked aspects of group behavior, boundary issues, gender-based countertransference in group treatment, and cross-cultural issues for women in groups. This excellent text serves as a scholarly marker about the complexities of group practice in a multicultural society.

There also may be differences in group dynamics among nations or by national origin. Yamaguchi (1986) described some differences between Western culture groups and those in Japan: Group leaders appear to have a more influential role and privacy issues are prominent (consistent with Japanese tradition related to "intimate" information). Counselors who work with culturally different individuals without knowledge of those cultural differences and without making an effort to understand them are counseling in a disadvantaged way. Such a disadvantage may, ultimately, be a disservice or even a detriment to clients.

The ACA and APA codes of ethics are clear on the issue of diversity. Counselors and psychologists do not condone or engage in discrimination. Counselors should actively attempt to understand the diverse cultural backgrounds of the clients with whom they work. In a culture that values equality in a context rich in human diversity, counseling must acknowledge difference nonjudgmentally. Group counselors should facilitate a nonjudgmental discourse on cross-cultural issues.

CHAPTER SUMMARY

Because of the presence of individuals other than a counselor and one client, group counseling poses some interesting ethical dilemmas. The general codes of the APA and the ACA give general guidance related to group work. However, the ASGW provides detailed and specific guidance in addressing issues typically faced in the practice of group counseling. Although group counseling does not clearly meet the criteria of a formal, designated specialty of counseling, it does have unique theory at its base and it has a set of methods or techniques that is not shared with individual, couples, or family therapies. Special training is required of the counselor who plans to provide group counseling services ethically and in the context of a multicultural society.

Specific ethical issues that are relevant to group practice include confidentiality and privileged communication, informed consent, potentially detrimental counselor-client relationships, responsibility, values, and counselor competence.

REFERENCES

Association for Specialists in Group Work. (1990). Ethical guidelines for group counselors—ASGW 1989 Revision. *The Journal for Specialists in Group Work, 15,* 119–126.

Association for Specialists in Group Work. (1998a). *Best practice guidelines.* Alexandria, VA: Author.

Association for Specialists in Group Work. (1998b). *Principles for diversity-competent group workers.* Alexandria, VA: Author.

Association for Specialists in Group Work. (2000). *Professional standards for the training of group workers.* Alexandria, VA: Author.

Brittain, D. E., & Merriam, K. (1988). Groups for significant others of survivors of child sexual abuse. *Journal of Interpersonal Violence, 3*(1), 90–101.

Corey, G., Corey, M. S., & Callanan, P. (1993). *Issues and ethics in the helping professions.* Pacific Grove, CA: Brooks/Cole.

Corey, G., Williams, G. T., & Moline, M. E. (1995). Ethical and legal issues in group counseling. *Ethics and Behavior, 5,* 161–183.

Corey, M. S., & Corey, G. (1997). *Groups: Process and practice.* Pacific Grove, CA: Brooks/Cole.

Council for Accreditation of Counseling and Related Educational Programs. (1994). *CACREP accreditation standards and procedures manual.* Alexandria, VA: Author.

Council for Accreditation of Counseling and Related Educational Programs. (2001). *CACREP accreditation manual.* Alexandria, VA: Author.

DeChant, B. (Ed.). (1996). *Women and group therapy: Theory and practice.* New York: Guilford.

Gazda, G. M. (1975). *Basic approaches to group psychotherapy and group counseling.* Springfield, IL: Charles C. Thomas.

Glass, T. A. (1998). Ethical issues in group work. In R. M. Anderson, T. L. Needels, & H. V. Hall (Eds.), *Avoiding ethical misconduct in psychology specialty areas*. Springfield, IL: Charles C. Thomas.

Gregory, J. C., & McConnell, S. C. (1986). Ethical issues with psychotherapy in group contexts. *Psychotherapy in Private Practice, 4*(1), 51–62.

Hoffman, L. (1981). *Foundations of family therapy*. New York: Basic.

Kotter, J. A. (1982). Ethics comes of age: Introduction to the special issue. *Journal*

for Specialists in Group Work, 7(3), 138–139.

Posey, E. C. (1988). Confidentiality in an AIDS support group. *Journal of Counseling and Development, 66,* 226–227.

Roback, H. B., & Purdon, S. E. (1992). Confidentiality dilemmas in group psychotherapy. *Small Group Research, 23,* 169–185. (Accessed through the MasterFILE Elite database, pp. 1–10).

Rogers, C. (1970). *On encounter groups*. New York: Harper & Row.

Sue, D. W., Arrendondo, P., & McDavis, R. J. (1992). Multicultural counseling competencies and standards: A call to the profession. *Journal of Counseling and Development, 70,* 477–486.

Sue, D. W., & Sue, D. (1990). *Counseling the culturally different: Theory and practice*. New York: Wiley.

Yamaguchi, T. (1986). Group psychotherapy in Japan today. *International Journal of Group Psychotherapy, 36*(4), 567–578.

APPENDIX 16-A

Association for Specialists in Group Work Best Practice Guidelines

The Association for Specialists in Group Work (ASGW) is a division of the American Counseling Association whose members are interested in and specialize in group work. We value the creation of community; service to our members, clients, and the profession; and value leadership as a process to facilitate the growth and development of individuals and groups.

The Association for Specialists in Group Work recognizes the commitment of its members to the Code of Ethics and Standards of Practice (as revised in 1995) of its parent organization, the American Counseling Association, and nothing in this document shall be construed to supplant that code. These Best Practice Guidelines are intended to clarify the application of the ACA Code of Ethics and Standards of Practice to the field of group work by defining Group Workers' responsibility and scope of practice involving those activities, strategies and interventions that are consistent and current with effective and appropriate professional ethical and community standards. ASGW views ethical process as being integral to group work and views Group Workers as ethical agents. Group Workers, by their very nature in being responsible and responsive to their group members, necessarily embrace a certain potential for ethical vulnerability. It is incumbent upon Group Workers to give considerable attention to the intent and context of their actions because the attempts of Group Workers to influence human behavior through group work always have ethical implications. These Best Practice Guidelines address Group Workers' responsibilities in planning, performing and processing groups.

SECTION A: BEST PRACTICE IN PLANNING

A.1. Professional Context and Regulatory Requirements

Group Workers actively know, understand and apply the ACA Code of Ethics and Standards of Best Practice, the ASGW

Professional Standards for the Training of Group Workers, the ASGW Best Practice Guidelines, the ASGW diversity competencies, the ACA Multicultural Guidelines, relevant state laws, accreditation requirements, relevant National Board for Certified Counselors Codes and Standards, their organization's standards, and insurance requirements impacting the practice of group work.

A.2. Scope of Practice and Conceptual Framework

These guidelines were approved by the association for specialists in Group Work (ASGW) Executive Board, March 29, 1998. Prepared by Lynn Rapin and Linda Keel, ASGW Ethics committee Co-Chairs.

Group Workers define the scope of practice related to the core and specialization competencies defined in the ASGW Training Standards. Group Workers are aware of personal strengths and weaknesses in leading groups. Group Workers develop and are able to articulate a general conceptual framework to guide practice and a rationale for use of techniques that are to be used. Group Workers limit their practice to those areas for which they meet the training criteria established by the ASGW Training Standards.

A.3. Assessment

a. *Assessment of self.* Group Workers actively assess their knowledge and skills related to the specific group(s) offered. Group Workers assess their values, beliefs and theoretical orientation and how these impact upon the group, particularly when working with a diverse and multicultural population.

b. *Ecological assessment.* Group Workers assess community needs, agency or organization resources, sponsoring organization mission, staff competency, attitudes regarding group work, professional training levels of potential group leaders regarding group work; client attitudes regarding group work, and multicultural and diversity considerations. Group Workers use this information as the basis for making decisions related to their group practice, or to the implementation of groups for which they have supervisory, evaluation, or oversight responsibilities.

A.4. Program Development and Evaluation

a. Group Workers identify the type(s) of group(s) to be offered and how they relate to community needs.
b. Group Workers concisely state in writing the purpose and goals of the group. Group Workers also identify the role of the group members in influencing or determining the group goals.
c. Group Workers set fees consistent with the organization's fee schedule, taking into consideration the financial status and locality of prospective group members.
d. Group Workers choose techniques and a leadership style appropriate to the type(s) of group(s) being offered.
e. Group Workers have an evaluation plan consistent with regulatory, organization and insurance requirements, where appropriate.
f. Group Workers take into consideration current professional guidelines when using technology, including but not limited to Internet communication.

A.5. Resources

Group Workers coordinate resources related to the kind of group(s) and group activities to be provided, such as: adequate funding; the appropriateness and availability of a trained co-leader; space and privacy requirements for the type(s) of group(s) being offered; marketing and recruiting; and appropriate collaboration with other community agencies and organizations.

A.6. Professional Disclosure Statement

Group Workers have a professional disclosure statement which includes information on confidentiality and exceptions to confidentiality, theoretical orientation, information on the nature, purpose(s) and goals of the group, the group services that can be provided, the role and responsibility of group members and leaders, group workers; qualifications to conduct the specific group(s), specific licenses, certifications and professional affiliations, and address of licensing/credentialing body.

A.7. Group and Member Preparation

a. Group Workers screen prospective group members if appropriate to the type of group being offered. When selection of group members is appropriate, Group Workers identify group members whose needs and goals are compatible with the goals of the group.

b. Group Workers facilitate informed consent. Group Workers provide in oral and written form to prospective members (when appropriate to group type): the professional disclosure statement; group purpose and goals; group participation expectations including voluntary and involuntary membership; role expectations of members and leader(s); policies related to entering and exiting the group; policies governing substance use; policies and procedures governing mandated groups (where relevant); documentation requirements; disclosure of information to others; implications of out-of-group contact or involvement among members; procedures for consultation between group leader(s) and group member(s); fees and time parameters; and potential impacts of group participation.
c. Group Workers obtain the appropriate consent forms for work with minors and other dependent group members.
d. Group Workers define confidentiality and its limits (for example, legal and ethical exceptions and expectations; waivers implicit with treatment plans, documentation and insurance usage). Group Workers have the responsibility to inform all group participants of the need for confidentiality, potential consequences of breaching confidentiality and that legal privilege does not apply to group discussions (unless provided by state statute).

A.8. Professional Development

Group Workers recognize that professional growth is a continuous, ongoing, developmental process throughout their career.

a. Group Workers remain current and increase knowledge and skill competencies through activities such as continuing education, professional supervision, and participation in personal and professional development activities.
b. Group Workers seek consultation and/or supervision regarding ethical concerns that interfere with effective functioning as a group leader. Supervisors have the responsibility to keep abreast of consultation, group theory, process, and adhere to related ethical guidelines.
c. Group Workers seek appropriate professional assistance for their own personal problems or conflicts that are likely to impair their professional judgment or work performance.
d. Group Workers seek consultation and supervision to ensure appropriate practice whenever working with a group for which all knowledge and skill competencies have not been achieved.
e. Group Workers keep abreast of group research and development.

A.9. Trends and Technological Changes

Group Workers are aware of and responsive to technological changes as they affect society and the profession. These include but are not limited to changes in mental health delivery systems; legislative and insurance industry reforms; shifting population demographics and client needs; and technological advances in Internet and other communication and delivery systems. Group Workers adhere to ethical guidelines related to the use of developing technologies.

SECTION B: BEST PRACTICE IN PERFORMING

B.1. Self Knowledge

Group Workers are aware of and monitor their strengths and weaknesses and the effects these have on group members.

B.2. Group Competencies

Group Workers have a basic knowledge of groups and the principles of group dynamics, and are able to perform the core group competencies, as described in the ASGW Professional Standards for the Training of Group Workers. Additionally, Group Workers have adequate understanding and skill in any group specialty area chosen for practice (psychotherapy, counseling, task, psychoeducation, as described in the ASGW Training Standards).

B.3. Group Plan Adaptation

a. Group Workers apply and modify knowledge, skills and techniques appropriate to group type and stage, and to the unique needs of various cultural and ethnic groups.
b. Group Workers monitor the group's progress toward the group goals and plan.
c. Group Workers clearly define and maintain ethical, professional, and social relationship boundaries with group members as appropriate to their role in the organization and the type of group being offered.

B.4. Therapeutic Conditions and Dynamics

Group Workers understand and are able to implement appropriate models of group development, process observation and therapeutic conditions.

B.5. Meaning

Group Workers assist members in generating meaning from the group experience.

B.6. Collaboration

Group Workers assist members in developing individual goals and respect group members as co-equal partners in the group experience.

B.7. Evaluation

Group Workers include evaluation (both formal and informal) between sessions and at the conclusion of the group.

B.8. Diversity

Group Workers practice with broad sensitivity to client differences including but not limited to ethnic, gender, religious, sexual, psychological maturity, economic class, family history, physical characteristics or limitations, and geographic location. Group Workers continuously seek information regarding the cultural issues of the diverse population with whom they are working both by interaction with participants and from using outside resources.

B.9. Ethical Surveillance

Group Workers employ an appropriate ethical decision making model in responding to ethical challenges and issues and in determining courses of action and behavior for self and group members. In addition, Group Workers employ applicable standards as promulgated by ACA, ASGW, or other appropriate professional organizations.

SECTION C: BEST PRACTICE IN GROUP PROCESSING

C.1. Processing Schedule

Group Workers process the workings of the group with themselves, group members, supervisors or other colleagues, as appropriate. This may include assessing progress on group and member goals, leader behaviors and techniques, group dynamics and interventions; developing understanding and acceptance of meaning. Processing may occur both within sessions and before and after each session, at time of termination, and later follow up, as appropriate.

C.2. Reflective Practice

Group Workers attend to opportunities to synthesize theory and practice and to incorporate learning outcomes into ongoing groups. Group Workers attend to session dynamics of members and their interactions and also attend to the relationship between session dynamics and leader values, cognition and affect.

C.3. Evaluation and Follow-Up

a. Group Workers evaluate process and outcomes. Results are used for ongoing program planning, improvement and revisions of current group and/or to contribute to professional research literature. Group Workers follow all applicable policies and standards in using group material for research and reports.

b. Group Workers conduct follow-up contact with group members, as appropriate, to assess outcomes or when requested by a group member(s).

C.4. Consultation and Training with Other Organizations

Group Workers provide consultation and training to organizations in and out of their setting, when appropriate. Group Workers seek out consultation as needed with competent professional persons knowledgeable about group work.

CHAPTER 17

Rehabilitation Counseling

Objectives

■ ■ ■ ■ ■ ■ ■ ■ ■ ■ ■

After reading this chapter, you should be able to:

- Describe the specialty of rehabilitation counseling, the historic trends in its evolution, and the political issues of importance to the field.
- Define the standards for a qualified rehabilitation counselor, including professional identity, training, and credentialing.
- Differentiate the roles and functions of rehabilitation counselors from those of other counseling specialties.
- Summarize the ethical issues of concern to rehabilitation counselors.
- Explain the newly revised Code of Professional Ethics for Rehabilitation Counselors and compare it to the ACA Code of Ethics.
- Discuss multiculturalism and diversity in rehabilitation counseling.

■ ■ ■ ■ ■ ■ ■ ■ ■ ■ ■

INTRODUCTION

The specialty of rehabilitation counseling (RC) has its origins in the tremendous interest in vocational guidance and counseling that began in the early decades of the 20th century. It evolved out of powerful events in the history of the United States: societal changes surrounding the Industrial Revolution and immigration patterns in the late 1800s and early 1900s, the Great Depression, and World Wars I and II. Vocational issues became leading concerns during these critical times. Whether those requiring guidance and counseling were students, adults with industrial injuries, or veterans, the need to understand the individual and how that person's individual needs and skills could be used to find a satisfying and satisfactory match with vocational opportunities became a powerful impetus to this field. Currently, rehabilitation counseling is defined as "a profession that assists persons with disabilities in adapting to the environment, assists environments in accommodating the needs of the individual and works toward full participation of persons with disabilities in all aspects of society, especially work" (Szymanski, 1985, p. 3).

There always has been significant social and political support for studying the world of work and training professionals to help people make vocational choices

---

Box 17.1   Exploring the Codes

According to the CRCC code, to whom does a rehabilitation counselor (RC) owe an obligation if the RC is providing forensic evaluations but has not conducted an examination?

Should an RC who holds a doctoral degree from a field other than counseling use the title "Dr."?

After how many years post-treatment may an RC engage in a sexually intimate relationship with a former client?

If disparities exist between laws and the CRCC code, what should the RC do?

According to the CRCC code, for what two purposes should RCs seek peer supervision or consultation?

According to the CRCC code, can RCs diagnose mental disorders?

According to the CRCC code, what three steps are required of a RC prior to disclosing to a third party that her client has a contagious, fatal disease if that third party is at high risk of contracting the disease from the client?

---

and adjust to problems of vocational placement. Rehabilitation counseling received significant legislative support for the emergence and continued growth of information and methods in this new field. The evolution of rehabilitation counseling has been influenced greatly by social and cultural forces affecting Americans' work lives and the legislation and programs created as a result of these forces.

As it evolved, rehabilitation counseling increasingly took on an individualized identity. Its services and professional development have been tailored to the needs of the populations it has specialized in serving. Historically, rehabilitation counselors have adapted their vocational approaches to meet the needs of people with disabilities across various settings. Clients of rehabilitation counselors may have a wide range of disabling conditions including physical (e.g., spinal cord injury or epilepsy), sensory (e.g., blindness or deafness), developmental (e.g., mental retardation or autism), cognitive (e.g., traumatic brain injury or learning disability), and emotional disabilities (e.g., schizophrenia or substance abuse). Rehabilitation counselors have had a long-standing tradition that incorporates philosophy and the practical importance of addressing clients holistically, even while addressing vocational concerns. They have long recognized that increasing the client's positive experiences and gains in emotional well-being, or in organizing an efficient, satisfying lifestyle in the community, can significantly enhance the individual's effectiveness and adjustment on the job. This phenomenon likely is due to the pervasive psychosocial effects of disability on all life areas

and the holistic nature of human functioning for all people. This knowledge has resulted in a dual focus on vocational and psychosocial adjustment counseling in rehabilitation counseling.

Since the 1970s, the independent living movement has stimulated use of rehabilitation counseling skills to provide community rehabilitation services for people with disabilities and, thus, has underscored the emphasis on addressing problems across all areas of individual and functioning environmental demands. Practitioners of rehabilitation counseling recognize that attitudinal and other social and economic barriers, as well as limited opportunities to access appropriate types of skills training, are often the most severely limiting aspects of disability and design and provide interventions to address these problems.

DEFINING THE SPECIALTY, SETTING, AND CLIENTS

Rehabilitation counseling practitioners most often are trained as generalist rehabilitation counselors and are conversant with the perspectives of both vocational and personal adjustment counseling. They possess basic skills that are useful in both areas. The profession's scope of practice statement has been endorsed by CRCC, ARCA, and NRCA (see *Scope of Practice for Rehabilitation Counseling* in Appendix 17-B at the end of this chapter), and involves a blending of the two points of view. The interventions and modalities used within the process of rehabilitation counseling offer a snapshot of the range and intensity of services used by these practitioners (CRCC, 1994):

■ Assessment and appraisal;
■ Diagnosis and treatment planning;
■ Career (vocational) counseling;
■ Individual and group counseling treatment interventions focused on facilitating adjustments to the medical and psychosocial impact of disability;
■ Case management, referral, and service coordination;
■ Program evaluation and research;
■ Interventions to remove environmental, employment, and attitudinal barriers;
■ Consultation services among multiple parties and regulatory systems;
■ Job analysis, job development, and placement services, including assistance with employment and job accommodations; and
■ The provision of consultation about, and access to, rehabilitation technology.

Often, it is only in increasingly specialized practice over the course of their careers that rehabilitation counselors may become more fully involved in one of the most differentiated modes of practice. Leahy (1997) summarized this blending of elements into a unique practice by stating the following:

> It is the specialized knowledge of disabilities and of environmental factors that interact with disabilities, as well as the range of knowledge and skills required in addition to counseling that serves to differentiate the rehabilitation counselor from social workers, other types of counselors (e.g., mental health counselors, school counselors, career counselors) and other rehabilitation practitioners (e.g., vocational evaluators, job placement specialists) in today's service delivery environments. (p. 97)

The discussion of individual scopes of practice in Chapter 3 is important to all counselors in discerning how they develop an appropriate and ethical specialty practice for themselves.

At first glance, rehabilitation counselors may seem to practice within a more restricted or specialized range of clients and settings than do other types of counselors. Nothing could be further from the truth. Rehabilitation counselors work with people who have physical, mental, developmental, cognitive, emotional, and addiction disabilities and help them achieve their personal, career, and independent living goals in the most integrated settings possible (CRCC, 1994). It has been estimated that more than 43 million Americans have disabilities that restrict some of their life activities and prevent them from attaining or maintaining jobs. The diversity of types, degrees, and combinations of disabilities that individuals bring to rehabilitation counselors is immense. Examples of clients served include people who have orthopedic work injuries, brain injuries sustained in an automobile crash, hearing or visual impairments, "invisible" disabilities such as epilepsy, AIDS, or pulmonary disease, developmental disabilities such as mental retardation or cerebral palsy, drug or alcohol addictions, or a psychiatric disorder such as schizophrenia or depression. In recent years, services to individuals with severe disabilities have been emphasized in many settings, and often individuals being served have combinations of several of these disabilities, thus providing more complex issues to the rehabilitation counselors with whom they work.

The primary employment settings for rehabilitation counselors are similarly diverse and include state rehabilitation agencies, alcohol and drug programs, hospitals, independent living centers, educational settings, private rehabilitation companies and practice settings, halfway houses, supported living and employment agencies, private rehabilitation facilities, and mental health centers. These facilities may be public, private nonprofit, or private-for-profit.

Due to the traditional emphasis on holistic practice, rehabilitation practice is typically conducted within a rehabilitation team context. The composition of the team is dictated by the nature of the treatment setting and disability-related needs of the clients. Whether the team is in-house or is physically dispersed, rehabilitation counselors have been trained to work within a collaborative team framework. They generally provide the coordination necessary to help the team function for the client's benefit. Often, they also provide the broader case management functions for this process to occur unless another team member has been formally designated to do so. *Case management* is "focused on interviewing, counseling, planning rehabilitation programs, coordinating services, interacting with significant others, placing clients in jobs and following up with them, monitoring a client's progress, and solving problems" (CRCC, 1994, p. 2). Case managers need to be knowledgeable in both medical and vocational case management, and rehabilitation counselors often perform functions in both of those areas, most frequently in vocational case management. These vocational case management services are often most intensely sought after within the private insurance and Worker's Compensation industry and involve these professionals in long-term disability, bodily injury liability, automobile no-fault claims, disability management, and life-care planning service provision.

In recent years, case management has grown tremendously as an area of advanced practice with a separate credential now offered to professionals who have their core professional education and wish to receive acknowledgement of advanced expertise in this particular area of service. Case management as a specific subfield has been intensely stimulated by the demand for professional case managers within the managed care industry. Its growth has been particularly clear since the successful initiation of the Certified Case Manager (CCM) credential by the Commission for Case Manager Certification (CCMC) in 1993. As of this writing, there are over 20,000 CCMs in the United States. Although the majority of those practitioners are nurses by training, a large number of rehabilitation counselors also seek this additional credential.

In recent years, a number of employment settings have begun to emerge as additionally important areas for rehabilitation counseling practice. These areas include employee assistance programs, employer-based disability management programs, school-based transition programs, disabled student services offices in post-secondary educational settings, and agencies that serve people with HIV and AIDS (Leahy & Szymanski, 1995). Recent developments in health care, legislation, technology, and the economic or business community have added demand for other new roles and function to the more traditional roles and functions of this diverse group of practitioners: psychiatric rehabilitation, life-care planning, functional capacity evaluation, genetic counseling, consultation on work motivation and organizational culture, late deafness rehabilitation, human resource management, and job re-design.

ISSUES OF SIGNIFICANCE TO THE SPECIALTY

Professional Differentiation

Rehabilitation counseling also has enjoyed prominence within the history of the counseling profession. The American Rehabilitation Counseling Association (ARCA) and the National Rehabilitation Counseling Association (NRCA) were founded in 1958, with ARCA as a division of the American Counseling Association, and NRCA a division of the National Rehabilitation Association. Rehabilitation counseling established both the first accreditation of professional educational programs and national certification of individual counseling practitioners in the profession of counseling. The Council on Rehabilitation Education (CORE) was incorporated in 1972 by a group that included ARCA and NRCA. CORE is based on an innovative multiple-stakeholder, field-tested approach to accreditation. There are 99 accredited rehabilitation counseling master's-degree programs (CORE, 2001). Similarly, the Commission on Rehabilitation Counselor Certification (CRCC), established in 1973, is the oldest and most well-established professional counselor certification. Both the CORE and CRCC processes continue to be at the forefront of credentialing in counseling. The ongoing CORE/CRCC Knowledge Validation Study provides continuous empirical validation of the professional standards of this professional group. CORE and CRCC are recognized by ACA as parallel to credentialing by the Council on Accreditation of Counseling and Related Education Programs (CACREP) and NBCC, respectively. More than 23,000 professionals have participated in the CRCC certification process in the United States and several foreign countries (Leahy & Holt, 1993). Estimates indicate that at a given point in time, there are likely to be over 25,000 professionals who identify their positions as "rehabilitation counselor" (Thomas, 1991) and, of these, approximately 15,000 are CRCs.

The issue of multiple professional constituencies has expressed itself in rehabilitation counseling. Rehabilitation counseling has arrived at unified professional credentials and standards through collaborative work among its major professional organizations—primarily ARCA and NRCA and the related rehabilitation organizations. This collaboration has resulted in unified accreditation (CORE), certification processes (CRCC), and a code of ethics (reprinted in Appendix 17-A at the end of this chapter). However, this historical duality of the major organizations has created problems of definition regarding which core identity underlies the profession of rehabilitation counseling—counseling or rehabilitation (Tarvydas & Leahy, 1993).

The first perspective historically casts rehabilitation counselors as counselors who work in a variety of rehabilitation and community counseling agencies with people who have disabilities. This perspective appears to be more aligned with an emphasis on counseling through ARCA and its parent organization, ACA (Salomone, 1996). The counseling point of view is grounded firmly in the developmental and psychoeducational counseling approaches that are so important to the profession. The alternate position adds emphasis on case management or coordination with rehabilitation counselors practicing within more of a medical model. This perspective emphasizes rehabilitation as the profession's core function and is seen as more closely related to NRCA and its parent group, the National Rehabilitation Association (Salomone, 1996). It allows for the incorporation of the clinical treatment perspective, and allows the use of medical information and collaboration with medical treatment systems that are important to serve clients with certain types of rehabilitation needs. The discussion in Chapter 9 described many of the specialized health care issues that exist for rehabilitation counselors and others working within a medical model of treatment. In many cases, rehabilitation counselors work with people who have mental health disabilities and deal with many of the same issues discussed in Chapter 14 on mental health counseling. In fact, the practice of psychiatric rehabilitation has been a long-term part of rehabilitation counseling training and practice. The Boston University approach is one of the most well-respected, effective, and widespread approaches to psychiatric rehabilitation. It was originated and developed for over 30 years by rehabilitation counselor Dr. Bill Anthony and his associates, who continue to provide leadership in this interesting area of practice to rehabilitation counselors and all professions. In addition, the many rehabilitation counselors who work with people who have drug and alcohol abuse disabilities will find Chapter 18 on addictions counseling to be helpful. All rehabilitation counselors have advanced expertise in vocational counseling and through this can be seen as linked to career counseling (see Chapter 15).

In terms of the organizational issues in rehabilitation counseling, Leahy and Szymanski (1995) have provided a reality-based analysis by noting that the two organizations (ARCA and NRCA) have often found methods to collaborate on important projects. Active discussions concerning merger began as early as 1979. In 1993, they formed the Alliance for Rehabilitation Counseling (ARC) as a stable, formal structure to continue this process of melding the two perspectives into an effective working structure for professional policy and strategic planning, while still preserving historic ties to their parent groups. The unified code of ethics and scope of practice documents were reviewed and jointly approved through this Alliance in conjunction with CRCC.

More recently, a major effort has been undertaken to merge these two organizations into one, unified organization that will remain affiliated as a division of ACA with a tentative target date of 2002. The newly merged organization will take advantage of the ACA policy adopted in the late 1990s to allow divisions to retain divisional affiliation and also to solicit freestanding members (members not affiliated with the ACA). This forward-looking option would allow individual rehabilitation counselors to signify their solidarity with the profession of counseling through ACA membership, and/or their interest in a more rehabilitation-specific base through maintaining membership in a rehabilitation organization such as the National Rehabilitation Association. In this manner, the independent choices of individual members can be pursued without impeding the professional organization of rehabilitation counselors from forwarding the advancement within the counseling professionalization movement. The potential merger into a single, ACA-affiliated organization, together with the recent adoption of a new code of ethics for rehabilitation counselors that is substantially based on the ACA ethics code, seems to further consolidate rehabilitation counseling as a specialty of counseling—albeit a unique and structurally and professionally complex one. This development will strengthen both rehabilitation counseling and the profession of counseling, and improve the representation of the needs of people with disabilities to the general professional, legislative, and lay communities (Leahy & Tarvydas, 2001). Any future development of some type of organizational tie would ensure its linkage with the rehabilitation movement and its advocacy agenda.

Rehabilitation counseling has a broad area of practice and diverse practitioner base, yet has clearly identified standards for what constitutes appropriate professional practice. The standards for a qualified rehabilitation counselor have been established by the professional organizations in RC including ARCA, NRCA, and the ARC. These standards require that rehabilitation counselors have (a) completed a master's degree in rehabilitation counseling or a closely related program (e.g., counseling), (b) achieved national certification as a CRC, and (c) attained the appropriate state licensure (e.g., Licensed Professional Counselor) in states that require this level of credential for counseling practice and that allow for the licensing of counselors with a rehabilitation counseling background. Both certification and licensure have requirements for supervised professional practice in rehabilitation counseling and for passing a knowledge-based national examination in counseling.

The agencies in the state-federal vocational rehabilitation system are mandated by a federal law to employ qualified staff. In the late 1990s, the federal government took aggressive steps to require that the states observe this requirement. According to the operationalization of qualifications, rehabilitation counselors must meet the requirements to be eligible for certification by CRCC, even though they are not required to become certified. In essence, then, these counselors must have completed a master's degree in rehabilitation counseling or a closely related program and have taken the core courses in rehabilitation counseling. Unfortunately, in most states, employees practicing only within state agencies are exempt from any licensure requirement to practice counseling in that state. Even though quite a number of rehabilitation counselors work in such exempted settings, a recent survey on the ethical beliefs of CRCs revealed that 22 percent of the respondents were licensed, indicating that a larger proportion of rehabilitation counselors is licensed than might be supposed (Tarvydas et al., 2001). In fact, as of this writing, 16 of the 46 states, including the District of Columbia, that regulate counseling also regulate rehabilitation counseling. These states regulate RCs either through the general credential of Licensed Professional Counselor (LPC), or separately, as in Louisiana, Massachusetts, and New Jersey (ACA, 2001).

Ethical Issues

Confidentiality and Privileged Communication.
Rehabilitation counselors may have particularly pressing issues regarding confidentiality in their work. Issues regarding confidentiality that emerged in a survey of CRCs (Patterson & Settles, 1992) were (a) maintaining confidentiality in institutional settings, (b) knowing that a client is driving with poorly controlled seizures, (c) recommending to an employer a client who is suspected of abusing substances, (d) sharing information with family members about a client with chronic mental illness, (e) conflicts between Workers' Compensation and state laws related to confidentiality, (f) the requirement to report client information to an agency that results in disciplinary action against the client, (g) learning that a client who has AIDS is not practicing safe sex, and (h) discussing clients with others without signed, written consent.

Many rehabilitation counselors are involved in legal and third-party consultant roles as vocational experts in civil court matters, administrative hearings, and Social Security or Workers' Compensation work (Blackwell, Martin, & Scalia, 1994). Practices involving vocational or forensic expert services often involve **indirect services** provision. CRCC (2001) defines indirect services in its revised Code of Ethics as services provided when rehabilitation counselors are employed by a third party, whether or not they engage in direct communication with the client, and where there is no intent to provide rehabilitation counseling services directly to the person with the disability. In such instances, they must clearly address confidentiality limitations with all the individuals involved. Havranek (1997) examined the application of ethical principles in forensic rehabilitation and noted the different demands of this practice in various settings and with specific populations. He further alerted rehabilitation counselors to the necessity of remaining objective despite expectations of the party who may have retained their services. The CRCC Code of Professional Ethics for Rehabilitation Counselors provides a rule that embodies well-accepted advice in such situations in the areas of informed consent and privileged communications, to involved individuals:

> Rehabilitation counselors who are employed by third parties as case consultants or expert witnesses, and who engage in communication with the individual with a disability, will fully disclose to the individual with a disability and/or his or her designee their role and limits of their relationship. (CRCC, 2001, p. 2)

The use of appropriate professional disclosure statements to enhance informed consent is recommended. (See Chapter 4 for elements of written professional disclosure.)

The clarity and timeliness of disclosure of role limitations is crucial to good ethical practice for the rehabilitation counselor. Unless so informed, it is not unreasonable that the client would assume that all information obtained would be held in confidence. If an uninformed client's benefits were cancelled as a result of the rehabilitation counselor's report provided to a third party that employs the rehabilitation counselor, the client justifiably feels that their trust and confidence was violated. Such situations are a common source of ethics complaints. To further assist in encouraging appropriate professional disclosure practice, the new code of ethics notes that "whether direct client contact occurs or whether indirect services are provided, rehabilitation counselors are obligated to adhere to the Code" (CRCC, 2001, Preamble). Rehabilitation counselors are further required to explain the limitations of confidentiality and any foreseeable situations that might limit confidentiality at the beginning of counseling and throughout the counseling process (see Case Scenario 17-1).

CASE SCENARIO 17-1

Indirect Services and Client Confusion

James is a new client being seen by Dawn, a vocational rehabilitation counselor working for the RehabCo Insurance Company in its long-term disability policy rehabilitation service program. James, a nurse, has been off on disability with a severe back injury that has resolved into a chronic back pain condition. Several different physicians and clinics made a variety of attempts to provide James with medical services, all resulting in no substantial improvement. James has been out of work for 12 months and his current physician says that he cannot carry out the physical requirements of his job. Dawn is assigned to assess whether James can benefit from rehabilitation services through a medical and vocational file review. During this process, she interviews James by phone and he states that he is not willing to consider alternative types of employment because he does not want to lose his benefits. James is still hopeful he can return to his old job as a nurse even though his employer is unwilling to consider job modification or light-duty employment. Dawn recommends an independent medical evaluation, after which James is declared medically able to return to work. As a result, James's benefits are terminated. James is angry with Dawn and lodges a complaint that she did not advocate for him. He expected that Dawn would work with him to assist him in returning to work with his previous employer. Was Dawn unethical?

MAYBE.   This scenario presents an all-too-frequent situation when rehabilitation counselors provide indirect services on behalf of a third party—the insurance company, in this case. The client who has a disability may not understand what to expect from this professional. The key issues here are whether or not proper professional disclosure and fully informed consent occurred at the onset of the involvement with James. He should have been fully informed that Dawn was only calling to verify information regarding his medical and vocational status and that she would not be providing direct services to him (professional disclosure). In addition, she should have told him that all information he gave her would be provided to the insurance company to determine the status of his disability claim. Dawn should have clearly explained to James his choices and the consequences of each choice for his benefits (informed consent). If she had done so and truthfully reported her opinion to the insurer based on objective facts, she would have been providing ethically appropriate services to James that unfortunately resulted in an outcome he did not desire.

Rehabilitation counselors should not assume that privileged communication status extends to their practices. Some may erroneously think that their national certification provides privilege to their counselor-client relationships. Rehabilitation counselors must carefully research the legal protections afforded them in their own jurisdictions (see Chapters 3 and 4). In cases where privileged communication is extended to counselors, it is only to those who hold a license in that jurisdiction. Unfortunately, rehabilitation counselors' involvement in the state-by-state counselor licensure movement has

been inconsistent and unintegrated compared with that of some counseling specialties, such as mental health counseling. Multidisciplinary or interdisciplinary teams are a frequent aspect of the rehabilitation counseling practice and tradition. They are an important asset to the client's counseling process, but offer an additional challenge to ethical practice. These teams may not necessarily work in physical proximity or have similar levels of training or understanding regarding ethical obligations to the client. Also, the rehabilitation counselor must communicate client information to team members involved in the client's treatment or employment plan. While this transfer of information is usually standard practice and done to benefit the client, clients must be fully informed of what type of information will be shared, when, how, and with whom it will be shared. Their consent to this disclosure should not be taken for granted nor obtained under pressure to give blanket permission.

Minimal disclosure is another important ethical practice intended to further safeguard client confidentiality. Minimal disclosure requires that even where client consent is given, the rehabilitation counselor only reveals the minimum amount of information necessary. Just being a member of the treatment team does not entitle one automatically to know whether a young man with a spinal cord injury is capable of erection and penile penetration while having sex, or that a student involved in a work-study placement through a high school is a victim of incest. The standard of minimum disclosure also applies to disclosure of case records and other client information provided to other team members or professionals. Whenever disclosure does occur, the rehabilitation counselor must take care that team members have specific rules they follow on confidentiality, that they reinforce the need to preserve client confidentiality, and that the client is informed of this disclosure to the team (Strein & Hershenson, 1991).

Confidentiality issues for rehabilitation counselors may be more prevalent or complex in certain settings or within particular groups of clients such as those with addictions, psychiatric, correctional, or HIV/AIDS disabilities. Certain types of services such as group counseling or treatment present extraordinary challenges to dealing with confidentiality. Rehabilitation counselors may offer group services ranging from skills training groups for job seeking or social skills training, to psychosocial treatment oriented groups that assist in the therapeutic or personal adjustment of their clients. While the rehabilitation counselor may take appropriate measures to set the expectation of confidentiality among group members, all clients must be informed that confidentiality cannot be guaranteed in a group setting. They must also be told that privileged communication is generally not extended to group counseling by the legal system. Some other confidentiality issues are specific to particular settings. Examples include: (a) legal restrictions placed on access to educational records of minor students provided by the federal Family and Educational Rights and Privacy Act (FERPA; see Chapter 13), (b) conflicting legal dictates in state and federal law regarding the privacy rights of people who are HIV-positive and the public's need to know about dangerous individuals with fatal, contagious diseases (see Chapter 4 and Anderson & Barret, 2001, for an excellent discussion), and (c) the laws extending stricter confidentiality to those in treatment in any addictions treatment facility receiving federal funding (see Chapters 4, 13, and 18, respectively).

Informed Consent.   The intent of informed consent procedures is that clients be provided with the information they need to make informed choices about their own counseling process and rehabilitation plan. The three elements of informed consent necessary to exercise autonomy through informed choice are: (a) capacity, (b) comprehension, and (c) voluntariness.

Rehabilitation counseling has a longstanding philosophical and political tradition that endorses the ideal of the client participating as an equal partner with the counselor in the counseling process. A keystone right in this movement is the normalization principle—the right of persons with disabilities to have access to informed choices. **Normalization** is a rehabilitation principle that dictates that people with disabilities "should be treated in a manner that allows them to participate both symbolically and actually in roles and lifestyles that are 'normal' for a person of their age and culture" (Greenspan & Love, 1995, p. 75). This tradition of client participation has become institutionalized in rehabilitation treatment settings in diverse ways, including the powerful accreditation standards for rehabilitation programs such as the Commission on Accreditation of Rehabilitation Facilities (CARF) and the Joint Commission on Accreditation of Healthcare Organizations (JCAHO).

Historically, this point of view is one of the values that differentiates rehabilitation service from the medical treatment model. It received resounding affirmation through the passage of the Rehabilitation Act of 1973, which emphasized consumer involvement of the client in the state-federal vocational rehabilitation process in a number of its provisions. The most striking example of this focus was the mandated involvement in the re-

habilitation services planning process through the completion of an Individual Written Rehabilitation Program (IWRP) (Rubin & Roessler, 1995). The Rehabilitation Act Amendments of 1998 elaborated on the concept of *informed choice* by stating: "individuals . . . must be active participants in their own rehabilitation programs, including making meaningful and informed choices about the selection of their vocational goals, objectives, and services" (section 100(a)(3)(c)). In this plan and its contemporary version—the Individualized Plan for Employment (IPE)— the plan is co-developed by counselor and client, written, and reviewed periodically by both as part of the ongoing evaluation of the services plan. The required elements of the plan are (a) a statement of the long-term goals for the client and intermediate steps related to it, (b) a statement of the particular rehabilitation services to be provided, (c) the methods to be used in determining whether the intermediate objectives or the long-term goals are being attained, and (d) information from the client regarding how the client was involved in choosing from among alternative goals (Rubin & Roessler, 1995).

It is important that the rehabilitation counselor consider it an aspect of the rehabilitation counseling process to *prepare* clients to participate in this collaborative rehabilitation process on a meaningful basis, rather than just offering an opportunity to decide. This process may involve some preparatory counseling, skill teaching, or motivation-enhancing techniques. Due to their disabilities, some clients may not have had a chance to develop decision-making skills; or they may have a limited base of life experiences or other cognitive or psychological limitations. In a recent study of counselors' perceptions of barriers to informed choice, participants identified the four most prominent barriers to choice as: (a) unrealistic consumer vocational goals; (b) consumers requesting more services than are necessary to achieve suitable employment; (c) the consumers' desire for the most expensive services rather than reasonable cost/professionally recommended services; and (d) finding ways to balance the expectations of consumers with reality (Patterson, Patrick, & Parker, 2000).

While rehabilitation philosophy clearly is in support of full informed consent and inclusion, it is a significant ethical challenge to rehabilitation counselors to fulfill the actual intent, rather than just the letter, of these guidelines. The determination of when a client is legally or ethically competent to provide informed consent is a critical consideration for rehabilitation counselors. If a client is a minor, but is psychosocially and cognitively mature, has a traumatic brain injury, or appears to be under the influence of a drug, the counselor must think carefully about whether informed consent is possible, or whether other measures are needed. The counselor might need to involve a parent or guardian, or wait until the client is in a better position to provide consent. Haffey (1989) and Stebnicki (1997) provided guidance on the assessment of clinical competency for rehabilitation interventions. Haffey differentiated the legal from the clinicoethical issues involved; Stebnicki utilized a functional assessment approach for determining mental capacity.

The rehabilitation client may have a legal guardian who has been court appointed to make decisions for them if they have been found to be legally incompetent to do this for themselves. There are a number of ways in which the legal requirements of achieving this consent can be reconciled with the ethical responsibility of respectfully allowing the client to participate in the decision as fully as her abilities allow (Stebnicki, 1999). Therefore, while clients with legal guardians may not be able to provide legal *consent* to a decision, ethically they should be able to *assent* to it. Often the client can be educated about this process over time. If the client undergoes involuntary commitment or has guardianship instituted on her behalf, the revised Code of Ethics for Rehabilitation Counselors directs the counselor to take such action only after careful deliberation and to advocate for resumption of client autonomy as quickly as possible (CRCC, 2001).

Potentially Detrimental Counselor-Client Interactions or Relationships. Some types of relationship counselors may have with clients outside of the counselor-client relationship may be detrimental to the well-being of the client—even if clients are desirous of pursuing them. These extra-counseling relationships are based on a power differential and may risk impairing the objectivity of the rehabilitation counselor (see Chapter 3). Sexual intimacy is strictly prohibited with current clients by the rehabilitation counseling code of ethics because the potential for serious harm to the client in such relationships has been documented as very high (see Case Scenario 17-2). Like the ACA ethics code, the new CRCC code discourages sexual relationships with former clients. However, the new CRCC code does allow the potential for such a relationship after a minimum of 5 years have passed. The ACA code allows such a relationship after only 2 years. The CRC code requires that the relationship occur only after full examination of its implications and thorough documentation of the evaluation undertaken to ensure it is not exploitative in nature. The counselor is also directed to seek peer consultation prior to entering into the relationship.

CASE SCENARIO 17-2

Allegations of Sex with a Client

Your colleague, Mary, has been hospitalized quite suddenly to have surgery for a ruptured appendix. She was quite ill and on medical leave, so you were assigned to cover some of her cases. Two of her clients tell you that Mary has been having sexual relations with them. You do not question Mary's intentions because you know her to be a conscientious rehabilitation counselor. On Mary's return, you ask her about these charges, and she replies that she has had a "very close personal relationship" with these individuals. However, she states that it is not a problem because she has only provided these clients limited case management services and purchased some vocationally required adaptive equipment—she is not counseling them. She assures you that she will not continue the relationships because she realizes that other counselors who do not see clients with disabilities in as positive a light might misconstrue these relationships. What should you do?

Mary clearly has engaged in serious, unethical conduct. Sexual contact with current clients is always unethical and is even a felony for licensed professionals in some states. Her position that the ethical standard did not apply because she was not "really" counseling these individuals is seriously inappropriate. The code of ethics makes no such distinction and case management services are counseling services, delivered as one of a potential range of rehabilitation counseling services. You must immediately report Mary's behavior to your supervisor, who will take steps to evaluate the well-being of these two clients, take appropriate action against Mary, and ensure the safety of any future clients of the agency. Mary herself may have emotional or personal issues for which she might be evaluated and for which she might need help herself. This course of action will be difficult for you because of your friendship and because you do not like being cast in the role of a whistleblower. However, it is essential that you act, or you yourself will be behaving in an unethical manner.

In rehabilitation counseling, involvements routinely may be incorporated into vocational, independent living skill, or behavioral interventions that may result in additional tensions around the issue of counselor-client relationships. By necessity, many of these interventions take place in natural social, recreational, residential, or vocational settings. For example, social skills training intentionally may simulate some behavioral elements of, but not the emotional content of, relationships such as friend or coworker. For a naive client or an emotionally needy counselor, the climate can create confusion about relationship boundaries. On the other hand, innovative and constructive intervention styles such as mentoring, coaching, and providing a personalized climate for successful achievement, such as that found in a job club, may be beneficial for many of the nontraditional, diverse clients needing vocational and life skills seen by these specialty counselors.

Some ethical relationship issues involve situations in which the rehabilitation counselor may have monetary, business, or personal interests with another party to the client's rehabilitation process. These other professionals may be such parties as attorneys, claims adjusters, or case managers involved in a long-term disability insurance case on which you are the client's rehabilitation counselor. These may be serious conflicts of interest affecting the rehabilitation counselor's judgement. Even if the rehabilitation counselor proceeds ethically, the appearance of such a conflict does exist and should be avoided. An example would be a counselor entering into a sexually intimate relationship with the plaintiff's attorney in a client's Workers' Compensation case, or becoming a business partner of this person. Such conflicting relationships may be difficult to avoid since it seems convenient and natural to hire experts and consultants who are familiar and well known. However, caution should be taken to fully evaluate the potential for conflict of interests and the appearance of conflict, even if no direct rehabilitation counseling services are provided.

Responsibility. The Code of Professional Ethics for Rehabilitation Counselors clearly asserts that the primary responsibility of the counselor is to the client. Interestingly, the code defines clients as "individuals with disabilities who are receiving services from rehabilitation counselors" (CRCC, 2001, Preamble) due to the sometimes uncritical use of the term "client" in contemporary counseling. It is clear that rehabilitation counselors have secondary responsibilities to other parties. For example, rehabilitation counselors are told to recognize that families are usually important to clients' rehabilitation and to enlist the families' understanding and positive involvement in rehabilitation, with client permission. Another relationship that is acknowledged is the rehabilitation counselor's need to "neither place nor participate in placing clients in positions that will result in damaging the interest and welfare of either clients, employers, or the public" (CRCC, 2001, p. 1). It would seem that the imperative need in contemporary

counseling is to acknowledge the important moral theme of interdependence as the true human condition rather than the traditional and excessive U.S. emphasis on the myth of possessive individualism and independence (Gatens-Robinson & Tarvydas, 1992). This view of interdependence is also more respectful of multiculturally diverse client groups who have a more collectivist worldview emphasizing central importance of family members for example.

Rehabilitation counseling has a long history of practicing primarily within agency or institutional settings. This fact is embodied by standards that enjoin counselors to respect the rights and responsibilities that they owe to their employing agencies and the need to try to resolve disputes with them through constructive, internal processes. However, they also have the responsibility to alert the employer to conditions that may be disruptive to their professional practice or limit their effectiveness (CRCC, 2001).

There has been substantial documentation on disability in the sociological, political science, and anthropological literatures that people with disabilities are often denied basic human rights. Even well-meaning individuals and institutions inadvertently deny these individuals equal opportunities for participation and inclusion. For that well-recognized reason, the rehabilitation counseling Code of Ethics contains a canon on the obligation of counselors to advocate on behalf of their clients and other people with disabilities, and to assist in ensuring accessibility of facilities and services. This provision is unique among professional codes of ethics and has become an important aspect of the self-definition for this profession. It requires the rehabilitation counselor to "strive to eliminate attitudinal barriers, including stereotyping and discrimination, toward individuals with disabilities and to increase their own awareness and sensitivity to such individuals" (CRCC, 2001, p. 6). The canon goes on to detail the many facets of this advocacy role. The concept is laudatory and was updated at revision of the code from an emphasis on only advocating for clients, to emphasizing the need to empower people with disabilities through providing appropriate information and supporting their efforts at self-advocacy. This change acknowledges the leadership and primary role of people with disabilities in advocating for their own interests, and the responsibilities of RCs to assist and teach self-advocacy skills as needed (Vash, 1987).

While the need to work for the best interests of the rehabilitation client is clear, the exact nature of the balance to be struck between the ethical principles of autonomy and beneficence in actual rehabilitation practice situations is not determined so easily. This tension centers on the temptation of paternalism, which originated within the tradition of medical practice in acute rehabilitation. This tendency toward paternalism is difficult to resolve. It originated in the observations of caregivers that clients, at some early points in their adjustment to disability, might not be able to discern what they might want or need at some later point in their recovery, when they are better equipped emotionally to make stable judgements regarding their needs and wishes. Unfortunately, the beneficence of the caregiver—wishing to influence the process for the good of the client through controlling information and decision making—clashes with the client's right to autonomous ability to exercise her discretion in her own matters (Gatens-Robinson & Tarvydas, 1992). Greenspan and Love (1995) provided a perspective on this issue:

> In disability services, the perception has been that a majority of persons with disabilities (particularly those with cognitive limitations) have sufficiently limited access to autonomy as to justify the substituted decision making of weak paternalism. The reality, however, is that the vast majority of people with disabilities (including cognitive limitations) do have access to autonomy (sometimes with assistance, but more often not). This fact suggests that much of the weak paternalism that is perceived as ethically permissible is, in reality, a form of strong paternalism that should be considered much less acceptable than it is. (p. 80)

The importance of work as a meaningful human activity is a central value shared by both career and rehabilitation counselors (see Chapter 15 for a broader discussion of work values). New employment and workforce development initiatives by the federal and state government provide a number of ethical challenges to rehabilitation counselors that are not dissimilar to other challenges faced throughout the years of the profession's evolution. Positive legislative reform driven by changes in disability policy has sought to remove barriers to work for people receiving Social Security Disability Insurance (SSDI) and Supplemental Security Income (SSI) programs through the Ticket to Work (TTW) program and in one-stop career services centers established under the Workforce Investment Act (WIA) of 1998. New pressures have been placed on the abilities of rehabilitation counselors to respond to their primary responsibilities to their own clients while at the same time honoring their responsibility to the welfare of their agencies and the need to serve new populations of clients. Counselors struggle to adapt to

new service models and methods are difficult to reconcile, and many issues are far from resolved and await the process of experience-based refinements of policies and procedures. Such periods of change are stressful for counselors, clients, and all agency personnel. Using the example of the TTW initiative, a number of potentially ethically troublesome issues must be discussed and resolved (see Figure 17–1 to see examples of some potential TTW dilemmas for discussion).

In addition to the other value issues that confront all counselors, RCs will be required to lead the professions in interpreting and supporting work-related values in collaboration with their clients.

Counselor Competence.   The work of rehabilitation counselors is extremely diverse, presenting counselors with many challenges to stay competent in the range of skills practiced, and add new skills in areas of evolving practice. It is an ethical requirement of rehabilitation counselors that they continuously monitor their levels of competency and practice only within the limits of their own individual scopes of practice (see Appendix 17-C). One new challenge to evaluating one's individual scope of practice is presented by the increasing involvement of rehabilitation counselors in psychiatric rehabilitation, mental health, and substance abuse counseling areas where diagnosis of mental disorders is a prominent responsibility (see Case Scenario 17-3). The revised Code of Ethics for Rehabilitation Counselors has a new section that establishes ethical standards for rehabilitation counselors to provide proper diagnosis of mental disorders. In addition, extensive standards address evaluation, assessment, and interpretation of various tests and psychometric instruments.

For some rehabilitation counselors, the issue of adopting a medically based diagnostic paradigm has profound, troubling implications for the long-valued, asset-focused, nonstigmatizing rehabilitation model that centered on functional assessment and not diagnosis of medical problems or pathologies as a basis for treatment. Other rehabilitation counselors do not find the task of reconciling a medical diagnostic framework as a background to functionally based treatment strategies to be problematic. The psychiatric rehabilitation model developed by Anthony, Cohen, and Farkas (1990) is an example of such a model. The model builds from a medical rehabilitation model used with physical disabilities, and allows for medical diagnosis; yet, it emphasizes rehabilitation intervention using a behaviorally oriented, highly supportive, client-directed, and positive model.

---

1. **Creaming** Employment networks (ENs) may select consumers with the best chances to be successful in the job market and discourage or be passive with other consumers.

2. **Informed Choice Issues** Consumers may not receive full information concerning the various aspects of the TTW program, ENs that might better serve their needs, and/or be subtly coerced into working with particular ENs. (Note: The regulations do not provide a definition or procedures to be observed related to informed consent even though the law requires it.)

3. **Competency of Staff** Since overhead costs to ENs will be punishing for long periods of time until monies are recouped for services provided, will administration/management provide sufficient staff and/or fully competent staff to serve the needs of consumers? (Note: Not specifically "qualified staff" related to rehabilitation counselors, but also other team members—such as job placement specialists or job coaches. Will competent benefits counseling be provided to consumers?)

4. **Rehabilitation Systems Competition** Concerns about marketing, the payment system, and business practices that will foster competitiveness rather than collaboration in consumer service planning and delivery.

5. **Ticketholder Confidentiality** There may be an increased tendency to erode consumers' confidentiality through such practices as providing ticketholders' names to ENs and one-stops and vice versa (without prior consumer consent).

6. **Above All "Do No Harm"** What will the responsibility be for services to consumers who are adversely impacted by receiving frightening or anxiety-provoking information and are negatively impacted? What will be the impact to some clients who attempt to work and fail? How will they be assisted? It is in the best interests of ENs to get consumers who are severely disabled off of long-term supports as soon as possible to get payment, but this may disrupt long-term systems of consumer support that have been reliable and may not be easily reinstituted if needed.

7. **Due Process** What will be the due process rights of consumers (outside of state VR systems and CAP programs) and how will they be provided? Will there be penalties to ENs that flagrantly violate consumer rights?

8. **Honesty of Outcome Data** There will be serious pressures on the agencies and their management to report favorable results for TTW efforts. Will outcome data be collected in such a way that accurately reflects both the positive and negative effects of the program on consumers (i.e., selection of quality of life and extra programmatic effects of the program as well as the traditional vocational/fiscal indicators).

9. **Professional Disclosure** Will professional staff members provide full disclosure of their qualifications, methods, and the nature of their approach to services (e.g., business-centered versus rehabilitation focus)? Will consumers be informed that "counseling" may not mean counseling in the sense the consumer understands it? It may be focused on education regarding program requirements, not on supporting the consumer or the consumer's psychosocial or vocational issues.

10. **Two-Tier System** Is there a potential that we may end up with the consumers having the most severe disabilities served by the state VR agencies? What are the implications for the consumers for the agencies?

FIGURE 17–1. Potential Ticket-to-Work Dilemmas

Rehabilitation counselor educators and the Council on Rehabilitation Education (CORE) should consider the increased demand for diagnostic and treatment planning competency on the part of their graduates in the revision of their curricula and standards. Similarly, individual practitioners wishing to gain or increase these competencies must carefully create individualized professional development plans that ethically and completely prepare them through such added experiences as coursework, continuing education workshops, and expertly supervised practice.

CASE SCENARIO 17-3

Can I Diagnose?

Sophie is a rehabilitation counselor who graduated two years ago from an excellent rehabilitation counselor education program that allowed her to specialize in psychiatric rehabilitation. Since graduation, she has been working in a psychiatric rehabilitation agency that provides a wide range of mental health and rehabilitation services for people with severe and long-term psychiatric disabilities; she finds it to be a fine environment in which to practice. Recently, the agency was purchased by a larger institution and Sophie was assigned to a new supervisor, Mike. Mike tells her that she will have to begin assessing and diagnosing the new clients who come to the agency, rather than referring clients out for evaluations to establish a diagnosis. The clients' records are reviewed once every three months by the consulting psychiatrist, but Sophie is very concerned that this cursory review will not provide sufficient oversight to her fledgling diagnostic attempts. She is worried that this might be unethical, and is also concerned about rumors that indicate those who are not "on board" with the new requirements will be fired. Is it unethical for Sophie to begin doing diagnostic evaluations?

PROBABLY. Given the limited information provided, Sophie is not likely to be capable of independently determining psychiatric diagnoses. She may, however, have a reasonable start in learning this skill. The Code of Ethics does allow for properly prepared individuals to do so with proper care. However, the difficulty is determining what is proper preparation in this area—very little consensus exists. First, counselors need to determine if mental health counselors are licensed in their particular state and the basic requirements for that license, and then actually work toward achieving those requirements. Generally, in addition to a strong basic preparation as a counselor, such credentials require specific courses in psychopathology and specialized assessment, and diagnosis and treatment planning at a minimum. Beyond that coursework, supervised practice under a properly credentialed, experienced diagnostician is critical. In most states, that is the equivalent of at least two, if not three, years of supervised practice. Obviously, supervised practice in diagnostics with diverse types of client conditions is essential. Sophie should contact the state licensure board to gather this basic information and form a professional development plan in consultation with Mike, her supervisor, to permit her to gain this expertise in an appropriate manner. Sophie is delighted to discover that she had the required courses during her master's education, but lacks the supervised experience needed for licensure and to do diagnoses. Mike may be willing to provide her with some access to proper supervision, but states that the agency cannot afford to provide the extensive supervision required. Sophie agrees to contract with a consulting supervisor, an appropriately credentialed psychololgist, who is acceptable to her and to the agency to provide the remaining necessary supervision hours. Mike agrees to allow Sophie to see this supervisor on agency time. While Sophie will have to pay this consultant and ensure that her clients give proper release of information for this consultation, she thinks this investment is well worthwhile to allow her to grow in her professional skills and to learn how to properly assess and diagnose her clients. If some type of satisfactory arrangement had not been reached, and Sophie had still been pressured to diagnose her new clients, she would have to

have considered leaving that position in the agency, or even leave the agency altogether.

The 2001 ethics code for rehabilitation counselors also emphasizes new standards for evaluation, assessment, and interpretation of various psychometric instruments. At present, the most authoritative set of guidelines for test users are probably the *Standards for Educational and Psychological Testing* (AERA, APA, NCME, 1999). Counselors should review and seek to conform to these qualification requirements for any and all tests they utilize in their practices. The CRCC (2001) code of ethics has specific and detailed requirements concerning the ethical obligations of its members in observing the competence standards for the use of these instruments and techniques. In addition, rehabilitation counselers must be knowledgeable of guidelines for the use and release of test data and be aware of relevant federal and state statutes and rules and regulations that relate to release of test data (Blackwell, Autry, & Guglielmo, 2001). For additional discussion of testing in career counseling see Chapter 15.

CODE COMPARISONS

The ethical practices of rehabilitation counselors are governed by the codes of the organizations to which they belong. However, in rehabilitation counseling, the professional organizations have provided a unified code of ethics through the endorsement by ARCA, NRCA, and CRCC of one code of ethics for the entire profession. Of course, rehabilitation counselors who are ARCA members are subject to enforcement of ethics through ACA, its parent organization. NRCA and ARCA do not provide disciplinary processes to enforce the rehabilitation counseling code within their organizations.

The CRCC does provide active enforcement of the code for all rehabilitation counselors who hold the CRC certification. CRCC is also an organizational affiliate of the American Association of State Counseling Boards and participates in its Disciplinary Information Network (DIN). This network allows for exchange of information about serious ethical disciplinary infractions for which adjudication has been completed among AASCB state counseling licensure boards and affiliate organizations. In that way, it enhances the ability of the counseling profession to protect consumers across state jurisdictions. The CRCC also provides advisory opinions to certificants regarding general ethical concerns to improve ethical practices and assist them in proactively avoiding ethical problems. Topics that arise most frequently in connection with either disciplinary or advisory cases are: potentially detrimental relationships (sexual or financial); lapses or failure in providing professional disclosure; confidentiality (failure to maintain or inform clients of its limitations); and informed consent (failure to obtain consent in a properly documented form) (C. Chapman, personal communication, June 15, 2001).

In early 1999, CRCC established an Ethics Taskforce to officially examine, review, and update the CRCC Code of Professional Ethics for Rehabilitation Counselors (Tarvydas & Cottone, 2000). The taskforce was directed to consider the core standards from the counseling profession as embodied by the ACA Code of Ethics and Standards of Practice and to develop supplemental standards specifically related to rehabilitation counseling. The rationale for this charge is related directly to the need to: (a) consolidate ethical standards; (b) avoid duplication and inconsistencies; and (c) directly relate the CRCC standards to the general counseling code used as an example or model by other credentialing bodies, such as state licensure boards and other certification agencies. This approach is also informed by analysis of the Scope of Practice for Rehabilitation Counseling (CRCC, 1994). The Scope of Practice reflects an understanding that "the field of rehabilitation counseling is a specialty within the rehabilitation profession with counseling at its core, and is differentiated from other related counseling fields" (CRCC, 1994, p. 1); as such, it is part of the profession of counseling.

The earliest systematic review of the then-new ACA Code and the 1989 Code for Professional Rehabilitation Counselors was undertaken in 1994 by the ARCA Ethical Standards Committee. The overall conclusion did not raise concerns about compatibility on basic concepts, but it did note that the ACA code was more specific and detailed in its treatment of the standards of practice and ethical standards (J. LaForge, personal communication, May 10, 1994). Beyond that general commentary, some areas of the two documents differed in the depth of coverage. The rehabilitation counseling code did not address the following topics: group counseling, experimental methods of treatment, fees and bartering, computer technology, groups and families, diagnosis of mental disorders, and test security. The report also described questions about the degree of adequacy of coverage in the re-

habilitation counseling code in areas related to client welfare, respecting diversity, personal needs and values, termination and referral, confidentiality versus privacy, records, credentials, and relationships with employers and employees and counselor educators and trainers (Tarvydas & Cottone, 2000). The rehabilitation counseling code was seen as having more specificity in treating concerns relating to testing, and a rule-by-rule analysis noted many instances wherein the rehabilitation standard was more definite or specific on a particular issue (J. LaForge, personal communication, May 10, 1994).

The CRCC Ethics Committee undertook an additional analysis of the rehabilitation counseling code during its 1996–1997 work year to review and supplement the ARCA analysis. The committee reviewed ethics literature and the issues raised within the committee during its processing of ethical complaints. Special note was taken of the particular need to provide more emphasis on addressing diversity and multicultural issues, dealing with business and financial issues in practice, client privacy and confidentiality rights, potentially detrimental relationships and relationship boundary issues, among other important areas, and preserving the specific disability-related issues and unique rehabilitation features needed by rehabilitation counselors. The initial draft of the code was refined by the Ethics Committee, underwent a year of public comment and review, was finally adopted in June 2001, and became effective January 1, 2002.

The 2001 code includes new standards in a number of areas including sexual intimacies with former clients; dealing with clients who have contagious, fatal diseases; confidentiality issues and other obligations in working with groups and families; expanded consideration of advertising and soliciting clients; sexual harrassment; proper diagnosis of mental disorders; expanded considerations for teaching, training, and supervision; use of fees and bartering; importance of ethics consultation; and unwarranted ethics complaints. Two other major changes are the infusion of a major emphasis on multicultural considerations and the addition of an entire section on electronic communication and emerging applications, including computers and Internet services. Many of these new areas are a result of the influence of the ACA Code of Ethics and place rehabilitation counseling practitioners in a consistent posture with the mainstream of counseling. However, there remains a number of unique rehabilitation counseling practices that are integral to its specialized requirements, including emphasis on client advocacy and concerns with accessibility; responsibilities in relationships to rehabilitation team members and employers of clients; issues of diminished client autonomy; provision of indirect services; responsibilities to ensure clients that assistants are instructed about client rights to confidentiality; and assurance of confidentiality in alternative communications means. See the edition of the *Journal for Applied Rehabilitation Counseling* for further discussion of code elements (Shaw & Tarvydas, 2001). In this exhaustive process, the Code of Professional Ethics for Rehabilitation Counselors has truly achieved the desired balance of adopting the ethical standards of the general profession of counseling while still retaining the specialized elements of its ethical traditions that are necessary to serve rehabilitation counselors in this unique area of counseling practice.

ISSUES OF DIVERSITY

Over the last decade, rehabilitation counseling has been struggling with the question of how to respond to the widespread movement in society and the professions to build its practice on a foundation of multicultural awareness, knowledge, and competencies. This focus has been prominent in all the helping professions, yet has been slower in developing in rehabilitation counseling until recently. This situation is ironic—rehabilitation counseling is a profession that is heavily invested in a specific, inclusive philosophy. It is based historically on the core rehabilitation, philosophical assumptions of valuing human differences and the basic dignity and worth of all persons. Rehabilitation counselors always have been keenly aware of the difficulties that politically oppressed and socially stigmatized individuals face in having the full opportunity to participate fully in their communities and have their basic human needs met. Therefore, it seems ironic that the field's scholars and practitioners were not at the forefront of explicitly incorporating multiculturalism into its professional literature, practice, and standards. The answer may lie partially in this fact—rehabilitation counselors have adopted an explicit, general value system that honors human diversity and are aware of the problems presented by social, vocational, economic, and political barriers to those who are not understood or those who are devalued. This groundwork may have been seen as automatically translating into appropriate competencies and adequate service when rehabilitation counselors serve others from ethnically or racially diverse groups.

In more recent years, greater awareness of the more particular needs of people from racially, culturally, or other types of diverse backgrounds has led to serious attempts to infuse a more explicit attention to multicultural issues within rehabilitation practice. The common foundations of the civil rights of persons with disability in the civil rights movement of the 1960s, and the subsequent development of affirmative action, cultural diversity, and disability policy reform are traced by Middleton, Harley, Rollins, and Solomon (1998). Based on their analysis of these forces, they make the following recommendations:

1. Explore alternative ways to enable the ACA to have a positive impact on racial and ethnic minority populations with disability.
2. Implementation should dominate outcomes. Local choices about how to put a policy into practice should be encouraged as it will have more significance for policy outcomes.
3. Reforms or policies that engage the natural networks of the rehabilitation can support change efforts in a more sustained fashion.
4. Competence matters as much as process. Policies and reforms intending to promote more effective rehabilitation practice must address both and acknowledge that working with multicultural populations required a specific set of competencies (Middleton et al., 1998, p. 16).

The challenge has been to meet these needs in a serious manner without detracting from the balance with the needs of people with disabilities—who come from all of these multicultural backgrounds. Unfortunately, in the contemporary politico-economic framework, disadvantaged populations of all types are often pitted against each other for the attention and resources they need.

The growing emphasis on multicultural aspects of practice has also extended to the critique of rehabilitation counseling's core professional institutions and standards. Rehabilitation counseling has lagged behind fields such as counseling psychology and counseling in its attention to infusing multicultural issues into its practice and standards, as noted in earlier rehabilitation literature on multicultural issues and discussed by McGinn, Flowers, and Rubin (1994). When comparing this literature to that of counseling psychology, they found less emphasis had been placed on multiculturalism and the need to incorporate these knowledge and competency elements into services to ethnic minorities. McGinn and colleagues subsequently turned their attention to analysis of the then-current Code of Ethics for Rehabilitation Counselors and found it seriously lacking. This lack has serious implications in that "by omission, however, the Code may encourage unethical behavior with culturally diverse populations" (Middleton et al., 2000). The obvious conclusion is that: "Although the authors of the Code of Professional Ethics for Rehabilitation Counselors deserve tremendous credit for their work, the absence of a multicultural perspective in the code suggests a need for modification of the document" (McGinn et al., 1994, pp. 264, 266).

In response to this need, the CRCC Ethics Taskforce and Ethics Committee committed to more emphasis on diversity and multicultural standards in the revision process that led to the current Code of Ethics (Tarvydas & Cottone, 2000). The specific mention of multicultural issues is infused in several places throughout the code. However, this focus is heralded early in the code with an entire section on respecting diversity. Among other things, it calls on rehabilitation counselors to "develop and adapt interventions and services to incorporate consideration of clients' cultural perspectives and recognition of barriers external to clients that may interfere with achieving effective rehabilitation outcomes" (CRCC, 2001, p. 1). Types of diversity directly mentioned in the code now include age, color, culture, disability, ethnic group, gender, race, religion, sexual orientation, marital status, and socioeconomic status. Attention to the needs of culturally diverse populations is also explicitly required by the standards in test selection, scoring, and interpretation. Examples of areas of multicultural emphasis in other ethical obligations noted in the code include enhancing diversity and sensitivity to the diversity issues in rehabilitation counselor education and training programs and research and scholarly

publications. It is hoped that these newly revised ethical standards will assist rehabilitation counseling in better fulfilling its obligations to the increasingly diverse and multicultural population of rehabilitation clients it serves.

CHAPTER SUMMARY

The counseling specialty of rehabilitation counseling is historically embedded in the vocational guidance, rehabilitation, and counseling movements. It has evolved in response to the specialized needs of its clients and settings of choice. Rehabilitation counseling continues to experience dynamic issues in its current ethical and professional issues, as do other counseling specialties. Most recently, these issues have been better reflected in the revised 2001 CRCC Code of Professional Ethics for Rehabilitation Counselors. Rehabilitation counseling has been complex in its evolutionary influences by counseling and rehabilitation-based knowledge and skills, as well as developing a strong involvement in the function of case management. The profession's scope of practice and the ethical standards reflect these various elements, as do the activities of its professional organizations. Recent developments in the relationship of these organizations include the consolidation around core standards shared with the counseling profession. The ethical issues that are commonly addressed by rehabilitation counselors include confidentiality and privileged communication, informed consent, potentially detrimental counselor-client relationships, responsibility, values, and counselor competence. Recent changes to the ethical standards for rehabilitation counseling stress greater awareness and emphasis on multicultural perspectives to supplement the traditional emphasis on disability and diversity.

REFERENCES

American Counseling Association. (2001). Licensure chart—Requirements for mental health counselor credentials (On-line). Available: http://www.counseling.org/members/licensureintro.cfm. Accessed on August 16, 2001.

American Educational Research Association, American Psychological Association, National Council on Measurement in Education. (1999). *Standards for educational and psychological testing*. Washington, D.C.: American Educational Research Association.

Anderson, J. R., & Barret, B. (Eds.). (2001). *Ethics in HIV-related psychotherapy: Clinical decision-making in complex cases*. Washington, D.C.: American Psychological Association.

Anthony, W., Cohen, M., & Farkas, M. (1990). *Psychiatric rehabilitation*. Boston: Center for Psychiatric Rehabilitation.

Blackwell, T. L., Autry, T. L., & Guglielmo, D. E. (2001). Ethical issues in disclosure of test data. *Rehabilitation Counseling Bulletin, 44*, 161–169.

Blackwell, T. L., Martin, W. E., & Scalia, V. A. (1994). *Ethics in rehabilitation*. Athens, GA: Elliott & Fitzpatrick.

Commission on Rehabilitation Counselor Certification (CRCC). (1994). *CRCC certification guide*. Rolling Meadows, IL: Author.

Commission on Rehabilitation Counselor Certification (CRCC). (2001). *Code of professional ethics for rehabilitation counselors.* Rolling Meadows, IL: Author.

Cottone, R. R., Pullen, J. R., & Wilson, W. C. (1983). Counselor licensure, confidentiality, and privileged communication: Implications for private practice in rehabilitation. *Journal of Applied Rehabilitation, 14,* 6–8.

Council on Rehabilitation Counselor Education. (2001). CORE accredited master's programs in rehabilitation counselor education: 2000–2001 academic year (Online). Retrieved August 27, 2001 from http://core-rehab.org.

Gatens-Robinson, E., & Rubin, S. E. (1995). Societal values and ethical commitments that influence rehabilitation service delivery behavior. In S. E. Rubin & R. T. Roessler (Eds.), *Foundations of the vocational rehabilitation process* (pp. 157–174). Austin, TX: Pro-Ed.

Gatens-Robinson, E., & Tarvydas, V. (1992). Ethics of care, women's perspectives and the status of the mainstream rehabilitation analysis. *Journal of Applied Rehabilitation Counseling, 23,* 26–33.

Greenspan, S., & Love, P. (1995). Ethical challenges in supporting persons with disabilities. In O. C. Karan & S. Greenspan (Eds.), *Community rehabilitation services for people with disabilities* (pp. 71–89). Boston: Butterworth-Heinemann.

Haffey, W. J. (1989). The assessment of clinical competency to consent to medical rehabilitation interventions. *Journal of Head Trauma Rehabilitation, 4,* 43–56.

Havranek, J. E. (1997). Ethical issues in forensic rehabilitation. *Journal of Applied Rehabilitation Counseling, 28,* 11–16.

Herlihy, B., & Corey, G. (1992). *Dual relationships in counseling.* Alexandria, VA: American Counseling Association.

Leahy, M. J. (1997). Qualified providers of rehabilitation counseling services. In D. R. Maki & T. F. Riggar (Eds.), *Rehabilitation counseling: Profession and practice* (pp. 95–110). New York: Springer.

Leahy, M. J., & Holt, E. (1993). Certification in rehabilitation counseling: History and process. *Rehabilitation Counseling Bulletin, 37,* 71–80.

Leahy, M. J., & Szymanski, E. M. (1995). Rehabilitation counseling: Evolution and current status. *Journal of Counseling & Development, 74,* 163–166.

Leahy, M. J., & Tarvydas, V. M. (2001). Transforming our professional organizations: A first step toward the unification of the rehabilitation counseling profession. *Journal of Applied Rehabilitation Counseling, 32,* 3–8.

McGinn, F., Flowers, C. R., & Rubin, S. E. (1994). In quest of an explicit multicultural emphasis in ethical standards for rehabilitation counselors. *Rehabilitation Education, 7,* 261–268.

Middleton, R. A., Harley, D. A., Rollins, C. W., & Solomon, T. (1998). Affirmative action, cultural diversity, and disability policy reform: Foundations to the civil rights of persons with disability. *Journal for Applied Rehabilitation Counseling, 29*(3), 9–18.

Middleton, R. A., Rollins, C. W., Sanderson, P. L., Leung, P., Harley, D. A., Ebener, D., & Leal-Idrogo, A. (2000). Endorsement of professional multicultural rehabilitation competencies and standards: A call to action. *Rehabilitation Counseling Bulletin, 43,* 219–240.

Niles, S. G., & Pate, R. H., Jr. (1989). Competency and training issues related to the integration of career counseling and mental health counseling. *Journal of Career Development, 16,* 63–71.

Patterson, J. B., & Settles, R. (1992). The ethics education of certified rehabilitation counselors. *Rehabilitation Education, 6,* 179–184.

Patterson, J. B., Patrick, A., & Parker, R. M. (2000). Choice: Ethical and legal rehabilitation challenges. *Rehabilitation Counseling Bulletin, 43,* 203–208.

Rehabilitation Act Amendments of 1998, 29 U.S.C. §2801 *et seq.*

Rubin, S. E., & Roessler, R. T. (1995). *Foundations of the vocational rehabilitation process.* Austin, TX: Pro-Ed.

Salomone, P. R. (1996). Career counseling and job placement: Theory and practice.

In E. M. Szymanski & R. M. Parker (Eds.), *Work and disability: Issues and strategies in career development and job placement* (pp. 365–420). Austin, TX: Pro-Ed.

Shaw, L. R., & Tarvydas, V. M. (Eds.). (2001). Special issue—Ethics. *Journal of Applied Rehabilitation, 32*(4), 3–37.

Stebnicki, M. A. (1997, October/November/December). A conceptual framework for utilizing a functional assessment approach for determining mental capacity: A new look at informed consent in rehabilitation. *Journal of Rehabilitation, 41,* 32–37.

Stebnicki, M. A. (1999). Ethical dilemmas in adult guardianship and substitute decision-making. *Journal of Rehabilitation, 43,* 23–27.

Strein, W., & Hershenson, D. (1991). Confidentiality in nondyadic counseling situations. *Journal of Counseling & Development, 69,* 312–316.

Szymanski, E. M. (1995). Rehabilitation counseling: A profession with a vision, an identity, and a future (Presidential address). *Rehabilitation Counseling Bulletin, 29*(1), 2–5.

Tarvydas, V. M., & Cottone, R. R. (2000). The code of ethics for rehabilitation counselors: What we have and what we need. *Rehabilitation Counseling Bulletin, 43,* 188–196.

Tarvydas, V. M., & Leahy, M. J. (1993). Licensure in rehabilitation counseling: A critical incident in professionalization. *Rehabilitation Counseling Bulletin, 37,* 92–108.

Tarvydas, V. M., Leahy, M., Saunders, J., Thielsen, V., Murray, G., & Chan, F. (2001). Beliefs about the ethics of practice among rehabilitation counselors: A national survey. *Journal of Applied Rehabilitation Counseling, 32*(2), 9–18.

Thomas, K. R. (1991). The future of rehabilitation counseling. In K. R. Thomas and Associates, *Rehabilitation counseling: A profession in transition* (pp. 170–194). Athens, GA: Elliot & Fitzpatrick.

Vash, C. (1987). Canon 3—Client advocacy: Fighting another's battles: Is it helpful? Professional? Ethical? *Journal of Applied Rehabilitation Counseling, 18,* 15–17.

APPENDIX 17-A

Code of Professional Ethics for Rehabilitation Counselors

Adopted in June 2001 by the Commission on Rehabilitation Counselor Certification for its Certified Rehabilitation Counselors. This Code is effective as of January 1, 2002.

PREAMBLE

Rehabilitation counselors are committed to facilitating the personal, social, and economic independence of individuals with disabilities. In fulfilling this commitment, rehabilitation counselors work with people, programs, institutions, and service delivery systems. Rehabilitation counselors provide services within the Scope of Practice for Rehabilitation Counseling (see the Scope of Practice document) and recognize that both action and inaction can be facilitating or debilitating. It is essential that rehabilitation counselors demonstrate adherence to ethical standards and ensure that the standards are enforced vigorously. The Code of Professional Ethics for Rehabilitation Counselors, henceforth referred to as the Code, is designed to facilitate these goals.

The fundamental spirit of caring and respect with which the Code is written is based upon five principles of ethical behavior.[1] These include autonomy, beneficence, nonmaleficence, justice, and fidelity, as defined below:

> Autonomy: To honor the right to make individual decisions.
> Beneficence: To do good to others.
> Nonmaleficence: To do no harm to others.

---

[1]Beauchamp, T. L., & Childress, J. F. (1994), 4th Ed. *Principles of Biomedical Ethics*. Oxford: Oxford University Press. Kitchener, K. S. (1984). Ethics in Counseling Psychology: Distinctions and Directions. *Counseling Psychologists, 12*(3), 43–55.

> Justice: To be fair and give equally to others.
> Fidelity: To be loyal, honest, and keep promises.

The primary obligation of rehabilitation counselors is to their clients, defined in the Code as individuals with disabilities who are receiving services from rehabilitation counselors. Regardless of whether direct client contact occurs or whether indirect services are provided, rehabilitation counselors are obligated to adhere to the Code. At times, rehabilitation counseling services may be provided to individuals other than those with disabilities, such as a student population. In all instances, the primary obligation remains with the client and adherence to the Code is required.

The basic objective of the Code is to promote public welfare by specifying ethical behavior expected of rehabilitation counselors. The Enforceable Standards within the Code are the exacting standards intended to provide guidance in specific circumstances and will serve as the basis for processing ethical complaints initiated against certificants.

Rehabilitation counselors who violate the Code are subject to disciplinary action. Since the use of the Certified Rehabilitation Counselor (CRC) designation is a privilege granted by the Commission on Rehabilitation Counselor Certification (CRCC), CRCC reserves unto itself the power to suspend or to revoke the privilege or to approve other penalties for a violation. Disciplinary penalties are imposed as warranted by the severity of the offense and its attendant circumstances. All disciplinary actions are undertaken in accordance with published procedures and penalties designed to assure the proper enforcement of the Code within the framework of due process and equal protection under the law.

APPENDIX 17-B

Enforceable Standards of Ethical Practice

SECTION A: THE COUNSELING RELATIONSHIP

A.1. Client Welfare

a. **Definition of Client.** The primary obligation of rehabilitation counselors will be to their clients, defined as individuals with disabilities who are receiving services from rehabilitation counselors.

b. **Rehabilitation and Counseling Plans.** Rehabilitation counselors will work jointly with their clients in devising and revising integrated, individual rehabilitation and counseling plans that contain realistic and mutually agreed upon goals and are consistent with abilities and circumstances of clients.

c. **Career and Employment Needs.** Rehabilitation counselors will work with their clients in considering employment that is consistent with the overall abilities, vocational limitations, physical restrictions, psychological limitations, general temperament, interest and aptitude patterns, social skills, education, general qualifications, and cultural and other relevant characteristics and needs of clients. Rehabilitation counselors will neither place nor participate in placing clients in positions that will result in damaging the interest and the welfare of clients, employers, or the public.

d. **Autonomy.** Rehabilitation counselors will respect the autonomy of the client if actions such as involuntary commitment or initiation of guardianship are taken that diminish client autonomy. The assumption of responsibility for decision-making on behalf of the client will be taken only after careful deliberation. The rehabilitation counselor will advocate for client resumption of responsibility as quickly as possible.

A.2. Respecting Diversity

a. **Respecting Culture.** Rehabilitation counselors will demonstrate respect for clients' cultural backgrounds.
b. **Interventions.** Rehabilitation counselors will develop and adapt interventions and services to incorporate consideration of clients' cultural perspectives and recognition of barriers external to clients that may interfere with achieving effective rehabilitation outcomes.
c. **Non-Discrimination.** Rehabilitation counselors will not condone or engage in discrimination based on age, color, culture, disability, ethnic group, gender, race, religion, sexual orientation, marital status, or socioeconomic status.

A.3. Client Rights

a. **Disclosure to Clients.** When counseling is initiated, and throughout the counseling process as necessary, rehabilitation counselors will inform clients, preferably through both written and oral means, of their credentials, the purposes, goals, techniques, procedures, limitations, potential risks, and benefits of services to be performed, and other pertinent information. Rehabilitation counselors will take steps to ensure that clients understand the implications of diagnosis, the intended use of tests and reports, fees, and billing arrangements. Clients have the right to (1) expect confidentiality will be provided with an explanation of its limitations, including disclosure to supervisors and/or treatment team professionals; (2) obtain clear information about their case records; (3) actively participate in the development and implementation of rehabilitation counseling plans; and (4) refuse any recommended services and be advised of the consequences of such refusal.
b. **Third Party Referral.** Rehabilitation counselors who have direct contact with a client at the request of a third party will define the nature of their relationships and role to all rightful, legal parties with whom they have direct contact. Direct contact is defined as any written, oral, or electronic communication. Legal parties may include clients, legal guardians, referring third parties, and attorneys actively involved in a matter directly related to rehabilitation services.
c. **Indirect Service Provision.** Rehabilitation counselors who are employed by third parties as case consultants or expert witnesses, and who engage in communication with the individual with a disability, will fully disclose to the individual with a disability and/or his or her designee their role and limits of their relationship. Communication includes all forms of written or oral interactions regardless of the type of communication tool used. When there is no pretense or intent to provide rehabilitation counseling services directly to the individual with a disability, and where there will be no communication, disclosure by the rehabilitation counselor is not required. When serving as case consultants or expert witnesses, rehabilitation counselors will provide unbiased, objective opinions. Rehabilitation counselors acting as expert witnesses will generate written documentation, either in the form of case notes or a report, as to their involvement and/or conclusions.
d. **Freedom of Choice.** To the extent possible, rehabilitation counselors will offer clients the freedom to choose whether to enter into a counseling relationship and to determine which professional(s) will provide counseling. Restrictions that limit choices of clients will be fully explained. Rehabilitation counselors will honor the rights of clients to consent to participate and the right to make decisions with regard to rehabilitation services. Rehabilitation counselors will inform clients or the clients' legal guardians of factors that may affect decisions to participate in rehabilitation services, and they will obtain written consent or will acknowledge consent in writing after clients or legal guardians are fully informed of such factors.
e. **Inability to Give Consent.** When counseling minors or persons unable to give voluntary informed consent, rehabilitation counselors will obtain written informed consent from legally responsible parties. Where no legally responsible parties exist, rehabilitation counselors will act in the best interest of clients.
f. **Involvement of Significant Others.** Rehabilitation counselors will attempt to enlist family understanding and involvement of family and/or significant others as a positive resource if (or when) appropriate. The client or legal guardian's permission will be secured prior to any involvement of family and/or significant others.

A.4. Personal Needs and Values

In the counseling relationship, rehabilitation counselors will be aware of the intimacy and responsibilities inherent in the counseling relationship, maintain respect for clients, and avoid actions that seek to meet their personal needs at the expense of clients.

A.5. Sexual Intimacies with Clients

a. **Current Clients.** Rehabilitation counselors will not have any type of sexual intimacies with clients and will not counsel persons with whom they have had a sexual relationship.

b. **Former Clients.** Rehabilitation counselors will not engage in sexual intimacies with former clients within a minimum of five years after terminating the counseling relationship. Rehabilitation counselors who engage in such relationship after five years following termination will have the responsibility to examine and document thoroughly that such relations do not have an exploitative nature, based on factors such as duration of counseling, amount of time since counseling, termination circumstances, client's personal history and mental status, adverse impact on the client, and actions by the counselor suggesting a plan to initiate a sexual relationship with the client after termination. Rehabilitation counselors will seek peer consultation prior to engaging in a sexual relationship with a former client.

A.6. Non-Professional Relationships with Clients

a. **Potential for Harm.** Rehabilitation counselors will be aware of their influential positions with respect to clients, and will avoid exploiting the trust and dependency of clients. Rehabilitation counselors will make every effort to avoid non-professional relationships with clients that could impair professional judgement or increase the risk of harm to clients. (Examples of such relationships include, but are not limited to, familial, social, financial, business, close personal relationships with clients, or volunteer or paid work within an office in which the client is actively receiving services.) When a non-professional relationship cannot be avoided, rehabilitation counselors will take appropriate professional precautions such as informed consent, consultation, supervision, and documentation to ensure that judgement is not impaired and no exploitation occurs.

b. **Superior/Subordinate Relationships.** Rehabilitation counselors will not accept as clients, superiors or subordinates, with whom they have administrative, supervisory, or evaluative relationships.

A.7. Multiple Clients

When rehabilitation counselors agree to provide counseling services to two or more persons who have a relationship (such as husband and wife, or parents and children), rehabilitation counselors will clarify at the outset which person or persons are clients, and the nature of the relationships they will have with each involved person. If it becomes apparent that rehabilitation counselors may be called upon to perform potentially conflicting roles, they will clarify, adjust, or withdraw from such roles appropriately.

A.8. Group Work

a. **Screening.** Rehabilitation counselors will screen prospective group counseling/therapy participants. To the extent possible, rehabilitation counselors will select members whose needs and goals are compatible with goals of the group, who will not impede the group process, and whose well being will not be jeopardized by the group experience.

b. **Protecting Clients.** In a group setting, rehabilitation counselors will take reasonable precautions to protect clients from physical or psychological trauma.

A.9. Termination and Referral

a. **Abandonment Prohibited.** Rehabilitation counselors will not abandon or neglect clients in counseling. Rehabilitation counselors will assist in making appropriate arrangements for the continuation of treatment, when necessary, during interruptions such as vacations, and following termination.

b. **Inability to Assist Clients.** If rehabilitation counselors determine an inability to be of professional assistance to clients, they will avoid entering or immediately terminate a counseling relationship.

c. **Appropriate Termination.** Rehabilitation counselors will terminate a counseling relationship, securing client agreement when possible, when it is reasonably clear that the client is no longer benefiting, when services are no longer required, when counseling no longer serves the client's needs or interests, or when there is failure to pay fees according to Section J of this document.

d. **Referral Upon Termination.** Rehabilitation counselors will be knowledgeable about referral resources and suggest appropriate alternatives. If clients decline the suggested referral, rehabilitation counselors have the right to discontinue the relationship.

A.10. Computer Technology

a. **Use of Computers.** When computer applications are used in counseling services, rehabilitation counselors will ensure that (1) the client is intellectually, emotionally, and physically capable of using the computer application; (2) the computer application is appropriate for the needs of the client; (3) the client understands the purpose and operation of the computer applications; and (4) a follow-up of client use of a computer application is provided to correct possible misconceptions, discover inappropriate use, and assess subsequent needs.

b. **Explanation of Limitations.** Rehabilitation counselors will ensure that clients are provided information as a part of the counseling relationship that adequately explains the limitations of computer technology.

c. **Access to Computer Applications.** Rehabilitation counselors will provide reasonable access to computer applications in counseling services.

SECTION B: CONFIDENTIALITY

B.1. Right to Privacy

a. **Respect for Privacy.** Rehabilitation counselors will respect clients' rights to privacy and will avoid illegal and unwarranted disclosures of confidential information.

b. **Client Waiver.** Rehabilitation counselors will respect the right of the client or his/her legally recognized representative to waive the right to privacy.

c. **Exceptions.** When disclosure is required to prevent clear and imminent danger to the client or others, or when legal requirements demand that confidential information be revealed, the general requirement that rehabilitation counselors keep information confidential will not apply. Rehabilitation counselors will consult with other professionals when in doubt as to the validity of an exception.

d. **Contagious, Fatal Diseases.** Rehabilitation counselors will become aware of the legal requirements for disclosure of contagious and fatal diseases in their jurisdiction. In jurisdictions where allowable, a rehabilitation counselor who receives information will confirm that a client has a disease known to be communicable and/or fatal. If allowable by law, the rehabilitation counselor will disclose this information to a third party, who by his or her relationship with the client is at high risk of contracting the disease. Prior to disclosure, the rehabilitation counselor will ascertain that the client has not already informed the third party about his or her disease and that the client is not intending to inform the third party in the immediate future.

e. **Court-Ordered Disclosure.** When court ordered to release confidential information without a client's permission, rehabilitation counselors will request to the court that the disclosure not be required due to potential harm to the client or counseling relationship.

f. **Minimal Disclosure.** When circumstances require the disclosure of confidential information, rehabilitation counselors will endeavor to reveal only essential information. To the extent possible, clients will be informed before confidential information is disclosed.

g. **Explanation of Limitations.** When counseling is initiated and throughout the counseling process as necessary, rehabilitation counselors will inform clients of the limitations of confidentiality and will identify foreseeable situations in which confidentiality must be breached.

h. **Work Environment.** Rehabilitation counselors will make every effort to ensure that a confidential work environment exists and that subordinates including employees, supervisees, clerical assistants, and volunteers maintain the privacy and confidentiality of clients.

i. **Treatment Teams.** If client treatment will involve the sharing of client information among treatment team members, the client will be advised of this fact and will be informed of the team's existence and composition.

j. **Client Assistants.** When a client is accompanied by an individual providing assistance to the client (e.g., interpreter, personal care assistant, etc.), rehabilitation counselors will ensure that the assistant is apprised of the need to maintain confidentiality.

B.2. Groups and Families

a. **Group Work.** In group work, rehabilitation counselors will clearly define confidentiality and the parameters for the specific group being entered, explain its importance, and discuss the difficulties related to confidentiality involved in group work. The fact that confidentiality cannot be guaranteed will be clearly communicated to group members.

b. **Family Counseling.** In family counseling, unless otherwise directed by law, information about one family member will not be disclosed to another member without permission. Rehabilitation counselors will protect the privacy rights of each family member.

B.3. Records

a. **Requirement of Records.** Rehabilitation counselors will maintain records necessary for rendering professional services to their clients and as required by laws, regulations, or agency or institution procedures.

b. **Confidentiality of Records.** Rehabilitation counselors will be responsible for securing the safety and confidentiality of any counseling records they create, maintain, transfer, or destroy whether the records are written, taped, computerized, or stored in any other medium.

c. **Permission to Record or Observe.** Rehabilitation counselors will obtain and document written or recorded permission from clients prior to electronically recording or observing sessions. When counseling clients who are minors or individuals who are unable to give voluntary, informed consent, written or recorded permission of guardians must be obtained.

d. **Client Access.** Rehabilitation counselors will recognize that counseling records are kept for the benefit of clients, and therefore provide access to records and copies of records when requested by clients, unless prohibited by law. In instances where the records contain information that may be sensitive or detrimental to the client, the rehabilitation counselor has a responsibility to adequately interpret such information to the client. In situations involving multiple clients, access to records will be limited to those parts of records that do not include confidential information related to another client.

e. **Disclosure or Transfer.** Rehabilitation counselors will obtain written permission from clients to disclose or transfer records to legitimate third parties unless exceptions to confidentiality exist as listed in Section B.1.

B.4. Consultation

a. **Respect for Privacy.** Information obtained in a consulting relationship will be discussed for professional purposes only with persons clearly concerned with the case. Written and oral reports will present data germane to the purposes of the consultation, and every effort will be made to protect client identity and to avoid undue invasion of privacy.

b. **Cooperating Agencies.** Before sharing information, rehabilitation counselors will make efforts to ensure that there are defined policies in other agencies serving the counselor's clients that effectively protect the confidentiality of information.

B.5. Alternative Communication

Rehabilitation counselors will make every effort to ensure that methods of exchanging information that utilize alternative means of communication (i.e., facsimile, cellular telephone, computer, or videoconferencing) will be conducted in such a manner that ensures protection of client confidentiality. If confidentiality cannot be ensured, client or guardian permission must be obtained.

SECTION C: ADVOCACY AND ACCESSIBILITY

C.1. Advocacy

a. **Attitudinal Barriers.** Rehabilitation counselors will strive to eliminate attitudinal barriers, including stereotyping and discrimination, toward individuals with disabilities and to increase their own awareness and sensitivity to such individuals.

b. **Advocacy with Cooperating Agencies.** Rehabilitation counselors will remain aware of actions taken by cooperating agencies on behalf of their clients and will act as advocates of such clients to ensure effective service delivery.

c. **Empowerment.** Rehabilitation counselors will provide the client with appropriate information and will support their efforts at self-advocacy both on an individual and an organizational level.

C.2. Accessibility

a. **Counseling Practice.** Rehabilitation counselors will demonstrate, in their practice, an appreciation of the need to provide necessary accommodations, including accessible facilities and services, to individuals with disabilities.

b. **Barriers to Access.** Rehabilitation counselors will identify physical, communication, and transportation barriers to clients and will communicate information on barriers to public and private authorities to facilitate removal of barriers to access.

c. **Referral Accessibility.** Rehabilitation counselors, as advocates for individuals with disabilities, will ensure, prior to referring clients to programs, facilities, or employment settings, that they are appropriately accessible.

SECTION D: PROFESSIONAL RESPONSIBILITY

D.1. Professional Competence

a. **Boundaries of Competence.** Rehabilitation counselors will practice only within the boundaries of their competence, based on their education, training, supervised experience, state and national professional credentials, and appropriate professional experience. Rehabilitation counselors will demonstrate a commitment to gain knowledge, personal awareness, sensitivity, and skills pertinent to working with a diverse client population. Rehabilitation counselors will not misrepresent their role or competence to clients.

b. **Referral.** Rehabilitation counselors will refer clients to other specialists as the needs of the clients dictate.

c. **New Specialty Areas of Practice.** Rehabilitation counselors will practice in specialty areas new to them only after appropriate education, training, and supervised experience. While developing skills in new specialty areas, rehabilitation counselors will take steps to ensure the competence of their work and to protect clients from possible harm.

d. **Resources.** Rehabilitation counselors will ensure that the resources used or accessed in counseling are credible and valid (e.g., web link, books used in Bibliotherapy, etc.).

e. **Qualified for Employment.** Rehabilitation counselors will accept employment only for positions for which they are qualified by education, training, supervised experience, state and national professional credentials, and appropriate professional experience. Rehabilitation counselors will hire only individuals who are qualified and competent for professional rehabilitation counseling positions.

f. **Monitor Effectiveness.** Rehabilitation counselors will take reasonable steps to seek peer supervision to evaluate their efficacy as rehabilitation counselors.

g. **Ethical Issues Consultation.** Rehabilitation counselors will take reasonable steps to consult with other rehabilitation counselors or related professionals when they have questions regarding their ethical obligations or professional practice.

h. **Continuing Education.** Rehabilitation counselors will engage in continuing education to maintain a reasonable level of awareness of current scientific and professional information in their fields of activity. They will take steps to maintain competence in the skills they use, will be open to new techniques, and will develop and maintain competence for practice with the diverse and/or special populations with whom they work.

i. **Impairment.** Rehabilitation counselors will refrain from offering or rendering professional services when their physical, mental, or emotional problems are likely to harm the client or others. They will seek assistance for problems, and, if necessary, will limit, suspend, or terminate their professional responsibilities.

D.2. Legal Standards

a. **Legal Versus Ethical.** Rehabilitation counselors will obey the laws and statutes of the legal jurisdiction in which they practice unless there is a conflict with the Code, in which case they should seek immediate consultation and advice.

b. **Legal Limitations.** Rehabilitation counselors will be familiar with and observe the legal limitations of the services they offer to clients. They will discuss these limitations as well as all benefits available to clients they serve in order to facilitate open, honest communication and avoid unrealistic expectations.

D.3. Advertising and Soliciting Clients

a. **Accurate Advertising.** Advertising by rehabilitation counselors shall not be restricted. Rehabilitation counselors will advertise or will represent their services to the public by identifying their credentials in an accurate manner that is not false, misleading, deceptive, or fraudulent. Rehabilitation counselors will only advertise the highest degree earned which is in counseling or a closely related field from a college or university that was accredited when the degree was awarded by one of the regional accrediting bodies recognized by the Council on Higher Education Accreditation.

b. **Testimonials.** Rehabilitation counselors who use testimonials will not solicit them from clients or other persons who, because of their particular circumstances, may be vulnerable to undue influence. Full disclosure of uses and the informed consent of the client or guardian will be obtained. Use of testimonials will be for a specified and agreed upon period of time.

c. **Statements by Others.** Rehabilitation counselors will make reasonable efforts to ensure that statements made by others about them or the profession of rehabilitation counseling are accurate.

d. **Recruiting through Employment.** Employed rehabilitation counselors will not use their institutional affiliations or relationship with their employers to recruit clients, supervisees, or consultees for their separate private practices.

e. **Products and Training Advertisements.** Rehabilitation counselors who develop products related to their profession or conduct workshops or training events will ensure that the advertisements concerning these products or events are accurate and disclose adequate information for consumers to make informed choices.

f. **Promoting to Those Served.** Rehabilitation counselors will not use counseling, teaching, training, or supervisory relationships to promote their products or training events in a manner that is deceptive or would exert undue influence on individuals who may be vulnerable. Rehabilitation counselors may adopt textbooks they have authored for instructional purposes.

D.4. Credentials

a. **Credentials Claimed.** Rehabilitation counselors will claim or will imply only professional credentials possessed and are responsible for correcting any known misrepresentations of their credentials by others. Professional credentials include graduate degrees in counseling or closely related fields, accreditation of graduate programs, national voluntary certifications, government-issued certifications or licenses, or any other credential that might indicate to the public specialized knowledge or expertise in counseling.

b. **Credential Guidelines.** Rehabilitation counselors will follow the guidelines for use of credentials that have been established by the entities that issue the credentials.

c. **Misrepresentation of Credentials.** Rehabilitation counselors will not attribute more to their credentials than the credentials represent, and will not imply that other rehabilitation counselors are not qualified because they do not possess certain credentials.

d. **Doctoral Degrees from Other Fields.** Rehabilitation counselors who hold a master's degree in counseling or a closely related field, but hold a doctoral degree from other than counseling or a closely related field, will not use the title "Dr." in their practices and will not announce to the public in relation to their practice or status as a rehabilitation counselor that they hold a doctorate.

D.5. CRC Credential

a. **Acting on Behalf of CRCC.** Certified Rehabilitation Counselors will not write, speak, nor act in ways that lead others to believe the counselor is officially representing CRCC unless the Commission has granted permission in writing.

b. **Support of Candidates.** Certified Rehabilitation Counselors will not initiate or support the candidacy of an individual for certification by CRCC if the individual is known to engage in professional practices that violate the Code of Professional Ethics for Rehabilitation Counselors.

D.6. Public Responsibility

a. **Sexual Harassment.** Rehabilitation counselors will not engage in sexual harassment. Sexual harassment is defined as sexual solicitation, physical advances, or verbal or nonverbal conduct that is sexual in nature, that occurs in connection with professional activities or roles, and that either (1) the rehabilitation counselor knows or is told the act is unwelcome, offensive, or creates a hostile workplace environment; or (2) is sufficiently severe or intense to be perceived as harassment to a reasonable person within the context in which it occurs. Sexual harassment may consist of a single intense or severe act or multiple persistent or pervasive acts.

b. **Reports to Third Parties.** Rehabilitation counselors will be accurate, timely, and objective in reporting their professional activities and opinions to appropriate third parties including courts, health insurance companies, those who are the recipients of evaluation reports, and others.

c. **Media Presentations.** When rehabilitation counselors provide advice or comment by means of public lectures, demonstrations, radio or television programs, prerecorded tapes, printed articles, mailed material, or other media, they will take reasonable precautions to ensure that (1) the statements are based on appropriate professional counseling literature and practice; (2) the statements are otherwise consistent with the Code of Professional Ethics for Rehabilitation Counselors; and (3) the recipients of the information are not encouraged to infer that a professional rehabilitation counseling relationship has been established.

d. **Conflicts of Interest.** Rehabilitation counselors will not use their professional positions to seek or receive unjustified personal gains, sexual favors, unfair advantage, or unearned goods or services.

e. **Dishonesty.** Rehabilitation counselors will not engage in any act or omission of a dishonest, deceitful, or fraudulent nature in the conduct of their professional activities.

D.7. Responsibility to Other Professionals

a. **Disparaging Comments.** Rehabilitation counselors will not discuss in a disparaging way the competency of other professionals or agencies, or the findings made, the methods used, or the quality of rehabilitation plans.

b. **Personal Public Statements.** When making personal statements in a public context, rehabilitation counselors will clarify that they are speaking from their personal perspectives and that they are not speaking on behalf of all rehabilitation counselors or the profession.

c. **Clients Served by Others.** When rehabilitation counselors learn that their clients have an ongoing professional relationship with another rehabilitation or treating professional, they will request release from clients to inform the other professionals and strive to establish positive and collaborative professional relationships. File reviews, second-opinion services, and other indirect services are not considered ongoing professional services.

SECTION E: RELATIONSHIPS WITH OTHER PROFESSIONALS

E.1. Relationships with Employers and Employees

a. **Negative Conditions.** Rehabilitation counselors will alert their employers to conditions that may be potentially disruptive or damaging to the counselor's professional responsibilities or that may limit their effectiveness.

b. **Evaluation.** Rehabilitation counselors will submit regularly to professional review and evaluation by their supervisor or the appropriate representative of the employer.

c. **Discrimination.** Rehabilitation counselors, as either employers or employees, will engage in fair practices with regard to hiring, promotion, or training.

d. **Exploitative Relationships.** Rehabilitation counselors will not engage in exploitative relationships with individuals over whom they have supervisory, evaluative, or instructional control or authority.

e. **Employer Policies.** In those instances where rehabilitation counselors are critical of policies, they will attempt to affect change through constructive action within the organization. Where such change cannot be affected, rehabilitation counselors will take appropriate further action. Such action may include referral to appropriate certification, accreditation, or state licensure organizations or termination of employment.

E.2. Consultation

a. **Consultation as an Option.** Rehabilitation counselors may choose to consult with professionally competent persons about their clients. In choosing consultants, rehabilitation counselors will avoid placing the consultant in a conflict of interest situation that will preclude the consultant from being a proper party to the counselor's efforts to help the client. If rehabilitation counselors are engaged in a work setting that compromises this consultation standard, they will consult with other professionals whenever possible to consider justifiable alternatives.

b. **Consultant Competency.** Rehabilitation counselors will be reasonably certain that they have, or the organization represented has, the necessary competencies and resources for giving the kind of consulting services needed and that appropriate referral resources are available.

E.3. Agency and Team Relationships

a. **Client as a Team Member.** Rehabilitation counselors will ensure that clients and/or their legally recognized representative are afforded the opportunity for full participation in their own treatment team.

b. **Communication.** Rehabilitation counselors will ensure that there is fair mutual understanding of the rehabilitation plan by all agencies cooperating in the rehabilitation of clients and that any rehabilitation plan is developed with such mutual understanding.

c. **Dissent.** Rehabilitation counselors will abide by and help to implement team decisions in formulating rehabilitation plans and procedures, even when not personally agreeing with such decisions, unless these decisions breach the Code.

d. **Reports.** Rehabilitation counselors will attempt to secure from other specialists appropriate reports and evaluations, when such reports are essential for rehabilitation planning and/or service delivery.

SECTION F: EVALUATION, ASSESSMENT, AND INTERPRETATION

F.1. Informed Consent

a. **Explanation to Clients.** Prior to assessment, rehabilitation counselors will explain the nature and purposes of assessment and the specific use of results in language the client (or other legally authorized person on behalf of the client) can understand. Regardless of whether scoring and interpretation are completed by rehabilitation counselors, by assistants, or by computer or other outside services, rehabilitation counselors will take reasonable steps to ensure that appropriate explanations are given to the client.

b. **Recipients of Results.** The client's welfare, explicit understanding, and prior agreement will determine the recipients of test results. Rehabilitation counselors will include accurate and appropriate interpretations with any release of test results.

F.2. Release of Information to Competent Professionals

a. **Misuse of Results.** Rehabilitation counselors will not misuse assessment results, including test results and interpretations, and will take reasonable steps to prevent the misuse of such by others.

b. **Release of Raw Data.** Rehabilitation counselors will ordinarily release data (e.g., protocols, counseling or interview notes, or questionnaires) in which the client is identified only with the consent of the client or the client's legal representative. Such data will be released only to persons recognized by rehabilitation counselors as competent to interpret the data.

F.3. Research and Training

a. **Data Disguise Required.** Use of data derived from counseling relationships for purposes of training, research, or publication will be confined to content that is disguised to ensure the anonymity of the individuals involved.

b. **Agreement for Identification.** Identification of a client in a presentation or publication will be permissible only when the client has agreed in writing to its presentation or publication.

F.4. Proper Diagnosis of Mental Disorders

a. **Proper Diagnosis.** Rehabilitation counselors qualified to provide proper diagnosis of mental disorders will take special care when doing so. Assessment techniques (including personal interview) used to determine client care (e.g., locus of treatment, type of treatment, or recommended follow-up) will be carefully selected and appropriately used.

b. **Cultural Sensitivity.** Disability, socioeconomic, and cultural experience of clients will be considered when diagnosing mental disorders.

F.5. Competence to Use and Interpret Tests

a. **Limits of Competence.** Rehabilitation counselors will recognize the limits of their competence and perform only those testing and assessment services for which they have been trained. They will be familiar with reliability, validity,

related standardization, error of measurement, and proper application of any technique utilized. Rehabilitation counselors using computer-based test interpretations will be trained in the construct being measured and the specific instrument being used prior to using this type of computer application. Rehabilitation counselors will take reasonable measures to ensure the proper use of psychological assessment techniques by persons under their supervision.

b. **Appropriate Use.** Rehabilitation counselors will be responsible for the appropriate application, scoring, interpretation, and use of assessment instruments, whether they score and interpret such tests themselves or use computerized or other services.

c. **Decisions Based on Results.** Rehabilitation counselors will be responsible for decisions involving individuals or policies that are based on assessment results and will have a thorough understanding of educational and psychological measurement, including validation criteria, test research, and guidelines for test development and use.

d. **Accurate Information.** Rehabilitation counselors will provide accurate information and avoid false claims or misconceptions when making statements about assessment instruments or techniques. Special efforts will be made to avoid utilizing test results to make inappropriate diagnoses or inferences.

F.6. Test Selection

a. **Appropriateness of Instruments.** Rehabilitation counselors will carefully consider the validity, reliability, psychometric limitations, and appropriateness of instruments when selecting tests for use in a given situation or with a particular client.

b. **Referral Information.** If a client is referred to a third party provider for testing, the rehabilitation counselor will provide specific referral questions and sufficient objective data about the client so as to ensure that appropriate test instruments are utilized.

c. **Culturally Diverse Populations.** Rehabilitation counselors will be cautious when selecting tests for disability or culturally diverse populations to avoid inappropriateness of testing that may be outside of socialized behavioral or cognitive patterns or functional abilities.

d. **Norm Divergence.** Rehabilitation counselors will be cautious in using assessment techniques, making evaluations, and interpreting the performance of populations not represented in the norm group on which an instrument was standardized and will disclose such information.

F.7. Conditions of Test Administration

a. **Administration Conditions.** Rehabilitation counselors will administer tests under the same conditions that were established in the test standardization. When tests are not administered under standard conditions, as may be necessary to accommodate modifications for clients with disabilities or when unusual behavior or irregularities occur during the testing session, those conditions will be noted in interpretation.

b. **Computer Administration.** When a computer or other electronic methods are used for test administration, rehabilitation counselors will be responsible for ensuring that programs function properly to provide clients with accurate results.

c. **Unsupervised Test-Taking.** Rehabilitation counselors will not permit unsupervised or inadequately supervised use of tests or assessments unless the tests or assessments are designed, intended, and validated for self-administration and/or scoring.

F.8. Test Scoring and Interpretation

a. **Reporting Reservations.** In reporting assessment results, rehabilitation counselors will indicate any reservations that exist regarding validity or reliability because of the circumstances of the assessment or the inappropriateness of the norms for the person tested.

b. **Diversity in Testing.** Rehabilitation counselors will place test results and their interpretations in proper perspective considering other relevant factors including age, color, culture, disability, ethnic group, gender, race, religion, sexual orientation, marital status, and socioeconomic status.

c. **Research Instruments.** Rehabilitation counselors will exercise caution when interpreting the results of research instruments possessing insufficient technical data to support respondent results. The specific purposes for the use of such instruments will be stated explicitly to the examinee.

d. **Testing Services.** Rehabilitation counselors who provide test scoring and test interpretation services to support the assessment process will confirm the validity of such interpretations. The interpretation of assessment data will be related to the particular goals of evaluation. Rehabilitation counselors will accurately describe the purpose, norms, validity, reliability, and applications of the procedures and any special qualifications applicable to their use.

e. **Automated Testing Services.** The public offering of an automated test interpretation service will be considered a professional-to-professional consultation. The formal responsibility of the consultant will be to the consultee, but the ultimate and overriding responsibility will be to the client.

F.9. Test Security

Rehabilitation counselors will maintain the integrity and security of tests and other assessment techniques consistent with legal and contractual obligations. Rehabilitation counselors will not appropriate, reproduce, or modify published tests or parts thereof without acknowledgment and permission from the publisher.

F.10. Obsolete Tests and Outdated Test Results

Rehabilitation counselors will not use data or test results that are obsolete or outdated for the current purpose. Rehabilita-

tion counselors will make every effort to prevent the misuse of obsolete measures and test data by others.

F.11. Test Construction

Rehabilitation counselors will use established scientific procedures, relevant standards, and current professional knowledge for test design in the development, publication, and utilization of educational and psychological assessment techniques.

F.12. Forensic Evaluation

When providing forensic evaluations, the primary obligation of rehabilitation counselors will be to produce objective findings that can be substantiated based on information and techniques appropriate to the evaluation, which may include examination of the individual with a disability and/or review of records. Rehabilitation counselors will define the limits of their reports or testimony, especially when an examination of the individual with a disability has not been conducted.

SECTION G: TEACHING, TRAINING, AND SUPERVISION

G.1. Rehabilitation Counselor Educators and Trainers

a. **Relationship Boundaries with Students and Supervisees.** Rehabilitation counselors will clearly define and maintain ethical, professional, and social relationship boundaries with their students and supervisees. They will be aware of the differential in power that exists and the student or supervisee's possible incomprehension of that power differential. Rehabilitation counselors will explain to students and supervisees the potential for the relationship to become exploitive.

b. **Sexual Relationships.** Rehabilitation counselors will not engage in sexual relationships with students or supervisees and will not subject them to sexual harassment.

c. **Supervision Preparation.** Rehabilitation counselors will supervise only within the boundaries of their competence, based on their education, training, supervised experience, state and national professional credentials, and appropriate professional experience. Rehabilitation counselors who are doctoral students serving as practicum or internship supervisors will be adequately prepared and supervised by the training program.

d. **Responsibility for Services to Clients.** Rehabilitation counselors who supervise the rehabilitation counseling services of others will perform direct supervision sufficient to ensure that rehabilitation counseling services provided to clients are adequate and do not cause harm to the client.

e. **Endorsement.** Rehabilitation counselors will not endorse students or supervisees for certification, licensure, employment, or completion of an academic or training program if they believe students or supervisees are not qualified for the endorsement. Rehabilitation counselors will take reasonable steps to assist students or supervisees who are not qualified for endorsement to become qualified.

G.2. Rehabilitation Counselor Education and Training Programs

a. **Orientation.** Prior to admission, rehabilitation counselor educators will orient prospective students to the counselor education or training program's expectations, including but not limited to the following: (1) the type and level of skill acquisition required for successful completion of the training, (2) subject matter to be covered, (3) basis for evaluation, (4) training components that encourage self-growth or self-disclosure as part of the training process, (5) the type of supervision settings and requirements of the sites for required clinical field experiences, (6) student evaluation and dismissal policies and procedures, and (7) up-to-date employment prospects for graduates.

b. **Evaluation.** Rehabilitation counselor educators will clearly state, in advance of training, to students and internship supervisees, the levels of competency expected, appraisal methods, and timing of evaluations for both didactic and experiential components. Rehabilitation counselor educators will provide students and internship supervisees with periodic performance appraisal and evaluation feedback throughout the training program.

c. **Teaching Ethics.** Rehabilitation counselor educators will teach students and internship supervisees the ethical responsibilities and standards of the profession and the students' and supervisees' professional ethical responsibilities.

d. **Peer Relationships.** When students are assigned to lead counseling groups or provide clinical supervision for their peers, rehabilitation counselor educators will take steps to ensure that students placed in these roles do not have personal or adverse relationships with peers and that they understand they have the same ethical obligations as counselor educators, trainers, and supervisors. Rehabilitation counselor educators will make every effort to ensure that the rights of peers are not compromised when students are assigned to lead counseling groups or provide clinical supervision.

e. **Varied Theoretical Positions.** Rehabilitation counselor educators will present varied theoretical positions so that students may make comparisons and have opportunities to develop their own positions. Rehabilitation counselor educators will provide information concerning the scientific bases of professional practice.

f. **Field Placements.** Rehabilitation counselor educators will develop clear policies within their training program regarding field placement and other clinical experiences. Rehabilitation counselor educators will provide clearly stated roles and responsibilities for the student and the site

supervisor. Rehabilitation counselor educators will confirm that site supervisors will be qualified to provide supervision and are informed of their professional and ethical responsibilities in this role. Rehabilitation counselor educators will not accept any form of professional services, fees, commissions, reimbursement, or remuneration from a site for student placement.

g. **Diversity in Programs.** Rehabilitation counselor educators will respond to their institution and program's recruitment and retention needs for training program administrators, faculty, and students with diverse backgrounds and special needs.

G.3. Students and Supervisees

a. **Limitations.** Rehabilitation counselors, through ongoing evaluation and appraisal, will be aware of the academic and personal limitations of students and supervisees that might impede performance. Rehabilitation counselors will assist students and supervisees in securing remedial assistance when needed, and will dismiss students or supervisees who are unable to provide competent service due to academic or personal limitations. Rehabilitation counselors will seek professional consultation and document their decision to dismiss or to refer students or supervisees for assistance. Rehabilitation counselors will advise students and supervisees of appeals processes as appropriate.

b. **Self-Growth Experiences.** Rehabilitation counselor educators, when designing training groups or other experiences conducted by the rehabilitation counselor educators themselves, will inform students of the potential risks of self-disclosure. Rehabilitation counselor educators will respect the privacy of students by not requiring self-disclosure that could reasonably be expected to be harmful and student evaluation criteria will not include the level of the student's self-disclosure.

c. **Counseling for Students and Supervisees.** If students or supervisees request counseling, supervisors or rehabilitation counselor educators will provide them with acceptable referrals. Supervisors or rehabilitation counselor educators will not serve as rehabilitation counselors to students or supervisees over whom they hold administrative, teaching, or evaluative roles unless this is a brief role associated with a training experience.

d. **Clients of Students and Supervisees.** Rehabilitation counselors will make every effort to ensure that clients are aware of the services rendered and the qualifications of the students and supervisees rendering those services. Clients will receive professional disclosure information and will be informed of the limits of confidentiality. Client permission will be obtained in order for the students and supervisees to use any information concerning the counseling relationship in the training process.

e. **Professional Development.** Rehabilitation counselors who employ or supervise individuals will provide appropriate working conditions, timely evaluations, constructive consultations, and suitable opportunities for experience and training.

SECTION H: RESEARCH AND PUBLICATION

H.1. Research Responsibilities

a. **Use of Human Participants.** Rehabilitation counselors will plan, design, conduct, and report research in a manner that reflects cultural sensitivity, is culturally appropriate, and is consistent with pertinent ethical principles, federal and state/provincial laws, host institutional regulations, and scientific standards governing research with human participants.

b. **Deviation from Standard Practices.** Rehabilitation counselors will seek consultation and observe stringent safeguards to protect the rights of research participants when a research problem suggests a deviation from standard acceptable practices.

c. **Precautions to Avoid Injury.** Rehabilitation counselors who conduct research with human participants will be responsible for the participants' welfare throughout the research and will take reasonable precautions to avoid causing injurious psychological, physical, or social effects to their participants.

d. **Principal Researcher Responsibility.** While ultimate responsibility for ethical research practice lies with the principal researcher, rehabilitation counselors involved in the research activities will share ethical obligations and bear full responsibility for their own actions.

e. **Minimal Interference.** Rehabilitation counselors will take precautions to avoid causing disruptions in participants' lives due to participation in research.

f. **Diversity.** Rehabilitation counselors will be sensitive to diversity and research issues with culturally diverse populations and they will seek consultation when appropriate.

H.2. Informed Consent

a. **Topics Disclosed.** In obtaining informed consent for research, rehabilitation counselors will use language that is understandable to research participants and that (1) accurately explains the purpose and procedures to be followed; (2) identifies any procedures that are experimental or relatively untried; (3) describes the attendant discomforts and risks; (4) describes the benefits or changes in individuals or organizations that might reasonably be expected; (5) discloses appropriate alternative procedures that would be advantageous for participants; (6) offers to answer any inquiries concerning the procedures; (7) describes any limitations of confidentiality; and (8) instructs that participants are free to withdraw their consent and to discontinue participation in the project at any time.

b. **Deception.** Rehabilitation counselors will not conduct research involving deception unless alternative procedures are not feasible and the prospective value of the research justifies the deception. When the methodological requirements of a study necessitate concealment or deception, the investigator will be required to explain clearly the reasons for this action as soon as possible.

c. **Voluntary Participation.** Participation in research is typically voluntary and without any penalty for refusal to participate. Involuntary participation will be appropriate only when it can be demonstrated that participation will have no harmful effects on participants and is essential to the investigation.

d. **Confidentiality of Information.** Information obtained about research participants during the course of an investigation will be confidential. When the possibility exists that others may obtain access to such information, ethical research practice requires that the possibility, together with the plans for protecting confidentiality, will be explained to participants as a part of the procedure for obtaining informed consent.

e. **Persons Incapable of Giving Informed Consent.** When a person is incapable of giving informed consent, rehabilitation counselors will provide an appropriate explanation, obtain agreement for participation, and obtain appropriate consent from a legally authorized person.

f. **Commitments to Participants.** Rehabilitation counselors will take reasonable measures to honor all commitments to research participants.

g. **Explanations After Data Collection.** After data are collected, rehabilitation counselors will provide participants with full clarification of the nature of the study to remove any misconceptions. Where scientific or human values justify delaying or withholding information, rehabilitation counselors will take reasonable measures to avoid causing harm.

h. **Agreements to Cooperate.** Rehabilitation counselors who agree to cooperate with another individual in research or publication will incur an obligation to cooperate as agreed.

i. **Informed Consent for Sponsors.** In the pursuit of research, rehabilitation counselors will give sponsors, institutions, and publication channels the same opportunity for giving informed consent that they accord to individual research participants. Rehabilitation counselors will be aware of their obligation to future researchers and will ensure that host institutions are given feedback information and proper acknowledgment.

H.3. Reporting Results

a. **Information Affecting Outcome.** When reporting research results, rehabilitation counselors will explicitly mention all variables and conditions known to the investigator that may have affected the outcome of a study or the interpretation of data.

b. **Accurate Results.** Rehabilitation counselors will plan, conduct, and report research accurately and in a manner that minimizes the possibility that results will be misleading. They will provide thorough discussions of the limitations of their data and alternative hypotheses. Rehabilitation counselors will not engage in fraudulent research, distort data, misrepresent data, or deliberately bias their results.

c. **Obligation to Report Unfavorable Results.** Rehabilitation counselors will make available the results of any research judged to be of professional value even if the results reflect unfavorably on institutions, programs, services, prevailing opinions, or vested interests.

d. **Identity of Participants.** Rehabilitation counselors who supply data, aid in the research of another person, report research results, or make original data available will take due care to disguise the identity of respective participants in the absence of specific authorization from the participants to do otherwise.

e. **Replication Studies.** Rehabilitation counselors will be obligated to make sufficient original research data available to qualified professionals who may wish to replicate the study.

H.4. Publication

a. **Recognition of Others.** When conducting and reporting research, rehabilitation counselors will be familiar with and give recognition to previous work on the topic, observe copyright laws, and give full credit to those to whom credit is due.

b. **Contributors.** Rehabilitation counselors will give credit through joint authorship, acknowledgment, footnote statements, or other appropriate means to those who have contributed significantly to research or concept development in accordance with such contributions. The principal contributor will be listed first and minor technical or professional contributions are acknowledged in notes or introductory statements.

c. **Student Research.** For an article that is substantially based on a student's dissertation or thesis, the student will be listed as the principal author.

d. **Duplicate Submission.** Rehabilitation counselors will submit manuscripts for consideration to only one journal at a time. Manuscripts that are published in whole or in substantial part in another journal or published work will not be submitted for publication without acknowledgment and permission from the previous publication.

e. **Professional Review.** Rehabilitation counselors who review material submitted for publication, research, or other scholarly purposes will respect the confidentiality and proprietary rights of those who submitted it.

SECTION I: ELECTRONIC COMMUNICATION AND EMERGING APPLICATIONS

I.1. Communication

a. **Communication Tools.** Rehabilitation counselors will be held to the same level of expected behavior as defined by the Code of Professional Ethics for Rehabilitation Counselors regardless of the form of communication they choose to use (i.e., cellular phones, electronic mail, facsimile, video, audio-visual).

b. **Imposters.** In situations where it is difficult to verify the identity of the rehabilitation counselor, the client, or the client's guardian, rehabilitation counselors will take steps to address imposter concerns, such as using code words, numbers, or graphics.

c. **Confidentiality.** Rehabilitation counselors will ensure that clients are provided sufficient information to adequately address and explain the limits of: (1) computer technology in the counseling process in general; and (2) the difficulties of ensuring complete client confidentiality of information transmitted through electronic communication over the Internet through on-line counseling.

I.2. Counseling Relationship

a. **Ethical/Legal Review.** Rehabilitation counselors will review pertinent legal and ethical codes for possible violations emanating from the practice of distance counseling and supervision. Distance counseling is defined as any counseling that occurs at a distance through electronic means, such as web-counseling, tele-counseling, or video-counseling.

b. **Security.** Rehabilitation counselors will use encryption methods whenever possible. If encryption is not made available to clients, clients must be informed of the potential hazards of unsecured communication on the Internet. Hazards may include authorized or unauthorized monitoring of transmissions and/or records of sessions.

c. **Records Preservation.** Rehabilitation counselors will inform clients whether the records are being preserved, how they are being preserved, and how long the records are being maintained.

d. **Self-Description.** Rehabilitation counselors will provide information about themselves as would be available if the counseling were to take place face-to-face (e.g., possibly ethnicity or gender).

e. **Consumer Protection.** Rehabilitation counselors will provide information to the client regarding all appropriate certification bodies and licensure boards to facilitate consumer protection, such as links to Web sites.

f. **Crisis Contact.** Rehabilitation counselors will provide the name of at least one agency or counselor-on-call for purposes of crisis intervention within the client's geographical region.

g. **Unavailability.** Rehabilitation counselors will provide clients with instructions for contacting them when they are unavailable through electronic means.

h. **Inappropriate Use.** Rehabilitation counselors will mention at their Web sites or in their initial contacts with potential clients those presenting problems they believe to be inappropriate for distance counseling.

i. **Technical Failure.** Rehabilitation counselors will explain to clients the possibility of technology failure and will provide an alternative means of communication.

j. **Potential Misunderstandings.** Rehabilitation counselors will explain to clients how to prevent and address potential misunderstandings arising from the lack of visual cues and voice intonations from the counselor or client.

SECTION J: BUSINESS PRACTICES

J.1. Billing

Rehabilitation counselors will establish and maintain billing records that accurately reflect the services provided and the time engaged in the activity, and that clearly identify who provided the service.

J.2. Termination

Rehabilitation counselors in fee for service relationships may terminate services with clients due to nonpayment of fees under the following conditions: a) the client was informed of payment responsibilities and the effects of nonpayment or the termination of payment by a third party, and b) the client does not pose an imminent danger to self or others. As appropriate, rehabilitation counselors will refer clients to another qualified professional to address issues unresolved at the time of termination.

J.3. Client Records

a. **Accurate Documentation.** Rehabilitation counselors will establish and will maintain documentation that accurately reflects the services provided and that identifies who provided the service. If case notes need to be altered, it will be done so in a manner that preserves the original note and will be accompanied by the date of change, information that identifies who made the change, and the rationale for the change.
b. **Sufficient Documentation.** Rehabilitation counselors will provide sufficient documentation in a timely manner (e.g., case notes, reports, plans).
c. **Privacy.** Documentation generated by rehabilitation counselors will protect the privacy of clients to the extent that it is possible and appropriate, and will include only relevant information.
d. **Maintenance.** Rehabilitation counselors will maintain records necessary for rendering professional services to their clients and as required by applicable laws, regulations, or agency/institution procedures. Subsequent to file closure, records will be maintained for the number of years consistent with jurisdictional requirements or for a longer period during which maintenance of such records is necessary or helpful to provide reasonably anticipated future services to the client. After that time, records will be destroyed in a manner assuring preservation of confidentiality.

J.4. Fees and Bartering

a. **Advance Understanding.** Rehabilitation counselors will clearly explain to clients, prior to entering the counseling relationship, all financial arrangements related to professional services including the use of collection agencies or legal measures for nonpayment.
b. **Establishing Fees.** In establishing fees for professional rehabilitation counseling services, rehabilitation counselors will consider the financial status and locality of clients. In the event that the established fee structure is inappropriate for a client, assistance will be provided in attempting to find comparable services of acceptable cost.
c. **Bartering Discouraged.** Rehabilitation counselors will ordinarily refrain from accepting goods or services from clients in return for rehabilitation counseling services because such arrangements create inherent potential for conflicts, exploitation, and distortion of the professional relationship. Rehabilitation counselors will participate in bartering only if the relationship is not exploitative, if the client requests it, if a clear written contract is established, and if such arrangements are an accepted practice in the client's community or culture.

J.5. Fees for Referral

a. **Accepting Fees from Agency Clients.** Rehabilitation counselors will not accept a private fee or other remuneration for rendering services to persons who are entitled to such services through the rehabilitation counselor's employing agency or institution. However, the policies of a particular agency may make explicit provisions for agency clients to receive rehabilitation counseling services from members of its staff in private practice. In such instances, the clients will be informed of other options open to them should they seek private rehabilitation counseling services.
b. **Referral Fees.** Rehabilitation counselors will neither give nor receive commissions, rebates or any other form of remuneration when referring clients for professional services.

SECTION K: RESOLVING ETHICAL ISSUES

K.1. Knowledge of Standards

Rehabilitation counselors are responsible for learning the Code and should seek clarification of any standard that is not understood. Lack of knowledge or misunderstanding of an ethical responsibility will not be used as a defense against a charge of unethical conduct.

K.2. Suspected Violations

a. **Consultation.** When uncertain as to whether a particular situation or course of action may be in violation of the Code of Professional Ethics for Rehabilitation Counselors, rehabilitation counselors will consult with other rehabilitation counselors who are knowledgeable about ethics, with colleagues, and/or with appropriate authorities, such as CRCC, state licensure boards, or legal counsel.

b. **Organization Conflicts.** If the demands of an organization with which rehabilitation counselors are affiliated pose a conflict with the Code of Professional Ethics for Rehabilitation Counselors, rehabilitation counselors will specify the nature of such conflicts and express to their supervisors or other responsible officials their commitment to the Code of Professional Ethics for Rehabilitation Counselors. When possible, rehabilitation counselors will work toward change within the organization to allow full adherence to the Code of Professional Ethics for Rehabilitation Counselors.

c. **Informal Resolution.** When rehabilitation counselors have reasonable cause to believe that another rehabilitation counselor is violating an ethical standard, they will attempt to resolve the issue informally with the other rehabilitation counselor if feasible, providing that such action does not violate confidentiality rights that may be involved.

d. **Reporting Suspected Violations.** When an informal resolution is not appropriate or feasible, rehabilitation counselors, upon reasonable cause, will take action such as reporting the suspected ethical violation to state or national ethics committees or CRCC, unless this action conflicts with confidentiality rights that cannot be resolved.

e. **Unwarranted Complaints.** Rehabilitation counselors will not initiate, participate in, or encourage the filing of ethics complaints that are unwarranted or intended to harm a rehabilitation counselor rather than to protect clients or the public.

K.3. Cooperation with Ethics Committees

Rehabilitation counselors will assist in the process of enforcing the Code of Professional Ethics for Rehabilitation Counselors. Rehabilitation counselors will cooperate with investigations, proceedings, and requirements of the CRCC Ethics Committee or ethics committees of other duly constituted associations or boards having jurisdiction over those charged with a violation.

A copy of CRCC's Guidelines and Procedures for Processing Complaints along with a Complaint Form may be obtained from CRCC's Web site at www.crccertification.com or by contacting CRCC at:

CRCC
1835 Rohlwing Road, Suite E
Rolling Meadows, IL 60008
(847) 394-2104, extension 121

Acknowledgements—CRCC recognizes the American Counseling Association for permitting the Commission to adopt, in part, the ACA Code of Ethics and Standards of Practice.

APPENDIX 17-C

Scope of Practice for Rehabilitation Counseling

I. ASSUMPTIONS

■ The Scope of Practice Statement identifies knowledge and skills required for the provision of effective rehabilitation counseling services to persons with physical, mental, developmental, cognitive, and emotional disabilities as embodied in the standards of the profession's credentialing organizations.

■ The several rehabilitation disciplines and related processes (e.g., vocational evaluation, job development and job placement, work adjustment, case management) are tied to the central field of rehabilitation counseling. The field of rehabilitation counseling is a specialty within the rehabilitation profession with counseling at its core, and is differentiated from other related counseling fields.

■ The professional scope of rehabilitation counseling practice is also differentiated from an individual scope of practice, which may overlap, but is more specialized than the professional scope. An individual scope of practice is based on one's own knowledge of the abilities and skills that have been gained through a program of education and professional experience. A person is ethically bound to limit his/her practice to that individual scope of practice.

II. UNDERLYING VALUES

■ Facilitation of independence, integration, and inclusion of people with disabilities in employment and the community.

■ Belief in the dignity and worth of all people.

■ Commitment to a sense of equal justice based on a model of accommodation to provide and equalize the opportunities to participate in all rights and privileges available to all people; and a commitment to supporting persons with disabilities in advocacy activities to enable them to achieve this status and empower themselves.

■ Emphasis on the holistic nature of human function which is procedurally facilitated by the utilization of such techniques as:

1. interdisciplinary teamwork.
2. counseling to assist in maintaining a holistic perspective.
3. a commitment to considering individuals within the context of their family systems and communities.

■ Recognition of the importance of focusing on the assets of the person.

■ Commitment to models of service delivery that emphasize integrated, comprehensive services which are mutually planned by the consumer and the rehabilitation counselor.

III. SCOPE OF PRACTICE STATEMENT

Rehabilitation counseling is a systematic process which assists persons with physical, mental, developmental, cognitive, and emotional disabilities to achieve their personal, career, and independent living goals in the most integrated setting possible through the application of the counseling process. The counseling process involves communication, goal setting, and beneficial growth or change through self-advocacy, psychological, vocational, social, and behavioral interventions. The specific techniques and modalities utilized within this rehabilitation counseling process may include, but are not limited to:

■ assessment and appraisal;
■ diagnosis and treatment planning;
■ career (vocational) counseling;
■ individual and group counseling treatment interventions focused on facilitating adjustments to the medical and psychosocial impact of disability;
■ case management, referral, and service coordination;
■ program evaluation and research;
■ interventions to remove environmental, employment, and attitudinal barriers;
■ consultation services among multiple parties and regulatory systems;
■ job analysis, job development, and placement services, including assistance with employment and job accommodations; and
■ the provision of consultation about, and access to, rehabilitation technology.

IV. SELECTED DEFINITIONS

The following definitions are provided to increase the understanding of certain key terms and concepts used in the Scope of Practice Statement for Rehabilitation Counseling.

Appraisal: Selecting, administering, scoring, and interpreting instruments designed to assess an individual's attitudes, abilities, achievements, interests, personal characteristics, disabilities, and mental, emotional, or behavioral disorders as well as the use of methods and techniques for understanding human behavior in relation to coping with, adapting to, or changing life situations.

Diagnosis and Treatment Planning: Assessing, analyzing, and providing diagnostic descriptions of mental, emotional, or behavioral conditions or disabilities; exploring possible solutions; and developing and implementing a treatment plan for mental, emotional, and psychosocial adjustment or development. Diagnosis and treatment planning shall not be construed to permit the performance of any act which rehabilitation counselors are not educated and trained to perform.

Counseling Treatment Intervention: The application of cognitive, affective, behavioral, and systemic counseling strategies which include developmental, wellness, pathologic, and multicultural principles of human behavior. Such interventions are specifically implemented in the context of a professional counseling relationship and may include, but are not limited to: appraisal; individual, group, marriage, and family counseling and psychotherapy; the diagnostic description and treatment of persons with mental, emotional, and behavioral disorders or disabilities; guidance and consulting to facilitate normal growth and development, including educational and career development; the utilization of functional assessments and career counseling for persons requesting assistance in adjusting to a disability or handicapping condition; referrals; consulting; and research.

Referral: Evaluating and identifying the needs of a counselee to determine the advisability of referrals to other specialists, advising the counselee of such judgments, and communicating as requested or deemed appropriate to such referral sources.

Case Management: A systematic process merging counseling and managerial concepts and skills through the application of techniques derived from intuitive and researched methods, thereby advancing efficient and effective decision-making for functional control of self, client, setting, and other relevant factors for anchoring a proactive practice. In case management, the counselor's role is focused on interviewing, counseling, planning rehabilitation programs, coordinating services, interacting with significant others, placing clients and following up with them, monitoring a client's progress, and solving problems.

Program Evaluation: The effort to determine what changes occur as a result of a planned program by comparing actual changes (results) with desired changes (stated goals), and by identifying the degree to which the activity (planned program) is responsible for those changes.

Research: A systematic effort to collect, analyze, and interpret quantitative or qualitative data that describe how social characteristics, behavior, emotions, cognition, disabilities, mental disorders, and interpersonal transactions among individuals and organizations interact.

Consultation: The application of scientific principles and procedures in counseling and human development to provide assistance in understanding and solving current or potential problems that the consultee may have in relation to a third party, be it an individual, group, or organization.

Source: From the Commission on Rehabilitation Counselor Certification. Reprinted with permission.

CHAPTER 18

Addiction Counseling

Susan Robine McGuire
R. Rocco Cottone

Objectives
■ ■ ■ ■ ■ ■ ■ ■ ■ ■ ■

After reading this chapter, you should be able to:

• Describe the specialty of addiction counseling.

• Explain the ethical considerations in the counseling needs of addicted clients.

■ ■ ■ ■ ■ ■ ■ ■ ■ ■ ■

INTRODUCTION

Addiction counselors serve individuals with addictive behaviors who have sets of behaviors that seriously disrupt their own functioning and, in some instances, the functioning of others and of society in general. Unique ethical issues are relevant to assessment and treatment of addicted individuals. In most cases, individuals seek services because an addiction or pattern of behavior has caused significant difficulty in a social or legal context. Typically, the difficulty is of such a significant level that third-party intervention is necessary. In recognition of this counseling specialization, the ACA has an affiliate group, the International Association of Addictions and Offender Counselors (IAAOC), which operates under the ACA ethics code (see Appendix at the end of this text).

Great debates have occurred regarding diagnosis of "dependency" versus "abuse" as related to addictive disorders. According to Peele and Brodsky (1991), addictions are habits the individual believes cannot be changed or controlled—habits that are detrimental to the individual's lifestyle, self-esteem, and employment. Whether the addictive object is alcohol, drugs, tobacco, food, shopping, gambling, work, excessive exercise, relationships, sex, criminal activities, or aggression, the behavioral patterns are similar. Symptomatic addiction crosses many behavior patterns. To become more familiar with the common symptoms associated with addictions, the following list of symptoms developed by Zuckerman (1995) provides a useful working definition (focusing on chemical addictions): (a) increased tolerance (needing more and more to get the effect experienced in initial stages of the addiction); (b) withdrawal (a substance-specific syndrome that manifests itself in symptoms of discomfort when the addictive substance or object is removed); (c) addictive activity or substance use to control withdrawal symptoms; (d) preoccupation with the object of the addiction—drinking/drug use—more time is spent on activities associated with the addiction; (e) continued use despite physical/medical disorder or social problem made worse by use; (f) consumption pattern that is impulsive, gulping, in inappropriate circumstances, solitary, rationalized as medicinal, secret/hidden, out of control, or with use of drugs and alcohol together; (g) guilt over the addiction; (h) periodic attempts at abstinence or cutting down; (i) social avoidance/isolation, (j) frequent intoxication/impairment when expected to fulfill social or occupational obligations; (k) missing appointments, work, or recreation, etc. in order to drink/use or to pursue addictive objects; (l) daily use, morning tremor, morning drinking/use; (m) use of addictive substance to the point of intoxication/unconsciousness; (n) arrests for driving while intoxicated, driving under the influence, public intoxication, violence, or other legal problems associated with use. Although these symptoms focus on chemical addictions, the pattern of dysfunctional behavior is consistent regardless of the object of obsession. Not all of the symptoms listed must be present for a diagnosis of an addiction.

Researchers are only now learning the full extent of the physiological aspects of chemical addictions; it is now postulated that addictive behaviors, in addition to chemical dependency, may be attributed to defects in an individual's physiology (Maraizzilli et al., 1993). However, the question still remains, does brain chemistry alter behavior, or does behavior bring about a change in brain chemistry?

The four-step addiction cycle as presented by Carnes (1992) clearly illustrates the repetitive nature of self-destructive behaviors. The first step in developing an addiction is preoccupation, during which individuals experience obsessions that center on obtaining gratification through the object of their addiction. The second step is ritualization, a series of behaviors designed to obtain the addictive object. In observing ex-offender or addicted individuals, one quickly notices a unique language, nonverbal communications, and behavioral patterns that communicate membership in this special group. The gambler gaslights, the pedophile grooms, the burglar cases, the drug addict scores, the alcoholic gets trashed, and the list goes on. The third step is acting out the compulsive behavior. At this stage, the individual is unable to refrain from obtaining gratification. The addicted individual describes this as a "craving," or poor impulse control of an "urge." Regardless of semantics, a compulsion to act out in a possibly self-destructive manner occurs. The fourth and final step in an addiction is despair and the feeling of powerlessness, which is characterized by condemning self-talk and in-ternalized guilt. Although there may be an effort to regain a sense of personal control and inner harmony (Balint, 1979; Kohut, 1971), the cycle takes hold, and there is a return to preoccupied and obsessive behavior.

A high correlation exists between addictive behaviors and criminal activity. Yochelson and Samenow (1986) explained this correlation by postulating that it is not the addictive object, but the individual's view of life as dull or constrained without such activities, that affects recovery. Thus, personal choice, more than physical addiction, is emphasized in recovery.

Another issue unique to addictions is the prevalence of the role of group counseling in programs such as Alcoholics Anonymous (AA), Narcotics Anonymous (NA), Overeaters Anonymous (OA), Gamblers Anonymous (GA), Relationships Anonymous (RA), and Sexaholics Anonymous (SA). Many treatment programs may rely (or over-rely) on group treatment at the expense of individual or family treatment models. Additionally, group treatment through self-help organizations is not supervised by licensed professionals and, thus, may not afford group members the protection of the professional license, especially as related to confidentiality or privileged communications. (See Chapter 16 for a related discussion on group counseling.)

Addiction counseling is also known for its high "burnout" rate, meaning that many counselors suffer dissatisfaction in their jobs or change jobs frequently. George (1990) stated the following, related to work with chemically dependent individuals:

> One of the disturbing aspects of chemical-dependency counseling is the high turnover of treatment staff. This results from counselors choosing to find other work, as well as from a great deal of switching from one treatment program to another. Such a turnover is generally the result of individuals becoming frustrated and unhappy in their current job. Frustration is most likely the response of *burnout* that occurs with many helping professionals, but is particularly found among chemical-dependency counselors. (p. 224)

Part of the burnout may relate to a high relapse rate, or recidivism, among individuals who complete structured treatment programs for addictions—this rate is generally understood to be as high as 70 percent over the long term (George, 1990; Hester & Miller, 1989). Counselors who work with such treatment-resistant groups may show the signs of stress or even exasperation related to treatment success, dealing primarily with revolving door phenomena—treating people who have already been unsuccessfully treated, or seeing

Box 18.1   Exploring the Codes

Do the ACA and APA ethics codes specifically address addiction in the area of counselor or psychologist impairment or personal problems?

Are there any sections of the ACA or APA ethics codes that directly relate or refer to addiction?

first-time treatment clients soon returning as relapsed cases. Counselors entering the field of addictions counseling should be alert to the personal and emotional risks involved in such work.

There is some noteworthy controversy in the field of chemical dependency treatment related to the qualifications necessary to adequately provide chemical dependency treatment. As George (1990) stated:

> The ongoing question of whether one is adequately trained to be a chemical-dependency counselor is a source of difficulty in the field. Unfortunately, those who currently work as chemical-dependency counselors have tended to adopt one of two extreme positions: that chemical dependency counselors must be recovering addicts (or, at the very least, have a recovery program as codependents), or that chemical dependency counselors must have a minimum of a master's degree in such related fields as counseling, social work, or psychology. Unfortunately, this polarization often results in unnecessary conflict among counselors and a lack of respect and appreciation for what each group offers to the treatment process. (p. 216)

Although George (1990) recommended an emphasis on skills, the position taken here is a strictly professional counselor position—that is, professionals providing front-line addiction treatment first should be master's-level-educated practitioners who, in addition, have adequate coursework and experience related to serving individuals with addictions. Regardless, counselors must understand that many individuals who do not hold professional academic credentials perform addictions counseling and, specifically, chemical dependency counseling. In fact, some states exempt addiction treatment personnel from licensure or other standards, and some states have developed separate standards for individuals who counsel clients with chemical dependency or pathological gambling concerns. So long as other professionals have legal sanction to perform addiction treatment services, it is the counselor's ethical obligation to work with these professionals in a way that does not strain professional relations if the services provided by the other professionals are provided competently and within applicable ethical standards.

DEFINING THE SPECIALTY, SETTING, AND CLIENTS

Once individuals are trained in the general field of counseling, they may seek credentials to further identify themselves as specialists in the field of addictions or chemical dependency. The term *addiction counselor* has gained prominence recently; however, the term *addiction counselor* implies a treatment professional who is competently trained and experienced in working with addictions in general. Addictions are not limited to substances—some individuals are addicted to gambling, overeating, sex, or other activities. There is some similarity regardless of the object of addiction. Some individuals are recurrent perpetrators of sexual abuse of children (pedophiles) who show classic signs of addictive behavior, although this behavior is not usually diagnosed as an addiction. Yet, it would not be advisable for a generally trained addiction counselor to attempt treatment of this population. Treatment of pedophilia is a highly specialized area of counseling that necessitates specific training. It is unreasonable to believe that addiction counselors should be able to treat individuals demonstrating an addictive behavior, regardless of the nature of the addiction.

Individuals who are chemically dependent show symptoms or signs unique to chemical dependency (Shearer & King, 2001). A duly trained and experienced chemical dependency counselor should be able to demonstrate some competence in the diagnosis and treatment of individuals with substance abuse problems across a broad spectrum of substances. In-depth knowledge of chemical effects (short- and long-term) and signs of intoxication or recent use is critical. Specialized knowledge of treatment approaches related to chemical dependency treatment is necessary (Hester & Miller, 1989). Although treatment is similar across many addictions, differences also exist, and chemical dependency does represent a subcategory of addictions requiring special knowledge and training.

Most chemical dependency treatment begins with a hospitalization of the identified patient. In-patient treatment initially attempts to detoxify the individual who is physically addicted and may suffer withdrawal symptoms. At the detoxification stage, physicians and nurses are involved to oversee the individual's physical response to drug use cessation. Medications may ease the discomfort associated with the withdrawal syndrome. Initial detoxification may take from two to four (or in some cases more) days under close medical oversight. Once detoxification is complete, psychologists or psychiatrists may become involved to assess the mental status of the individual and to make a diagnosis. Additional mental disorders are often associated with chemical dependency, such as organic brain disorders or other emotional or personality disorders. When a person is diagnosed with chemical dependency and additionally meets the diagnostic criteria for a second or even third mental disorder, he is considered a "dual" or "multiple" diagnosis case. It is common for individuals to be dually diagnosed. Chemical dependency may facilitate the development of a mental disorder. Data suggest that individuals with mental disabilities are also more prone to substance abuse and dependence (Evans & Sullivan, 1990). Chemical dependency counselors must be alert to the signs and symptoms of compounding mental disturbance so that other professionals may be involved. The diagnostic process, undertaken usually by a psychiatrist or psychologist, helps to identify initial signs of other difficulties.

In recent years, legal sanctions have mandated treatment of alcohol-related problems. Most states now require that individuals convicted of driving while intoxicated or under the influence of substances seek treatment prior to regaining driving privileges. This government involvement in the treatment field has opened a variety of outpatient education and treatment programs.

Once diagnoses are made, the counselor and the social worker begin to provide treatments. Counselors are usually involved in individual counseling related to the chemical dependency or other problems that may arise. Social workers may provide group treatment and arrange for services once hospitalization ends (e.g., referral for vocational rehabilitation services or housing assistance). Couple or family counseling may be provided by a professional trained to deal with family and relationship problems. However, the chemical dependency counselor is often viewed as the front-line professional in providing counseling and psychotherapy for individuals in in-patient treatment programs. Out-patient treatment programs (those provided without hospitalization of the individual) are often staffed by counselors who perform a wide range of diagnostic and treatment services, except for diagnostic or treatment services of a medical nature.

Chemical dependency does not appear to be gender specific, associated with one race and not another, or localized to one geographic locale. Some studies, however, have shown different prevalence rates among nationalities or ethnicities (Ray, 1983), although no sweeping generalizations appear warranted. Overall, rich and poor, young and old, male or female, chemical dependency appears to be a prevalent problem.

ISSUES OF SIGNIFICANCE TO THE SPECIALTY

Professional Differentiation

Controversy exists over the professional credential necessary to be involved in chemical dependency or other addiction treatment. The position taken in this text is that counselors providing chemical dependency or other addiction treatment should be duly trained to the master's-degree level, and where required or available, they should meet licensure standards as professional counselors. In regard to further specialty designation, several professional credentials can be sought by counselors wishing to specialize in chemical dependency or addictions treatment. Two that are closely linked to the professional organizations representing counseling professionals are (a) the National Board of Certified Counselors (NBCC) specialty designation of Master Addictions Counselor (MAC); and (b) the Commission on Rehabilitation Counselor Certification (CRCC) specialty designation credential titled Substance Abuse Credential (SAC). Both of these credentials require the broader certification of the sponsoring certifying board (the NCC or the CRC, respectively) and, in addition, candidates must have specialty coursework or continuing education related to addictions or chemical dependency treatment, experience under supervision in a setting where addictions are treated, and/or a passing score on a specialty examination developed by the board. Both the NBCC and CRCC specialty designations would serve a professional counselor well, identifying that individual as a highly trained counseling professional who has additionally sought specialty certification (beyond general counseling criteria) in a field often staffed with individuals who are less professionally trained.

Ethical Issues

Confidentiality and Privileged Communication.

Confidential communications in the area of addictions counseling is complicated by several factors. First, in addition to state law requiring confidential relations between individuals treated by licensed professionals, a federal law limits release of information related to chemical dependency treatments. For example, federal laws regulate service providers who receive federal funds directly, by way of state distribution, or by way of tax-exempt status. Any provider receiving such funding is bound by federal confidentiality laws. The federal confidentiality laws protect information about any client applying for or receiving services, including assessment, diagnosis, counseling, group counseling, or referral for other treatment. Information about a client protected by federal confidentiality laws may be disseminated only with client consent. In several situations, client consent is not needed, such as in cases of medical emergencies, child abuse, or when program staff members are involved. Federal law prohibits the use of information in criminal investigation or prosecution of a patient unless a court order has been issued according to federal guidelines, *even if client consent is obtained*. Federal law protects the chemically dependent client beyond what is offered by licensure statute confidentiality or privileged communication provisions. Even when consent is granted, federal guidelines require consent forms to meet federal standards. Consent forms must include (a) the name of the disclosing program, (b) the name and titles of the party receiving the information, (c) the client's name, (d) the purpose of the information disclosure, (e) a statement allowing the client to revoke the consent at any time, (f) a date at which the consent will expire if not revoked, (g) the signature of the client, and (h) the date the consent was signed. The rules were developed to prevent the disclosure of information about a client's past chemical dependency treatment and to protect the client's privacy rights. The intent of these laws is to engage people in treatment for chemical dependency problems who otherwise might be cautious about the legal implications of seeking such treatment. In effect, treatment of a chemically dependent client in a program that directly or indirectly receives federal funds requires additional ethical precautions.

An additional concern related to confidentiality and privileged communication in treatment of individuals with addictions is confidentiality in group treatment. Depending on state statute or federal regulation, communications made in a group setting, even if a licensed professional is involved, may not be considered confidential or privileged in the classic sense of these terms. If group treatment is referenced in a licensure statute, the licensed professional is usually bound to keep what is communicated confidential. However, other group members, being peers to each other and nonprofessionals (in their roles as group members), are not bound by law to keep information secret. Group members may gossip about other group members without repercussion. They may also report to others, even authorities, information communicated at group meetings. Therefore, if a group member confesses a crime in a group meeting, other group members can take this information to authorities, and even testify as to what was said, without legal repercussion. If a counselor is present, the counselor may be bound to confidentiality if, in fact, group counseling is within the purview of the license that is held, and if the crime reported does not come under an exception to the statute's confidentiality provision (such as child abuse). However, even if there is a confidential relationship in a group context for the counselor, privileged communication may not stand because, in many state laws, there is privileged communication for civil court cases but not for criminal court cases. Counselors should study their state statutes closely in this regard. Counselors may be compelled to testify on criminal allegations, even if a revelation of such was made in a confidential counseling context. In most cases, counselors have group members sign an agreement about keeping group-disclosed information confidential, but such agreements may not be legally binding and may serve only as a promise to not discuss group information in other settings. Accordingly, group members should know, before they enter a group, that there are limits to the confidentiality of what is disclosed in counseling sessions. Likewise, chemically dependent clients should know that federal laws provide them extra protections if they seek treatment in a program that is obligated to honor federal confidentiality law.

CASE SCENARIO 18-1

A private practice, Licensed Professional Counselor who conducts group therapy was informed by the local police that one of his patients allegedly committed a felony. This particular client was seen in a group treatment setting. He sought treatment to address issues associated with addictive behaviors, and, in fact, he used his attendance in group therapy as an alibi. Police officers requested the names, addresses, and case files of all clients who attended group with the suspect. The counselor refused to provide this information. Did the counselor act appropriately?

Yes. In an actual case (*State of Missouri v. Anthony Genovese*), a counselor refused to turn over the files of other group clients to authorities, which resulted in the police standing outside of the counselor's office requesting identification from anyone attempting to enter her office. The counselor immediately contacted an attorney, who filed a protest with the police department. The police did leave the entrance of the counselor's office. The counselor was then served with a subpoena to provide all group members' information to the police. Clients of counselors in the state are afforded privileged communication in civil cases, but not criminal cases. The counselor requested that her case files of clients not under investigation be considered confidential and privileged. The court ruled in her favor. Approximately five months later, when the original felony charge was being tried, the counselor's records of all group members were again subpoenaed. Again, the counselor requested the court view her files as confidential and privileged communications, but this time the court ordered all group members' names, addresses, and phone numbers to be released—they were considered public information and crucial to the defendant's alibi. The counselor appealed this decision, and the court's ruling was overturned.

Informed Consent.   Clients have the right to consent to counseling services, and they must be fully informed of the nature of the service, alternative treatments, the qualifications of the professionals involved, or other information that would help them make an educated decision. Informed consent with ex-offenders and addicted clients is complicated by the fact that treatment services are often initiated when a person is not in a condition or state to make an informed decision. Treatment services are most needed when individuals are under direct or recent effects of drugs or alcohol or in the throes of an addictive episode. Under the influence of substances or blinded by an addiction, it is questionable whether a person can make an educated decision of his or her own accord. Often, other family members must be consulted and it may be necessary to involve their cooperation in directing an individual to in-patient or outpatient treatment. Regardless, once a client has been treated initially (especially detoxified in cases of chemical dependency), it is incumbent upon the counselor to respect the client's right to further consent to treatment or to withdraw from treatment on his or her own accord.

It is no secret that addicted clients are highly resistant to treatment. There is a denial process related to the individual's recognition of dependency on drugs or alcohol (George, 1990), as with other addictions. Initial treatment must address the denial process in resistant clients and should also encourage continued treatment.

Unfortunately, some chemical dependency treatment programs have been implicated for unusual tactics in seeking patients. One such program in Kansas City in the 1980s was the focus of a television expose: Counselors were visiting potential patients' homes and arm-twisting family members to admit the identified patient without a reasonable screening of the person for chemical dependency. Tactics that result in hasty admissions without adequate screening and without the educated permission of the client may be considered breaches of professional responsibility and informed consent.

Of course, there are numerous referrals for addictions or ex-offender treatment that can be considered compulsory. Many states mandate treatment for traffic offenders identified as substance abusers. Judges may also order treatment for other offenders before making decisions such as child custody or sentencing. In many cases, treatment is mandated as part of a judicial sentence or condition of parole. In these cases, it must be understood that the client—no matter how the client is referred—still has the right to refuse treatment. It is not the counselor's responsibility to persuade clients sent for compulsory treatment that they must remain in treatment. It would, however, be appropriate to explore the alternatives and possible consequences if compulsory counseling clients choose to terminate counseling prematurely. The counselor should then simply report to the referral source, with client consent, that clients have or have not initiated treatment or have ceased treatment. In such cases, it is important for the counselor to obtain consent (from the beginning of treatment) to report (release information) at least on the client's compliance with mandated treatment.

Some states make provisions for minors to receive chemical dependency treatment without the consent of parents or guardians. In most cases, however, states require the consent of parents or guardians before treatment can be initiated. Also, parents or guardians have the right to review assessment or treatment files. In cases in which minors do not have the right to consent to their own treatment or are not provided confidentiality protection by law, they should be informed from the outset of treatment that the information they provide is subject to review by parents or legal guardians. Informed consent in addiction treatment, then, has some special circumstances that require ethical sensitivity on the part of the counselor.

Potentially Detrimental Counselor-Client Relationships. The potentially detrimental relationship issue is complicated in addictions treatment when a counselor is also recovering. When a counselor is in the role of a therapist, but is also a peer in groups such as Alcoholics Anonymous, anonymity is obviously compromised, forming a complex web of nonprofessional relationships. Recovering treatment professionals should make efforts to avoid nonprofessional relationships with clients and they should seek treatment in contexts that will decrease the likelihood of nontreatment contacts with clients. Addicted individuals or ex-offenders may live in small communities, and inadvertent contacts outside of treatment may be unavoidable. In such cases, the intention of such contacts is the critical issue, and the counselor is obligated to make efforts to avoid such contacts or to ensure that future contacts are prevented.

The issue of sexual relations with current or recent clients is the same for addictions and ex-offender treatment as with any area of counseling: It is unethical. Most ethical codes and ethical standards in licensure statutes prohibit such contacts during active treatment and for up to two to five years after treatment has ceased.

Responsibility. The responsibility of addiction counselors is first and foremost to their clients. Clients hold the highest priority in terms of the actions of the counselor. Additionally, counselors are obligated to their employers and their profession. If there is a conflict between a counselor's responsibility to a client and to a third party (such as an employer), the counselor must act to rectify the conflict. In the end, however, the counselor should take actions in accordance with a client's welfare.

A client's welfare is a responsibility of the treating counselor. Counselors must do their best to serve their clients, recognizing that services may not provide the intended purpose. If a counselor recognizes that his or her client is not benefiting from services, it is the counselor's responsibility to cease treatment and, if necessary, to refer the client to appropriate services provided by other professionals or in other treatment contexts.

Even in cases of family treatment of an individual with an addiction, if the individual with the addiction is the identified patient and has sought treatment primarily for the addiction, the counselor must advocate for the individual with the addiction. The counselor should not compromise the client's treatment progress even with the intent of serving the larger system of relationships in the family. If treatment is undertaken primarily as a means of assisting in the recovery of the addicted or offending individual, that individual's welfare is the focus of counselor responsibility.

Values. Individuals treating clients with chemical dependency should clearly define their values related to use of alcohol or drugs in society. There is controversy in the field about the issue of abstinence. Some programs require that clients maintain total abstinence. Other programs attempt to produce a pattern of controlled drinking (Hester & Miller, 1989). The traditional wisdom, especially following the 12-step programs of AA or NA, holds that abstinence is an absolute necessity. Twelve-step programs value abstinence and also have a spiritual foundation (Alcoholics Anonymous, 1953, 1976). When referring clients to AA, counselors should be aware of the 12 traditions of AA (Alcoholics Anonymous, 1976, p. 564):

One. Our common welfare should come first; personal recovery depends upon A.A. unity.

Two. For our group purpose there is but one ultimate authority—a loving God as He may express Himself in our group conscience. Our leaders are but trusted servants; they do not govern.

Three. The only requirement for A.A. membership is a desire to stop drinking.

Four. Each group should be autonomous except in matters affecting other groups or A.A. as a whole.

Five. Each group has but one primary purpose—to carry its message to the alcoholic who still suffers.

Six. An A.A. group ought never endorse, finance or lend the A.A. name to any related facility or outside enterprise, lest problems of money, property and prestige divert us from our primary purpose.

Seven. Every A.A. group ought to be fully self-supportive, declining outside contributions.

Eight. Alcoholics Anonymous should remain forever nonprofessional, but our service centers may employ special workers.

Nine. A.A., as such, ought never be organized; but we may create service boards or committees directly responsible to those they serve.

Ten. Alcoholics Anonymous has no opinion on outside issues; hence the A.A. name ought never be drawn into public controversy.

Eleven. Our public relations policy is based on attraction rather than promotion; we need always maintain personal anonymity at the level of press, radio and films.

Twelve. Anonymity is the spiritual foundation of all our Traditions, ever reminding us to place principles before personalities. (p. 564)

These 12 traditions of AA clearly reflect the values of the alliance. It is spiritual, anonymous, voluntary, non-financially focused, and primarily intended to help people who wish to remain sober.

The 12 steps of AA are different from the 12 traditions, but follow from them philosophically—the 12 steps are the individual's self-commitments in accordance with AA philosophy. Not all addiction treatment programs follow the traditions of AA or even encourage involvement in a 12-step program. Some programs may even discourage involvement in a 12-step program.

Another issue that is unique to addictions or ex-offender treatment involves philosophy related to the use of specialized techniques that may cause the client some pain or discomfort. These include antidipsotropic medications, which deter the alcoholic from drinking by producing an unpleasant physical reaction if alcohol is ingested (Fuller, 1989) and aversion therapies (Rimmele, Miller, & Dougher, 1989). These types of therapies typically produce nausea, apnea, electric shock, or unpleasant imagery. Counselors involved in such programs may experience discomfort themselves over the type of treatment being administered.

The values and philosophy of the program within which the professional counselor works should be thoroughly analyzed and studied to ensure that the counselor can assess program philosophy against his or her personal philosophy.

Value issues come to the fore when dealing with ex-offenders who have committed crimes that are objectionable, heinous, or that seriously challenge the counselor's personal values. For example, working with pedophiles (individuals charged or convicted of sexually molesting or abusing children) may be abhorrent to a counselor. The counselor has an obligation to refer such individuals to specialists who are trained and experienced with these issues. In circumstances in which no alternative mental health treatment is available, counselors must fully inform the client of their concerns, respecting the right of the client to consent to treatment. Further, counselors must act as objectively as possible to prevent punitive or condemning responses. The ACA ethics code clearly allows clients the freedom to choose whether to enter into a counseling relationship and to determine which professional will provide counseling. Any restrictions that limit choices of clients should be fully explained. Counselors need to address any value restrictions before beginning counseling.

Counselor Competence.   It is not enough for a counselor to receive a general or community counseling degree and then to practice primarily as an addiction counselor without additional training and specialized supervision. The intricacies of addiction treatment, especially related to chemical effects, the denial process, specialized treatment approaches, and adjunctive involvement of 12-step or other self-help groups, requires in-depth knowledge (best gained in academic settings or accredited continuing education) and supervision under the direction of a counselor well versed in treating addictions.

However, the competence issue is more complex than the adequacy of preparation of the treating counselor. It also relates to counselors' relations with other professionals (including physicians, social workers, lawyers, judges, probation officers, and vocational rehabilitation counselors) who are almost always involved in cases in which clients receive treatment for addictions or are charged with legal offenses. The competence issue relates to the boundaries of professional practice—counselors must be cautious not to overstep their professional bounds because other professionals have valid and important roles in the treatment of individuals with complex addictive disorders.

Finally, due to the high burnout rate of professionals who serve clients with addictions or legal offenses, counselors must be alert to their own limitations. If counselors recognize they are becoming impatient or uncompromising, they should consider methods for professional rejuvenation, including linkage to a professional organization, continuing education, or even a sabbatical from addiction treatment. This is especially true of counselors who are recovering themselves. The counseling role should not be so stressful as to produce undue distress in the treating professional.

CODE COMPARISONS

Membership in the International Association of Addictions and Offender Counselors is not independent of the ACA. Members are bound to the ACA ethics code. The IAAOC has an Ethics Committee that is responsible to communicate ethical problems faced by its membership to the ACA Ethics Committee. There is no freestanding, mandatory ethical code of the IAAOC, although the Ethics Committee is charged with developing aspirational standards of conduct.

ISSUES OF DIVERSITY

Addictions cross all cultures and individuals of diverse economic status, so counselors are wise to reflect on the need for cultural sensitivity. Clients may represent diverse cultures, and each culture may have specific or ritualistic behaviors associated with the addiction in question. Counselors need to be alert to cultural differences, for instance, in the use and acceptability of alcoholic beverages or illicit drugs. Sensitivity to cultural nuances surrounding the addiction is critical to establishing a therapeutic alliance or bond with the addicted individual. Some people believe also that only addicted individuals (recovered from their addiction) are competent or credible in service to other addicted individuals in need. Although credibility is an issue, it is important for clients to understand that the counselor's role is that of facilitating abstinence and healthy fit in a cultural context that is not supportive of the addictive behavior. In that regard, someone closely linked to the nonaddicted cultural context can provide important information and resources to those seeking abstinence.

CHAPTER SUMMARY

Working with individuals who manifest addictive behavior patterns presents ethical challenges that are unique and require special knowledge and ethical awareness. The competent professional counselor will ensure that a client's rights are respected, no matter how uncomfortable the counselor may be with the individual's past behaviors. It is incumbent upon the counselor to maintain current knowledge, ongoing training, skill assessment, and ethical sensitivity. Because burnout is common among counselors who work with individuals with addictive behaviors, counselors must also be aware of their own limitations and stress levels. In circumstances in which the counselor experiences serious burnout, the counselor should seek professional guidance, continuing education, or counseling.

Addictions are not limited to chemical dependency and affect all cultural groups. Specific ethical challenges are unique to the addiction treatment field and specialized professional issues apply to those who wish to pursue work in the addiction area. Specific federal laws also address addictions, requiring addiction counselors to be alert and knowledgeable about the legal parameters of their work.

REFERENCES

Alcoholics Anonymous. (1953). *Twelve steps and twelve traditions.* New York: Author.

Alcoholics Anonymous. (1976). *Alcoholics Anonymous.* New York: Author.

Balint, M. (1979). *The basic fault: Therapeutic aspects of regression.* New York: Brunner & Mazel.

Carnes, P. (1992). *Out of the shadows.* Minneapolis, MN: CompCare.

Evans, K., & Sullivan, M. J. (1990). *Dual diagnosis: Counseling the mentally ill substance abuser.* New York: Guilford.

Fuller, R. K. (1989). Antidipsotropic medications. In R. K. Hester & W. R. Miller (Eds.), *Handbook of alcoholism treatment approaches* (pp. 117–127). Boston: Allyn & Bacon.

George, R. L. (1990). *Counseling the chemically dependent: Theory and practice.* Boston: Allyn & Bacon.

Hester, R. K., & Miller, W. R. (1989). *Handbook of alcoholism treatment approaches: Effective alternatives.* Boston: Allyn & Bacon.

Kohut, H. (1971). *The analysis of the self: A systematic approach to the psychoanalytic treatment of narcissistic personality disorder.* New York: University International Press.

Maraizzilli, D., Rotondo, A., Presta, S., Pnacioli-Guadagnucci, M., Pagleo, L., & Conti, L. (1993). Role of serotonin in human aggression behavior. *Aggressive Behavior, 19,* 347–353.

Peele, S., & Brodsky, A. (1991). *The truth about addiction and recovery.* New York: Simon & Schuster.

Ray, O. (1983). *Drugs, society, and human behavior.* St. Louis, MO: Mosby.

Rimmele, C. T., Miller, W. R., & Dougher, M. J. (1989). Aversive therapies. In R. K. Hester & W. R. Miller (Eds.), *Handbook of alcoholism treatment approaches* (pp. 128–140). Boston: Allyn & Bacon.

Shearer, R., & King, P. (2001). The powerless-empowerment scale: Measurement of substance abuse counseling orientation. *Journal of Addictions & Offender Counseling, 21.*

State of Missouri v. Anthony Genovese (April 14, 1999). Associate Circuit Court, County of St. Charles, Missouri, No. CR199-875F.

Yochelson, S., & Samenow, S. (1986). *The criminal personality: Volume III: The drug user.* New York: Jason Aronson.

Zuckerman, E. (1995). *Clinician's thesaurus* (4th ed.). New York: Guilford Press.

CHAPTER 19

The Ethics of Clinical Supervision

Dennis R. Maki
Janine M. Bernard

Objectives

■ ■ ■ ■ ■ ■ ■ ■ ■ ■ ■

After reading this chapter, you should be able to:

- Define clinical supervision and discuss it as an area of specialization and a mainstream activity across all specialties within counseling.
- Discuss the specific ethical codes, standards, and issues relevant to clinical supervision.
- Explain the ethical violations and the legal issues and strategies for their prevention in clinical supervision.
- Discuss issues of diversity in clinical supervision and suggest guidelines for ethical multicultural supervision.

■ ■ ■ ■ ■ ■ ■ ■ ■ ■ ■

INTRODUCTION

Clinical supervision is both an area of specialization and a mainstream activity across all specialties within counseling. Clinical supervision earns its status as a specialty due to the sizable literature describing the practice of supervision, research verifying its distinctiveness from counseling, and credentialing/licensing bodies that acknowledge clinical supervision as a separate and specialized professional activity. Unlike other specialties, however, clinical supervision is an area of professional activity that most counselors will encounter in their careers. Thus, although most specialties define one's practice (e.g., addictions counseling), clinical supervision defines one's "professional maturity," so to speak. While such professional maturity was considered both necessary and sufficient in years past, the last 25 years have clearly demonstrated that supervision is a unique activity requiring discrete knowledge, skills, and sensitivities.

DEFINING THE SPECIALTY, SETTINGS, AND CLIENTS

The evolution of clinical supervision can be seen as reflecting two paradigms—one ancient and the other parallel to the evolution of the helping professions. For virtually all professions and throughout history, fledgling professionals have relied on

---

Box 19.1 Exploring the Codes

Which ethical guidelines and/or Standards for Ethical Practice for Clinical/Counseling Supervisors apply to these issues?

1. Records of the counseling relationship
2. Training in supervision
3. Endorsement
4. Access to the supervisee's performance evaluation
5. Priority for resolving conflicts among the needs of client, supervisee, and agency/program
6. Professional status and conditions of supervision
7. Potentially detrimental relationships
8. Informed consent
9. Cultural issues
10. Laws and legal standards
11. Continuing education

---

those senior to them to mentor them to a level of acceptable competence (Bernard & Goodyear, 1998). For most of the history of counseling, this mentoring/apprenticeship paradigm has greatly influenced the practice of clinical supervision. Additionally (and, to some extent, separately), the early practice of clinical supervision paralleled that of counseling and psychotherapy (Leddick & Bernard, 1980). Even within psychoanalysis wherein supervision was stressed early on, clinical supervision took the form of analyzing the supervisee, an intervention that did not necessarily require supervisors to stretch beyond their training as psychoanalysts. Until recent years, clinical supervision was viewed primarily as an extension of counseling and reflected counseling skills and values. The personal growth of the supervisee was often targeted and when supervisees floundered in their clinical work, social modeling and counseling were most likely to be the supervisor interventions of choice.

In the mid-1970s to early 1980s, models of supervision that required a conceptual and technical shift from counseling began to appear (e.g., Bernard, 1979; Kagan, 1976; Loganbill, Hardy, & Delworth, 1982; Stoltenberg, 1981). Since those early contributions, other models and model refinements have enriched the practice of clinical supervision (e.g., Hawkins & Shohet, 1989; Holloway, 1995; Maki & Delworth, 1995). Additionally, research efforts that address process variables have helped to illuminate the complex supervision interaction.

Although there are a variety of ways to conduct clinical supervision, the nature of the contract between supervisor and supervisee is foundational and is different from other professional relationships within counseling. Bernard and Goodyear (1998) defined **supervision** as:

> An intervention provided by a more senior member of a profession to a more junior member or members of that same profession. This relationship is evaluative, extends over time, and has the simultaneous purposes of enhancing the professional functioning of the more junior person(s), monitoring the quality of professional services offered to the client(s) she, he, or they see(s), and serving as a gatekeeper of those who are to enter the particular profession. (p. 6)

This definition distinguishes clinical supervision from counseling, consultation, and administrative supervision. Neither counseling nor consultation is an evaluative relationship. Counselors attempt to assist clients in ways that they request—counseling's success, or lack of success, is ultimately determined by the client. Consultation is a nonhierarchical relationship—it is understood that the advice offered by the consultant can be rejected by the consultee. The key distinction between administrative supervision and clinical supervision is the focus of the activity. The administrative supervisor oversees case management and the professionalism of services offered by counseling staff. However, this person does not focus on the process of counseling itself and, therefore, is not in a position to make a judgement about the counseling or assist in the development of the counselor as clinician.

Most counselors first encounter clinical supervision in their training programs to become entry-level professional counselors, usually as part of a practicum. At this early juncture, standard practice (and requirements of pertinent accrediting bodies) includes both individual supervision and group supervision. (It is beyond the capacity of this chapter to explain the intricacies of these different supervision methods or the many approaches that can be used within each. For coverage of these methods, see Bernard and Goodyear [1998].) Although the clinical supervision within accredited training programs has been regulated and most training programs offer sound supervision, postdegree supervision is far more random. It is still the case that many, if not most, clinical supervisors in the field have not received formal training in supervision. This situation is changing, albeit slowly. Furthermore, the growth of licensure/certification in individual states and national certification have required that counselors receive postdegree supervision. Counselors who do not seek certification or licensure may receive virtually no additional clinical supervision once they are employed. This situation results in a heavy responsibility on the new professional counselor to make an accurate assessment regarding her competence and to be aware of a multitude of complicating issues that may affect the counseling process.

Postdegree supervision is usually conducted at a counselor's employment site; for example, a counselor in a community agency is expected to acquire licensure as soon possible. Because a license to practice counseling requires a certain amount of time postdegree under supervision, the agency expects to offer that supervision to the new employee. Despite the distinctions made earlier, supervisors often have more than one role with supervisees. It is not uncommon for a clinical supervisor to be a counselor's administrative supervisor as well. This is not an ideal situation because it makes it more difficult for trust to be established and for the supervisee to express her doubts and/or vulnerabilities. For example, a supervisor may encourage the supervisee to disclose personal views toward others that may block supervisee development. In doing so, the supervisee may share information that leads the supervisor to conclude that the supervisee is not as mature or introspective as she initially thought. This knowledge will most certainly influence the supervisor when it is time to review staff for contract re-

newal. In this instance, therefore, the clinical and administrative responsibilities of the supervisor are in direct conflict with each other.

Occasionally, counselors seek clinical supervision privately. If it is within the counselor's financial means to do so, this can be the best option because it eliminates any role ambiguity within the workplace. Further, a privately sought clinical supervisor clearly focuses on the supervisee's development and is obliged only to act on the gatekeeper role if she feels that the supervisee's counseling is substandard and poses potential harm to clients.

While employment or licensure/certification requirements may mandate supervision, there are many reasons why counselors seek clinical supervision throughout their careers. Among these are a desire to develop an expertise in a new clinical area, overall professional development, and as a means to avoid professional burnout. It is indicative of those who are most engaged in their professional lives that they continually seek opportunities to learn and to improve their craft. The process of clinical supervision is perhaps most fruitful when approached with the motive of professional development.

Professionalization of Clinical Supervision

Clinical supervision has been performed at some level since the inception of psychotherapy and counseling. For most of this history, however, the practice of supervision did not benefit from standards of practice. The American Association for Marriage and Family Therapy (AAMFT) formalized standards for training clinical supervisors as early as 1971 (Falvey, 2002). The first counseling group to establish standards for clinical supervision training was the National Academy for Certified Clinical Mental Health Counselors (NACCMHC), the credentialing arm of the American Mental Health Counselors Association (AMHCA), which established its Approved Supervisor designation in 1989. The Academy's Approved Supervisor designation was available to CCMHCs until the Academy's merger with the National Board for Certified Counselors (NBCC) in 1994.

Beginning in the mid-1980s, the Association for Counselor Education and Supervision (ACES), through its Supervision Interest Network, sought to professionalize clinical supervision for all specialties within the counseling profession. As a result of its efforts, several key publications emerged that greatly advanced the general knowledge and regard for counselor supervision and its parameters. These publications included the *Standards for Preparation and Practice of Counseling Supervisors* (Supervision Interest Network, 1990), a curriculum guide for training counseling supervisors (Borders et al., 1991), and *Ethical Guidelines for Clinical Supervisors* (ACES, 1993) (see Appendix 19-A). The efforts of the ACES Supervision Interest Network over the years culminated in 1998 when, in collaboration with NBCC, the Approved Clinical Supervisor (ACS) credential was established by NBCC. Although eligibility for the ACS was initially restricted to National Certified Counselors, the NBCC Board passed a resolution in 2000 opening up access to the credential to any mental health professional who meets the training and experience criteria. The ACS stipulates nine content areas that training in clinical supervision must include (see Appendix 19-B). Among these is a focus on legal and ethical tenets that affect supervision. The ACS Standards for the Ethical Practice of Clinical Supervision (1998) are listed in Appendix 19-C. In addition, recent revisions of codes of ethics that previously included little or nothing on supervision now have expanded their coverage or included sections specifically dedicated to the topic (ASGW, 1998; CRCC, 2001).

Licensure or certification of counselors in individual states has also affected the professionalization of clinical supervision. All jurisdictions (i.e., state boards and the District of Columbia board) that regulate the profession of counseling call for postdegree supervision as a stipulation for licensure/certification. Additionally, 17 of these jurisdictions obligate supervisors to receive training in supervision prior to providing supervision (Sutton, Nielson, & Essex, 1998). A small number of states currently require either state licensure as a clinical supervisor or a national credential in clinical supervision as a prerequisite to offering supervision to counselors seeking licensure. It is quite likely that this trend will continue and that clinical supervision will be increasingly regulated by counseling licensure boards (Sutton, 2000).

ISSUES OF SIGNIFICANCE TO CLINICAL SUPERVISION

Professional Differentiation

Supervision is an inherently hierarchical relationship, involving supervisor, supervisee(s), and client(s). The professional responsibilities of the supervisor, therefore, are twofold: (1) to enhance the professional functioning of the supervisee and (2) to monitor client care (Bernard & Goodyear, 1998). Although careful case management typically ensures that these two responsibilities are noncontradictory, occasionally this is not the case. This, then, adds a third critical responsibility of clinical supervision—monitoring the fit between the needs of the supervisee and the needs of the client.

Assisting the supervisee to become a better counselor involves assigning clients within the counselor's current level of competence. At the same time, the supervisee must be challenged to learn. This may include assigning clients that represent the upper edge of the counselor's ability and perhaps are beyond the counselor's comfort level. Additionally, the supervisor must be cognizant of different learning styles, cultural issues, and personal characteristics, all of which influence how efficiently the supervisee will become more expert. Williams (1995) suggested that clinical wisdom be a supervision goal—an ambitious goal indeed! In light of all of these factors, the supervisor must determine what can be accomplished within the time devoted to supervision (e.g., one semester or open-ended) and what types of interventions will maximize the desired outcomes. Finally, the supervisor must monitor progress, give regular feedback, and often evaluate the level of competence at the end of the supervision contract.

Clinical supervision will fail if there is insufficient focus on the supervisee. There is no reason to believe that a counselor will become more expert without the kind of feedback routinely offered by supervisors. It is essential that the supervisor not lose sight of the welfare of the client(s) in working with the supervisee. In fact, the original purpose of supervision was to monitor client care (Bernard & Goodyear, 1998). Only later did the focus expand to include a deliberate focus on the supervisee. Professional responsibility continues to dictate that the clinical supervisor monitor the counseling being performed *in light of the client's needs* as well as in deference to training goals. Ultimately, if close supervision is not adequate to ensure that the client is being served at a minimally acceptable level, the supervisor must intervene. As Rubin (1997) aptly stated, "When the supervisor's responsibilities to the evolving supervisee/therapist and the client do not lend themselves to reconciliation, the clinical, ethical and training aspects of the supervisory process all fall on the side of client welfare" (p. 1).

Ethical Issues

Supervisors have ethical obligations both to clients and to supervisees. However, Bernard and Goodyear (1998) described two major problems with regard to supervisors executing their ethical responsibilities. First, most codes of ethics for practitioners have limited references to supervision. Counselor educators and counseling supervisors often encounter situations that require more specific guidelines than provided by the ACA Code of Ethics. Secondly, complex, multidimensional thinking is required by the supervisor's obligations to consider simultaneously the ethical issues that affect both the supervisee and the client. These two problems can lead to ethical issues for both the supervisor and the counselor being supervised.

To address the first problem, ACES and NBCC (ACS) adopted specific supervision codes and standards. The Standards for Preparation and Practice of Counseling Supervisors (Supervision Interest Network, 1990), the ACS Standards for the Ethical Practice of Clinical Supervision (1998), and the Ethical Guidelines for Clinical Supervisors (ACES, 1993; see Appendix 19-A) assist supervisors by helping them (1) ensure ethical and legal protection of clients' and supervisees' rights; (2) meet the training and professional development needs of supervisees in ways consistent with clients' welfare and programmatic requirements; and (3) establish policies, procedures, and standards for implementing programs. To facilitate ethical knowledge and behavior in supervisees, supervisors at a minimum must possess a thorough knowledge of the ethical and regulatory codes in their professions and jurisdictions.

In addition to the ethical codes and standards, ethical principles and decision-making models have been proposed to address the second problem—the multidimensional thinking required by the supervisor to consider simultaneously the ethical issues that affect both the supervisee and their client. Kitchener (1984) suggested that ethical codes are inadequate for deliberation, instead; ethical principles must be considered when ethical dilemmas surface. Kitchener's five principles can be used to evaluate dilemmas. Specifically, she proposed that consideration of these issues with regard to the principles of autonomy, nonmaleficence, beneficence, justice, and fidelity can provide a basis to assess possible harm to the client and growth of the counselor. The ethical decision-making process involves a direct, evaluative process of deciding the morally appropriate option for resolving an ethical dilemma.

Models of ethical decision making have been developed for counseling. These models can be adapted to provide a framework for ethical decision making in supervision. These models generally incorporate consideration of the issue or dilemma in relation to the pertinent ethical codes and principles. They provide a cognitive map to process the issue from determination

of a potential dilemma to its resolution. One such model to guide this process is Tarvydas's Integrative Decision-Making Model of Ethical Behavior in Counseling (1997), which is presented in its updated form in Chapter 6. Knowledge of ethical decision-making models, especially when shared by the supervisee, can assist with the multidimensional thinking required by the supervisor to consider simultaneously the ethical issues that affect both the supervisee and their client.

The following discussion describes the ethical issues that present themselves in the process of clinical supervision. These issues are not unique to clinical supervision; however, the supervisor's obligation to consider simultaneously both the supervisee and the client requires unique considerations. Credit is given to Bernard and Goodyear (1998), whose text has provided a framework and primary reference for the following discussion. Although the discussion is organized by the concept of ethical issues, the primary strategy developed in each section focuses on guidelines provided by codes and standards. The intention here is to direct both supervisor and supervisee in the direction of prevention or containment of ethical issues as they present themselves in the complex, though natural, course of supervision.

Issues of Confidentiality in Clinical Supervision

Confidentiality in supervision must be considered from the perspective of both the client and the supervisee. From either perspective, the definition is comparable to confidentiality as traditionally referenced in counseling—that is, "confidentiality involves professional ethics rather than legalism and indicates an explicit promise or contract to reveal nothing about an individual except under conditions agreed to by the source or subject" (Siegel, 1979, p. 251). The following discussion will first consider confidentiality as it relates to the client of the supervisee and then the counselor as supervisee.

Issues of Client Confidentiality

Supervisors should make supervisees aware of clients' rights, including protecting clients' right to privacy and confidentiality in the counseling relationship and the information resulting from it. Clients also should be informed that their right to privacy and confidentiality will not be violated by the supervisory relationship (ACES, 1993). Thus, the supervisor must ensure that the counselor has informed her clients of their rights to confidentiality and privileged communication. Clients also should be informed of the limits of confidentiality and privileged communication. The general limits of confidentiality are when harm to self or others is threatened; when the abuse of children, elders, or persons with disabilities is suspected; and in cases when a court compels the counselor to testify and break confidentiality. These are generally accepted limits to confidentiality and privileged communication, but they may be modified by state or federal statute.

Supervisors must also be sure that their supervisees keep confidential all client information, except for purposes of supervision. Because supervision allows for third-party discussion, the supervisee must be reminded that this type of discourse cannot be repeated elsewhere (Bernard & Goodyear, 1998). In group supervision, the supervisor must reiterate this point and take the extra precaution of presenting cases using first names only, with as few demographic details as possible (Strein & Hershenson, 1991).

With video, electronic, or live supervision, the supervisor needs to re-emphasize the importance of confidentiality. When supervisees tape, they must be reminded they possess confidential documents. Notes should use code numbers rather than names and be guarded with care. Records of the counseling relationship, including interview notes, test data, correspondence, the electronic storage of these documents, and audio- and videotape recordings, are considered confidential professional information. Supervisors should verify these materials are used in counseling, research, and training and supervision of counselors with the full knowledge of the clients and with permission granted by the applied counseling setting that is offering service to the client. This professional information is to be used for full protection of the client. Written consent from the client (or legal guardian, if a minor) should be secured prior to using such information for instructional, supervisory, and/or research purposes. Policies of the applied counseling setting regarding client records also should be followed (ACES, 1993).

Issues of Supervisee Confidentiality

It is the supervisor's responsibility to keep information obtained during supervision regarding the counselor-supervisee confidential and to protect the supervisee's right to privacy. The supervisor must keep and secure supervision records and consider all information gained in supervision as confidential. The supervisee should understand the circumstances under which information obtained in supervision can be revealed. Supervisees can make more informed decisions about what to re-veal in supervision if they understand that evaluative information from supervision may be passed along or any particular issues troubling the supervisor may be discussed with colleagues (Sherry, 1991).

Informed Consent Issues in Clinical Supervision

It is essential that both clients and supervisees understand and agree to the procedures of counseling and supervision prior to these activities. Actively involving all parties throughout the decision-making processes or providing for informed consent throughout these processes enhances the likelihood of attaining successful and ethical outcomes for both the client and the counselor being supervised. Informed consent is not a one-time event; rather, it is a continuing concern that needs to be revisited throughout the counseling and supervision process. Bernard and Goodyear (1998) noted that the supervisor has three levels of responsibility: (1) The supervisor must determine that the supervisee has informed clients regarding the parameters of counseling; (2) the supervisor must be sure that the clients are aware of the parameters of supervision that will affect them; and (3) the supervisor must provide the supervisee with the opportunity for informed consent.

Informed Consent with Clients.   Counseling and supervision codes of ethics specify that counselors-in-training or in practice make every effort to ensure clients are aware of the services rendered and the qualifications of the person rendering those services. The supervisor must ensure that supervisees inform clients of their professional status. Supervisors need to ensure that supervisees inform their clients of any status other than being fully qualified for independent practice or licensed. For example, supervisees need to inform their clients if they are a student, intern, trainee or, if licensed with restrictions, the nature of those restrictions (ACES, 1993).

The types of services and the risks and benefits of counseling also need to be discussed. This discussion by the supervisee should include such specifics as the number and length of sessions, the cost for service, and the opportunity for telephone consultations. The type of services the client will be offered, preferred alternatives, and the risk of receiving no treatment should also be explained to ensure informed consent by the supervisee.

Informed   Consent   Regarding   Supervision. Supervisors should have supervisees inform their clients that they are being supervised and explain all the conditions of their supervision. The client must be informed of the supervision procedures, whether sessions will be taped or observed, who will be involved, and how close the supervision will be. Clients should be informed of the limits of confidentiality. Client permission must be obtained before students and supervisees can use any information concerning the counseling relationship in the training process (ACA).

Confidentiality should be fully explained as it applies to both the process of counseling and to supervision. This discussion must also include when confidentiality will be breached. Disney and Stephens (1994) noted, "Supervisees place themselves in a position to be sued for invasion of privacy and breach of it if they do not inform their clients that they will be discussing sessions with their supervisor" (p. 50). A written form to alert clients of the conditions of supervision is a strategy to avoid possible misunderstandings later.

Informed Consent with Supervisee.   Just as the supervisee has a responsibility to secure the client's informed consent, the supervisor is obligated to ensure that the supervisee understands and consents to the conditions of her supervision. Supervisees should enter the supervisory experience knowing the conditions that dictate their success or advancement. The responsibilities of both the supervisor and the supervisee should be clear. Supervisors should incorporate the principles of informed consent and participation with clarity of requirements, expectations, roles, and rules in the establishment of policies and procedures for their institutions, program, courses, and individual supervisory relationships. Mechanisms for due process appeal of individual supervisory actions should be established and made available to all supervisees. Supervisors should also inform supervisees of the goals, policies, theoretical orientations toward counseling, training, and supervision model or approach on which the supervision is based (ACES, 1993).

Whiston and Emerson (1989) stated all trainees entering a program should be cognizant that personal counseling may be recommended. Trainees should also be informed regarding the choice of supervisor, the form of supervision, the time allotted for supervision, the expectations of the supervisor, the theoretical orientation of the supervisor, and the type of documentation required for supervision. A written agreement can articulate a supervisory relationship in detail to avoid later misunderstandings. It serves to formalize the relationship, educate the supervisee regarding the nature of supervision, provide a model of how to approach informed consent with clients, and provide se-

curity for both parties by structuring the relationship (McCarthy et al., 1995).

Issues of Due Process in Clinical Supervision

Supervisees have due process rights. Borders (2001) noted that supervisees must be afforded due process, ranging from timely feedback to opportunities for remediation to avenues to report dissatisfaction with supervision. To be ethically and legally sound, supervisors must employ a process that is neither arbitrary nor capricious (Disney & Stephens, 1994). The ACES Guidelines are very clear on this issue. Supervisors should incorporate the principles of due process and appeal into the policies and procedures of their institutions, program, courses, and individual supervisory relationships. Mechanisms for due process appeal of individual supervisory actions should be established and made available to all supervisees (ACES, 1993).

The ACES Guidelines further specify that supervisors of counselors should meet regularly in face-to-face sessions with their supervisees and provide supervisees with ongoing feedback on their performance. This feedback should take a variety of forms, both formal and informal, and should include verbal and written evaluations. It should be formative during the supervisory experience and summative at the conclusion of the experience. Supervisors should also establish and communicate to supervisees and field supervisors specific procedures regarding consultation, performance review, and evaluation of supervisees (ACES, 1993).

The ACA Code of Ethics addresses the issue of due process with regard to counselor education and training programs. It states that prior to admission, counselors should orient prospective students to the counselor education or training program's expectations, including but not limited to the following: (1) the type and level of skill acquisition required for successful completion of the training, (2) subject matter to be covered, (3) basis for evaluation, (4) training components that encourage self-growth or self-disclosure as part of the training process, (5) the type of supervision settings and requirements of the sites for required clinical field experiences, (6) student and supervisee evaluation and dismissal policies and procedures, and (7) up-to-date employment prospects for graduates. Counselor education and training programs should integrate academic study and supervised practice. Such programs also are required to clearly state to students and supervisees, in advance of training, the levels of competency expected, appraisal methods, and timing of evaluations for both didactic and experiential components. Supervisors are also required to provide students and supervisees with periodic performance evaluations.

Bridge and Bascue (1990) noted the importance of proper documentation of supervision. It is critical that supervisors document the periodic formative as well as the summative evaluations that provide direct feedback to supervisees. Specific competencies and behaviors that are not adequate with behavioral indicators of the target performance to be attained should be noted. The supervision records should be dated and signed. This information should be available to the supervisee so that sufficient time is provided to correct any deficiency. Established notification and grievance procedures should provide recourse for supervisees who are unsuccessful in this process. Evaluations of supervisee performance in universities and in applied counseling settings should be available to supervisees in ways consistent with the Family Rights and Privacy Act and the Buckley Amendment (ACES, 1993).

Potentially Detrimental Relationship Issues in Supervision

Supervision is complicated when supervisors have potentially detrimental roles with their supervisees. These relationships occur when counselors or supervisors take on two or more roles, either professional or personal, simultaneously or sequentially with each other or with the clients served (Herlihy & Corey, 1997). These relationships may be intimate, therapeutic, and/or social in nature. Examples of such relationships include, but are not limited to, familial, social, financial, business, therapeutic, or close personal relationships with clients or supervisees. Borders (2001) has noted that potentially detrimental relationships may be a particularly challenging area in supervision because there is a high probability that many supervisors and supervisees will have such relationships. Bernard and Goodyear (1998) noted that these relationships between supervisors and supervisees have proven to be a difficult issue to resolve, as evidenced by much debate in the literature. Such relationships should be anticipated and, when they occur, handled with care (Herlihy & Corey, 1997).

All relevant ethical codes for counseling professionals make some reference to potentially detrimental relationships between supervisors and supervisees. The factors that make such a relationship unethical are: (1) the likelihood that it will impair the supervisor's judgment, and (2) the risk of exploitation to the supervisee (Hall, 1988). The primary risk factor is a power differen-

tial; misuse of this power is exploitive and could cause harm. Kitchener and Harding (1990) identified two additional factors that create the risk of harm: (1) incompatible expectations of the counselor or supervisor in different roles, and (2) incompatible responsibilities of the counselor or supervisor. Whatever the rationale, it is the consensus of the profession that all potentially detrimental relationships should be avoided if at all possible.

The ACES Ethical Guidelines for Counseling Supervisors give the most attention to these relationships. Specifically, these guidelines provide the following directives: Supervisors who have multiple roles (e.g., teacher, clinical supervisor, administrative supervisor, etc.) with supervisees should minimize potential conflicts. Whenever possible, the roles should be divided among several supervisors. When this is not possible, supervisors should convey carefully the expectations and responsibilities associated with each supervisory role. Stoltenberg, McNeill, and Delworth (1998) noted that the supervisor needs to be alert to inappropriate relations between supervisee and client and to avoid multiple relations in supervisory assignments. Specifically, when a potentially detrimental relationship cannot be avoided, counselors and supervisors should take appropriate professional precautions such as informed consent, consultation, supervision, and documentation to ensure that their judgment is not impaired and that no exploitation occurs (ACA).

Bernard and Goodyear (1998) provided a detailed review of potentially detrimental relationship issues related to supervisee-supervisor. The following is drawn from their discussion:

Sexual Attraction.   Ellis and Douce (1994) identified sexual attraction between the supervisee-supervisor as one of eight recurring issues in supervision. Ladany, Hill, Corbett, and Nutt (1996) found counselor-client and supervisor-supervisee attractions among the topics that trainees were unwilling to disclose in supervision. This topic needs to be discussed openly, ethically, and viewed as a relatively normal part of supervision and therapy.

Sexual Harassment.   Unlike sexual attraction, sexual harassment is an aberration of the supervision process. It is never acceptable to put the supervisor's own needs and wants in the foreground to the detriment of the professional development needs of the supervisee (Peterson, 1993). The ACA code clearly states that counselors and supervisors do not engage in sexual relationships with students or supervisees and do not subject them to sexual harassment.

Hidden Consensual Sexual Relationship. Brodsky (1980) asserted "when one person in a relationship has a position of power over the other, there is no true consent for the acceptance of a personal relationship" (p. 516). Bartell and Rubin (1990) advised "sexual involvement may further a human relationship, but it does so at the expense of the professional relationship" (p. 446). Supervisors should not participate in any form of sexual contact with supervisees nor engage in any form of social contact or interaction that would compromise the supervisor-supervisee relationship. Again, potentially detrimental relationships with supervisees that might impair the supervisor's objectivity and professional judgment should be avoided and/or the supervisory relationship terminated (ACES, 1993).

Nonsexual Relationships. Goodyear and Sinnett (1984) argued that it is inevitable that supervisors and their supervisees will have potentially detrimental relationships. Supervisors should not establish a therapeutic relationship as a substitute for supervision. Personal issues should be addressed in supervision only in terms of the impact of these issues on clients and on professional functioning (ACES, 1993). If students or supervisees request counseling, supervisors or counselor educators should provide them with acceptable referrals. Supervisors or counselor educators should not serve as a counselor to students or supervisees over whom they hold administrative, teaching, or evaluative roles unless this is a brief role associated with a training experience (ACA). In addition to personal counseling, a supervisor may recommend participation in activities such as personal growth groups when it has been determined that a supervisee has deficits in the areas of self-understanding and problem resolution that impede her professional functioning. Again, supervisors should not be the direct provider of these activities for the supervisee (ACES, 1993).

Strategy to Resolve Potentially Detrimental Relationships. Bernard and Goodyear (1998) proposed the following strategy when a potentially detrimental relationship emerges within the context of supervision: (1) The supervisee should get a new supervisor in a manner that will not negatively affect clients being served or the professional growth of the trainee. If it is not possible to replace the supervisor, an additional supervisor should be involved to monitor the supervisory relationship. (2) If it is not possible to remove the supervisor, both the supervisor and the supervisee should document their work together with audio/video examples of the supervisee's work to enable a second opinion.

The topics covered in supervision should be recorded; the supervisor should request consultation with colleagues; and if group supervision is used, personal relationships should be made known to the group.

Potentially detrimental relationships exist on a continuum. Peterson (1993) cautioned that these relationship challenges abound in supervisory relationships and cannot be regulated out of existence. The ACA Code of Ethics states that counselors must clearly define and maintain ethical, professional, and social relationship boundaries with their students and supervisees. Boundaries in this relationship must be carefully managed because supervisors have considerable power in the relationship.

CASE SCENARIO 19-1

Brett, a doctoral student in counselor education, is on a graduate student volleyball team with Jim, a master's student. When Brett sees the list of master's students to supervise, he immediately asks to supervise Jim, without mentioning the volleyball team. Their outside activity is not private, so is there any problem with Brett's decision? What are the ethical issues?

This relationship may not cause any issues for Brett or for Jim. At the same time, because there was a choice of supervisees, Brett should not have asked to supervise Jim because of their ongoing athletic team relationship. It is difficult to know a priori what type of potentially detrimental relationship can become problematic. Furthermore, this could also be seen as a violation of Jim's informed consent rights in that he was not consulted before the choice was made.

ISSUES OF COMPETENCE IN CLINICAL SUPERVISION

The ACA Code of Ethics states that counselors must practice only within the boundaries of their competence. The ACES Guidelines (1993) extend this concept to supervision, stating that supervisors should teach courses and/or supervise clinical work only in areas in which they are fully competent and experienced. Thus, the capacity of the supervisor to perform the essential functions of both counselor and supervisor is fundamental to the ethical practice of supervision. Competence, existing on a continuum, means having the ability to perform a task at an acceptable level (Cramton, 1981).

Essential Competencies for the Counselor Supervisor

The essential competencies for the counselor supervisor have been established by ACES. The following provides an abstracted listing of these 11 core areas. A detailed description of these competencies can be found in the source document, *Supervision Interest Network* (1990).

Supervisors: (1) are effective counselors themselves; (2) demonstrate attitudes and traits consistent with the supervisory role, such as sensitivity to individual differences, motivation, commitment to supervision, and comfort with the authority inherent in the supervisory role; (3) are knowledgeable of and can skillfully apply the ethical, legal, and regulatory dimensions of supervision; (4) demonstrate conceptual knowledge of the professional and personal nature of the supervisory relationship and the impact of supervision on the supervisee; (5) understand and are skilled in the methods and techniques of supervision; (6) understand the process of counselor development and can apply it to supervision; (7) are competent in case conceptualization and management; (8) are competent in client assessment and evaluation; (9) are knowledgeable about oral and written reporting and recording; (10) can evaluate a supervisee's counseling performance fairly and accurately and provide feedback to facilitate growth; and (11) are knowledgeable of the rapidly expanding body of theory and research concerning counseling and counselor supervision and incorporate it in their practice.

Counselor and Supervisor Competence

ACES standards require that the supervisor first be an effective counselor. Importantly, the supervisor must be more advanced than the supervisee in all areas of counseling practice. Counselors must assess their counseling competencies and then determine the kinds of clients they would not supervise, the settings that are out of their scopes of expertise, and the kinds of clients they would supervise only working under supervision or in conjunction with a consultant.

Being a competent counselor does not necessarily mean an individual is also a competent supervisor. The ACES guidelines state that supervisors should have training in supervision prior to initiating their role as supervisors. The guidelines go on to state that supervisors should be knowledgeable regarding the ethical, legal, and regulatory aspects of the profession. They also must be skilled in applying that knowledge and in making students and supervisees aware of their responsibilities. Again, as supervisors, professionals must assess their competencies.

Supervisee Competence

Supervisors have the oversight responsibility for supervisees' work in relation to their competence. Su-

pervisors should therefore assess their supervisees' skills and experience to establish the level of their supervisees' competence. Supervisors should then restrict their supervisees' activities to those that are commensurate with their current level of skills and experiences (ACES, 1993). The only way for supervisors to have confidence in their assessment is to use direct forms of supervision, at least on an intermittent basis. The task for supervisors and supervisees is to recognize when they are and are not qualified to serve prospective clients and to accept clients who will challenge them to stretch the boundaries of their competence with consultation.

Stoltenberg, McNeill, and Delworth (1998) also spoke to the ethical mandate to permit supervisees to provide only those services within their competence. They noted that supervisors must select the type and number of clients to match the supervisee's level of competence. Supervisors then need to be vigilant to monitor client welfare and base their level of monitoring on the level of education and experience of the supervisee. In addition, the amount of time supervisors have available to supervise and their competency relative to pertinent issues must be factored into ethical supervisory decisions.

Impairment of Competence

The ACES guidelines speak directly to the issue of supervisee impairment by stating that supervisors, through ongoing supervisee assessment and evaluation, should be aware of any personal or professional limitations of supervisees that are likely to impede future professional performance. Lamb, Cochran, and Jackson (1991) defined the impairment of competence as an inability or unwillingness (a) to acquire and integrate one's repertoire of professional standards into one's repertoire of professional behavior; (b) to acquire professional skills and reach an accepted level of competency; and/or (c) to control personal stress, psychological dysfunction, or emotional reactions that may affect professional functioning. Any one or combination of these factors requires responsible action on the part of the supervisor.

Supervisors have the responsibility of recommending remedial assistance to the supervisee and of screening from the training program, applied counseling setting, or state licensure those supervisees who are unable to provide competent professional services. These recommendations should be clearly and professionally explained in writing to the supervisees who are so evaluated (ACES, 1993). Stoltenberg and Delworth (1988) described the reciprocal ethical responsibility on the part of supervisees to recognize personal problems that may interfere with their practice, to let the supervisor know of them, and to seek appropriate assistance.

Ultimately, supervisors should not endorse a supervisee for certification, licensure, completion of an academic training program, or continued employment if the supervisor believes the supervisee is impaired in any way that would interfere with the performance of counseling duties. The presence of any such impairment should begin a process of feedback and remediation wherever possible, so the supervisee understands the nature of the impairment and has the opportunity to remedy the problem and continue with her professional development (ACES, 1993).

CASE SCENARIO 19-2

Alex has been Jaime's post-master's supervisor as part of the requirements for seeking licensure in her state. Alex has been both supportive and challenging in his supervision. Now that Jaime has completed her required hours, she gives Alex an endorsement form for Alex to fill out and file with the state. A week later, Jaime receives an e-mail from Alex that he has studied the form and he does not feel comfortable endorsing her at this time. Alex recommends that Jaime seek additional supervision from another supervisor. What are the ethical issues?

Alex might actually believe (and it could be argued) that he is behaving in an ethical manner by withholding endorsement from a supervisee for whom he has marginal confidence. At the same time, Jaime has due process rights that Alex has violated. Because Alex knew that Jaime was interested in seeking licensure, he needed to share his reservations earlier in the supervisory relationship and to stipulate exactly what those reservations were. By doing so, Jaime would have had an opportunity to work on her deficits and perhaps ultimately receive Alex's endorsement. It is also possible that Alex's expectations are higher than reasonable. By informing Jaime sooner about his evaluation, Jaime would have had an opportunity to seek another supervisor with whom to work.

Remaining Competent

Competence is not a static concept; counselors and supervisors need to participate in continuing education activities to maintain their competence (ACA). In addition, a supervisor must remain competent as both counselor and supervisor. The issue of competence for both the supervisor and the supervisee is central to the most pressing ethical responsibility—that of monitoring client welfare (Sherry, 1991). The ACES

code speaks directly to this issue, stating that supervisors should pursue professional and personal continuing education activities such as advanced courses, seminars, and professional conferences on a regular and ongoing basis. These activities should include both counseling and supervision topics and skills. Supervisors are also expected to be active participants in peer review and peer supervision procedures (ACES, 1993).

Supervisors must be committed to continuing education. They need to keep current in their own specialty areas and be aware of advances in the area of clinical supervision. Many professionals become complacent with their degree of competence and wean themselves from professional literature and/or attendance at professional meetings or workshops (Campbell, 1994). In addition to continuing education, liberal use of consultation with peers is important to prevent the kind of isolation that diminishes competence (Sherry, 1991).

The ethical considerations for supervisor and supervisee are complex and ever present. The ACES Ethical Guidelines for Counseling Supervisors and the ACS Standards for the Ethical Practice of Clinical Supervision, in conjunction with the ethical principles and an ethical decision-making model, assist both parties in identifying and strategizing to best ensure client welfare in the course of counselor development. If supervisors and supervisees do not deal with these issues in a proactive, systematic manner, ethical violations can result, with implications for both.

CASE SCENARIO 19-3

Alice is the faculty member assigned to Teresa's practicum class. Teresa conceptualizes her cases adequately and seems to have good technical skills, but she is not available emotionally to her clients. In fact, she appears "shut down" in all of her interactions with her clients, with Alice, and with her peers. During one particular supervision session, Alice challenges Teresa more than usual about her affective unavailability. Teresa cries and shares that she was emotionally and sexually abused as a child. She shares that she is in counseling, but, obviously, she still has difficulty trusting others and allowing herself to feel emotions during counseling. She asks Alice to keep her background in confidence. What are the ethical issues?

This example is laden with ethical issues. First, there is the issue of informed consent. Was there a supervision contract that made it clear that Alice would not keep in confidence information that was relevant to Teresa's standing in the program? If not, and Alice feels obliged to share this information, she has denied Teresa informed consent. Second, if Alice keeps the confidence, she is in danger of forming an inappropriate, potentially detrimental relationship with Teresa by treating her more like a client than a student. Finally, the issue of competence must be addressed. If Teresa is not able to assess her own feelings or to deal with the feelings of clients, Alice must question her competence at this time. To ignore this limitation in evaluation would be an ethical concern.

ETHICAL VIOLATIONS

It is quite likely that most ethical violations in clinical supervision go unreported. The professional literature points to the fact that ethical violations committed by supervisors occur (e.g., Lamb & Catanzaro, 1998; Miller and Larabee, 1995). Yet, there is also evidence that mental health professionals are reluctant to report ethical violations of peers when they become aware of them (e.g., Bernard & Jara, 1986). Furthermore, a recent study of counseling supervisors (Erwin, 2000) found that 67 percent of supervisors in the sample received low scores on moral sensitivity when the ethical issue presented to them was ambiguous (having to do with a potentially detrimental relationship). Even when the ethical issue was considered less ambiguous (breach of confidentiality), 35 percent received low moral sensitivity scores. In light of social modeling, therefore, it should not be surprising that in a national survey of graduate trainees (of clinical psychology), over half of the training directors who responded reported that they had dealt with an ethical transgression of a trainee (Fry, Van Bark, Weinman, Kitchener, & Lang, 1997).

Definitions

It is important to distinguish terms when entering the quagmire of unethical behavior of supervisees and supervisors. An **ethical violation** is just that—a behavior that violates the letter or perhaps the spirit of an ethical standard of practice. If a supervisee violates an ethical standard and it becomes known, the consequences will probably occur within the supervisory context. If the supervisee is in a training program, the consequences may range from a confrontation with the supervisor to dismissal from the program, often depending on the egregiousness of the violation (Fry et al., 1997).

An **ethical complaint** is a more formal process and is far more public. A complaint of ethical violation appeals to the professional group that endorses the violated ethical standards. There are three categories of such groups: professional membership associations (e.g., the American Counseling Association [ACA]), voluntary certification organizations (e.g., the Commission of Rehabilitation Counselor Certification [CRCC]), and state boards for the licensure or certification of counselors. There is nothing to prohibit a complainant from appealing to more than one group—for example, if a supervisor is a member of the ACA, a certified rehabilitation counselor, and a licensed clinical mental health counselor in the state of Maine, complaints could be made to the ACA, the CRCC, and the state of Maine. Each group would independently evaluate the complaint and determine its validity and, if valid, impose appropriate sanctions. Professional membership groups and certification groups have jurisdiction only over their members/certificants. State boards are similar unless a mental health professional commits an act specifically prohibited by the law in the state that granted licensure/certification (e.g., practicing without a license, which may or may not be considered an ethical violation). In such a case, the state's attorney general's office can order the mental health professional to "cease and desist." Typically, however, state counseling boards operate similarly to professional membership and certification boards.

Just as a complainant can appeal to different boards, a complainant may also initiate both a complaint and a malpractice lawsuit. (The latter involves the civil court and will be addressed under legal issues in this chapter and, more generally, in Chapter 4.)

Supervisee Violations

Supervisors are responsible for their own behaviors as well as the behavior of their supervisees. When there is **layered supervision** (e.g., doctoral students supervising master's students who are themselves being supervised by faculty), supervisors must attend to this additional layer. Welfel (1998) cautioned that, in this case, "the professionals who have ultimate responsibility for the client find more and more distance between them and the client" (p. 276). Welfel advised supervisors to develop careful and consistent data-gathering methods to compensate for this vulnerability.

The ethical issue that has received the most attention in the literature (e.g., Hamilton & Spruill, 1999; Lamb & Catanzaro, 1998) is sexual boundary violations between trainees and their clients. The investigation of ethical violations of psychology students (Fry et al., 1997) would justify this concern. Of the eight categories of ethical transgressions, professional boundary transgressions (sexual and nonsexual) ranked as the second most likely trainee transgression, after violations of confidentiality. (These two types of transgressions together represented 45 percent of the total reported by training directors.) Because it is not uncommon for persons in the mental health fields to have unresolved personal issues of one sort or another, supervisors should be vigilant regarding boundary transgressions. To this point, Jackson and Nuttall (2001) found that three out of five mental health practitioners with severe childhood sexual abuse in their backgrounds reported sexual boundary violations with clients. Jackson and Nuttall strongly recommended that clinicians with this profile avoid private practice and seek ongoing clinical supervision. Supervisors, therefore, need to be prepared to work not only with novice supervisees, but also with more seasoned, yet high-risk, clinicians.

Supervisor Violations

Using primarily the ACES Ethical Standards for Counselor Supervisors as their template, Ladany, Lehrman-Waterman, Molinaro, and Wolgast (1999) surveyed 151 counselors or psychologists-in-training regarding the behavior of their supervisors. A startling 51 percent reported at least one ethical violation by their supervisors. The most frequently violated standards involved adequate performance evaluation, confidentiality issues having to do with supervision, and the supervisor's ability/willingness to work with alternative perspectives. Although Ladany et al. (1999) found sexual boundary violations to represent only 1.3 percent of reported breaches, other authors have focused on such violations

and have found evidence that they pose some risk within the supervisor/supervisee dyad (e.g., Bonosky, 1995; Miller & Larabee, 1995; Slimp & Burian, 1994).

Preventing Ethical Violations

In light of Erwin's (2000) finding that moral sensitivity appears to be less than robust for counselor supervisors, it would be wise for supervisors to look for ways to increase their ethical foresight—for themselves and as models for their supervisees. It appears that coursework in ethics is not sufficient to prevent ethical transgressions (Fry et al., 1997) and more attention on ethical behavior needs to be placed within the supervision dialogue itself.

Hamilton and Spruill (1999) asserted that a decline in concern over transference and countertransference within training programs has increased the risk of problematic potentially detrimental relationships occurring. They also advised supervisors to deal straightforwardly with trainees about sexual attraction between clients and counselors and counselors and supervisors, a strategy also proposed by Bridges and Wohlberg (1999). Hamilton and Spruill (1999) developed an excellent risk management checklist for supervisees and supervisors to help them identify feelings and motives and to confront inappropriate behaviors (Figure 19–1).

Cobia and Boes (2000) suggested the use of professional disclosure statements and formal supervision

---

Therapist Responses to Clients

■ Do you find it difficult to set limits on the demands your client makes of you?
■ Do you accept phone calls from your client at home or your office when the client needs you to (a) help with a "crisis," (b) deal with minor problems, or (c) alleviate his or her loneliness or meet his or her need to talk to someone who "understands"?
■ Do you make statements such as "This is not my usual practice; I ordinarily don't do this, but, in your case…" or "Under the circumstances, it seems OK to…"?
■ Do you find yourself wanting to rescue your client from some situation or behavior that is detrimental to him or her?
■ Do you find yourself talking about your client to others?
■ Does your client occupy your thoughts outside office hours?
■ Do you hope you will "run into" your client at the grocery store, social settings, and so forth?
■ Is it becoming progressively easier and more satisfying to share intimate details of your own life with your client?
■ Do you find opportunities to talk about nontherapy issues with your client?
■ Do you take care to dress or look more attractive than usual for a particular client?
■ Do you find yourself wondering what the client thinks about you?
■ Do you make excuses to talk with your client by phone?
■ Do you accept friends of your client as therapy clients, and then find yourself spending a lot of the session talking about the original client to the current client rather than focusing on the current client's problems?
■ Do you find yourself looking forward to seeing a particular client (or type of client) and feeling disappointed if he or she cancels the session?

continued

FIGURE 19–1. Risk Management: A Checklist for Trainees and Supervisors
Hamilton & Spruill (1999)

Therapist Needs

■ Does your primary satisfaction come from your work with therapy clients?
■ Do you have more clients than required or more than your fellow practicum students?
■ Are you lonely and feeling as if your needs are not being met by anyone?
■ Do you have a circle of friends with whom you engage in pleasurable social activities?
■ Do you have a circle of friends to whom you can turn for support?
■ Do you have one or more close friends in whom you could confide about fears, anxieties, and self-doubts?
■ What are the important stressors in your life, and what steps are you taking to resolve or to cope with them?

Session Characteristics

■ Do you regularly extend the session for one client but not for others?
■ Do you regularly start the session early, end it late, or both for one client?
■ Do you schedule a particular client at times that afford the opportunity to linger, or to walk out of the clinic together, and so forth?
■ Do you schedule the client after regular office hours because your schedule or the client's schedule does not permit regular office hours?

Accountability

■ Do you find yourself forgetting to document phone calls from your client?
■ Do you find yourself getting defensive about particular clients or certain issues (e.g., you bristle when a supervisor suggests that there is no progress being made and a referral is in order)?
■ Are you reluctant to talk about transference or boundary issues, particularly feelings related to sexual attraction by or to the client?
■ Do you find it difficult to tell your treatment team or supervisor some details related to your client?
■ Is there anything that you "try not to talk about" concerning a particular client?
■ Do you find yourself putting off seeking supervision or consultation about a particular client or issue?
■ Does the tape always run out or mess up at a "sensitive" point in the session? Does the therapy session regularly extend beyond the length of the tape?
■ If you make phone calls, extend sessions, and so forth, how much of this information is recorded in the client's file? Do you find yourself unwilling, or "forgetting," to document information with regard to a particular client?

Other

■ Have the secretaries or other people commented about your behavior toward a client?
■ Have you offered to do such things as give the client a ride home, give tutoring in a difficult class, or arrange a meeting outside the therapy hour or place?
■ Are you concerned about the client's feelings toward you, or your feelings toward the client?

Checklist for Supervisors

■ Have I discussed how to establish a professional therapist-client relationship with my practicum students?
■ Have I reviewed the issue of sexual attraction to clients and shared my own experiences with my practicum students? If I am unwilling to share my own feelings, what have I done about this?
■ Have I created an atmosphere of openness and willingness to discuss the fears, uncertainties, and so forth of my practicum students?
■ Do my practicum students know about boundary violations and the reasons for establishing boundaries?
■ Have I discussed the checklist for students with them?

FIGURE 19–1. Risk Management: A Checklist for Trainees and Supervisors—*continued*
Hamilton & Spruill (1999)

plans as strategies to reduce the risk of ethical conflicts within supervision. Both of these documents will give the supervisee a great deal of information about the supervisor and about the process of supervision. They serve not only as a guideline for the supervisee but also as an aid to the supervisor in planning ahead (e.g., choosing an evaluation plan) and covering a variety of issues that could potentially lead to an ethical breach (e.g., informed consent).

LEGAL ISSUES

Any ethical violation becomes a legal issue when a claim of malpractice is made. Such a claim does not mean that a different kind of egregious behavior has been committed. Rather, it simply means that the harmed party has appealed to a civil court rather than (or in addition to) a professional body (such as state counseling board) for reparation. As noted by Montgomery, Cupit, and Wimberley (1999), it is not uncommon for the same claim to result in both a complaint to a regulatory body and a malpractice lawsuit. At the same time, it is safe to assume that there are many more complaints made to regulatory boards than suits for malpractice. Whereas a professional peer review board that would investigate a complaint is interested primarily in whether the professional has breached professional ethics, the civil court's role is quite different. It is restricted by tort law and is an appropriate venue only if negligence can be proved to have caused harm by the defendant.

Malpractice

Although there are two types of torts (i.e., civil wrongs other than breach of contract)—intentional and unintentional (Swenson, 1997)—it is highly unlikely (though possible) that a supervisor would be sued for an intentional tort or for deliberately causing harm to a supervisee and/or client. An example of such a Machiavellian act might be a supervisor suggesting that a supervisee develop a strategy in counseling that the supervisor believes would increase the suicide risk of a client. Or, less dramatic, a supervisor might place a disliked intern in a clinical setting where the supervisor is fairly sure that the intern will fail. In both of these cases, the offense could be argued under intentional tort.

Virtually all malpractice cases in the mental health professions, however, are negligence cases, and are therefore unintentional torts (Swenson, 1997). Disney and Stephens (1994) defined malpractice as "harm to another individual due to negligence consisting of the breach of a professional duty or standard of care" (p. 7). Although the definition seems fairly straightforward, there are actually four elements that must be present for a successful malpractice suit (Ogloff & Olley, 1998): (1) There must be what is called a fiduciary relationship. Within the supervisory context, this means that the supervisor can be trusted to be working in the best interests of the supervisee and her clients rather than in her own interests (Remley & Herlihy, 2001). In short, there is an acknowledged duty of care based on a professional relationship. (2) The professional (supervisor) must act in a way that falls below the standard established by her profession. (3) The client (and/or supervisee) must suffer some harm. (4) A relationship between the harm and the supervisor's (or supervisee's) act must be established.

It generally is agreed that the crux of liability is whether the professional acted outside the bounds of accepted practice (Ogloff & Olley, 1998; Remley & Herlihy, 2001). Guest and Dooley (1999) made the astute point that until recently it was difficult to get a handle on "acceptable practice" where clinical supervision was concerned. However, with the emergence of training requirements, standards of practice, and ethical guidelines, supervisors have become more accountable to a standard and, consequently, are more vulnerable to being held liable. At the same time, supervisors who follow sanctioned practice and ethical standards for clinical supervision are protected by their presence.

Direct Liability

Because supervision involves two levels of oversight, liability can be both direct and indirect. **Direct liability** occurs when the harm that is done is a result of supervision itself. Any harm done to the supervisee within supervision would most likely be direct. Results reported by Montgomery, Cupit, and Wimberley (1999) suggested that direct liability is still rare for supervisors, though two reported malpractice suits did, indeed, involve supervisory issues (supervisee performance evaluation and a billing/payment issue). When faulty evaluation is claimed, a violation of due process is most likely the grounds on which the suit stands. All areas outlined in clinical supervision standards, however, could potentially lead to a malpractice suit of direct liability, including competence to supervise an individual supervisee (including an inability to work with cultural differences); violations of informed consent, the supervision contract, or confidentiality; or an inappropriate potentially detrimental relationship.

Direct liability can also be claimed if the harm is done to the client, and the cause of the harm directly traces to the supervisor. For example, if an inadequately informed supervisor suggested an intervention to the supervisee that led to client harm, this could be argued as direct liability. Liability can be argued for actions or omissions of the supervisor (Falvey, 2002). Therefore, a lack of adequate recordkeeping by the supervisor could lead to additional vulnerability should a client be harmed.

Vicarious Liability

Vicarious liability is perhaps more feared by clinical supervisors. Based on the legal concept of *respondeat superior,* supervisors are considered liable "for the negligent acts of supervisees if these acts are performed in the course and scope of the supervisory relationship" (Disney & Stephens, 1994, p. 15). Falvey (2002) further clarified that three conditions must be met for vicarious liability: (1) Supervisees must agree to work under the direction of the supervisor and act in ways that benefit the supervisor; (2) supervisees must act within a scope of tasks endorsed by the supervisor; and (3) the supervisor must have the power to control and direct the work of the supervisee. Falvey pointed out that administrative supervisors may be more likely to be considered vicariously liable because of the condition that supervisee acts "benefit the supervisor," as would be the case if a supervisor received part of a fee paid by the client to the supervisee. Finally, Disney and Stephens (1994) added one more important component in defining whether an action falls within the scope of supervisory relationships: "whether the supervisor could have reasonably expected the supervisee to commit the act" (p. 16). Ignorance of the supervisee's behavior is not a strong defense if it is reasonable to expect that the supervisor could have predicted the likelihood of the action occurring. The courts do not expect supervisors to be infallible, but they do expect that reasonable care will be applied to the activity of clinical supervision.

Remley and Herlihy (2001) cautioned that exact facts of each situation are different and call for unique interpretations. They underscore the fact that the amount of control that a supervisor has over a counselor would be important to determine in arriving at a judgment of vicarious liability. In this light, they further suggested that supervisors on-site are more likely to be held accountable for a counselor's negligence than those who supervise from elsewhere (e.g., within a university training program setting).

Preventing the Malpractice Lawsuit

It is no surprise to anyone living in the United States that we are a litigious culture. Within this broad context, it must be noted that there is no way to make an individual invulnerable to a lawsuit, or as Swenson (1997) asserted, "the courthouse is a place that cannot always be avoided" (p. 165). There are ways to avoid being found guilty of malpractice and this is where supervisors' energies are constructively placed. First and foremost, the supervisor who stays abreast of the field, seeks consultation when necessary, and is particularly vigilant about standards for ethical practice of both counseling and supervision is highly unlikely to ever

be found guilty of malpractice. Although professional regulatory bodies and the courts remain very separate entities, there is evidence that courts typically support decisions made by bodies such as licensing boards (Ogloff & Olley, 1998). Therefore, following the lead of the certification and licensing bodies is totally warranted as a measure to prevent liability.

Falvey, Caldwell, and Cohen (2002) developed a comprehensive supervision documentation system as a strategy for risk management. Their supervision record forms ask the supervisor to review 19 risk management issues (e.g., duty to warn, potentially detrimental relationships) for each supervision session as a means to keep these important matters in the forefront of the supervisor's attention. Although time-consuming, this kind of system necessarily leads to increased command over both client and supervisee issues.

Woodworth (2000) concurred that recordkeeping is an important risk management strategy. She includes six other strategies for counselors that are equally relevant to supervisors, including: staying within one's area(s) of competence; attending to communication issues and the therapeutic (or supervisory) relationship; seeking supervision or consultation when needed; carrying liability insurance; staying abreast of ethics and relevant law; and practicing self-care to maintain physical and emotional well-being.

"Avoiding the courthouse," then, involves a unique blend of professional wisdom and human wisdom. In addition to some distinct knowledge, skill, and good work habits, healthy, respectful relationships and keen, unencumbered self-knowledge add significant protection to the clinical supervisor. In short, insight, integrity, and goodwill are enormous barriers to professional difficulty.

CODE COMPARISONS

Clinical supervision is a unique specialty in that it is not tied to any particular clientele or setting. All counselors receive supervision throughout their training, and most receive supervision early in their careers. The ACA has 17 divisions, many of which have separate ethical codes, and counseling has two certifying organizations (NBCC and CRCC), each with separate ethical codes. All of these conceivably refer to the practice of clinical supervision.

Prior to the ethical standards that were formulated primarily for counselors, two were written specifically for supervision—those of ACES and the ACS. The ACES Ethical Guidelines (1993; Appendix 19-A) are divided into three sections: client welfare and rights; supervisory role; and program administration role. The first two sections are very much in synchrony with the ACS Standards of Ethical Practice (Appendix 19-C). This is not surprising in light of the coordination that took place between ACES and NBCC in creating the ACS designation. The "program administration role" section of the ACES guidelines refers primarily to issues within training programs and the ethical practice of supervision when, for example, off-campus sites are involved, supervisees are also students, and evaluations translate to academic grades. These two publications are essential for practicing clinical supervisors and underscore the sometimes illusive, yet profoundly important, differences in responsibilities between counselors and supervisors.

Most ethical guidelines for counselors make only cursory reference to supervision and tend to single out one standard (e.g., regarding potentially detrimental relationships) for which to include a statement about supervisors and supervisees. There are four exceptions to this practice: The codes of the American Counseling Association (ACA), the American Mental Health Counseling Association (AMHCA), the International Association for Marriage and Family Counselors (IAMFC), and the Commission on Rehabilitation Counselor Certification (CRCC) have sections devoted to supervision. Members of these organizations should read these guidelines and those of ACES and the ACS prior to conducting supervision.

ISSUES OF DIVERSITY AND MULTICULTURAL SUPERVISION

All practitioners have an ethical mandate to increase their competence in working with diverse populations; supervisors are no exception (Stoltenberg & Delworth, 1988). Cross/multicultural counseling has been defined as "any counseling relationship in which two or more of the participants differ with respect to cultural background, values, and lifestyle" (Sue et al., 1982, p. 47). Sue went on to conclude that if these distinguishing characteristics of the supervisor and the counselor or supervisee are acknowledged and incorporated into practice, it becomes clear that all supervision is, by definition, cross-cultural. Framing supervision cross-culturally acknowledges the diverse backgrounds of each individual in the supervision/counseling triad and promotes culturally sensitive, ethical counseling and supervision practice (Terrell & Cheatman, 1996).

Given this, it would not be ethical for counselors or supervisors to attempt to provide services to culturally diverse clients or supervisees without appropriate training and experience. The ACA Code of Ethics in fact requires counselors to strive actively to understand the diverse cultural backgrounds of their clients and to gain skills and current knowledge in working with diverse client populations. Recognizing the importance of counselor self-awareness, the code also obligates counselors to learn how their own cultural/racial/ethnic identities impact their own values and beliefs about counseling. The importance of recognizing and appreciating parallel diversity issues for the supervisor's self-understanding, knowledge, and skills follows logically from this (Bernard & Goodyear, 1998; Leong & Wagner, 1994). If supervisors are not equipped adequately to deal with diversity, they are likely to overlook or even reinforce inadvertently biased attitudes and behaviors of their supervisees that could result in potential harm to clients.

Terrell and Cheatman (1996) noted that writers addressing multicultural supervision suggest that multicultural supervision dyads may be more conflicted in nature. They noted that this conclusion might indicate a predisposition on the part of the ethnic minority counselors and majority supervisors to anticipate difficulty in the supervisory relationship. These anticipated difficulties might also be explained by the minority counselors' anticipation of being evaluated by majority supervisors based on criteria rooted in cultural norms not shared in the supervision dyad. Ethical supervision demands that the supervisor be aware of these factors and proceed with sensitivity and a model of multicultural supervision.

Given the cross-cultural nature of all counseling and counseling supervision, the supervisor is involved consistently in cross-cultural supervision of cross-cultural counseling. The challenge for ethical and effective practice is the capacity for the supervisor to share simultaneously the worldview of the counselor and those of the counselor's clients. The culturally effective supervisor is able to generate the widest repertoire of supervisory skills and interventions appropriate to the counselor and the counselor's skill level. She may, in turn, facilitate the counselor's development of the widest repertoire of counseling skills and interventions appropriate to the client and the client's issues. This approach is best ethical practice.

Ethical Multicultural Supervision

Terrell and Cheatman (1996) outlined the following guidelines for multicultural supervision as a strategy to enhance effective and ethical multicultural supervision.

First, supervisors need to develop an understanding and awareness of self as a cultural being (McCrae & Johnson, 1991) in the supervision process. Supervisors should then undertake self-education about cultural groups that may influence a counselor's worldview. From this perspective, it is suggested that effective cross-cultural supervision should be process-oriented rather than client-oriented. This method will often include the use of new and creative supervisory interventions to meet the needs of the counselor. This guideline is consistent with Ivey's (1994) call to "cultural intentionality"—generating counseling and supervisory "alternatives from different vantage points, using a variety of skills and personal qualities within a culturally appropriate framework" (p. 19). Supervisees should have the experience of being supervised by culturally different and culturally similar supervisors. Finally, effective multicultural supervision should use multiple or tiered supervisory consultation.

D'Andrea and Daniels (1997) contended supervisors are acting in an ethical manner when they acknowledge their limitations in issues related to multicultural counseling regardless of their supervisory competencies. They noted supervisors should emphasize their interest and commitment to learn about multicultural issues from others, especially from their nonmajority and culturally diverse supervisees. This approach will "often necessitate an increased level of collaboration between supervisor and supervisee" (p. 307).

In the context of supervision, the task becomes one of creating an environment in which supervisees, clients, and supervisors can speak the truth of their respective experiences. Gonzalez (1997) suggested that supervisees find it permissible to be imperfect with regard to multiculturalism and be allowed to reveal ignorance and misunderstandings. In supervision, he suggested supervisors assess what contingencies hinder or facilitate both personal and social constructions that allow for shifts in perspectives, meanings, interpretations, evaluations, and explanations. In this way, he believes, supervisees will not experience guilt but will take personal responsibility for best practice.

Issues of diversity have often been perceived as an obstacle to overcome rather than an opportunity to enhance ethical practice in counseling and supervision. Effective cross-cultural supervisors are sensitive to diversity in both the client-supervisee and supervisor-supervisee relationships. Collaborations between supervisor and supervisee often take place within a multicultural context. This context can involve supervisees and supervisors who are affiliated in a variety of ways with different or similar cultural groups. An attitude of discovery, explo-

ration, and critical thinking in clinical work as opposed to political correctness in approaching multicultural issues has been proposed to enhance the ethical practice of both counseling and supervision (Stone, 1997).

CHAPTER SUMMARY

Clinical supervision is both an area of specialization and a mainstream activity across all specialties within counseling. Given that supervision is an inherently hierarchical relationship involving supervisor, supervisee(s), and client(s), the ethical and legal considerations are complex. Counseling supervisors encounter situations that challenge the help given by the general ethical standards of the profession at large. To address the problem, ACES and NBCC (ACS) have specific supervision codes and standards. The ACS Standards for the Ethical Practice of Clinical Supervision (1998) and the Ethical Guidelines for Clinical Supervisors (ACES, 1993) are intended to assist supervisors by helping them observe ethical and legal protection of clients' and supervisees' rights.

The ethical standards for supervision provide guidelines for best practice.

Supervisors should make supervisees aware of clients' rights, including protecting clients' right to privacy and confidentiality in the counseling relationship and the information resulting from it. It is also the supervisor's responsibility to keep the supervisee's information confidential and to protect her right to privacy. The supervisee should understand the circumstances under which information obtained in supervision will be revealed.

The client must be informed of the supervision procedures, whether sessions will be taped or observed, who will be involved, and how close the supervision will be. Just as the supervisee has a responsibility to secure the client's informed consent, the supervisor is obligated to ensure that the supervisee understands and consents to the conditions of supervision. Supervisors should incorporate the principles of informed consent and participation; clarity of requirements, expectations, roles, and rules; and due process and appeal into the establishment of policies and procedures of their institutions, programs, courses, and individual supervisory relationships.

Supervision is complicated when supervisors have multiple roles, such as teacher, supervisor, and administrator. All guidelines in the ACA Code of Ethics regarding potentially detrimental relationships between counselor educators and students apply equally to the supervisory relationship. The primary risk factor is a power differential; misuse of this power is exploitive and could cause harm. Potential issues related to the supervisee-supervisor relationships include sexual attraction, harassment, and relationships, as well as acting as counselor or other relationships with supervisees that might impair the supervisor's objectivity and professional judgment.

Being a competent counselor does not necessarily mean one is also a competent supervisor. Counselors must refrain from offering professional services when their physical, mental, or emotional problems are likely to harm clients or others. Supervisors have the responsibility of recommending remedial assistance to the supervisee and of screening from the training program, applied counseling setting, or state licensure those supervisees who are unable to provide competent professional services. Supervisors need to participate in continuing education activities to maintain their competence.

An ethical violation is a behavior that violates the letter or perhaps the spirit of an ethical standard of practice. A complaint of ethical violation appeals to the professional group that endorses the ethical standards

that have been violated. Just as a complainant can appeal to different boards, a complainant may also initiate both a complaint and a malpractice lawsuit. Supervisors are responsible for their own behaviors as well as the behavior of their supervisees. Professional disclosure statements and formal supervision plans are strategies to reduce the risk of ethical conflicts within supervision. Any ethical violation becomes a legal issue when a claim of malpractice is made. Because supervision involves two levels of oversight, liability can be both direct and indirect.

Effective cross-cultural supervisors are sensitive to diversity in both the client-supervisee and supervisor-supervisee relationships. Given the cross-cultural nature of all counseling and counseling supervision, the supervisor is consistently involved in cross-cultural supervision of cross-cultural counseling. The challenge for ethical and effective practice is the capacity for the supervisor to share simultaneously the worldview of the counselor and the counselor's clients.

REFERENCES

American Counseling Association. (1998). *Code of ethics and standards of practice.* Alexandria, VA: Author.

Association for Counselor Education and Supervision. (1990). Standards for counseling supervisors. *Journal of Counseling and Development, 69,* 30–32.

Association for Counselor Education and Supervision. (1993). ACES ethical guidelines for counseling supervisors. *ACES Spectrum, 53,* 5–8.

Association for Specialists in Group Work. (1998). Best practice guidelines. *Journal for Specialists in Group Work, 23*(3), 237–244.

Bartell, P. A., & Rubin, L. J. (1990). Dangerous liaisons: Sexual intimacies in supervision. *Professional Psychology: Research and Practice, 21,* 442–450.

Bernard, J. L., & Jara, C. S. (1986). The failure of clinical psychology graduate students to apply understood ethical principles. *Professional Psychology: Research and Practice, 17,* 313–315.

Bernard, J. M. (1979). Supervisor training: A discrimination model. *Counselor Education and Supervision, 19,* 60–68.

Bernard, J. M., & Goodyear, R. K. (1998). *Fundamentals of clinical supervision* (2nd ed.). Boston: Allyn & Bacon.

Bonosky, N. (1995). Boundary violations in social work supervision: Clinical, educational and legal implications. *The Clinical Supervisor, 13*(2), 79–95.

Borders, L. D. (2001). Counseling supervision: A deliberate educational process. In D. Locke, J. Myers, & E. Herr (Eds.), *Handbook of counseling* (pp. 417–432). Thousand Oaks, CA: Sage.

Borders, L. D., Bernard, J. M., Dye, H. A., Fong, M. L., Henderson, P., & Nance, D. W. (1991). Curriculum guide for training counseling supervisors: Rationale, development, and implementation. *Counselor Education and Supervision, 31,* 58–82.

Bridge, P., & Bascue, L. O. (1990). Documentation of psychotherapy supervision. *Psychotherapy in Private Practice, 8,* 79–86.

Bridges, N. A., & Wohlberg, J. W. (1999). Sexual excitement in therapeutic relationships: Clinical and supervisory management. *The Clinical Supervisor, 18*(2), 123–141.

Brodsky, A. (1980). Sex role issues in the supervision of therapy. In A. K. Hess (Ed.), *Psychotherapy supervision: Theory, research, and practice* (pp. 509–524). New York: Wiley.

Campbell, T. W. (1994). Psychotherapy and malpractice exposure. *American Journal of Forensic Psychology, 12,* 5–41.

Cobia, D. C., & Boes, S. R. (2000). Professional disclosure statements and formal plans for supervision: Two strategies for minimizing the risk of ethical conflict in post-master's supervision. *Journal of Counseling & Development, 78,* 293–296.

Cramton, R. (1981). Incompetence: The North American experience. In L. E. Trak-

man & D. Watters (Eds.), *Professional competence and the law* (pp. 158–163). Halifax, Nova Scotia, Canada: Dalhousie University.

CRCC. 2001. *Code of ethics for rehabilitation counselors.* Rolling Meadows, IL: Author.

D'Andrea, M., & Daniels, J. (1997). Multicultural counseling supervision: Central issues, theoretical considerations, and practical strategies. In D. Pope-Davis & H. Coleman (Eds.), *Multicultural counseling competencies: Assessment, education and training, and supervision. Multicultural aspects of counseling series: Vol. 7.* Thousand Oaks, CA: Sage.

Disney, M. J., & Stephens, A. M. (1994). *Legal issues in clinical supervision.* Alexandria, VA: ACA Press.

Ellis, M. V., & Douce, L. A. (1994). Group supervision of novice clinical supervisors: Eight recurring issues. *Journal of Counseling and Development, 72,* 520–525.

Erwin, W. J. (2000). Supervisor moral sensitivity. *Counseling Education and Supervision, 40,* 115–127.

Falvey, J. E. (2002). *Managing clinical supervision: Ethical practice and legal risk management.* Pacific Grove, CA: Brooks/Cole.

Falvey, J. E., Caldwell, C. F., & Cohen, C. R. (2002). *Documentation in supervision: The focused risk management supervision system.* Pacific Grove, CA: Brooks/Cole.

Fry, B. J., van Bark, W. P., Weinman, L., Kitchener, K. S., & Lang, P. R. (1997). Ethical transgressions of psychology graduate students: Critical incidents with implications for training. *Professional Psychology: Research and Practice, 28,* 492–495.

Gonzalez, R. C. (1997). Postmodern supervision: Issues for the white supervisor. In D. Pope-Davis & H. Coleman (Eds.), *Multicultural counseling competencies: Assessment, education and training, and supervision. Multicultural aspects of counseling series: Vol. 7.* Thousand Oaks, CA: Sage.

Goodyear, R. K., & Sinnett, E. D. (1984). Current and emerging ethical issues for counseling psychologists. *Counseling Psychologist, 12,* 87–98.

Guest, C. L., Jr., & Dooley, K. (1999). Supervisor malpractice: Liability to the supervisee in clinical supervision. *Counselor Education and Supervision, 38,* 269–279.

Hall, J. E. (1988). Dual relationships in supervision. *Register Report, 15,* 5–6.

Hamilton, J. C., & Spruill, J. (1999). Identifying and reducing risk factors related to trainee-client sexual misconduct. *Professional Psychology: Research and Practice, 30,* 318–327.

Hawkins, P., & Shohet, R. (1989). *Supervision in the helping professions.* Milton Keynes, UK: Open University Press.

Herlihy, B., & Corey, G. (1997). Codes of ethics as catalysts for improving practice. In B. Herlihy & G. Corey (Eds.), *Ethics in therapy* (pp. 37–56). New York: Hatherleigh.

Holloway, E. L. (1995). *Clinical supervision: A systems approach.* Thousand Oaks, CA: Sage.

Ivey, A. E. (1994). *Intentional interviewing and counseling: Facilitating client development in a multicultural society.* Pacific Grove, CA: Brooks/Cole.

Jackson, H., & Nuttal, R. L. (2001). A relationship between childhood sexual abuse and professional sexual misconduct. *Professional Psychology: Research and Practice, 32,* 200–204.

Kagan, N. (1976). *Influencing human interaction.* Mason, MI: Mason Media, Inc.; or Washington, D.C.: American Counseling Association.

Kitchener, K. S. (1984). Intuition, critical evaluation and ethical principles: The foundation for ethical decisions in counseling psychology. *The Counseling Psychologist, 12,* 43–55.

Kitchener, K. S., & Harding, S. S. (1990). Dual role relationships. In B. Herlihy & L. Golden (Eds.), *Ethical standards casebook* (4th ed., pp. 145–148). Alexandria, VA: American Counseling Association.

Ladany, N., Hill, C. E., Corbett, M., & Nutt, E. A. (1996). Nature, extent, and importance of what psychotherapy trainees do not disclose to their supervisors. *Journal of Counseling Psychology, 43,* 10–24.

Ladany, N., Lehrman-Waterman, D., Molinaro, M., & Wolgast, B. (1999). Psychotherapy supervisor ethical practices: Adherence to guidelines, the supervisory working alliance, and supervisee satisfaction. *The Counseling Psychologist, 27,* 443–475.

Lamb, D. H., & Catanzaro, S. J. (1998). Sexual and nonsexual boundary violations involving psychologists, clients, supervisees, and students: Implications for professional practice. *Professional Psychology: Research and Practice, 29,* 498–503.

Lamb, D. H., Cochran, D. J., & Jackson, V. R. (1991). Training and organizational issues associated with identifying and responding to intern impairment. *Professional Psychology: Research and Practice, 22,* 291–296.

Leddick, G. R., & Bernard, J. M. (1980). The history of supervision: A critical review. *Counselor Education and Supervision, 19,* 186–196.

Leong, F. T., & Wagner, N. S. (1994). Cross-cultural counseling supervision: What do we know? What do we need to know? *Counselor Education and Supervision, 34,* 117–131.

Loganbill, C., Hardy, E., & Delworth, U. (1982). Supervision: A conceptual model. *Counseling Psychologist, 10,* 3–42.

Maki, D., & Delworth, U. (1995). Clinical supervision: A definition and model for the rehabilitation counseling profession. *Rehabilitation Counseling Bulletin, 38*(4), 282–293.

McCarthy, P., Sugden, S., Koker, M., Lamendola, F., Maurer, S., & Renninger, S. (1995). A practical guide to informed consent in clinical supervision. *Counselor Education and Supervision, 35,* 130–138.

McCrae, M. B., & Johnson, S. D. (1991). Toward training for competence in multicultural counselor education. *Journal of Counseling & Development, 70,* 131–135.

Miller, G. M., & Larrabee, M. J. (1995). Sexual intimacy in counselor education and supervision: A national survey. *Counselor Education and Supervision, 34,* 332–343.

Montgomery, L. M., Cupit, B. E., & Wimberley, T. K. (1999). Complaints, malpractice, and risk management: Professional issues and personal experiences. *Professional Psychology: Research and Practice, 30,* 402–410.

National Board for Certified Counselors. (1998). *Standards for the ethical practice of clinical supervision.* Greensboro, NC: Author.

Ogloff, J. R. P., & Olley, M. C. (1998). The interaction between ethics and the law: The ongoing refinement of ethical standards for psychologists in Canada. *Professional Psychology: Research and Practice, 39,* 221–230.

Peterson, M. (1993). Covert agendas in supervision. *Supervision Bulletin, 6,* 7–8.

Remley, T. R., Jr., & Herlihy, B. (2001). *Ethical, legal, and professional issues in counseling.* Upper Saddle River, NJ: Prentice-Hall.

Rubin, S. S. (1997). Balancing duty to client and therapist in supervision: Clinical, ethical and training issues. *The Clinical Supervisor, 16*(1), 1–23.

Sherry, P. (1991). Ethical issues in the conduct of supervision. *The Counseling Psychologist, 19,* 566–585.

Siegel, M. (1979). Privacy, ethics, and confidentiality. *Professional Psychology, 10,* 249–258.

Slimp, P. A. O., & Burian, B. K. (1994). Multiple role relationships during internship: Consequences and recommendations. *Professional Psychology: Research and Practice, 25,* 39–45.

Stoltenberg, C. (1981). Approaching supervision from a developmental perspective: The counselor-complexity model. *Journal of Counseling Psychology, 28,* 59–65.

Stoltenberg, C. D., & Delworth, U. (1988). Developmental models of supervision: It is development—Response to Holloway. *Professional Psychology: Research and Practice, 19,* 134–137.

Stoltenberg, C. D., McNeill, B., & Delworth, U. (1998). *IDM supervision: An integrated developmental model for supervising counselors and therapists.* San Francisco: Jossey-Bass.

Stone, G. L. (1997). Multiculturalism as a context for supervision: Perspectives, limitations, and implications. In D. Pope-Davis & H. Coleman (Eds.), *Multicultural counseling competencies: Assessment, education and training, and supervision.* Thousand Oaks, CA: Sage.

Strein, W., & Hershenson, D. B. (1991). Confidentiality in non-dyadic counseling situations. *Journal of Counseling and Development, 69,* 312–316.

Sue, D. W., Bernier, J. E., Duran, A., Feinberg, L., Pederson, P., Smith, E. G., & Vasquez-Nuttall, E. (1982). Position paper: Cross-cultural counseling competencies. *The Counseling Psychologist, 10,* 45–52.

Supervision Interest Network, Association for Counselor Education and Supervision. (1990). Standards for counseling supervisors. *Journal of Counseling and Development, 69,* 30–32.

Supervision Interest Network, Association for Counselor Education and Supervision. (1993, Summer). ACES ethical guidelines for counseling supervisors. *ACES Spectrum, 53*(4), 5–8.

Sutton, J. M., Jr. (2000). Counselor licensure. In H. Hackney (Ed.). *Practice issues for the beginning counselor* (pp. 55–78). Boston: Allyn & Bacon.

Sutton, J. M., Jr., Nielson, R., & Essex, M. (1998). *A descriptive study of the ethical standards related to supervisory behavior employed by counselor licensing boards.* Paper presented at the annual conference of the American Association of State Counseling Boards, Tucson, AZ.

Swenson, L. C. (1997). *Psychology and law for the helping professions.* Pacific Grove, CA: Brooks/Cole.

Tarvydas, V. M. (1997). Ethical and legal standards of practice in rehabilitation counseling. In D. R. Maki & T. F. Riggar (Eds.), *Rehabilitation counseling: Profession and practice.* New York: Springer, 72–94.

Terrell, Y. L., & Cheatman, H. E. (1996). Creating a therapeutic alliance: A multicultural perspective. In J. L. DeLucia-Waack (Ed.), *Multicultural counseling competencies: Implications for training and practice.* Alexandria, VA: Association for Counselor Education and Supervision, 63–88.

Welfel, E. R. (1998). *Ethics in counseling and psychotherapy: Standards, research, and emerging issues.* Pacific Grove, CA: Brooks/Cole.

Whiston, S. C., & Emerson, S. (1989). Ethical implications for supervisors in counseling of trainees. *Counselor Education and Supervision, 28,* 318–325.

Williams, A. (1995). *Visual and active supervision: Roles, focus, and technique.* New York: W. W. Norton.

Woodworth, C. B. (2000). Legal issues in counseling practice. In H. Hackney (Ed.), *Practice issues for the beginning counselor* (pp. 119–136). Boston: Allyn & Bacon.

APPENDIX 19-A

ACES Ethical Guidelines

ETHICAL GUIDELINES FOR COUNSELING SUPERVISORS ASSOCIATION FOR COUNSELOR EDUCATION AND SUPERVISION

Adopted by ACES Executive Counsel and Delegate Assembly March, 1993

Preamble

The Association for Counselor Education and Supervision (ACES) is composed of people engaged in the professional preparation of counselors and people responsible for the ongoing supervision of counselors. ACES is a founding division of the American Counseling Association for (ACA) and as such adheres to ACA's current ethical standards and to general codes of competence adopted throughout the mental health community.

ACES believes that counselor educators and counseling supervisors in universities and in applied counseling settings, including the range of education and mental health delivery systems, carry responsibilities unique to their job roles. Such responsibilities may include administrative supervision, clinical supervision, or both. Administrative supervision refers to those supervisory activities that increase the efficiency of the delivery of counseling services; whereas, clinical supervision includes the supportive and educative activities of the supervisor designed to improve the application of counseling theory and technique directly to clients.

Counselor educators and counseling supervisors encounter situations that challenge the help given by general ethical standards of the profession at large. These situations require more specific guidelines that provide appropriate guidance in everyday practice.

The Ethical Guidelines for Counseling Supervisors are intended to assist professionals by helping them:

1. Observe ethical and legal protection of clients' and supervisees' rights;
2. Meet the training and professional development needs of supervisees in ways consistent with clients' welfare and programmatic requirements; and
3. Establish policies, procedures, and standards for implementing programs.

The specification of ethical guidelines enables ACES members to focus on and to clarify the ethical nature of responsibilities held in common. Such guidelines should be reviewed formally every five years, or more often if needed, to meet the needs of ACES members for guidance.

The Ethical Guidelines for Counselor Educators and Counseling Supervisors are meant to help ACES members in conducting supervision. ACES is not currently in a position to hear complaints about alleged non-compliance with these guidelines. Any complaints about the ethical behavior of any ACA member should be measured against the ACA Ethical Standards and a complaint lodged with ACA in accordance with its procedures for doing so.

One overriding assumption underlying this document is that supervision should be ongoing throughout a counselor's career and not stop when a particular level of education, certification, or membership in a professional organization is attained.

DEFINITIONS OF TERMS

Applied Counseling Settings—Public or private organizations of counselors such as community mental health centers, hospitals, schools, and group or individual private practice settings.

Supervisees—Counselors-in-training in university programs at any level who work with clients in applied settings as part of their university training program, and counselors who have completed their formal education and are employed in an applied counseling setting.

Supervisors—Counselors who have been designated within their university or agency to directly oversee the professional clinical work of counselors. Supervisors also may be persons who offer supervision to counselors seeking state licensure and so provide supervision outside of the administrative aegis of an applied counseling setting.

1. Client Welfare and Rights

   1.01 The primary obligation of supervisors is to train counselors so that they respect the integrity and promote the welfare of their clients. Supervisors should have supervisees inform clients that they are being supervised and that observation and/or recordings of the session may be reviewed by the supervisor.

   1.02 Supervisors who are licensed counselors and are conducting supervision to aid a supervisee to become licensed should instruct the supervisee not to communicate or in any way convey to the supervisee's clients or to other parties that the supervisee is himself/herself licensed.

   1.03 Supervisors should make supervisees aware of clients' rights, including protecting clients' right to privacy and confidentiality in the counseling relationship and the information resulting from it. Clients also should be informed that their right to privacy and confidentiality will not be violated by the supervisory relationship.

   1.04 Records of the counseling relationship, including interview notes, test data, correspondence, the electronic storage of these documents, and audio and videotape recordings, are considered to be confidential professional information. Supervisors should see that these materials are used in counseling, research, and training and supervision of counselors with the full knowledge of the clients and that permission to use these materials is granted by the applied counseling setting offering service to the client. This professional information is to be used for full protection of the client. Written consent from the client (or legal guardian, if a minor) should be secured prior to the use of such information for instructional, supervisory, and/or research purposes. Policies of the applied counseling setting regarding client records also should be followed.

   1.05 Supervisors shall adhere to current professional and legal guidelines when conducting research with human participants such as Section D-1 of the ACA Ethical Standards.

   1.06 Counseling supervisors are responsible for making every effort to monitor both the professional actions, and failures to take action, of their supervisees.

2. Supervisory Role

   Inherent and integral to the role of supervisor are responsibilities for:

   a. monitoring client welfare;
   b. encouraging compliance with relevant legal, ethical, and professional standards for clinical practice;
   c. monitoring clinical performance and professional development of supervisees; and
   d. evaluating and certifying current performance and potential of supervisees for academic, screening, selection, placement, employment, and credentialing purposes.

   2.01 Supervisors should have had training in supervision prior to initiating their role as supervisors.

   2.02 Supervisors should pursue professional and personal continuing education activities such as advanced courses, seminars, and professional conferences on a regular and ongoing basis. These activities should include both counseling and supervision topics and skills.

   2.03 Supervisors should make their supervisees aware of professional and ethical standards and legal responsibilities of the counseling profession.

   2.04 Supervisors of post-degree counselors who are seeking state licensure should encourage these counselors to adhere to the standards for practice established by the state licensure board of the state in which they practice.

   2.05 Procedures for contacting the supervisor, or an alternative supervisor, to assist in handling crisis situations should be established and communicated to supervisees.

   2.06 Actual work samples via audio and/or video tape or live observation in addition to case notes should be reviewed by the supervisor as a regular part of the ongoing supervisory process.

   2.07 Supervisors of counselors should meet regularly in face-to-face sessions with their supervisees.

   2.08 Supervisors should provide supervisees with ongoing feedback on their performance. This feedback should take a variety of forms, both formal and informal, and should include verbal and written evaluations. It should be formative during the supervisory experience and summative at the conclusion of the experience.

   2.09 Supervisors who have multiple roles (e.g., teacher, clinical supervisor, administrative supervisor, etc.) with supervisees should minimize potential conflicts. Where possible, the roles should be divided among several supervisors. Where this is not possible, careful explanation should be conveyed to the supervisee as to the expectations and responsibilities associated with each supervisory role.

2.10 Supervisors should not participate in any form of sexual contact with supervisees. Supervisors should not engage in any form of social contact or interaction which would compromise the supervisor-supervisee relationship. Dual relationships with supervisees that might impair the supervisor's objectivity and professional judgment should be avoided and/or the supervisory relationship terminated.

2.11 Supervisors should not establish a psychotherapeutic relationship as a substitute for supervision. Personal issues should be addressed in supervision only in terms of the impact of these issues on clients and on professional functioning.

2.12 Supervisors, through ongoing supervisee assessment and evaluation, should be aware of any personal or professional limitations of supervisees which are likely to impede future professional performance. Supervisors have the responsibility of recommending remedial assistance to the supervisee and of screening from the training program, applied counseling setting, or state licensure those supervisees who are unable to provide competent professional services. These recommendations should be clearly and professionally explained in writing to the supervisees who are so evaluated.

2.13 Supervisors should not endorse a supervisee for certification, licensure, completion of an academic training program, or continued employment if the supervisor believes the supervisee is impaired in any way that would interfere with the performance of counseling duties. The presence of any such impairment should begin a process of feedback and remediation wherever possible so that the supervisee understands the nature of the impairment and has the opportunity to remedy the problem and continue with his/her professional development.

2.14 Supervisors should incorporate the principles of informed consent and participation; clarity of requirements, expectations, roles and rules; and due process and appeal into the establishment of policies and procedures of their institutions, program, courses, and individual supervisory relationships. Mechanisms for due process appeal of individual supervisory actions should be established and made available to all supervisees.

3. Program Administration Role

3.01 Supervisors should ensure that the programs conducted and experiences provided are in keeping with current guidelines and standards of ACA and its divisions.

3.02 Supervisors should teach courses and/or supervise clinical work only in areas where they are fully competent and experienced.

3.03 To achieve the highest quality of training and supervision, supervisors should be active participants in peer review and peer supervision procedures.

3.04 Supervisors should provide experiences that integrate theoretical knowledge and practical application. Supervisors also should provide opportunities in which supervisees are able to apply the knowledge they have learned and understand the rationale for the skills they have acquired. The knowledge and skills conveyed should reflect current practice, research findings, and available resources.

3.05 Professional competencies, specific courses, and/or required experiences expected of supervisees should be communicated to them in writing prior to admission to the training program or placement/employment by the applied counseling setting and, in case of continued employment, in a timely manner.

3.06 Supervisors should accept only those persons as supervisees who meet identified entry level requirements for admission to a program of counselor training or for placement in an applied counseling setting. In the case of private supervision in search of state licensure, supervisees should have completed all necessary prerequisites as determined by the state licensure board.

3.07 Supervisors should inform supervisees of the goals, policies, theoretical orientations toward counseling, training, and supervision model or approach on which the supervision is based.

3.08 Supervisees should be encouraged and assisted to define their own theoretical orientation toward counseling, to establish supervision goals for themselves, and to monitor and evaluate their progress toward meeting these goals.

3.09 Supervisors should assess supervisees' skills and experience in order to establish standards for competent professional behavior. Supervisors should restrict supervisees' activities to those that are commensurate with their current level of skills and experiences.

3.10 Supervisors should obtain practicum and fieldwork sites that meet minimum standards for preparing students to become effective counselors. No practicum or fieldwork setting should be approved unless it truly replicates a counseling work setting.

3.11 Practicum and fieldwork classes would be limited in size according to established professional standards to ensure that each student has ample opportunity for individual supervision and feedback. Supervisors in applied counseling settings should have a limited number of supervisees.

3.12 Supervisors in university settings should establish and communicate specific policies and procedures regarding field placement of students. The respective roles of the student counselor, the university supervisor, and the field supervisor should be clearly differentiated in areas such as evaluation, requirements, and confidentiality.

3.13   Supervisors in training programs should communicate regularly with supervisors in agencies used as practicum and/or fieldwork sites regarding current professional practices, expectations of students, and preferred models and modalities of supervision.

3.14   Supervisors at the university should establish clear lines of communication among themselves, the field supervisors, and the students/supervisees.

3.15   Supervisors should establish and communicate to supervisees and to field supervisors specific procedures regarding consultation, performance review, and evaluation of supervisees.

3.16   Evaluations of supervisee performance in universities and in applied counseling settings should be available to supervisees in ways consistent with the Family Rights and Privacy Act and the Buckley Amendment.

3.17   Forms of training that focus primarily on self understanding and problem resolution (e.g., personal growth groups or individual counseling) should be voluntary. Those who conduct these forms of training should not serve simultaneously as supervisors of the supervisees involved in the training.

3.18   A supervisor may recommend participation in activities such as personal growth groups or personal counseling when it has been determined that a supervisee has deficits in the areas of self understanding and

problem resolution which impede his/her professional functioning. The supervisors should not be the direct provider of these activities for the supervisee.

3.19   When a training program conducts a personal growth or counseling experience involving relatively intimate self disclosure, care should be taken to eliminate or minimize potential role conflicts for faculty and/or agency supervisors who may conduct these experiences and who also serve as teachers, group leaders, and clinical directors.

3.20   Supervisors should use the following prioritized sequence in resolving conflicts among the needs of the client, the needs of the supervisee, and the needs of the program or agency. Insofar as the client must be protected, it should be understood that client welfare is usually subsumed in federal and state laws such that these statutes should be the first point of reference. Where laws and ethical standards are not present or are unclear, the good judgment of the supervisor should be guided by the following list.

   a. Relevant legal and ethical standards (e.g., duty to warn, state child abuse laws, etc.);
   b. Client welfare;
   c. Supervisee welfare;
   d. Supervisor welfare; and
   e. Program and/or agency service and administrative needs.

Source: Reprinted by permission of the Association for Counselor Education and Supervisor.

APPENDIX 19-B

Required Content Areas for Training in Clinical Supervision

Approved Clinical Supervisor (ACS)

1.   *Roles and Functions of Clinical Supervision*—Includes the unique purposes, goals, and foci of supervision, the appropriate conditions for supervision, and the distinction between supervision and other professional roles.

2.   *Models of Clinical Supervision*—Includes the major approaches for conceptualizing supervision (e.g., psychotherapy theory-based models of supervision, developmental models, and social models).

3.   *Counselor Development*—Includes topics such as individual learning styles, cognitive developmental levels, differences in experience levels, stages of counselor development, and critical transition points, as well as how to create an appropriate educational environment or climate based on developmental differences.

4.   *Methods and Techniques in Clinical Supervision*—Includes supervision methods for assessing and intervening with supervisees (e.g., audiotape review, live supervision, self-report), as well as the appropriate use of, and benefits and limitations of, each supervision method.

5.   *Supervisory Relationship Issues*—Includes the inter- and intrapersonal variables that affect supervision such as the parameters of a working alliance, conflict within supervision, supervisee anxiety, social influence, and parallel process.

6.   *Cultural Issues in Supervision*—Includes the implications of cultural differences and/or similarities between supervisee and supervisor such as race, gender, sexual orientation, and belief systems, and how these impact the process and outcome of supervision.

7.   *Group Supervision*—Includes topics such as the structure and processes of group supervision, the unique tasks of the supervisor in the group context, ground rules and stages of group supervision, and the advantages and limitations of the group modality.

8.   *Legal and Ethical Issues*—Includes major ethical and legal tenets that affect supervision such as due process, confidentiality, informed consent, dual relationships, competence, duty to warn, and direct and vicarious liability, and the implications of these tenets for supervisees, clients, and the supervisor.

9.   *Evaluation*—Includes studies that address the role of evaluation as central to supervision, criteria for evaluation, sources of feedback, the process and outcomes of evaluation, and the role of documentation in evaluation, as well as procedures for the evaluation of the supervision experience.

Source: Reprinted with permission of the National Board for Certified Counselors, Inc. and Affiliates, 3 Terrace Way, Suite D., Greensboro, NC 27403-3660.

APPENDIX 19-C

ACS Standards for the Ethical Practice of Clinical Supervision

In addition to following the NBCC Code of Ethics pertaining to the practice of professional counseling, clinical supervisors shall:

1.   Ensure that supervisees inform clients of their professional status (e.g., intern) and of all conditions of supervision.

Supervisors need to ensure that supervisees inform their clients of any status other than being fully qualified for independent practice of licensed. For example, supervisees need to inform their clients if they are a student, intern, trainee or, if licensed with restrictions, the nature of those restrictions (e.g., associate or conditional). In addition, clients must be informed of the requirements of supervision (e.g., the audiotaping of all counseling sessions for purposes of supervision).

2.   Ensure that clients have been informed of their rights to confidentiality and privileged communication when applicable. Clients also should be informed of the limits of confidentiality and privileged communication.

The general limits of confidentiality are when harm to self or others is threatened; when the abuse of children, elders or disabled persons is suspected, and in cases when the court compels the counselor to testify and break confidentiality. These are generally accepted limits to confidentiality and privileged communication, but they may be modified by state or federal statute.

3.   Inform supervisees about the process of supervision, including supervision goals, case management procedures, and the supervisor's preferred supervision model(s).

4.   Keep and secure supervision records and consider all information gained in supervision as confidential.

5.   Avoid all dual relationships with supervisees that may interfere with the supervisor's professional judgment or exploit the supervisee.

Although all dual relationships are not in and of themselves inappropriate, any sexual relationship is considered to be a violation. Sexual relationships mean sexual contact, sexual harassment, or sexual bias toward a supervisee by a supervisor.

6.   Establish procedures with their supervisees for handling crisis situations.

7.   Provide supervisees with adequate and timely feedback as part of an established evaluation plan.

8.   Render assistance to any supervisee who is unable to provide competent counseling services to clients.

9.   Intervene in any situation where the supervisee is impaired and the client is at risk.

10.   Refrain from endorsing an impaired supervisee when such impairment deems it unlikely that the supervisee can provide adequate counseling services.

11.   Refrain from offering supervision outside of their area(s) of competence.

12.   Ensure that supervisees are aware of the current ethical standards related to their professional practice, as well as legal standards that regulate the practice of counseling.

Current ethical standards would mean standards published by the National Board for Certified Counselors (NBCC) and other appropriate entities such as the American Counseling Association (ACA). In addition, it is the supervisor's responsibility to ensure that the supervisee is aware that state and federal laws might regulate the practice of counseling and to inform the supervisee of key laws that affect counseling in the supervisee's jurisdiction.

13. Engage supervisees in an examination of cultural issues that might affect supervision and/or counseling.

14. Ensure that both supervisees and clients are aware of their rights and of due process procedures.

ADOPTED BY THE NBCC BOARD OF DIRECTORS: June 12, 1998

Source: Reprinted with permission of the National Board for Certified Counselors, Inc. and Affiliates, 3 Terrace Way, Suite D., Greensboro, NC 27403-3660.

PART VI
Conclusion

20.   The Ethical Professional Counselor

CHAPTER 20

The Ethical Professional Counselor

Objectives

■ ■ ■ ■ ■ ■ ■ ■ ■ ■ ■

After reading this chapter, you should be able to:

- Describe ethical practice in counseling.
- Provide current statistics on ethical complaint adjudication.
- Explain what a counselor should do when confronted with an allegation of ethical misconduct.
- Describe the counselor's response to an ethical challenge in the context of potential legal and professional scrutiny.
- Explain the consequences for clients who are victims of unethical professional conduct.

■ ■ ■ ■ ■ ■ ■ ■ ■ ■ ■

INTRODUCTION

The study of ethics is like a journey. After an individual first reads a code of ethics, he or she may feel confident about his or her knowledge and have a sense that nothing can create a serious ethical crisis in his or her professional life. However, as the journey progresses, it becomes clearer that the practice of counseling is complex. Often, no easy answers emerge. At the end of the journey, there is the realization that ethical dilemmas do arise, and they challenge even the most sophisticated and ethically sensitive practitioner.

No professional is immune to ethical dilemmas—no matter how ethically sensitive counselors may be, circumstances will always arise that place them in a quandary. It is important, however, that counselors recognize when they are facing a serious ethical challenge. With such recognition, wise counselors protect themselves from a naive decision and a possible breach of ethical standards.

No professional is immune from being accused of ethical misconduct. Complaints against mental health professionals have increased dramatically in recent years. Bass et al. (1996) reported a 500 percent increase in disciplinary actions by state and provincial licensing boards in psychology over a 10-year period. They stated:

Box 20.1   Exploring the Codes

What sections of the ACA and APA codes address how to resolve ethical dilemmas?
What sections of the ACA and APA ethical codes specifically address how to report ethical violations?

A wide range of behaviors and practices may lead to disciplinary or legal action before a regulatory board, professional association, or court of law. . . . Common problem areas include (a) competence, (b) informed consent and confidentiality, (c) dual relationships, and (d) financial arrangements. (p. 71)

Even counselor educators are concerned about the ethics of educating counselors (Schwab & Neukrug, 1994). Clients and students of counseling are becoming more sophisticated about their rights. Licensure and regulatory boards are more experienced at addressing complaints, and there may be a tendency among licensure board members to assume guilt rather than innocence when a licensed professional is accused (Peterson, 2001). American society is also a litigious culture. It can be expected that a good percentage of counselors will be accused formally of unethical or illegal practice during their careers. Innocent or not, the consequences can be serious. Professional careers can be ruined by poor decisions made in the moments of an ethical dilemma or in the face of an ethical complaint.

CONSEQUENCES OF A BREACH OF ETHICS FOR THE COUNSELOR

The professional consequences of a breach of an ethical standard can range from no formal repercussions to serious repercussions, such as professional and personal censure and the loss of a license to practice. Chauvin and Remley (1996) recommended that once confronted with an allegation of unethical conduct, it is wise for counselors not to discuss the complaint openly with family or friends, to contact their malpractice insurance carrier, and to retain the services of an attorney. Chauvin and Remley stated:

The immediate reaction of most counselors would be shock and disbelief accompanied by deep sorrow, embarrassment, or extreme anger, or very likely a combina-

tion of all three. A first inclination of most counselors would be to call a best friend or family member and describe the details of the accusation and lament the injustice of what has been alleged. A lawyer most likely would advise against such a response. (p. 565)

To consult other individuals (for personal rather than professional reasons) with details of a client's allegation of impropriety is, in effect, a breach of the client's confidentiality and/or privacy; such action essentially compounds an already tenuous professional situation. Personal needs must be dealt with in a way that will not complicate the situation. Chauvin and Remley (1996) recommended that counselors suffering serious emotional pain over an allegation of unethical behavior should seek confidential treatment by mental health professionals. Even then, what is said should be said carefully, because the mental health professional may not be able to guarantee privileged communications in certain cases (especially those of a criminal nature).

Revelation of serious unethical practice can be devastating to the professional—guilt may prevent an unfettered return to practice. Remorseful counselors will be faced with guilt over possible damage done to any victims involved in the ethical breach. They may feel anxiety over the professional consequences related to licensure board or other certifying board actions. Legal problems may arise, such as malpractice. Malpractice insurance companies, valued by counselors as shields against financial ruin, may be untrusting and unwilling participants in defense of charges of unethical conduct.

There are always cases of professional counselors who are accused falsely of serious ethical misconduct, adding the issue of anger. If cleared of all allegations of misconduct, the exonerated counselors may have done themselves serious professional damage by having communicated to others about the complaint. Trusted colleagues from the past may view them with suspicion or disdain. For their own benefit, counselors are well advised to maintain the secrecy of an ethical complaint against them or be willing to suffer the consequence of professional stigmatization, even in cases of total innocence. In many cases, licensure or certifying bodies will keep the complaint confidential, unless legal standards exist that require public knowledge or public hearing of such complaints (Chauvin & Remley, 1996). It is possible that the complaint will be dismissed by the licensure board as unfounded, without merit, or poorly supported. In cases in which a certifying or licensing authority dismisses a case, the dismissal may signify the end of the charge, unless the client brings legal action (e.g., malpractice charges). According to a 1994 report of the ACA Ethics Committee (Garcia, Glosoff, & Smith, 1994), 32 complaints were processed, but only 11 decisions were made on those complaints. Of the 11 decisions, eight were decisions of "no violation." For the reporting period of 1 July 1999 to 30 June 2000, the ACA Ethics Committee reported that it received five complaints, and none of those complaints was accepted for adjudication (Brown, 2001). Brown (2001) stated: "All cases were denied adjudication due to lack of jurisdiction, lack of substance, or lack of response by claimants to requests for additional information" (p. 251). In effect, counselors should not panic; they should address complaints as a professional faced with a matter of professional business. If personal stress somehow affects the practitioner's judgment, professional counsel should be sought from an attorney and a mental health professional.

CONSEQUENCES OF A BREACH OF ETHICAL STANDARDS FOR THE CLIENT

Unethical situations are even more difficult for a client who suffers an injustice. Victimized clients have to deal with the unacceptable actions of the counselor, but they must also deal with a professional system that may be reluctant to discipline one of its own. The legal system may also become involved, and once the legal wheels begin to roll, it is difficult to steer a new direction. Financial and personal commitments may place a strain on the victim of unethical practice. In some cases, there may be degrees of embarrassment or public humiliation. Just the revelation of treatment by a mental health professional may be embarrassing to some individuals. The conduct of the professional also may be embarrassing to the client or may inadvertently or inappropriately reflect on the morals or judgment of the client. Friendships may be strained or destroyed. In

the end, the brave victims of serious unethical practice who file formal complaints may place themselves in positions of double or multiple victimization.

FILING A COMPLAINT TO A LICENSURE AUTHORITY

Procedures for filing complaints about unethical practitioners in the mental health field are fairly standard. Licensed professionals practicing in a particular state are bound legally to the ethical and administrative standards of practice as adopted by statute and regulation in that state. These standards and disciplinary procedures are usually available to the public through the state's department of regulation or licensure. Related to psychology licensure, Reaves (1996) stated:

> Virtually all jurisdictions require that complaints concerning psychologists' behavior be in writing. Unless a complaint is determined to be frivolous or made in bad faith, an investigation ensues. In some jurisdictions, trained investigators are employed to perform this task. In smaller jurisdictions, a board member may be assigned as an investigating officer. The method used to investigate a complaint varies with the type or substance of the complaint. For example, an allegation that a licensee has been convicted of a felony would involve obtaining documentation from the court where the conviction occurred, whereas an allegation of sexual intimacies with a client would likely involve interviews and possible collection of other evidence. (p. 102)

Reaves further noted that a license to practice a profession is considered a "property" and, therefore, a license cannot be taken away without due process of law.

If a professional is accused of unethical conduct and simply admits to the conduct, the case is uncontested. Settlement on such cases may be a matter of the regulatory board's disposition—in such cases the board may make a decision as to the consequences of the unethical conduct. Contested cases, wherein the professional essentially pleads innocent to some or all of the charges, typically leads to a civil court (versus criminal court) hearing or legal proceeding. In such cases, a hearing officer is present and attorneys may be involved. In some jurisdictions, hearings may be open to the public (Chauvin & Remley, 1996). Chauvin and Remley (1996) stated, "If a hearing is held, the complainant, the witnesses, and the accused counselor would be given an opportunity to present their positions and would be questioned by the board members"

(p. 565). After a hearing, the board most typically makes a decision, which could include the following consequences: reprimand, probation, suspension of a certificate or license, or revocation of a certificate or a license. The counselor or psychologist is allowed to appeal. According to Chauvin and Remley (1996), "After an appeal, if the counselor still disagrees with the board's findings, he or she could sue the board in court in an effort to have the board's decision overturned" (p. 565).

Clients or involved laypersons who desire to file complaints should be provided adequate information to file such complaints. Responsible counselors who are knowledgeable about the questionable or unethical practices of colleagues are obligated by law (in most cases) and by mandatory professional ethical standards to file complaints. Filing of a complaint is required if direct, informal attempts to resolve the issue with the offending professional fail or if the conduct is either serious or repetitive.

It is standard procedure for a complaint to be filed in writing. Any member of the public or the profession may file a complaint, regardless of residence (inside or outside of the state of the alleged ethical violation). Complaints can be based on personal knowledge, public record, or information received from third-party sources. The complainant and the individual filing the complaint (often the same person) must be identified fully in the complaint by name and address and in writing. Complaints typically are logged by the date and nature of the complaint. Each complaint will be acknowledged by the board in writing and the complainant will be notified of the ultimate disposition of the complaint. Complaints may be dismissed on several grounds, including insufficient evidence or information, noncooperation of the complainant, or inability to prove or to refute charges due to lack of probable corroboration (e.g., hearsay evidence only).

Complainants to licensure boards may file complaints against a suspected unethical practitioner simultaneously with the professional associations to which the practitioner belongs (e.g., the ACA or APA). Counselors are obligated to disclose information about their professional qualifications and affiliations to interested parties. Withholding such information, especially to clients, may be considered a breach of ethics in and of itself, depending on state statute or professional ethical standards. The important issue is the availability of information so that complainants can make informed complaints to appropriate authorities; concerned individuals should not be impeded in their attempts to file complaints.

Counselors who are guilty of unethical conduct and who have the intention of practicing again have a responsibility to "rehabilitate" themselves and to seek guidance so they never repeat their actions (Chauvin & Remley, 1996). There is nothing more repulsive to the public or to professional colleagues than a repeat offender, especially in cases of serious ethical misconduct. In those instances, it becomes obvious that the unethical practitioner has become a predator, is incompetent, or is simply interested in personal gain. Such activity reflects badly on the profession of counseling, and all professionals have an obligation to prevent such activity.

THE DEVELOPMENT OF THE ETHICAL PROFESSIONAL COUNSELOR

Professional associations such as the ACA and the APA have a special role in helping to develop ethical behavior in practitioners. In a survey of certified counselors who were asked to rate 16 sources of ethical information (Gibson & Pope, 1993), the ACA ethical code, the ACA Ethics Committee, and the ACA *Journal of Counseling and Development* were given the highest ratings. But good information may not be enough. The development of the ethically sensitive counselor is a complex process. It is not simply a matter of information, education, supervision, and training. As Pettifor (1996) stated:

> Psychologists who maintain high levels of professional conduct are encouraged by aspirational ethics to practice appropriately and . . . the measures they take to maintain competence are voluntary and targeted to specific professional needs. Aspirational ethics are based on moral principles that always place the well-being of the other, the consumer, above self-interest, as opposed to codes of conduct that define minimal levels of acceptable behavior. (pp. 91–92)

Professional training may not be enough. The works of Kohlberg (1964, 1971, 1981) demonstrated that the application of moral thinking stems from a developmental process. It may be that training, no matter how targeted to moral development, may not inspire moral choice adequately in certain counselors. In the end, even the most trained counselor or psychologist may choose to act unethically. Therefore, it is as important to study what prevents unethical conduct as it is to study the correlates of unethical conduct. It may be that what prevents unethical conduct, as Pettifor implied, is a moral standard and moral directives that supersede even the most powerful motivations to breach an accepted ethical standard. Counselors must have the constitution to make moral choices when other needs enter into decisions.

One approach, deriving from the "positive psychology" movement (Seligman & Csikszentmihalyi, 2000) is to address ethical issues in a positive light—focusing on building strengths against ethical breaches rather than approaching ethics as a crisis and remedial concern. Handelsman, Knapp, and Gottlieb (2002) make a compelling argument for positive ethics:

> Our view of positive ethics encompasses a broad context of ethical behavior—including aspirational elements that range from the personal to the societal in nature—which goes beyond a focus on rules and risk. We propose that the morality of professional actions can be explored without emphasizing the prohibitions or potential sanctions found within psychology's disciplinary codes. At the same time, we are not advocating the abandonment of ethical rules and prohibitions; they do have a basis in morality that psychologists need to understand. Likewise, psychologists should know the laws that govern the practice of psychology and the ways to reduce legal risk. We are suggesting that whereas rules and good risk management strategies are not antithetical to positive ethics, they are not sufficient to ensure optimal ethical practice. What is necessary is an awareness of several interacting perspectives. (p. 734)

Handelsman et al. (2002) recommended "seven themes of positive ethics," which are: (a) values and virtues; (b) sensitivity and integration; (c) ethics as ongoing self-care; (d) ethical reasoning and decision-making; (e) appreciation of the moral traditions underlying ethical principles; (f) prevention of misconduct and promotion of positive behaviors; and (g) sensitivity to larger professional contexts. With the positive psychology movement, there is an opportunity to redefine professional ethics around a positive developmental process rather than a remedial post-crisis event.

On the other hand, some might argue that no matter how sophisticated the profession becomes, there always will be practitioners who consciously breach or challenge the limits of ethical behavior. Also, if a profession is struggling—that is, if trained professionals are having difficulty making a living—temptations to sell clients short of ethical services may become more common. In this light, it is important for the leaders of the profession to ensure that ethical professionals are rewarded adequately in their professional practices; otherwise, the fringe ethical behaviors of desperate practitioners may erode the reputation of the profession as a whole.

Ideally, counselors should make the best of their education to take ethics to heart and develop a moral stance. A profession devoted to helping others should facilitate a personal, as well as academic, interest in defining what is right and wrong in the treatment of individuals in need. The clients of counselors deserve no less.

CHAPTER SUMMARY

This text has been organized to provide the student of counseling and practicing counselors with a clear and concise overview of ethical issues in counseling and psychology. The intent of the book is to provide a thorough and scholarly foundation, defining ethical concepts and practice, legal issues, methods for clarifying values, decision-making models, and contemporaneous and emerging issues. Additionally, the book addresses issues related to some of the largest specialties of counseling. It is hoped that this text will inspire ethically sensitive counselors who will reflect before acting and who will consult with educated colleagues at those moments when ethical dilemmas arise. In the end, ethical counselors are those who have the best interests of their clients at heart, and who also respect the rights that derive from being professionals.

REFERENCES

Bass, L. J., DeMers, S. T., Ogloff, J. R., Peterson, C., Pettifor, J. L., Reaves, R. P., Retfalvi, T., Simon, N. P., Sinclair, C., & Tipton, R. M. (1996). *Professional conduct and discipline in psychology.* Washington, D.C.: American Psychological Association.

Brown, S. P. (2001). Report of the ACA Ethics Committee: 1999–2000. *Journal of Counseling and Development, 79,* 251–252.

Chauvin, J. C., & Remley, T. P. (1996). Responding to allegations of unethical conduct. *Journal of Counseling and Development, 74,* 563–568.

Garcia, J., Glosoff, H. L., & Smith, J. L. (1994). Report of the ACA Ethics Committee: 1993–1994. *Journal of Counseling and Development, 73,* 253–256.

Gibson, W. T., & Pope, K. S. (1993). The ethics of counseling: A national survey of certified counselors. *Journal of Counseling and Development, 71,* 330–336.

Handelsman, M. M., Knapp, S., & Gottlieb, M. C. (2002). Positive ethics. In C. R. Snyder & S. J. Lopez (Eds.), *Handbook of positive psychology* (pp. 731–744). New York: Oxford University Press.

Kohlberg, L. (1964). Development of moral character and moral ecology. In M. L. Hoffman & L. W. Hoffman (Eds.), *Review of child development research* (Vol. 1). New York: Russell Sage Foundation.

Kohlberg, L. (1971). Moral development and the education of adolescents. In R. Purnell (Ed.), *Adolescents and the American high school*. New York: Holt, Rinehart & Winston.

Kohlberg, L. (1981). *Philosophy of moral development*. San Francisco: Harper & Row.

Peterson, M. B. (2001). Recognizing concerns about how some licensing boards are treat-

ing psychologists. *Professional Psychology: Research and Practice, 32*, 339–340.

Pettifor, J. L. (1996). Maintaining professional conduct in daily practice. In Bass et al. (Eds.), *Professional conduct and discipline in psychology* (pp. 91–100). Washington, D.C.: American Psychological Association.

Reaves, R. P. (1996). Enforcement of codes of conduct by regulatory boards and professional associations. In Bass et al.

(Eds.), *Professional conduct and discipline in psychology* (pp. 101–108). Washington, D.C.: American Psychological Association.

Schwab, R., & Neukrug, E. (1994). A survey of counselor educators' ethical concerns. *Counseling and Values, 39,* 42–54.

Seligman, M. E. P., & Csikszentmihalyi, M. (2000). Positive psychology: An introduction. *American Psychologist, 55,* 5–14.

APPENDIX A

ACA Code of Ethics and Standards of Practice

ACA CODE OF ETHICS PREAMBLE

The American Counseling Association is an educational, scientific, and professional organization whose members are dedicated to the enhancement of human development throughout the life-span. Association members recognize diversity in our society and embrace a cross-cultural approach in support of the worth, dignity, potential, and uniqueness of each individual.

The specification of a code of ethics enables the association to clarify to current and future members, and to those served by members, the nature of the ethical responsibilities held in common by its members. As the code of ethics of the association, this document establishes principles that define the ethical behavior of association members. All members of the American Counseling Association are required to adhere to the Code of Ethics and the Standards of Practice. The Code of Ethics will serve as the basis for processing ethical complaints initiated against members of the association.

ACA CODE OF ETHICS

Section A: The Counseling Relationship

A.1. Client Welfare

a. *Primary Responsibility.* The primary responsibility of counselors is to respect the dignity and to promote the welfare of clients.
b. *Positive Growth and Development.* Counselors encourage client growth and development in ways that foster the clients' interest and welfare; counselors avoid fostering dependent counseling relationships.
c. *Counseling Plans.* Counselors and their clients work jointly in devising integrated, individual counseling plans that offer reasonable promise of success and are consistent with abilities and circumstances of clients. Counselors and clients regularly review counseling plans to ensure their continued viability and effectiveness, respecting clients' freedom of choice. (See A.3.b.)
d. *Family Involvement.* Counselors recognize that families are usually important in clients' lives and strive to enlist family understanding and involvement as a positive resource, when appropriate.
e. *Career and Employment Needs.* Counselors work with their clients in considering employment in jobs and circumstances that are consistent with the clients' overall abilities, vocational limitations, physical restrictions, general temperament, interest and aptitude patterns, social skills, education, general qualifications, and other relevant characteristics and needs.

Counselors neither place nor participate in placing clients in positions that will result in damaging the interest and the welfare of clients, employers, or the public.

A.2. Respecting Diversity

a. *Nondiscrimination.* Counselors do not condone or engage in discrimination based on age, color, culture, disability, ethnic group, gender, race, religion, sexual orientation, marital status, or socioeconomic status. (See C.5.a., C.5.b., and D.1.i.)

b. *Respecting Differences.* Counselors will actively attempt to understand the diverse cultural backgrounds of the clients with whom they work. This includes, but is not limited to, learning how the counselor's own cultural/ethnic/racial identity impacts her or his values and beliefs about the counseling process. (See E.8. and F.2.i.)

A.3. Client Rights

a. *Disclosure to Clients.* When counseling is initiated, and throughout the counseling process as necessary, counselors inform clients of the purposes, goals, techniques, procedures, limitations, potential risks, and benefits of services to be performed, and other pertinent information. Counselors take steps to ensure that clients understand the implications of diagnosis, the intended use of tests and reports, fees, and billing arrangements. Clients have the right to expect confidentiality and to be provided with an explanation of its limitations, including supervision and/or treatment team professionals; to obtain clear information about their case records; to participate in the ongoing counseling plans; and to refuse any recommended services and be advised of the consequences of such refusal. (See E.5.a. and G.2.)

b. *Freedom of Choice.* Counselors offer clients the freedom to choose whether to enter into a counseling relationship and to determine which professional(s) will provide counseling. Restrictions that limit choices of clients are fully explained. (See A.1.c.)

c. *Inability to Give Consent.* When counseling minors or persons unable to give voluntary informed consent, counselors act in these clients' best interests. (See B.3.)

A.4. Clients Served by Others

If a client is receiving services from another mental health professional, counselors, with client consent, inform the professional persons already involved and develop clear agreements to avoid confusion and conflict for the client. (See C.6.c.)

A.5. Personal Needs and Values

a. *Personal Needs.* In the counseling relationship, counselors are aware of the intimacy and responsibilities inherent in the counseling relationship, maintain respect for clients, and avoid actions that seek to meet their personal needs at the expense of clients.

b. *Personal Values.* Counselors are aware of their own values, attitudes, beliefs, and behaviors and how these apply in a diverse society, and avoid imposing their values on clients. (See C.5.a.)

A.6. Dual Relationships

a. *Avoid When Possible.* Counselors are aware of their influential positions with respect to clients, and they avoid exploiting the trust and dependency of clients. Counselors make every effort to avoid dual relationships with clients that could impair professional judgment or increase the risk of harm to clients. (Examples of such relationships include, but are not limited to, familial, social, financial, business, or close personal relationships with clients.) When a dual relationship cannot be avoided, counselors take appropriate professional precautions such as informed consent, consultation, supervision, and documentation to ensure that judgment is not impaired and no exploitation occurs. (See F.1.b.)

b. *Superior/Subordinate Relationships.* Counselors do not accept as clients superiors or subordinates with whom they have administrative, supervisory, or evaluative relationships.

A.7. Sexual Intimacies With Clients

a. *Current Clients.* Counselors do not have any type of sexual intimacies with clients and do not counsel persons with whom they have had a sexual relationship.

b. *Former Clients.* Counselors do not engage in sexual intimacies with former clients within a minimum of 2 years after terminating the counseling relationship. Counselors who engage in such relationship after 2 years following termination have the responsibility to examine and document thoroughly that such relations did not have an exploitative nature, based on factors such as duration of counseling, amount of time since counseling, termination circumstances, client's personal history and mental status, adverse impact on the client, and actions by the counselor suggesting a plan to initiate a sexual relationship with the client after termination.

A.8. Multiple Clients

When counselors agree to provide counseling services to two or more persons who have a relationship (such as husband and wife, or parents and children), counselors clarify at the outset which person or persons are clients and the nature of the relationships they will have with each involved person. If it becomes apparent that counselors may be called upon to perform potentially conflicting roles, they clarify, adjust, or withdraw from roles appropriately. (See B.2. and B.4.d.)

A.9. Group Work

a. *Screening.* Counselors screen prospective group counseling/therapy participants. To the extent possible, counselors select members whose needs and goals are compatible with goals of the group, who will not impede the group process, and whose well-being will not be jeopardized by the group experience.

b. *Protecting Clients.* In a group setting, counselors take reasonable precautions to protect clients from physical or psychological trauma.

A.10. Fees and Bartering (See D.3.a. and D.3.b.)

a. *Advance Understanding.* Counselors clearly explain to clients, prior to entering the counseling relationship, all financial arrangements related to professional services including the use of collection agencies or legal measures for nonpayment. (A.11.c.)

b. *Establishing Fees.* In establishing fees for professional counseling services, counselors consider the financial status of clients and locality. In the event that the established fee structure is inappropriate for a client, assistance is provided in attempting to find comparable services of acceptable cost. (See A.10.d., D.3.a., and D.3.b.)

c. *Bartering Discouraged.* Counselors ordinarily refrain from accepting goods or services from clients in return for counseling services because such arrangements create inherent potential for conflicts, exploitation, and distortion of the professional relationship. Counselors may participate in bartering only if the relationship is not exploitative, if the client requests it, if a clear written contract is established, and if such arrangements are an accepted practice among professionals in the community. (See A.6.a.)

d. *Pro Bono Service.* Counselors contribute to society by devoting a portion of their professional activity to services for which there is little or no financial return (pro bono).

A.11. Termination and Referral

a. *Abandonment Prohibited.* Counselors do not abandon or neglect clients in counseling. Counselors assist in making appropriate arrangements for the continuation of treatment, when necessary, during interruptions such as vacations, and following termination.

b. *Inability to Assist Clients.* If counselors determine an inability to be of professional assistance to clients, they avoid entering or immediately terminate a counseling relationship. Counselors are knowledgeable about referral resources and suggest appropriate alternatives. If clients decline the suggested referral, counselors should discontinue the relationship.

c. *Appropriate Termination.* Counselors terminate a counseling relationship, securing client agreement when possible, when it is reasonably clear that the client is no longer benefiting, when services are no longer required, when counseling no longer serves the client's needs or interests, when clients do not pay fees charged, or when agency or institution limits do not allow provision of further counseling services. (See A.10.b. and C.2.g.)

A.12. Computer Technology

a. *Use of Computers.* When computer applications are used in counseling services, counselors ensure that (1) the client is intellectually, emotionally, and physically capable of using the computer application; (2) the computer application is appropriate for the needs of the client; (3) the client understands the purpose and operation of the computer applications; and (4) a follow-up of client use of a computer application is provided to correct possible misconceptions, discover inappropriate use, and assess subsequent needs.

b. *Explanation of Limitations.* Counselors ensure that clients are provided information as a part of the counseling relationship that adequately explains the limitations of computer technology.

c. *Access to Computer Applications.* Counselors provide for equal access to computer applications in counseling services. (See A.2.a.)

Section B: Confidentiality

B.1. Right to Privacy

a. *Respect for Privacy.* Counselors respect their clients right to privacy and avoid illegal and unwarranted disclosures of confidential information. (See A.3.a. and B.6.a.)

b. *Client Waiver.* The right to privacy may be waived by the client or his or her legally recognized representative.

c. *Exceptions.* The general requirement that counselors keep information confidential does not apply when disclosure is required to prevent clear and imminent danger to the client or others or when legal requirements demand that confidential information be revealed. Counselors consult with other professionals when in doubt as to the validity of an exception.

d. *Contagious, Fatal Diseases.* A counselor who receives information confirming that a client has a disease commonly known to be both communicable and fatal is justified in disclosing information to an identifiable third party, who by his or her relationship with the client is at a high risk of contracting the disease. Prior to making a disclosure the counselor should ascertain that the client has not already informed the third party about his or her disease and that the client is not intending to inform the third party in the immediate future. (See B.1.c and B.1.f.)

e. *Court-Ordered Disclosure.* When court ordered to release confidential information without a client's permission, counselors request to the court that the disclosure not be required due to potential harm to the client or counseling relationship. (See B.1.c.)

f. *Minimal Disclosure.* When circumstances require the disclosure of confidential information, only essential information is revealed. To the extent possible, clients are informed before confidential information is disclosed.

g. *Explanation of Limitations.* When counseling is initiated and throughout the counseling process as necessary, counselors inform clients of the limitations of confidentiality and identify foreseeable situations in which confidentiality must be breached. (See G.2.a.)

h. *Subordinates.* Counselors make every effort to ensure that privacy and confidentiality of clients are maintained by subordinates including employees, supervisees, clerical assistants, and volunteers. (See B.1.a.)

i. *Treatment Teams*. If client treatment will involve a continued review by a treatment team, the client will be informed of the team's existence and composition.

B.2. Groups and Families

a. *Group Work*. In group work, counselors clearly define confidentiality and the parameters for the specific group being entered, explain its importance, and discuss the difficulties related to confidentiality involved in group work. The fact that confidentiality cannot be guaranteed is clearly communicated to group members.

b. *Family Counseling*. In family counseling, information about one family member cannot be disclosed to another member without permission. Counselors protect the privacy rights of each family member. (See A.8., B.3., and B.4.d.)

B.3. Minor or Incompetent Clients

When counseling clients who are minors or individuals who are unable to give voluntary, informed consent, parents or guardians may be included in the counseling process as appropriate. Counselors act in the best interests of clients and take measures to safeguard confidentiality. (See A.3.c.)

B.4. Records

a. *Requirement of Records*. Counselors maintain records necessary for rendering professional services to their clients and as required by laws, regulations, or agency or institution procedures.

b. *Confidentiality of Records*. Counselors are responsible for securing the safety and confidentiality of any counseling records they create, maintain, transfer, or destroy whether the records are written, taped, computerized, or stored in any other medium. (See B.1.a.)

c. *Permission to Record or Observe*. Counselors obtain permission from clients prior to electronically recording or observing sessions. (See A.3.a.)

d. *Client Access*. Counselors recognize that counseling records are kept for the benefit of clients, and therefore provide access to records and copies of records when requested by competent clients, unless the records contain information that may be misleading and detrimental to the client. In situations involving multiple clients, access to records is limited to those parts of records that do not include confidential information related to another client. (See A.8., B.1.a., and B.2.b.)

e. *Disclosure or Transfer*. Counselors obtain written permission from clients to disclose or transfer records to legitimate third parties unless exceptions to confidentiality exist as listed in Section B.1. Steps are taken to ensure that receivers of counseling records are sensitive to their confidential nature.

B.5. Research and Training

a. *Data Disguise Required*. Use of data derived from counseling relationships for purposes of training, research, or publication is confined to content that is disguised to ensure the anonymity of the individuals involved. (See B.1.g. and G.3.d.)

b. *Agreement for Identification*. Identification of a client in a presentation or publication is permissible only when the client has reviewed the material and has agreed to its presentation or publication. (See G.3.d.)

B.6. Consultation

a. *Respect for Privacy*. Information obtained in a consulting relationship is discussed for professional purposes only with persons clearly concerned with the case. Written and oral reports present data germane to the purposes of the consultation, and every effort is made to protect client identity and avoid undue invasion of privacy.

b. *Cooperating Agencies*. Before sharing information, counselors make efforts to ensure that there are defined policies in other agencies serving the counselor's clients that effectively protect the confidentiality of information.

Section C: Professional Responsibility

C.1. Standards Knowledge

Counselors have a responsibility to read, understand, and follow the Code of Ethics and the Standards of Practice.

C.2. Professional Competence

a. *Boundaries of Competence*. Counselors practice only within the boundaries of their competence, based on their education, training, supervised experience, state and national professional credentials, and appropriate professional experience. Counselors will demonstrate a commitment to gain knowledge, personal awareness, sensitivity, and skills pertinent to working with a diverse client population.

b. *New Specialty Areas of Practice*. Counselors practice in specialty areas new to them only after appropriate education, training, and supervised experience. While developing skills in new specialty areas, counselors take steps to ensure the competence of their work and to protect others from possible harm.

c. *Qualified for Employment*. Counselors accept employment only for positions for which they are qualified by education, training, supervised experience, state and national professional credentials, and appropriate professional experience. Counselors hire for professional counseling positions only individuals who are qualified and competent.

d. *Monitor Effectiveness*. Counselors continually monitor their effectiveness as professionals and take steps to improve when necessary. Counselors in private practice take reasonable steps to seek out peer supervision to evaluate their efficacy as counselors.

e. *Ethical Issues Consultation*. Counselors take reasonable steps to consult with other counselors or related professionals when they have questions regarding their ethical obligations or professional practice. (See H.1.)

f. *Continuing Education*. Counselors recognize the need for continuing education to maintain a reasonable level of awareness of current scientific and professional information in their fields of activity. They take steps to maintain competence in the skills they use, are open to new procedures, and keep current with the diverse and/or special populations with whom they work.

g. *Impairment.* Counselors refrain from offering or accepting professional services when their physical, mental, or emotional problems are likely to harm a client or others. They are alert to the signs of impairment, seek assistance for problems, and, if necessary, limit, suspend, or terminate their professional responsibilities. (See A.11.c.)

C.3. Advertising and Soliciting Clients

a. *Accurate Advertising.* There are no restrictions on advertising by counselors except those that can be specifically justified to protect the public from deceptive practices. Counselors advertise or represent their services to the public by identifying their credentials in an accurate manner that is not false, misleading, deceptive, or fraudulent. Counselors may only advertise the highest degree earned which is in counseling or a closely related field from a college or university that was accredited when the degree was awarded by one of the regional accrediting bodies recognized by the Council on Postsecondary Accreditation.

b. *Testimonials.* Counselors who use testimonials do not solicit them from clients or other persons who, because of their particular circumstances, may be vulnerable to undue influence.

c. *Statements by Others.* Counselors make reasonable efforts to ensure that statements made by others about them or the profession of counseling are accurate.

d. *Recruiting Through Employment.* Counselors do not use their places of employment or institutional affiliation to recruit or gain clients, supervisees, or consultees for their private practices. (See C.5.e.)

e. *Products and Training Advertisements.* Counselors who develop products related to their profession or conduct workshops or training events ensure that the advertisements concerning these products or events are accurate and disclose adequate information for consumers to make informed choices.

f. *Promoting to Those Served.* Counselors do not use counseling, teaching, training, or supervisory relationships to promote their products or training events in a manner that is deceptive or would exert undue influence on individuals who may be vulnerable. Counselors may adopt textbooks they have authored for instruction purposes.

g. *Professional Association Involvement.* Counselors actively participate in local, state, and national associations that foster the development and improvement of counseling.

C.4. Credentials

a. *Credentials Claimed.* Counselors claim or imply only professional credentials possessed and are responsible for correcting any known misrepresentations of their credentials by others. Professional credentials include graduate degrees in counseling or closely related mental health fields, accreditation of graduate programs, national voluntary certifications, government-issued certifications or licenses, ACA professional membership, or any other credential that might indicate to the public specialized knowledge or expertise in counseling.

b. *ACA Professional Membership.* ACA professional members may announce to the public their membership status. Regular members may not announce their ACA membership in a manner that might imply they are credentialed counselors.

c. *Credential Guidelines.* Counselors follow the guidelines for use of credentials that have been established by the entities that issue the credentials.

d. *Misrepresentation of Credentials.* Counselors do not attribute more to their credentials than the credentials represent, and do not imply that other counselors are not qualified because they do not possess certain credentials.

e. *Doctoral Degrees from Other Fields.* Counselors who hold a master's degree in counseling or a closely related mental health field, but hold a doctoral degree from other than counseling or a closely related field, do not use the title "Dr." in their practices and do not announce to the public in relation to their practice or status as a counselor that they hold a doctorate.

C.5. Public Responsibility

a. *Nondiscrimination.* Counselors do not discriminate against clients, students, or supervisees in a manner that has a negative impact based on their age, color, culture, disability, ethnic group, gender, race, religion, sexual orientation, or socioeconomic status, or for any other reason. (See A.2.a.)

b. *Sexual Harassment.* Counselors do not engage in sexual harassment. Sexual harassment is defined as sexual solicitation, physical advances, or verbal or nonverbal conduct that is sexual in nature, that occurs in connection with professional activities or roles, and that either (1) is unwelcome, is offensive, or creates a hostile workplace environment, and counselors know or are told this; or (2) is sufficiently severe or intense to be perceived as harassment to a reasonable person in the context. Sexual harassment can consist of a single intense or severe act or multiple persistent or pervasive acts.

c. *Reports to Third Parties.* Counselors are accurate, honest, and unbiased in reporting their professional activities and judgments to appropriate third parties including courts, health insurance companies, those who are the recipients of evaluation reports, and others. (See B.1.g.)

d. *Media Presentations.* When counselors provide advice or comment by means of public lectures, demonstrations, radio or television programs, prerecorded tapes, printed articles, mailed material, or other media, they take reasonable precautions to ensure that (1) the statements are based on appropriate professional counseling literature and practice; (2) the statements are otherwise consistent with the Code of Ethics and the Standards of Practice; and (3) the recipients of the information are not encouraged to infer that a professional counseling relationship has been established. (See C.6.b.)

e. *Unjustified Gains.* Counselors do not use their professional positions to seek or receive unjustified personal gains, sexual favors, unfair advantage, or unearned goods or services. (See C.3.d.)

C.6. Responsibility to Other Professionals

a. *Different Approaches.* Counselors are respectful of approaches to professional counseling that differ from their own. Counselors know and take into account the traditions and practices of other professional groups with which they work.

b. *Personal Public Statements.* When making personal statements in a public context, counselors clarify that they are speaking from their personal perspectives and that they are not speaking on behalf of all counselors or the profession. (See C.5.d.)

c. *Clients Served by Others.* When counselors learn that their clients are in a professional relationship with another mental health professional, they request release from clients to inform the other professionals and strive to establish positive and collaborative professional relationships. (See A.4.)

Section D: Relationships with Other Professionals

D.1. Relationships with Employers and Employees

a. *Role Definition.* Counselors define and describe for their employers and employees the parameters and levels of their professional roles.

b. *Agreements.* Counselors establish working agreements with supervisors, colleagues, and subordinates regarding counseling or clinical relationships, confidentiality, adherence to professional standards, distinction between public and private material, maintenance and dissemination of recorded information, work load, and accountability. Working agreements in each instance are specified and made known to those concerned.

c. *Negative Conditions.* Counselors alert their employers to conditions that may be potentially disruptive or damaging to the counselor's professional responsibilities or that may limit their effectiveness.

d. *Evaluation.* Counselors submit regularly to professional review and evaluation by their supervisor or the appropriate representative of the employer.

e. *In-Service.* Counselors are responsible for in-service development of self and staff.

f. *Goals.* Counselors inform their staff of goals and programs.

g. *Practices.* Counselors provide personnel and agency practices that respect and enhance the rights and welfare of each employee and recipient of agency services. Counselors strive to maintain the highest levels of professional services.

h. *Personnel Selection and Assignment.* Counselors select competent staff and assign responsibilities compatible with their skills and experiences.

i. *Discrimination.* Counselors, as either employers or employees, do not engage in or condone practices that are inhumane, illegal, or unjustifiable (such as considerations based on age, color, culture, disability, ethnic group, gender, race, religion, sexual orientation, or socioeconomic status) in hiring, promotion, or training. (See A.2.a. and C.5.b.)

j. *Professional Conduct.* Counselors have a responsibility both to clients and to the agency or institution within which services are performed to maintain high standards of professional conduct.

k. *Exploitative Relationships.* Counselors do not engage in exploitative relationships with individuals over whom they have supervisory, evaluative, or instructional control or authority.

l. *Employer Policies.* The acceptance of employment in an agency or institution implies that counselors are in agreement with its general policies and principles. Counselors strive to reach agreement with employers as to acceptable standards of conduct that allow for changes in institutional policy conducive to the growth and development of clients.

D.2. Consultation (See B.6.)

a. *Consultation as an Option.* Counselors may choose to consult with any other professionally competent persons about their clients. In choosing consultants, counselors avoid placing the consultant in a conflict of interest situation that would preclude the consultant being a proper party to the counselor's efforts to help the client. Should counselors be engaged in a work setting that compromises this consultation standard, they consult with other professionals whenever possible to consider justifiable alternatives.

b. *Consultant Competency.* Counselors are reasonably certain that they have or the organization represented has the necessary competencies and resources for giving the kind of consulting services needed and that appropriate referral resources are available.

c. *Understanding with Clients.* When providing consultation, counselors attempt to develop with their clients a clear understanding of problem definition, goals for change, and predicted consequences of interventions selected.

d. *Consultant Goals.* The consulting relationship is one in which client adaptability and growth toward self-direction are consistently encouraged and cultivated. (See A.1.b.)

D.3. Fees for Referral

a. *Accepting Fees from Agency Clients.* Counselors refuse a private fee or other remuneration for rendering services to persons who are entitled to such services through the counselor's employing agency or institution. The policies of a particular agency may make explicit provisions for agency clients to receive counseling services from members of its staff in private practice. In such instances, the clients must be informed of other options open to them should they seek private counseling services. (See A.10.a., A.11.b., and C.3.d.)

b. *Referral Fees.* Counselors do not accept a referral fee from other professionals.

D.4. Subcontractor Arrangements

When counselors work as subcontractors for counseling services for a third party, they have a duty to inform clients of the limitations of confidentiality that the organization may place on counselors in providing counseling services to clients. The limits of such confidentiality ordinarily are discussed as part of the intake session. (See B.1.e. and B.1.f.)

Section E: Evaluation, Assessment, and Interpretation

E.1. General

a. *Appraisal Techniques.* The primary purpose of educational and psychological assessment is to provide measures that are objective and interpretable in either comparative or absolute terms. Counselors recognize the need to interpret the statements in this section as applying to the whole range of appraisal techniques, including test and nontest data.

b. *Client Welfare.* Counselors promote the welfare and best interests of the client in the development, publication, and utilization of educational and psychological assessment techniques. They do not misuse assessment results and interpretations and take reasonable steps to prevent others from misusing the information these techniques provide. They respect the client's right to know the results, the interpretations made, and the bases for their conclusions and recommendations.

E.2. Competence to Use and Interpret Tests

a. *Limits of Competence.* Counselors recognize the limits of their competence and perform only those testing and assessment services for which they have been trained. They are familiar with reliability, validity, related standardization, error of measurement, and proper application of any technique utilized. Counselors using computer-based test interpretations are trained in the construct being measured and the specific instrument being used prior to using this type of computer application. Counselors take reasonable measures to ensure the proper use of psychological assessment techniques by persons under their supervision.

b. *Appropriate Use.* Counselors are responsible for the appropriate application, scoring, interpretation, and use of assessment instruments, whether they score and interpret such tests themselves or use computerized or other services.

c. *Decisions Based on Results.* Counselors responsible for decisions involving individuals or policies that are based on assessment results have a thorough understanding of educational and psychological measurement, including validation criteria, test research, and guidelines for test development and use.

d. *Accurate Information.* Counselors provide accurate information and avoid false claims or misconceptions when making statements about assessment instruments or techniques. Special efforts are made to avoid unwarranted connotations of such terms as IQ and grade equivalent scores. (See C.5.c.)

E.3. Informed Consent

a. *Explanation to Clients.* Prior to assessment, counselors explain the nature and purposes of assessment and the specific use of results in language the client (or other legally authorized person on behalf of the client) can understand, unless an explicit exception to this right has been agreed upon in advance. Regardless of whether scoring and interpretation are completed by counselors, by assistants, or by computer or other outside services, counselors take reasonable steps to ensure that appropriate explanations are given to the client.

b. *Recipients of Results.* The examinee's welfare, explicit understanding, and prior agreement determine the recipients of test results. Counselors include accurate and appropriate interpretations with any release of individual or group test results. (See B.1.a. and C.5.c.)

E.4. Release of Information to Competent Professionals

a. *Misuse of Results.* Counselors do not misuse assessment results, including test results, and interpretations, and take reasonable steps to prevent the misuse of such by others. (See C.5.c.)

b. *Release of Raw Data.* Counselors ordinarily release data (e.g., protocols, counseling or interview notes, or questionnaires) in which the client is identified only with the consent of the client or the client's legal representative. Such data are usually released only to persons recognized by counselors as competent to interpret the data. (See B.1.a.)

E.5. Proper Diagnosis of Mental Disorders

a. *Proper Diagnosis.* Counselors take special care to provide proper diagnosis of mental disorders. Assessment techniques (including personal interview) used to determine client care (e.g., locus of treatment, type of treatment, or recommended follow-up) are carefully selected and appropriately used. (See A.3.a. and C.5.c.)

b. *Cultural Sensitivity.* Counselors recognize that culture affects the manner in which clients' problems are defined. Clients' socioeconomic and cultural experience is considered when diagnosing mental disorders.

E.6. Test Selection

a. *Appropriateness of Instruments.* Counselors carefully consider the validity, reliability, psychometric limitations, and appropriateness of instruments when selecting tests for use in a given situation or with a particular client.

b. *Culturally Diverse Populations.* Counselors are cautious when selecting tests for culturally diverse populations to avoid inappropriateness of testing that may be outside of socialized behavioral or cognitive patterns.

E.7. Conditions of Test Administration

a. *Administration Conditions.* Counselors administer tests under the same conditions that were established in their standardization. When tests are not administered under standard conditions or when unusual behavior or irregularities occur during the testing session, those conditions are noted in interpretation, and the results may be designated as invalid or of questionable validity.

b. *Computer Administration.* Counselors are responsible for ensuring that administration programs function properly to provide clients with accurate results when a computer or other electronic methods are used for test administration. (See A.12.b.)

c. *Unsupervised Test Taking.* Counselors do not permit unsupervised or inadequately supervised use of tests or assessments unless the tests or assessments are designed, intended, and validated for self-administration and/or scoring.

d. *Disclosure of Favorable Conditions.* Prior to test administration, conditions that produce most favorable test results are made known to the examinee.

E.8. Diversity in Testing
Counselors are cautious in using assessment techniques, making evaluations, and interpreting the performance of populations not represented in the norm group on which an instrument was standardized. They recognize the effects of age, color, culture, disability, ethnic group, gender, race, religion, sexual orientation, and socioeconomic status on test administration and interpretation and place test results in proper perspective with other relevant factors. (See A.2.a.)

E.9. Test Scoring and Interpretation
a. *Reporting Reservations.* In reporting assessment results, counselors indicate any reservations that exist regarding validity or reliability because of the circumstances of the assessment or the inappropriateness of the norms for the person tested.

b. *Research Instruments.* Counselors exercise caution when interpreting the results of research instruments possessing insufficient technical data to support respondent results. The specific purposes for the use of such instruments are stated explicitly to the examinee.

c. *Testing Services.* Counselors who provide test scoring and test interpretation services to support the assessment process confirm the validity of such interpretations. They accurately describe the purpose, norms, validity, reliability, and applications of the procedures and any special qualifications applicable to their use. The public offering of an automated test interpretations service is considered a professional-to-professional consultation. The formal responsibility of the consultant is to the consultee, but the ultimate and overriding responsibility is to the client.

E.10. Test Security
Counselors maintain the integrity and security of tests and other assessment techniques consistent with legal and contractual obligations. Counselors do not appropriate, reproduce, or modify published tests or parts thereof without acknowledgment and permission from the publisher.

E.11. Obsolete Tests and Outdated Test Results
Counselors do not use data or test results that are obsolete or outdated for the current purpose. Counselors make every effort to prevent the misuse of obsolete measures and test data by others.

E.12. Test Construction
Counselors use established scientific procedures, relevant standards, and current professional knowledge for test design in the development, publication, and utilization of educational and psychological assessment techniques.

Section F: Teaching, Training, and Supervision

F.1. Counselor Educators and Trainers
a. *Educators as Teachers and Practitioners.* Counselors who are responsible for developing, implementing, and supervising educational programs are skilled as teachers and practitioners. They are knowledgeable regarding the ethical, legal, and regulatory aspects of the profession, are skilled in applying that knowledge, and make students and supervisees aware of their responsibilities. Counselors conduct counselor education and training programs in an ethical manner and serve as role models for professional behavior. Counselor educators should make an effort to infuse material related to human diversity into all courses and/or workshops that are designed to promote the development of professional counselors.

b. *Relationship Boundaries with Students and Supervisees.* Counselors clearly define and maintain ethical, professional, and social relationship boundaries with their students and supervisees. They are aware of the differential in power that exists and the student's or supervisee's possible incomprehension of that power differential. Counselors explain to students and supervisees the potential for the relationship to become exploitive.

c. *Sexual Relationships.* Counselors do not engage in sexual relationships with students or supervisees and do not subject them to sexual harassment. (See A.6. and C.5.b)

d. *Contributions to Research.* Counselors give credit to students or supervisees for their contributions to research and scholarly projects. Credit is given through coauthorship, acknowledgment, footnote statement, or other appropriate means, in accordance with such contributions. (See G.4.b. and G.4.c.)

e. *Close Relatives.* Counselors do not accept close relatives as students or supervisees.

f. *Supervision Preparation.* Counselors who offer clinical supervision services are adequately prepared in supervision methods and techniques. Counselors who are doctoral students serving as practicum or internship supervisors to master's level students are adequately prepared and supervised by the training program.

g. *Responsibility for Services to Clients.* Counselors who supervise the counseling services of others take reasonable measures to ensure that counseling services provided to clients are professional.

h. *Endorsement.* Counselors do not endorse students or supervisees for certification, licensure, employment, or completion of an academic or training program if they believe students or supervisees are not qualified for the endorsement. Counselors take reasonable steps to assist students or supervisees who are not qualified for endorsement to become qualified.

F.2. Counselor Education and Training Programs

a. *Orientation.* Prior to admission, counselors orient prospective students to the counselor education or training program's expectations, including but not limited to the following: (1) the type and level of skill acquisition required for successful completion of the training, (2) subject matter to be covered, (3) basis for evaluation, (4) training components that encourage self-growth or self-disclosure as part of the training process, (5) the type of supervision settings and requirements of the sites for required clinical field experiences, (6) student and supervisee evaluation and dismissal policies and procedures, and (7) up-to-date employment prospects for graduates.

b. *Integration of Study and Practice.* Counselors establish counselor education and training programs that integrate academic study and supervised practice.

c. *Evaluation.* Counselors clearly state to students and supervisees, in advance of training, the levels of competency expected, appraisal methods, and timing of evaluations for both didactic and experiential components. Counselors provide students and supervisees with periodic performance appraisal and evaluation feedback throughout the training program.

d. *Teaching Ethics.* Counselors make students and supervisees aware of the ethical responsibilities and standards of the profession and the students' and supervisees' ethical responsibilities to the profession. (See C.1. and F.3.e.)

e. *Peer Relationships.* When students or supervisees are assigned to lead counseling groups or provide clinical supervision for their peers, counselors take steps to ensure that students and supervisees placed in these roles do not have personal or adverse relationships with peers and that they understand they have the same ethical obligations as counselor educators, trainers, and supervisors. Counselors make every effort to ensure that the rights of peers are not compromised when students or supervisees are assigned to lead counseling groups or provide clinical supervision.

f. *Varied Theoretical Positions.* Counselors present varied theoretical positions so that students and supervisees may make comparisons and have opportunities to develop their own positions. Counselors provide information concerning the scientific bases of professional practice. (See C.6.a.)

g. *Field Placements.* Counselors develop clear policies within their training program regarding field placement and other clinical experiences. Counselors provide clearly stated roles and responsibilities for the student or supervisee, the site supervisor, and the program supervisor. They confirm that site supervisors are qualified to provide supervision and are informed of their professional and ethical responsibilities in this role.

h. *Dual Relationships as Supervisors.* Counselors avoid dual relationships such as performing the role of site supervisor and training program supervisor in the student's or supervisee's training program. Counselors do not accept any form of professional services, fees, commissions, reimbursement, or remuneration from a site for student or supervisee placement.

i. *Diversity in Programs.* Counselors are responsive to their institution's and program's recruitment and retention needs for training program administrators, faculty, and students with diverse backgrounds and special needs. (See A.2.a.)

F.3. Students and Supervisees

a. *Limitations.* Counselors, through ongoing evaluation and appraisal, are aware of the academic and personal limitations of students and supervisees that might impede performance. Counselors assist students and supervisees in securing remedial assistance when needed, and dismiss from the training program supervisees who are unable to provide competent service due to academic or personal limitations. Counselors seek professional consultation and document their decision to dismiss or refer students or supervisees for assistance. Counselors ensure that students and supervisees have recourse to address decisions made to require them to seek assistance or to dismiss them.

b. *Self-Growth Experiences.* Counselors use professional judgment when designing training experiences conducted by the counselors themselves that require student and supervisee self-growth or self-disclosure. Safeguards are provided so that students and supervisees are aware of the ramifications their self-disclosure may have on counselors whose primary role as teacher, trainer, or supervisor requires acting on ethical obligations to the profession. Evaluative components of experiential training experiences explicitly delineate predetermined academic standards that are separate and do not depend on the student's level of self-disclosure. (See A.6.)

c. *Counseling for Students and Supervisees.* If students or supervisees request counseling, supervisors or counselor educators provide them with acceptable referrals. Supervisors or counselor educators do not serve as counselor to students or supervisees over whom they hold administrative, teaching, or evaluative roles unless this is a brief role associated with a training experience. (See A.6.b.)

d. *Clients of Students and Supervisees.* Counselors make every effort to ensure that the clients at field placements are aware of the services rendered and the qualifications of the students and supervisees rendering those services. Clients receive professional disclosure information and are informed of the limits of confidentiality. Client permission is obtained in order for the students and supervisees to use any information concerning the counseling relationship in the training process. (See B.1.e.)

e. *Standards for Students and Supervisees.* Students and supervisees preparing to become counselors adhere to the Code of Ethics and the Standards of Practice. Students and supervisees have the same obligations to clients as those required of counselors. (See H.1.)

Section G: Research and Publication

G.1. Research Responsibilities

a. *Use of Human Subjects.* Counselors plan, design, conduct, and report research in a manner consistent with pertinent ethical principles, federal and state laws, host institutional regulations, and scientific standards governing research with human subjects. Counselors design and conduct research that reflects cultural sensitivity appropriateness.

b. *Deviation from Standard Practices.* Counselors seek consultation and observe stringent safeguards to protect the rights of research participants when a research problem suggests a deviation from standard acceptable practices. (See B.6.)

c. *Precautions to Avoid Injury.* Counselors who conduct research with human subjects are responsible for the subjects' welfare throughout the experiment and take reasonable precautions to avoid causing injurious psychological, physical, or social effects to their subjects.

d. *Principal Researcher Responsibility.* The ultimate responsibility for ethical research practice lies with the principal researcher. All others involved in the research activities share ethical obligations and full responsibility for their own actions.

e. *Minimal Interference.* Counselors take reasonable precautions to avoid causing disruptions in subjects' lives due to participation in research.

f. *Diversity.* Counselors are sensitive to diversity and research issues with special populations. They seek consultation when appropriate. (See A.2.a. and B.6.)

G.2. Informed Consent

a. *Topics Disclosed.* In obtaining informed consent for research, counselors use language that is understandable to research participants and that (1) accurately explains the purpose and procedures to be followed; (2) identifies any procedures that are experimental or relatively untried; (3) describes the attendant discomforts and risks; (4) describes the benefits or changes in individuals or organizations that might be reasonably expected; (5) discloses appropriate alternative procedures that would be advantageous for subjects; (6) offers to answer any inquiries concerning the procedures; (7) describes any limitations on confidentiality; and (8) instructs that subjects are free to withdraw their consent and to discontinue participation in the project at any time. (See B.1.f.)

b. *Deception.* Counselors do not conduct research involving deception unless alternative procedures are not feasible and the prospective value of the research justifies the deception. When the methodological requirements of a study necessitate concealment or deception, the investigator is required to explain clearly the reasons for this action as soon as possible.

c. *Voluntary Participation.* Participation in research is typically voluntary and without any penalty for refusal to participate. Involuntary participation is appropriate only when it can be demonstrated that participation will have no harmful effects on subjects and is essential to the investigation.

d. *Confidentiality of Information.* Information obtained about research participants during the course of an investigation is confidential. When the possibility exists that others may obtain access to such information, ethical research practice requires that the possibility, together with the plans for protecting confidentiality, be explained to participants as a part of the procedure for obtaining informed consent. (See B.1.e.)

e. *Persons Incapable of Giving Informed Consent.* When a person is incapable of giving informed consent, counselors provide an appropriate explanation, obtain agreement for participation, and obtain appropriate consent from a legally authorized person.

f. *Commitments to Participants.* Counselors take reasonable measures to honor all commitments to research participants.

g. *Explanations After Data Collection.* After data are collected, counselors provide participants with full clarification of the nature of the study to remove any misconceptions. Where scientific or human values justify delaying or withholding information, counselors take reasonable measures to avoid causing harm.

h. *Agreements to Cooperate.* Counselors who agree to cooperate with another individual in research or publication incur an obligation to cooperate as promised in terms of punctuality of performance and with regard to the completeness and accuracy of the information required.

i. *Informed Consent for Sponsors.* In the pursuit of research, counselors give sponsors, institutions, and publication channels the same respect and opportunity for giving informed consent that they accord to individual research participants. Counselors are aware of their obligation to future research workers and ensure that host institutions are given feedback information and proper acknowledgment.

G.3. Reporting Results

a. *Information Affecting Outcome.* When reporting research results, counselors explicitly mention all variables and conditions known to the investigator that may have affected the outcome of a study or the interpretation of data.

b. *Accurate Results.* Counselors plan, conduct, and report research accurately and in a manner that minimizes the possibility that results will be misleading. They provide thorough discussions of the limitations of their data and alternative hypotheses. Counselors do not engage in fraudulent research, distort data, misrepresent data, or deliberately bias their results.

c. *Obligation to Report Unfavorable Results.* Counselors communicate to other counselors the results of any research judged to be of professional value. Results that reflect unfavorably on institutions, programs, services, prevailing opinions, or vested interests are not withheld.

d. *Identity of Subjects*. Counselors who supply data, aid in the research of another person, report research results, or make original data available take due care to disguise the identity of respective subjects in the absence of specific authorization from the subjects to do otherwise. (See B.1.g. and B.5.a.)

e. *Replication Studies*. Counselors are obligated to make available sufficient original research data to qualified professionals who may wish to replicate the study.

G.4. Publication

a. *Recognition of Others*. When conducting and reporting research, counselors are familiar with and give recognition to previous work on the topic, observe copyright laws, and give full credit to those to whom credit is due. (See F.1.d. and G.4.c.)

b. *Contributors*. Counselors give credit through joint authorship, acknowledgment, footnote statements, or other appropriate means to those who have contributed significantly to research or concept development in accordance with such contributions. The principal contributor is listed first and minor technical or professional contributions are acknowledged in notes or introductory statements.

c. *Student Research*. For an article that is substantially based on a student's dissertation or thesis, the student is listed as the principal author. (See F.1.d. and G.4.a.)

d. *Duplicate Submission*. Counselors submit manuscripts for consideration to only one journal at a time. Manuscripts that are published in whole or in substantial part in another journal or published work are not submitted for publication without acknowledgment and permission from the previous publication.

e. *Professional Review*. Counselors who review material submitted for publication, research, or other scholarly purposes respect the confidentiality and proprietary rights of those who submitted it.

Section H: Resolving Ethical Issues

H.1. Knowledge of Standards

Counselors are familiar with the Code of Ethics and the Standards of Practice and other applicable ethics codes from other professional organizations of which they are member, or from certification and licensure bodies. Lack of knowledge or misunderstanding of an ethical responsibility is not a defense against a charge of unethical conduct. (See F.3.e.)

H.2. Suspected Violations

a. *Ethical Behavior Expected*. Counselors expect professional associates to adhere to the Code of Ethics. When counselors possess reasonable cause that raises doubts as to whether a counselor is acting in an ethical manner, they take appropriate action. (See H.2.d. and H.2.e.)

b. *Consultation*. When uncertain as to whether a particular situation or course of action may be in violation of the

Code of Ethics, counselors consult with other counselors who are knowledgeable about ethics, with colleagues, or with appropriate authorities.

c. *Organization Conflicts*. If the demands of an organization with which counselors are affiliated pose a conflict with the Code of Ethics, counselors specify the nature of such conflicts and express to their supervisors or other responsible officials their commitment to the Code of Ethics. When possible, counselors work toward change within the organization to allow full adherence to the Code of Ethics.

d. *Informal Resolution*. When counselors have reasonable cause to believe that another counselor is violating an ethical standard, they attempt to first resolve the issue informally with the other counselor if feasible, providing that such action does not violate confidentiality rights that may be involved.

e. *Reporting Suspected Violations*. When an informal resolution is not appropriate or feasible, counselors, upon reasonable cause, take action such as reporting the suspected ethical violation to state or national ethics committees, unless this action conflicts with confidentiality rights that cannot be resolved.

f. *Unwarranted Complaints*. Counselors do not initiate, participate in, or encourage the filing of ethics complaints that are unwarranted or intend to harm a counselor rather than to protect clients or the public.

H.3. Cooperation with Ethics Committees

Counselors assist in the process of enforcing the Code of Ethics. Counselors cooperate with investigations, proceedings, and requirements of the ACA Ethics Committee or ethics committees of other duly constituted associations or boards having jurisdiction over those charged with a violation. Counselors are familiar with the ACA Policies and Procedures and use it as a reference in assisting the enforcement of the Code of Ethics.

ACA STANDARDS OF PRACTICE

All members of the American Counseling Association (ACA) are required to adhere to the Standards of Practice and the Code of Ethics. The Standards of Practice represent minimal behavioral statements of the Code of Ethics. Members should refer to the applicable section of the Code of Ethics for further interpretation and amplification of the applicable Standard of Practice.

Section A: The Counseling Relationship

Standard of Practice One (SP-1)

Nondiscrimination

Counselors respect diversity and must not discriminate against clients because of age, color, culture, disability, ethnic group, gender, race, religion, sexual orientation, marital status, or socioeconomic status. (See A.2.a.)

Standard of Practice Two (SP-2)

Disclosure to Clients

Counselors must adequately inform clients, preferably in writing, regarding the counseling process and counseling relationship at or before the time it begins and throughout the relationship. (See A.3.a.)

Standard of Practice Three (SP-3)

Dual Relationships

Counselors must make every effort to avoid dual relationships with clients that could impair their professional judgment or increase the risk of harm to clients. When a dual relationship cannot be avoided, counselors must take appropriate steps to ensure that judgment is not impaired and that no exploitation occurs. (See A.6.a. and A.6.b.)

Standard of Practice Four (SP-4)

Sexual Intimacies with Clients

Counselors must not engage in any type of sexual intimacies with current clients and must not engage in sexual intimacies with former clients within a minimum of 2 years after terminating the counseling relationship. Counselors who engage in such relationship after 2 years following termination have the responsibility to examine and document thoroughly that such relations did not have an exploitative nature.

Standard of Practice Five (SP-5)

Protecting Clients During Group Work

Counselors must take steps to protect clients from physical or psychological trauma resulting from interactions during group work. (See A.9.b.)

Standard of Practice Six (SP-6)

Advance Understanding of Fees

Counselors must explain to clients, prior to their entering the counseling relationship, financial arrangements related to professional services. (See A.10. a.-d. and A.11.c.)

Standard of Practice Seven (SP-7)

Termination

Counselors must assist in making appropriate arrangements for the continuation of treatment of clients, when necessary, following termination of counseling relationships. (See A.11.a.)

Standard of Practice Eight (SP-8)

Inability to Assist Clients

Counselors must avoid entering or immediately terminate a counseling relationship if it is determined that they are unable to be of professional assistance to a client. The counselor may assist in making an appropriate referral for the client. (See A.11.b.)

Section B: Confidentiality

Standard of Practice Nine (SP-9)

Confidentiality Requirement

Counselors must keep information related to counseling services confidential unless disclosure is in the best interest of clients, is required for the welfare of others, or is required by law. When disclosure is required, only information that is essential is revealed and the client is informed of such disclosure. (See B.1. a.–f.)

Standard of Practice Ten (SP-10)

Confidentiality Requirements for Subordinates

Counselors must take measures to ensure that privacy and confidentiality of clients are maintained by subordinates. (See B.1.h.)

Standard of Practice Eleven (SP-11)

Confidentiality in Group Work

Counselors must clearly communicate to group members that confidentiality cannot be guaranteed in group work. (See B.2.a.)

Standard of Practice Twelve (SP-12)

Confidentiality in Family Counseling

Counselors must not disclose information about one family member in counseling to another family member without prior consent. (See B.2.b.)

Standard of Practice Thirteen (SP-13)

Confidentiality of Records

Counselors must maintain appropriate confidentiality in creating, storing, accessing, transferring, and disposing of counseling records. (See B.4.b.)

Standard of Practice Fourteen (SP-14)

Permission to Record or Observe

Counselors must obtain prior consent from clients in order to record electronically or observe sessions. (See B.4.c.)

Standard of Practice Fifteen (SP-15)

Disclosure or Transfer of Records

Counselors must obtain client consent to disclose or transfer records to third parties, unless exceptions listed in SP-9 exist. (See B.4.e.)

Standard of Practice Sixteen (SP-16)

Data Disguise Required

Counselors must disguise the identity of the client when using data for training, research, or publication. (See B.5.a.)

Section C: Professional Responsibility

Standard of Practice Seventeen (SP-17)

Boundaries of Competence

Counselors must practice only within the boundaries of their competence. (See C.2.a.)

Standard of Practice Eighteen (SP-18)

Continuing Education

Counselors must engage in continuing education to maintain their professional competence. (See C.2.f.)

Standard of Practice Nineteen (SP-19)

Impairment of Professionals

Counselors must refrain from offering professional services when their personal problems or conflicts may cause harm to a client or others. (See C.2.g.)

Standard of Practice Twenty (SP-20)

Accurate Advertising

Counselors must accurately represent their credentials and services when advertising. (See C.3.a.)

Standard of Practice Twenty-One (SP-21)

Recruiting Through Employment

Counselors must not use their place of employment or institutional affiliation to recruit clients for their private practices. (See C.3.d.)

Standard of Practice Twenty-Two (SP-22)

Credentials Claimed

Counselors must claim or imply only professional credentials possessed and must correct any known misrepresentations of their credentials by others. (See C.4.a.)

Standard of Practice Twenty-Three (SP-23)

Sexual Harassment

Counselors must not engage in sexual harassment. (See C.5.b.)

Standard of Practice Twenty-Four (SP-24)

Unjustified Gains

Counselors must not use their professional positions to seek or receive unjustified personal gains, sexual favors, unfair advantage, or unearned goods or services. (See C.5.e.)

Standard of Practice Twenty-Five (SP-25)

Clients Served by Others

With the consent of the client, counselors must inform other mental health professionals serving the same client that a counseling relationship between the counselor and client exists. (See C.6.c.)

Standard of Practice Twenty-Six (SP-26)

Negative Employment Conditions

Counselors must alert their employers to institutional policy or conditions that may be potentially disruptive or damaging to the counselor's professional responsibilities, or that may limit their effectiveness or deny clients' rights. (See D.1.c.)

Standard of Practice Twenty-Seven (SP-27)

Personnel Selection and Assignment

Counselors must select competent staff and must assign responsibilities compatible with staff skills and experiences. (See D.1.h.)

Standard of Practice Twenty-Eight (SP-28)

Exploitative Relationships with Subordinates

Counselors must not engage in exploitative relationships with individuals over whom they have supervisory, evaluative, or instructional control or authority. (See D.1.k.)

Section D: Relationship with Other Professionals

Standard of Practice Twenty-Nine (SP-29)

Accepting Fees from Agency Clients

Counselors must not accept fees or other remuneration for consultation with persons entitled to such services through the counselor's employing agency or institution. (See D.3.a.)

Standard of Practice Thirty (SP-30)

Referral Fees

Counselors must not accept referral fees. (See D.3.b.)

Section E: Evaluation, Assessment and Interpretation

Standard of Practice Thirty-One (SP-31)

Limits of Competence

Counselors must perform only testing and assessment services for which they are competent. Counselors must not allow the use of psychological assessment techniques by unqualified persons under their supervision. (See E.2.a.)

Standard of Practice Thirty-Two (SP-32)

Appropriate Use of Assessment Instruments

Counselors must use assessment instruments in the manner for which they were intended. (See E.2.b.)

Standard of Practice Thirty-Three (SP-33)

Assessment Explanations to Clients

Counselors must provide explanations to clients prior to assessment about the nature and purposes of assessment and the specific uses of results. (See E.3.a.)

Standard of Practice Thirty-Four (SP-34)

Recipients of Test Results

Counselors must ensure that accurate and appropriate interpretations accompany any release of testing and assessment information. (See E.3.b.)

Standard of Practice Thirty-Five (SP-35)

Obsolete Tests and Outdated Test Results

Counselors must not base their assessment or intervention decisions or recommendations on data or test results that are obsolete or outdated for the current purpose. (See E.11.)

Section F: Teaching, Training, and Supervision

Standard of Practice Thirty-Six (SP-36)

Sexual Relationships with Students or Supervisees

Counselors must not engage in sexual relationships with their students and supervisees. (See F.1.c.)

Standard of Practice Thirty-Seven (SP-37)

Credit for Contributions to Research

Counselors must give credit to students or supervisees for their contributions to research and scholarly projects. (See F.1.d.)

Standard of Practice Thirty-Eight (SP-38)

Supervision Preparation

Counselors who offer clinical supervision services must be trained and prepared in supervision methods and techniques. (See F.1.f.)

Standard of Practice Thirty-Nine (SP-39)

Evaluation Information

Counselors must clearly state to students and supervisees in advance of training the levels of competency expected, appraisal methods, and timing of evaluations. Counselors must provide students and supervisees with periodic performance appraisal and evaluation feedback throughout the training program. (See F.2.c.)

Standard of Practice Forty (SP-40)

Peer Relationships in Training

Counselors must make every effort to ensure that the rights of peers are not violated when students and supervisees are assigned to lead counseling groups or provide clinical supervision. (See F.2.e.)

Standard of Practice Forty-One (SP-41)

Limitations of Students and Supervisees

Counselors must assist students and supervisees in securing remedial assistance, when needed, and must dismiss from the training program students and supervisees who are unable to provide competent service due to academic or personal limitations. (See F.3.a.)

Standard of Practice Forty-Two (SP-42)

Self-Growth Experiences

Counselors who conduct experiences for students or supervisees that include self-growth or self-disclosure must inform participants of counselors' ethical obligations to the profession and must not grade participants based on their nonacademic performance. (See F.3.b.)

Standard of Practice Forty-Three (SP-43)

Standards for Students and Supervisees

Students and supervisees preparing to become counselors must adhere to the Code of Ethics and the Standards of Practice of counselors. (See F.3.e.)

Section G: Research and Publication

Standard of Practice Forty-Four (SP-44)

Precautions to Avoid Injury in Research

Counselors must avoid causing physical, social, or psychological harm or injury to subjects in research. (See G.1.c.)

Standard of Practice Forty-Five (SP-45)

Confidentiality of Research Information

Counselors must keep confidential information obtained about research participants. (See G.2.d.)

Standard of Practice Forty-Six (SP-46)

Information Affecting Research Outcome

Counselors must report all variables and conditions known to the investigator that may have affected research data or outcomes. (See G.3.a.)

Standard of Practice Forty-Seven (SP-47)

Accurate Research Results

Counselors must not distort or misrepresent research data, nor fabricate or intentionally bias research results. (See G.3.b.)

Standard of Practice Forty-Eight (SP-48)

Publication Contributors

Counselors must give appropriate credit to those who have contributed to research. (See G.4.a. and G.4.b.)

Section H: Resolving Ethical Issues

Standard of Practice Forty-Nine (SP-49)

Ethical Behavior Expected

Counselors must take appropriate action when they possess reasonable cause that raises doubts as to whether counselors or other mental health professionals are acting in an ethical manner. (See H.2.a.)

Standard of Practice Fifty (SP 50)

Unwarranted Complaints

Counselors must not initiate, participate in, or encourage the filing of ethics complaints that are unwarranted or intended to harm a mental health professional rather than to protect clients or the public. (See H.2.f.)

Standard of Practice Fifty-One (SP-51)

Cooperation with Ethics Committees

Counselors must cooperate with investigations, proceedings, and requirements of the ACA Ethics Committee or ethics committees of other duly constituted associations or boards having jurisdiction over those charged with a violation. (See H.3.)

REFERENCES

The following documents are available to counselors as resources to guide them in their practices. These resources are not a part of the *Code of Ethics and the Standards of Practice.*

American Association for Counseling and Development/Association for Measurement and Evaluation in Counseling and Development. (1989). *The responsibilities of users of standardized tests (revised).* Washington, DC: Author.

American Counseling Association. (1988). (Note: This is ACA's previous edition of its ethics code). *Ethical standards.* Alexandria, VA: Author.

American Psychological Association. (1985). *Standards for educational and psychological testing (revised).* Washington, DC: Author.

Joint Committee on Testing Practices. (1988). Code of fair testing practices in education. Washington, DC: Author.

National Board for Certified Counselors. (1989). National Board for Certified Counselors code of ethics. Alexandria, VA: Author.

Prediger, D. J. (Ed.). (1993, March). Multicultural assessment standards. Alexandria, VA: Association for Assessment in Counseling.

APPENDIX B

Ethical Principles of Psychologists and Code of Conduct

CONTENTS

INTRODUCTION

The American Psychological Association's (APA's) Ethical Principles of Psychologists and Code of Conduct (hereinafter referred to as the Ethics Code) consists of an Introduction, a Preamble, six General Principles (A–F), and specific Ethical Standards. The Introduction discusses the intent, organization, procedural considerations, and scope of application of the Ethics Code. The Preamble and General Principles are *aspirational* goals to guide psychologists toward the highest ideals of psychology. Although the Preamble and General Principles are not themselves enforceable rules, they should be considered by psychologists in arriving at an ethical course of action and may be considered by ethics bodies in interpreting the Ethical Standards. The Ethical Standards set forth *enforceable* rules for conduct as psychologists. Most of the Ethical Standards are written broadly, in order to apply to psychologists in varied roles, although the application of an Ethical Standard may vary depending on the context. The Ethical Standards are not exhaustive. The fact that a given conduct is not specifically addressed by the Ethics Code does not mean that it is necessarily either ethical or unethical.

Membership in the APA commits members to adhere to the APA Ethics Code and to the rules and procedures used to implement it. Psychologists and students, whether or not they are APA members, should be aware that the Ethics Code may be applied to them by state psychology boards, courts, or other public bodies.

This Ethics Code applies only to psychologists' work-related activities, that is, activities that are part of the psychologists' scientific and professional functions or that are psychological in nature. It includes the clinical or counseling practice of psychology, research, teaching, supervision of trainees, development of assessment instruments, conducting assessments, educational counseling, organizational consulting, social intervention, administration, and other activities as well. These work-related activities can be distinguished from the purely private conduct of a psychologist, which ordinarily is not within the purview of the Ethics Code.

The Ethics Code is intended to provide standards of professional conduct that can be applied by the APA and by other bodies that choose to adopt them. Whether or not a psychologist has violated the Ethics Code does not by itself determine whether he or she is legally liable in a court action, whether a contract is enforceable, or whether other legal consequences occur. These results are based on legal rather than ethical rules. However, compliance with or violation of the Ethics Code may be admissible as evidence in some legal proceedings, depending on the circumstances.

In the process of making decisions regarding their professional behavior, psychologists must consider this Ethics Code, in addition to applicable laws and psychology board regulations. If the Ethics Code establishes a higher standard of conduct than is required by law, psychologists must meet the higher ethical standard. If the Ethics Code standard appears to conflict with the requirements of law, then psychologists make known their commitment to the Ethics Code and take steps to resolve the conflict in a responsible manner. If neither law nor the Ethics Code resolves an issue, psychologists should consider other professional materials and the dictates of their own conscience, as well as seek consultation with others within the field when this is practical.

The procedures for filing, investigating, and resolving complaints of unethical conduct are described in the current Rules and Procedures of the APA Ethics Committee. The actions that APA may take for violations of the Ethics Code include actions such as reprimand, censure, termination of APA membership, and referral of the matter to other bodies. Complainants who seek remedies such as monetary damages in alleging ethical violations by a psychologist must resort to private negotiation, administrative bodies, or the courts. Actions that violate the Ethics Code may lead to the imposition of sanctions on a psychologist by bodies other than APA, including state psychological associations, other professional groups, psychology boards, other state or federal agencies, and payors for health services. In addition to actions for violation of the Ethics Code, the APA Bylaws provide that APA may take action against a member after his or her conviction of a felony, expulsion or suspension from an affiliated state psychological association, or suspension or loss of licensure.

PREAMBLE

Psychologists work to develop a valid and reliable body of scientific knowledge based on research. They may apply that knowledge to human behavior in a variety of contexts. In doing so, they perform many roles, such as researcher, educator, diagnostician, therapist, supervisor, consultant, administrator, social interventionist, and expert witness. Their goal is to broaden knowledge of behavior and, where appropriate, to apply it pragmatically to improve the condition of both the individual and society. Psychologists respect the central importance of freedom of inquiry and expression in research, teaching, and publication. They also strive to help the public in developing informed judgments and choices concerning human behavior. This Ethics Code provides a common set of values upon which psychologists build their professional and scientific work.

This Code is intended to provide both the general principles and the decision rules to cover most situations encountered by psychologists. It has as its primary goal the welfare and protection of the individuals and groups with whom psychologists work. It is the individual responsibility of each psychologist to aspire to the highest possible standards of conduct. Psychologists respect and protect human and civil rights, and do not knowingly participate in or condone unfair discriminatory practices.

The development of a dynamic set of ethical standards for a psychologist's work-related conduct requires a personal commitment to a lifelong effort to act ethically; to encourage ethical behavior by students, supervisees, employees, and colleagues, as appropriate; and to consult with others, as needed, concerning ethical problems. Each psychologist supplements, but does not violate, the Ethics Code's values and rules on the basis of guidance drawn from personal values, culture, and experience.

GENERAL PRINCIPLES

Principle A: Competence

Psychologists strive to maintain high standards of competence in their work. They recognize the boundaries of their particular competencies and the limitations of their expertise. They provide only those services and use only those techniques for which they are qualified by education, training, or experience. Psychologists are cognizant of the fact that the competencies required in serving, teaching, and/or studying groups of people vary with the distinctive characteristics of those groups. In those areas in which recognized professional standards do not yet exist, psychologists exercise careful judgment and take appropriate precautions to protect the welfare of those with whom they work. They maintain knowledge of relevant scientific and professional information related to the services they render, and they recognize the need for ongoing education. Psychologists make appropriate use of scientific, professional, technical, and administrative resources.

Principle B: Integrity

Psychologists seek to promote integrity in the science, teaching, and practice of psychology. In these activities psychologists are honest, fair, and respectful of others. In describing or reporting their qualifications, services, products, fees, research, or teaching, they do not make statements that are false, misleading, or deceptive. Psychologists strive to be aware of their own belief systems, values, needs, and limitations and the effect of these on their work. To the extent feasible, they attempt to clarify for relevant parties the roles they are performing and to function appropriately in accordance with those roles. Psychologists avoid improper and potentially harmful dual relationships.

Principle C: Professional and Scientific Responsibility

Psychologists uphold professional standards of conduct, clarify their professional roles and obligations, accept appropri-

ate responsibility for their behavior, and adapt their methods to the needs of different populations. Psychologists consult with, refer to, or cooperate with other professionals and institutions to the extent needed to serve the best interests of their patients, clients, or other recipients of their services. Psychologists' moral standards and conduct are personal matters to the same degree as is true for any other person, except as psychologists' conduct may compromise their professional responsibilities or reduce the public's trust in psychology and psychologists. Psychologists are concerned about the ethical compliance of their colleagues' scientific and professional conduct. When appropriate, they consult with colleagues in order to prevent or avoid unethical conduct.

Principle D: Respect for People's Rights and Dignity

Psychologists accord appropriate respect to the fundamental rights, dignity, and worth of all people. They respect the rights of individuals to privacy, confidentiality, self-determination, and autonomy, mindful that legal and other obligations may lead to inconsistency and conflict with the exercise of these rights. Psychologists are aware of cultural, individual, and role differences, including those due to age, gender, race, ethnicity, national origin, religion, sexual orientation, disability, language, and socioeconomic status. Psychologists try to eliminate the effect on their work of biases based on those factors, and they do not knowingly participate in or condone unfair discriminatory practices.

Principle E: Concern for Others' Welfare

Psychologists seek to contribute to the welfare of those with whom they interact professionally. In their professional actions, psychologists weigh the welfare and rights of their patients or clients, students, supervisees, human research participants, and other affected persons, and the welfare of animal subjects of research. When conflicts occur among psychologists' obligations or concerns, they attempt to resolve these conflicts and to perform their roles in a responsible fashion that avoids or minimizes harm. Psychologists are sensitive to real and ascribed differences in power between themselves and others, and they do not exploit or mislead other people during or after professional relationships.

Principle F: Social Responsibility

Psychologists are aware of their professional and scientific responsibilities to the community and the society in which they work and live. They apply and make public their knowledge of psychology in order to contribute to human welfare. Psychologists are concerned about and work to mitigate the causes of human suffering. When undertaking research, they strive to advance human welfare and the science of psychology. Psychologists try to avoid misuse of their work. Psychologists comply with the law and encourage the development of law and social policy that serve the interests of their patients and clients and the public. They are encouraged to contribute a portion of their professional time for little or no personal advantage.

ETHICAL STANDARDS

1. General Standards

These General Standards are potentially applicable to the professional and scientific activities of all psychologists.

1.01 Applicability of the Ethics Code.
The activity of a psychologist subject to the Ethics Code may be reviewed under these Ethical Standards only if the activity is part of his or her work-related functions or the activity is psychological in nature. Personal activities having no connection to or effect on psychological roles are not subject to the Ethics Code.

1.02 Relationship of Ethics and Law.
If psychologists' ethical responsibilities conflict with law, psychologists make known their commitment to the Ethics Code and take steps to resolve the conflict in a responsible manner.

1.03 Professional and Scientific Relationship.
Psychologists provide diagnostic, therapeutic, teaching, research, supervisory, consultative, or other psychological services only in the context of a defined professional or scientific relationship or role. (See also Standards 2.01, Evaluation, Diagnosis, and Interventions in Professional Context, and 7.02, Forensic Assessments.)

1.04 Boundaries of Competence.
a. Psychologists provide services, teach, and conduct research only within the boundaries of their competence, based on their education, training, supervised experience, or appropriate professional experience.

b. Psychologists provide services, teach, or conduct research in new areas or involving new techniques only after first undertaking appropriate study, training, supervision, and/or consultation from persons who are competent in those areas or techniques.

c. In those emerging areas in which generally recognized standards for preparatory training do not yet exist, psychologists nevertheless take reasonable steps to ensure the competence of their work and to protect patients, clients, students, research participants, and others from harm.

1.05 Maintaining Expertise.
Psychologists who engage in assessment, therapy, teaching, research, organizational consulting, or other professional activities maintain a reasonable level of awareness of current scientific and professional information in their fields of activity, and undertake ongoing efforts to maintain competence in the skills they use.

1.06 Basis for Scientific and Professional Judgments.
Psychologists rely on scientifically and professionally derived knowledge when making scientific or professional judgments or when engaging in scholarly or professional endeavors.

1.07 Describing the Nature and Results of Psychological Services.
a. When psychologists provide assessment, evaluation, treatment, counseling, supervision, teaching, consultation, research, or other psychological services to an individual, a group, or an organization, they provide, using language that is reasonably understandable to the recipient of those services, appropriate information beforehand about the nature of such services and appropriate information later about results and conclusions. (See also Standard 2.09, Explaining Assessment Results.)

b. If psychologists will be precluded by law or by organizational roles from providing such information to particular individuals or groups, they so inform those individuals or groups at the outset of the service.

1.08 Human Differences.
Where differences of age, gender, race, ethnicity, national origin, religion, sexual orientation, disability, language, or socioeconomic status significantly affect psychologists' work concerning particular individuals or groups, psychologists obtain the training, experience, consultation, or supervision necessary to ensure the competence of their services, or they make appropriate referrals.

1.09 Respecting Others.
In their work-related activities, psychologists respect the rights of others to hold values, attitudes, and opinions that differ from their own.

1.10 Nondiscrimination.
In their work-related activities, psychologists do not engage in unfair discrimination based on age, gender, race, ethnicity, national origin, religion, sexual orientation, disability, socioeconomic status, or any basis proscribed by law.

1.11 Sexual Harassment.
a. Psychologists do not engage in sexual harassment. Sexual harassment is sexual solicitation, physical advances, or verbal or nonverbal conduct that is sexual in nature, that occurs in connection with the psychologist's activities or roles as a psychologist, and that either: (1) is unwelcome, is offensive, or creates a hostile workplace environment, and the psychologist knows or is told this; or (2) is sufficiently severe or intense to be abusive to a reasonable person in the context. Sexual harassment can consist of a single intense or severe act or of multiple persistent or pervasive acts.

b. Psychologists accord sexual-harassment complainants and respondents dignity and respect. Psychologists do not participate in denying a person academic admittance or advancement, employment, tenure, or promotion, based solely upon their having made, or their being the subject of, sexual harassment charges. This does not preclude taking action based upon the outcome of such proceedings or consideration of other appropriate information.

1.12 Other Harassment.

Psychologists do not knowingly engage in behavior that is harassing or demeaning to persons with whom they interact in their work based on factors such as those persons' age, gender, race, ethnicity, national origin, religion, sexual orientation, disability, language, or socioeconomic status.

1.13 Personal Problems and Conflicts.

a. Psychologists recognize that their personal problems and conflicts may interfere with their effectiveness. Accordingly, they refrain from undertaking an activity when they know or should know that their personal problems are likely to lead to harm to a patient, client, colleague, student, research participant, or other person to whom they may owe a professional or scientific obligation.

b. In addition, psychologists have an obligation to be alert to signs of, and to obtain assistance for, their personal problems at an early stage, in order to prevent significantly impaired performance.

c. When psychologists become aware of personal problems that may interfere with their performing work-related duties adequately, they take appropriate measures, such as obtaining professional consultation or assistance, and determine whether they should limit, suspend, or terminate their work-related duties.

1.14 Avoiding Harm.

Psychologists take reasonable steps to avoid harming their patients or clients, research participants, students, and others with whom they work, and to minimize harm where it is foreseeable and unavoidable.

1.15 Misuse of Psychologists' Influence.

Because psychologists' scientific and professional judgments and actions may affect the lives of others, they are alert to and guard against personal, financial, social, organizational, or political factors that might lead to misuse of their influence.

1.16 Misuse of Psychologists' Work.

a. Psychologists do not participate in activities in which it appears likely that their skills or data will be misused by others, unless corrective mechanisms are available. (See also Standard 7.04, Truthfulness and Candor.)

b. If psychologists learn of misuse or misrepresentation of their work, they take reasonable steps to correct or minimize the misuse or misrepresentation.

1.17 Multiple Relationships.

a. In many communities and situations, it may not be feasible or reasonable for psychologists to avoid social or other nonprofessional contacts with persons such as patients, clients, students, supervisees, or research participants. Psychologists must always be sensitive to the potential harmful effects of other contacts on their work and on those

persons with whom they deal. A psychologist refrains from entering into or promising another personal, scientific, professional, financial, or other relationship with such persons if it appears likely that such a relationship reasonably might impair the psychologist's objectivity or otherwise interfere with the psychologist's effectively performing his or her functions as a psychologist, or might harm or exploit the other party.

b. Likewise, whenever feasible, a psychologist refrains from taking on professional or scientific obligations when preexisting relationships would create a risk of such harm.

c. If a psychologist finds that, due to unforeseen factors, a potentially harmful multiple relationship has arisen, the psychologist attempts to resolve it with due regard for the best interests of the affected person and maximal compliance with the Ethics Code.

1.18 Barter (With Patients or Clients).

Psychologists ordinarily refrain from accepting goods, services, or other nonmonetary remuneration from patients or clients in return for psychological services because such arrangements create inherent potential for conflicts, exploitation, and distortion of the professional relationship. A psychologist may participate in bartering only if (1) it is not clinically contraindicated, and (2) the relationship is not exploitative. (See also Standards 1.17, Multiple Relationships, and 1.25, Fees and Financial Arrangements.)

1.19 Exploitative Relationships.

a. Psychologists do not exploit persons over whom they have supervisory, evaluative, or other authority such as students, supervisees, employees, research participants, and clients or patients. (See also Standards 4.05–4.07 regarding sexual involvement with clients or patients.)

b. Psychologists do not engage in sexual relationships with students or supervisees in training over whom the psychologist has evaluative or direct authority, because such relationships are so likely to impair judgment or be exploitative.

1.20 Consultations and Referrals.

a. Psychologists arrange for appropriate consultations and referrals based principally on the best interests of their patients or clients, with appropriate consent, and subject to other relevant considerations, including applicable law and contractual obligations. (See also Standards 5.01, Discussing the Limits of Confidentiality, and 5.06, Consultations.)

b. When indicated and professionally appropriate, psychologists cooperate with other professionals in order to serve their patients or clients effectively and appropriately.

c. Psychologists' referral practices are consistent with law.

1.21 Third-Party Requests for Services.

a. When a psychologist agrees to provide services to a person or entity at the request of a third party, the psychologist clarifies to the extent feasible, at the outset of the service, the nature of the relationship with each party. This clarification includes the role of the psychologist (such as therapist, organizational consultant, diagnostician, or expert witness), the probable uses of the services provided or the information obtained, and the fact that there may be limits to confidentiality.

b. If there is a foreseeable risk of the psychologist's being called upon to perform conflicting roles because of the involvement of a third party, the psychologist clarifies the nature and direction of his or her responsibilities, keeps all parties appropriately informed as matters develop, and resolves the situation in accordance with this Ethics Code.

1.22 Delegation to and Supervision of Subordinates.

a. Psychologists delegate to their employees, supervisees, and research assistants only those responsibilities that such persons can reasonably be expected to perform competently, on the basis of their education, training, or experience, either independently or with the level of supervision being provided.

b. Psychologists provide proper training and supervision to their employees or supervisees and take reasonable steps to see that such persons perform services responsibly, competently, and ethically.

c. If institutional policies, procedures, or practices prevent fulfillment of this obligation, psychologists attempt to modify their role or to correct the situation to the extent feasible.

1.23 Documentation of Professional and Scientific Work.

a. Psychologists appropriately document their professional and scientific work in order to facilitate provision of services later by them or by other professionals, to ensure accountability, and to meet other requirements of institutions or the law.

b. When psychologists have reason to believe that records of their professional services will be used in legal proceedings involving recipients of or participants in their work, they have a responsibility to create and maintain documentation in the kind of detail and quality that would be consistent with reasonable scrutiny in an adjudicative forum. (See also Standard 7.01, Professionalism, under Forensic Activities.)

1.24 Records and Data.

Psychologists create, maintain, disseminate, store, retain, and dispose of records and data relating to their research, practice, and other work in accordance with law and in a manner that permits compliance with the requirements of this Ethics Code. (See also Standard 5.04, Maintenance of Records.)

1.25 Fees and Financial Arrangements.

a. As early as is feasible in a professional or scientific relationship, the psychologist and the patient, client, or other appropriate recipient of psychological services reach an agreement specifying the compensation and the billing arrangements.

b. Psychologists do not exploit recipients of services or payors with respect to fees.

c. Psychologists' fee practices are consistent with law.

d. Psychologists do not misrepresent their fees.

e. If limitations to services can be anticipated because of limitations in financing, this is discussed with the patient, client, or other appropriate recipient of services as early as is feasible. (See also Standard 4.08, Interruption of Services.)

f. If the patient, client, or other recipient of services does not pay for services as agreed, and if the psychologist wishes to use collection agencies or legal measures to collect the fees, the psychologist first informs the person that such measures will be taken and provides that person an opportunity to make prompt payment. (See also Standard 5.11, Withholding Records for Nonpayment.)

1.26 Accuracy in Reports to Payors and Funding Sources.

In their reports to payors for services or sources of research funding, psychologists accurately state the nature of the research or service provided, the fees or charges, and where applicable, the identity of the provider, the findings, and the diagnosis. (See also Standard 5.05, Disclosures.)

1.27 Referrals and Fees.

When a psychologist pays, receives payment from, or divides fees with another professional other than in an employer-employee relationship, the payment to each is based on the services (clinical, consultative, administrative, or other) provided and is not based on the referral itself.

2. Evaluation, Assessment, or Intervention

2.01 Evaluation, Diagnosis, and Interventions in Professional Context.

a. Psychologists perform evaluations, diagnostic services, or interventions only within the context of a defined professional relationship. (See also Standards 1.03, Professional and Scientific Relationship.)

b. Psychologists' assessments, recommendations, reports, and psychological diagnostic or evaluative statements are based on information and techniques (including personal interviews of the individual when appropriate) sufficient to provide appropriate substantiation for their findings. (See also Standard 7.02, Forensic Assessments.)

2.02 Competence and Appropriate Use of Assessments and Interventions.

a. Psychologists who develop, administer, score, interpret, or use psychological assessment techniques, interviews, tests, or instruments do so in a manner and for purposes that are appropriate in light of the research on or evidence of the usefulness and proper application of the techniques.

b. Psychologists refrain from misuse of assessment techniques, interventions, results, and interpretations and take reasonable steps to prevent others from misusing the information these techniques provide. This includes refraining from releasing raw test results or raw data to persons, other than to patients or clients as appropriate, who are not qualified to use such information. (See also Standards 1.02, Relationship of Ethics and Law, and 1.04, Boundaries of Competence.)

2.03 Test Construction.

Psychologists who develop and conduct research with tests and other assessment techniques use scientific procedures and current professional knowledge for test design, standardization, validation, reduction or elimination of bias, and recommendations for use.

2.04 Use of Assessment in General and with Special Populations.

a. Psychologists who perform interventions or administer, score, interpret, or use assessment techniques are familiar with the reliability, validation, and related standardization or outcome studies of, and proper applications and uses of, the techniques they use.

b. Psychologists recognize limits to the certainty with which diagnoses, judgments, or predictions can be made about individuals.

c. Psychologists attempt to identify situations in which particular interventions or assessment techniques or norms may not be applicable or may require adjustment in administration or interpretation because of factors such as individuals' gender, age, race, ethnicity, national origin, religion, sexual orientation, disability, language, or socioeconomic status.

2.05 Interpreting Assessment Results.

When interpreting assessment results, including automated interpretations, psychologists take into account the various test factors and characteristics of the person being assessed that might affect psychologists' judgments or reduce the accuracy of their interpretations. They indicate any significant reservations they have about the accuracy or limitations of their interpretations.

2.06 Unqualified Persons.

Psychologists do not promote the use of psychological assessment techniques by unqualified persons. (See also Standard 1.22, Delegation to and Supervision of Subordinates.)

2.07 Obsolete Tests and Outdated Test Results.

a. Psychologists do not base their assessment or intervention decisions or recommendations on data or test results that are outdated for the current purpose.

b. Similarly, psychologists do not base such decisions or recommendations on tests and measures that are obsolete and not useful for the current purpose.

2.08 Test Scoring and Interpretation Services.

a. Psychologists who offer assessment or scoring procedures to other professionals accurately describe the purpose,

norms, validity, reliability, and applications of the procedures and any special qualifications applicable to their use.

b. Psychologists select scoring and interpretation services (including automated services) on the basis of evidence of the validity of the program and procedures as well as on other appropriate considerations.

c. Psychologists retain appropriate responsibility for the appropriate application, interpretation, and use of assessment instruments, whether they score and interpret such tests themselves or use automated or other services.

2.09 Explaining Assessment Results.

Unless the nature of the relationship is clearly explained to the person being assessed in advance and precludes provision of an explanation of results (such as in some organizational consulting, pre-employment or security screenings, and forensic evaluations), psychologists ensure that an explanation of the results is provided using language that is reasonably understandable to the person assessed or to another legally authorized person on behalf of the client. Regardless of whether the scoring and interpretation are done by the psychologist, by assistants, or by automated or other outside services, psychologists take reasonable steps to ensure that appropriate explanations of results are given.

2.10 Maintaining Test Security.

Psychologists make reasonable efforts to maintain the integrity and security of tests and other assessment techniques consistent with law, contractual obligations, and in a manner that permits compliance with the requirements of this Ethics Code. (See also Standard 1.02, Relationship of Ethics and Law.)

3. Advertising and Other Public Statements

3.01 Definition of Public Statements.

Psychologists comply with this Ethics Code in public statements relating to their professional services, products, or publications or to the field of psychology. Public statements include but are not limited to paid or unpaid advertising, brochures, printed matter, directory listings, personal resumes or curriculum vitae, interviews or comments for use in media, statements in legal proceedings, lectures and public oral presentations, and published materials.

3.02 Statements by Others.

a. Psychologists who engage others to create or place public statements that promote their professional practice, products, or activities retain professional responsibility for such statements.

b. In addition, psychologists make reasonable efforts to prevent others whom they do not control (such as employers, publishers, sponsors, organizational clients, and representatives of the print or broadcast media) from making deceptive statements concerning psychologists' practice or professional or scientific activities.

c. If psychologists learn of deceptive statements about their work made by others, psychologists make reasonable efforts to correct such statements.

d. Psychologists do not compensate employees of press, radio, television, or other communication media in return for publicity in a news item.

e. A paid advertisement relating to the psychologist's activities must be identified as such, unless it is already apparent from the context.

3.03 Avoidance of False or Deceptive Statements.

a. Psychologists do not make public statements that are false, deceptive, misleading, or fraudulent, either because of what they state, convey, or suggest or because of what they omit, concerning their research, practice, or other work activities or those of persons or organizations with which they are affiliated. As examples (and not in limitation) of this standard, psychologists do not make false or deceptive statements concerning (1) their training, experience, or competence; (2) their academic degrees; (3) their credentials; (4) their institutional or association affiliations; (5) their services; (6) the scientific or clinical basis for, or results or degree of success of, their services; (7) their fees; or (8) their publications or research findings. (See also Standards 6.15, Deception in Research, and 6.18, Providing Participants with Information About the Study.)

b. Psychologists claim as credentials for their psychological work, only degrees that (1) were earned from a regionally accredited educational institution or (2) were the basis for psychology licensure by the state in which they practice.

3.04 Media Presentations.

When psychologists provide advice or comment by means of public lectures, demonstrations, radio or television programs, prerecorded tapes, printed articles, mailed material, or other media, they take reasonable precautions to ensure that (1) the statements are based on appropriate psychological literature and practice, (2) the statements are otherwise consistent with this Ethics Code, and (3) the recipients of the information are not encouraged to infer that a relationship has been established with them personally.

3.05 Testimonials.

Psychologists do not solicit testimonials from current psychotherapy clients or patients or other persons who because of their particular circumstances are vulnerable to undue influence.

3.06 In-Person Solicitation.

Psychologists do not engage, directly or through agents, in uninvited in-person solicitation of business from actual or potential psychotherapy patients or clients or other persons who because of their particular circumstances are vulnerable to undue influence. However, this does not preclude attempting to implement appropriate collateral contacts with significant others for the purpose of benefiting an already engaged therapy patient.

4. Therapy

4.01 Structuring the Relationship.

a. Psychologists discuss with clients or patients as early as is feasible in the therapeutic relationship appropriate issues, such as the nature and anticipated course of therapy, fees, and confidentiality. (See also Standards 1.25, Fees and Financial Arrangements, and 5.01, Discussing the Limits of Confidentiality.)

b. When the psychologist's work with clients or patients will be supervised, the above discussion includes that fact, and the name of the supervisor, when the supervisor has legal responsibility for the case.

c. When the therapist is a student intern, the client or patient is informed of that fact.

d. Psychologists make reasonable efforts to answer patients' questions and to avoid apparent misunderstandings about therapy. Whenever possible, psychologists provide oral and/or written information, using language that is reasonably understandable to the patient or client.

4.02 Informed Consent to Therapy.

a. Psychologists obtain appropriate informed consent to therapy or related procedures, using language that is reasonably understandable to participants. The content of informed consent will vary depending on many circumstances; however, informed consent generally implies that the person (1) has the capacity to consent, (2) has been informed of significant information concerning the procedure, (3) has freely and without undue influence expressed consent, and (4) consent has been appropriately documented.

b. When persons are legally incapable of giving informed consent, psychologists obtain informed permission from a legally authorized person, if such substitute consent is permitted by law.

c. In addition, psychologists (1) inform those persons who are legally incapable of giving informed consent about the proposed interventions in a manner commensurate with the persons' psychological capacities, (2) seek their assent to those interventions, and (3) consider such persons' preferences and best interests.

4.03 Couple and Family Relationships.

a. When a psychologist agrees to provide services to several persons who have a relationship (such as husband and wife or parents and children), the psychologist attempts to clarify at the outset (1) which of the individuals are patients or clients and (2) the relationship the psychologist will have with each person. This clarification includes the role of the psychologist and the probable uses of the services provided or the information obtained. (See also Standard 5.01, Discussing the Limits of Confidentiality.)

b. As soon as it becomes apparent that the psychologist may be called on to perform potentially conflicting roles (such as marital counselor to husband and wife, and then witness for one party in a divorce proceeding), the psychologist attempts to clarify and adjust, or withdraw from, roles appropriately. (See also Standard 7.03, Clarification of Role, under Forensic Activities.)

4.04 Providing Mental Health Services to Those Served by Others.

In deciding whether to offer or provide services to those already receiving mental health services elsewhere, psychologists carefully consider the treatment issues and the potential patient's or client's welfare. The psychologist discusses these issues with the patient or client, or another legally authorized person on behalf of the client, in order to minimize the risk of confusion and conflict, consults with the other service providers when appropriate, and proceeds with caution and sensitivity to the therapeutic issues.

4.05 Sexual Intimacies with Current Patients or Clients.

Psychologists do not engage in sexual intimacies with current patients or clients.

4.06 Therapy with Former Sexual Partners.

Psychologists do not accept as therapy patients or clients persons with whom they have engaged in sexual intimacies.

4.07 Sexual Intimacies with Former Therapy Patients.

a. Psychologists do not engage in sexual intimacies with a former therapy patient or client for at least two years after cessation or termination of professional services.
b. Because sexual intimacies with a former therapy patient or client are so frequently harmful to the patient or client, and because such intimacies undermine public confidence in the psychology profession and thereby deter the public's use of needed services, psychologists do not engage in sexual intimacies with former therapy patients and clients even after a two-year interval except in the most unusual circumstances. The psychologist who engages in such activity after the two years following cessation or termination of treatment bears the burden of demonstrating that there has been no exploitation, in light of all relevant factors, including (1) the amount of time that has passed since therapy terminated, (2) the nature and duration of the therapy, (3) the circumstances of termination, (4) the patient's or client's personal history, (5) the patient's or client's current mental status, (6) the likelihood of adverse impact on the patient or client and others, and (7) any statements or actions made by the therapist during the course of therapy suggesting or inviting the possibility of a post-termination sexual or romantic relationship with the patient or client. (See also Standard 1.17, Multiple Relationships.)

4.08 Interruption of Services.

a. Psychologists make reasonable efforts to plan for facilitating care in the event that psychological services are interrupted by factors such as the psychologist's illness, death, unavailability, or relocation or by the client's relocation or financial limitations. (See also Standard 5.09, Preserving Records and Data.)
b. When entering into employment or contractual relationships, psychologists provide for orderly and appropriate resolution of responsibility for patient or client care in the event that the employment or contractual relationship ends, with paramount consideration given to the welfare of the patient or client.

4.09 Terminating the Professional Relationship.

a. Psychologists do not abandon patients or clients. (See also Standard 1.25e, under Fees and Financial Arrangements.)
b. Psychologists terminate a professional relationship when it becomes reasonably clear that the patient or client no longer needs the service, is not benefiting, or is being harmed by continued service.
c. Prior to termination for whatever reason, except where precluded by the patient's or client's conduct, the psychologist discusses the patient's or client's views and needs, provides appropriate pretermination counseling, suggests alternative service providers as appropriate, and takes other reasonable steps to facilitate transfer of responsibility to another provider if the patient or client needs one immediately.

5. Privacy and Confidentiality

These Standards are potentially applicable to the professional and scientific activities of all psychologists.

5.01 Discussing the Limits of Confidentiality.

a. Psychologists discuss with persons and organizations with whom they establish a scientific or professional relationship (including, to the extent feasible, minors and their legal representatives) (1) the relevant limitations on confidentiality, including limitations where applicable in group, marital, and family therapy or in organizational consulting, and (2) the foreseeable uses of the information generated through their services.
b. Unless it is not feasible or is contradicated, the discussion of confidentiality occurs at the outset of the relationship and thereafter as new circumstances may warrant.
c. Permission for electronic recording of interviews is secured from clients and patients.

5.02 Maintaining Confidentiality.

Psychologists have a primary obligation and take reasonable precautions to respect the confidentiality rights of those with whom they work or consult, recognizing that confidentiality may be established by law, institutional rules, or professional or scientific relationships. (See also Standard 6.26, Professional Reviewers.)

5.03 Minimizing Intrusions on Privacy.

a. In order to minimize intrusions on privacy, psychologists include in written and oral reports, consultations, and the like, only information germane to the purpose for which the communication is made.

b. Psychologists discuss confidential information obtained in clinical or consulting relationships, or evaluative data concerning patients, individual or organizational clients, students, research participants, supervisees, and employees, only for appropriate scientific or professional purposes and only with persons clearly concerned with such matters.

5.04 Maintenance of Records.

Psychologists maintain appropriate confidentiality in creating, storing, accessing, transferring, and disposing of records under their control, whether these are written, automated, or in any other medium. Psychologists maintain and dispose of records in accordance with law and in a manner that permits compliance with the requirements of this Ethics Code.

5.05 Disclosures.

a. Psychologists disclose confidential information without the consent of the individual only as mandated by law, or where permitted by law for a valid purpose, such as (1) to provide needed professional services to the patient or the individual or organizational client, (2) to obtain appropriate professional consultations, (3) to protect the patient or client or others from harm, or (4) to obtain payment for services, in which instance disclosure is limited to the minimum that is necessary to achieve the purpose.

b. Psychologists also may disclose confidential information with the appropriate consent of the patient or the individual or organizational client (or of another legally authorized person on behalf of the patient or client), unless prohibited by law.

5.06 Consultations.

When consulting with colleagues, (1) psychologists do not share confidential information that reasonably could lead to the identification of a patient, client, research participant, or other person or organization with whom they have a confidential relationship unless they have obtained the prior consent of the person or organization or the disclosure cannot be avoided, and (2) they share information only to the extent necessary to achieve the purposes of the consultation. (See also Standard 5.02, Maintaining Confidentiality.)

5.07 Confidential Information in Databases.

a. If confidential information concerning recipients of psychological services is to be entered into databases or systems of records available to persons whose access has not been consented to by the recipient, then psychologists use coding or other techniques to avoid the inclusion of personal identifiers.

b. If a research protocol approved by an institutional review board or similar body requires the inclusion of personal identifiers, such identifiers are deleted before the information is made accessible to persons other than those of whom the subject was advised.

c. If such deletion is not feasible, then before psychologists transfer such data to others or review such data collected by others, they take reasonable steps to determine that ap-

propriate consent of personally identifiable individuals has been obtained.

5.08 Use of Confidential Information for Didactic or Other Purposes.

a. Psychologists do not disclose in their writings, lectures, or other public media, confidential, personally identifiable information concerning their patients, individual or organizational clients, students, research participants, or other recipients of their services that they obtained during the course of their work, unless the person or organization has consented in writing or unless there is other ethical or legal authorization for doing so.

b. Ordinarily, in such scientific and professional presentations, psychologists disguise confidential information concerning such persons or organizations so that they are not individually identifiable to others and so that discussions do not cause harm to subjects who might identify themselves.

5.09 Preserving Records and Data.

A psychologist makes plans in advance so that confidentiality of records and data is protected in the event of the psychologist's death, incapacity, or withdrawal from the position or practice.

5.10 Ownership of Records and Data.

Recognizing that ownership of records and data is governed by legal principles, psychologists take reasonable and lawful steps so that records and data remain available to the extent needed to serve the best interests of patients, individual or organizational clients, research participants, or appropriate others.

5.11 Withholding Records for Nonpayment.

Psychologists may not withhold records under their control that are requested and imminently needed for a patient's or client's treatment solely because payment has not been received, except as otherwise provided by law.

6. Teaching, Training Supervision, Research, and Publishing

6.01 Design of Education and Training Programs.

Psychologists who are responsible for education and training programs seek to ensure that the programs are competently designed, provide the proper experiences, and meet the requirements for licensure, certification, or other goals for which claims are made by the program.

6.02 Descriptions of Education and Training Programs.

a. Psychologists responsible for education and training programs seek to ensure that there is a current and accurate description of the program content, training goals and objectives, and requirements that must be met for satisfactory completion of the program. This information must be made readily available to all interested parties.

b. Psychologists seek to ensure that statements concerning their course outlines are accurate and not misleading, particularly regarding the subject matter to be covered, bases for evaluating progress, and the nature of course experiences. (See also Standard 3.03, Avoidance of False or Deceptive Statements.)

c. To the degree to which they exercise control, psychologists responsible for announcements, catalogs, brochures, or advertisements describing workshops, seminars, or other non-degree-granting educational programs ensure that they accurately describe the audience for which the program is intended, the educational objectives, the presenters, and the fees involved.

6.03 Accuracy and Objectivity in Teaching.

a. When engaged in teaching or training, psychologists present psychological information accurately and with a reasonable degree of objectivity.

b. When engaged in teaching or training, psychologists recognize the power they hold over students or supervisees and therefore make reasonable efforts to avoid engaging in conduct that is personally demeaning to students or supervisees. (See also Standards 1.09, Respecting Others, and 1.12, Other Harassment.)

6.04 Limitation on Teaching.

Psychologists do not teach the use of techniques or procedures that require specialized training, licensure, or expertise, including but not limited to hypnosis, biofeedback, and projective techniques, to individuals who lack the prerequisite training, legal scope of practice, or expertise.

6.05 Assessing Student and Supervisee Performance.

a. In academic and supervisory relationships, psychologists establish an appropriate process for providing feedback to students and supervisees.

b. Psychologists evaluate students and supervisees on the basis of their actual performance on relevant and established program requirements.

6.06 Planning Research.

a. Psychologists design, conduct, and report research in accordance with recognized standards of scientific competence and ethical research.

b. Psychologists plan their research so as to minimize the possibility that results will be misleading.

c. In planning research, psychologists consider its ethical acceptability under the Ethics Code. If an ethical issue is unclear, psychologists seek to resolve the issue through consultation with institutional review boards, animal care and use committees, peer consultations, or other proper mechanisms.

d. Psychologists take reasonable steps to implement appropriate protections for the rights and welfare of human participants, other persons affected by the research, and the welfare of animal subjects.

6.07 Responsibility.

a. Psychologists conduct research competently and with due concern for the dignity and welfare of the participants.

b. Psychologists are responsible for the ethical conduct of research conducted by them or by others under their supervision or control.

c. Researchers and assistants are permitted to perform only those tasks for which they are appropriately trained and prepared.

d. As part of the process of development and implementation of research projects, psychologists consult those with expertise concerning any special population under investigation or most likely to be affected.

6.08 Compliance with Law and Standards.

Psychologists plan and conduct research in a manner consistent with federal and state law and regulations, as well as professional standards governing the conduct of research, and particularly those standards governing research with human participants and animal subjects.

6.09 Institutional Approval.

Psychologists obtain from host institutions or organizations appropriate approval prior to conducting research, and they provide accurate information about their research proposals. They conduct the research in accordance with the approved research protocol.

6.10 Research Responsibilities.

Prior to conducting research (except research involving only anonymous surveys, naturalistic observations, or similar research), psychologists enter into an agreement with participants that clarifies the nature of the research and the responsibilities of each party.

6.11 Informed Consent to Research.

a. Psychologists use language that is reasonably understandable to research participants in obtaining their appropriate informed consent (except as provided in Standard 6.12, Dispensing with Informed Consent). Such informed consent is appropriately documented.

b. Using language that is reasonably understandable to participants, psychologists inform participants of the nature of the research; they inform participants that they are free to participate or to decline to participate or to withdraw from the research; they explain the foreseeable consequences of declining or withdrawing; they inform participants of significant factors that may be expected to influence their willingness to participate (such as risks, discomfort, adverse effects, or limitations on confidentiality, except as provided in Standard 6.15, Deception in Research); and they explain other aspects about which the prospective participants inquire.

c. When psychologists conduct research with individuals such as students or subordinates, psychologists take special care to protect the prospective participants from adverse consequences of declining or withdrawing from participation.

d. When research participation is a course requirement or opportunity for extra credit, the prospective participant is given the choice of equitable alternative activities.

e. For persons who are legally incapable of giving informed consent, psychologists nevertheless (1) provide an appropriate explanation, (2) obtain the participant's assent, and (3) obtain appropriate permission from a legally authorized person, if such substitute consent is permitted by law.

6.12 Dispensing with Informed Consent.

Before determining that planned research (such as research involving only anonymous questionnaires, naturalistic observations, or certain kinds of archival research) does not require the informed consent of research participants, psychologists consider applicable regulations and institutional review board requirements, and they consult with colleagues as appropriate.

6.13 Informed Consent in Research Filming or Recording.

Psychologists obtain informed consent from research participants prior to filming or recording them in any form, unless the research involves simply naturalistic observations in public places and it is not anticipated that the recording will be used in a manner that could cause personal identification or harm.

6.14 Offering Inducements for Research Participants.

a. In offering professional services as an inducement to obtain research participants, psychologists make clear the nature of the services, as well as the risks, obligations, and limitations. (See also Standard 1.18, Barter [With Patients or Clients].)

b. Psychologists do not offer excessive or inappropriate financial or other inducements to obtain research participants, particularly when it might tend to coerce participation.

6.15 Deception in Research.

a. Psychologists do not conduct a study involving deception unless they have determined that the use of deceptive techniques is justified by the study's prospective scientific, educational, or applied value and that equally effective alternative procedures that do not use deception are not feasible.

b. Psychologists never deceive research participants about significant aspects that would affect their willingness to participate, such as physical risks, discomfort, or unpleasant emotional experiences.

c. Any other deception that is an integral feature of the design and conduct of an experiment must be explained to participants as early as is feasible, preferably at the conclusion of their participation, but no later than at the conclusion of the research. (See also Standard 6.18, Providing Participants with Information About the Study.)

6.16 Sharing and Utilizing Data.

Psychologists inform research participants of their anticipated sharing or further use of personally identifiable research data and of the possibility of unanticipated future uses.

6.17 Minimizing Invasiveness.

In conducting research, psychologists interfere with the participants or milieu from which data are collected only in a manner that is warranted by an appropriate research design and that is consistent with psychologists' roles as scientific investigators.

6.18 Providing Participants with Information About the Study.

a. Psychologists provide a prompt opportunity for participants to obtain appropriate information about the nature, results, and conclusions of the research, and psychologists attempt to correct any misconceptions that participants may have.

b. If scientific or humane values justify delaying or withholding this information, psychologists take reasonable measures to reduce the risk of harm.

6.19 Honoring Commitments.

Psychologists take reasonable measures to honor all commitments they have made to research participants.

6.20 Care and Use of Animals in Research.

a. Psychologists who conduct research involving animals treat them humanely.

b. Psychologists acquire, care for, use, and dispose of animals in compliance with current federal, state, and local laws and regulations, and with professional standards.

c. Psychologists trained in research methods and experienced in the care of laboratory animals supervise all procedures involving animals and are responsible for ensuring appropriate consideration of their comfort, health, and humane treatment.

d. Psychologists ensure that all individuals using animals under their supervision have received instruction in research methods and in the care, maintenance, and handling of the species being used, to the extent appropriate to their role.

e. Responsibilities and activities of individuals assisting in a research project are consistent with their respective competencies.

f. Psychologists make reasonable efforts to minimize the discomfort, infection, illness, and pain of animal subjects.

g. A procedure subjecting animals to pain, stress, or privation is used only when an alternative procedure is unavailable and the goal is justified by its prospective scientific, educational, or applied value.

h. Surgical procedures are performed under appropriate anesthesia; techniques to avoid infection and minimize pain are followed during and after surgery.

i. When it is appropriate that the animal's life be terminated, it is done rapidly, with an effort to minimize pain, and in accordance with accepted procedures.

6.21 Reporting of Results.

a. Psychologists do not fabricate data or falsify results in their publications.

b. If psychologists discover significant errors in their published data, they take reasonable steps to correct such errors in a correction, retraction, erratum, or other appropriate publication means.

6.22 Plagiarism.

Psychologists do not present substantial portions or elements of another's work or data as their own, even if the other work or data source is cited occasionally.

6.23 Publication Credit.

a. Psychologists take responsibility and credit, including authorship credit, only for work they have actually performed or to which they have contributed.

b. Principal authorship and other publication credits accurately reflect the relative scientific or professional contributions of the individuals involved, regardless of their relative status. Mere possession of an institutional position, such as Department Chair, does not justify authorship credit. Minor contributions to the research or to the writing for publications are appropriately acknowledged, such as in footnotes or in an introductory statement.

c. A student is usually listed as principal author on any multiple-authored article that is substantially based on the student's dissertation or thesis.

6.24 Duplicate Publication of Data.

Psychologists do not publish, as original data, data that have been previously published. This does not preclude republishing data when they are accompanied by proper acknowledgment.

6.25 Sharing Data.

After research results are published, psychologists do not withhold the data on which their conclusions are based from other competent professionals who seek to verify the substantive claims through reanalysis and who intend to use such data only for that purpose, provided that the confidentiality of the participants can be protected and unless legal rights concerning proprietary data preclude their release.

6.26 Professional Reviewers.

Psychologists who review material submitted for publication, grant, or other research proposal review respect the confidentiality of and the proprietary rights in such information of those who submitted it.

7. Forensic Activities

7.01 Professionalism.

Psychologists who perform forensic functions, such as assessments, interviews, consultations, reports, or expert testimony, must comply with all other provisions of this Ethics Code to the extent that they apply to such activities. In addition, psychologists base their forensic work on appropriate knowledge of and competence in the areas underlying such work, including specialized knowledge concerning special populations. (See also Standards 1.06, Basis for Scientific and Professional Judgments; 1.08, Human Differences; 1.15, Misuse of Psychologists' Influence; and 1.23, Documentation of Professional and Scientific Work.)

7.02 Forensic Assessments.

a. Psychologists' forensic assessments, recommendations, and reports are based on information and techniques (including personal interviews of the individual, when appropriate) sufficient to provide appropriate substantiation for their findings. (See also Standards 1.03, Professional and Scientific Relationship; 1.23, Documentation of Professional and Scientific Work; 2.01, Evaluation, Diagnosis, and Interventions in Professional Context; and 2.05, Interpreting Assessment Results.)

b. Except as noted in (c), below, psychologists provide written or oral forensic reports or testimony of the psychological characteristics of an individual only after they have conducted an examination of the individual adequate to support their statements or conclusions.

c. When, despite reasonable efforts, such an examination is not feasible, psychologists clarify the impact of their limited information on the reliability and validity of their reports and testimony, and they appropriately limit the nature and extent of their conclusions or recommendations.

7.03 Clarification of Role.

In most circumstances, psychologists avoid performing multiple and potentially conflicting roles in forensic matters. When psychologists may be called on to serve in more than one role in a legal proceeding—for example, as consultant or expert for one party or for the court and as a fact witness—they clarify role expectations and the extent of confidentiality in advance to the extent feasible, and thereafter as changes occur, in order to avoid compromising their professional judgment and objectivity and in order to avoid misleading others regarding their role.

7.04 Truthfulness and Candor.

a. In forensic testimony and reports, psychologists testify truthfully, honestly, and candidly and, consistent with applicable legal procedures, describe fairly the bases for their testimony and conclusions.

b. Whenever necessary to avoid misleading, psychologists acknowledge the limits of their data or conclusions.

7.05 Prior Relationships.

A prior professional relationship with a party does not preclude psychologists from testifying as fact witnesses or from testifying to their services to the extent permitted by applicable law. Psychologists appropriately take into account ways in which the prior relationship might affect their professional objectivity or opinions and disclose the potential conflict to the relevant parties.

7.06 Compliance with Law and Rules.

In performing forensic roles, psychologists are reasonably familiar with the rules governing their roles. Psychologists are aware of the occasionally competing demands placed upon them by these principles and the requirements of the court system, and attempt to resolve these conflicts by making known their commitment to this Ethics Code and taking steps to resolve the conflict in a responsible manner. (See also Standard 1.02, Relationship of Ethics and Law.)

8. Resolving Ethical Issues

8.01 Familiarity with Ethics Code.

Psychologists have an obligation to be familiar with this Ethics Code, other applicable ethics codes, and their application to psychologists' work. Lack of awareness or misunderstanding of an ethical standard is not itself a defense to a charge of unethical conduct.

8.02 Confronting Ethical Issues.

When a psychologist is uncertain whether a particular situation or course of action would violate this Ethics Code, the psychologist ordinarily consults with other psychologists knowledgeable about ethical issues, with state or national psychology ethics committees, or with other appropriate authorities in order to choose a proper response.

8.03 Conflicts Between Ethics and Organizational Demands.

If the demands of an organization with which psychologists are affiliated conflict with this Ethics Code, psychologists clarify the nature of the conflict, make known their commitment to the Ethics Code, and to the extent feasible, seek to resolve the conflict in a way that permits the fullest adherence to the Ethics Code.

8.04 Informal Resolution of Ethical Violations.

When psychologists believe that there may have been an ethical violation by another psychologist, they attempt to resolve the issue by bringing it to the attention of that individual if an informal resolution appears appropriate and the intervention does not violate any confidentiality rights that may be involved.

8.05 Reporting Ethical Violations.

If an apparent ethical violation is not appropriate for informal resolution under Standard 8.04 or is not resolved properly in that fashion, psychologists take further action appropriate to the situation, unless such action conflicts with confidentiality rights in ways that cannot be resolved. Such action might include referral to state or national committees on professional ethics or to state licensing boards.

8.06 Cooperating with Ethics Committees.

Psychologists cooperate in ethics investigations, proceedings, and resulting requirements of the APA or any affiliated state psychological association to which they belong. In doing so, they make reasonable efforts to resolve any issues as to confidentiality. Failure to cooperate is itself an ethics violation.

8.07 Improper Complaints.

Psychologists do not file or encourage the filing of ethics complaints that are frivolous and are intended to harm the respondent rather than to protect the public.

Source: Effective date December 1, 1992. Copyright © 1992 by the American Psychological Association. Reprinted with permission. All rights reserved.

Glossary

This Glossary Defines Boldfaced Terms From The Text.

Abuse (child)   the infliction by other than accidental means of physical harm upon the body of a child, continual psychological damage, or denial of emotional needs.

Accreditation (general)   the process whereby a college, university, or academic program voluntarily undergoes review by a recognized accrediting body. Accreditation allows for clear recognition of an institution's or a program's nature, intent, and quality. Accreditation is often used to designate that a degree program meets acceptable standards; typically accreditation is sought by one of the regional accrediting agencies acceptable to the United States Department of Education as a legitimate evaluator of the quality of the program.

Accreditation (professional)   the process whereby an educational program meets high standards for preparation of professionals beyond standards required for offering a degree.

Accrediting bodies (professional)   organizations that qualify educational programs as meeting standards beyond those required of colleges or universities to offer degrees. Professional accreditation of graduate counseling degrees occurs through the Council on Accreditation of Counseling and Related Educational Programs (CACREP) or the Council on Rehabilitation Education (CORE). In psychology, the American Psychological Association accredits doctoral programs.

Active euthanasia   the intentional termination of life, also referred to as mercy killing or assisted suicide.

Advance directives   (1) living wills, which are specific substantive directives regarding medical procedures that should be provided or forgone in specific circumstances; or (2) durable power of attorney (DPA) for health care, or proxy directive, giving someone else the right to make such decisions.

Alternative medicine   nontraditional medical approaches that are used instead of traditional medical practices.

Arbitrating   a process wherein a negotiator or negotiators seek the judgement of individuals (alone or in groups) who are socially approved as representatives of sociolegal consensus—arbitrators.

Aspirational ethics   See "Ethics, aspirational."

Assent   the process of consulting with and informing a person incapable of giving legal informed consent regarding his or her preferences regarding the actions to be taken by the counselor to fulfill ethical obligations to this person for informed consent.

Assessment   the process that involves the collection and evaluation of information to address a client's counseling or rehabilitation concern or problem. Typically, an individual is assessed against a normative standard, or a set of criteria, for diagnosis, case planning, or treatment. Objective or projective testing may be involved.

Asynchronous learning   distance learning in which students are not learning at the same time that live instruction occurs (e.g., use of Web-based, software-packaged instruction units).

Attributions (multicultural)   inferences or characteristics assigned to an individual that result in assigning cause and effects to behavior.

Autonomy   the principle that involves having a right to self-determination of choice and freedom from the control of others.

Balancing   involves weighing which ethical or moral principles are more applicable or important in an analysis.

Beneficence   the principle that guides actions consistent with contributing to the well-being of others; it implies doing good to others.

Benevolence   the experience of sharing, helping, and acting generously toward others.

Biomedical ethics   a way of understanding ethical complexity and examining life as it pertains to the biological sciences, medicine, and health care.

Breach of contract   a failure to provide agreed-on services considered to be contracted services.

Burnout   an emotional state experienced by some counselors; characterized by an emotional exhaustion in which the professional no longer has any positive feelings, sympathy, or respect for clients.

CAM   an abbreviation used for "complementary and alternative medicine." (See "Complementary medicine" and "Alternative medicine.")

Capacity   ability, often related specifically to making a rational decision or giving informed consent.

Career counseling   counseling that focuses on a certain realm of the client's life—the world of work.

Case law   legal precedence deriving from past legal judgements, relevant to a law's interpretation in specific circumstances and jurisdictions.

Case manager   an individual who focuses on interviewing, planning rehabilitation, medical, or educational programs; coordinating services; interacting with significant others; placing clients in facilities, organizations, or jobs; following and monitoring a client's progress; and solving problems. Counseling may or may not be a part of case management, depending on the context of employment.

Certification (board) see "Certification, specialty."

Certification (specialty) a voluntary means of identifying oneself as a trained and qualified specialist in counseling, psychology, or other professions. Certification usually requires meeting national standards of expertise beyond those required for state licensure.

Civil law involves the obligation of citizens to one another and the obligation must be asserted by the individual before the obligation is enforced by the government. A civil action may or may not be related to a crime. Typically, divorce cases and Workers' Compensation cases are addressed in a civil court.

Competence (client) the capability of clients to make decisions—a precondition to consent autonomously to services.

Competence (counselor) a counselor's capability to provide a minimum quality of service within the counselor's (and his or her profession's) scope of practice.

Complaint (ethical) a formal grievance by an individual (complainant) that expresses dissatisfaction with a counselor's action and appeals to the professional group that endorses the ethical standards that an ethical standard or standards have been violated.

Complementary medicine nontraditional medical practices that are used with traditional medical practices.

Comprehension having sufficient information and being able to understand it; a necessary condition of informed consent.

Compulsory therapy therapy initiated and/or demanded by a third party, usually as a form of rehabilitation or ongoing assessment of a client.

Confidentiality akin to an antigossip guarantee to clients; the obligation of professional counselors to respect the privacy of clients specifically related to the information communicated during counseling sessions. Legal confidentiality carries the penalty of law should there be a breach of confidentiality. Professional (nonlegal) confidentiality does not carry the weight of law, but it carries the weight of sanctions by the professional associations or certifying organizations with which the counselor affiliates.

Conformity the following of rules and observation of societal regulations.

Consensualizing a process whereby at least two individuals act in agreement and in coordination on an issue.

Consultation (professional) a paid, formal arrangement wherein a consulting counselor obtains a second opinion, advice, or supervision on an issue or issues of concern from a knowledgeable, competent colleague.

Corporal punishment an act of physical force upon a student for the purpose of punishing the student.

Counseling psychology a specialty of psychology that focuses on: (a) intact personalities, (b) assets and strengths, (c) emphasis on brief intervention, (d) emphasis on person-environment interactions, and (e) educational and career development of individuals.

Criminal law the area of law that involves conduct required of all citizens or prohibited to all, and is enforced by the government's legal authorities.

Critical-evaluative level a level of reasoning that involves three hierarchically arranged stages or tiers of examination to resolve a moral dilemma; involves the evaluation of the implications of laws, ethical principles, and ethical theories for the ethical decision to be made.

Cross-cultural counseling counseling between two individuals from different cultural backgrounds.

Cultural deficit an outdated, harmful term used in the past to describe some aspects of attributes of a diverse group from a deficit viewpoint.

Cultural encapsulation a tendency for people to treat others relative to their own cultural perspective, disregarding important cultural differences.

Culturally disadvantaged an outdated, harmful term utilized in counseling to describe some aspect of a diverse or multicultural population.

Culture a psychological construct that is a socially learned set of constructs encompassing affective styles and values regarding personal control, communication, familial patterns, and societal norms.

Cybercounseling counseling on the Internet.

Differential diagnosis the process of describing a client whereby one mental disorder is used over another disorder with similar diagnostic signs, symptoms, or course.

Diplomate the term used by some professions such as psychology to denote the attainment of specialty credentials within a specific area of advanced practice.

Direct liability liability that occurs when the harm that is done by the supervisor is a result of supervision itself.

Disability an identifiable physical or mental condition whose functional limitations, when manifested, are recognized and often overcome with appropriate accommodations.

Distance learning the use of technical equipment or media in place of live teachers to deliver education or training.

Double effect the circumstance wherein unacceptable consequences such as death are deemed acceptable under certain circumstances; a concept often considered in the context of using medication with a terminally ill patient that is intended to alleviate pain but also hastens or causes death.

Downcoding giving a client a less serious or severe diagnosis to obtain treatment.

Dual relationship   a professional (treatment or supervisory) relationship and, additionally, a simultaneous or contiguous personal and nonprofessional relationship.

Durable Power of Attorney for Health Care   a proxy directive for health care that allows individuals to select substitute decision makers empowered to make health care decisions on their behalf should they be incapacitated.

Duty to protect   the counselor's responsibility to protect the intended victims of a client or others who may be harmed.

Duty to warn   the counselor's responsibility to inform an endangered party or parties when it is believed a client poses a serious danger to an identifiable, potential victim.

Equivalence (assessment)   psychometric similarity of two different versions of an assessment device.

Ethical climate   one facet of an organizational climate that describes the shared perceptions that colleagues hold concerning ethical procedures and practices occurring within an organization.

Ethical dilemma   a circumstance involving an ethical question that stymies or confuses the counselor because there are: (a) competing or conflicting ethical standards that apply; (b) a conflict between moral and ethical standards; (c) complexities that make the application of specific standards unclear; (d) other circumstances that prevent a clear application of standards.

Ethical principles   higher-order norms or fundamental assumptions that develop within society that are consistent with moral principles and constitute higher standards of moral behavior. In counseling, five ethical principles are often referred to: autonomy, beneficence, fidelity, nonmaleficence, and justice.

Ethical violation   a behavior that violates the letter or perhaps the spirit of an ethical standard of practice.

Ethics   See "Ethics, professional."

Ethics (applied)   See "Ethics, professional."

Ethics (aspirational)   a level of ethical guidance above mandatory ethics that involves consideration of the welfare of clients and the effects of actions on the profession as a whole. Aspirational standards specify *ideals* for the profession, and are not enforceable.

Ethics (mandatory)   the most basic level of professional ethical guidance focusing on compliance with laws and dictates of professional codes of ethics.

Ethics (philosophical)   a branch of study in philosophy concerning theories of what is "good," "right," or "worthy." Philosophical ethics is theoretical.

Ethics (professional)   agreed on rules or standards established by a profession that define what is acceptable or "good" practice.

Ethics of care   an ethics approach that emphasizes human connectedness, or a relational perspective.

Ethnicity   people who share a common origin and a unique social and cultural heritage.

Eugenics   the use of a scientific strategy for orchestrating human evolution through methods of encouraging transmission of "desirable" traits and discouraging transmission of "undesirable" traits.

Euthanasia   term originally derived from two Greek words meaning "good death"; generally refers to the process of facilitating the painless death of a person who has a terminal/incurable disease. *Active euthanasia* means there was an intentional act taken to produce the death, sometimes described as mercy killing or assisted suicide. *Passive* or *indirect euthanasia* involves the withdrawal or withholding of life-sustaining treatments.

Fidelity   the principle that directs people to keep commitments or promises.

Gene therapy   an approach in which researchers and medical professionals prevent, treat, and cure disease processes through the alteration of an individual's genes.

Genetic testing   specific techniques that are used to seek genetic mutation or an altered gene protein that may indicate a genetic condition or a predisposition.

Genetics   the study of inherited traits.

Genomics   the study of the entire set of human genes.

Hastened death   any process by which people speed up the dying process.

Hierarchical model (four-level)   model of ethical practice that introduces an extended consideration of the contextual forces acting on ethical practice beyond the singular focus on the individual practitioner in relationship to the individual client.

HMO   an abbreviation for "health maintenance organization"; a type of managed care organization.

Holistic care   the use of complementary and alternative methods in health care.

Hospital privileges   the right of a professional to admit and/or to treat patients in a hospital.

Impairment   a covert, often insidious condition that suggests a level of diminished function (obtained by documented evidence) that may be manifested on a continuum by varying degrees of loss of optimal function and may be caused by many reasons.

Independence   being free to make one's own decisions and to act autonomously.

Independent practice   the practice of counseling in a private setting based on the right to practice provided by a license of a profession and free from other institutional oversight.

Indirect services   services provided when a counselor is employed by a third party whether or not he or she engages in direct communication with the client, and where there is no intent to provide counseling services directly to the person.

Informed consent the client's right to agree to participate in counseling, assessment, or professional procedures or services after such services are fully described and explained in a manner that is comprehensible to the client.

Intentionality acting with a sense of capability and deciding from among a range of alternative actions.

Intuitive level a level of reasoning that incorporates the richness and influence of the everyday personal and professional moral wisdom of the counselor in the process of ethical decision making.

Justice the ethical principle that involves the idea of fairness and equality in terms of access to resources and treatment by others.

Layered supervision doctoral students supervising master's students who are themselves being supervised by faculty.

Leadership having responsibility, power, and authority over others, with recognition of such by the others.

Legal guardian a person who is appointed by the court to make decisions regarding an individual's person and /or property.

Licensure a type of professional regulation that restricts both the use of a professional title, such as "counselor," and the practice of counseling.

Limits of practice the boundaries that demarcate the acceptable activities associated with a profession.

Living will specific, substantive directives regarding medical procedures that should be provided or forgone in specific circumstances.

Malpractice a violation of duty, requiring a determination of what constitutes "good professional practice" as applied to the actions of a professional.

Managed care provision of health services through medical insurance managed or overseen by a contracted company (a managed care company) that serves as a mediator between insurance carriers and health professionals.

Managed care contract an agreement between a managed care company and the provider of counseling services; the contract usually defines the type of services that can be provided, the maximum fee, and other limitations of services.

Mandatory ethics See "Ethics, mandatory."

MCO an abbreviation used to denote the general term for "managed care organizations."

Mental status examination a structured interview designed to provide a controlled, interpersonal setting for the emergence and observation of symptoms and signs of mental disorder.

Minority any identifiable group with differential power and a history of mistreatment.

Mobbing workplace expulsion through emotional abuse.

Morality (morals) the principles that guide an individual, sometimes deriving from a religious standard; sometimes referred to as "moral principles."

Morality (philosophical) the branch of philosophy dealing with the assessment of actions of a person against a theory in philosophical ethics. Philosophical morality always refers to an act.

Multicultural counseling a helping relationship involving two or more individuals with differing, socially constructed worldviews.

Multiculturalism an individual's or an organization's underlying beliefs, attitudes, and values that are employed for the formulation of attributions of others in a multicultural context. (See "Attributions.")

Negotiating the process of discussing and debating an issue wherein at least two individuals indicate some degree of disagreement.

Neglect (child) the failure to provide necessary food, care, clothing, supervision, or medical attention for a child.

Nonmaleficence the principle that requires that individuals refrain from any action that might cause harm.

Normalization a rehabilitation principle that dictates that persons with disabilities should be treated in a manner that allows them to participate both symbolically and actually in roles and lifestyles that are normal for persons of their age and culture.

On-line forums (of counseling) counseling on the Internet; these forums typically offer group interaction on the Internet.

Organizational climate the outward manifestation of culture and the way people would characterize a system's (agency's or business's) atmosphere related to practices and procedures.

Over-diagnosis a diagnosis that is more severe than diagnostically justified that ensures adequate insurance coverage for the anticipated treatment.

Passive (indirect) euthanasia See "Euthanasia."

Personal counseling counseling that involves professional helpers who assist clients to understand, accept, and resolve their problems by using basic counseling techniques so that their clients can lead more satisfying, well-adjusted lives.

Pirating the illegal and unethical copying and use of software.

Plagiarism the act of stealing or passing off the ideas or words of another author or person as one's own original work.

Portability   the ability of counselors who are licensed in one state to move to another state and have their credentials accepted.

Potentially detrimental counselor-client relationships   counselor-client relationships that involve either serious potential or actual harmful or illegal interactions or relationships between counselor and client. This newer term is more clearly descriptive of the ethical issue than the older, increasingly outmoded term, "dual relationships."

PPA   an abbreviation for "preferred provider agreement"; used to establish a preferred provider organization relationship.

PPO   an abbreviation for "preferred provider organization," a type of managed care organization.

Prima facie   Latin phrase meaning that the obligation in question must be considered in every case and set aside only if valid and compelling reasons are present to do so in a specific instance.

Principle ethics   objectively applying a system of ethical rules and principles to determine what is the right decision when an ethical dilemma arises. It focuses on the objective, rational and cognitive aspects of the decision-making process (compare to "Virtue ethics").

Privacy   the client's right to keep the counseling relationship to oneself (e.g., as a secret). Privacy is more inclusive than confidentiality, which addresses communications in the counseling context.

Privileged communication   a client's right that prevents the revelation of confidential information in a legal proceeding (e.g., a legal hearing or courtroom).

Pro bono publico   for the public good (usually meaning providing a service for no fee to those in need).

Race   an anthropological classification based on classification by physical appearance.

Rational suicide   the act of an individual, following a sound decision-making process, and without being coerced by others, to end his or her life because of unbearable suffering associated with a terminal illness.

Reciprocity   the process whereby a licensed counselor's credentials in one state (licensure) are recognized by another state for licensure purposes without additional imposed requirements.

Recognition   the attraction of favorable notice and being considered important.

Residency (specialty)   a three-year or more, hospital-based training that prepares a physician to practice diagnosis, general treatment, and specialty procedures in a specific area of medical practice.

Responsibility (professional)   a counselor's obligation to clients and his or her profession to act in an appropriate and considerate manner.

Revocation (of a professional license)   the loss of the right to practice in a licensing jurisdiction.

Scapegoating   a process whereby one member of a group is placed in an "odd-person-out" position or is treated by others as deviant, thereby receiving negative messages from other members of the group.

Scope of practice   the extent and limits of activities performed by a licensed or certified individual in a profession defined as acceptable practice by the profession. Scope of practice also refers to a recognized area of proficiency or competence gained through appropriate education and experience.

Sliding fee scale   requiring clients to pay a certain amount for a service based on their income.

Slippery slope argument   An argument that a certain course of action will lead to the progressive erosion of moral restraints.

Social constructivism   a philosophical framework that proposes that reality is a creation of individuals in interaction—a socially, consensually agreed-on definition of what is real.

Specialty certification   see "Certification, specialty."

Specialty designation   certification through a national specialty certifying board.

Specialty residency   see "Residency, specialty."

Specifying   determining and naming the principles that are involved in a situation being considered.

Subpoena   a document issued under authority of a court that compels the appearance of a witness at a legal proceeding. Disobeying a subpoena may result in punishment based on "contempt of court."

Supervision   an intervention provided by a more senior member of a profession to a more junior member or members of that same profession. It is evaluative, extends over time, and has the purposes of enhancing the professional functioning of the more junior person, monitoring the quality of services offered to clients, and serving as a gatekeeper for entrance to the profession.

Support   the receiving of encouragement, understanding, and kindness from others.

Suspension (of a professional license)   a temporary loss of the right to practice a profession within a jurisdiction.

Synchronous learning   distance learning in which students learn at the same time that the instruction occurs.

Technoanxious   fearful and avoiding computerization of a profession.

Technocentered   comfortable with computer technology.

Telehealth   remote electronic consultation between consumers and providers in the health care professions.

Testing   use of a specific tool or instrument used to gather information or measure some individual quality, characteristic, or level of knowledge.

Third party   an individual or organization that is somehow involved with a case (e.g., a referral source or payor) but is not the counselor or the client.

Upcoding   diagnosing a client with a more serious or severe diagnosis than is diagnostically justified.

UR   an abbreviation for "utilization review."

Value(s)   the quality that makes something desirable, useful, or an object of interest. A value is esteemed, prized, and considered worthwhile. Values also may be viewed as objective, relative to a social context, or relative to an individual (subjective).

Value system   a particular hierarchical rank-ordering of the degree of preference for the values expressed by a particular person or social entity.

Valuing   the process of negotiating values with a client or other individual.

Vicarious liability   the legal responsibility of another professional or organization for the potential negligence of another or an employee. In supervision, supervisors are considered liable for the negligent acts of supervisees if these acts are performed in the course and scope of the supervisory relationship.

Virtue ethics   considering the characteristics of counselors themselves as the critical element for responsible practice. (Compare to "Principle ethics.")

Voluntariness   giving consent by acting freely in the decision-making process, such as in giving informed consent.

WebCounseling   the practice of professional counseling and information delivery over the Internet.

Whistle-blowing   the ethical reporting of unethical behavior.

Worldview   view constituted by the observable artifacts, values, and underlying assumptions held by an individual.

Name Index

Subject Index

ongoing counseling issues, 52–55
on-line counseling and, 197
school counseling, 244–251
termination phase issues, 57
Layered supervision, 400
Leadership, 67
Legal confidentiality, 26–27
Legal guardian, 304
Legal issues. *See* Law
Legal mechanisms, 47–48. *See also* Law
Lesbian clients, 309
Liability
    direct, 403
    vicarious, 159, 403–404
Licensure, 5, 17, 197
Limits of practice, 16
Literature, for career counseling, 296,
    315–318
Living wills, 151
Local area network (LAN), 171
Loyalties, conflicted, 142

Malpractice, 10, 142–143, 403, 404
Managed care, 139–146
Managed care contract, 261
Mandatory ethics, 8
Marriage and family therapy, 21–22, 218–219
    chat-based couple Internet
        counseling, 196
    diversity issues, 225–226
    ethical codes, 225, 227–235
    ethical issues, 220–225
    professional differentiation, 220
    specialty, setting, and clients, 219
    telephone-based couple counseling, 195
    video-based couple Internet counseling
Master career counselor, 300–301
Master career development professional, 302
MCOs. *See* Managed care organizations
Medical model, 112
Mental health counseling, 260–261
    assessment, 270
    diversity issues, 271–272
    ethical codes, 270–271, 273–283
    ethical issues, 265–270
    professional differentiation, 264–265
    specialty, setting, and clients, 261–263
    standardized tests, 283–288
Mental-health injury, 124
Mental health nursing. *See* Psychiatric nursing
Mental health professions, 16–17
    counseling, 17–18
    marriage and family therapy, 21–22
    psychiatric nursing, 22–23
    psychiatry, 18–20
    psychology, 20–21
    social work, 23–24
Mental health services, on-line, 178–182.
    See also specific services
Mental status examination, 263
Mercy killing. *See* Active euthanasia

Minorities, 206
Mission, 187
Mobbing, 121–122, 124, 125
Morality/morals, 3–4
    CAM and, 159–160
    clarification of, 5
    discussion and development, 72–74
    philosophical, 4
    values and, 63
Multicultural counseling, 203, 205
Multiculturalism, 203
    addiction counseling, 387–388
    career counseling, 297, 308–309
    clinical supervision, 405–406
    ethical issues, 211–212
    ethical standards, 212–215
    evolution of, 204–207
    group counseling, 340–341
    marriage and family therapy, 225–226
    mental health counseling, 271–272
    professional issues, 207–211
    rehabilitation counseling, 360–361
    school counseling, 252
    values and, 68–69
Multicultural supervision, 405–406
Multiple relationships, 31–32

National Board of Certified Counselors
    (NBCC), 179–180, 194–197
National Career Development Association
    (NCDA), 181, 199–202, 294–299,
    310–331
National credentialing, for career
    counseling, 299
Neglect, 250
Negotiating, 104–106
Nonharmful interactions, 32–33
Nonmaleficence, 26, 75–76, 78
Nonprofessional staff members, 131–132
Nonsexual relationships, 397. *See also* Dual
    relationships
Normalization, 353
Nursing. *See* Psychiatric nursing

Objectivity, 101–103
Occupational counseling. *See* Career
    counseling
Office, layout of, 128–129
On-line counseling, 176–182
    ethical standards, 197–199
    practice of, 194–197
On-line supervision, 185
Oppressed populations, 206
Organizational climate, 113–115
Organizational culture, 111–113
Organ transplantation, 165–166

Parents, school counseling, 241–242
Passive euthanasia, 151
Performance indicators, career counseling,
    294–299

Personal blind spots, 94–95
Personal computers. *See* Computers
Personal counseling, 290
Personal development, 237
Personal self-care skills, 117
Philosophical ethics, 4
Philosophically-based ethical decision
    making models, 84–86
Philosophical morality, 4
Pirating, 189
Plans
    on-line counseling, 199–202
    school counseling, 239
Portability, 49
Potentially detrimental counselor-client
    relationships, 31–36
    addiction counseling, 386
    career counseling, 304–305
    clinical supervision, 396–397
    group counseling, 337–338
    marriage and family therapy, 222–223
    mental health counseling, 268
    rehabilitation counseling, 354–355
    school counseling, 240
PPAs. *See* Preferred provider agreements
PPOs. *See* Preferred provider organizations
Practica, virtual, 185
Practice-based ethical decision making
    models, 86–89
    negotiating, consensualizing, and
        arbitrating, 104–106
    social constructivism model, 100–104, 106
    Tarvydas integrative model, 89–100
Practices, 77
Preferred provider organizations (PPOs),
    139. *See also* Managed care
Prejudices, 94–95
Prima facie, 46
Principle analysis, 94
Principle ethics, 74, 89. *See also* Ethical
    principles
Principle orientation, 73
Principles, 77, 435. *See also* Ethical principles
Privacy, 26–29
    mental health counseling, 265–266
    on-line counseling, 196
Privileged communication, 29–30
    addiction counseling, 384–385
    career counseling, 303–304
    group counseling, 334–336
    legal issues, 52–53
    marriage and family therapy, 220–221
    mental health counseling, 266
    rehabilitation counseling, 351–353
    school counseling, 244
Pro bono publico, 268
Professional accreditation, 9
Professional accrediting bodies, 9
Professional associates, and school
    counseling, 242
Professional boundaries, 117–120